Shākta Upaniṣats

(*Upaniṣats* about *Sri Devi*)

*

Dr. Ramamurthy N.
M.Sc., B.G.L., CAIIB, CCP, DSADP, CISA, PMP, CGBL, Ph.D.

*

*

Title: *Shākta Upaniṣats*
(*Upaniṣats* about *Sri Devi*)

First Edition: 2020
Second Edition: 2021

Author: **Dr. Ramamurthy N,**
http://ramamurthy.jāgruti.co.in/

Number of pages: 380

ISBN (13): 978-93-82237-66-2

Price: ₹ 500

*****

Table of Contents

*****

Dedication

मातृ देवो भव

या देवी सर्वभूतेषु मातृरूपेण संस्थिता।
नमस्तस्यै नमस्तस्यै नमस्तस्यै नमो नमः ॥

Mātru Devo Bhava

Yā Devī Sarvabhooteshu Mātru Roopena Samstitā I
Namastasyai Namastasyai Namastasyai Namo Nama: II

This book is dedicated with devotion to all the *upasakas* of *Sri Devi*. There cannot be even an iota of doubt that all will be blessed by *Sri Ambikai*.

Dr. Ramamurthy N

*****

SRI JAYADURGAYAI NAMAHA STD : 0431

SRIMATH POOJYA GURU PRANAVANANDHA SWAMIGAL
SRIVIDYA MAHA SOWBHAGYA PARAMBIKA PEETAM

SRI JAYADURGA SAPARYA SAMAJAM TRUST
ANDANALLUR (POST) TRICHY - 639 101.

Blessings - 1

The learned opines that the Vedas are the root of Vedic Dharma. *Upaniṣats* are the Head of those Vedas. Among those *Upaniṣats* the *Ishaadhi Ashtotra Shata Upaniṣats* are the most famous. The "*Shakta Upaniṣats*" in that order are the ones that can give direct benefit in this Kaliyuga.

Having the forethat that it would be difficult for the common people to follow the *Parama Vaidheeka dharma* during this period, *Sri Adi Shankara Bhagavat Bhadar* divided the worship as *Shanmadha* into Poojas, Homam, Japam, Tarpanam, Marjanam, etc. For our convenience we are worshiping briefly and still reaping the benefits. There is no doubt that the *Shakta Upaniṣats* are the easiest way to attan full benefits – to give peace of mind, cleansing of mind and moksha also.

Dr. Ramamurthy has compiled and written this book "*Shakta Upaniṣats*" with the aim of making it possible for everyone to read, comprehend and benefit from the *Upaniṣats*.

We pray for the full grace and compassion to him and his family and to everyone reading this book, of the Almighty - *Srividya Lalita Para Shodashi Devi* and all our *Gurus*.

Ahimsa Truth Bliss Auspciousness

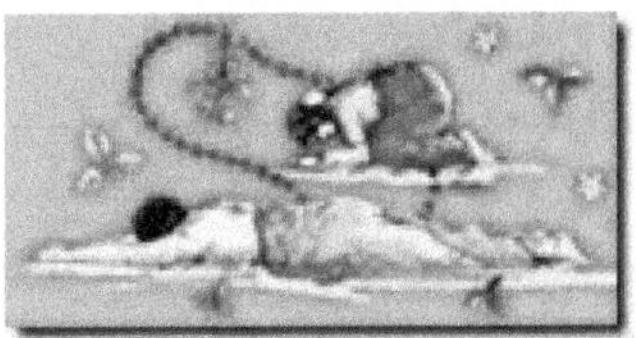

*****

Blessings – 2

'Jai Sri Mouna Guru'
SRI MOUNANDA TAPOVANAM
SRI SOWBHAGYA BHUWANESWARI PEETAM
D.No : 50-53-11/4, MIG-3, Seethammadhara North Extn.
Visakhapatnam, Andhra Pradesh-530013
Ph: +91-9963532728, Email : rajasimham123@gmail.com

Śrī Gurubhyo Namaḥ I

Panivutaiyan Insolan Aadal Oruvarku
Aniyalla Marrup Pira (*Kural* 95)

Yādevī Sarvabhūteśu Buddhi Rūpeṇa Samstitā |
Namastasyai Namastasyai Namastasyai Namo Namaḥ | |

Yādevī Sarvabhūteśu Śraddhā Rūpeṇa Samstitā |
Namastasyai Namastasyai Namastasyai Namo Namaḥ | |

The *Upaniṣats* are the head of the *Vedas*. *Upaniṣats* can also be called *Atmanjnānam*. *Brahma Vidyā* and *Ātma Vidyā* are one and the same. The *Upaniṣats* are the epitome of "*Aham Brahmāsmi*" (I am in the form Brahmam) and *'Tatvamasi'* (you are the same).

There are a total of 108 *Upaniṣats*. Among them main are the *Aitreya Upaniṣat, Taitreeya Upaniṣat, Katopanishat, Swetashvadhara Upaniṣat, Brahadaranyaka Upaniṣat, Prashnopanishat, Kenopanishat, Mundakapanishat* and *Chantokya Upaniṣat*. For these 10 *Upaniṣats Sri Adi Shankara* wrote the *Bhashyam* initially followed by *Ramanujar, Vidyaranyar* and *Ananda Teertar*.

The word *Upaniṣat* is derived from the word *Sat*. *Sat* contains many ingredients. The divine enlightenment *Upaniṣat*, which frees us from the impermanent of samsara life, is to destroy the ignorance that obscures our true nature and lead us to the *Brahmam*. The *Upaniṣats* are the epitome of biblical thought.

No philosophy or class of Indian history can be without the influence of these *Upaniṣats*. The *Muktikopaniṣats* says that *Sri Rama* taught the *Upaniṣats* to *Anjaneya*. *Shakti* is the worship of *Ambikai*, which explains the principle that *Shakti*. *Devi Jaganmata* is the Absolute God and that the omnipotent and omnipresent *Shakti* creates, protects and oppresses the universe. Some of these *Upaniṣats* are in the category of *Shakta Upaniṣats*.

If one is to do good deeds, he must have the blessings of the Guru and the perfect grace of *Sri Devi*. Thus Dr. Ramamurthy N., has a great privilege to have these two together. In that sense Ayyarmalai Poojyasree Pranavananda Swamy has helped him to write this book with blessings and support.

This book is very good and useful for Shakta devotees and to others as well. The author of this book, has composed these Shakta (about Sri Devi) *Upaniṣats* taking much of hard work. Our blessings to him and to his family. The grace of Mother Sri Saubakya Bhuvaneshwari and the grace of Gurunath Sri Sri Sri Mauna Swami to bestow all the benefits to all.

Nārāyana *Nārāyana* *Nārāyana*

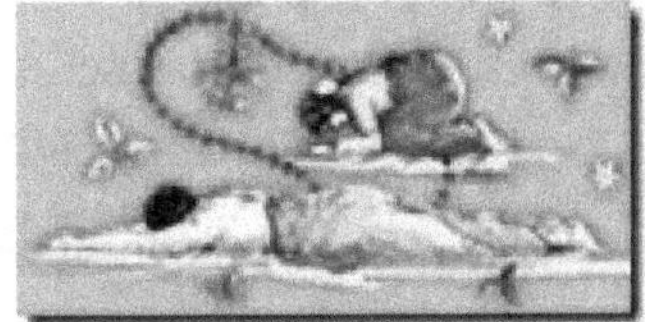

*****

Introduction

ॐ श्री गुरुभ्यो नमः । *Oṃ Śrī Gurubhyo Namaḥ* ।

गुरुर्ब्रह्मा गुरुर्विष्णुः गुरुर्देवो महेश्वरः । गुरु साक्षात् परं ब्रह्म तस्मै श्रीगुरवे नमः ॥

Gururbrahma Gururvishnuḥ Gururdevo Maheshvaraḥ ।
Guru Sākshāt Parabrahma Tasmai Shrīgurave Namaḥ ॥

गुरुवे सर्वलोकानां भिषजे भवरोगिनां। निधये सर्व विद्यानां दक्षिणा मूर्तये नमः॥

Guruve Sarvloksansam Bhishje Bhavaroginām ।

Nidhaye Sarva Vidyānām Dakshina Moortaye Nama: ॥

सदाशिव समारंभां शङ्कराचार्य मध्यमां । अस्मद आचार्य पर्यन्तां वन्दे गुरु परंपराम्॥

Sadāshiva Samārambām Shankarāchārya Madhyamām ।

Asmad Achārya Paranthām Vande Guru Paramparām ॥

श्रुति स्मृति पुराणानामालयं करुणालयम्। नमामि भगवत्पादशंकरं लोकशंकरम्॥

Shruti Smruti Purānānām Ālayam Karunālayam ।
Namāmi Bhagavatapādam Shankaram Lokashankaram ॥

वागर्थाविव सम्प्रुक्तौ वागर्थ प्रतिपत्तये। जगतः पितरौ वन्दे पार्वती परमेश्वरौ ॥

Vāgarthāviva Sampruktakou Vāgartha Pratipaye ।
Jagataḥ Pitarou Vande Pārvati Parameshwarou ॥

We all originated from *Brahmam*[1]. We reach that *Brahmam* – We merge with that *Brahmam*. That is actually *liam-samāti*. This rhythm cannot be exercised without the use or support of an appropriate instructor. The *Upasana* is aimed at an idol. It is both *Suguna* (with qualities) and (without qualities) *Nirguna*. A person is capable of doing *Nirguna Upasana* only after he has attained *Sagunopasana*. Suddenly, it is impossible for one to get involved in *Nirgunobasana* straight away.

Sri Adi Shankarar has written a comprehensive commentary (*Bhashyam*) for *Upaniṣats*. After writing commentary for 10 *Upaniṣats* he has started

---

[1] *Brahmam* is different from *Brahma*. *Brahma* is the chief of *Devas*. *Brahmam* is the top most one – *Parabrahmam*.

writing commentary for *Brahma Sutra*. His followers, *Shankarānanda*, *Narayana Saraswathi*, *Upaniṣat* Brahma-yogi, Appayya Dīkshatar, and others also addressed the 108 *Upaniṣats*.

Further, some *Upaniṣats* describe the soul and the others describe *Brahmam*, Atom, *Shiva*, *Narayana*, *Shakti*, *Yoga*, Body, etc. In order to understand each and every matter in particular, we must realize that there is no bias among them.

One should properly worship Lord Shiva in the morning and Sri Devi in the evening, with pure inner mind. Then the worshipper can obtain the shakti, Mukti, yoga and enlightenment. Further worship is essential in addition to reading and hearing.

Therefore, as many people have clearly explained that the puja of the earliest Mother *Parāshakti* is the best and recitation is also necessary as part of the same. As *Upaniṣats* are recited, the praises of the marital qualities of the mother of *Ādi Shakti* are meditated upon in the minds of the lovers. Further, understanding the meaning and reciting is conducive to developing knowledge and wisdom.

More mature wisdom and experience is required to do these things. Wisdom does not come from simply reading the book. That is the specialty of the *Upaniṣats*. The *Upaniṣats* are not simply recited, but they can live the great life of understanding, embracing and experiencing their substance and philosophy. After completing life in this world, attain liberation also.

Legends have indicated that the four Vedas are the four gates (as detailed below) of Srinagaram, which is the seat of *Sri Lalita Parameshwari Parābatatārikai*, the supreme form of *Sri Paraashakti*. This is what Sri Goutapādar refers to in his Sri Vidya Ratna Sutras as "*Tanmantrasya Rigvedādi Chaturdvare*";

- *Rig* Veda - East
- *Yajur* Veda - South
- *Sama* Veda - West
- *Atharva* Veda - North

There are 33 *Upaniṣats* related to the Shāktam, listed in a later chapter. The purpose of this book is to give the mantras of all of them with commentaries (*Bhashyam*). However, the commentaries of 6 *Devi Upaniṣats* only are reachable and considered in this book alongwith moola mantras both in Samskrutam and English. The commentaries of other *Upaniṣats* will be tried in next edition.

The general rule is that the Vedic *mantras* should be recited with Swara. However, the Swara is not emphasized for the *Upaniṣats*. Hence it is not given importance here.

Generally, it is very difficult to read Samskruta words in English with proper pronunciation. It is apt to read them in Samskruta script itself. But to benefit those who cannot read Samskruta script the mantras have been given in English also. The Samskruta words, when transliterated in English are given in *italics*. Also, whenever She denotes Goddess *Sri Devi*, it is written as **She** or **Her**. Normally diacritical marks will be used for transliteration of Samskruta words into English. But general readers are not fully conversant with diacritical marks and hence they find it difficult to read. Hence, it not been used in this book in normal texts. But for proper pronunciation it has been completely used in mantras.

Humble pranāms are due to Pujyasri Pranavananda Swamiji of Ayyarmalai, who provided various inputs to this book. Hearty thanks to all the good-hearted souls who enabled this book to be presented in this fashion.

Attempts have been made to give this book as much error free as possible. Still if there are any errors, apologies are sought. If the errors given as feedback, it will the next edition to be fault free.

Our humble pranāms with thanks are offered to Pujyashree Pranavanunda Swamijee who has given some blessings and pleasantries about the author and the book.

This book has been simultaneously published in Tamil language also.

There is no doubt that Sri Devi will shower her compassion and blessings to all those who read this book.

Chennai *Dr. Ramamurthy N.*
2020

*****

Upaniṣats

The *Upaniṣats* are the head of the *Vedas*. *Upaniṣat* means soul wisdom. Vedanta is the name for the principle, which is the end of scriptures. *'Upaniṣat'* is the same as "*Brahma Vidya*" and "*Atman Vidya*" though. The doctrines of the scriptures are certainly the *Upaniṣats*.

There is contradictory opinion, even about the total number of *Upaniṣats* – 108 is the mostly accepted number, but still some schools list 188[2]. *Muktikopaniṣats* says that *Sri Rama* has advised 108 *Upaniṣats* to *Sri Anjaneya*. Out of these 10 are considered as most important ones.

In *Vedas*, *Upaniṣats* are found at the end of *Aranyaka*. If *Samhitas* are considered as a tree, *Brahmanas* are flowers, *Āranyakas* are raw-unripe fruits and *Upaniṣats* are the ultimate ripe fruits, the result. In the path of knowledge (*jnana marga*) *Upaniṣats* are meant to show us the difference between *Jīvātma* and *Paramātma*. *Samhitas*, *Brahmanas* and *Āranyakas* are steps to reach us there. Different *Vidyas*, worshipping methods, *yagnas*, etc., are mentioned in some places in *Upaniṣats*. But importance is given to philosophical discussions. The essence of *Upaniṣats* is to unbind us from all bondages like rituals. Based on the main subject dealt with, *Vedas* have been bifurcated into *Karma Kanda* and *Jnana Kanda*. This is also respectively called as *Poorva Mīmāmsa* and *Uttara Mīmāmsa*.

After doing research on *Karma Kanda*, Sage *Jaiminī* summarized his conclusions as a *Shastra* and named it is *Poorva Mīmāmsa*. In the same way, aiming at the *Jnana Kanda*, *Vyasa's* book *Brahma Sutra* is called *Uttara Mīmāmsa*. When compared to *Karma Kanda*, the *Jnana Kanda* containing *Upaniṣats* is very small. Proportionately, *Jaiminī Sutra* has 1,000 parts and hence called as *"Sahasra Adikarani"* and *Brahma Sutra* has less than 200 parts. A tree may contain lot many leaves, but will contain very little flowers and fruits. Similarly, in the tree of *Vedas*, *Karma Kanda* is bigger and *Upaniṣats* part is smaller.

For a human being to live, the basic necessities are four viz., - *Artha*, *Kama*, *Dharma*, and *Moksha* (conventional order is *Dharma*, *Artha*, *Kama*

---

[2] 188 *Upaniṣads* are listed at the end of this chapter.

and *Moksha*[3]. It has been consciously given in different order in this context.)

Artha denotes necessaries that are required for our livelihood. The holdings what we accumulate for the nourishment of our body and mind. *Kama* is the enjoyment of our body and mind. For instance, if we go for a food to satisfy our hunger, then it is *artha*. If we go for a tasty food to satisfy our tongue then it is *kama* (in the present days the word *Kama* is used to denote one particular desire only). *Dharma* is virtue. These un-visible virtues can be reached by performing the rituals prescribed by *Vedas* and by all acts not against the *Dharma*.

The early part of *Vedas* called *Karma Kanda* suggest various ways and methods to attain *Artha, Kama* and *Dharma*. Having suggested different methods to attain, at the end, the shortcomings are also listed. Each delight is mixed with sorrow. Protecting the wealth, losing them, etc., will always lead to sorrow, though enjoying the wealth is a joy. No pleasure can give complete satisfaction for the mind, excepting Bliss. Having introduced the blemish-less Bliss, the path to reach this is also shown by *Vedas*. That is *Vedanta*, more in particular *Upaniṣats* called as *Jnana Kanda*.

The philosophical discussions of *Upaniṣats* do not end like the research done on other subjects by others in the logical perspective or evidence based. The research done by the mind and brain should be experienced. If one says that Mentioning that Halwa is so sweet that is of no use to anyone. One has to taste it to enjoy the sweetness. The greatness of *Upaniṣats*, that is not available to other philosophies, is that this contains *mantras*. Whatever be the philosophy conveyed, with the power of *mantras*, the chanter (not a simple reader) can experience it. To experience this, different lifestyles are prescribed in the *Karma Kanda* of *Vedas*. If one lives strictly as prescribed, cleanse himself internally, leaving all the rituals and then comprehend the communication of *Upaniṣats* then he can realize that the philosophies are not only

---

[3] Note: There are texts containing 700 verses (*Saptashatee*) dealing with each one of these four viz., *Dharma – Manu Smruti, Artha – Devi Mahaatmeeyam, Kaama – Kaama Sootram* and *Moksha – Shreemad Bhagavad* Gita.

intellectual related, but also part and parcel of the soul. The peak of these philosophies is the unity of the soul with *Brahmam* (*advaita*).

To climb that peak of inter-mixing of *Jīvātma-Paramātma*, a person having matured with all the rituals, becomes a *Sanyasi*. At that time of getting sainthood, he will be advised with the *Maha* (great) sentences of the four *Vedas*. These four sentences describe the indifferences between *Jīvātma* and *Paramātma*. He can attain the peak, if he meditates upon these four sentences. These four sentences are taken from four *Upaniṣats* – each for one *Veda*. How many ever rituals, prayers, life styles, etc., are all prescribed and explained in *Samhita* and *Brahmana* parts of *Vedas*, the ultimate goal is achieved only through the great sentences of *Upaniṣats*. Though they are called as sentences, typically they are phrases only. These four great sentences are briefed below:

1. प्रज्ञानं ब्रह्मा – *"Prajnānam Brahma"* – the highest experience of the knowledge is **the** *Brahmam*. This sentence forms part of *Aitreya Upaniṣat*. This belongs to *Rig Veda*.
2. अहं ब्रह्मास्मि – *"Aham Brahmāsmi"* – I am **the** *Brahmam*. This sentence forms part of *Bruhadāranyaka Upaniṣat*. This belongs to *Yajur Veda*.
3. तत् त्वं असि – *"Tat Tvam Asi"* – That thou art – The *guru* advises to his disciple as "you and the *paramaatma* are one and the same". This sentence forms part of *Cāndogya Upaniṣat*. This belongs to *Sama Veda*.
4. अयं आत्मा ब्रह्मा – *"Ayam Atmā Brahma"* – This soul is **the** *Brahmam*. This sentence forms part of *Mandukya Upaniṣat*. This belongs to *Atharva Veda*.

Thus, the special sentences of each of *Vedas* are found in the concerned *Upaniṣats* pertaining to that *Veda* itself.

Sri Adi Shankara, in his book called *"Shobāna Pancakam"*, which is an essence of advises, starts his book as – "Chant *Vedas*, i.e. *Samhitas* and perform all the rituals prescribed in the *Brahmanas*". He ends his book with "get these great sentences initiated, practice and meditate upon them. Reach the *Brahmam*".

The final stage of all the *Vedas* are all mentioned only in *Upaniṣats*. They are only called as *Vedanta*. As already mentioned, '*anta*' means end; they are the end part of *Vedas* and hence *Vedanta's*. In two ways they are the end part.

When we consider each *Shāka*, the order of the texts, is *Samhita*, *Brahmana*, *Āranyaka* and at last *Upaniṣats*. That is, *Upaniṣats* are the last part of *Vedas*. Again, in the connotation perspective the final goal is mentioned only in *Upaniṣats*. Hence, both in the order of texts and connotation angles *Upaniṣats* are the end part of *Vedas*.

Every town has a temple. A temple has a tower. A tower has a peak. This is the way they are rising. In the same way *Upaniṣats* are the peak of philosophies, that is the concluding part of *Vedas*.

Upaniṣat = *Upa* + *ni* + *shat* – literally this means sitting by the side. The *Guru* advises the *Upaniṣats*, by making his disciple sit by his side. It can also mean "to enable to go near the *Brahmam*". We have all heard of the ritual called '*Upanayanam*' – this means "taking the child near the *guru*". It can also mean "taking the child near the *Brahmam*". In the same manner, *Upaniṣats* can also mean both the above ways.

- *Upa* – going near (to *guru*).
- *Ni* – definite - getting the knowledge of real truth
- *Shat* – removes (*Shātayati*) – what is removed? The sorrows of the birth and death.

The *Upaniṣats* form the end of *Vedas* and hence they are called *Vedanta* (*Anta* means end). Hence, they are also called as the Head of the *Vedas*.

When it is mentioned "as advising by sitting the side of the disciple", it means that it is very secretive. It is not to be advised to the immature, who do not know its value. That is the reason, even within the *Upaniṣats*, while talking about subtle philosophies and not stories kind of messages, it is specifically mentioned as "*ItUpaniṣat* – this is *Upaniṣat*". The secret parts of *Vedas* are mentioned as '*Rahasya*' and the secret parts of *Vedanta's* are mentioned as '*Upaniṣat*'.

Table of 188 *Upaniṣats*

The first ten are important *Upaniṣats*. It is told that in earlier days the *Upaniṣats* were 108 in number. Further 12 more were added and 120 is called first part. Later 68 more *Upaniṣats* were added as second part. The "*Brahma Vidya*" is the internal essence of the first part of 120 *Upaniṣats*. The second part of 68 *Upaniṣats* are divided into 5 as - *Yoga*, *Vedanta*, *Vaishnava*, *Shaiva* and *Shākta*.

#	*Upaniṣat*	
First Part		
1.	*Īshāvāsya Upaniṣat*	ईशावास्य उपनिषत्
2.	*Kena Upaniṣat*	केन उपनिषत्
3.	*Katha Upaniṣat*	कठ उपनिषत्
4.	*Prashna Upaniṣat*	प्रश्न पनिषत्
5.	*Mundaka Upaniṣat*	मुण्डक उपनिषत्
6.	*Māndukya Upaniṣat*	माण्डुक्य उपनिषत्
7.	*Taittirīya Upaniṣat*	तैत्तिरीय उपनिषत्
8.	*Aitreya Upaniṣat*	ऐत्रेय उपनिषत्
9.	*Chāndogyo Upaniṣat*	छान्दोग्य उपनिषत्
10.	*Bṛhadāranyako Upaniṣat*	बृह्दारण्यक उपनिषत्
11.	*Brahma Upaniṣat*	ब्रह्म उपनिषत्
12.	*Kaivalya Upaniṣat*	कैवल्य उपनिषत्
13.	*Jābāla Upaniṣat*	जाबाल पनिषत्
14.	*Shvetāshvatara Upaniṣat*	श्वेताश्वतर उपनिषत्
15.	*Hamsa Upaniṣat*	हंस उपनिषत्
16.	*Ārunya Upaniṣat*	आरुण्य उपनिषत्
17.	*Garba Upaniṣat*	गर्भ उपनिषत्
18.	*Nārāyana Upaniṣat*	नारायण उपनिषत्
19.	*Mahā Nārāyana Upaniṣat*	महा नारायण उपनिषत्
20.	*Paramahamsa Upaniṣat*	परमहंस उपनिषत्
21.	*Amrutabindu Upaniṣat*	अमृतबिन्दु उपनिषत्
22.	*Amrutanāda Upaniṣat*	अमृतनाद उपनिषत्
23.	*Atarvashika Upaniṣat*	अतर्वशिक उपनिषत्

#	*Upaniṣat*	
24.	*Atarvashira Upaniṣat*	अतर्वशिर उपनिषत्
25.	*Maitrāyanī Upaniṣat*	मैत्रायणी उपनिषत्
26.	*Koushītakī Upaniṣat*	कौशीतकी उपनिषत्
27.	*Bruhajjābāla Upaniṣat*	बृहज्जाबाल उपनिषत्
28.	*Nrusimha Pūrvatāpanīya Upaniṣat*	नृसिम्ह पूर्वतापनीय उपनिषत्
29.	*Nrusimha Uttaratāpanīya Upaniṣat*	नृसिम्ह उत्तरतापनीय उपनिषत्
30.	*Maitreyī Upaniṣat*	मैत्रेयी उपनिषत्
31.	*Subāla Upaniṣat*	सुबाला उपनिषत्
32.	*Kshurika Upaniṣat*	क्षुरिकपनिषत्
33.	*Mantrika Upaniṣat*	मन्त्रिक उपनिषत्
34.	*Sarvasāra Upaniṣat*	सर्वसार उपनिषत्
35.	*Nirālamba Upaniṣat*	निरालंब उपनिषत्
36.	*Shuka Rahasya Upaniṣat*	शुक रहस्य उपनिषत्
37.	*Vajrasūcika Upaniṣat*	वज्रसूचिक उपनिषत्
38.	*Vajrabinjarā Upaniṣat*	वज्रबिंजर उपनिषत्
39.	*Tejobindu Upaniṣat*	तेजोबिन्दु उपनिषत्
40.	*Nādabindu Upaniṣat*	नादबिन्दु उपनिषत्
41.	*Dhyānabindu Upaniṣat*	ध्यानबिन्दु उपनिषत्
42.	*Brahmavidyā Upaniṣat*	ब्रह्मविद्या उपनिषत्
43.	*Yogatatva Upaniṣat*	योगतत्व पनिषत्
44.	*Ātmapraboda Upaniṣat*	आत्मप्रबोद उपनिषत्
45.	*Nārada Parivrājaka Upaniṣat*	नारद परिव्राजक उपनिषत्
46.	*Trishikhi Brahmana Upaniṣat*	त्रिशिखि उपनिषत्
47.	*Tripādvibhūti Upaniṣat*	त्रिपाद्विभूति उपनिषत्
48.	*Yoga Cūdāmani Upaniṣat*	योग चूडामणि उपनिषत्
49.	*Nirvāna Upaniṣat*	निर्वाण उपनिषत्
50.	*Mandala Brahmana Upaniṣat*	मण्डल ब्राह्मण उपनिषत्

#	*Upaniṣat*	
51.	*Dakshināmoorti Upaniṣat*	दक्षिणामूर्ति उपनिषत्
52.	*Sharabha Upaniṣat*	शरभ उपनिषत्
53.	*Skanda Upaniṣat*	स्कन्द पनिषत्
54.	*Tripādvibhooti Mahā Nārāyana Upaniṣat*	त्रिपाद्विभूति महा नारायण उपनिषत्
55.	*Advayatāraka Upaniṣat*	अद्वयतारक उपनिषत्
56.	*Rāmarahasya Upaniṣat*	रामरहस्य उपनिषत्
57.	*Shrīrāma Poorvatāpinya Upaniṣat*	श्रीरामपूर्वतापिन्य उपनिषत्
58.	*Shrīrāma Uttaratāpinya Upaniṣat*	श्रीराम उत्तरतापिन्य उपनिषत्
59.	*Vāsudeva Upaniṣat*	वासुदेव उपनिषत्
60.	*Mudgala Upaniṣat*	मुद्गल उपनिषत्
61.	*Shāndilya Upaniṣat*	शाण्डिल्य उपनिषत्
62.	*Paiṅkala Upaniṣat*	पैङ्कल उपनिषत्
63.	*Bikshuka Upaniṣat*	भिक्षुक पनिषत्
64.	*Mahā Upaniṣat*	महा उपनिषत्
65.	*Shārīraka Upaniṣat*	शारीरक उपनिषत्
66.	*Yogashika Upaniṣat*	योगशिख उपनिषत्
67.	*Turīyātīta Upaniṣat*	तुरीयातीत उपनिषत्
68.	*Sanyāsa Upaniṣat*	सन्यास उपनिषत्
69.	*Paramahamsapari-vrājaka Upaniṣat*	परमहंसपरिव्राजक उपनिषत्
70.	*Akshamālika Upaniṣat*	अक्षमालिक उपनिषत्
71.	*Avyakta Upaniṣat*	अव्यक्त उपनिषत्
72.	*Ekākshara Upaniṣat*	एकाक्षर पनिषत्
73.	*Soorya Upaniṣat*	सूर्य उपनिषत्
74.	*Akshyu Upaniṣat*	अक्ष्यु उपनिषत्
75.	*Adyātma Upaniṣat*	अध्यात्म उपनिषत्
76.	*Kundika Upaniṣat*	कुण्डिक उपनिषत्
77.	*Ātma Upaniṣat*	आत्म उपनिषत्
78.	*Pāshupatabrahma Upaniṣat*	पाशुपतब्रह्म उपनिषत्

#	Upaniṣat	
79.	*Parabrahma Upaniṣat*	परब्रह्म उपनिषत्
80.	*Avadoota Upaniṣat*	अवधूत पनिषत्
81.	*Tiripura Upaniṣat*	त्रिपुर उपनिषत्
82.	*Yoga Kundalya Upaniṣat*	योगकुन्डलय उपनिषत्
83.	*Basmajābāla Upaniṣat*	भस्मजाबाल उपनिषत्
84.	*Rudrākshajābālo Upaniṣat*	रुद्राक्षजाबाल उपनिषत्
85.	*Ganapaty Upaniṣat*	गणपति उपनिषत्
86.	*Jābāladarshano Upaniṣat*	जाबालदर्शन उपनिषत्
87.	*Tārasāro Upaniṣat*	तारसार उपनिषत्
88.	*Mahāvākyo Upaniṣat*	महावाक्य उपनिषत्
89.	*Pancabrahmo Upaniṣat*	पञ्चब्रह्म उपनिषत्
90.	*Prānāgnihotra Upaniṣat*	प्राणाग्निहोत्र उपनिषत्
91.	*Gopālapoorvatāpinya Upaniṣat*	गोपाल पूर्वतापिन्य उपनिषत्
92.	*Gopālouttaratāpinya Upaniṣat*	गोपाल उत्तरतापिन्य उपनिषत्
93.	*Krishna Upaniṣat*	कृष्ण उपनिषत्
94.	*Yāgñayavalkya Upaniṣat*	याज्ञवल्क्य उपनिषत्
95.	*Varāha Upaniṣat*	वराह उपनिषत्
96.	*Shātyāyanīya Upaniṣat*	शाट्यायनीय उपनिषत्
97.	*Hayagrīva Upaniṣat*	हयग्रीव उपनिषत्
98.	*Dattātreya Upaniṣat*	दत्तात्रेय उपनिषत्
99.	*Garuda Upaniṣat*	गरुड उपनिषत्
100.	*Kalisantarana Upaniṣat*	कलिसन्तरण उपनिषत्
101.	*Ganesha Poorvatāpinya Upaniṣat*	गणेश पूर्वतापिन्य उपनिषत्
102.	*Ganesha Uttaratāpinya Upaniṣat*	गणेश उत्तरतापिन्य उपनिषत्
103.	*Gopīcandana Upaniṣat*	गोपीचन्दन उपनिषत्
104.	*Āshrama Upaniṣat*	आश्रम उपनिषत्

#	Upaniṣat	
105.	*Sarasvatīrahasya Upaniṣat*	योगराज उपनिषत्
106.	*Advaita Upaniṣat*	अद्वैत उपनिषत्
107.	*Ācamana Upaniṣat*	आचमन उपनिषत्
108.	*Kātyāyana Upaniṣat*	कात्यायन उपनिषत्
109.	*Pinda Upaniṣat*	पिण्ड उपनिषत्
110.	*Mrutyukānkoola Upaniṣat*	मृत्युकांकूल उपनिषत्
111.	*Ātmapooja Upaniṣat*	आत्मपूज उपनिषत्
112.	*Ārsheya Upaniṣat*	आर्षेय उपनिषत्
113.	*Itihāsa Upaniṣat*	इतिहास उपनिषत्
114.	*Caturveda Upaniṣat*	चतुर्वेद उपनिषत्
115.	*Cākshusha Upaniṣat*	चाक्षुष उपनिषत्
116.	*Chāgaleya Upaniṣat*	छागलेय उपनिषत्
117.	*Turīya Upaniṣat*	तुरीय उपनिषत्
118.	*Pranava Upaniṣat*	प्रणव उपनिषत्
119.	*Dvaya Upaniṣat*	द्वय उपनिषत्
120.	*Nirukta Upaniṣat*	निरुक्त उपनिषत्
Second Part		
Yoga Upaniṣats		
Ordinary *Vedanta Upaniṣats*		
121.	*Bāshkalamantra Upaniṣat*	बाष्कलमन्त्र उपनिषत्
122.	*Matāmnaya Upaniṣat*	मठाम्नाय उपनिषत्
123.	*Vishrāma Upaniṣat*	विश्राम उपनिषत्
124.	*Shounakā Upaniṣat*	शौनक उपनिषत्
125.	*Sooryatāpinya Upaniṣat*	सूर्यतापिन्य उपनिषत्
126.	*Svasamvedya Upaniṣat*	स्वसंवेद्य उपनिषत्
127.	*Kshurikā Upaniṣat*	क्षुरिका उपनिषत्
128.	*Mantrikā Upaniṣat*	मन्त्रिका उपनिषत्
Vaishnava Upaniṣats		
129.	*Oordva Pundarīka Upaniṣat*	ऊर्ध्वपुण्ड्र उपनिषत्

#	*Upaniṣat*	
130.	*Sri Krishna Puruşotama Siddhānta Upaniṣat*	श्रीकृष्ण पुरुषोत्तम सिद्धान्त उपनिषत्
131.	*Nārada Upaniṣat*	नारद उपनिषत्
132.	*Nārāyana Poorvatāpanīya Upaniṣat*	नारायण पूर्वतापनीय उपनिषत्
133.	*Nārāyana Uttaratāpanīya Upaniṣat*	नारायण उत्तरतापनीय उपनिषत्
134.	*Nrusimha Shatcakra Upaniṣat*	नृसिंह षट्चक्र उपनिषत्
135.	*Pāramātmia Upaniṣat*	पारमात्मिक उपनिषत्
136.	*Yajnopavīta Upaniṣat*	यज्ञोपवीत उपनिषत्
137.	*Rāga Upaniṣat*	राघ उपनिषत्
138.	*Lāngoola Upaniṣat*	लाङ्गूल उपनिषत्
139.	*Sankarshana Upaniṣat*	सङ्कर्षण उपनिषत्
140.	*Sāmarahasya Upaniṣat*	सामरहस्य उपनिषत्
141.	*Sudarshana Upaniṣat*	सुदर्शन उपनिषत्
	Shaiva Upaniṣats	
142.	*Nīlarudra Upaniṣat*	नीलरुद्र उपनिषत्
143.	*Katha Rudra Upaniṣat*	कठरुद्र उपनिषत्
144.	*Kālāgni Rudra Upaniṣat*	कालाग्नि रुद्र उपनिषत्
145.	*Rudra Hrudaya Upaniṣat*	रुद्रहृदय उपनिषत्
146.	*Pārāyana Upaniṣat*	पारायण उपनिषत्
147.	*Bilva Upaniṣat*	बिल्व उपनिषत्
148.	*Rudra Upaniṣat*	रुद्र उपनिषत्
149.	*Linga Upaniṣat*	लिङ्ग उपनिषत्
150.	*Vatuka Upaniṣat*	वटुक उपनिषत्
151.	*Shivasaṅkalpa Upaniṣat*	शिवसङ्कल्प उपनिषत्
152.	*Shiva Upaniṣat*	शिव उपनिषत्
153.	*Sadānanda Upaniṣat*	सदानन्द उपनिषत्
154.	*Siddhāntashika Upaniṣat*	सिद्धान्तशिख उपनिषत्
155.	*Heramba Upaniṣat*	हेरम्ब उपनिषत्

#	*Upaniṣat*	
Shākta Upaniṣats		
156.	*Atharvanadvitīya Upaniṣat*	अथर्वणद्वितीय उपनिषत्
157.	*Atharvashika Upaniṣat*	अथर्वशिकोपनिषत्
158.	*Aruno Upaniṣat*	अरुणोपनिषत्
159.	*Allā Upaniṣat*	अल्ला उपनिषत्
160.	*Annapoorṇa Upaniṣat*	अन्नपूर्णोपनिषत्
161.	*Ārunika Upaniṣat*	आरुणिकोपनिषत्
162.	*Kāmarāja Kīlitoddhāra Upaniṣat*	कामराजकीलितोद्धार उपनिषत्
163.	*Gāyatree Upaniṣat Guhyakāḷi Upaniṣat*	गायत्री उपनिषत्
164.	*Gāyatree Rahasya Upaniṣat*	गायत्री रहस्य उपनिषत्
165.	*Kālikā Upaniṣat*	काळिका उपनिषत्
166.	*Kālīmedhādīkshta Upaniṣat*	काळीमेधादीक्षित उपनिषत्
167.	*Guhyakāli Upaniṣat*	गुह्यकाळी उपनिषत्
168.	*Guhyashodhānyāsa Upaniṣat*	गुह्यषोढान्यास उपनिषत्
169.	*Shrīcakra Upaniṣat*	तुलसि उपनिषत्
170.	*Shrīvidyātāraka Upaniṣat*	त्रिपुरातापिन्य उपनिषत्
171.	*Shodasha Upaniṣat*	त्रिपुरोपनिषत्
172.	*Sumukhya Upaniṣat*	बह्वृचोपनिषत्
173.	*Hamsa Ṣodasha Upaniṣat*	भावनोपनिषत्
174.	*Pitāmbara Upaniṣat*	पीताम्बर उपनिषत्
175.	*Muktika Upaniṣat*	मुख्तिकोपनिषत्
176.	*Rājashyāmala Rahasya Upaniṣat*	राजश्यामळा रहस्य उपनिषत्
177.	*Vanadurgā Upaniṣat*	वनदुर्गा उपनिषत्
178.	*Sarasvatī Rahasya Upaniṣat*	सरस्वती रहस्योपनिषत्
179.	*Sāvitri Upaniṣat*	सावित्रि उपनिषत्
180.	*Sita Upaniṣat*	सीतोपनिषत्
181.	*Sumukhya Upaniṣat*	सुमुख्य उपनिषत्

#	*Upaniṣat*	
182.	*Soubhāgya Lakśmi Upaniṣat*	सौभाग्यलक्ष्मि उपनिषत्
183.	*Shyāma Upaniṣat*	श्याम उपनिषत्
184.	*Sri Devi Upaniṣat* or *Sri Devi Atharva Shīrsham*	श्री देवि उपनिषत् or श्री देवी अथर्व शीर्शम्
185.	*Sri Cakra Upaniṣat*	श्रीचक्र उपनिषत्
186.	*Sri Vidyā Tāraka Upaniṣat*	श्रीविद्यातारक उपनिषत्
187.	*Shodasha Upaniṣat*	षोढश उपनिषत्
188.	*Hamsa Shodasha Upaniṣat*	हंसषोढश उपनिषत्

*****

Ādi Śankara – Establisher of *Śaṇmatas*

Sri *Adi Shankara Bhagwat Pādar*, the greatest philosopher and thinker, in a short life span of 32 years, has created a collection of art-essays Indian culture and the intellectual and emotional integration of this sub-continent.

He called for the abolition of superstitions and practices and the supremacy of radical reasoning. The hard philosophies of the *Upaniṣats* were easily described by him for the benefit of those who were involved in unnecessary and useless verbal arguments.

Having traveled many times from east to west and south to North of India, he succeeded in convincing his opponents, not by sword or threats or charms, but by persuasive arguments about the teachings of the Vedas and especially the *Upaniṣats*. Such things can be achieved in such a short time only by an incarnation of the God. That is why, he is believed to be the incarnation of the Supreme Being of all the people of the world. He is the embodiment of the *Dakshinamoorti* manifestation and the supreme spiritual knowledge. The supreme beauty of his teaching is that it applies to all human beings irrespective of religion or race, caste or creed or nationality. That is the reason, he is aptly called as *'Jagadguru'* – teacher of the entire universe.

There is one name as *"Shanmada Stāpakar"* in the ashtotram of Adi Shankarar – the founder of *Shanmada*. He has sub-divided our religion of Hinduism, into six sub-religion kind of as;

1. *Gānapatyam* – People who primarily worship Lord *Ganapati*
2. *Shouram* – People who primarily worship Lord *Soorya*
3. *Shaivam* – People who primarily worship Lord *Shiva*
4. *Vaishnavam* – People who primarily worship Lord *Vishnu*
5. *Koumāram* – People who primarily worship Lord *Subramanya* (*Muruga or Kumara*)
6. *Shāktam* – People who primarily worship Goddess *Sri Devi* (*Shakti*)

Each of these *Shanmata* deities is found in various forms. Such variants differ in terms of image, clan customs, patriotism and the need of the devotee. For instance;

- *Ganapati – Mahā Ganapati, Ucchishta Ganapati, Vallabha Ganapati, Siddhi Bhuddhi Ganapati, Ganapati* with two hands, *Ganapati* with five heads and so on.
- *Subrahmanyar – Muruga, Kumāra, Bāla Subrahmanyar, Subrahmanyar* with *Devasena, Subrahmanyar* with *Valli* and *Devasena* and so on.
- *Shiva – Rudra, Sarabeshwara, Bhairavar, Arddhanārīshwara, Shankara Narayana* and so on.
- *Vishnu – Ranganatha, Srinivasan, Rama, Krishna, Narasimha* and lot many names.
- *Shakti – Durga, Ashta Lakshmi, Sarasvati, Chāmundī, Dasha Maha Vidyas, Bhuvaneshwari, Tripurasundari, Shodashī, Maha Shodashī, Para Shodashī* and thousands of similar names.

Moreover, we cannot ignore the family deities, clan goddesses, Lord Iyyappa, Santoshi Mata, Kubera, etc. which do not fall within the above defined limits.

Although the worship of these deities had already been existing, Sri Adi Shankarar brought a system into play. These six religions are considered to be the branches of Hinduism. Later, the *Smārtas*, which is not present in the six branches, appear to be a branch of the religion, which in some sense is associated with *Shaivam*. In one perspective, they can be called smārtas because all the gods are worshipped in the same sense by them – *sama + artha.*

Even before *Sri Adi Shankara* worshipping of these Gods were existing. Devi Bhagavatam (7.39.30) reads as;

शिवाश्च वैष्णवाश्चैव सौरा: शाक्तास्तथैव च ।

गाणपत्या आगमाश्च प्रणीता: शङ्करेण तु ॥

Śivāśca Vaiṣṇavāścaiva Sourāḥ Śāktāstathaiva Ca I

Gānapatyaa Āgamāśca Praṇītāḥ Śankarena Tu II

To bring back those brahmins, who have gone against the path of *Vedas*, in the proper route, the auspicious scriptures like *Shaivam*, *Vaishnavam*, *Shaaktam*, *Souram* and *Gaanapatyam* were created properly. It may be worth noting that *Koumaaram* is not listed here.

Worshipping of these Gods were there even before *Sri Adi Shankara*. However, he only structured them and hence called as the author of Shanmada and Advaita doctrines. He also included one more sub-religion called *Koumaaram*. Hence the Advaita concepts are common to all the six sub-religions.

*****

Śāktam

There is nowhere else in the world where perfect love can be found, such as motherhood. Even if the child does not replicate his love, the mother has continued to make perfect love. Tamil proverb reads - "Mother's mind is manic, the child's is like a stone" - "பெற்ற மனம் பித்து, பிள்ளை மனம் கல்லு".

We can enjoy the perfect love and selfless labour only with a mother. When the child calls 'mother!', the pleasure of the mother is unique. This love is more enduring to the cow-clan than to the human race - the mother of the calf!

Let us enjoy Paramacharya's a little speech about Ambikai, possibly in his own words.

Our mother is the only for this body. After this birth then next birth – another mother. Destruction of the body does not kill *Atma*. There is only one mother for the *Atma*. *Sri Lalita Sahasranama* starts with "*Sri Mātre Namaḥ*" Ambikai is the *Jaganmata* – mother of this entire universe. All the energy we have is hers.

Continuously, the fragments of her energy are exhibited to all living organisms. Whatever we do, it is all hers. We cannot do anything. It is wrong to be arrogant thinking that we only did it.

Even if anything is not asked for, **she** will automatically grant them gimmicks, wealth, shine, etc., in the world and then bless them with the bliss also. When we have the supreme Advaita bliss, we become blissful. On the other hand, it is a condition that **she** will settle our *karma* and give liberation one day. Let it be available when it is available. We have a mother who loves us. It is now possible for us to remember her love and pray for her love. Is there anything more to enjoy? The entire world and all living beings will always be happy to think of the dear *Ambika* as a love.

Let us surrender the golden feet of the *Paramacharya*.

Shāktam - Worshipping *Sri Devi* as the primary Goddess. Among the *Shanamadas,* after *Shaivam* and *Vaishnavism,* the most popular god(dess) is *Shakti*. Even the followers of *Shiva,* have a practice of worshipping *Shakti*. *Navaratri* festival is meant for exclusively worshipping *Sri Devi*. *Shakti* worship is practiced and **she** is an important deity who is worshiped all-day, irrespective of religion, male, female and caste.

Ancient Tamil poetess Aouvaiyār also said "அன்னையும் பிதாவும் முன்னறித் தெய்வம் – Mother and father are the primary gods". She kept the mother first before even father. In the sequence "*Mata* (Mother), *Pita* (Father), *Guru* (teacher), *Deivam* (God)" also mother is given the top priority. Subramanya Bharathi also says, "ஆதிப் பரம் பொருளின் ஊக்கம் – அதை அன்னையெனப் பணிதல் ஆக்கம்". *Upaniṣat* also says "*Mātru Devo Bhava*". Thus, Mother is given importance in all places and father only secondary.

The thought of mother as a goddess, it is turned into – Goddess as mother - we worship "*Ambāl - Ambikai*". When *Paramātma* form is thought as a mother more than any other form, the happiness overflows as bliss.

No matter how old are we, we become a baby to mother. We cling to absolute belief and surrender. To obtain the divine nature through the childish nature, we assume the *Paramātma* form into our mother. Hunger or any other desire we cling to the mother as '*amma*' – must hold her strongly.

If we presume *Paramātma* as a *Jagatjanani*, it is not that we enjoy something that does not exist. In fact, *Paramātma*, who is truly in love with all the qualities of the virtues, is the absolute motherhood. The *Paramātma* is everything, hence it blesses us in whatever form, we imagine. In the same way that *Parabrahmam* becomes a mother and with compassion, definitely it comes and satisfies our needs, when we pray, imagining it as a mother.

Why do we need a form when it is formless? We have a body, we are all born from that root, it is our mother, we are its children – as long as we have this in mind, we need a form for the Parabrahmam also. When we have matured enough to understand that we do not have a form – we are all *Atma* only – once we have realized this, we do not need any form or shape for the *Parabrahmam*.

We do not need to pray to *Devi*, "you give me this or that". Doesn't the mother know what to give to us, based on our eligibility? However, this is not the case in practice. We have not yet got that prudence. We have been asking, "Please give me this – give me that and so on". That is why we do puja, *Upasana*, *japam*, etc. This is also not wrong. But this cannot be a permanent one. We need to get out of the worldly pleasures and move on to eternal bliss. We need to Pray to Mother God this maturity also.

Sri Devi is;

- *Nāyaki* as **she** is the consort of *Lord Shiva*
- *Nānmukkī* as **she** is the consort of *Lord Brahma* (four faced)
- *Nārāyanī* as **she** is the consort of *Lord Narayanan*
- *Shāmbhavī*, holding five flowers in hand, the world's greenest greenery.
- *Varāhi*, who destroys bad elements
- *Shoolini* holding a trident (*shoolam*)
- *Mātangī*, the daughter of sage Matangar

Thus, **she** is worshipped with different names, different forms, different actions, etc. However, it is this same *Shakti*, who creates, protects, destroys, covers and blesses this world – thus **she** plays. The entire universe originated from **her** and merges with **her** at the end. The name *'Uma'* is same as the *Praṇava Mantra 'Om'*. *'Hrīm'* is the *Shākta Praṇava Mantra*.

It is the unique feature of our Hindu religion to pray the God treating as a mother of all the creatures. The knowledge about the mother God is called *Sri Vidya*. The knowledge about the *Brahmam* is called *Brahma Vidya*. The sages used to say both *Srividya* and *Brahmavidya* are one and the same. The *Paramatma* signified by *'Om'* in *Brahmavidya*, is signified by *'Hrīm'* in *Sri Vidya*. The root letter *'Hrīm* is called *Maya Bījam* (root letter) - *Bījam* means seed. The seed becomes a plant then becomes a *tree*. In the same manner the *Mahakali, Mahalakshmi* and *Mahasaraswati*, originate from this *Maya Bījam*.

The energy of the amorphous material is the female aspect. When the energy is formed, it becomes the mother. Swamy Vivekananda would say, "*Shakti* is the tidal wave in the calm waters of *Paramporul*". In the *Tantra Shastras*, the so-called *Shiva-Shakti* are respectively *Purusha-prakruti*, according to the Vedic system. In Advaita, they are called *Brahmam-Maya*. "By nature, both are the same. Every living thing is blissfully-sensitive" says Arthur Avalon.

The practice of worshipping god as a mother is not only in Hinduism but also in Vajrayana Buddhism and in Jainism.

The way of worshipping such *Ambika* is called *Srividya*. According to the *Srividya* practice of worship, it is very pleasing to Goddess *Sridevi*, if *Mahameru* or *Sri Chakra* Puja is performed.

Mahesha, Madhava, Vidhatru, Manmatha (Cupid), *Skanda, Nandi* (Bull God), *Indra, Manu, Chandra* (Moon), *Kubera, Agastya*, Lopamudra (wife of *Agastya*) and *Krota Bhattāraka* are the 12 major *Sri Vidya upasakas*. It is worth noting that Lord *Shiva* and *Vishnu* are also included in the list. They do not have any *gurus* (teachers). They only originated the method of worshipping *Sri Devi*.

The mother of all the *Yantras* or *Chakras* is the *Sri Chakra*. The word *'Sri'* is a symbol of greatness, passion and great prosperity.

Adi Shankarar, all over the Bharat that he visited, made everyone feel the pride of *Sri Chakra* and the cult of *Srividya*. Although seemingly he equally treated all the deities, he seems to have given importance to the worship of *Shakti*. He has gracefully authored commentary to *Sri Lalita Trishati* and also given us the noble beings of the *Soundaryalahari*.

*****

Śākta **Texts**

There are many texts related to *Shāktam*. Some of these are listed below. This is not a comprehensive list. Some of the important texts are recorded.

- *Tantra Rāja Tantram*
- *Vāmakeshwara Tantram* (part of *Nityā Shodashikārnavam*)
- *Kulārnavam*
- *Jnānārnavam*
- *Tattātreya Samhita*
- *Sharadā Tilakam*
- *Prapancha Sāram* (By *Adi Shankarar*)
- *Paramānanda Tantram*
- *Chitkagana Candrika*
- *Panchāshtavam* (by *Kālidāsa*)
- *Shakti Mahimnā Stotram*
- *Lalita Stavaratnam* (By *Doorvāsa*)
- *Parashurāma Kalpa Sootram*
- *Tripurā Rahasyam*
- *Srividya Ratna Sutra*-s (By *Sri Gowdabādar*)
- *Soundaryalaharī* (By *Adi Shankarar*)
- *Sri Lalita Sahasranamam* and *Sri Lalita Trishatī* – mid of *Brahmānda Puranam*
- *Sri Devi Bhagavatam*
- *Sri Devi Narayanīyam* – abridged form of *Sri Devi Bhagavatam* - By Pāleli Sri Narayana Namboothiri – with 41 *Dashakams* and 430 verses
- *Sri Devi Khadgamala Stotram* – amidst *Sri Vāmakeshwara Tantram* as a dialogue between *Uma* and *Maheswar*
- *Varivasya Rahasyam* (commentary for *Sri Lalita Sahasranamam* by *Sri Bhāskararāya*[4])
- *Gowrī Tantram* amidst *Rudra Yāmalam*
- Commentary for *Sri Lalita Trishatī* by *Adi Shankarar*[5]
- *Kāmakalā Vilāsam*

---

[4] The author of this book has translated this commentary into English as a separate book.

[5] The author of this book has translated this commentary into English and Tamil as separate books.

- *Sri Vidya Tantram*
- Lot many *Suktas* within *Rig Veda* like *Sri Suktam, Durga Suktam, Bhagya Suktam, Saraswathi Suktam, Sri Devi Suktam*, etc.
- *Sri Devi Bhāgavata Mahatmyam* amidst *Sri Skanda Purāṇam*.
- *Sri Devi Māhātmyam* amidst *Sri Mārkandeya Purāṇam*.
- Tantric Texts (around 22) by Sir John Woodroffe (Arthur Avalon)
- 33 *Shākta Upaniṣats* as listed below.

#	*Veda*	*Upaniṣat*
Popular *Upaniṣats*		
1.	*Rig Veda*	*Bahvrochopaniṣats* *
2.		*Tripuropaniṣats*
3.		*Sowbhāgya Lakshmi Upaniṣat*
4.	*Krishna Yajur Veda*	*Saraswathi Rahasya Upaniṣat*
5.	*Sama Veda*	*Ārunikopaniṣats*
6.	*Atharva Veda*	*Arunopaniṣats* *
7.		*Sitopaniṣats* *
8.		*Sri Devi Atharva Shīrsham or Sri Devi Upaniṣat* *
9.		*Annapoornopaniṣats*
10.		*Tripurā Tāpinīya Upaniṣat*
11.		*Bhāvanopaniṣats*
Not so Popular *Upaniṣats*		
12.	*Atharva Veda*	*Atharvashikopaniṣats* *
13.		*Sri Chakra Upaniṣat* *
14.		*Atharva Dvitīya Upaniṣat*
15.		*Alla Upaniṣat*
16.		*Kāmarāja Kīlidottāra Upaniṣat*
17.		*Gāyatri Upaniṣat*
18.		*Gāyatri Rahasya Upaniṣat*
19.		*Kālikā Upaniṣat*
20.		*Kālī Medādīkshita Upaniṣat*
21.		*Guhyakālī Upaniṣat*
22.		*Guhya Shodānyāsa Upaniṣat*
23.		*Tulasi Upaniṣat*
24.		*Pītāmbara Upaniṣat*
25.		*Muktikopaniṣats*

#	Veda	Upaniṣat
26.	*Atharva Veda*	*Rājashyāmalā Rahasya Upaniṣat*
27.		*Vanadurgā Upaniṣat*
28.		*Sāvitri Upaniṣat*
29.		*Sumukhya Upaniṣat*
30.		*Shyāma Upaniṣat*
31.		*Sri Vidyātāraka Upaniṣat*
32.		*Shodasha Upaniṣat*
33.		*Hamsashodasha Upaniṣat*

* The commentaries for these 6 *Upaniṣats*, alongwith mantras both in Samskrutam and English are given as separate chapters. The verses/ mantras both in English and Samskrutam have been provided. The commentaries are not readily available. Probably they will be included in next editions.

It is apparent, in many ways, that *Sri Adi Shankarar* gave great importance to *Shāktam*. Let us look at just a few examples. We may know by a handful the whole sack.

The writings of *Sri Adi Shankarar* include *Soundaryalaharī*, which is the epitome of the philosophy of the religion. It has 100 verses.

From the very words of Kanchi *Paramacharya* - *Sri Adi Shankarar* files an allegation on *Ambal* of stealing, in the 25th verse of his *Soundaryalahari*;

I mean - I close my eyes and try to meditate on you. I expected half male and half female body (*Ardhanārīshwara* form), because Lord *Parameshwara* has already given his half body to you. But you were seen in full female form – stealing the remaining half body also of Lord *Parameshwara* and seen in full female form.

As a young child, Thirugnana Sambandar started singing Thevāram "God with an ear ring" while singing the hymn of God. It was then itself, that he realized the Arddhanārīshwara form - the Siva-Shakti unified form.

Even in the very first verse of *Soundaryalaharī*, *Adi Shankara* says - It is only if the Lord *Mahadeva* is joined with you, the Supreme Being, he gets the power to make the universe. Otherwise he does not even be able to get the energy to move in the gutter. If that is the case with *Mahadeva*, how about deities like *Vishnu, Rudran, Brahma* and so on. Only with virtues of earlier births one can be able to worship you.

In the same way, in the 4th verse of *Soundaryalaharī*, he says – ordinarily Gods show the non-fearing and boon signets through their hands. But you display the signets through your legs in the dancing posture. Because your golden feet are the ones capable of saving the devotees from fear and giving them more than asked for.

Similar to *Soundaryalaharī, Sri Adi Shankara* has also written 100 verses on *Lord Shiva* called *'Sivānandalaharī'*. *Sri Adi Shankara* has never praised Lord *Shiva* in his *Soundaryalaharī*. On the other hand, he talks about *Devi* in the very first verse of *Sivānandalaharī*. He says *pranāms* to Lord *Shiva* and his consort *Sri Devi*. Our Holy Mother (*Shivā*) is the repository of all knowledge, the arts, and the offers benefits of all. She is the offer of greatest blessing. She raises again and again in my heart and spreads highest happiness. Even when he wants to talk about the father, he could not forget mother.

In the same way, in the 61st verse of the same *Sivānandalaharī* he says – the minds of the devotees are attracted, becomes dependent, and merges together, towards the lotus feet of the *Sri Devi* alongwith *Pashupati*. He gives various comparisons in this regard – how the seeds of *Angola* tree are attracted back towards the tree – how a needle is attracted by a magnet – how a *Sumangali* lady is attracted towards her loving husband – how climbers are dependent on the trees – how the rivers merge themselves in the oceans.

In the 7th verse of *Devi Aparādha Kshamāpana Stotram* written by *Sri Adi Shankarar*, he says – only because he is wedded to you, he gets the role of *Jagadīshan* (Lord of this universe). Otherwise, he was just a watchman in a burial ground having the garland of skulls and the ashes throughout the body.

In this way, we can read 'n' number of examples. *Sri Adi Shankarar*, continues to compare Lord *Shiva* and *Sri Devi* – both wear the crescent moon on the crown. Both do not have origin neither end. Both are merged as two soul and a single body.

Kālidāsa, the greatest Samskruta poet declares, Lord *Shiva* and *Sri Devi* as the parent of the universe – he does not say that they are mother and father – but addresses with a single word 'Parent' – "*Jagata Pitarou*".

In our houses also, even though small children have a great respect towards their father, they do not take that much right as they take with their mother. In the same fashion, we, the children of our mother of universe take lots of rights with **her.** We cannot take comparatively that much rights with Lord *Shiva*.

Therefore, the elders have said that the *Shākta Upasana* is the transcendental device to attain liberation. We also feel it in many ways. Thus, let us all continue to worship *Sri Devi* and live a life of prosperity.

This in no way mean that worshipping the other deities is being belittled. *Shākta* worship is an easy tool for moksha. Further, all the gods are one and the same - only one. Whatever form of deity pleases him, let him worship that god and attain all kinds of attractions.

*****

Bahvruchopaniṣats

बह्वृचोपनिषत्

This *Bahvruchopaniṣats* belongs to *Rig Veda*. This has nine *mantras*, Praising the greatness of the Goddess *Sri Devi*.

It is normal practice to chant *Śānti Mantraḥ* before any *Veda Mantra* and ends with the same. Depending on the Veda and practice in that region the *Śānti Mantraḥ* may vary.

शान्ति मन्त्रः । *Śānti Mantraḥ* ।

ॐ वाङ्मे मनसि प्रतिष्ठिता । मनो मे वाचि प्रतिष्ठितम् ।

Om Vāngme Manasi Pratiṣṭitā I *Mano Me Vāci Pratiṣṭitam* I

आविरावीर्म एधि । वेदस्य म आणीस्थः । श्रुतं मे मा प्रहासीः ।

Āvirāvīrma Edhi I *Vedasya Ma Āṇīsthaḥ* I *Śrutam Me Mā Prahāsīḥ* I

अनेनाधीतेनाहोरात्रान्सन्दधामि । ऋतं वदिष्यामि ।

Anenādhī Tenāhorātrānsandadhāmi I *Rutam Vadhiṣyāmi* I

सत्यं वदिष्यामि । तन्मामवतु । तद्वक्तारमवतु ।

Satyam Vadhiṣyāmi I *Tanmāmavatu* I *Tadvaktāramavatu* I

अवतु माम् । अवतु वक्तारम् । अवतु वक्तारम् ।

Avatu Mām I *Avatu Vaktāram* I *Avatu Vaktāram* I

ॐ शान्तिः शान्तिः शान्तिः II *Oṃ Śāntiḥ Śāntiḥ Śāntiḥ* II

बह्वृचाख्य ब्रह्म विद्या महा खण्डार्थ वैभवम् ।

Bahvrucākhya Brahma Vidyā Mahākhaṇḍārtha Vaibhavam I

अखण्डानन्दसाम्राज्यं रामचन्द्रपदं भजे ॥

Akhaṇḍā Nanda Sāmrājyam Rāmacandra Padam Bhaje ॥

हरिः ॐ ॥ *Hariḥ Oṃ* ॥

1. देवी ह्येकाग्र एवासीत् । सैव जगदण्डमसृजत् ।

Devī Hyekāgra Evāsīt । *Saiva Jagadaṇḍamasṛjat* ।

कामकलेति विज्ञायते । शृंगारकलेति विज्ञायते ॥

Kāmakaleti Vijñāyate । *Śṛṃgārakaleti Vijñāyate* ॥

The form of *Chitshakti* is being explained here. It is that *Devi*, who created this dynamic and static world through her glory. That greatest is the *Chitshakti*. **She** was the only one who existed before the even appearance of the world. **She** is the creator of the universe. **She** is known by the *Upasakas* as *Kamakala* due to her *saguna* feature. **She** is also known as *Shrungaarakala* because of the shape of the *Ardha-Maatra*, like the peak of *Akaara-Makaara-Ukaara*-s.

2. तस्या एव ब्रह्मा अजीजनत् । विष्णुरजीजनत् ।

Tasyā Eva Brahmā Ajījanat । *Viṣṇurajījanat* ।

रुद्रोऽजीजनत् । सर्वे मरुद्गणा अजीजनत् ।

Rudro'jījanat । *Sarve Marudgaṇā Ajījanat* ।

गन्धर्वाप्सरसः किन्नरा वादित्रवादिनः समन्तादजीजनत् ।

Gandharvāpsarasaḥ Kinnarā Vāditravādinaḥ Samantādajījanat ।

भोग्यमजीजनत्। सर्वमजीजनत् । सर्वं शाक्तमजीजनत् ।

Bhogyamajījanat । *Sarvamajījanat* । *Sarvaṃ Śāktamajījanat* ।

अण्डजं स्वेदजमुद्भिज्जं जरायुजम् यत्किंचैतत्

Aṇḍajaṃ Svedajamudbhijjaṃ Jarāyujam Yatkiṃcaitat

प्राणि स्थावरजंगमं मनुष्यमजीजनत् ॥

Prāṇi Sthāvarajaṃgamaṃ Manuṣyamajījanat ॥

The origin of *Brahma* and the like is attributed to the *Chitshakti*. *Brahma* was created by that Chitshakti. Likewise, *Vishnu*, *Shiva* and all kinds of *Maruts*, *Gandharvas*, *Apsaras*, *Kinneras*, rhythmists and singers and all the enjoyments appearing in this world. All the motives for this power were there. *Andjajam* (from the egg), *Uppijjam* (from the earth), *Swetajajam* (from the sweating), *Irajujam* (from the nucleus), etc., which are the objects of the universe, with *prana*.

3. सैषा परा शक्तिः । सैषा शांभवीविद्या

Saiṣā Parā Śaktiḥ I *Saiṣā Śāṃbhavīvidyā*

कादिविद्येति वा हादिविद्येति वा सादिविद्येति वा । रहस्यमोमों वाचि प्रतिष्ठा ॥

Kādividyeti Vā Hādividyeti Vā Sādividyeti Vā I

Rahasyamomom Vāci Pratiṣṭhā II

This *mantra* says – that *Chitshakti* is the one in the form of the meaning for all sounds. That great one is the *Paraashakti*. **She** is in the form of the first one-third part of *Sri Panchadashaaksharee mantra*, called *Kaadhi vidya*. This *mantra* is connecting *Sri Devi* and *Lord Shiva*. **She** is also in the form of the second one-third part of *Sri Pancha-dashaaksharee mantra*, called *Haadhi vidya* and **She** is again in the form of the third one-third part of *Sri Panchadashaaksharee mantra*, called *Saadhi vidya* as well. **She** is in the form of the most secret *Parabrahmam*. **She** is also in the form of the *Pranavam*. **She** is again in the form of the *Vaag* originated from *Pranavam* and the permanently in the form of the meaning of the *Vaag* also.

5. सैव पुरत्रयं शरीरत्रयं व्याप्य बहिरन्तरवभासयन्ती

Saiva Puratrayaṃ Śarīratrayaṃ Vyāpya Bahirantaravabhāsayantī

देशकालवस्त्वन्तरसंगान्महात्रिपुरसुन्दरीवै प्रत्यक्चितिः ॥

Deśakālavastvantarasaṃgānmahātripurasundarī Vai Pratyakcitiḥ ॥

That energy (*shakti*) called *Chit*, is differently showing as individual, group and individual-group – all the three types of bodies *Stoola*, *Sookshma* and *Beejam*. **She** is shining both inside and outside of the three bodies. Still **she** shines alone and has no connection with time, place and thing. Hence, **she** is called as *Mahaa Tripura Sundaree*, who is in the form of knowledge.

Since, **she** is the ignorance in all the three bodies and she is involved in all the activities of the bodies, **she** is aptly called great (*mahaa*) and called as *Mahaa Tripura Sundaree*.

5. सैवात्मा ततोऽन्यमसत्यमनात्मा । अत एषा ब्रह्मासंवित्तिर्भावभावकलाविनिर्मुक्ता चिद्विद्याऽद्वितीय ब्रह्मसंवित्तिः सच्चिदानन्द

Saivātmā Tato'nyamasatyamanātmā । *Ata Eṣā Brahmā saṃvittir bhava bhava kalāvi nirmuktā Cidvidyā'dvitīya Brahmasaṃvittiḥ Saccidānanda*

लहरी महात्रिपुरसुन्दरी बहिरन्तरनुप्रविश्य स्वयमेकैव विभाति ।

LaharīMahātripurasundarī Bahirantaranupraviśya Svayamekaiva Vibhāti

यदस्ति सन्मात्रम् । यद्विभाति चिन्मात्रम् ।

Yadasti Sanmātram । *Yadvibhāti Cinmātram* ।

यत्प्रियमानन्दं तदेतत् पूर्वाकारा महात्रिपुरसुन्दरी ।

Yatpriyamānandaṃ Tadetat Pūrvākārā Mahātripurasundarī ।

त्वं चाहं च सर्वं विश्वं सर्वदेवता इतरत् सर्वं महात्रिपुरसुन्दरी ।

Tvaṃ Cāhaṃ Ca Sarvaṃ Viśvaṃ Sarvadevatā Itarat Sarvaṃ Mahātripurasundarī ।

सत्यमेकं ललिताख्यं वस्तु तदद्वितीयमखण्डार्थं परं ब्रह्म ॥

Satyamekaṃ Lalitākhyaṃ Vastu Tadadvitīyamakhaṇḍārthaṃ Paraṃ Brahma ॥

It is advised here that *Chitshakti* herself is a no-two Advaita. That *Chitshakti* is the soul form. Nothing else is more true than this *Chit*; Not even the soul; Therefore, **she** is the knowledge of *Brahmam*. **She** is the embodiment of the enlightenment and the art of being and non-existence. The *Mahaa Tripura Sundari* is also known as the flowing form of *Sat-Chit-Aanandam*. **She** is a self-proclaimed person, both outside and inside creation. Whatever substance is, it is *Sat*. Whatever shines is the *Chit*. Whatever is dear it is the pleasure (*Aanandam*).

It is conceived that *Sri Maha Tripura Sundari* is the form of the universal universe. And you and I, all the worlds, all the angels and all others are in the form of the *Sri Maha Tripura Sundari*. The name Lalita is also the same. That object is non-dual - the metaphorical form. It is that *Brahmam* excelling all things.

6. पञ्चरूपपरित्यागा दर्वरूपप्रहाणतः ।

Pañcarūpaparityāgā Darvarūpaprahāṇataḥ ।

अधिष्ठानं परं तत्त्वमेकं सच्छिष्यते महत् ॥ इति ॥

Adhiṣṭhānaṃ Paraṃ Tattvamekaṃ Sacchiṣyate Mahat ॥ *Iti* ॥

The most powerful philosophy, *Sat* and *Mahat*, is an object of love and merging with the Goddess. Therefore, the only thing that stands out above all else is the remains of *Sat*.

7. प्रज्ञानं ब्रह्मेति वा अहं ब्रह्मास्मीति वा भाष्यते ।

Prajñānaṃ Brahmeti Vā Ahaṃ Brahmāsmīti Vā Bhāṣyate ।

तत्त्वमसीत्येव संभाष्यते । *Tattvamasītyeva Saṃbhāṣyate* ।

अयमात्मा ब्रह्मेति वा ब्रह्मैवाहमस्मीति वा ॥

Ayamātmā Brahmeti Vā Brahmaivāhamasmīti Vā ॥

Brahma, Vishnu, Rudran, Eeshvaran and *Sadashiivan*, the five fives, are in a state of misery and are in the fourth stage, but still with qualities (*saguna*).

To enable them to perform their five duties, they have the energy (*shakti*) in the form of *Vaani*, *Ramaa*, *Uma*, *Samanaa* and *Ummanaa* respectively. Their activities, *Srushti, Stiti, Samhaaram, Aaviribaavam* and *Thirobhavam* cannot take place without these energies. Without the energies they are in *saguna* form. They are all slaves to the power called *Tureeya*.

शान्ति मन्त्रः । *Śānti Mantraḥ* ।

ॐ वाङ्मे मनसि प्रतिष्ठिता । मनो मे वाचि प्रतिष्ठितम् ।

Om Vāngme Manasi Pratiştitā I *Mano Me Vāci Pratiştitam* I

आविरावीर्म एधि । वेदस्य म आणीस्थः । श्रुतं मे मा प्रहासीः ।

Āvirāvīrma Edhi I *Vedasya Ma Āṇīsthaḥ* I *Śrutam Me Mā Prahāsīḥ* I

अनेनाधीतेनाहोरात्रान्सन्दधामि । ऋतं वदिष्यामि ।

Anenādhī Tenāhorātrānsandadhāmi I *Rutam Vadhişyāmi* I

सत्यं वदिष्यामि । तन्मामवतु । तद्वक्तारमवतु ।

Satyam Vadhişyāmi I *Tanmāmavatu* I *Tadvaktāramavatu* I

अवतु माम् । अवतु वक्तारम् । अवतु वक्तारम् ।

Avatu Mām I *Avatu Vaktāram* I *Avatu Vaktāram* I

ॐ शान्तिः शान्तिः शान्तिः ॥ *Oṃ Śāntiḥ Śāntiḥ Śāntiḥ* ॥

॥ Thus ends *Bahvruchopanişats* ॥

Arunopaniṣats

अरुणोपनिषत्

This *Arunopaniṣats* is a small *Upaniṣat*, explaining the *shaktis* (energies) of *Sri Devi* called *Arunaa*. It is in the midst of the *Taitreeya Aaranyaka* of *Krishna Yajur Veda*. The 27th *Anuvaakam* of *Aruna Prashnam* also called as *Surya Namaskara Mantra* is given as a separate *Upaniṣat* with 25 *mantras*.

With the intention of everyone to grasp the gist of this *Upaniṣat*, it has been nicely explained in *Rudra Yaamalam*, how the sages called *Prushnis* worshipped *Sri Arunaa Devi*;

प्रश्नयो नाम मुनयः सर्वे चक्रसमाश्रयाः । सेवमानाश्चक्रविद्यां देवगन्धर्व पूजिताम् ॥

Praśnayo Nāma Munayaḥ Sarve Cakrasamāśrayāḥ ।

Sevamānāścakravidyām Devagandharva Pūjitām ॥

अग्नीषोमात्मकं चक्रमग्नीषोममयं जगत् । अह्नावन्तर्बभौ बानुरघीषोममयं स्मृतम् ॥

AgnīşOmātmakam CakramagnīşOmamayam Jagat ।

Ahnāvantarbabhou BānuraghīşOmamayam smrutam ॥

त्रिखण्डं मातृकाचक्रम् सोमसूर्यानलात्मकम् ।

Trikhanḍam mātrukācakram SOmasūryānalātmakam ।

त्रिकोणं बैन्दवं सौम्यमष्टकोणं च मिश्रकम् ॥

Trikoṇam Baindavam Soumyamaşţakoṇam Ca Miśrakam ॥

चक्रं चन्द्रमयं चैव दशारद्वितयं तथा । चतुर्दशारं वह्नेस्तु चतुश्चक्रं च भानुमत् ॥

Cakram Candramayam Caiva Daśāradvitayam Tathā ।

Caturdaśāram Vahnestu catuścakram Ca Bhānumat ॥

एतत्प्रसादादिन्द्राद्या वसवोऽष्टौ मरुद्गणाः ।

Etatprasādādindrādyā VasavoşStou Marudgaṇāḥ ।

ये ये समृद्धा लोकेऽस्मिन् त्रिपुराचक्रसेवका ॥
Ye Ye Samruddhā LokeSsmin Tripurācakrasevakā ॥

पुरत्रयं च चक्रस्य सोमसूर्यानलात्मकम् ।
Puratrayam Ca Cakrasya SOmasūryānalātmakam ।

महालक्ष्म्या: पुरं चक्रं तत्रैवास्ते सदाशिव: ॥
Mahālakśmyāḥ Puram Cakram Tatraivāste Sadāśivaḥ ॥

The *Prashni* sages, who surrendered the *Chakras*, started to do *Upasana* of the *Sri Chakra*, which was worshipped by *Devas* and *Gandharvas*. This entire world is in form of Fire (*Agni*) and Moon (*Chandran*). Since, the Sun is in contained within *Agni*, it is called as *Agnieeshomeeyam*.

The *Sri Chakra* is in three parts – in the form of Moon, Sun and Fire. The organs of *Sri Chakra* viz., *Triangular chakra* and *Bindu Chakra* are in the form of Moon. *Ashtakona* (Eight cornered) *Chakra* is *Mishram*, i.e. in the combined form of both Sun and Moon. Thus, the two *Dashakona* (ten cornered) *chakras* are in the form of Moon. *Chaturdasharam* (14 cornered) is in the form of Fire and the remaining four are in the form of Sun.

By the blessings of *Sri Chakra Vidya Upasana*, all the devas including *Indra*, Eight *Vasus*, Seven *Maruts* and all reached the dwelling place of *Sri Devi*. And the ones who has attained complete perfection in this world is the art of *Sri Tripura Sundari*. Moon-Sun-Fire also live in the abode of the Sri Mahalakshmi. *Sadashiivan* also lives there.

Since this small *Upaniṣat* describes the glories of *Sri Arunaa Devi*, it is called *Arunopaniṣats*. Also, it is told that, this was originally found out by a sage called *Arunaketu* and hence it is called as *Arunopaniṣats*.

1. इमानुकं भुवना सीषधेम ॥ *Imānukam Bhuvanā Sīşadhema* ॥

The concept is that we (the *Upaniṣats*) feel that these worlds are in a state of devotion to the *Sri Chakra* Ritual. Or we may mean this three-wheeler

Vicaram-Vimarsham-Pariseelanam, system globally and that we are hearing-critical.

2. इन्द्रश्च विश्वे च देवा: ॥ *Indraśca Viśve ca Devāḥ* ॥

Indra and *Vishvedevas* were upheld by surrendering to this *Sri Chakra Vidya*.

3. यज्ञं च नस्ततन्वं च प्रजां च । आदित्यैरिन्द्र: सह सीषधातु ॥
Yajnam Ca Nastanvanḥ Ca Prajān Ca । *Ādityairindraḥ Saha Sīşadhātu* ॥

Indra, who has practiced this *Sri Chakra Vidya* and achieved all the wealth with the *Adityas*. Let him teach us this *Vidya*, the fire-rituals (*yagas*) like *Agnishtomam*, etc. Let us earn, the wife – who is half of my body, children, friends, pouches and other gatherings.

4. आदित्यैरिन्द्र: सगणो मरुद्भि: । अस्माकं भूत्ववितता तनूनाम् ॥
Ādityairindraḥ Sagaṇo Marudbhiḥ । *Asmākam Bhūtvavitā Tanūnām* ॥

Indra with *Adityas, Maruts* and all goddesses, let us guard our spouse, our people, cows, friends and all other wealth.

5. आप्लवस्व प्रप्लवस्व । *Āplavasva Praplavasva* ।

Oh Mother! Please soak us from head to toe with the rain of nectar. And soak our 72,000 nerves in our body with your nectar.

6. आण्डी भव ज मा मुहु: ॥ *Āṇḍī Bhava Ja Mā Muhuḥ* ॥

My body is made of fetus and the egg (*Pindaandam*). Yours is made of the greatest (*Brahmaandam*) universes. Hence, please give me the status of your immortal bliss, which is a form of *saayujya*. You will feel this prayer of mine often.

7. सुखादीन्दु: खनिधनाम् ॥ *Sukhādīnduḥ Khanidhanām* ॥

This *mantra* can have many meanings; The word "*Sukhādīndu*" can mean pleasure or enjoyment. *Indu* – Moon is the one who bestows the thrills. Hence the word *Chandran* (Moon) means place of *Baindavasthanam* – the *Bindu*.

Similarly, the letter *'ka'* in *Kanidanaam* also means *Baindavam*. *'ni'* - meaning continuation of the prefix - always means. *Dhanam* - means wealth. Therefore, *"Sukhādīnduḥ Khanidhanām"* means the occurrence of *Baindavastanam* is the ceaseless place of *Sridevi*.

Or the term *'Sukhaadim'* may mean "the first". Or **She** is in the form of happiness; It can mean the goddess defeating the misfortune – is attributed to the word "*Dukhanidhanām*" is the *Khanidhanām*.

Therefore, the notion that the Supreme Being is the embodiment of happiness and the destroyer of sorrow, or the absence of sorrow.

The letter *'su'* in the phrase *'Sukhaadeem'*, may mean propitious – in the form of auspicious – *'kham'* means organ that is mind. *Aadeem* means the first to expose - It is said that **She** is the first senses of the mind. It is, therefore, first known by the eye. Similarly, *Dukanithanam* means destruction and the letter *'tu'* in the sentence is evil, and *'k'* means the organ, *'Nithanam'* can also mean that **She** cannot be identified by the evil senses such as eyes, ears and mind.

8. प्रतिमुञ्चस्व स्वां पुरम् ll *Pratimuncasva Svām Puram* ll

The sense communicated here is that you get the dwelling place of *Sri Paraashakti*. It means that you have to imagine that you and *Sri Devi* are one and the same.

9. मरीचय: स्वायं भुवा: ll *Marīcayaḥ Svāyam Bhuvāḥ*: ll

The spontaneous illumination from the Goddess encompasses all the earth. *Soma-Surya-Agni*, get their illumination from the rays of this *Shakti* only.

10. ये शरीराण्य कल्पयन् ll *Ye Śarīrāṇya Kalpayan* ll

The rays that originate from the presence of *Sri Paraashakti* have the count of time viz. 360. Hence, we have a year having 360 days. The essence of the Goddess of the time is that the goddess is in the form of the year, *ayanam*, *rudu*, month, *paksha*, day, etc.

11. ते ते देहं कल्पयन्तु ॥ *Te Te Deham Kalpayantu* ॥

May all of these ecstasies be blessed with *Sridevi's* divine form. The word *'Deha'* in this place is meant to be the feet, an organ of the body of *Devi*. It is therefore conceivable that these rays originated from the divine lotus feet of *Sri Devi*.

12. मा च ते क्यास्म तीरिषत् ॥ *Mā Ca Te Khyāsma Tīriṣat* ॥

May the glory of thy body not always ignore us. The idea of staying with us is not always ignored.

It is explained by this *mantra* that *Sri Vidya* should be followed with the concentration and effort.

13. उत्तिष्ट मा स्वप्त । अग्निमिच्छध्वं भारता: । राज्ञ: सोमस्य तृप्तास: ।
सूर्येण सयुजोषस:

Uttiṣṭa Mā Svapta I *Agnimichchadhvam Bhāratāḥ* I

Rājnaḥ Somasya Truptāsaḥ I *Sūryeṇa Sayujoṣasaḥ* II

Oh *Upasakas*! you are in the form of the light of the *Sri Chakra Vidya*. (*Bhaaratao*: the term can be interpreted as *upaasakas* of *Sri Vidya mantra*). You wake up. Begin the *Upaasana*. Do not neglect.

By this mantra, the *Prashni* sages teach puja devices;

14. युवा सुवासा: ॥ *Yuvā Suvāsāḥ* ॥

It is conceivable that one who is bound, i.e. who is healthy, observes the celibacy and practices sincerity, who wears pure white garments, wears pure ornaments and garlands has to perform the *upaasana* (worship).

This mantra explains the format of *Sri Chakra*[6];

15. अष्टाचक्रा नवद्वारा ॥ *Aşţācakrā Navadvārā* ॥

The format of Sri Chakra is being described here. Eight triangles, two ten cornered, 14 four cornered, 8 petaled, 14 petaled, three circular lines, and three *Bhoopuras* (border lines) – thus alongwith eight chakras and nine entrances.

16. देवानां पूरयोध्या ॥ *Devānām Pūrayodhyā* ॥

The marvelous city of *Srividya* is illuminated forms of the 25 philosophical wonders (dwelling) of the Sun, the Moon, Agni, etc., because they are worshiped by the gods like Indra, etc. The marvelous city of fire forms, *Thejomurti*. That is to say that the tricycle is a form of sunspot. It is therefore necessary to know that the singularity of the word *Ayodhya* is used in conjunction with the three *Bhoopuras* in *Sri Chakra*. Ayodhya here means that no one can attain the position of *Sridevi*.

17. तस्यां हिरण्मयः कोशः । स्वर्गो लोको ज्योतिषावृतः ॥
Tasyām Hiraṇmayaḥ Kośaḥ । *Svargo Loko Jyotişāvrutaḥ* ॥

In the middle of the city of *Srividya* - the center of a thousand petalled lotus - that is, the *Baindavastanam*. The 1000 petalled sheath is surrounded by the astrological *Jyotisha Swargaloka*. Here the heaven is referred to as the astral world.

In this *mantra*, the fruit of *Sri Vidya upasana* is explained;

18. यो वै तां ब्रह्मणो वेद । अमृतेनावृतां पुरीम् ।
Yo Vai Tām Brahmaṇo Veda । *Amrutenāvrutām Purīm* ।

तस्मै ब्रह्म च ब्रह्मा च । आयुः कीर्तिं प्रजां ददुः ॥
Tasmai Brahma Ca Brahmā Ca । *Āyuḥ Kīrtim Prajām Daduḥ* ॥

---

[6] The author of this book has written a book ***"Śree Chakra - An Esoteric Approach"*** explaining the mathematical construction to draw *Sri Chakra*.

The *Upasaka*, who realizes the city of *Srividya*, the formerly mentioned, surrounded by the image of the *Parabrahma* form of *Sridevi* alongwith *Sadaashiva*, as already mentioned, as gives long life, glory, children and prosperity.

The two '*ca*-s' mentioned here means *Shiva-Shakti* unison. The couple, who live in *Chintaamani* house, in the midst of the Amruta (nectar) Ocean in the thousand petalled Lotus in the Baindavasthanam, have given themselves a long life, widespread fame and growing prosperity.

19. विभ्राजमानां हरिणीम् । यशसा संपरीवृताम् ।

Vibhrājamānām Hariṇīm | *Yaśasā Samparīvrutām* |

पुरं हिरण्मयीं ब्रह्मा । विवेशापराजिता ॥

Puram Hiraṇmayīm Brahmā || *Viveşāparājitā* |

Sadaashivan entered the *Chintamani* house, which is shining like gold and well-surrounded. *Sridevi*, a moonlike form of *Saadaa* (also entered). Previously it was mentioned that, the Chintamani house was surrounded by gold and glory, it is believed that **he** is living with *Sridevi*.

Vibraajamaanam means countless millions of rays. Whatever things are famous in this world for being *Yashas* (pride), they are all meant to be the blessings of *Sridevi*. *Harineem* means the substance of the *Sree Sooktam* "*Hiranyavarnaam Harineem* ..." to mean the dream. *Brahma* means the masculinity described in the verse "*Brahma Shivo Me Astu SadhaashiOm*", which emphasizes that *Brahma* is the same thing as *Brahma* and *Sadaashiva*.

The verb 'pravesh' is used for both sentences. Therefore, it is often said that Sri *Sadaashivan* always resides in the Chintamani house in *Baindavasthanam*. The *Kundalinee* energy called as *Aparaajitaa* or *Saadaa* often breaks the six chakras and reaches the *Baindavastaanam*.

In this *mantra*, the status of *Shiva-Shakti* in the *Baindava chakra* is explained.

20. पराङे त्यज्यामयी । पराङे त्ययनाशकी ॥

Parānge Tyajyāmayī | *Parānge Tyayanāśakī* ||

Downward *Shakti* triangles[7] indicate that **She** is immortal, i.e., eternal and is in the form of pleasure. Or in the phrase *Ajyaamayee-jyaa-bhoOmi* – the word earth indicates all five elements, hence *panchabhootas* are available. The letter *'a'* in the word *Ajyaamayee* gives negative sense.

Therefore, there are those who are above the philosophical form of the five-elements and the rhythmic *Chakras*, being the opposite of the lower part of the pillar, are the form of the four *yoni*-s of the divine force. *Anaaskakee* = immortal, the five *Yoni*-s, the form of the *Shakti Chakras*, are the downward looking and the *Paraang* = Upward facing – the *Shiva-Yonis* and the downward facing are the *Shakti Yonis*. Thus the *Shiva-Shakti* yonis are mutually portrayal of the rhythm and the octaveon.

In this mantra, the benefit of those who are enlightened by *Srividya Upasana*;

21. इह चामुत्र चान्वेति । विद्वान् देवासुरानु भयान् ॥

Iha Chāmutra Chānveti | *Vidvān Devāsurānu Bhayān* ||

Here the word *Deva* (Gods) has to be construed to mean 11 organs and the word *Asuraa*: (Demons) has to be construed to mean 5 gases (*Praanan* and others). Hence the *maayaa* both in the form of Devas and Demons, hides *Shuddha Vidya*, *Maheshwara*, *Sadashiva*-s and the 25 philosophies. The upaasaka, realizing the hidden philosophies and further the 26th philosophy, which is the unison of *Shiva-shakti*, enjoys in this world and also gets the liberation to reach other world – *Saaloka*, *Saameepya* and *Saayujya* – reaching the other world, goes near and merges with the *Brahmam*.

This mantra advises both the knowledge of Gods and Demons;

22. यत्कुमारी मन्द्रयते । यद्योषिद्यत्पतिव्रता ।

---

[7] In the *Sri Chakra*, upward triangles are considered to be male (*Shiva*) triangles and downward are female (*Shakti*) triangles.

Yatkumārī Mandrayate I *Yadyoşidyatpativratā* I

अरिष्टं यत् किं च क्रियते । अग्निस्तदनुवेधति ॥

Ariştam Yat Kim Ca Kriyate I *Agnistadanuvedhati* II

There are three different stages of the sound viz. – *mantra, madhyama* and *taara*. The *Kundalinee* energy also goes through The three different stages. This is being explained here. In the *Sri Chakra*, the *Kundalinee* energy is in the childhood stage. It gets up from sleep and wakes up the *mantra svara*. This is the first stage. Hence when we wake up in the morning we could hear a mild sound and that is the mild *mantra svara* of *Kundalinee* energy. This could be felt by anyone, in general.

Again the *Kundalinee* energy makes a sound after reaching the *Vishnu Granti* (knot). It has been mentioned in *Sanatkumara Samhita* also that *Kundalinee* energy makes a sound after reaching the *Vishnu Granti* from its original place. This is the second stage.

Further, the same *Kundalinee* energy reaches the *Sahasraaram* – the 1000 petalled lotus, unifies with *Sadaashivan*, enjoys the nectar and does other activies. These are followed by *Kundalinee* fire right from its place *Moolaadhaaram*.

By practice, with the help of gas, the fire in the *Svaadhishtaanam*, is well lit. With the heat of this flame of the fire, the nectar from the Moon in the *Sahasraaram* melts and flows. When the performer (*saadhaka*) enjoys this, then he could realize the *Paraapattarikaa Devi* called '*Saadhaa*'. The command of the learned is that all these are to be learnet from an appropriate teacher.

It has been explained in this *mantra* that *Sri Chakra Upaasana* satisfies all the needs and requirements of Bachelors, others, learned, ignorant and all;

23. अश्रुतासः श्रुतासश्च । यज्वानो येप्य यज्वनः । स्वर्यन्तो नापेक्षन्तो ॥

Aśrutāsa Śrutāsaśca I *Yajvāno Yepya Yajvanaḥ* I

Svaryanto Nāpekśante II

Those who know the *Sri Chakra Vidya* – whether they are matured or not, whether they have performed any holy-rituals or not, will not like to go to heaven.

Here not matured indicate that those who have cleansed their mind.

In the same way those who are so matured, are those who have cleared the dirt of the mind. The seers who perform the holy fire all the time - the three *Ashramis*. Therefore, the benefits of the rituals, yagas, etc., and the benefits of them, such as paradise, are avoided.

It is also the essence of the belief that only the surrender to *Sri Aruna Devi* is capable of immortal bliss.

It is explained that in this mantra, the worship of Gods other than Sri Chakra Upaasana does not bestow welfare;

24. इन्द्रमग्निं च ये विदुः । सिकता इव संयन्ति ।

Indramagnin Ca Ye Viduḥ | *Sikatā Iva Samyanti* |

रश्मिभिः समुदीरिताः । अस्माल्लोकादमुष्माच्च ॥

Raśmibhiḥ Samudīritāḥ | *Asmāllokādamuşmācca* ||

If anybody does not worship *Sri Chakra*, who is always worshipped by *Devas* and demons; always surrender to the golden feet of *Sri Devi*; **She** is hidden in every living being; **She** is the absolute cause of creation, destruction, merger, etc.; If anyone worship and other God like *Indra*, *Yama*, *Agni* and so on, other than this *Devi*, they are like a bunch of sand slipping and not attaching with each other. Further they are bound by the *pasha* rope of *yama*.

They are also rejected both in this and the world. They worship *Indra* and others against the path of knowledge (*gnaana maarga*); against Brahma Vidya; they are idiots trying to reach the dark world.

25. ऋषिभिरदात् पृश्निभिः ॥ *Ṛşibhiradāt Pṛşnibhiḥ* ||

This secret *Upaniṣat* has been guided by the *Prushni* sages for the *Upaasakas*.

इत्यरुणोपनिषत् । *Iti Arunopaniṣats* ।

Thus ends *Arunopaniṣats*.

*****

Sitopaniṣats

सीतोपनिषत्

This is one of the *Upaniṣats* belonging to *Atharva Veda*.

शान्ति मन्त्रः । *Śānti Mantraḥ* ।

ॐ भद्रं कर्णेभिः शृणुयाम देवाः । भद्रं पश्येमाक्षभिर्यजत्राः ।
Om Bhadraṃ Karṇebhiḥ Śruṇuyāma Devāḥ ।
Bhadraṃ Paśyemākṣabhiryajatrāḥ ।

स्थिरैरङ्गैस्तुष्टुवाँसस्तनूभिः । व्यशेम देवहितं यदायुः ॥
Sthirairaṅgaistuṣṭuvāg̃sastanūbhiḥ । *Vyaśema Devahitaṃ Yadāyuḥ* ॥

स्वस्ति न इन्द्रो वृद्धश्रवाः । स्वस्ति नः पूषा विश्ववेदाः ।
Svasti Na Indro Vṛddhaśravāḥ । *Svasti Naḥ Pūṣā Viśvavedāḥ* ।

स्वस्ति नस्तार्क्ष्यो अरिष्टनेमिः । स्वस्ति नो बृहस्पतिर्दधातु ॥
Svasti Nastārkṣyo Ariṣṭanemiḥ । *Svasti No Bṛhaspatirdadhātu* ॥

ॐ शान्तिः शान्तिः शान्तिः ॥ *Oṃ Śāntiḥ Śāntiḥ Śāntiḥ* ॥

Oh *Devas*! Let our ears listen only auspicious sound; Oh Gods worthy of worship! Let our eyes see only the good things; Let our body do prayers through the organs of consciousness (through hearing and seeing the holiness). Let me spend the rest of my life devoted to the gods. Let great *Indra*, grant us well-being. *Pusha*, who knows all things, please grant us well-being. *Dharkshan*, who is a security circle, let us do well. *Brahaspati* (and) let us be peaceful life.

Om, peace, tranquility, tranquility.

1. देवा ह वै प्रजापतिमब्रुवन्का सीता किं रूपमिति ।
Devā Ha Vai Prajāpatimabruvankā Sītā Kiṃ Rūpamiti ।

स होवाच प्रजापतिः सा सीतेति । *Sa Hovāca Prajāpatiḥ Sā Sīteti* ।

मूलप्रकृतिरूपत्वात्सा सीता प्रकृतिः स्मृता ।
Mūlaprakṛtirūpatvātsā Sītā Prakṛtiḥ Smṛtā ।

प्रणवप्रकृतिरूपत्वात्सा सीता प्रकृतिरुच्यते ।
Praṇavaprakṛtirūpatvātsā Sītā Prakṛtirucyate ।

सीता इति त्रिवर्णात्मा साक्षान्मायामयी भवेत् ।
Sītā Iti Trivarṇātmā Sākṣānmāyāmayī Bhavet ।

Devas asked *Brahma* – who is Sita? What is her form? *Brahma* replied – **She** is the form of *Moolaprakruti* (base nature). Hence **she** is called as *Sita Prakruti*. The *Mahaamaayaa*, who is in an unmanifested form displays herself in manifested form.

2. श्रीरामसान्निध्यवशाज्जगदानन्दकारिणी । उत्पत्तिस्थितिसंहारकारिणी सर्वदेहिनाम् ।
Srīrāmasānnidhya Vaśājjagadānandakāriṇī ।
Utpattisthitisamhārakāriṇī Sarvadehinām ।

सीता भगवती ज्ञेया मूलप्रकृतिसंज्ञिता । सर्वाधारकार्यकारणमयी महालक्ष्मीर्देवेशस्य

Sītā Bhagavatī Jneyā Mūlaprakrutisamjnitā ।
Sarvādhārakāryakāraṇamayī Mahālakśmīrdeveśasya

भिन्नाभिन्नरूपा चेतनाचेतनात्मिका भूतेन्द्रियमनःप्राणरूपेति च विज्ञायते ।
Bhinnābhinnarūpā Cetanācetanātmikā
Bhūtendriyamanaḥ Prāṇarūpeti Ca Vijnāyate ।

Because **she** is with Rama **she** could bestow happiness to the world. **She** is the one who performs creation, protection and destruction of all the living beings. *Bhagavati Sita* is the *Moolaprakruti*. **She** is *Mahalakshmi*, the root cause of all things, alongwith and also devoid of divine love. She is in the form of moving and static things. Everyone must realize that everything is her form – five elements, the senses, the mind, the *prana*.

3. सा देवी त्रिविधा भवति । शक्त्यासना इच्छाशक्तिः क्रियाशक्तिः साक्षाच्छक्तिरिति ।

Sā Devī Trividhā Bhavati **|** *Śaktyāsanā*

Icchāśaktiḥ Kriyāśaktiḥ Sākśācchaktiriti **|**

इच्छाशक्तिस्त्रिविधा भवति । *Icchāśaktistrividhā Bhavati* ।
श्रीभूमिनीलात्मिका भद्ररूपिणी प्रभावरूपिणी। सोमसूर्याग्निरूपा भवति ।

Srībhūminīlātmikā Bhadrarūpiṇī Prabhāvarūpiṇī|
SOmasūryāgnirūpā Bhavati ।

सोमात्मिका ओषधीनां प्रभवति । *SOmātmikā Oşadhīnām Prabhavati* ।

सूर्यादिसकलभुवनप्रकाशिनी दिवा च रात्रिः कालकला भवति ।
Sūryādisakalabhuvana-Prakāśinī Divā Ca Rātriḥ Kālakalā Bhavati ।

अग्निरूपा अन्नपानादिप्राणिनां क्षुत्तृष्णात्मिका देवानां मुखरूपा वनौषधीनां
Agnirūpā Annapānādiprāṇinām Kśuttruşṇātmikā
Devānām Mukharūpā Vanouşadhīnām

शीतोष्णरूपा काष्ठेष्वन्तर्बहिश्च नित्यानित्यरूपा भवति ।
Sītośṇarūpā Kāşţheşvantarbahiśca Nityānityarūpā Bhavati ।

That *Devi* is of three forms – *Icchaashakti, Kriyaashakti* and *Jnaanashakti. Icchaashakti* is again three forms – *Sree, BhoOmi* and *Neelaa* – Auspicious form, enlightened form and form of brightness of *SOm*a, Surya and fire. **She** creates plants and trees in the form of *SOma*. In the enlightened form – form of time – **she** illuminates the Sun and other stars. In the form of fire she is hunger-thirst in the living beings, food-water, face of Devas, the weather for the plants and trees, inclusive of wood. At the same time **she** appears and conceals herself.

4. श्रीदेवी त्रिविधं रूपं कृत्वा भगवत्सङ्कल्पानु गुण्येन लोकरक्षणार्थं रूपं धारयति ।
Srīdevī Trividham Rūpam Krutvā Bhagavatsankalpānu
Guṇyena Lokarakśṇārtham Rūpam Dhārayati ।

श्रीरिति लक्ष्मीरिति लक्ष्यमाणा भवतीति विज्ञायते ।

Śrīriti Lakśmīriti Lakśyamāṇā Bhavatīti Vijnāyate ।

भूदेवी ससागरांभः सप्तद्वीपा वसुन्धरा भूरादिचतुर्दश

Bhūdevī Sasāgarāmbhaḥ Saptadvīpā Vasundharā Bhūrādicaturdaśa

भुवनानामाधाराधेया प्रणवात्मिका भवति ।

Bhuvanānāmādhārādheyā Praṇavātmikā Bhavati ।

नीला च मुखविद्युन्मालिनी सर्वौषधीनां सर्वप्राणिनां पोषणार्थं सर्वरूपा भवति ।

Nīlā Ca Mukhavidyunmālinī Sarvouşadhīnām Sarvaprāṇinām Poşaṇārtham Sarvarūpā Bhavati ।

Sri Devi takes three different forms and protects this world. **She** is the one who is seen as *Sri* or *Lakshmi*.

Bhoo Devi is in the form of Pranavam, surrounded by the oceans and source for seven peninsula and 14 worlds including the earth.

Neela Devi is in the form of lightning energy and She accepts a wide variety of images for the nutrietion of the all plant plants and all herbs.

5. क्रियाशक्तिस्वरूपं हरेर्मुखान्नादः । तन्नादाद्बिन्दुः । बिन्दोरोङ्कारः ।

Kriyāśaktisvarūpam Harermukhānnādaḥ ।
Tannādādbinduḥ । *Bindoronkāraḥ* ।

ओङ्कारात्परतो राम वैखानसपर्वतः । तत्पर्वते कर्मज्ञानमयीभिर्बहुशाखा भवन्ति ।

Onkārātparato Rāma Vaikhānasaparvataḥ ।
Tatparvate Karmajnānamayībhirbahuśākhā Bhavanti ।

तत्र त्रयीमयं शास्त्रमाद्यं सर्वार्थदर्शनम् । वैखानसऋषेः पूर्वं विष्णोर्वाणी समुद्भवेत् ।

Tatra Trayīmayam Śāstramādyam Sarvārthadarśanam ।
Vaikhānasaruşeḥ Pūrvam Vişṇorvāṇī Samudbhavet ।

Brahma explains the *Kriyaashakti* form – the *naadam* originates from the face of *Hari*. Fr*Om* that *naadam* originates the *Bindu*. Fr*Om* the *Bindu* the *Onkaaram*. Beyond the *Onkaaram* is the mountain called *Raama Vaikaanasa*. There are many parts in the form of *Karma Gnaanam* in that mountain. The first of them and explaining all the things is the scripture – the *Veda* called *Thrayee*. The *vaag* of *Vishnu* originated from sage *Vaikaanasa*.

6. साक्षाच्छक्तिर्भगवतः स्मरणमात्ररूपाविर्भावप्रादुर्भावात्मिका निग्रहानुग्रहरूपा

Sākśācchaktirbhagavataḥ Smaraṇa Mātra Rūpāvir Bhāvaprādur Bhāvātmikā Nigrahānugraharūpā

भगवत्सहचारिणी अनपायिनी अनवरतसहाश्रयिणी उदितानुदिताकारा

Bhagavatsahacāriṇī Anapāyinī Anavaratasahāśrayiṇī Uditānuditākārā

निमेषोन्मेषसृष्टिस्थितिसंहारतिरोधानानुग्रहादिसर्वशक्तिसामर्थ्यात्साक्षाच्छक्तिरिति गीयते ।

Nimeşonmeşasruşţisthiti Samhāratirodhānānugrahādi Sarvaśakti Sāmarthyātsākśācchaktiriti Gīyate ।

The real energy of the God originates just by the thought – in the form of creation and blessing – in the form of peace and brightness. Emerges from hiding. To be different and not to be different with all the experiences, to go along without separation – performing all the five activities like creation, protection, destruction, complete dissolution and blessing – hence **she** is aptly called as *Shakti* (energy).

7. इच्छाशक्तिस्त्रिविधा प्रलयावस्थायां विश्रमणार्थं भगवतो दक्षिणवक्षः स्थले श्रीवत्साकृतिर्भूत्वा विश्राम्यतीति सा योगशक्तिः ।

Icchāśaktistrividhā Pralayāvasthāyām Viśramaṇārtham Bhagavato Dakśiṇavakśaḥ Sthale Śrīvatsākrutirbhūtvā Viśrāmyatīti Sā Yogaśaktiḥ ।

भोगशक्ति र्भोगरूपा कल्पवृक्ष कामधेनु चिन्तामणि शङ्ख पद्मनिध्यादि नवनिधि समाश्रिता भगवदुपासकानां कामनया अकामनया वा सर्वं क्रियते ।

Bhogaśaktir Bhogarūpā Kalpavrukśa Kāmadhenu Cintāmaṇi Śankha Padmanidhyādi Navanidhi Samāśritā Bhagavadupāsakānām Kāmanayā Akāmanayā Vā Sarvam Kriyate ।

The *Icchaashakti,* who is in the three forms, during the complete dissolution period, in order to relax rests in the right chest of the Lord becomes *Srivatsam,* a yogic body.

When **she** is the enjoyable energy form, **she** becomes the dwelling place of the - h*Om*e to - charitable tree *Kamadhenu, Chintamani, Sanganidhi, Padumanidhi,* etc. **She** offers whatever is their need for the worshippers or even without they seeking for.

8. अथातो वीरशक्ति श्चतुर्भुजाऽभय वरदपद्मधरा किरीटाभरणयुता सर्वदेवैः परिवृता
Athāto Vīraśakti Ścaturbhujāऽbhaya Varadapadmadharā Kirīṭābharaṇayutā Sarvadevaiḥ Parivrutā
कल्पतरु मूले चतुर्भिर्गजै रत्नघटै रमृत जलै-रभिषिच्यमाना सर्वदैवतैर्ब्रह्मादिभिर्वन्द्यमाना
Kalpataru Mūle Caturbhirgajai Ratnaghaṭai Ramruta Jalai-Rabhiṣicyamānā Sarvadaivatairbrahmādibhirvandyamānā

अणिमाद्यष्टैश्वर्ययुता भृगुपुण्यादिभिरभ्यर्च्यमाना देवी दिव्यसिंहासने पद्मासनरूढा सकल
Aṇimādyaṣṭaiśvaryayutā Bhrugupuṇyādibhirabhyarcyamānā Devī Divyasimhāsane Padmāsanarūḍhā Sakala

कारण कार्यकरी वीरलक्ष्मीरिति विज्ञायत इत्युपनिषत् ॥
Kāraṇa Kāryakarī Vīralakśmīriti Vijnāyata Ityupaniṣat ॥

Veerashakthi is decorated with ornaments and crowns, bearing no-fear and boon signets and lotus in the four hands, surrounded by all the *devas,* beneath the *karpaga* tree. Four elephants in a festive mood anointed with precious holy water filled with jewel pots, with *Ashta Aishwarya* (eight types of wealth). Worshipped by the saintly souls like *Bruku* and others – **She** is the Goddess of all causes – she is seated in *padmaasana* on the Divine Throne. **She** is known as *Veeralakshmi* by the *Upaniṣats.*

शान्ति मन्त्रः । *Śānti Mantraḥ* ।

ॐ भद्रं कर्णेभिः शृणुयाम देवाः । भद्रं पश्येमाक्षभिर्यजत्राः ।

Om Bhadraṃ Karṇebhiḥ Śruṇuyāma Devāḥ ।

Bhadraṃ Paśyemākṣabhiryajatrāḥ ।

स्थिरैरङ्गैस्तुष्टुवाँसस्तनूभिः । व्यशेम देवहितं यदायुः ॥

Sthirai], raṅgaistuṣṭuvāg̃sastanūbhiḥ । *Vyaśema Devahitaṃ Yadāyuḥ* ॥

स्वस्ति न इन्द्रो वृद्धश्रवाः । स्वस्ति नः पूषा विश्ववेदाः ।

Svasti Na Indro Vṛddhaśravāḥ । *Svasti Naḥ Pūṣā Viśvavedāḥ* ।

स्ति नस्तार्क्ष्यो अरिष्टनेमिः । स्वस्ति नो बृहस्पतिर्दधातु ॥

Svasti Nastārkṣyo Ariṣṭanemiḥ । *Svasti No Bṛhaspatirdadhātu* ॥

ॐ शान्तिः शान्तिः शान्तिः ॥ *Oṃ Śāntiḥ Śāntiḥ Śāntiḥ* ॥

इति सीतोपनिषत्समाप्ता ॥ *Iti Sitopaniṣats* ॥

*****

Śrī Devī Atharvaśīrsha Upaniṣat (Śrī Devī Upaniṣat)

देवी अथर्वशिर उपनिषत् or देवी उपनिषत्

This is also called as *Sri Devi Upaniṣat*. This also belongs to *Atharva Veda*, containing 32 mantras. It talks about *Sri Devi* and **her** glories. Once chant it immediately bestows wisd*Om*.

शान्ति मन्त्रः । *Śānti Mantraḥ* ।

ॐ भद्रं कर्णेभिः शृणुयाम देवाः । भद्रं पश्येमाक्षभिर्यजत्राः ।
Om Bhadraṃ Karṇebhiḥ Śruṇuyāma Devāḥ ।
Bhadraṃ Paśyemākṣabhiryajatrāḥ ।

स्थिरैरङ्गैस्तुष्टुवाँसस्तनूभिः । व्यशेम देवहितं यदायुः ॥
Sthirairaṅgaistuṣṭuvāğsastanūbhiḥ । *Vyaśema Devahitaṃ Yadāyuḥ* ॥

स्वस्ति न इन्द्रो वृद्धश्रवाः । स्वस्ति नः पूषा विश्ववेदाः ।
Svasti Na Indro Vṛddhaśravāḥ । *Svasti Naḥ Pūṣā Viśvavedāḥ* ।

स्वस्ति नस्तार्क्ष्यो अरिष्टनेमिः । स्वस्ति नो बृहस्पतिर्दधातु ॥
Svasti Nastārkṣyo Ariṣṭanemiḥ । *Svasti No Bṛhaspatirdadhātu* ॥

ॐ शान्तिः शान्तिः शान्तिः ॥ *Oṃ Śāntiḥ Śāntiḥ Śāntiḥ* ॥

1. ॐ सर्वे वै देवा देवीमुपतस्थुः कासि त्वं महादेवीति ॥
Om Sarve Vai Devā Devīmupatasthuḥ Kāsi Tvaṃ Mahādevīti ॥
All the *devas*, reaching *Sri Devi* asked **her** – Oh *Mahaadevi*! Who are you?

2. साब्रवीत्-अहं ब्रह्मस्वरूपिणी । मत्तः प्रकृतिपुरुषात्मकं जगत् शून्यं चाशून्यम् च ।
Sābravīdahaṃ Brahmasvarūpiṇī ।
Mattaḥ Prakṛtipuruṣātmakaṃ Jagat Śūnyaṃ Cāśūnyaṃ Ca ।

अहमानन्दानानन्दाः । विज्ञानाविज्ञानेऽहं ।
Ahamānandānānandau । *Ahaṃ Vijñānāvijñāne* ।

ब्रह्माब्रह्मणी वेदितव्ये । इत्याहाथर्वणी श्रुतिः ॥

Ahaṃ Brahmābrahmaṇī Veditavye I Iti Cātharvaṇī Śrutiḥ II

That *Devi* replied – I am in the form of *Parabrahmam*. I am the nature in the male form – vacuam or filled everything originated from me. All the happy and unhappy forms are mine. I am the vivid and the vague form of wisdo and the vivid enlightenment. *Brahmam* and non-*brahmam* should be perceived as myself.

3. अहं पञ्चभूतान्यपञ्चभूतानि। अहमखिलं जगत् ॥

Ahaṃ Pañcabhūtāni Ahaṃ Pañcatanmātrāṇi I Ahamakhilaṃ Jagat II

वेदोऽहमवेदोऽहम्। विद्याहमविद्याहम्। अजाहमनजाहम् । अधश्चोर्ध्वं च तिर्यक्चाहम् ।

Vedo'hamavedo'ham I Vidyāhamavidyāham I

Ajāhamanajāham I Adhaścordhvaṃ Ca Tiryakcāham II

I am the great five elements and as well non-elements; I am the mundane world that appears; I am the *vedas* myself; I am the non-*vedas* also; I am the form of vidya (knowledge) and ignorance as well. I have no origin and I have birth also. The ones below are me too and the above and cross also myself;

4. अहं रुद्रेभिर्वसुभिश्चरामि । अहमादित्यैरुत विश्वदेवैः ।

Ahaṃ Rudrebhirvasubhiścarāmi I Ahamādityairuta Viśvadevaiḥ I

अहं मित्रावरुणावुभौ बिभर्मि । अहमिन्द्राग्नी अहमश्विनावुभौ ॥

Ahaṃ Mitrāvaruṇāvubhau Bibharmi I

Ahamindrāgnī Ahamaśvināvubhau II

The 11 *rudras*, 8 *vasus*, 12 *aadityas*, 13 *vishwedevas* and all originated from me. I have been travelling alongwith them. Further I am wearing – the two *Mitra* and *Varuna*; the two *Indra* and *Agni*; in the same fashion the *Ashwini Devas*;

5. अहं सोमं त्वष्टारं पूषणं भगं दधामि। अहं विष्णुमुरुक्रमं ब्रह्माणमुत प्रजापतिं दधामि ॥

Ahaṃ Somaṃ Tvaṣṭāraṃ Pūṣaṇaṃ Bhagaṃ Dadhāmi ।
Ahaṃ Viṣṇumurukramaṃ Brahmāṇamuta Prajāpatiṃ Dadhāmi ॥

I am wearing the *devas* called *Soman*, *Tvashtaa*, *Pooshan* and six types of wealth[8]. Further I wear *Vishnu*, who has great valour, *Brahma* and *Prajapati*.

6. अहं दधामि द्रविणं हविष्मते सुप्राव्ये उ यजमानाय सुन्वते ।

Ahaṃ Dadhāmi Draviṇaṃ Haviṣmate Suprāvye Yajamānāya Sunvate ।

अहं राष्ट्री सङ्गमनी वसूनां अहं सुवे पितरमस्य मूर्धन् ।
Ahaṃ Rāṣṭī Saṅgamanī Vasūnāṃ Aham Suve Pitaramasya Mūrdhan ॥

I bestow wealth or good knowledge to those with good will, who perform *yagnam* with good offerings and those who worship with good prayers. I am the apt place for the 8 *Vasus* to move on. I, in the form of the head for this world (both moving and static) to prevail, create *Parameshwaran*, who is the father of the entire universe.

7. मम योनिरप्स्वन्तः समुद्रे । य एवम् वेद। स देवीं सम्पदमाप्नोति ।

Mama Yonirapsvantaḥ Samudre ।*Ya Evaṃ Veda* ।
Sa Daivīṃ Sampadamāpnoti ।

My place of origination is the middle of the water in the ocean. Or, in the, in the shape of a lotus bud and the form of five elements. The concept is that I am in the form of *Jeevan*, the form of *Jeeva* consciousness, etc. Whoever knows me thus, attains the position of the mine, that is, the form of the *Chith*.

8. ते देवा अब्रुवन् - *Te Devā Abruvan* ।

नमो देव्यै महादेव्यै शिवायै सततं नमः ।

---

[8] The six types of wealth - the undiminishing money, the *Dharma*, the pride, the Supreme, the Enlightenment and *Vairagya*.

Namo Devyai Mahādevyai Śivāyai Satataṃ Namaḥ I

नमः प्रकृत्यै भद्रायै नियताः प्रणताः स्म ताम् ॥८॥
Namaḥ Prakṛtyai Bhadrāyai Niyatāḥ Praṇatāḥ Sma Tām II

Those *devas* having greatly understood the glories of *Sri Devi*, through her own words, prayed to **her** after bowing – our *pranams* to you. Oh Mother shining with the creation of *tri-moorthis*! You have the auspicious form. Regular *pranaamas* to you, the consort of *Sarvadevan*. You have the form of *Moola-prakruti*. We bow to you, such a great goddess, again and again.

9. तामग्निवर्णां तपसा ज्वलन्तीं वैरोचनीं कर्मफलेषु जुष्टाम् ।
Tāmagnivarṇāṃ Tapasā Jvalantīṃ Vairocanīṃ Karmaphaleṣu Juṣṭām I

दुर्गां देवीं शरणं प्रपद्यामहेऽसुरान्नाशयित्र्यै ते नमः ॥
Durgāṃ Devīṃ Śaraṇaṃ Prapadyāmahe'surānnāśayitryai Te Namaḥ II

She has the brightness like fire – **she** can be realised only through penance. She shines by her own illumination. That Durga is so connected to the results of *karmas*. We surrender. Her compassion will definitely remove our ignorance.

10. देवीं वाचमजनयन्त देवास्तां विश्वरूपाः पशवो वदन्ति
Devīṃ Vācamajanayanta Devāstāṃ Viśvarūpāḥ Paśavo Vadanti I

सा नो मन्द्रेषमूर्जं दुहाना धेनुर्वागस्मानुपसुष्टुतैतु ॥
Sā No Mandreṣamūrjaṃ Duhānā Dhenurvāgasmānupa Suṣṭutaitu II

Whatever speech created by *Devas*, is constantly used by all the creatures in this moving and static world. May the Goddess taking the *Kamadhenu*, give the image of the sweet and agreeable sustenance, the speech proportion to the power of *Karma*,. That is, let us serve her well.

11. कालरात्रीं ब्रह्मस्तुतां वैष्णवीं स्कन्दमातरम् ।

Kālarātreeṃ Brahmastutāṃ Vaiṣṇavīṃ Skandamātaram I

सरस्वतीमदितिं दक्षदुहितरं नमामः पावनां शिवाम् ॥

Sarasvatīmaditiṃ Dakṣaduhitaraṃ Namāmaḥ Pāvanāṃ Śivām II

She is recognized as *Kaalaraatri* on account of ignorance; **She** is worshipped by *Brahma*; **She** is the in the form of *Vishnu Maya* (illusion);

She is so pure, as daughter of *Daksha Prajapati*, mother of *Skanda*, in the form *Atiti Devata*, bestowing auspiciousness – **she** is the *Saraswati* and we all bow **her**.

12. महालक्ष्म्यै च विद्महे सर्वशक्त्यै च धीमहि । तन्नो देवी प्रचोदयात् ॥

Mahālakṣmyai Ca Vidmahe Sarvaśaktyai Ca Dhīmahi I

Tanno Devī Pracodayāt II

We all very well know you as *Mahalakshmi*. We meditate upon you in the form of *Sarvasiddhi*. Hence, you have to stimulate us to perform all good deeds.

13. अदितिर्ह्यजनिष्ट दक्ष या दुहिता तव । तां देवा अन्वजायन्त भद्रा अमृतबन्धवः ॥

Aditirhyajaniṣṭa Dakṣa Yā Duhitā Tava I

Tāṃ Devā Anvajāyanta Bhadrā Amṛtabandhavaḥ II

Atitidevi originated by you, *Daakshaayanee*. Hence she can be considered as your daughter. All the Devas, who drank *Amruta*, were born to her. Hence we can be considered as grand sons (sons of your daughter) and hence, you have to eradicate us from ignorance.

The greatness of *Pancadashee Mantra*

14. कामो योनिः कमला वज्रपाणिर्गुहा हसा मातरिश्वाभ्रमिन्द्रः ।

Kāmo Yoniḥ Kamalā Vajrapāṇirguhā Hasā Mātariśvābhramindraḥ I

पुनर्गुहासकला मायया च पुरूच्यैषा विश्वमातादिविद्योम् ॥
Punarguhā Sakalā Māyayā Ca Purūcyaiṣā Viśvamātādividyom ॥

The origin of *Aadi Vidya* is being described through this *mantra*. It is a combinaton of the letters '*Ka, A, Ee, La, Hreem, Ha, Sa, Ka, Ha, La, Hreem, Sa, Ka, La, Hreem* – This is the oldest *Aadi Vidya*, cause of the creation of this world – This, alongwith the *pranava mantra*, is called the great *Panchadashee* or *Panchadashaasharee mantra*.

15. एषात्मशक्तिः । एषा विश्वमोहिनी । पाशाङ्कुशधनुर्बाणधरा । एषा श्रीमहाविद्या ।
Eṣā''tmaśaktiḥ I *Eṣā Viśvamohinī* I *Pāśāṅkuśadhanurbāṇadharā* I
Eṣā Śrīmahāvidyā ॥

This *Aadi Vidya* is the *Atma Shakti* (self-energy). This is the illusion making the world faint. **She** is the earliest energy (*Aadi shakti*). **She** is armed in **her** hands with goad, noose, bow and arrow. **She** is the *Sree Mahaa Vidya*.

16. य एवं वेद स शोकं तरति ॥ *Ya Evaṃ Veda Sa Śokaṃ Tarati* ॥

He, who realizes the *Sree Mahaa Vidya*, crosses all the tragedies.

17. नमस्ते अस्तु भगवति मातरस्मान् पाहि सर्वतः ॥
Namaste I*Stu Bhagavati Mātarasmānpāhi Sarvataḥ* ॥

Oh mother, filled with six qualities (wealth and others)! *Pranaams* to you in all the ways. Please protect us.

18. सैषाष्टौ वसवः। सैषैकादशरुद्राः । सैषा द्वादशादित्याः ।
Saiṣā Vaiṣṇavyaṣṭau Vasavaḥ I *Saiṣaikādaśa Rudrāḥ* I
Saiṣā Dvādaśādityāḥ I

सैषा विश्वेदेवाः सोमपा असोमपाश्च । सैषा यातुधाना असुरा रक्षांसि पिशाचा यक्षाः सिद्धाः ।

Saiṣā Viśvedevāḥ SOmapā AsOmapāśca ।

Saiṣā Yātudhānā Asurā Rakṣāṃsi Piśācā Yakṣā Siddhāḥ ।

सैषा सत्त्वरजस्तमांसि । सैषा ब्रह्मविष्णुरुद्ररूपिणी। सैषा प्रजापतीन्द्रमनवः ।

Saiṣā Sattvarajastamāṃsi । *Saiṣā Brahmaviṣṇurudrarūpiṇī* ।

Saiṣā Prajāpatīndramanavaḥ ।

सैषा ग्रहनक्षत्रज्योतींषि । कला काष्ठादिकालरूपिणी। तामहं प्रणौमि नित्यम् ।

Saiṣā Grahanakṣatrajyotiḥkalākāṣṭhādiviśvarūpiṇī ।

Kalākāṣṭhādiviśvarūpiṇī । *Tāmahaṃ Praṇaumi Nityam* ।

Thus, this great mother is the 8 *Vasus*; She is the 11 *Rudras*; She is the 12 *Aadityaas*; She is also the *Vishvedevas*; **She** is those who drink *Soma* drink or who do not; **She** is the demons, *pishasas*, *yakshas*, *siddhas* and all; **She** is in the form of the three qualities – *Satva*, *Rajas* and *Tamas*; **She** is the *Prajaapati*, *Indra* and *Manus*; **She** is the nine-planets and 27 stars; Hence, I all always bow to that *Aadi Mahaa Shakti*. The sense we all bow to **her** individually, is conveyed here by the singular phrase *"Aham Prnoumi"*.

19. तापापहारिणीं देवीं भुक्तिमुक्तिप्रदायिनीम् ।

Tāpāpahāriṇīṃ Devīṃ Bhuktimuktipradāyinīm ।

अनन्तां विजयां शुद्धां शरण्यां शिवदां शिवाम्॥

Anantāṃ Vijayāṃ Śuddhāṃ Śaraṇyāṃ Śivadāṃ Śivām ॥

She is the one who removes all the three types of sins – *Adiyaatmikam*, *Aadi Bhoudikam* and *Adi Daivikam*; **She** bequeaths all the desires of the worshippers in this world and also the liberation in the other world; **She** is in the form of the endless success in all the three times; **She** is so pure and auspicious. Let us all surrender to that *Mahadevi*, who is rising star.

Bhuvaneshwari (*Shaakta Pranava*) *Mantra*

20. वियदीकारसंयुक्तं वीतिहोत्रसमन्वितम् । अर्धेन्दु लसितं देव्या बीजं सर्वार्थसाधकम् ॥

Viyadīkārasaṃyuktaṃ Vītihotrasamanvitam I
Ardhendulasitaṃ Devyā Bījaṃ Sarvārthasādhakam II

Sri Devi shines with the combination of *ha* – the root letter of ether, *ra* – the root letter of *agni* (the fire god), alongwith *'Ee'*, the half moon *'m'*. The combined root letter *'Hreem'* of *Sri Devi*, has the power of to do anything and everything. This is single letter mantra, that is explained here, of Sri *Bhuvaneshwari*.

21. एवमेकाक्षरं ब्रह्म यतयः शुद्धचेतसः । ध्यायन्ति परमानन्दमया ज्ञानाम्बुराशयः ॥
Evamekākṣaraṃ Mantraṃ Yatayaḥ Śuddhacetasaḥ I
Dhyāyanti Paramānandamayā Jñānāmburāśayaḥ II

Thus the *Yogis* who are pure-minded and are like the sea of spiritual enlightenment, meditate on the *Bhuvaneswari Devi's* monastic *mantra*.

Navaaksharee Mantra

22. वाङ्माया ब्रह्मसूस्तस्मात् षष्ठं वक्त्रसमन्वितम्
Vāṅmāyā Brahmasūstasmāt Ṣaṣṭhaṃ Vaktrasamanvitam I

सुर्योऽवामश्रोत्रबिन्दुसंयुक्तष्टात्तृतीयकम् ।
Sūryo'vāmaśrotrabindusaṃyuktāṣṭāttṛtīyakam II

23. नारायणेन संयुक्तो वायुश्चाधरसंयुत: । विच्चे नवार्णकोऽर्णः स्यान्महदानन्ददायकः ॥
Nārāyaṇena Saṃmiśro Vāyuścādhārayuktataḥ I
Vicce Navārṇako'rṇaḥ Syānmahadānandadāyakaḥ II

The *Navaaksharee Mantra* of *Sri Chandika Devi*, "*Aim-Hreem-Kleem-Chaamundaayai-Vicche*" is got like this – the combination of;

- *'Aim'*, the *Vaagbhava* root letter
- *'Kleem'*, the *Shakti* root letter

- *'Caa'*, the sixth from the first letter *'Ka'* of *Kaamaraaja* root letter conjoined with 'a'
- *'Mum'*, *'Ma'* the root letter of Sun, merged with *'u'* and bindu
- *'Daa'* – the third letter in the *'ta'* family joined with *'a'*

All the above conjoined with the *svara 'ai'* form the great *mantra*. It is the usual practice that the *pranava mantra 'Om'* is prefixed and the word *'Namaha'* is suffixed. Thus we get the glorified *Navaaksharee Mantra* "*Om Aim-Hreem-Kleem-Chaamundaayai-Vicche Namaha*"; It is beyond doubt sure that this *mantra* is capable of offering increased happiness to the *upaasakas*.

24. हृत्पुण्डरीकमध्यस्थां प्रातः सूर्यसमप्रभां ।

Hṛtpuṇḍarīkamadhyasthāṃ Prātaḥsūryasamaprabhām I

पाशाङ्कुशधरां सौम्यां वरदाभयहस्तकाम् । त्रिनेत्रां रक्तवसनां भक्तकामदुघां भजे ॥

Pāśāṅkuśadharāṃ Saumyāṃ Varadābhayahastakām I

Trinetrāṃ Raktavasanāṃ Bhaktakāmadughāṃ Bhaje II

I bow to that *Mahaadevi*, who is situated in the middle of the (*Hrudaya Kamala*) lotus heart, shining like a rising Sun during the dawn; wearing the hoad and noose in the hands; showing the boon and no-fear signets; having a stunning form; wearing a red dress; ready to bequeath the lusts of the devotees' like *Kamadhenu*; in giving the lusts no less.

25. नमामि त्वां महादेवीं महाभयविनाशिनीम् । महादुर्गप्रशमनीं महाकारुण्यरूपिणीम् ॥

Namāmi Tvāṃ Mahādevīṃ Mahābhayavināśinim I

Mahādurgapraśamanīṃ Mahākāruṇyarūpiṇīm II

She removes the increasing fear and mounting difficulties. **She** is of growing compassion and has a shining form. I bow you.

26. यस्याः स्वरूपं ब्रह्मादयो न जानन्ति तस्मादुच्यते अज्ञेया ।

Yasyāḥ Svarūpaṃ Brahmādayo Na Jānanti Tasmāducyate Ajñeyā I

यस्या अन्तो न लभ्यते तस्मादुच्यते अनन्ता ।

Yasyā Anto Na Labhyate Tasmāducyate Anantā ।

यस्या लक्ष्यं नोपलक्ष्यते तस्मादुच्यते अलक्ष्या ।

Yasyā Lakṣyaṃ Nopalakṣyate Tasmāducyate Alakṣyā ।

यस्या जननं नोपलभ्यते तस्मादुच्यते अजा । एकैव सर्वत्र वर्तते तस्मादुच्यते एका ।

Yasyā Jananaṃ Nopalakṣyate Tasmāducyate Ajā ।
Ekaiva Sarvatra Vartate Tasmāducyate Ekā ।

एकैव विश्वरूपिणी तस्मादुच्यते नैका । अत एवोच्यते अज्ञेयानन्तालक्ष्याजैका नैकेति ॥

Ekaiva Viśvarūpiṇī Tasmāducyate Naikā ।
Ata Evocyate Ājñeyānantālakṣyājaikā Naiketi ॥

Since the goddess could not be recognized by Brahma and all, she is said to be unaware by all. Since she does not have any birth, she is mentioned as originless. Since she does not have termination, she is endless. Her sight is rare to get and hence she is said to invisible. She destroys everything during complete devastation and she is shining alone and hence she is the single in the universe. She creates the moving and static world and she is merged in the Jeevan and shows herself in that unmanifested form, she is said to be in different forms. Hence, that *Devi* is unidentifiable, originless, endless, invisible – she is alone and she has many a form. She is praised in all these ways.

27. मन्त्राणां मातृका देवी शब्दानां ज्ञानरूपिणी ।

Mantrāṇāṃ Mātṛkā Devī Śabdānāṃ Jñānarūpiṇī ।

ज्ञानानां चिन्मयातीता शून्यानां शून्यसाक्षिणी ।

Jñānānāṃ Cinmayātītā Śūnyānāṃ Śūnyasākṣiṇī ॥

Sri Devi is in the form of the great *Maatruka Mantra* (in the form of typescripts) among the *mantras*; **She** is the in form of wisdom among the sounds; She is beyond wisdom; She is the witness of all that unseen; She is praised in all these ways.

28. यस्याः परतरं नास्ति सैषा दुर्गा प्रकीर्तिता ॥

Yasyāḥ Parataraṃ Nāsti Saiṣā Durgā Prakīrtitā ।

तां दुर्गां दुर्गमां देवीं दुराचारविघातिनीम् । नमामि भवभीतोऽहं संसारार्णवतारिणीम् ॥

Tāṃ Durgāṃ Durgamāṃ Devīṃ Durācāravighātinīm ।

Namāmi Bhavabhīto'haṃ Saṃsārārṇavatāriṇīm ॥

There is nothing more in the world than this goddess. That great goddess is called *Durga*. The idea that she destroys the bad etiquette. Those who worship her is devoid of birth-death cycle. It is emphasized that it is not possible to attain the darshan of that *Devi*, unless they are given *Deekasha* as per procedures, by an appropriate teacher (*guru*). I am worshiping that *Durga Devi*, who is attainable with great difficulty in the ocean of *samsaara*.

Results/ fruits

29. इदमथर्वशीर्षं योऽधीते स पञ्चाथर्वशीर्षजपफलमाप्नोति ।

Idamatharvaśīrṣaṃ Yo'dhīte Sa Pañcātharvaśīrṣaphalamāpnoti ।

इदमथर्वशीर्षमज्ञात्वा योऽर्चां स्थापयति

Idamatharvaśīrṣamajñātvā Yo'rcāṃ Sthāpayati ।

Whoever, chants this *Atharvashiras*, he gets the fruits of chanting *Narsayana Atharvashiras* like five *Atharvashiras*[9]. Whoever worships with this *Atharvashiras*, as prescribed, he gets growing fame in this world.

30. शतलक्षं प्रजप्त्वाऽपि सोऽर्चासिद्धिं न विन्दति ।

[9] *Ganapati Atharvashiras*, *Naaraayana Atharvashiras*, *Devi Atharvashiras*, *Atharvashikham* and *Bhavanopanishat* are the five *Atharvashiras*.

Śatalakṣaṃ PrajaptvāSpi SoSrcāsiddhiṃ Na Vindati ।

शतमष्टोत्तरं चास्य पुरश्चर्याविधिः स्मृतः ।

Śatamaṣṭottaraṃ Cāsya Puraścaryāvidhiḥ Smṛtaḥ ॥

Even after chanting for 100 lakhs times, one may not be able to get the fruits, because there are various procedures prescribed by the sages for this *Mahaa Vidyaa*. This mantra has to be chant alongwith 108 times *purashcaram*, that have been set by the sages.

31. दशवारं पठेद्यस्तु सद्यः पापैः प्रमुच्यते । महादुर्गाणि तरति महादेव्याः प्रसादतः ॥

Daśavāraṃ Paṭhedyastu Sadyaḥ Pāpaiḥ Pramucyate ।

Mahādurgāṇi Tarati Mahādevyāḥ Prasādataḥ ॥

Whichever *upaasakan*, chants this mantra alongwith 108 times *purashcaram*, he is immediately bereft of all the sins. Further with the blessings of Sri Devi, he is removed from all the abstacles and crosses the growing woes easily.

32. प्रातरधीयानो रात्रिकृतं पापं नाशयति । सायमधीयानो दिवसकृतं पापं नाशयति।

Prātaradhīyāno Rātrikṛtaṃ Pāpaṃ Nāśayati ।

Sāyamadhīyāno Divasakṛtaṃ Pāpaṃ Nāśayati ।

सायं प्रातः प्रयुञ्जानो अपापो भवति।निशीथे तुरीयसन्ध्यायां जप्त्वा वाक्सिद्धिर्भवति ।

Sāyaṃ Prātaḥ Prayuñjāno'pāpo Bhavati ।

Niśīthe Turīyasaṃdhyāyāṃ Japtvā Vāksiddhirbhavati ।

नूतनायां प्रतिमायां जप्त्वा देवतासान्निध्यं भवति ।

Nūtanāyāṃ Pratimāyāṃ Japtvā Devatāsāṃnidhyaṃ Bhavati ।

प्राणप्रतिष्ठायां जप्त्वा प्राणानां प्रतिष्ठा भवति ।

Prāṇapratiṣṭhāyāṃ Japtvā Prāṇānāṃ Pratiṣṭhā Bhavati ।

भौमाश्विन्यां महादेवीसन्निधौ जप्त्वा महामृत्युं तरति ।

स महामृत्युं तरति य एवं वेद। इत्युपनिषत् ॥

Bhaumāśvinyāṃ Mahādevīsaṃnidhau Japtvā Mahāmṛtyuṃ Tarati Sa Mahāmṛtyuṃ Tarati ॥ *Ya Evaṃ Veda* ॥ *Ityupaniṣat* ॥

If this *Upaniṣat* is chant in the morning all the sins done during night are removed. In the same manner, if this is chant in the evening all the sins done during day-time are removed. If this is chant both in the morning and evening, the chanter is devoid of all the sins. If this is chant in the fourth quarter of the night, the chanter becomes an expert in the speech. If this is chant before a new sculpture, that image becomes a full fledged God as if the *Praanapratishta* has been performed. If this is chant on Tuesday with Ashwini star, then the chanter can able to cross the fear of the crude death. It is the command of this *Devi Upaniṣat* of, that one who realizes the truth of this *Upaniṣat,* he has all the hallucinations of the blessings of *Srimahaadevi*.

शान्ति मन्त्रः ॥ *Śānti Mantraḥ* ॥

ॐ भद्रं कर्णेभिः शृणुयाम देवाः । भद्रं पश्येमाक्षभिर्यजत्राः ।
Om Bhadraṃ Karṇebhiḥ Śruṇuyāma Devāḥ ।
Bhadraṃ Paśyemākṣabhiryajatrāḥ ।
स्थिरैरङ्गैस्तुष्टुवाँसस्तनूभिः । व्यशेम देवहितं यदायुः ॥
Sthirairaṅgaistuṣṭuvāĝsastanūbhiḥ । *Vyaśema Devahitaṃ Yadāyuḥ* ॥
स्वस्ति न इन्द्रो वृद्धश्रवाः । स्वस्ति नः पूषा विश्ववेदाः ।
Svasti Na Indro Vṛddhaśravāḥ । *Svasti Naḥ Pūṣā Viśvavedāḥ* ।

स्वस्ति नस्तार्क्ष्यो अरिष्टनेमिः । स्वस्ति नो बृहस्पतिर्दधातु ॥
Svasti Nastārkṣyo Ariṣṭanemiḥ । *Svasti No Bṛhaspatirdadhātu* ॥

ॐ शान्तिः शान्तिः शान्तिः ॥ *Oṃ Śāntiḥ Śāntiḥ Śāntiḥ* ॥

॥ *Iti Sri DevyUpaniṣat Samaaptaa* ॥
Om Tat Sat

*****

Śrī Chakropaniṣat

श्रीचक्रोपनिषत्

This *Sri Chakropaniṣats* explains the glory of *Sri Kaameshwara* and *Kaameshwari* surrounded by *Titi Nitya Devis*. This assurs that if the God and Goddess are properly worshipped and puja is done as per procedure, then the *upaasaka* will get all the siddhis. He will be adored by all the people in the world. This is one small *Upaniṣat* belonging to *Atharva Veda*.

शान्ति मन्त्रः || *Śānti Mantraḥ* ||

ॐ भद्रं कर्णेभिः शृणुयाम देवाः । भद्रं पश्येमाक्षभिर्यजत्राः ।
Om Bhadraṃ Karṇebhiḥ Śruṇuyāma Devāḥ ।
Bhadraṃ Paśyemākṣabhiryajatrāḥ ।

स्थिरैरङ्गैस्तुष्टुवाँसस्तनूभिः । व्यशेम देवहितं यदायुः ॥
Sthirairaṅgaistuṣṭuvāg̃sastanūbhiḥ । *Vyaśema Devahitaṃ Yadāyuḥ* ॥

स्वस्ति न इन्द्रो वृद्धश्रवाः । स्वस्ति नः पूषा विश्ववेदाः ।
Svasti Na Indro Vṛddhaśravāḥ । *Svasti Naḥ Pūṣā Viśvavedāḥ* ।

स्वस्ति नस्तार्क्ष्यो अरिष्टनेमिः । स्वस्ति नो बृहस्पतिर्दधातु ॥
Svasti Nastārkṣyo Ariṣṭanemiḥ । *Svasti No Bṛhaspatirdadhātu* ॥

ॐ शान्तिः शान्तिः शान्तिः || *Oṃ Śāntiḥ Śāntiḥ Śāntiḥ* ||

1. ॐ अथाह वै श्रीचक्रे नित्याक्रान्ते ।
Om Athāha Vai Śrīcakre Nityākrānte ।

Then when the *Sri Chakram* was surrounded by the famous *Titi Nityaa Devis*;

2. गौरीर्मियाय सलिलानि तक्षत्येकपदी द्विपदी सा चतुष्पदी ।

Gaurīrmiyāya Salilāni Takṣatyekapadī Dvipadī Sā Catuṣpadī I

अष्टापदी नवपदी बभूवुषी सहस्राक्षरा परमे व्योमन् ॥

Aṣṭāpadī Navapadī Babhūvuṣī Sahasrākṣarā Parame VyOman II

The *Sri Chakra* is surrounded by 15 *Titi Nityaa Devatai*-s. Lord *Sri Kaameshwara* and *Devi Sri Kaameshwari* have to be initiated in the *Sri Chakra* and daily puja has to be performed as per Veda procedures with the mantra '*Gaurīrmiyāya...*'.

She makes water and all the things originate from water, look like so small. **She** is in the form of *mantras* with one quarter (*paada*); **She** is in the form of *mantras* with two quarters; **She** is in the form of *mantras* with four quarters; **She** is in the form of *mantras* with eight quarters; **She** is in the form of *mantras* with nine quarters; **She** is in the form of *mantras* with many letters; That great *Devi* is in white colour and seen alongwith *Brahmam*;

The earlierst to be created is water. Before creation of any movable object, Lord *Parameshwara* created water and then remaining four of the five primary elements. Hence the entire moving world has instigated from the water only.

Further this universe is divided into two viz., Sound (*Shabda*) and Meaning (*Artha*). In these the Sound universe is in much expanded form than the Meaning universe. This can be understood like this – in any language to indicate anything there could be many words. Thus taking into consideration many a language, then there will be infinite words to specify anything. Thus the meaning universe becomes very small when compared to sound universe.

Hence, *Sri Devi*, spreading across the world, peforms the five great tasks, taking the form of Sound universe. Further, **she** takes the form of single quarter mantra till mantas with 'n' number of letters. Hence the mother is called as *Vaidheeka Shabda Prapancham*.

Further **she** is in the form of *Parabrahmam*, who is the cause of the origin of this universe. That great Mother Devi, in white colour, the energy of this universe, is within all the things of this world in the form of *Shabdaartha* – sound and meaning. **She** integrates and also splits all the things in the world.

3. इति प्रत्यहं ससङ्गति सहस्रं कलशान् स्थाप्य शतं वा नव वा सर्वाभावे पूर्णाभिषेकं चरेत्।

Iti Pratyahaṃ Sasaṅgati Sahasraṃ Kalaśān Sthāpya Śataṃ Vā Nava Vā Sarvābhāve Pūrṇābhiṣekaṃ Caret I *Aṣṭāṣṭakaṃ Caret* I

Daily *puja* has to be performed with 1000 holy-pots (*kalasa*), or 100 holy-pots, or at least 9 holy-pots – abhishekam (bathing the gods) has to be performed from the holy pots.

4. अष्टाष्टकं चरेत् । पञ्चपञ्चकं वा चरेत् । सर्वाभावे शतं पूजयेत् । अमृतत्वं गच्छति ।

Aṣṭāṣṭakaṃ Caret I *Pañcapañcakaṃ Vā Caret* I *Sarvābhāve Śataṃ Pūjayet* I *Amṛtatvaṃ Gacchati* I

Sixty-four *upacaaras*[10] (offerings) have to be done; or at least 25. 100 times puja have to be performed. Thus worshipper will reach the liberation at the end.

5. श्रीचक्रन्यासं चरेत् । स व्यापकत्वं गच्छति ।

Śrīcakranyāsaṃ Caret I *Sa Vyāpakatvaṃ Gacchati* I

The *nyaasa* of *Sri Chakra* has to be performed as per procedure. Any worshiper doing this will become omniscient. He get all the eight siddhies starting *Animaa*.

6. मूलाधाराद्बिलान्तं क्रमेण न्यसेत् ।

Mūlādhārādbilāntaṃ Krameṇa Nyaset I

स्वराट्चक्रं विराट्चक्रं समाट्चक्रं विराज्यचक्रं विश्वरूपचक्रं

[10] 235th name of *Sri Lalita Sahasranama* - *Chatushshashṭiyupacārādhyā* is worth comparing here.

शत्रुजिच्चक्रं क्रमेण सप्तकलामयं न्यसेत् ।

Svarāṭcakraṃ Virāṭcakraṃ Samāṭcakraṃ Virājyacakraṃ Viśvarūpacakraṃ Śatrujiccakraṃ Krameṇa Saptakalāmayaṃ Nyaset ।

स शिवो भवेत् । स कविर्भवेत् । स सर्वसिद्धीश्वरो भवेत् ।

Sa Śivo Bhavet । Sa Kavirbhavet । Sa Sarvasiddhīśvaro Bhavet ।

स नवनाथाधिष्ठितो भवेत् । स भुवनाराधितो भवेत् ।

Sa Navanāthādhiṣṭhito Bhavet । Sa Bhuvanārādhito Bhavet ।

Puja has to be performed in all the *chakras* assuming with *nyaasa*;

- *Moolaadhaara* as *Svaraat Chakra*
- *Svaadhishtaaana* as *Viraat Chakra*
- *Manipooraka* as *Samraat Chakra*
- *Anaahata* as *Viraajya Chakra*
- *Vishddhi* as *Vishvaroopa Chakra*
- *Agnaa* as *Chatrujit Chakra*
- *Sahasraara* as *Shiva-Shakti* unison

Such a worshipper becomes lord *Shiva* himself. He becomes a poet. He becomes expert in all the eight *siddhis* starting from *Animaa*. He has blessed by all nine planets. The entire world will admire his intelligence.

7. निर्विकल्पेन मनसा यश्चरेच्छक्तिदेहे स कालीरूपो भवेत् ।

Nirvikalpena Manasā Yaścarecchaktidehe Sa Kālīrūpo Bhavet ।

विना शक्तिं न मोक्षो न ज्ञानं न सत्यं न धर्मो न तपो न हरिर्न हरो न विरिञ्चिः ।

Vinā Śaktiṃ Na Mokṣo Na Jñānaṃ Na Satyaṃ Na Dharmo Na Tapo Na Harirna Haro Na Viriñciḥ ।

सर्वं शक्तियुक्तं भवेत् । तत्संयोगात् सिद्धीश्वरो भवेत् । इति शिवम् ॥

Sarvaṃ Śaktiyuktaṃ Bhavet ।

Tatsaṃyogāt Siddhīśvaro Bhavet | *Iti Śivam* ||

That *Upasaka* who worships *Sri Chakam* with a pure mind, becomes the form of *Kaali* in the body of *Shakti*. There is no liberation without *Shakti*; no wisdom; No truth; No *dharma*; No penance. The trinities *Brahma*, *Vishnu* and *Rudra* who perform the three actions viz. creation, protection and destruction cannot exist with *shakti*. Therefore all the things that appear in the world are full of energy. All that is involved in the power of the *shakti*, the nature of the will.

शान्ति मन्त्रः || *Śānti Mantraḥ* ||

ॐ भद्रं कर्णेभिः शृणुयाम देवाः । भद्रं पश्येमाक्षभिर्यजत्राः ।

Om Bhadraṃ Karṇebhiḥ Śruṇuyāma Devāḥ |

Bhadraṃ Paśyemākṣabhiryajatrāḥ |

स्थिरैरङ्गैस्तुष्टुवाँसस्तनूभिः । व्यशेम देवहितं यदायुः ॥

Sthirairaṅgaistuṣṭuvāg̃sastanūbhiḥ | *Vyaśema Devahitaṃ Yadāyuḥ* ||

स्वस्ति न इन्द्रो वृद्धश्रवाः । स्वस्ति नः पूषा विश्ववेदाः ।

Svasti Na Indro Vṛddhaśravāḥ | *Svasti Naḥ Pūṣā Viśvavedāḥ* |

स्वस्ति नस्ताक्ष्यो अरिष्टनेमिः । स्वस्ति नो बृहस्पतिर्दधातु ॥

Svasti Nastārkṣyo Ariṣṭanemiḥ | *Svasti No Bṛhaspatirdadhātu* ||

ॐ शान्तिः शान्तिः शान्तिः || *Oṃ Śāntiḥ Śāntiḥ Śāntiḥ* ||

इत्याथर्वणे सौभाग्यकाण्डे श्रीचक्रोपनिषत् समाप्ता ।

Ityaatharvane Soubhaagyakaande Sricakropaniṣats Samaaptaa |

Atharvashikopaniṣats

अथर्वशिखोपनिषत्

ओङ्कारार्थतया भातं तुर्योङ्काराग्रभासुरम्। तुर्यतुर्यंत्रिपाद्रामं स्वमात्रं कलयेऽन्वहम्॥

Oṅkārārthatayā Bhātaṃ Turyoṅkārāgrabhāsuram ।

Turyaturyaṃtripādrāmaṃ Svamātraṃ Kalaye'nvaham ॥

This *Upaniṣat* also belonging to Athava Veda and explains the meaning of *Onkaaram* (*Om*). At the top of Oṃ Devi shines as the fourth (*tureeyam*) quarter. She is tureeya of tureeya – and merging with other three quarters. I meditate upon that *Paramprorul* continously.

शान्ति मन्त्रः ॥ *Śānti Mantraḥ* ॥

ॐ भद्रं कर्णेभिः शृणुयाम देवाः । भद्रं पश्येमाक्षभिर्यजत्राः ।

Om Bhadraṃ Karṇebhiḥ Śruṇuyāma Devāḥ ।

Bhadraṃ Paśyemākṣabhiryajatrāḥ ।

स्थिरैरङ्गैस्तुष्टुवाँसस्तनूभिः । व्यशेम देवहितं यदायुः ॥

Sthirairaṅgaistuṣṭuvāg̃sastanūbhiḥ । *Vyaśema Devahitaṃ Yadāyuḥ* ॥

स्वस्ति न इन्द्रो वृद्धश्रवाः । स्वस्ति नः पूषा विश्ववेदाः ।

Svasti Na Indro Vṛddhaśravāḥ । *Svasti Naḥ Pūṣā Viśvavedāḥ* ।

स्वस्ति नस्ताक्ष्यों अरिष्टनेमिः । स्वस्ति नो बृहस्पतिर्दधातु ॥

Svasti Nastārkṣyo Ariṣṭanemiḥ । *Svasti No Bṛhaspatirdadhātu* ॥

ॐ शान्तिः शान्तिः शान्तिः ॥ *Oṃ Śāntiḥ Śāntiḥ Śāntiḥ* ॥

1.1 ॐ अथ हैनं पैप्पलादोऽङ्गिराः सनत्कुमारश्चाथर्वणमुवाच भगवन्किमादौ प्रयुक्तं

Om Atha Hainaṃ Paippalādo'ṅgirāḥ

Sanatkumāraścātharvaṇamuvāca Bhagavankimādau Prayuktaṃ

ध्यानं ध्यायितव्यं किं तद्ध्यानं को वा ध्याता कश्च ध्येयः ।
Dhyānaṃ Dhyāyitavyaṃ Kiṃ Taddhyānaṃ Ko
Vā Dhyātā Kaśca Dhyeyaḥ ।

Om. Sages like *Pippalada*, *Aangirasa* and *Sanatkumara* jointly asked Sage *Atharva* – Oh God! What is the type of important meditation that has been instructed? What is the mantra for meditation? Who can perform meditation? Which is the God who can be meditated upon?

1.2 स एभ्योथर्वा प्रत्युवाच । ओमित्येतदक्षरमादौ प्रयुक्तं ध्यानं ध्यायितव्यमित्येतदक्षरं
Sa Ebhyotharvā Pratyuvāca । *Omityetadakṣaramādau Prayuktaṃ*
Dhyānaṃ Dhyāyitavyamityetadakṣaraṃ

परं ब्रह्मास्य पादाश्चत्वारो वेदाश्चतुष्पादिदमक्षरं परं ब्रह्म ।
Paraṃ Brahmāsya Pādāścatvāro Vedāścatuṣ
Pādidamakṣaraṃ Paraṃ Brahma ।

Sage *Atharva* replied them – Oṃ is the single letter *mantra* is the one which is important to meditate upon. That is what meditation is all about. The four quarters of the *mantra*, the four *devas*, the *Vedas*, the meditation, the *Parabrahma* should be meditated.

1.3. पूर्वास्य मात्रा पृथिव्यकारः ऋग्भिरृग्वेदो ब्रह्मा वसवो गायत्री गार्हपत्यः ।
Pūrvāsya Mātrā Pṛthivyakāraḥ Ṛgbhirṛgvedo
Brahmā Vasavo Gāyatree Gārhapatyaḥ ।

Its first *maatra*, *'A'*, refers to the Earth (*Prithvi*), the mantra-shaped *Rig Veda*, the Lord *Brahma* (the Lord of the universe), the *Ashta vasus* in the deities, the *Gaayatri* in the chantas and the *Kaarhabatya* in the *Agni* – holy fire. This is how it has to be meditated upon.

1.4 द्वितीयान्तरिक्षं स उकारः स यजुभिर्यजुर्वेदो विष्णुरुद्रास्त्रिष्टुब्दक्षिणाग्निः ।
Dvitīyāntarikṣaṃ Sa Ukāraḥ Sa
Yajubhiryajurvedo Viṣṇurudrāstriṣṭubdakṣiṇāgniḥ ।

Its second *maatra, 'U'*, refers to the Ether (*Antariksha*), the *yajur*-shaped *Yajur Veda*, the Lord *Rudra* (the Lord of destruction), the 11 *Rudras* in the deities, the *Trishtup* in the chantas and the *Dakshinaagni* in the *Agni* – holy fire. This is how it has to be meditated upon.

1.5 तृतीयः द्यौः स मकारः स सामभिः सामवेदो रुद्रा आदित्या जगत्याहवनीयः ।

Tṛtīyaḥ Dyauḥ Sa Makāraḥ Sa Sāmabhiḥ

Sāmavedo Rudrā Ādityā Jagatyāhavanīyaḥ ।

Its third *maatra, 'Ma'*, refers to the upper world, the song type of *Saama Veda*, the Lord *Vishnu* (the Lord of protecction), the 12 *Aadityaas* in the deities, the *Jagatee* in the chantas and the *Aahavaneeyaagni* in the *Agni* – holy fire. This is how it has to be meditated upon.

1.6 यावसानेऽस्य चतुर्थ्यर्धमात्रा सा सोमलोक ओङ्कारः साथर्वणमन्त्रैरथर्ववेदः

Yāvasāne'sya Caturthyardhamātrā Sā SOmaloka
Oṅkāraḥ Sātharvaṇamantrairatharvavedaḥ

संवर्तकोऽग्निर्मरुतो विराडेकर्षिर्भास्वती स्मृता ।

Saṃvartako'gnirmaruto Virāḍekarṣirbhāsvatī Smṛtā ।

Its fourth half *maatra*, hidden-*'Ma'*, refers to the *Athara Veda,* the Lord *Vishnu* (the Lord of protecction), the *Marutganaaas* in the deities, (since it is half *maatra* no *chantas*) and the *Samvartaka* in the *Agni* – holy fire. The *Brahmam* is astounding by itself, looking at everything.

1.7 प्रथमा रक्तपीता महद्ब्रह्म दैवत्या । द्वितीया विद्युमती कृष्णा विष्णुदैवत्या ।

Prathamā Raktapītā Mahadbrahma Daivatyā ।

Dvitīyā Vidyumatī Kṛṣṇā Viṣṇudaivatyā ।

तृतीया शुभाशुभा शुक्ला रुद्रदैवत्या ।

Tṛtīyā Śubhāśubhā Śuklā Rudradaivatyā ।

यावासानेऽस्य चतुर्थ्यर्धमात्रा सा विद्युमती सर्ववर्णा पुरुषदैवत्या ।

Yāvāsāne'sya Caturthyardhamātrā Sā

Vidyumatī Sarvavarṇā Puruṣadaivatyā ।

- First is red in colour – *Brahma's* action of creation with *Brahma* himself as deity.
- Second is beautiful white in colour – *Rudra's* action of destruction with *Rudra* as deity.
- Third one is black in colour – *Vishnu's* action of protection with *Vishnu* as deity.
- Fourth is like lightning shining in all colours – having *Eeshwara*, who is the lord of all the worlds as deity.

The usual order is *Brahma*, *Vishnu* and *Rudra*. However in some places it is indicated as *Brahma*, *Rudra* and *Vishnu*. All are said to be the same *Brahmam*.The *Saanthokhya Upaniṣat* says – *Vasu* form in the morning, *Rudra* forms in noon and *Aaditya* form in the evening have to be worshipped. One of the Adityas, *Vishnu* is omniscient (*Antaryaami*).

1.8 स एष ह्योङ्कारश्चतु रक्षरश्चतुष्पादश्चतुः शिरश्चतुर्थमात्रः
Sa Eṣa Hyoṅkāraścatu Rakṣaraścatuṣpādaścatuḥ Śiraścaturthamātraḥ

स्थूलमेतद्ह्रस्वदीर्घप्लुत इति ॥ ॐ ॐ ॐ इति त्रिरुक्त्वा ॥
Sthūlametadhrasvadīrghapluta Iti ॥ *Oṃ Oṃ Oṃ Iti Triruktvā* ॥

The *Onkaaram* shines like having four quarters and four fire heads. The fourth half *maatra* is a hidden form of *'ma'*. It will be pronounced narrowly, stretched and stretched too long. This will be pronounced Oṃ with one *maatra*, two *maatras* and three long *maatras* as *Om*.

1.9 चतुर्थः शान्त आत्माप्लुतप्रणवप्रयोगेण समस्तमोमिति प्रयुक्त आत्मज्योतिः
Caturthaḥ Śānta Ātmāplutapraṇavaprayogeṇa
SamastamOmiti Prayukta Ātmajyotiḥ

सकृदावर्तते सकृदुच्चारितमात्रः स एष ऊर्ध्वमन्नमयतीत्योङ्कारः ।
Sakṛdāvartate Sakṛduccāritamātraḥ
Sa Eṣa Ūrdhvamannamayatītyoṅkāraḥ ।

The fourth half *maatra* in a peaceful form is hidden in the long sound. It is an incomparable soul torch. It is the same (*anaahata*) light that never existed before. That is, without pronouncing a single passage, the *Sushumna Naadi* takes all the *praanas* up to the *Sahasraaram*.

2.1 प्रणवः सर्वान् प्राणान् प्रणामयति नामयति चैतस्मात् प्रणवश्चतुर्धाऽवस्थित इति वेद देव
Prāṇva Sarvān Prāṇān Praṇāmayatī Nāmayati Caitasmāt Praṇavaścaturdhāvasthita Iti Veda Deva

योनिर्ध्येयाश्चेति सन्धर्ता सर्वेभ्यो दुःख भयेभ्यः सन्तारयति तारणात् तानि सर्वाणीति विष्णुः
Yonirdheyāśceti Sandhartā Sarvebhyo Duḥkha Bhayebhyaḥ Santārayati Tāraṇāt Tāni Sarṇīti Viṣṇuḥ ।

सर्वा जयति ब्रह्माऽबृहत् सर्व कारणानि संप्रतिष्टाप्य ध्यानाद्विष्णुर्मनसि नादान्ते
Sarvā Jayati Brahmā Sbruhat Sarva Kāraṇāni Sampratiştāpya Dhyānādviṣṇurmanasi Nādānte

परमात्मनि स्थाप्य ध्येयमीशाने प्रध्यायन्तीशा वा सर्वमिदं प्रयुक्तम् ॥
Paramātmani Sthāpya Dhyeyamīśāne Pradyāyantīśā Vā Sarvamidam Prayuktam ॥

Pranavam makes all the *praanans* to *pranaam* (bow). It should be meditated on as the four *Vedas*, the gods and their birthplaces. The meditator, thus meditating, is the one who has the power to protect himself from all fears and sorrows. And he gets the power of protecting others also. It is through this meditation that *Vishnu* (omnipresent) wins over everything. *Brahma* also attained the status of great *Brahma* as he meditated on all the senses. Vishnu also meditates on the mind (meditating on the meditation of the *Akara-Ukara-Makara-Bindu* – the integration of all the five), in the place of *Paramatma*, which is the state of worship. All of this applies to *Eeshaanan* also.

2.2 ब्रह्मविष्णुरुद्रेन्द्रास्ते सम्प्रसूयन्ते सर्वाणि चेन्द्रियाणि
Brahmaviṣnurudrendrāste Samprasūyante Sarvāṇi Cendriyāṇi

सह भूतैर्न कारणं कारणानां ध्याता कारणं तु ध्येयः

Saha Bhūtairna Kāraṇam Kāraṇānām Dhyātā Kāraṇam Tu Dhyeyaḥ

सर्वैश्वर्यसम्पन्नः शंभुराकाशमध्येध्रुवंस्तम्

Sarvaiśvaryasampannaḥ Śambhurākāśamadhye Druvam Stam

Brahma, *Vishnu*, *Rudra* and *Indra* create all the giants, all the senses and *karmas*. They have the power to rule them. On the other hand, the *Parashivam* is keeping mum and static among the celestial body of them.

2.3 ब्रह्मा विष्णुश्च रुद्रश्च ईश्वरः शिव एव च । पंचधा पंचदेवत्यः प्रणवः परिपठ्यते ॥

Bramā Viṣṇuśca Rudraśca Eśvaraḥ Śiva Eva Ca I

Pancadhā Pancadevatyaḥ Pranavaḥ Paripaṭhyate II

It is preached that *Pranava* should be meditated on in the form of five deities viz. *Brahma, Vishnu, Rudran, Eeshvaran* and *Jeevan* (*A + U + Ma + Nada + Bindu*).

2.4 तत्राधिकं क्षणमेकमास्थाय क्रतुशतस्यापि फलमवाप्नोति ।

Tatrādhikam Kśaṇamekamāsthāya Kratuśatasyāpi Phalamavāpnoti I

कृत्स्नमोंकारगतं च सर्वज्ञानेन योगध्यानाना शिव एको ध्येयः शिवंकरः ।

Kṛtsnamoṅkāragatiṃ Ca Sarvadhyāna Yogajñānānā

Śiva Eko Dhyeyaḥ Śivaṃkaraḥ I

सर्वमन्यत् परित्यज्य ऐतामधीत्य द्विजो गर्भ वासान्मुच्युत इति ॥

Sarvamanyat Parityajya Aitāmadhītya Dvijo Garbha Vāsānmucyuta Iti II

Even if a person meditates upon one quarter of this mantra for one second he gets more results than a person performing 100 *yagnas*.

With full focus and attention on *Parashivam*, the *mantra Om*, it has to be meditated upon. Then everything that are sought for can be reached.
By sacrificing everything else and learning one thing, it is certain that meditator will get rid of the birth-death cycle and reach the liberation.

शान्ति मन्त्रः । *Śānti Mantraḥ* ।

ॐ भद्रं कर्णेभिः शृणुयाम देवाः । भद्रं पश्येमाक्षभिर्यजत्राः ।
Om Bhadraṃ Karṇebhiḥ Śruṇuyāma Devāḥ ।
Bhadraṃ Paśyemākṣabhiryajatrāḥ ।

स्थिरैरङ्गैस्तुष्टुवाँसस्तनूभिः । व्यशेम देवहितं यदायुः ॥
Sthirairaṅgaistuṣṭuvāg̐sastanūbhiḥ । *Vyaśema Devahitaṃ Yadāyuḥ* ॥

स्वस्ति न इन्द्रो वृद्धश्रवाः । स्वस्ति नः पूषा विश्ववेदाः ।
Svasti Na Indro Vṛddhaśravāḥ । *Svasti Naḥ Pūṣā Viśvavedāḥ* ।

स्वस्ति नस्तार्क्ष्यो अरिष्टनेमिः । स्वस्ति नो बृहस्पतिर्दधातु ॥
Svasti Nastārkṣyo Ariṣṭanemiḥ । *Svasti No Bṛhaspatirdadhātu* ॥

ॐ शान्तिः शान्तिः शान्तिः ॥ *Oṃ Śāntiḥ Śāntiḥ Śāntiḥ* ॥

॥ इति अथर्ववेदीय अथर्वशिखोपनिषत्समाप्ता ॥

॥ *Iti Atharvavedeeya Atharvashikopaniṣats Samaaptaa* ॥

*****

Tripuropaniṣats
त्रिपुरोपनिषत्

This is one of the *Upaniṣats* belonging to *Rig Veda*.

त्रिपुरोपनिषद्वेद्यपारमैश्वर्यवैभवम् । अखण्डानन्दसाम्राज्यं रामचन्द्रपदं भजे ॥

Tripuropaniṣadvedyapāramaiśvaryavaibhavam ।
Akhaṇḍānandasāmrājyaṃ Rāmacandrapadaṃ Bhaje ॥

शान्ति मन्त्रः - *Shanti Mantra*:

ॐ वाङ्मे मनसि प्रतिष्ठिता । मनो मे वाचि प्रतिष्ठितम् ।
Oṃ Vāṅme Manasi Pratiṣṭhitā । *Mano Me Vāci Pratiṣṭhitam* ।
आविरावीर्म एधि । वेदस्य म आणीस्थः । श्रुतं मे मा प्रहासीः ।
Āvirāvīrma Edhi । *Vedasya Ma Āṇīsthaḥ* । *Śrutaṃ Me Mā Prahāsīḥ* ।
अनेनाधीतेनाहोरात्रान् संदधामि । ऋतं वदिष्यामि ।
Anenādhītenāhorātrān Saṃdadhāmi । *Ṛtaṃ Vadiṣyāmi* ।
सत्यं वदिष्यामि । तन्मामवतु । तद्वक्तारमवतु । अवतु माम् ।
Satyaṃ Vadiṣyāmi । *Tanmāmavatu* । *Tadvaktāramavatu* । *Avatu Mām* ।
अवतु वक्तारम् । अवतु वक्तारम् । *Avatu Vaktāram* । *Avatu Vaktāram* ।

ॐ शान्तिः शान्तिः शान्तिः ॥ *Oṃ Śāntiḥ Śāntiḥ Śāntiḥ* ॥

1. ॐ तिस्रः पुरास्त्रिपथा विश्वचर्षणा अत्राकथा अक्षराः सन्निविष्टाः ।
Oṃ Tisraḥ Purāstripathā Viśvacarṣaṇā Atrākathā Akṣarāḥ Sanniviṣṭāḥ ।
अधिष्ठायैना अजरा पुराणी महत्तरा महिमा देवतानाम् ॥
Adhiṣṭhāyainā Ajarā Purāṇī Mahattarā Mahimā Devatānām ॥

2. नवयोनिर्नवचक्राणि दधिरे नवैव योगा नव योगिन्यश्च ।
Navayonirnavacakrāṇi Dadhire Navaiva Yogā Nava Yoginyaśca ।
नवानां चक्रा अधिनाथाः स्योना नव मुद्रा नव भद्रा महीनाम् ॥
Navānāṃcakrā Adhināthāḥ Syonānava Mudrā Nava Bhadrā Mahīnām ॥

3. एका सा आसीत् प्रथमा सा नवासीदासोनविंशादासोनत्रिंशत्।
Ekā Sā Āsīt Prathamā Sā Navāsīdāsonaviṃśādāsonatriṃśat ।

चत्वारिंशादथ तिस्रः समिधा उशतीरिव मातरो मा विशन्तु ॥

Catvāriṃśādatha Tisraḥ Samidhā Uśatīriva Mātaro Mā Viśantu ॥

4. ऊर्ध्वज्वलज्ज्वलनं ज्योतिरग्रे तमो वै तिरश्चीनमजरं तद्रजोऽभूत् ।

Ūrdhvajvalajvalanaṃ Jyotiragre Tamo Vai Tiraśścīnamajaraṃ Tadrajo'bhūt ।

आनन्दनं मोदनं ज्योतिरिन्दो रेता उ वै मण्डला मण्डयन्ति ॥

Ānandanaṃ Modanaṃ Jyotirindo Retā U Vai Maṇḍalā Maṇḍayanti ॥

5. तिस्रश्च [यास्तिस्रो] रेखाः सदनानि भूमेस्त्रिविष्टपास्त्रिगुणास्त्रिप्रकाराः ।

Tisraśca [Yāstisro] Rekhāḥ Sadanāni Bhūmestriviṣṭapāstriguṇāstriprakārāḥ ।

एतत्पुरं [एतत्त्रयं] पूरकं पूरकाणामत्र [पूरकाणां मन्त्री] प्रथते मदनो मदन्या ॥

Etatpuraṃ [Etattrayaṃ] Pūrakaṃ Pūrakāṇāmatra [Pūrakāṇāṃ Mantrī] Prathate Madano Madanyā ॥

6. मदन्तिका मानिनी मंगला च सुभगा च सा सुन्दरी सिद्धिमत्ता ।

Madantikā Māninī Maṃgalā Ca Subhagā Ca Sā Sundarī Siddhimattā ।

लज्जा मतिस्तुष्टिरिष्टा च पुष्टा लक्ष्मीरुमा ललिता लालपन्ती ॥

Lajjā Matistuṣṭiriṣṭā Ca Puṣṭā Lakṣmīrumā Lalitā Lālapantī ॥

7. इमां विज्ञाय सुधया मदन्ती परिसृता तर्पयन्तः स्वपीठम् ।

Imāṃ Vijñāya Sudhayā Madantī Parisṛtā Tarpayantaḥ Svapīṭham ।

नाकस्य पृष्ठे वसन्ति परं धाम त्रैपुरं चाविशन्ति ॥

Nākasya Pṛṣṭhe Vasanti Paraṃ Dhāma Traipuraṃ Cāviśantic ॥

8. कामो योनिः कामकला व्रजपाणिर्गुहा हसा मातरिश्वाभ्रमिन्द्रः ।

Kāmo Yoniḥ Kāmakalā Vrajapāṇirguhā Hasā Mātariśvābhramindraḥ ।

पुनर्गुहा सकला मायया च पूरूच्येषा विश्वमातादिविद्या ॥

Punarguhā Sakalā Māyayā Ca Pūrūcyeṣā Viśvamātādividyā ॥

9. षष्ठं सप्तममथ वह्निसारथिमस्या मूलत्रिक्रमा देशयन्तः ।

Ṣaṣṭhaṃ Saptamamatha Vahnisārathimasyā Mūlatrikramā Deśayantaḥ।

कथ्यं कविं कल्पकं काममीशं तुष्टुवांसो अमृतत्वं भजन्ते ॥

Kathyaṃ Kaviṃ Kalpakaṃ Kāmamīśaṃ Tuṣṭuvāṃso Amṛtatvaṃ Bhajante ॥

10. त्रिविष्टपं त्रिमुखं विश्वमातुर्नवरेखाः स्वरमध्यं तदीले ।
Triviṣṭapaṃ Trimukhaṃ Viśvamāturnavarekhāḥ Svaramadhyaṃ Tadīle।
[पुरं हन्त्रीमुखं विश्वमातू रवे रेखा स्वरमध्यं तदेषा ।]
Puraṃ Hantrīmukhaṃ Viśvamātū Rave Rekhā Svaramadhyaṃ Tadeṣā।]
बृहत्तिथिर्दशा पञ्चादि नित्या सा षोडशी पुरमध्यं बिभर्ति ॥
Bṛhattithirdaśā Pañcādi Nityā Sā Ṣoḍaśī Puramadhyaṃ Bibharti ॥

11. यद्वा मण्डलाद्वा स्तनबिंबमेकं मुखं चाधस्त्रीणि गुहा सदनानि ।
Yadvā Maṇḍalādvā Stanabiṃbamekaṃ Mukhaṃ Cādhastrīṇi Guhā Sadanāni ।
कामी कलां काम्यरूपां विदित्वा [चिकित्वा] नरो जायते कामरूपश्च काम्यः [कामः] ॥
Kāmī Kalāṃ Kāmyarūpāṃ Viditvā [Cikitvā] Naro Jāyate Kāmarūpaśca Kāmyaḥ [Kāmaḥ] ॥

12. परिसृतम् झषमाद्यं [झषमाजं] फलं च भक्तानि योनीः सुपरिष्कृताश्च।
Parisṛtam Jhaṣamādyaṃ [Jhaṣamājaṃ] Phalaṃ Ca Bhaktāni Yonīḥ Supariṣkṛtāśca ।
निवेदयन्देवतायै महत्यै स्वात्मीकृते सुकृते सिद्धिमेति ॥
Nivedayandevatāyai Mahatyai Svātmīkṛte Sukṛte Siddhimeti ॥

13. सृण्येव सितया विश्वचर्षणिः पाशेनैव प्रतिबध्नात्यभीकाम् ।
Sṛṇyeva Sitayā Viśvacarṣaṇiḥ Pāśenaiva Pratibadhnātyabhīkām ।
इषुभिः पञ्चभिर्धनुषा च विध्यत्यादिशक्तिररुणा विश्वजन्या ॥
Iṣubhiḥ Pañcabhirdhanuṣā Ca Vidhyatyādiśaktiraruṇā Viśvajanyā ॥

14. भगः शक्तिर्भगवान्काम ईश उभा दाताराविह सौभगानाम् ।
Bhagaḥ Śaktirbhagavānkāma Īśa Ubhā Dātārāviha Saubhagānām ।
समप्रधानौ समसत्वौ समोजौ तयोः शक्तिरजरा विश्वयोनिः ॥
Samapradhānau Samasatvau Samojau Tayoḥ Śaktirajarā Viśvayoniḥ ॥

15. परिस्रुता हविषा भावितेन प्रसङ्कोचे गलिते वैमनस्कः ।
Parisrutā Haviṣā Bhāvitena Prasaṅkoce Galite Vaimanaskaḥ ।
शर्वः सर्वस्य जगतो विधाता धर्ता हर्ता विश्वरूपत्वमेति ॥
Śarvaḥ Sarvasya Jagato Vidhātā Dhartā Hartā Viśvarūpatvameti ॥

16. इयं महोपनिषत्त्रैपुर्या यामक्षरं परमो गीर्भिरीट्टे ।
Iyaṃ Mahopaniṣattraipuryā Yāmakṣaraṃ Paramo Gīrbhirīṭṭe ।
एषर्ग्यजुः परमेतच्च सामायमथर्वेयमन्या च विद्या ॥
Eṣargyajuḥ Parametacca Sāmāyamatharveyamanyā Ca Vidyā ॥

ॐ ह्रीम् ॐ ह्रीमित्युपनिषत् ॥ *Oṃ Hrīm Oṃ Hrīmityupaniṣat* ॥

शान्ति मन्त्र: - *Shanti Mantra*:

ॐ वाङ्मे मनसि प्रतिष्ठिता । मनो मे वाचि प्रतिष्ठितम् ।
Oṃ Vāṅme Manasi Pratiṣṭhitā । *Mano Me Vāci Pratiṣṭhitam* ।
आविरावीर्म एधि । वेदस्य म आणीस्थः । श्रुतं मे माप्रहासीः ।
Āvirāvīrma Edhi । *Vedasya Ma Āṇīsthaḥ* । *Śrutaṃ Me Mā Prahāsīḥ* ।
अनेनाधीतेनाहोरात्रान् संदधामि । ऋतं वदिष्यामि ।
Anenādhītenāhorātrān Saṃdadhāmi । *Ṛtaṃ Vadiṣyāmi* ।
सत्यं वदिष्यामि । तन्मामवतु । तद्वक्तारमवतु । अवतु माम् ।
Satyaṃ Vadiṣyāmi । *Tanmāmavatu* । *Tadvaktāramavatu* । *Avatu Mām* ।
अवतु वक्तारम् । अवतु वक्तारम् ।*Avatu Vaktāram* । *Avatu Vaktāram* ।

ॐ शान्तिः शान्तिः शान्तिः ॥ *Oṃ Śāntiḥ Śāntiḥ Śāntiḥ* ॥

॥ इति त्रिपुरोपनिषत् ॥ ॥ *Iti Tripuropaniṣat* ॥

*****

Saubhāgyalakṣmyupaniṣat
सौभाग्यलक्ष्म्युपनिषत्

This is one of the *Upaniṣats* belonging to *Rig Veda*.

सौभाग्यलक्ष्मीकैवल्यविद्यावेद्यसुखाकृति। त्रिपान्नारायणानन्दरमचन्द्रपदं भजे ॥
Saubhāgyalakṣmīkaivalyavidyāvedyasukhākṛti |
Tripānnārāyaṇānandaramacandrapadaṃ Bhaje ||

शान्ति मन्त्रः - *Shanti Mantra*:

ॐ वाङ्मे मनसि प्रतिष्ठिता। मनो मे वाचि प्रतिष्ठितम्।
Oṃ Vāṅme Manasi Pratiṣṭhitā I *Mano Me Vāci Pratiṣṭhitam* I
आविरावीर्म एधि। वेदस्य म आणीस्थः। श्रुतं मे मा प्रहासीः।
Āvirāvīrma Edhi I *Vedasya Ma Āṇīsthaḥ* I *Śrutaṃ Me Mā Prahāsīḥ* I
अनेनाधीतेनाहोरात्रान् संदधामि। ऋतं वदिष्यामि।
Anenādhītenāhorātrān Saṃdadhāmi I *Ṛtaṃ Vadiṣyāmi* I
सत्यं वदिष्यामि। तन्मामवतु। तद्वक्तारमवतु। अवतु माम्।
Satyaṃ Vadiṣyāmi I *Tanmāmavatu* I *Tadvaktāramavatu* I *Avatu Mām* I
अवतु वक्तारम्। अवतु वक्तारम् I*Avatu Vaktāram* I *Avatu Vaktāram* I

ॐ शान्तिः शान्तिः शान्तिः ॥ *Oṃ Śāntiḥ Śāntiḥ Śāntiḥ* ||

(सौभाग्यलक्ष्मीविद्याजिज्ञासा - *Saubhāgyalakṣmīvidyājijñāsā*)

1. हरिः ॐ ॥ अथ भगवन्तं देवा ऊचुर्हे भगवन्नः कथय सौभाग्यलक्ष्मीविद्याम्।
Hariḥ Oṃ || *Atha Bhagavantaṃ Devā Ūcurhe*
Bhagavannaḥ Kathaya Saubhāgyalakṣmīvidyām |

तथेत्यवोचद्भगवानादिनारायणः सर्वे देवा यूयं सावधानमनसो भूत्वा शृणुत
Tathetyavocadbhagavānādinārāyaṇaḥ Sarve Devā
Yūyaṃ Sāvadhānamanaso Bhūtvā Śṛṇuta

तुरीयरूपां तुरीयातीतान् सर्वोत्कटां सर्वमन्त्रासनगतां पीठोपपीठदेवतापरिवृतां
Tathetyavocadbhagavānādinārāyaṇaḥ Sarve Devā
Yūyaṃ Sāvadhānamanaso Bhūtvā Śṛṇuta

चतुर्भुजां श्रियं हिरण्यवर्णामिति पञ्चदशर्ग्भिर्ध्यायेत्।

Caturbhujāṃ Śriyaṃ Hiraṇyavarṇāmiti

Pañcadaśargbhirdhyāyet ।

अथ पञ्चदश ऋगात्मकस्य श्रीसूक्तस्यानन्दकर्दमचिक्लीतेन्दिरासुता ऋषयः ।

Atha Pañcadaśa Ṛgātmakasya

Śrīsūktasyānandakardamaciklītendirāsutā Ṛṣayaḥ ।

श्रीऋष्याद्या ऋचः चतुर्दशानमृचामानन्दाद्यृषयः ।

Śrīṛṣyādyā Ṛcaḥ Caturdaśānamṛcāmānandādyṛṣayaḥ ।

हिरण्यवर्णाद्याद्यत्रयस्यानुष्टुप् छन्दः । कांसोस्मीत्यस्य बृहती छन्दः ।

Hiraṇyavarṇādyādyatrayasyānuṣṭup Chandaḥ ।

Kāṃsosmītyasya Bṛhatī Chandaḥ ।

तदन्ययोर्द्वयोस्त्रिष्टुप् । पुनरष्टकस्यानुष्टुप् । शेषस्य प्रस्तारपङ्क्तिः । श्र्यग्निर्देवता ।

Tadanyayordvayostriṣṭup । *Punaraṣṭakasyānuṣṭup* ।

Śeṣasya Prastārapaṅktiḥ । *Śryagnirdevatā* ।

हिरण्यवर्णामिति बीजम् । कांसोऽस्मीति शक्तिः ।

Hiraṇyavarṇāmiti Bījam । *Kāṃso'smīti Śaktiḥ* ।

हिरण्मया चन्द्रा रजतस्रजा हिरण्या हिरण्यवर्णेति प्रणवादिनमोन्तैश्चतुर्थ्यन्तैरङ्गन्यासः ।

Hiraṇmayā Candrā Rajatasrajā Hiraṇyā Hiraṇyavarṇeti

Praṇavādinamontaiścaturthyantairaṅganyāsaḥ ।

अथ वक्त्रत्रयैरङ्गन्यासः । *Atha Vaktratrayairaṅganyāsaḥ* ।

मस्तकलोचनश्रुतिघ्राणवदनकण्ठबाहुद्वयहृदयनाभिगुह्यपायूरुजानुजङ्घेषुश्रीसूक्तैरेव क्रमशो न्यसेत् ।

Mastakalocanaśrutighrāṇa Vadanakaṇṭha Bāhu Dvayahṛdaya Nābhi Guhya Pāyūrujānujaṅgheṣu

अरुणकमलसंस्था तद्रजःपुञ्जवर्णा करकमलधृतेष्टाऽभीतियुग्माम्बुजा च ।

Śrīsūktaireva Kramaśo Nyaset । *Aruṇakamalasaṃsthā*

Tadrajaḥpuñjavarṇā Karakamaladhṛteṣṭā'bhītiyugmāmbujā Ca ।

मणिकटकविचित्रालङ्कृताकल्पजालैः सकलभुवनमाता सन्ततं श्रीः श्रियै नः ॥

Maṇikaṭakavicitrālaṅkṛtākalpajālaiḥ Sakalabhuvanamātā Santataṃ Śrīḥ Śriyai Naḥ ॥

(सौभाग्यलक्ष्मीचक्रम् - *Saubhagyalakṣmīcakram*)

1. तत्पीठकर्णिकायां ससाध्यं श्रीबीजम् । वस्वादित्यकलापद्मेषु श्रीसूक्तगतार्धार्धर्चा

Tatpīṭhakarṇikāyāṃ Sasādhyaṃ Śrībījam ।
Vasvādityakalāpadmeṣu Śrīsūktagatārdhārdharcā
तद्बहिर्यः शुचिरिति मातृकया च श्रियं यन्त्राङ्गदशकं च विलिख्य श्रियमावाहयेत् ।

Tadbahiryaḥ Śuciriti Mātṛkayā Ca Śriyaṃ Yantrāṅgadaśakaṃ Ca Vilikhya Śriyamāvāhayet ।

अङ्गैः प्रथमा वृत्तिः । *Aṅgaiḥ Prathamā Vṛttiḥ* ।

पद्मादिभिर्द्वितीया । सोकेशैस्तृतीया । तदायुधैस्तुरीया

Padmādibhirdvitīyā । *Sokeśaistṛtīyā* । *Tadāyudhaisturīyā*
वृत्तिर्भवति । श्रीसूक्तैरावाहनादि। षोडशसहस्रजपः ।

Vṛttirbhavati । *Śrīsūktairāvāhanādi* । *Ṣoḍaśasahasrajapaḥ* ।

(एकाक्षरीमन्त्रस्य ऋष्यादि - *Ekākṣarīmantrasya Ṛṣyādi*)

1. सौभाग्यरमैकाक्षर्या भृगुनिचृद्गायत्री । श्रिय ऋष्यादयः ।

Saubhāgyaramaikākṣaryā Bhṛgunicṛdgāyatrī । *Śriya Ṛṣyādayaḥ* ।

शमिति बीजशक्तिः । श्रीमित्यादि षडङ्गम् ।

Śamiti Bījaśaktiḥ । *Śrīmityādi Ṣaḍaṅgam* ।
भूयाद्भूयोद्विपद्माभयवरदकरा तप्तकार्तस्वराभा शुभ्राभ्राभेभयुग्मद्वय कर धृत कुम्भाद्भिरा सिच्यमाना ।

Bhūyādbhūyo Dvipadmābhayavaradakarā Taptakārtasvarābhā
Śubhrābhrābhebhayugma Dvayakaradhṛtakumbhādbhirāsicyamānā ।

रक्तौघाबद्धमौलिर्विमलतरदुकूलार्तवालेपनाढ्या पद्माक्षी

Raktaughābaddhamauli Rvimalataradukūlārtavālepanāḍhyā Padmākṣī
पद्मनाभोरसि कृतवसतिः पद्मगा श्रीः श्रियै नः ॥

Padmanābhorasi Kṛtavasatiḥ Padmagā Śrīḥ Śriyai Naḥ ॥

(एकाक्षरीचक्रम् - *Ekākṣarīcakram*)

1. तत्पीठम् । अष्टपत्रं वृत्तत्रयं द्वादशराशिखण्डं

Tatpīṭham | Aṣṭapatraṃ Vṛttatrayaṃ Dvādaśarāśikhaṇḍaṃ
चतुरस्रं रमापीठं भवति। कर्णिकायां ससाध्यं श्रीबीजम्।

Caturasraṃ Ramāpīṭhaṃ Bhavati | Karṇikāyāṃ Sasādhyaṃ Śrībījam |
विभूतिरुन्नतिः कान्तिः सृष्टिः कीर्तिः सन्नतिर्व्युष्टिः
Vibhūtirunnatiḥ Kāntiḥ Sṛṣṭiḥ Kīrtiḥ Sannatirvyuṣṭiḥ
सत्कृष्टिरृद्धिरिति प्रणवादिनमो तैश्चतुर्थ्यन्तैर्नवशक्तिं यजेत्।

Satkṛṣṭirṛddhiriti Praṇavādinamo Taiścaturthyantairnavaśaktiṃ Yajet |
अङ्गे प्रथमा वृतिः। वासुदेवाभिर्द्वितीया। बालाक्यादिभिस्तृतीया।

Aṅge Prathamā Vṛtiḥ | Vāsudevābhirdvitīyā | Bālākyādibhistṛtīyā |
इन्द्रादिभिश्चतुर्थी भवति। द्वादशलक्षजपः।

Indrādibhiścaturthī Bhavati | Dvādaśalakṣajapaḥ |

(लक्ष्मीमन्त्रविशेषाः - *Lakṣmīmantraviśeṣāḥ*)

1. श्रीलक्ष्मीर्वरदा विष्णुपत्नी वसुप्रदा हिरण्यरूपा
Śrīlakṣmīrvaradā Viṣṇupatnī Vasupradā Hiraṇyarūpā
स्वर्णमालिनी रजतस्रजा स्वर्णप्रभा स्वर्णप्राकारा
Svarṇamālinī Rajatasrajā Svarṇaprabhā Svarṇaprākārā
पद्मवासिनी पद्महस्ता पद्मप्रिया मुक्तालङ्कारा चन्द्रसूर्या बिल्वप्रिया ईश्वरी
Padmavāsinī Padmahastā Padmapriyā Muktālaṅkārā Candrasūryā Bilvapriyā Īśvarī
भुक्तिर्मुक्तिर्विभूतिरृद्धिः समृद्धिः कृष्टिः पुष्टिर्धनदा धनेश्वरी
Bhuktirmuktirvibhūtirṛddhiḥ Samṛddhiḥ Kṛṣṭiḥ Puṣṭirdhanadā Dhaneśvarī
श्रद्धा भोगिनी भोगदा सावित्री धात्री
Śraddhā Bhoginī Bhogadā Sāvitrī Dhātrī
विधात्रीत्यादिप्रणवादिनमोन्ताश्चतुर्थ्यन्ता मन्त्राः।

Vidhātrītyādipraṇavādinamontāścaturthyantā Mantrāḥ |
एकाक्षरवदङ्गादिपीठम्। लक्षजपः। दशांशं तर्पणम्।

Ekākṣaravadaṅgādipīṭham | Lakṣajapaḥ | Daśāṃśaṃ Tarpaṇam |
दशांशं हवनम्। द्विजतृप्तिः। निष्कामानामेव श्रीविद्यासिद्धिः।

Daśāṃśaṃ Havanam | Dvijatṛptiḥ | Niṣkāmānāmeva Śrīvidyāsiddhiḥ |
न कदापि सकामानामिति॥ *Na Kadāpi Sakāmānāmiti* ॥

द्वितीयः खण्डः - *Dvitīyaḥ Khaṇḍaḥ*

(उत्तमाधिकारिणां ज्ञानयोगः - *Uttamādhikāriṇāṃ Jñānayogaḥ*)

1. अथ हैनं देवा ऊचुस्तुरीयया मायया निर्दिष्टं तत्त्वं ब्रूहीति। तथेति स होवाच।

Atha Hainaṃ Devā Ūcusturīyayā Māyayā Nirdiṣṭaṃ Tattvaṃ Brūhīti |

Tatheti Sa Hovāca |

योगेन योगो ज्ञातव्यो योगो योगात्प्रवर्धते। योऽप्रमत्तस्तु योगेन स योगी रमते चिरम्॥

Yogena Yogo Jñātavyo Yogo Yogātpravardhate |
Yo'pramattastu Yogena Sa Yogī Ramate Ciram ||

2. समापय्य निद्रां सिजीर्णेऽल्पभोजी श्रमत्याज्यबाधे विविक्ते प्रदेशे।

Samāpayya Nidrāṃ Sijīrṇe'lpabhojī Śramatyājyabādhe Vivikte Pradeśe |
सदा शीतनिस्तृष्ण एष प्रयत्नोऽथ वा प्राणरोधो निजाभ्यासमार्गात्॥
Sadā Śītanistṛṣṇa Eṣa Prayatno'tha Vā Prāṇarodho Nijābhyāsamārgāt ||

3. वक्त्रेणापूर्य वायुं हुतवलनिलयेऽपानमाकृष्य धृत्वा स्वाङ्गुष्ठाद्यङ्गुलीभिर्वरकरतलयोः षड्भिरेवं निरुध्य।

Vaktreṇāpūrya Vāyuṃ Hutavalanilaye'pānamākṛṣya Dhṛtvā

Svāṅguṣṭhādyaṅgulībhirvarakaratalayoḥ Ṣaḍbhirevaṃ Nirudhya |
श्रोत्रे नेत्रे च नासापुटयुगलमतोऽनेन मार्गेण सम्यक् पश्यन्ति प्रत्ययाशं प्रणव बहुविध ध्यान संलीन चित्ताः॥

Śrotre Netre Ca Nāsāpuṭayugalamato'nena Mārgeṇa Samyak-
Paśyanti Pratyayāśaṃ Praṇavabahuvidhadhyānasaṃlīnacittāḥ ||

(नादाविर्भावपूर्वको ग्रन्थित्रयभेदः *Nādāvirbhāvapūrvako Granthitrayabhedaḥ*)

4. श्रवणमुखनयननासानिरोधनेनैव कर्तव्यम्। शुद्धसुषुम्नासरणौस्फुटममलं श्रूयते नादः॥
Śravaṇamukhanayananāsānirodhanenaiva Kartavyam |
Śuddhasuṣumnāsaraṇau Sphuṭamamalaṃ Śrūyate Nādaḥ ||

5. विचित्रघोषसंयुक्तानाहतेश्रूयते ध्वनिः। दिव्यदेहश्च तेजस्वी दिव्यगन्धोऽप्यरोगवान्॥

Vicitraghoṣasaṃyuktānāhate Śrūyate Dhvaniḥ |
Divyadehaśca Tejasvī Divyagandho'pyarogavān ||

6. सम्पूर्णहृदयः शून्ये त्वारम्भे योगवान्भवेत् । द्वितीया विघटीकृत्य वायुर्भवति मध्यगः ॥

Sampūrṇahṛdayaḥ Śūnye Tvārambhe Yogavānbhavet |
Dvitīyā Vighaṭīkṛtya Vāyurbhavati Madhyagaḥ ||

7. दृढासनो भवेद्योगी पद्माद्यासनसंस्थितः । विष्णुग्रन्थेस्ततो भेदात्परमानन्दसम्भवः ॥

Dṛḍhāsano Bhavedyogī Padmādyāsanasaṃsthitaḥ |
Viṣṇugranthestato Bhedātparamānandasambhavaḥ ||

8. अतिशून्यो विमर्दश्च भेरीशब्दस्ततो भवेत् । तृतीयां यत्नतो भित्त्वा निनादो मर्दलध्वनिः

Atiśūnyo Vimardaśca Bherīśabdastato Bhavet |
Tṛtīyāṃ Yatnato Bhittvā Ninādo Mardaladhvaniḥ ||

(अखण्डब्रह्माकारवृत्तिः - *Akhaṇḍabrahmākāravṛttiḥ*)

9. महाशून्यं ततो याति सर्वसिद्धिसमाश्रयम् । चित्तानन्दं ततो भित्त्वा सर्वपीठगतानिलः ॥

Mahāśūnyaṃ Tato Yāti Sarvasiddhisamāśrayam |
Cittānandaṃ Tato Bhittvā Sarvapīṭhagatānilaḥ ||

10. निष्पत्तौ वैष्णवः शब्दः क्वणतीति क्वणो भवेत् । एकीभूतं तदा चित्तं सनकादिमुनीडितम् ॥

Niṣpattau Vaiṣṇavaḥ Śabdaḥ Kvaṇatīti Kvaṇo Bhavet |
Ekībhūtaṃ Tadā Cittaṃ Sanakādimunīḍitam ||

11. अन्तेऽनन्तं समारोप्य खण्डेऽखण्डं समर्पयन् । भूमानं प्रकृतिं ध्यात्वा कृतकृत्योऽमृतो भवेत् ॥

Ante'nantaṃ Samāropya Khaṇḍe'khaṇḍaṃ Samarpayan |
Bhūmānaṃ Prakṛtiṃ Dhyātvā Kṛtakṛtyo'mṛto Bhavet ||

(निर्विकल्पभावः - *Nirvikalpabhāvaḥ*)

12. योगेन योगं संरोध्य भावं भावेन चाञ्जसा । निर्विकल्पं परं तत्त्वं सदा भूत्वा परं भवेत् ॥

Yogena Yogaṃ Saṃrodhya Bhāvaṃ Bhāvena Cāñjasā |
Nirvikalpaṃ Paraṃ Tattvaṃ Sadā Bhūtvā Paraṃ Bhavet ||

13. अहंभावं परित्यज्य जगद्भावमनीदृशम् । निर्विकल्पे स्थितो विद्वान्भूयो नाप्यनुशोचति

Ahaṃbhāvaṃ Parityajya Jagadbhāvamanīdṛśam ।
Nirvikalpe Sthito Vidvānbhūyo Nāpyanuśocati ॥

14. सलिले सैन्धावं यद्वत्साम्यं भवति योगतः । तथात्ममनसौरैक्यं समाधिरभिधीयते ॥

Salile Saindhāvaṃ Yadvatsāmyaṃ Bhavati Yogataḥ ।
Tathātmamanasaurekyaṃ Samādhirabhidhīyate ॥

15. यदा संक्षीयते प्राणो मानसं च प्रलीयते । तदा समरसत्वं यत्समाधिरभिधीयते ॥

Yadā Saṃkṣīyate Prāṇo Mānasaṃ Ca Pralīyate ।
Tadā Samarasatvaṃ Yatsamādhirabhidhīyate ॥

16. यत्समत्वं तयोरत्र जीवात्मपरमात्मनोः । समस्तनष्टसङ्कल्पः समाधिरभिधीयते ॥

Yatsamatvaṃ Tayoratra Jīvātmaparamātmanoḥ ।
Samastanaṣṭasaṅkalpaḥ Samādhirabhidhīyate ॥

17. प्रभाशून्यं मनःशून्यं बुद्धिशून्यं निरामयम् । सर्वशून्यं निराभासं समाधिरभिधीयते ॥

Prabhāśūnyaṃ Manaḥśūnyaṃ Buddhiśūnyaṃ Nirāmayam ।
Sarvaśūnyaṃ Nirābhāsaṃ Samādhirabhidhīyate ॥

तृतीय खण्डः *Tṛtīya Khaṇḍaḥ*

(आधारचक्रम् - *Ādhāracakam*)

18. स्वयमुच्चलिते देहे देही नित्यसमाधिना । निश्चलं तं विजानीयात्समाधिरभिधीयते ॥

Svayamuccalite Dehe Dehī Nityasamādhinā ।
Niścalaṃ Taṃ Vijānīyātsamādhirabhidhīyate ॥

19. यत्रयत्र मनो याति तत्रतत्र परं पदम् । तत्रतत्र परं ब्रह्म सर्वत्र समवस्थितम् ॥

Yatrayatra Mano Yāti Tatratatra Paraṃ Padam ।
Tatratatra Paraṃ Brahma Sarvatra Samavasthitam ॥

20. अथ हैनं देवा ऊचुर्नवचक्रविवेकमनुब्रूहीति।

Atha Hainaṃ Devā Ūcurnavacakravivekamanubrūhīti ।
तथेति स होवाच आधारे ब्रह्मचक्रं त्रिरावृत्तं भगमण्डलाकारम् ।
Tatheti Sa Hovāca Ādhāre Brahmacakraṃ Trirāvṛttaṃ

तत्र मूलकन्दे शक्तिः पावकाकारं ध्यायेत्। तत्रैव कामरूपपीठं सर्वकामप्रदं भवति।

Bhagamaṇḍalākāram ।

Tatra Mūlakande Śaktiḥ Pāvakākāraṃ Dhyāyet ।

Tatraiva Kāmarūpapīṭhaṃ Sarvakāmapradaṃ Bhavati ।

इत्याधारचक्रम्। द्वितीयं स्वाधिष्ठानचक्रं षड्दलम्।

Ityādhāracakram । *Dvitīyaṃ Svādhiṣṭhānacakraṃ Ṣaḍdalam* ।

तन्मध्ये पश्चिमाभिमुखं लिङ्गं प्रवालाङ्कुरसदृशं ध्यायेत्।

Tanmadhye Paścimābhimukhaṃ Liṅgaṃ Pravālāṅkurasadṛśaṃ Dhyāyet

तत्रैवोड्याणपीठं जगदाकर्षणसिद्धिदं भवति।

Tatraivoḍyāṇapīṭhaṃ Jagadākarṣaṇasiddhidaṃ Bhavati ।

तृतीयं नाभिचक्रं पञ्चावर्तं सर्पकुटिलाकारम्।

Tṛtīyaṃ Nābhicakraṃ Pañcāvartaṃ Sarpakuṭilākāram ।

तन्मध्ये कुण्डलिनीं बालार्ककोटिप्रभां तनुमध्यां ध्यायेत्।

Tanmadhye Kuṇḍalinīṃ Bālārkakoṭiprabhāṃ Tanumadhyāṃ Dhyāyet ।

सामर्थ्यशक्तिः सर्वसिद्धिप्रदा भवति। मणिपूरचक्रं हृदयचक्रम्।

Sāmarthyaśaktiḥ Sarvasiddhipradā Bhavati ।

Maṇipūracakraṃ Hṛdayacakram ।

अष्टदलमधोमुखम्। तन्मध्ये ज्योतिर्मयलिङ्गाकारं ध्यायेत्।

Aṣṭadalamadhomukham । *Tanmadhye Jyotirmayaliṅgākāraṃ Dhyāyet* ।

सैव हंसकला सर्वप्रिया सर्वलोकवश्यकरी भवति। कण्ठचक्रं चतुरङ्गुलम्।

Saiva Haṃsakalā Sarvapriyā Sarvalokavaśyakarī Bhavati ।

Kaṇṭhacakraṃ Caturaṅgulam ।

तत्र वामे इडा चन्द्रनाडी दक्षिणे पिङ्गला सूर्यनाडी तन्मध्ये सुषुम्नां श्वेतवर्णां ध्यायेत्।

Tatra Vāme Iḍā Candranāḍī Dakṣiṇe Piṅgalā Sūryanāḍī Tanmadhye Suṣumnāṃ Śvetavarṇāṃ Dhyāyet ।

य एवं वेदानाहता सिद्धिदा भवति। तालुचक्रम्। तत्रामृतधाराप्रवाहः।

Ya Evaṃ Vedānāhatā Siddhidā Bhavati ।

Tālucakram । *Tatrāmṛtadhārāpravāhaḥ* ।

घण्टिकालिङ्गमूलचक्ररन्ध्रे राजदन्तावलम्बिनीविवरं दशद्वादशारम्।

Ghaṇṭikāliṅgamūlacakrarandhre Rājadantāvalambinīvivaraṃ Daśadvādaśāram I

तत्र शून्यं ध्यायेत्। चित्तलयो भवति। सप्तमं भ्रूचक्रमङ्गुष्ठमात्रम्।

Tatra Śūnyaṃ Dhyāyet I *Cittalayo Bhavati* I

Saptamaṃ Bhrūcakramaṅguṣṭhamātram I

तत्र ज्ञाननेत्रं दीपशिखाकारं ध्यायेत्। तदेव कपालकन्दवाक्सिद्धिदं भवति।

Tatra Jñānanetraṃ Dīpaśikhākāraṃ Dhyāyet I

Tadeva Kapālakandavāksiddhidaṃ Bhavati I

आज्ञाचक्रमष्टमम्। ब्रह्मरन्ध्रं निर्वाणचक्रम्।

Ājñācakramaṣṭamam I *Brahmarandhraṃ Nirvāṇacakram* I

तत्र सूचिकागृहेतरं धूम्रशिखाकारं ध्यायेत्।

Tatra Sūcikāgṛhetaraṃ Dhūmraśikhākāraṃ Dhyāyet I

तत्र जालन्धरपीठं मोक्षप्रदं भवतीति परब्रह्मचक्रम्।

Tatra Jālandharapīṭhaṃ Mokṣapradaṃ Bhavatīti Parabrahmacakram I

नवममाकाशचक्रम्। तत्र षोडशदलपद्ममूर्ध्वमुखं तन्मध्यकर्णिकात्रिकूटाकारम्।

Navamamākāśacakram I *Tatra Ṣoḍaśadalapadmamūrdhvamukhaṃ*

तन्मध्ये ऊर्ध्वशक्तिः। तां पश्यन्ध्यायेत्।

Tanmadhyakarṇikātrikūṭākāram I *Tanmadhye Ūrdhvaśaktiḥ* I

Tāṃ Paśyandhyāyet I *Tatraiva Pūrṇagiripīṭhaṃ*

तत्रैव पूर्णगिरिपीठं सर्वेच्छासिद्धिसाधनं भवति।

Sarvecchāsiddhisādhanaṃ Bhavati I *Saubhāgyalakṣmyupaniṣadaṃ*

सौभाग्यलक्ष्म्युपनिषदं नित्यमधीते योऽग्निपूतो भवति। स वायुपूतो भवति।

Nityamadhīte Yo'gnipūto Bhavati I *Sa Vāyupūto Bhavati* I

स सकल धन धान्य सत्पुत्र कलत्र हयभूग जप शुमहिषीदासीदास योगज्ञानवान्भवति।

Sa Sakala Dhana Dhānya Satputra Kalatrahaya Bhūga Japa Śumahi Ṣīdāsīdāsa Yogajñānavānbhavati I

न स पुनरावर्तते न स पुनरावर्तत इत्युपनिषत्।

Na Sa Punarāvartate Na Sa Punarāvartata Ityupaniṣat I

शान्ति मन्त्रः - *Shanti Mantra*:

ॐ वाङ्मे मनसि प्रतिष्ठिता । मनो मे वाचि प्रतिष्ठितम् ।

Oṃ Vāṅme Manasi Pratiṣṭhitā । *Mano Me Vāci Pratiṣṭhitam* ।

आविरावीर्म एधि । वेदस्य म आणीस्थः । श्रुतं मे मा प्रहासीः ।

Āvirāvīrma Edhi । *Vedasya Ma Āṇīsthaḥ* । *Śrutaṃ Me Mā Prahāsīḥ* ।

अनेनाधीतेनाहोरात्रान् संदधामि । ऋतं वदिष्यामि ।

Anenādhītenāhorātrān Saṃdadhāmi । *Ṛtaṃ Vadiṣyāmi* ।

सत्यं वदिष्यामि । तन्मामवतु । तद्वक्तारमवतु । अवतु माम् ।

Satyaṃ Vadiṣyāmi । *Tanmāmavatu* । *Tadvaktāramavatu* । *Avatu Mām* ।

अवतु वक्तारम् । अवतु वक्तारम् ।*Avatu Vaktāram* । *Avatu Vaktāram* ।

ॐ शान्तिः शान्तिः शान्तिः ॥ *Oṃ Śāntiḥ Śāntiḥ Śāntiḥ* ॥

इति श्रीसौभाग्यलक्ष्म्युपनिषत्समाप्ता ॥
Iti Śrīsaubhāgyalakṣmyupaniṣatsamāptā ॥

*****

Śrī Sarasvatī Rahasyopaniṣat

श्रीसरस्वतीरहस्योपनिषत्

This *Upaniṣat* belongs to *Krişņa Yajur Veda*.

प्रतियोगिविनिर्मुक्तब्रह्मविद्यैकगोचरम् । अखण्डनिर्विकल्पं तद्रामचन्द्रपदं भजे ॥

Pratiyogivinirmuktabrahmavidyaikagocaram ।

Akhaṇḍanirvikalpaṃ Tadrāmacandrapadaṃ Bhaje ॥

शान्ति मन्त्र: - *Shanti Mantra*:

ॐ वाङ्मे मनसि प्रतिष्ठिता । मनो मे वाचि प्रतिष्ठितम् ।

Oṃ Vāṅme Manasi Pratiṣṭhitā । *Mano Me Vāci Pratiṣṭhitam* ।

आविरावीर्म एधि । वेदस्य म आणीस्थः । श्रुतं मे मा प्रहासीः ।

Āvirāvīrma Edhi । *Vedasya Ma Āṇīsthaḥ* । *Śrutaṃ Me Mā Prahāsīḥ* ।

अनेनाधीतेनाहोरात्रान् संदधामि । ऋतं वदिष्यामि ।

Anenādhītenāhorātrān Saṃdadhāmi । *Ṛtaṃ Vadiṣyāmi* ।

सत्यं वदिष्यामि । तन्मामवतु । तद्वक्तारमवतु। अवतु माम् ।

Satyaṃ Vadiṣyāmi । *Tanmāmavatu* । *Tadvaktāramavatu* । *Avatu Mām* ।

अवतु वक्तारम् । अवतु वक्तारम् ।*Avatu Vaktāram* । *Avatu Vaktāram* ।

ॐ शान्तिः शान्तिः शान्तिः ॥ *Oṃ Śāntiḥ Śāntiḥ Śāntiḥ* ॥

1. हरिः ॐ ॥ ऋषयो ह वै भगवन्तमाश्वलायनं सम्पूज्य पप्रच्छुः केनोपायेन तज्ज्ञानं तत्पदार्थावभासकम् ।

Hariḥ Oṃ ॥ *Ṛṣayo Ha Vai Bhagavantamāśvalāyanaṃ Sampūjya Papracchuḥ Kenopāyena Tajjñānaṃ Tatpadārthāvabhāsakam* ।

यदुपासनया तत्त्वं जानासि भगवन्वद ॥

Yadupāsanayā Tattvaṃ Jānāsi Bhagavanvada ॥

2. सरस्वती दशश्लोक्या सऋचा बीजमिश्रया ।

Sarasvatī Daśaślokyā Saṛcā Bījamiśrayā ।

स्तुत्वा जप्त्वा परां सिद्धिमलभं मुनिपुङ्गवाः॥

Stutvā Japtvā Parāṃ Siddhimalabhaṃ Munipuṅgavāḥ ॥

3. ऋषय ऊचुः । *Ṛṣaya Ūcuḥ* ।

कथं सारस्वतप्राप्तिः केन ध्यानेन सुव्रत। महासरस्वती येन तुष्टा भगवती वद ॥

Katham Sārasvataprāptiḥ Kena Dhyānena Suvrata ।

Mahāsarasvatī Yena Tuṣṭā Bhagavatī Vada ॥

स होवाचाश्वलायनः । अस्य श्रीसरस्वतीदशश्लोकीमहामन्त्रस्य ।

Sa Hovācāśvalāyanaḥ । *Asya Śrīsarasvatīdaśaślokīmahāmantrasya* ।
अहमाश्वलायन ऋषिः । अनुष्टुप् छन्दः । श्री वागीश्वरी देवता ।

Ahamāśvalāyana Ṛṣiḥ । *Anuṣṭup Chandaḥ* । *Śrī Vāgīśvarī Devatā* ।
यद्वागिति बीजम् । देवीं वाचमिति शक्तिः । प्रणो देवीति कीलकम् ।

Yadvāgiti Bījam । *Devīṃ Vācamiti Śaktiḥ* । *Praṇo Devīti Kīlakam* ।
विनियोगस्तत्प्रीत्यर्थे । श्रद्धा मेधा प्रज्ञा धारणा वाग्देवता महासरस्वतीत्येतैरङ्गन्यासः ॥

Viniyogastatprītyarthe । *Śraddhā Medhā Prajñā Dhāraṇā Vāgdevatā Mahāsarasvatītyetairaṅganyāsaḥ* ॥

1. नीहारहारघनसारसुधाकराभां कल्याणदां कनकचम्पकदामभूषाम् ।
Nīhārahāraghanasārasudhākarābhāṃ Kalyāṇadāṃ Kanakacampakadāmabhūṣām ।
उत्तुङ्गपीनकुचकुम्भ मनोहराङ्गीं वाणीं नमामि मनसा वचसा विभूत्यै ॥
Uttuṅgapīnakucakumbha Manoharāṅgīṃ Vāṇīṃ Namāmi Manasā Vacasā Vibhūtyai ॥
ॐ प्रणोदेवीत्यस्य मन्त्रस्य भरद्वाज ऋषिः । गायत्री छन्दः ।

Oṃ Praṇodevītyasya Mantrasya Bharadvāja Ṛṣiḥ । *Gāyatrī Chandaḥ* ।

श्रीसरस्वती देवता । प्रणवेन बीजशक्तिः कीलकम् । इष्टार्थे विनियोगः ।

Śrīsarasvatī Devatā । *Praṇavena Bījaśaktiḥ Kīlakam* । *Iṣṭārthe Viniyogaḥ* ।
मन्त्रेण न्यासः ॥ या वेदान्तार्थतत्त्वैकस्वरूपा परमार्थतः ।

Mantreṇa Nyāsaḥ ॥ *Yā Vedāntārthatattvaikasvarūpā Paramārthataḥ* ।
नामरूपात्मना व्यक्ता सा मां पातु सरस्वती ॥

Nāmarūpātmanā Vyaktā Sā Māṃ Pātu Sarasvatī ॥
ॐ प्रणो देवी सरस्वती वाजेभिर्वाजिनीवती ॥

Oṃ Praṇo Devī Sarasvatī Vājebhirvājinīvatī ||

धीनामवित्र्यवतु || *Dhīnāmavitryavatu* ||

आ नो दिव इति मन्त्रस्य अत्रिरृषिः । त्रिष्टुप् छन्दः ।

Ā No Diva Iti Mantrasya Atrirṛṣiḥ | *Triṣṭup Chandaḥ* |
सरस्वती देवता । ह्रीमिति बीजशक्तिः कीलकम् ।

Sarasvatī Devatā | *Hrīmiti Bījaśaktiḥ Kīlakam* |
इष्टार्थे विनियोगः । मन्त्रेण न्यासः ॥ या साङ्गोपाङ्गवेदेषु चतुर्ष्वेकैव गीयते ।

Iṣṭārthe Viniyogaḥ | *Mantreṇa Nyāsaḥ* || *Yā Sāṅgopāṅgavedeṣu*

Caturṣvekaiva Gīyate |
अद्वैता ब्रह्मणः शक्तिः सा मां पातु सरस्वती ॥

Advaitā Brahmaṇaḥ Śaktiḥ Sā Māṃ Pātu Sarasvatī ||

2. ह्रीं आ नो दिवो बृहतः पर्वतादा सरस्वती यजतागं तु यज्ञम् ।

Hrīṃ Ā No Divo Bṛhataḥ Parvatādā Sarasvatī Yajatāgaṃ Tu Yajñam |
हवं देवी जुजुषाणा घृताची शग्मां नो वाचमुशती श्रुणोतु ॥

Havaṃ Devī Jujuṣāṇā Ghṛtācī Śagmāṃ No Vācamuśatī Śruṇotu ||

3. पावका न इति मन्त्रस्य । मधुच्छन्द ऋषिः । गायत्री छन्दः ।

Pāvakā Na Iti Mantrasya | *Madhucchanda Ṛṣiḥ* | *Gāyatrī Chandaḥ* |
सरस्वती देवता । श्रीमिति बीजशक्तिः कीलकम् ।

Sarasvatī Devatā | *Śrīmiti Bījaśaktiḥ Kīlakam* |
इष्टार्थे विनियोगः । मन्त्रेण न्यासः ॥ या वर्णपदवाक्यार्थ-

Iṣṭārthe Viniyogaḥ | *Mantreṇa Nyāsaḥ* || *Yā Varṇapadavākyārtha-*
स्वरूपेणैव वर्तते । अनादिनिधनानन्ता सा मां पातु सरस्वती ॥

Svarūpeṇaiva Vartate | *Anādinidhanānantā Sā Māṃ Pātu*

Sarasvatī ||
श्रीं पावका नः सरस्वती वाजेभिर्वाजिनीवती । यज्ञं वष्टु धिया वसुः ॥

Śrīṃ Pāvakā Naḥ Sarasvatī Vājebhirvājinīvatī | *Yajñaṃ*

Vaṣṭu Dhiyā Vasuḥ ||

4. चोदयित्रीति मन्त्रस्य मधुच्छन्द ऋषिः । गायत्री छन्दः ।

Codayitrīti Mantrasya Madhucchanda Ṛṣiḥ | Gāyatrī Chandaḥ |
सरस्वती देवता। ब्लूमिति बीजशक्तिः कीलकम्। मन्त्रेण न्यासः॥

Sarasvatī Devatā | Blūmiti Bījaśaktiḥ Kīlakam | Mantreṇa Nyāsaḥ ||
अध्यात्ममधिदैवं च देवानां सम्यगीश्वरी। प्रत्यगास्ते वदन्ती या सा मां पातु सरस्वती॥

Adhyātmamadhidaivaṃ Ca Devānāṃ Samyagīśvarī |

Pratyagāste Vadantī Yā Sā Māṃ Pātu Sarasvatī ||
ब्लूं चोदयित्री सूनृतानां चेतन्ती सुमतीनाम्। यज्ञं दधे सरस्वती॥

Blūṃ Codayitrī Sūnṛtānāṃ Cetantī Sumatīnām |

Yajñaṃ Dadhe Sarasvatī ||

5. महो अर्ण इति मन्त्रस्य। मधुच्छन्द ऋषिः। गायत्री छन्दः।

Maho Arṇa Iti Mantrasya | Madhucchanda Ṛṣiḥ | Gāyatrī Chandaḥ |
सरस्वती देवता। सौरिति बीजशक्तिः कीलकम्। मन्त्रेण न्यासः।

Sarasvatī Devatā | Sauriti Bījaśaktiḥ Kīlakam | Mantreṇa Nyāsaḥ |
अन्तर्याम्यात्मना विश्वं त्रैलोक्यं या नियच्छति।

Antaryāmyātmanā Viśvaṃ Trailokyaṃ Yā Niyacchati |

रुद्रादित्यारूपस्था यस्यामावेश्य तां पुनः। ध्यायन्ति सर्वरूपैका सा मां पातु सरस्वती।

Rudrādityārūpasthā Yasyāmāveśya Tāṃ Punaḥ | Dhyāyanti

Sarvarūpaikā Sā Māṃ Pātu Sarasvatī |
सौः महो अर्णः सरस्वती प्रचेतयति केतुना। धियो विश्वा विराजति॥

Sauḥ Maho Arṇaḥ Sarasvatī Pracetayati Ketunā | Dhiyo Viśvā Virājati ||

6. चत्वारि वागिति मन्त्रस्य उचथ्यपुत्र ऋषिः। त्रिष्टुप् छन्दः।

Catvāri Vāgiti Mantrasya Ucathyaputra Ṛṣiḥ | Triṣṭup Chandaḥ |
सरस्वती देवता। ऐमिति बीजशक्तिः कीलकम्। मन्त्रेण न्यासः।

Sarasvatī Devatā | Aimiti Bījaśaktiḥ Kīlakam | Mantreṇa Nyāsaḥ |
या प्रत्यग्दृष्टिभिर्जीवैर्व्यज्यमानानुभूयते। व्यापिनी ज्ञप्तिरूपैका सा मां पातु सरस्वती॥

Yā Pratyagdṛṣṭibhirjīvairvyajyamānānubhūyate |

Vyāpinī Z`Naptirūpaikā Sā Māṃ Pātu Sarasvatī ||
ऐं चत्वारि वाक् परिमिता पदानि तानि विदुर्ब्राह्मणा ये मनीषिणः।

Aiṃ Catvāri Vāk Parimitā Padāni Tāni Vidurbrāhmaṇā Ye Manīṣiṇaḥ ।

गुहा त्रीणि निहिता नेङ्गयन्ति तुरीयं वाचो मनुष्या वदन्ति ॥

Guhā Trīṇi Nihitā Neṅgayanti Turīyaṃ Vāco Manuṣyā Vadanti ॥

7. यद्वाग्वदन्तीति मन्त्रस्य भार्गव ऋषिः । त्रिष्टुप् छन्दः ।

Yadrāgvadantīti Mantrasya Bhārgava Ṛṣiḥ । *Triṣṭup Chandaḥ* ।
सरस्वती देवता । क्लीमिति बीजशक्तिः कीलकम् । मन्त्रेण न्यासः ।

Sarasvatī Devatā । *Klīmiti Bījaśaktiḥ Kīlakam* । *Mantreṇa Nyāsaḥ* ।
नामजात्यादिभिर्भेदैरष्टधा या विकल्पिता । निर्विकल्पात्मना व्यक्ता सा मां पातु सरस्वती ॥

Nāmajātyādibhirbhedairaṣṭadhā Yā Vikalpitā ।

Nirvikalpātmanā Vyaktā Sā Māṃ Pātu Sarasvatī ॥
क्लीं यद्वाग्वदन्त्यविचेतनानि राष्ट्री देवानां निषसाद मन्द्रा ।

Klīṃ Yadvāgvadantyavicetanāni Rāṣṭrī Devānāṃ Niṣasāda Mandrā ।
चतस्र ऊर्जं दुदुहे पयांसि क्व स्विदस्याः परमं जगाम ॥

Catasra Ūrjaṃ Duduhe Payāṃsi Kva Svidasyāḥ Paramaṃ Jagāma ॥

8. देवीं वाचमिति मन्त्रस्य भार्गव ऋषिः । त्रिष्टुप् छन्दः ।

Devīṃ Vācamiti Mantrasya Bhārgava Ṛṣiḥ । *Triṣṭup Chandaḥ* ।
सरस्वती देवता । सौरिति बीजशक्तिः कीलकम् । मन्त्रेण न्यासः ।

Sarasvatī Devatā । *Sauriti Bījaśaktiḥ Kīlakam* । *Mantreṇa Nyāsaḥ* ।
व्यक्ताव्यक्तगिरः सर्वे वेदाद्या व्याहरन्ति याम् ।

Vyaktāvyaktagiraḥ Sarve Vedādyā Vyāharanti Yām ।
सर्वकामदुधा धेनुः सा मां पातु सरस्वती ॥

Sarvakāmadudhā Dhenuḥ Sā Māṃ Pātu Sarasvatī ॥
सौः देवीं वाचमजनयन्त देवास्ता विश्वरूपाः पशवो वदन्ति ।

Sauḥ Devīṃ Vācamajanayanta Devāstā Viśvarūpāḥ Paśavo Vadanti ।
सा नो मन्द्रेषमूर्जं दुहाना धेनुर्वागस्मानुपसुष्टुतैतु॥

Sā No Mandreṣamūrjaṃ Duhānā Dhenurvāgasmānupasuṣṭutaitu ॥

9. उत त्व इति मन्त्रस्य बृहस्पतिरृषिः । त्रिष्टुप् छन्दः ।

Uta Tva Iti Mantrasya Bṛhaspatirṛṣiḥ | *Triṣṭup Chandaḥ* |
सरस्वती देवता। समिति बीजशक्तिः कीलकम्। मन्त्रेण न्यासः।

Sarasvatī Devatā | *Samiti Bījaśaktiḥ Kīlakam* | *Mantreṇa Nyāsaḥ* |
यां विदित्वाखिलं बन्धं निर्मथ्याखिलवर्त्मना। योगी याति परं स्थानं सा मां पातु सरस्वती॥

Yāṃ Viditvākhilaṃ Bandhaṃ Nirmathyākhilavartmanā |

Yogī Yāti Paraṃ Sthānaṃ Sā Māṃ Pātu Sarasvatī ||
सं उत त्वः पश्यन्न ददर्श वाचमुत त्वः श्रुण्वन्न श्रुणोत्येनाम्।
Saṃ Uta Tvaḥ Paśyanna Dadarśa Vācamuta Tvaḥ Śruṇvanna Śruṇotyenām |
उतो त्वस्मै तन्वं (१) विसस्रे जायेव पत्य उशती सुवासाः॥

Uto Tvasmai Tanvaṃ (1) *Visasre Jāyeva Patya Uśatī Suvāsāḥ* ||

10. अम्बितम इति मन्त्रस्य गृत्समद ऋषिः। अनुष्टुप् छन्दः।

Ambitama Iti Mantrasya Gṛtsamada Ṛṣiḥ | *Anuṣṭup Chandaḥ* |
सरस्वती देवता। ऐमिति बीजशक्तिः कीलकम्। मन्त्रेण न्यासः।

Sarasvatī Devatā | *Aimiti Bījaśaktiḥ Kīlakam* | *Mantreṇa Nyāsaḥ* |
नामरूपात्मकं सर्वं यस्यामावेश्य तां पुनः। ध्यायन्ति ब्रह्मरूपैका सा मां पातु सरस्वती॥

Nāmarūpātmakaṃ Sarvaṃ Yasyāmāveśya Tāṃ Punaḥ |

Dhyāyanti Brahmarūpaikā Sā Māṃ Pātu Sarasvatī ||
ऐं अम्बितमे नदीतमे देवितमे सरस्वती। अप्रशस्ता इव स्मसि प्रशस्तिमम्ब नस्कृधि॥

Aiṃ Ambitame Nadītame Devitame Sarasvatī |

Apraśastā Iva Smasi Praśastimamba Naskṛdhi ||

11. चतुर्मुखमुखाम्भोजवनहंसवधूर्मम। मानसे रमतां नित्यं सर्वशुक्ला सरस्वती॥

Caturmukhamukhāmbhojavanahaṃsavadhūrmama |

Mānase Ramatāṃ Nityaṃ Sarvaśuklā Sarasvatī ||

12. नमस्ते शारदे देवि काश्मीरपुरवासिनि। त्वामहं प्रार्थये नित्यं विद्यादानं च देहि मे॥

Namaste Śārade Devi Kāśmīrapuravāsini |

Tvāmahaṃ Prārthaye Nityaṃ Vidyādānaṃ Ca Dehi Me ||

13. अक्षसूत्राङ्कुशधरा पाशपुस्तकधारिणी। मुक्ताहारसमायुक्ता वाचि तिष्ठतु मे सदा॥

Akṣasūtrāṅkuśadharā Pāśapustakadhāriṇī |

Muktāhārasamāyuktā Vāci Tiṣṭhatu Me Sadā ||

14. कम्बुकण्ठी सुताम्रोष्ठी सर्वाभरणभूषिता। महासरस्वती देवी जिह्वाग्रे संनिविश्यताम्॥

Kambukaṇṭhī Sutāmroṣṭhī Sarvābharaṇabhūṣitā |

Mahāsarasvatī Devī Jihvāgre Saṃniviśyatām ||

15. या श्रद्धा धारणा मेधा वाग्देवी विधिवल्लभा। भक्तजिह्वाग्रसदना शमादिगुणदायिनी॥

Yā Śraddhā Dhāraṇā Medhā Vāgdevī Vidhivallabhā |

Bhaktajihvāgrasadanā Śamādiguṇadāyinī ||

16. नमामि यामिनीनाथलेखालङ्कृतकुन्तलाम्। भवानीं भवसन्तापनिर्वापणसुधानदीम्॥

Namāmi Yāminīnāthalekhālaṅkṛtakuntalām |

Bhavānīṃ Bhavasantāpanirvāpaṇasudhānadīm ||

17. यः कवित्वं निरातङ्कं भुक्तिमुक्ती च वाञ्छति।
सोऽभैर्च्यैनां दशश्लोक्या नित्यं स्तौति सरस्वतीम्॥

Yaḥ Kavitvaṃ Nirātaṅkaṃ Bhuktimuktī Ca Vāñchati |

So'bhaircyaināṃ Daśaślokyā Nityaṃ Stauti Sarasvatīm ||

18. तस्यैवं स्तुवतो नित्यं समभ्यर्च्य सरस्वतीम्।
भक्तिश्रद्धाभियुक्तस्य षण्मासात्प्रत्ययो भवेत्॥

Tasyaivaṃ Stuvato Nityaṃ Samabhyarcya Sarasvatīm |

Bhaktiśraddhābhiyuktasya Ṣaṇmāsātpratyayo Bhavet ||

19. ततः प्रवर्तते वाणी स्वेच्छया ललिताक्षरा। गद्यपद्यात्मकैः शब्दैरप्रमेयैर्विवक्षितैः॥

Tataḥ Pravartate Vāṇī Svecchayā Lalitākṣarā |

Gadyapadyātmakaiḥ Śabdairaprameyairvivakṣitaiḥ ||

20. अश्रुतो बुध्यते ग्रन्थः प्रायः सारस्वतः कविः। इत्येवं निश्चयं विप्राः सा होवाच सरस्वती

Aśruto Budhyate Granthaḥ Prāyaḥ Sārasvataḥ Kaviḥ |

Ityevaṃ Niścayaṃ Viprāḥ Sā Hovāca Sarasvatī ||

21. आत्मविद्या मया लब्ध्वा ब्रह्मणैव सनातनी। ब्रह्मत्वं मे सदा नित्यं सच्चिदानन्दरूपतः

Ātmavidyā Mayā Labdhvā Brahmaṇaiva Sanātanī |

Brahmatvaṃ Me Sadā Nityaṃ Saccidānandarūpataḥ ||

22. प्रकृतित्वं ततः सृष्टं सत्त्वादिगुणसाम्यतः । सत्यमाभाति चिच्छाया दर्पणे प्रतिबिम्बवत्

Prakṛtitvaṃ Tataḥ Sṛṣṭaṃ Sattvādiguṇasāmyataḥ |

Satyamābhāti Cicchāyā Darpaṇe Pratibimbavat ||

23. तेन चित्प्रतिबिम्बेन त्रिविधा भाति सा पुनः । प्रकृत्यवच्छिन्नतया पुरुषत्वं पुनश्च ते ॥

Tena Citpratibimbena Trividhā Bhāti Sā Punaḥ |

Prakṛtyavacchinnatayā Puruṣatvaṃ Punaśca Te ||

24. शुद्धसत्त्वप्रधानायां मायायां बिम्बितो ह्यजः । सत्त्वप्रधाना प्रकृतिर्मायेति प्रतिपाद्यते ॥

Śuddhasattvapradhānāyāṃ Māyāyāṃ Bimbito Hyajaḥ |

Sattvapradhānā Prakṛtirmāyeti Pratipādyate ||

25. सा माया स्ववशोपाधिः सर्वज्ञस्येश्वरस्य हि । वश्यमायत्वमेकत्वं सर्वज्ञत्वं च तस्य तु ॥

Sā Māyā Svavaśopādhiḥ Sarvajñasyeśvarasya Hi |

Vaśyamāyatvamekatvaṃ Sarvajñatvaṃ Ca Tasya Tu ||

26. सात्विकत्वात्समष्टित्वात्साक्षित्वाज्जगतामपि । जगत्कर्तुमकर्तुं वा चान्यथा कर्तुमीशते ॥

Sātvikatvātsamaṣṭitvātsākṣitvājjagatāmapi |

Jagatkartumakartuṃ Vā Cānyathā Kartumīśate ||

27. यः स ईश्वर इत्युक्तः सर्वज्ञत्वादिभिर्गुणैः । शक्तिद्वयं हि मायाया विक्षेपावृतिरूपकम् ॥

Yaḥ Sa Īśvara Ityuktaḥ Sarvajñatvādibhirguṇaiḥ |

Śaktidvayaṃ Hi Māyāyā Vikṣepāvṛtirūpakam ||

28. विक्षेपशक्तिर्लिङ्गादिब्रह्माण्डान्तं जगत्सृजेत् । अन्तर्दृग्दृश्ययोर्भेदं बहिश्च ब्रह्मसर्गयोः ॥

Vikṣepaśaktirliṅgādibrahmāṇḍāntaṃ Jagatsṛjet |

Antardṛgdṛśyayorbhedaṃ Bahiśca Brahmasargayoḥ ||

29. आवृणोत्यपरा शक्तिः सा संसारस्य कारणम् । साक्षिणः पुरतो भातं लिङ्गदेहेन संयुतम्

Āvṛṇotyaparā Śaktiḥ Sā Saṃsārasya Kāraṇam |

Sākṣiṇaḥ Purato Bhātaṃ Liṅgadehena Saṃyutam ||

29. चितिच्छायासमावेशाज्जीवः स्याद्व्यावहारिकः ।
अस्य जीवत्वमारोपात्साक्षिण्यप्यवभासते ॥

Citicchāyāsamāveśājjīvaḥ Syādvyāvahārikaḥ |

Asya Jīvatvamāropātsākṣiṇyapyavabhāsate ||

31. आवृतौ तु विनष्टायां भेदे भातेऽपयाति तत् । तथा सर्गब्रह्मणोश्च भेदमावृत्य तिष्ठति ॥

Āvṛtau Tu Vinaṣṭāyāṃ Bhede Bhāte'payāti Tat |

Tathā Sargabrahmaṇośca Bhedamāvṛtya Tiṣṭhati ||

32. या शक्तिस्त्वद्वशाद्ब्रह्म विकृतत्वेन भासते । अत्राप्यावृतिनाशेन विभाति ब्रह्मसर्गयोः ॥

Yā Śaktistvadvaśādbrahma Vikṛtatvena Bhāsate |

Atrāpyāvṛtināśena Vibhāti Brahmasargayoḥ ||

34. भेदस्तयोर्विकारः स्यात्सर्गे न ब्रह्मणि क्वचित् ।
अस्ति भाति प्रियं रूपं नाम चेत्यंशपञ्चकम् ॥

Bhedastayorvikāraḥ Syātsarge Na Brahmaṇi Kvacit |

Asti Bhāti Priyaṃ Rūpaṃ Nāma Cetyaṃśapañcakam ||

35. आद्यत्रयं ब्रह्मरूपं जगद्रूपं ततो द्वयम् । अपेक्ष्य नामरूपद्वे सच्चिदानन्दतत्परः ॥

Ādyatrayaṃ Brahmarūpaṃ Jagadrūpaṃ Tato Dvayam |

Apekṣya Nāmarūpadve Saccidānandatatparaḥ ||

36. समाधिं सर्वदा कुर्याधृदये वाथ वा बहिः । सविकल्पो निर्विकल्पः समाधिर्द्विविधो हृदि

Samādhiṃ Sarvadā Kuryādhṛdaye Vātha Vā Bahiḥ |

Savikalpo Nirvikalpaḥ Samādhirdvividho Hṛdi ||

37. दृश्यशब्दानुभेदेन स विकल्पः पुनर्द्विधा । कामाद्याश्चित्तगा दृश्यास्तत्साक्षित्वेन चेतनम्

Dṛśyaśabdānubhedena Sa Vikalpaḥ Punardvidhā |

Kāmādyāścittagā Dṛśyāstatsākṣitvena Cetanam ||

38. ध्यायद्दृश्यानुविद्धोऽयंसमाधिः सविकल्पकः ।
स्वानुभूतिरसावेशाद्दृश्यशब्दा द्यपेक्षितुः ॥

Dhyāyaddṛśyānuviddho'yaṃ Samādhiḥ Savikalpakaḥ |

Svānubhūtirasāveśāddṛśyaśabdādyapekṣituḥ ||

39. निर्विकल्पः समाधिः स्यान्निवान्तस्थितदीपवत् ।
हृदीव बाह्यदेशेऽपि यस्मिन्कस्मिंश्च वस्तुनि ॥

Nirvikalpaḥ Samādhiḥ Syānnivāntasthitadīpavat |

Hṛdīva Bāhyadeśe'pi Yasminkasmiṃśca Vastuni ||

40. समाधिराद्यसन्मात्रान्नामरूपपृथक्कृतिः । स्तब्धीभावो रसास्वादात्तृतीयः पूर्ववन्मतः ॥

Samādhirādyasanmātrānnāmarūpapṛthakkṛtiḥ |

Stabdhībhāvo Rasāsvādāttṛtīyaḥ Pūrvavanmataḥ ||

41. एतैः समाधिभिः षड्भिर्नयेत्कालं निरन्तरम् । देहाभिमाने गलिते विज्ञाते परमात्मनि ।

Etaiḥ Samādhibhiḥ Ṣaḍbhirnayetkālaṃ Nirantaram |

Dehābhimāne Galite Vijñāte Paramātmani |
यत्र यत्र मनो याति तत्र तत्र परामृतम् ॥

Yatra Yatra Mano Yāti Tatra Tatra Parāmṛtam ||

42. भिद्यते हृदयग्रन्थिश्छिद्यन्ते सर्वसंशयाः । क्षीयन्ते चास्य कर्माणि तस्मिन्दृष्टे परावरे ॥

Bhidyate Hṛdayagranthiśchidyante Sarvasaṃśayāḥ |

Kṣīyante Cāsya Karmāṇi Tasmindṛṣṭe Parāvare ||

43. मयि जीवत्वमीशत्वं कल्पितं वस्तुतो नहि । इति यस्तु विजानाति स मुक्तो नात्र संशयः

Mayi Jīvatvamīśatvaṃ Kalpitaṃ Vastuto Nahi |

Iti Yastu Vijānāti Sa Mukto Nātra Saṃśayaḥ ||

इत्युपनिषत् ॥ *Ityupaniṣat* ||

शान्ति मन्त्र: - *Shanti Mantra*:

ॐ वाङ्मे मनसि प्रतिष्ठिता । मनो मे वाचि प्रतिष्ठितम् ।

Oṃ Vāṅme Manasi Pratiṣṭhitā | *Mano Me Vāci Pratiṣṭhitam* |

आविरावीर्म एधि । वेदस्य म आणीस्थः । श्रुतं मे मा प्रहासीः ।

Āvirāvīrma Edhi | *Vedasya Ma Āṇīsthaḥ* | *Śrutaṃ Me Mā Prahāsīḥ* |

अनेनाधीतेनाहोरात्रान् संदधामि। ऋतं वदिष्यामि।

Anenādhītenāhorātrān Saṃdadhāmi I Ṛtaṃ Vadiṣyāmi I

सत्यं वदिष्यामि। तन्मामवतु। तद्वक्तारमवतु। अवतु माम्।

Satyaṃ Vadiṣyāmi I Tanmāmavatu I Tadvaktāramavatu I Avatu Mām I

अवतु वक्तारम्। अवतु वक्तारम् I*Avatu Vaktāram I Avatu Vaktāram I*

ॐ शान्तिः शान्तिः शान्तिः ॥ *Oṃ Śāntiḥ Śāntiḥ Śāntiḥ* ॥

इति सरस्वतीरहस्योपनिषत्समाप्ता ॥ *Iti Sarasvatīrahasyopaniṣatsamāptā* ॥

*****

Āruṇikopaniṣat

आरुणिकोपनिषत्

This *Upaniṣat* belongs to *Sāma Veda*.

आरुणिकाख्योपनिषत्ख्यातसंन्यासिनोऽमलाः ।
यत्प्रबोधाद्यान्ति मुक्तिं तद्रामब्रह्म मे गतिः ॥

Āruṇikākhyopaniṣatkhyātasaṃnyāsino'malāḥ ।
Yatprabodhādyānti Muktiṃ Tadrāmabrahma Me Gatiḥ ॥

ॐ आप्यायन्त्विति शान्तिः ॥ *Oṃ Āpyāyantviti Śāntiḥ* ॥

1. ॐ आरुणिः प्राजापत्यः प्रजापतेर्लोकं जगाम । तं गत्वोवाच ।

Oṃ Āruṇiḥ Prājāpatyaḥ Prajāpaterlokaṃ Jagāma ।

Taṃ Gatvovāca ।
केन भगवन्कर्माण्यशेषतो विसृजामीति ।

Kena Bhagavankarmāṇyaśeṣato Visṛjāmīti ।
तं होवाच प्रजापतिस्तव पुत्रान्भ्रातॄन्बन्ध्वादीञ्छिखां यज्ञोपवीतं यागं स्वाध्यायं
Taṃ Hovāca Prajāpatistava Putrānbhrātṝnbandhvādīñchikhāṃ Yajñopavītaṃ Yāgaṃ Svādhyāyaṃ
भूर्लोकभुवर्लोकस्वर्लोकमहर्लोकजनोलोकतपोलोकसत्यलोकं
Bhūrlokabhuvarlokasvarlokamaharlokajanolokatapolokasatyalokaṃ
चातलतलातलवितलसुतलरसातलमहातलपातालं ब्रह्माण्डं च विसृजेत् ।
Cātalatalātalavitalasutalarasātalamahātalapātālaṃ Brahmāṇḍaṃ Ca Visṛjet ।
दण्डमाच्छादनं चैव कौपीनं च परिग्रहेत् । शेषं विसृजेदिति ॥

Daṇḍamācchādanaṃ Caiva Kaupīnaṃ Ca Parigrahet । *Śeṣaṃ Visṛjediti* ॥

2. गृहस्थो ब्रह्मचारी वा वानप्रस्थो वा उपवीतं भूमावप्सुवा विसृजेत् ।

Gṛhastho Brahmacārī Vā Vānaprastho Vā Upavītaṃ Bhūmāvapsu Vā Visṛjet ।

लौकिकाग्नीनुदराग्नौ समारोपयेत् । गायत्रीं च स्ववाचाग्नौ समारोपयेत् ।

Laukikāgnīnudarāgnau Samāropayet |

Gāyatrīṃ Ca Svavācāgnau Samāropayet |
कुटीचरो ब्रह्मचारी कुटुंबं विसृजेत् । पात्रं विसृजेत् ।

Kuṭīcaro Brahmacārī Kuṭumbaṃ Visṛjet | *Pātraṃ Visṛjet* |
पवित्रं विसृजेत् । दण्डां लोकां श्चविसृजेदिति होवाच। अत उर्ध्वममन्त्रवदाचरेत् । *Pavitraṃ Visṛjet* | *Daṇḍāæṃlokāṃśca Visṛjediti Hovāca* |

Ata Urdhvamamantravadācaret |
ऊर्ध्वगमनं विसृजेत् । औषधवदशनमाचरेत् । त्रिसन्ध्यादौ स्नानमाचरेत् ।

Ūrdhvagamanaṃ Visṛjet | *Auṣadhavadaśanamācaret* | *Trisandhyādau Snānamācaret* |
सन्धिं समाधावात्मन्याचरेत् । सर्वेषु वेदेष्वारण्यकमावर्तयेदुपनिषदमावर्तयेदुपनिषदमावर्तय् एदिति ॥

Sandhiṃ Samādhāvātmanyācaret | *SarveṣuVedeṣvāraṇyaka Māvartayedupaniṣada Māvartayedupaniṣadamāvartay Editi* ||

3. खल्वहं ब्रह्मसूचनात्सूत्रं ब्रह्मसूत्रमहमेव विद्वान्त्रिवृत्सूत्रं त्यजेद्विद्वान्य एवं वेद संन्यस्तं मया
Khalvahaṃ Brahmasūcanātsūtraṃ Brahmasūtramahameva Vidvāntrivṛtsūtraṃ Tyajedvidvānya Evaṃ Veda Saṃnyastaṃ Mayā
संन्यस्तं मया संन्यस्तं मयेति त्रिरुक्त्वाभयं सर्वभूतेभ्यो मत्तः सर्वं प्रवर्तते ।

Saṃnyastaṃ Mayā Saṃnyastaṃ Mayeti Triruktvābhayaṃ Sarvabhūtebhyo Mattaḥ Sarvaṃ Pravartate |
सखामागोपायोजः सखायोऽसीन्द्रस्य वज्रोऽसि वार्त्रघ्नः शर्म मे भव यत्पापं तन्निवारयेति ।

Sakhāmāgopāyojaḥ Sakhāyo'sīndrasya Vajro'si Vārtraghnaḥ Śarma Me Bhava Yatpāpaṃ Tannivārayeti |
अनेन मन्त्रेण कृतं वाइणवं दण्डं कौपीनं परिग्रहेदौषधवदशनमाचरेदौषधवदशनं प्राश्नीयाद्यथालाभमश्नीयात् ।

Anena Mantreṇa Kṛtaṃ Vāiṇavaṃ Daṇḍaṃ Kaupīnaṃ Parigrahedauṣadhavadaśanamācaredauṣadhavadaśanaṃ Prāśnīyādyathālābhamaśnīyāt |
ब्रह्मचर्यमहिंसा चापरिग्रहं च सत्यं च यत्नेन हे रक्षत हे रक्षत हे रक्षत इति ॥

Brahmacaryamahiṃsā Cāparigrahaṃ Ca Satyaṃ Ca Yatnena He Rakṣata He Rakṣata He Rakṣata Iti ||

4. अथातः परमहंसपरिव्राजकानामासनशयनादिकं भूमौ ब्रह्मचर्यं मृत्पात्रमलाम्बुपात्रं

Athātaḥ Paramahaṃsaparivrājakānāmāsanaśayanādikaṃ Bhūmau Brahmacaryaṃ Mṛtpātramalāmbupātraṃ

दारुपात्रं वा यतीनां कामक्रोधहर्षरोषलोभमोहदम्भदर्पेच्छासूयाममत्वाहङ्क् आरादीनपि परित्यजेत्।

Dārupātraṃ Vā Yatīnāṃ Kāma Krodhaharṣaroṣalobha Mohadambhadar Pecchāsūyāmamatvāhaṅk Ārādīnapi Parityajet ।

वर्षासु ध्रुवशीलोऽष्टौ मासानेकाकी यतिश्चरेत् द्वावेव वा विचरेद्द्वावेव वा विचरेदिति ॥

Varṣāsu Dhruvaśīlo'ṣṭau Māsānekākī Yatiścaret Dvāveva Vā Vicareddvāveva Vā Vicarediti ॥

5. स खल्वेवं यो विद्वान्सोपनयनादूर्ध्वमेतानि प्राग्वा त्यजेत्।

Sa Khalvevaṃ Yo Vidvānsopanayanādūrdhvametāni Prāgvā Tyajet ।

पित्रं पुत्रमग्न्युपवीतं कर्म कलत्रं चान्यदपीह यतयो भिक्षार्थं ग्रामं प्रविशन्ति पाणिपात्रमुदरपात्रं वा।

Pitraṃ Putramagnyupavītaṃ Karma Kalatraṃ Cānyadapīha Yatayo Bhikṣārthaṃ Grāmaṃ Praviśanti Pāṇipātramudarapātraṃ Vā ।

ॐ हि ॐ हि ॐ हीत्येतदुपनिषदं विन्यसेत् ॥

Oṃ Hi Oṃ Hi Oṃ Hītyetadupaniṣadaṃ Vinyaset ॥

6. खल्वेतदुपनिषदं विद्वान्य एवं वेद पालाशं बैल्वमाश्वत्थमौदुम्बरं दण्डं मौञ्जीं मेखलां यज्ञोपवीतं च त्यक्त्वा शूरो य एवं वेद।

Khalvetadupaniṣadaṃ Vidvānya Evaṃ Veda Pālāśaṃ Bailvamāśvatthamaudumbaraṃ Daṇḍaṃ Mauñjīṃ Mekhalāṃ Yajñopavītaṃ Ca Tyaktvā Śūro Ya Evaṃ Veda ।

तद्विष्णोः परमं पदं सदा पश्यन्ति सूरयः। दिवीव चक्षुराततम्।

Tadviṣṇoḥ Paramaṃ Padaṃ Sadā Paśyanti Sūrayaḥ । *Divīva Cakṣurātatam* ।

तद्विप्रासो विपन्यवो जागृवांसः समिन्धते। विष्णोर्यत्परमं पदमिति।

Tadviprāso Vipanyavo Jāgṛvāṃsaḥ Samindhate ।

Viṣṇoryatparamaṃ Padamiti ।

एवं निर्वाणानुशासनं वेदानुशासनं वेदानुशासनमिति ॥ ५॥

Evaṃ Nirvāṇānuśāsanaṃ Vedānuśāsanaṃ Vedānuśāsanamiti ॥

ॐ आप्यायन्त्विति शान्तिः ॥ *Oṃ Āpyāyantviti Śāntiḥ* ॥

Iti Sāmavedīyāruṇikopaniṣatsamāptā ॥

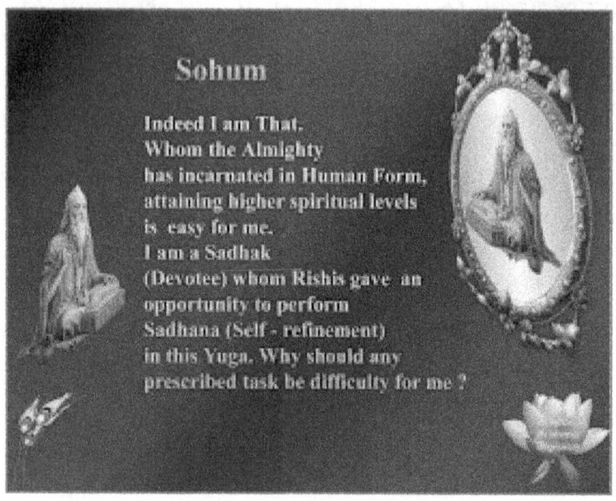

*****

Annapūrṇopaniṣat

अन्नपूर्णोपनिषत्

This *Upaniṣat* belongs to *Atharva Veda*. Probably one of the longest *Upaniṣats*.

सर्वापह्नवसंसिद्धब्रह्ममात्रतयोज्ज्वलम्। त्रैपदं श्रीरामतत्त्वं स्वमात्रमिति भावये ॥

Sarvāpahnavasaṃsiddhabrahmamātratayojjvalam ।

Traipadaṃ Śrīrāmatattvaṃ Svamātramiti Bhāvaye ॥

शान्ति मन्त्रः । *Śānti Mantraḥ* ।

ॐ भद्रं कर्णेभिः शृणुयाम देवाः । भद्रं पश्येमाक्षभिर्यजत्राः ।

Oṃ Bhadraṃ Karṇebhiḥ Śṛṇuyāma Devāḥ ॥

Bhadraṃ Paśyemākṣabhiryajatrāḥ ॥
स्थिरैरङ्गैस्तुष्टुवाँसस्तनूभिः । व्यशेम देवहितं यदायुः ।

Sthirairaṅgaistuṣṭuvāg̐Sastanūbhiḥ ॥ *Vyaśema Devahitaṃ Yadāyuḥ* ॥
स्वस्ति न इन्द्रो वृद्धश्रवाः । स्वस्ति नः पूषा विश्ववेदाः ।

Svasti Na Indro Vṛddhaśravāḥ ॥ *Svasti Naḥ Pūṣā Viśvavedāḥ* ॥
स्वस्ति नस्तार्क्ष्यो अरिष्टनेमिः । स्वस्ति नो बृहस्पतिर्दधातु ॥

Svasti Nastārkṣyo Ariṣṭanemiḥ ॥ *Svasti No Bṛhaspatirdadhātu* ॥
ॐ शान्तिः शान्तिः शान्तिः ॥ *Oṃ Śāntiḥ Śāntiḥ Śāntiḥ* ॥

First Chapter

1. हरिः ॐ निदाघो नाम योगीन्द्र ऋभुं ब्रह्मविदां वरम् ।
प्रणम्य दण्डवद्भूमावुत्थायस पुनर्मुनिः ॥

Hariḥ Oṃ Nidāgho Nāma Yogīndra Ṛbhuṃ Brahmavidāṃ Varam ।

Praṇamya Daṇḍavadbhūmāvutthāya Sa Punarmuniḥ ॥

2. आत्मतत्त्वमनुब्रूहीत्येवं पप्रच्छ सादरम् । कयोपासनया ब्रह्मन्नीदृशं प्राप्तवानसि ॥

Ātmatattvamanubrūhītyevaṃ Papraccha Sādaram ।

Kayopāsanayā Brahmannīdṛśaṃ Prāptavānasi ॥

3. तां मे ब्रूहि महाविद्यां मोक्षसाम्राज्यदायिनीम् ।
निदाघ त्वं कृतार्थोऽसि शृणु विद्यां सनातनीम् ॥

Tāṃ Me Brūhi Mahāvidyāṃ Mokṣasāmrājyadāyinīm |

Nidāgha Tvaṃ Kṛtārtho'si Śṛṇu Vidyāṃ Sanātanīm ||

4. यस्या विज्ञानमात्रेण जीवन्मुक्तो भविष्यसि। मूलशृङ्गाटमध्यस्था बिन्दुनादकलाश्रया ॥

Yasyā Vijñānamātreṇa Jīvanmukto Bhaviṣyasi |

Mūlaśṛṅgāṭamadhyasthā Bindunādakalāśrayā ||

5. नित्यानन्दा निराधारा विख्याता विलसत्कचा।
विष्टपेशी महालक्ष्मीः कामस्तारो नतिस्तथा॥

Nityānandā Nirādhārā Vikhyātā Vilasatkacā |

Viṣṭapeśī Mahālakṣmīḥ Kāmastāro Natistathā ||

6. भगवत्यन्नपूर्णेति ममाभिलषितं ततः। अन्नं देहि ततः स्वाहा मन्त्रसारेति विश्रुता॥

Bhagavatyannapūrṇeti Mamābhilaṣitaṃ Tataḥ |

Annaṃ Dehi Tataḥ Svāhā Mantrasāreti Viśrutā ||

7. सप्तविंशति वर्णात्मा योगिनीगणसेविता॥

Saptaviṃśati Varṇātmā Yoginīgaṇasevitā ||

8. ऐं ह्रीं सौं श्रीं क्लीमोन्नमो भगवत्यन्नपूर्णे ममाभिलषितमन्नं देहि स्वाहा।
इति पित्रोपदिष्टोऽस्मि तदादिनियमः स्थितः। कृतवान्स्वाश्रमाचारो मन्त्रानुष्ठानमन्वहम्॥

Aiṃ Hrīṃ Sauṃ Śrīṃ Klīmonnamo Bhagavatyannapūrṇe

Mamābhilaṣitamannaṃ Dehi Svāhā |

Iti Pitropadiṣṭo'smi Tadādiniyamaḥ Sthitaḥ |

Kṛtavānsvāśramācāro Mantrānuṣṭhānamanvaham ||

9. एवं गते बहुदिने प्रादुरासीन्ममाग्रतः। अन्नपूर्णा विशालाक्षी स्मयमानमुखाम्बुजा॥

Evaṃ Gate Bahudine Prādurāsīnmamāgrataḥ |

Annapūrṇā Viśālākṣī Smayamānamukhāmbujā ||

10. तां दृष्ट्वा दण्डवद्भूमौ नत्वा प्राञ्जलिरास्थितः।
अहो वत्स कृतार्थोऽसि वरं वरय मा चिरम्॥

Tāṃ Dṛṣṭvā Daṇḍavadbhūmau Natvā Prāñjalirāsthitaḥ |

Aho Vatsa Kṛtārtho'si Varaṃ Varaya Mā Ciram ||

11. एवमुक्तो विशालाक्ष्या मयोक्तं मुनिपुङ्गव। आत्मतत्त्वं मनसि मे प्रादुर्भवतु पार्वति ॥

Evamukto Viśālākṣyā Mayoktaṃ Munipuṅgava |

Ātmatattvaṃ Manasi Me Prādurbhavatu Pārvati ||

12. तथैवास्थिति मामुक्त्वा तत्रैवान्तरधीयत । तदा मे मतिरुत्पन्ना जगद्वैचित्र्यदर्शनात् ॥

Tathaivāsthiti Māmuktvā Tatraivāntaradhīyata |

Tadā Me Matirutpannā Jagadvaicitryadarśanāt ||

13. भ्रमः पञ्चविधो भाति तदेवेह समुच्यते। जीवेश्वरौ भिन्नरूपाविति प्राथमिको भ्रमः ॥

Bhramaḥ Pañcavidho Bhāti Tadeveha Samucyate |

Jīveśvarau Bhinnarūpāviti Prāthamiko Bhramaḥ ||

14. आत्मनिष्ठं कर्तृगुणं वास्तवं वा द्वितीयकः । शरीरत्रयसंयुक्तजीवः सङ्गी तृतीयकः ॥

Ātmaniṣṭhaṃ Kartṛguṇaṃ Vāstavaṃ Vā Dvitīyakaḥ |

Śarīratrayasaṃyuktajīvaḥ Saṅgī Tṛtīyakaḥ ||

15. जगत्कारणरूपस्य विकारित्वं चतुर्थकः । कारणाद्भिन्नजगतः सत्यत्वं पञ्चमो भ्रमः
पञ्चभ्रमनिवृत्तिश्च तदा स्फुरति चेतसि ॥

Jagatkāraṇarūpasya Vikāritvaṃ Caturthakaḥ |

Kāraṇādbhinnajagataḥ Satyatvaṃ Pañcamo Bhramaḥ |

Pañcabhramanivṛttiśca Tadā Sphurati Cetasi ||

16. बिम्बप्रतिबिम्बदर्शनेन भेदभ्रमो निवृत्तः ।
स्फटिकलोहितदर्शनेन पारमार्थिक कर्तृत्वभ्रमो निवृत्तः ।
घटमठाकाशदर्शनेन सङ्गीतिभ्रमो निवृत्तः ।
रज्जुसर्पदर्शनेन कारणाद्भिन्नजगतः सत्यत्वभ्रमो निवृत्तः ।
कनकरुचकदर्शनेन विकारित्वभ्रमो निवृत्तः । तदाप्रभृति मच्चित्तं ब्रह्माकारमभूत्स्वयम्।
निदाघ त्वमपीत्थं हि तत्त्वज्ञानमवाप्नुहि ॥

Bimbapratibimbadarśanena Bhedabhramo Nivṛttaḥ |

Sphaṭikalohitadarśanena Pāramārthikakartṛtvabhramo Nivṛttaḥ |

Ghaṭamaṭhākāśadarśanena Saṅgītibhramo Nivṛttaḥ |

Rajjusarpadarśanena Kāraṇādbhinnajagataḥ Satyatvabhramo Nivṛttaḥ |

Kanakarucakadarśanena Vikāritvabhramo Nivṛttaḥ ।

Tadāprabhṛti Maccittaṃ Brahmākāramabhūtsvayam ।

Nidāgha Tvamapītthaṃ Hi Tattvajñānamavāpnuhi ॥

17. निदाघः प्रणतो भूत्वा ऋभुं पप्रच्छ सादरम् । ब्रूहि मे श्रद्दधानाय ब्रह्मविद्यामनुत्तमाम् ॥

Nidāghaḥ Praṇato Bhūtvā Ṛbhuṃ Papraccha Sādaram ।

Brūhi Me Śraddadhānāya Brahmavidyāmanuttamām ॥

18. तथेत्याह ऋभुः प्रीतस्तत्त्वज्ञां वदामि ते । महाकर्ता महाभोक्ता महात्यागी भवानघ ।
स्वस्वरूपानुसन्धानमेवं कृत्वा सुखी भव ॥

Tathetyāha Ṛbhuḥ Prītastattvajñāṃ Vadāmi Te ।

Mahākartā Mahābhoktā Mahātyāgī Bhavānagha ।

Svasvarūpānusandhānamevaṃ Kṛtvā Sukhī Bhava ॥

19. नित्योदितं विमलमाद्यमनतरूपं ब्रह्मास्मि नेतरकलाकलनं हि किंचित् ।
इत्येव भावय निरञ्जनतामुपेतो निर्वाणमेहि सकलामलशान्तवृत्तिः ॥

Nityoditaṃ Vimalamādyamanatarūpaṃ

Brahmāsmi Netarakalākalanaṃ Hi Kiṃcit ।

Ityeva Bhāvaya Nirañjanatāmupeto

Nirvāṇamehi Sakalāmalaśāntavṛttiḥ ॥

20. यदिदं दृश्यते किंचित्तत्तन्नास्तीति भावय । यथा गन्धर्वनगरं यथा वारि मरुस्थले ॥

Yadidaṃ Dṛśyate Kiṃcittattannāstīti Bhāvaya ।

Yathā Gandharvanagaraṃ Yathā Vāri Marusthale ॥

21. यत्तु नो दृश्यते किंचिद्यन्नु किंचिदिव स्थितम् । मनःषष्ठेन्द्रियातीतं तन्मयो भव वै मुने ॥

Yattu No Dṛśyate Kiṃcidyannu Kiṃcidiva Sthitam ।

Manaḥṣaṣṭhendriyātītaṃ Tanmayo Bhava Vai Mune ॥

22. अविनाशि चिदाकाशं सर्वात्मकमखण्डितम् । नीरन्ध्रं भूरिवाशेषं तदस्मीति विभावय ॥

Avināśi Cidākāśaṃ Sarvātmakamakhaṇḍitam ।

Nīrandhraṃ Bhūrivāśeṣaṃ Tadasmīti Vibhāvaya ॥

23. यदा संक्षीयते चित्तमभावात्यन्तभावनात् । चित्सामान्यस्वरूपस्य सत्तासामान्यता तदा

Yadā Saṃkṣīyate Cittamabhāvātyantabhāvanāt |

Citsāmānyasvarūpasya Sattāsāmānyatā Tadā ||

24. नूनं चैत्यांशरहिता चिद्यदात्मनि लीयते । असद्रूपवदत्यच्छा सत्तासामान्यता तदा ॥

Nūnaṃ Caityāṃśarahitā Cidyadātmani Līyate |

Asadrūpavadatyacchā Sattāsāmānyatā Tadā ||

25. दृष्टिरेषा हि परमा सदेहादेहयोः समा । मुक्तयोः संभवत्येव तुर्यातीतपदाभिधा ॥

Dṛṣṭireṣā Hi Paramā Sadehādehayoḥ Samā |

Muktayoḥ Saṃbhavatyeva Turyātītapadābhidhā ||

26. व्युत्थितस्य भवत्येषा समाधिस्थस्य चानघ । ज्ञस्य केवलमज्ञस्य न भवत्येव बोधजा ।
अनानन्दसमानन्दमुग्धमुग्धमुखद्युतिः॥

Vyutthitasya Bhavatyeṣā Samādhisthasya Cānagha |

Jñasya Kevalamajñasya Na Bhavatyeva Bodhajā |

Anānandasamānandamugdhamugdhamukhadyutiḥ ||

27. चिरकालपरिक्षीणमननादिपरिभ्रमः । पदमासाद्यते पुण्यं प्रज्ञयैवैकया तथा ॥

Cirakālaparikṣīṇamananādiparibhramaḥ |

Padamāsādyate Puṇyaṃ Prajñayaivaikayā Tathā ||

28. इमं गुणसमाहारमनात्मत्वेन पश्यतः । अन्तःशीतलया यासौ समाधिरिति कथ्यते ॥

Imaṃ Guṇasamāhāramanātmatvena Paśyataḥ |

Antaḥśītalayā Yāsau Samādhiriti Kathyate ||

29. अवासनं स्थिरं प्रोक्तं मनोध्यानं तदेव च । तदेव केवलीभानं शान्ततैव च तत्सदा ॥

Avāsanaṃ Sthiraṃ Proktaṃ Manodhyānaṃ Tadeva Ca |

Tadeva Kevalībhānaṃ Śāntataiva Ca Tatsadā ||

30. तनुवासनमत्युच्चैः पदायोद्यतमुच्यते । अवासगं मनोऽकर्तृपदं तस्मादवाप्यते ॥

Tanuvāsanamatyuccaiḥ Padāyodyatamucyate |

Avāsagaṃ Mano'kartṛpadaṃ Tasmādavāpyate ||

31. घनवासनमेतत्तु चेतःकर्तृत्वभावनम् । सर्वदुःखप्रदं तस्माद्वासनां तनुतां नयेत् ॥

Ghanavāsanametattu Cetaḥkartṛtvabhāvanam |

Sarvaduḥkhapradaṃ Tasmādvāsanāṃ Tanutāṃ Nayet ||

32. चेतसा सम्परित्यज्य सर्वभावात्मभावनाम् । सर्वमाकाशतामेति नित्यमन्तर्मुखस्थितेः ॥

Cetasā Samparityajya Sarvabhāvātmabhāvanām |

Sarvamākāśatāmeti Nityamantarmukhasthiteḥ ||

33. यथा विपणगा लोका विहरन्तोऽप्यसत्समाः ।
असंबन्धात्तथा ज्ञस्य ग्रामोऽपि विपिनोपमः ॥

Yathā Vipaṇagā Lokā Viharanto'pyasatsamāḥ |

Asaṃbandhāttathā Jñasya Grāmo'pi Vipinopamaḥ ||

34. अन्तर्मुखतया नित्यं सुप्तो बुद्धो व्रजन्पठन् । पुरं जनपदं ग्राममरण्यमिव पश्यति ॥

Antarmukhatayā Nityaṃ Supto Buddho Vrajanpaṭhan |

Puraṃ Janapadaṃ Grāmamaraṇyamiva Paśyati ||

35. अन्तःशीतलतायां तु लब्धायां शीतलं जगत् । अन्तस्तृष्णोपतप्तानां दावदाहमयं जगत्

Antaḥśītalatāyāṃ Tu Labdhāyāṃ Śītalaṃ Jagat |

Antastṛṣṇopataptānāṃ Dāvadāhamayaṃ Jagat ||

36. भवत्यखिलजन्तूनां यदन्तस्तद्बहिः स्थितम् ॥

Bhavatyakhilajantūnāṃ Yadantastadbahiḥ Sthitam ||

37. यस्त्वात्मरतिरेवान्तः कुर्वन्कर्मेन्द्रियैः क्रियाः । न वशो हर्षशोकाभ्यां स समाहित उच्यते ।

Yastvātmaratirevāntaḥ Kurvankarmendriyaiḥ Kriyāḥ |
Na Vaśo Harṣaśokābhyāṃ Sa Samāhita Ucyate ||

38. आत्मवत्सर्वभूतानि परद्रव्याणि लोष्ठवत् । स्वभावादेव न भयाद्यः पश्यति स पश्यति ॥

Ātmavatsarvabhūtāni Paradravyāṇi Loṣṭhavat |

Svabhāvādeva Na Bhayādyaḥ Paśyati Sa Paśyati ||

39. अद्यैव मृतिरायातु कल्पान्तनिचयेन वा । नासौ कलङ्कमाप्नोति हेम पङ्कगतं यथा ॥

Adyaiva Mṛtirāyātu Kalpāntanicayena Vā |

Nāsau Kalaṅkamāpnoti Hema Paṅkagataṃ Yathā ||

40. कोऽहं कथमिदं किं वा कथं मरणजन्मनी। विचारयान्तरे वेत्थं महत्तत्फलमेष्यसि ॥

Ko'haṃ Kathamidaṃ Kiṃ Vā Kathaṃ Maraṇajanmanī |

Vicārayāntare Vetthaṃ Mahattatphalameṣyasi ||

41. विचारेण परिज्ञातस्वभावस्य सतस्तव। मनः स्वरूपमुत्सृज्य शममेष्यति विज्वरम् ॥

Vicāreṇa Parijñātasvabhāvasya Satastava |

Manaḥ Svarūpamutsṛjya Śamameṣyati Vijvaram ||

42. विज्वरत्वं गतं चेतस्तव संसारवृत्तिषु। न निमज्जति तद्ब्रह्मन्गोष्पदेष्विव वारणः ॥

Vijvaratvaṃ Gataṃ Cetastava Saṃsāravṛttiṣu |

Na Nimajjati Tadbrahmangoṣpadeṣviva Vāraṇaḥ ||

43. कृपणं तु मनो ब्रह्मन्गोष्पदेऽपि निमज्जति। कार्ये गोष्पदतोयेऽपि विशीर्णो मशको यथा ॥

Kṛpaṇaṃ Tu Mano Brahmangoṣpade'pi Nimajjati |

Kārye Goṣpadatoye'pi Viśīrṇo Maśako Yathā ||

44. यावद्यावन्मुनिश्रेष्ठ स्वयं संतज्यतेऽखिलम्। तावत्तावत्परालोकः परमात्मैव शिष्यते ॥

Yāvadyāvanmuniśreṣtha Svayaṃ Saṃtajyate'khilam |

Tāvattāvatparālokaḥ Paramātmaiva Śiṣyate ||

45. यावत्सर्वं न संत्यक्तं तावदात्मा न लभ्यते। सर्ववस्तुपरित्यागे शेष आत्मेति कथ्यते ॥

Yāvatsarvaṃ Na Saṃtyaktaṃ Tāvadātmā Na Labhyate |

Sarvavastuparityāge Śeṣa Ātmeti Kathyate ||

46. आत्मावलोकनार्थं तु तस्मात्सर्वं परित्यजेत्। सर्वं संत्यज्य दूरेण यच्छिष्टं तन्मयो भव ॥

Ātmāvalokanārthaṃ Tu Tasmātsarvaṃ Parityajet |

Sarvaṃ Saṃtyajya Dūreṇa Yacchiṣṭaṃ Tanmayo Bhava ||

47. सर्वं किंचिदिदं दृश्यं दृश्यते यज्जगद्गतम्। चिन्निष्पन्दांशमात्रं तन्नान्यत्किंचन शाश्वतम्

Sarvaṃ Kiṃcididaṃ Dṛśyaṃ Dṛśyate Yajjagadgatam ।

Cinniṣpandāṃśamātraṃ Tannānyatkiṃcana Śāśvatam ॥

48. समाहिता नित्यतृप्ता यथाभूतार्थदर्शिनी। ब्रह्मन्समाधिशब्देन परा प्रज्ञोच्यते बुधैः ॥

Samāhitā Nityatṛptā Yathābhūtārthadarśinī ।

Brahmansamādhiśabdena Parā Prajñocyate Budhaiḥ ॥

49. अक्षुब्धा निरहंकारा द्वन्द्वेष्वननुपातिनी। प्रोक्ता समाधिशब्देन मेरोः स्थिरतरा स्थितिः ॥

Akṣubdhā Nirahaṃkārā Dvandveṣvananupātinī ।

Proktā Samādhiśabdena Meroḥ Sthiratarā Sthitiḥ ॥

50. निश्चिता विगताभीष्टा हेयोपदेयवर्जिता। ब्रह्मन्समाधिशब्देन परिपूर्णा मनोगतिः ॥

Niścitā Vigatābhīṣṭā Heyopadeyavarjitā ।

Brahmansamādhiśabdena Paripūrṇā Manogatiḥ ॥

51. केवलं चित्प्रकाशांशकल्पिता स्थिरतां गता। तुर्या सा प्राप्यते दृष्टिर्महद्भिर्वेदवित्तमैः ॥

Kevalaṃ Citprakāśāṃśakalpitā Sthiratāṃ Gatā ।

Turyā Sā Prāpyate Dṛṣṭirmahadbhirvedavittamaiḥ ॥

52. अदूरगतसादृश्या सुषुप्तस्योपलक्ष्यते। मनोहंकारविलये सर्वभावान्तरस्थिता ॥

Adūragatasādṛśyā Suṣuptasyopalakṣyate ।

Manohaṃkāravilaye Sarvabhāvāntarasthitā ॥

53. समुदेति परानन्दा या तनुः पारमेश्वरी। मनसैव मनश्छित्त्वा सा स्वयं लभ्यते गतिः ॥

Samudeti Parānandā Yā Tanuḥ Pārameśvarī ।

Manasaiva Manaśchittvā Sā Svayaṃ Labhyate Gatiḥ ॥

54. तदनु विषयवासनाविनाशस्तदनु शुभः परमः स्फुटप्रकाशः।
तदनु च समतावशात्स्वरूपे परिणमनं महतामचिन्त्यरूपम् ॥

Tadanu Viṣayavāsanāvināśa Stadanu Śubhaḥ Paramaḥ Sphuṭaprakāśaḥ
Tadanu Ca Samatāvaśātsvarūpe Pariṇamanaṃ Mahatāmacintyarūpam॥

55. अखिलमिदमनन्तमनन्तमात्मतत्त्वं दृढपरिणामिनि चेतसि स्थितोऽन्तः ।
बहिरुपशमिते चराचरात्मास्वयमनुभूयत एव देवदेवः ॥

Akhilamidamanantamanantamātmatattvaṃ

Dṛḍhapariṇāmini Cetasi Sthito'ntaḥ ।

Bahirupaśamite Carācarātmā Svayamanubhūyata Eva Devadevaḥ ॥

56. असक्तं निर्मलं चित्तं युक्तं संसार्यविस्फुटम्। सक्तं तु दीर्घतपसा मुक्तमप्यतिबद्धवत्॥

Asaktaṃ Nirmalaṃ Cittaṃ Yuktaṃ Saṃsāryavisphuṭam ।

Saktaṃ Tu Dīrghatapasā Muktamapyatibaddhavat ॥

57. अन्तःसंसक्तिनिर्मुक्तो जीवो मधुरवृत्तिमान्।
बहिः कुर्वन्नकुर्वन्वा कर्ता भोक्ता न हि क्वचित् ॥

Antaḥsaṃsaktinirmukto Jīvo Madhuravṛttimān ।

Bahiḥ Kurvannakurvanvā Kartā Bhoktā Na Hi Kvacit ॥

इति प्रथमोऽध्यायः ॥ *Iti Prathamo'dhyāyaḥ* ॥

Second Chapter

निदाघ उवाच ॥ *Nidāgha Uvāca* ॥

1. सङ्गः कीदृश इत्युक्तः कश्च बन्धाय देहिनाम्।
कश्च मोक्षाय कथितः कथं त्वेष चिकित्स्यते ॥

Saṅgaḥ Kīdṛśa Ityuktaḥ Kaśca Bandhāya Dehinām ।

Kaśca Mokṣāya Kathitaḥ Kathaṃ Tveṣa Cikitsyate ॥

2. देहदेहिविभागैकपरित्यागेन भावना। देहमात्रे हि विश्वासः सङ्गो बन्धाय कथ्यते ॥

Dehadehivibhāgaikaparityāgena Bhāvanā ।

Dehamātre Hi Viśvāsaḥ Saṅgo Bandhāya Kathyate ॥

3. सर्वमात्मेदमत्राहं किं वाञ्छामि त्यजामि किम्।
इत्यसङ्गस्थितिं विद्धि जीवन्मुक्ततनुस्थिताम्॥

Sarvamātmedamatrāhaṃ Kiṃ Vāñchāmi Tyajāmi Kim ।

Ityasaṅgasthitiṃ Viddhi Jīvanmuktatanusthitām ॥

4. नाहमस्मि न चान्योस्ति न चायं न च नेतरः । सोऽसङ्ग इति सम्प्रोक्तो ब्रह्मास्मीत्येव सर्वदा॥

Nāhamasmi Na Cānyosti Na Cāyaṃ Na Ca Netaraḥ |

So'saṅga Iti Samprokto Brahmāsmītyeva Sarvadā ||

5. नाभिनन्दति नैष्कर्म्यं न कर्मस्वनुषज्जते। सुसमो यः परित्यागी सोऽसंसक्त इति स्मृतः ॥

Nābhinandati Naiṣkarmyaṃ Na Karmasvanuṣajjate |

Susamo Yaḥ Parityāgī So'saṃsakta Iti Smṛtaḥ ||

6. सर्वकर्मफलादीनां मनसैव न कर्मणा । निपुणो यः परित्यागी सोऽसंसक्त इति स्मृतः ॥

Sarvakarmaphalādīnāṃ Manasaiva Na Karmaṇā |

Nipuṇo Yaḥ Parityāgī So'saṃsakta Iti Smṛtaḥ ||

7. असंकल्पेन सकलाश्चेष्टा नाना विजृंभिताः । चिकित्सिता भवन्तीह श्रेयः सम्पादयन्ति हि ॥

Asaṃkalpena Sakalāśceṣṭā Nānā Vijṛṃbhitāḥ |

Cikitsitā Bhavantīha Śreyaḥ Sampādayanti Hi ||

8. न सक्तमिह चेष्टासु न चिन्तासु न वस्तुषु। न गमागमचेष्टासु न कालकलनासु च ॥

Na Saktamiha Ceṣṭāsu Na Cintāsu Na Vastuṣu |

Na Gamāgamaceṣṭāsu Na Kālakalanāsu Ca ||

9. केवलं चिति विश्रम्य किंचिच्चैत्यावलंब्यपि। सर्वत्र नीरसमिह तिष्ठत्यात्मरसं मनः ॥

Kevalaṃ Citi Viśramya Kiṃciccaityāvalaṃbyapi |

Sarvatra Nīrasamiha Tiṣṭhatyātmarasaṃ Manaḥ ||

10. व्यवहारमिदं सर्वं मा करोतु करोतु वा । अकुर्वन्वापि कुर्वन्वा जीवः स्वात्मरतिक्रियः ॥

Vyavahāramidaṃ Sarvaṃ Mā Karotu Karotu Vā |

Akurvanvāpi Kurvanvā Jīvaḥ Svātmaratikriyaḥ ||

11. अथवा तमपि त्यक्त्वा चैत्यांशं शान्तचिद्घनः ।
जीवस्तिष्ठति संशान्तो ज्वलन्मणिरिवात्मनि ॥

Athavā Tamapi Tyaktvā Caityāṃśaṃ Śāntacidghanaḥ |

Jīvastiṣṭhati Saṃśānto Jvalanmaṇirivātmani ||

12. चित्ते चैत्यदशाहीने या स्थितिः क्षीणचेतसाम्। सोच्यते शान्तकलना जाग्रत्येव सुषुप्तता॥

Citte Caityadaśāhīne Yā Sthitiḥ Kṣīṇacetasām |

Socyate Śāntakalanā Jāgratyeva Suṣuptatā ||

13. एषा निदाघ सौषुप्तस्थितिरभ्यासयोगतः। प्रौढा सती तुरीयेति कथिता तत्त्वकोविदैः॥

Eṣā Nidāgha Sauṣuptasthitirabhyāsayogataḥ |

Prauḍhā Satī Turīyeti Kathitā Tattvakovidaiḥ ||

14. अस्यां तुरीयावस्थायां स्थितिं प्राप्याविनाशिनीम्।
आनन्दैकान्तशीलत्वादनानन्दपदं गतः॥

Asyāṃ Turīyāvasthāyāṃ Sthitiṃ Prāpyāvināśinīm |

Ānandaikāntaśīlatvādanānandapadaṃ Gataḥ ||

15. अनानन्दमहानन्दकालातीतस्ततोऽपि हि। मुक्त इत्युच्यते योगी तुर्यातीतपदं गतः॥

Anānandamahānandakālātītastato'pi Hi |

Mukta Ityucyate Yogī Turyātītapadaṃ Gataḥ ||

16. परिगलितसमस्तजन्मपाशः सकलविलीनतमोमयाभिमानः।
परमरसमयीं परात्मसत्तां जलगतसैन्धवखण्डवन्महात्मा॥

Parigalitasamastajanmapāśaḥ Sakalavilīnatamomayābhimānaḥ |
Paramarasamayīṃ Parātmasattāṃ

Jalagatasaindhavakhaṇḍavanmahātmā ||

17. जडाजडदृशोर्मध्ये यत्तत्त्वं पारमार्थिकम्। अनुभूतिमयं तस्मात्सारं ब्रह्मेति कथ्यते॥

Jaḍājaḍadṛśormadhye Yattattvaṃ Pāramārthikam |

Anubhūtimayaṃ Tasmātsāraṃ Brahmeti Kathyate ||

18. दृश्यसंवलितो बन्धस्तन्मुक्तौ मुक्तिरुच्यते। द्रव्यदर्शनसंबन्धे यानुभूतिरनामया॥

Dṛśyasaṃvalito Bandhastanmuktau Muktirucyate |

Dravyadarśanasaṃbandhe Yānubhūtiranāmayā ||

19. तामवष्टभ्य तिष्ठ त्वं सौषुप्तीं भजते स्थितिम्। सैव तुर्यत्वमाप्नोति तस्यां दृष्टिं स्थिरां कुरु॥

Tāmavaṣṭabhya Tiṣṭha Tvaṃ Sauṣuptīṃ Bhajate Sthitim ।

Saiva Turyatvamāpnoti Tasyāṃ Dṛṣṭiṃ Sthirāṃ Kuru ॥

20. आत्मा स्थूलो न चैवाणुर्न प्रत्यक्षो न चेतरः । न चेतनो न च जडो न चैवासन्न सन्मयः ॥

Ātmā Sthūlo Na Caivāṇurna Pratyakṣo Na Cetaraḥ ।

Na Cetano Na Ca Jaḍo Na Caivāsanna Sanmayaḥ ॥

21. नाहं नान्यो न चैवैको न चानेकोऽद्वयोऽव्ययः ।
यदीदं दृश्यतां प्राप्तं मनः सर्वेन्द्रियास्पदम् ॥

Nāhaṃ Nānyo Na Caivaiko Na Cāneko'dvayo'vyayaḥ ।

Yadīdaṃ Dṛśyatāṃ Prāptaṃ Manaḥ Sarvendriyāspadam ॥

22. दृश्यदर्शनसंबन्धे यत्सुखं पारमार्थिकम् । तदतीतं पदं यस्मात्तन्न किंचिदिवैव तत् ॥

Dṛśyadarśanasaṃbandhe Yatsukhaṃ Pāramārthikam ।

Tadatītaṃ Padaṃ Yasmāttanna Kiṃcidivaiva Tat ॥

23. न मोक्षो नभसः पृष्ठे न पाताले न भूतले। सर्वाशासंक्षये चेतःक्षयो मोक्ष इतीष्यते ॥

Na Mokṣo Nabhasaḥ Pṛṣṭhe Na Pātāle Na Bhūtale ।

Sarvāśāsaṃkṣaye Cetaḥkṣayo Mokṣa Itīṣyate ॥

24. मोक्षो मेऽस्त्विति चिन्तान्तर्जाता चेदुत्थितं मनः ।
मननोत्थे मनस्यैष बन्धः सांसारिको दृढः ॥

Mokṣo Me'stviti Cintāntarjātā Cedutthitaṃ Manaḥ ।

Mananotthe Manasyaiṣa Bandhaḥ Sāṃsāriko Dṛḍhaḥ ॥

25. आत्मन्यतीते सर्वस्मात्सर्वरूपेऽथ वा तते । को बन्धः कश्च वा मोक्षो निर्मूलं मननं कुरु ॥

Ātmanyatīte Sarvasmātsarvarūpe'tha Vā Tate ।

Ko Bandhaḥ Kaśca Vā Mokṣo Nirmūlaṃ Mananaṃ Kuru ॥

26. अध्यात्मरतिराशान्तः पूर्णपावनमानसः। प्राप्तानुत्तमविश्रान्तिर्न किंचिदिह वाञ्छति ॥

Adhyātmaratirāśāntaḥ Pūrṇapāvanamānasaḥ ।

Prāptānuttamaviśrāntirna Kiṃcidiha Vāñchati ॥

27. सर्वाधिष्ठानसन्मात्रे निर्विकल्पे चिदात्मनि। यो जीवति गतस्नेहः स जीवन्मुक्त उच्यते॥

Sarvādhiṣṭhānasanmātre Nirvikalpe Cidātmani ।

Yo Jīvati Gatasnehaḥ Sa Jīvanmukta Ucyate ॥

28. नापेक्षते भविष्यच्च वर्तमाने न तिष्ठति। न संस्मरत्यतीतं च सर्वमेव करोति च॥

Nāpekṣate Bhaviṣyacca Vartamāne Na Tiṣṭhati ।

Na Saṃsmaratyatītaṃ Ca Sarvameva Karoti Ca ॥

29. अनुबन्धपरे जन्तावसंसर्गमनाः सदा। भक्ते भक्तसमाचरः शठे शठ इव स्थितः॥

Anubandhapare Jantāvasaṃsargamanāḥ Sadā ।

Bhakte Bhaktasamācaraḥ Śaṭhe Śaṭha Iva Sthitaḥ ॥

30. बालो बालेषु वृद्धेषु वृद्धो धीरेषु धैर्यवान्। युवा यौवनवृत्तेषु दुःखितेषु सुदुःखधीः॥

Bālo Bāleṣu Vṛddheṣu Vṛddho Dhīreṣu Dhairyavān ।

Yuvā Yauvanavṛtteṣu Duḥkhiteṣu Suduḥkhadhīḥ ॥

31. धीरधीरुदितानन्दः पेशलः पुण्यकीर्तनः। प्राज्ञः प्रसन्नमधुरो दैन्यादपगताशयः॥

Dhīradhīruditānandaḥ Peśalaḥ Puṇyakīrtanaḥ ।

Prājñaḥ Prasannamadhuro Dainyādapagatāśayaḥ ॥

32. अभ्यासेन परिस्पन्दे प्राणानां क्षयमागते। मनः प्रशममायाति निर्वाणमवशिष्यते॥

Abhyāsena Parispande Prāṇānāṃ Kṣayamāgate ।

Manaḥ Praśamamāyāti Nirvāṇamavaśiṣyate ॥

33. यतो वाचो निवर्तन्ते विकल्पकलनान्विताः। विकल्पसंक्षयाज्जन्तोः पदं तदवशिष्यते॥

Yato Vāco Nivartante Vikalpakalanānvitāḥ ।

Vikalpasaṃkṣayājjantoḥ Padaṃ Tadavaśiṣyate ॥

34. अनाद्यन्तावभासात्मा परमात्मैव विद्यते। इत्येतन्निश्चयं स्फारं सम्यग्ज्ञानं विदुर्बुधाः॥

Anādyantāvabhāsātmā Paramātmaiva Vidyate ।

Ityetanniścayaṃ Sphāraṃ Samyagjñānaṃ Vidurbudhāḥ ॥

35. यथाभूतार्थदर्शित्वमेतावद्भुवनत्रये। यदात्मैव जगत्सर्वमिति निश्चित्य पूर्णता॥

Yathābhūtārthadarśitvametāvadbhuvanatraye ।

Yadātmaiva Jagatsarvamiti Niścitya Pūrṇatā ॥

36. सर्वमात्मैव कौ दृष्टौ भावाभावौ क्व वा स्थितौ । क्व बन्धमोक्षकलने ब्रह्मैवेदं विजृम्भते ॥

Sarvamātmaiva Kau Dṛṣṭau Bhāvābhāvau Kva Vā Sthitau ।

Kva Bandhamokṣakalane Brahmaivedaṃ Vijṛmbhate ॥

37. सर्वमेकं परं व्योम को मोक्षः कस्य बन्धता । ब्रह्मेदं बृंहिताकारं बृहद्बृहदवस्थितम् ॥

Sarvamekaṃ Paraṃ Vyoma Ko Mokṣaḥ Kasya Bandhatā ।

Brahmedaṃ Bṛṃhitākāraṃ Bṛhadbṛhadavasthitam ॥

38. दूरादस्तमितद्वित्वं भवात्मैव त्वमात्मना । सम्यगालोकिते रूपे काष्ठपाषाणवाससाम् ॥

Dūrādastamitadvitvaṃ Bhavātmaiva Tvamātmanā ।

Samyagālokite Rūpe Kāṣṭhapāṣāṇavāsasām ॥

39. मनागपि न भेदोऽस्ति क्वासि संकल्पनोन्मुखः। आदावन्ते च संशान्तस्वरूपमविनाशि यत्

Manāgapi Na Bhedo'sti Kvāsi Saṃkalpanonmukhaḥ ।

Ādāvante Ca Saṃśāntasvarūpamavināśi Yat ॥

40. वस्तूनामात्मनश्चैतत्तन्मयो भव सर्वदा द्वैताद्वैतसमुद्भेदैर्जरामरणविभ्रमैः ॥

Vastūnāmātmanaścaitattanmayo Bhava Sarvadā ।

Dvaitādvaitasamudbhedairjarāmaraṇavibhramaiḥ ॥

41. स्फुरत्यात्मभिरात्मैव चित्तैरब्धीव वीचिभिः । आपत्करञ्जपरशुं पराया निर्वृतेः पदम् ॥

Sphuratyātmabhirātmaiva Cittairabdhīva Vīcibhiḥ ।

Āpatkarañjaparaśuṃ Parāyā Nirvṛteḥ Padam ॥

42. शुद्धमात्मानमालिङ्ग्य नित्यमन्तस्थया धिया ।
यः स्थितस्तं क आत्मेह भोगो बाधयितुं क्षमः ॥

Śuddhamātmānamāliṅgya Nityamantasthayā Dhiyā ।

Yaḥ Sthitastaṃ Ka Ātmeha Bhogo Bādhayituṃ Kṣamaḥ ॥

43. कृतस्फारविचारस्य मनोभोगादयोऽरयः । मनागपि न भिन्दन्ति शैलं मन्दानिला इव ॥

Kṛtasphāravicārasya Manobhogādayo'rayaḥ |

Manāgapi Na Bhindanti Śailaṃ Mandānilā Iva ||

44. नानात्वमस्ति कलनासु न वस्तुतोऽन्त र्नानाविधासु सरसीव जलादिवान्यत् ।
इत्येकनिश्चयमयः पुरुषो विमुक्त इत्युच्यते समवलोकितसम्यगर्थः ॥

Nānātvamasti Kalanāsu Na Vastuto'nta

Rnānāvidhāsu Sarasīva Jalādivānyat |

Ityekaniścayamayaḥ Puruṣo Vimukta

Ityucyate Samavalokitasamyagarthaḥ ||

इति द्वितीयोऽध्यायः ॥ *Iti Dvitīyo'dhyāyaḥ* ||

Third Chapter

1. विदेहमुक्तेः किं रूपं तद्वान्को वा महामुनिः । कं योगं समुपस्थाय प्राप्तवान्परमं पदम् ॥

Videhamukteḥ Kiṃ Rūpaṃ Tadvānko Vā Mahāmuniḥ |

Kaṃ Yogaṃ Samupasthāya Prāptavānparamaṃ Padam ||

2. सुमेरोर्वसुधापीठे माण्डव्यो नाम वै मुनिः । कौण्डिन्यात्तत्त्वमास्थाय जीवन्मुक्तो भवत्यसौ ॥

Sumerorvasudhāpīṭhe Māṇḍavyo Nāma Vai Muniḥ |

Kauṇḍinyāttattvamāsthāya Jīvanmukto Bhavatyasau ||

3. जीवन्मुक्तिदशां प्राप्य कदाचिद्ब्रह्मवित्तमः । सर्वेन्द्रियाणि संहर्तुं मनश्चक्रे महामुनिः ॥

Jīvanmuktidaśāṃ Prāpya Kadācidbrahmavittamaḥ |

Sarvendriyāṇi Saṃhartuṃ Manaścakre Mahāmuniḥ ||

4. बद्धपद्मासनस्तिष्ठन्नर्धोन्मीलितलोचनः । बाह्यानाभ्यान्तरांश्चैव स्पर्शान्परिहरञ्छनैः ॥

Baddhapadmāsanastiṣṭhannardhonmīlitalocanaḥ |

Bāhyānābhyāntarāṃścaiva Sparśānpariharañchanaiḥ ||

5. ततः स्वमनसः स्थैर्यं मनसा विगतैनसा । अहो नु चञ्चलमिदं प्रत्याहृतमपि स्फुटम् ॥

Tataḥ Svamanasaḥ Sthairyaṃ Manasā Vigatainasā |

Aho Nu Cañcalamidaṃ Pratyāhṛtamapi Sphuṭam ||

6. पटाद्घटमुपायाति घटाच्छकटमुत्कटम् । चित्तमर्थेषु चरति पादपेष्विव मर्कटः ॥

Paṭādghaṭamupāyāti Ghaṭācchakaṭamutkaṭam |

Cittamartheṣu Carati Pādapeṣviva Markaṭaḥ ||

7. पञ्च द्वाराणि मनसा चक्षुरादीन्यमून्यलम्। बुद्धीन्द्रियाभिधानानि तान्येवालोकयाम्यहम् ॥

Pañca Dvārāṇi Manasā Cakṣurādīnyamūnyalam |

Buddhīndriyābhidhānāni Tānyevālokayāmyaham ||

8. हन्तेन्द्रियगणा यूयं त्यजताकुलतां शनैः । चिदात्मा भगवान्सर्वसाक्षित्वेन स्थितोऽस्म्यहम् ॥

Hantendriyagaṇā Yūyaṃ Tyajatākulatāṃ Śanaiḥ |

Cidātmā Bhagavānsarvasākṣitvena Sthito'smyaham ||

9. तेनात्मना बहुज्ञेन निर्ज्ञाताश्चक्षुरादयः। परिनिर्वामि शान्तोऽस्मि दिष्ट्यास्मि विगतज्वरः ॥

Tenātmanā Bahujñena Nirjñātāścakṣurādayaḥ |

Parinirvāmi Śānto'smi Diṣṭyāsmi Vigatajvaraḥ ||

10. स्वात्मन्येवावतिष्ठेऽहं तुर्यरूपपदेऽनिशम्। अन्तरेव शशामास्य क्रमेण प्राणसन्ततिः ॥

Svātmanyevāvatiṣṭhe'haṃ Turyarūpapade'niśam |

Antareva Śaśāmāsya Krameṇa Prāṇasantatiḥ ||

11. ज्वालाजालपरिस्पन्दो दग्धेन्धन इवानलः । तदितोऽस्तं गत इव ह्यस्तं गत इवोदितः ॥

Jvālājālaparispando Dagdhendhana Ivānalaḥ |

Tadito'staṃ Gata Iva Hyastaṃ Gata Ivoditaḥ ||

12. समः समरसाभासस्तिष्ठामि स्वच्छतां गतः । प्रबुद्धोऽपि सुषुप्तिस्थः सुषुप्तिस्थः प्रबुद्धवान् ॥

Samaḥ Samarasābhāsastiṣṭhāmi Svacchatāṃ Gataḥ |

Prabuddho'pi Suṣuptisthaḥ Suṣuptisthaḥ Prabuddhavān ||

13. तुर्यमालम्ब्य कायान्तस्तिष्ठामि स्तम्भितस्थितिः ।
सबाह्याभ्यन्तरान्भावान्स्थूलान्सूक्ष्मतरानपि॥

Turyamālambya Kāyāntastiṣṭhāmi Stambhitasthitiḥ |

Sabāhyābhyantarānbhāvānsthūlānsūkṣmatarānapi ||

14. त्रैलोक्यसंभवांस्त्यक्त्वासंकल्पैकविनिर्मितान्। सह प्रणवपर्यन्तदीर्घनिःस्वनतन्तुना॥

Trailokyasaṃbhavāṃstyaktvā Saṃkalpaikavinirmitān |

Saha Praṇavaparyantadīrghaniḥsvanatantunā ||

15. जहाविन्द्रियतन्मात्रजालं खग इवानलः । ततोऽङ्गसंविदं स्वच्छां प्रतिभासमुपागताम् ॥

Jahāvindriyatanmātrajālaṃ Khaga Ivānalaḥ |

Tato'ṅgasaṃvidaṃ Svacchāṃ Pratibhāsamupāgatām ||

16. सद्योजातशिशुज्ञानं प्राप्तवान्मुनिपुङ्गवः। जहौ चित्तं चैत्यदशां स्पन्दशक्तिमिवानिलः ॥

Sadyojātaśiśujñānaṃ Prāptavānmunipuṅgavaḥ |

Jahau Cittaṃ Caityadaśāṃ Spandaśaktimivānilaḥ ||

17. चित्सामान्यमथासाद्य सत्तामात्रात्मकं ततः । सुषुप्तपदमालम्ब्य तस्थौ गिरिरिवाचलः ॥

Citsāmānyamathāsādya Sattāmātrātmakaṃ Tataḥ |

Suṣuptapadamālambya Tasthau Giririvācalaḥ ||

18. सुषुप्तस्थैर्यमासाद्य तुर्यरूपमुपाययौ। निरानन्दोऽपि सानन्दः सच्चासच्च बभूव सः ॥

Suṣuptasthairyamāsādya Turyarūpamupāyayau |

Nirānando'pi Sānandaḥ Saccāsacca Babhūva Saḥ ||

19. ततस्तु संबभूवासौ यद्गिरामप्यगोचरः । यच्छून्यवादिनां शून्यं ब्रह्म ब्रह्मविदां च यत् ॥

Tatastu Saṃbabhūvāsau Yadgirāmapyagocaraḥ |

Yacchūnyavādināṃ Śūnyaṃ Brahma Brahmavidāṃ Ca Yat ||

20. विज्ञानमात्रं विज्ञानविदां यदमलात्मकम् । पुरुषः सांख्यदृष्टीनामीश्वरो योगवादिनाम् ॥

Vijñānamātraṃ Vijñānavidāṃ Yadamalātmakam |

Puruṣaḥ Sāṃkhyadṛṣṭīnāmīśvaro Yogavādinām ||

21. शिवः शैवागमस्थानां कालः कालैकवादिनाम् । यत्सर्वशास्त्रसिद्धान्तं यत्सर्वहृदयानुगम् ॥

Śivaḥ Śaivāgamasthānāṃ Kālaḥ Kālaikavādinām |

Yatsarvaśāstrasiddhāntaṃ Yatsarvahṛdayānugam ||

22. यत्सर्वं सर्वगं वस्तु यत्तत्त्वं तदसौ स्थितः । यदनुक्तमनिष्पन्दं दीपकं तेजसामपि ॥

Yatsarvaṃ Sarvagaṃ Vastu Yattattvaṃ Tadasau Sthitaḥ |

Yadanuktamaniṣpandaṃ Dīpakaṃ Tejasāmapi ||

23. स्वानुभूत्यैकमानंच यत्तत्त्वं तदसौ स्थितः । यदेकं चाप्यनेकं च साञ्जनं च निरञ्जनम् ।
यत्सर्वं चाप्यसर्वं च यत्तत्त्वं तदसु स्थितः ॥

Svānubhūtyaikamānaṃ Ca Yattattvaṃ Tadasau Sthitaḥ |

Yadekaṃ Cāpyanekaṃ Ca Sāñjanaṃ Ca Nirañjanam |

Yatsarvaṃ Cāpyasarvaṃ Ca Yattattvaṃ Tadasu Sthitaḥ ||

24. अजममरमनाद्यमाद्यमेकं पदममलं सकलं च निष्कलं च ।
स्थित इति स तदा नभःस्वरूपा दपिविमलस्थितिरीश्वरः क्षणेन ॥

Ajamamaramanādyamādyamekaṃ

Padamamalaṃ Sakalaṃ Ca Niṣkalaṃ Ca |

Sthita Iti Sa Tadā Nabhaḥsvarūpā Dapivimalasthitirīśvaraḥ Kṣaṇena ||

इति तृतीयोऽध्यायः ॥ *Iti Tṛtīyo'dhyāyaḥ* ||

Fourth Chapter

1. जीवन्मुक्तस्य किं लक्ष्म ह्याकाशगमनादिकम् । तथा चेन्मुनिशार्दूल तत्र नैव प्रलक्ष्यते ॥

Jīvanmuktasya Kiṃ Lakṣma Hyākāśagamanādikam |

Tathā Cenmuniśārdūla Tatra Naiva Pralakṣyate ||

2. अनात्मविदमुक्तोऽपि नभोविहरणादिकम् । द्रव्यमन्त्रक्रियाकालशक्त्याप्नोत्येव स द्विजः ॥

Anātmavidamukto'pi Nabhoviharaṇādikam |

Dravyamantrakriyākālaśaktyāpnotyeva Sa Dvijaḥ ||

3. नात्मज्ञस्यैष विषय आत्मज्ञो ह्यात्ममात्रदृक् । आत्मनात्मनि संतृप्तो नाविद्यामनुधावति ॥

Nātmajñasyaiṣa Viṣaya Ātmajño Hyātmamātradṛk |

Ātmanātmani Saṃtṛpto Nāvidyāmanudhāvati ||

4. ये ये भावाः स्थिता लोके तानविद्यामयान्विदुः । त्यक्ताविद्यो महायोगी कथं तेषु निमज्जति

Ye Ye Bhāvāḥ Sthitā Loke Tānavidyāmayānviduḥ |

Tyaktāvidyo Mahāyogī Kathaṃ Teṣu Nimajjati ||

5. यस्तु मूढोऽल्पबुद्धिर्वा सिद्धिजालानि वाञ्छति । सिद्धिसाधनैर्योगैस्तानि साधयति क्रमात्

Yastu Mūḍho'lpabuddhirvā Siddhijālāni Vāñchati |

Siddhisādhanairyogaistāni Sādhayati Kramāt ||

6. द्रव्यमन्त्रक्रियाकालयुक्तयः साधुसिद्धिदाः। परमात्मपदप्राप्तौ नोपकुर्वन्ति काश्चन ॥

Dravyamantrakriyākālayuktayaḥ Sādhusiddhidāḥ |

Paramātmapadaprāptau Nopakurvanti Kāścana ||

7. यस्येच्छा विद्यते काचित्सा सिद्धिं साधयत्यहो।
निरिच्छोः परिपूर्णस्य नेच्छा संभवति क्वचित् ॥

Yasyecchā Vidyate Kācitsā Siddhiṃ Sādhayatyaho |

Niricchoḥ Paripūrṇasya Necchā Saṃbhavati Kvacit ||

8. सर्वेच्छाजालसंज्ञान्तावात्मलाभो भवेन्मुने। स कथं सिद्धिजालानि नूनं वाञ्छन्त्यचित्तकः

Sarvecchājālasaṃjñāntāvātmalābho Bhavenmune |

Sa Kathaṃ Siddhijālāni Nūnaṃ Vāñchantyacittakaḥ ||

9. अपि शीतरुचावर्के सुतीक्ष्णेऽपीन्दुमण्डले। अप्यधः प्रसरत्यग्नौ जीवन्मुक्तो न विस्मयी ॥

Api Śītarucāvarke Sutīkṣṇe'pīndumaṇḍale |

Apyadhaḥ Prasaratyagnau Jīvanmukto Na Vismayī ||

10. अधिष्ठाने परे तत्त्वे कल्पिता रज्जुसर्पवत्। कल्पिताश्चर्यजालेषु नाभ्युदेति कुतूहलम् ॥

Adhiṣṭhāne Pare Tattve Kalpitā Rajjusarpavat |

Kalpitāścaryajāleṣu Nābhyudeti Kutūhalam ||

11. ये हि विज्ञातविज्ञेया वीतरागा महाधियः। विच्छिन्नग्रन्थयः सर्वे ते स्वतन्त्रास्तनौ स्थितः

Ye Hi Vijñātavijñeyā Vītarāgā Mahādhiyaḥ |

Vicchinnagranthayaḥ Sarve Te Svatantrāstanau Sthitaḥ ||

12. सुखदुःखदशाधीरंसाम्यान्न प्रोद्धरन्ति यम्। निश्वासा इव शैलेन्द्रं चित्तं तस्य मृतं विदुः ॥

Sukhaduḥkhadaśādhīraṃ Sāmyānna Proddharanti Yam |

Niśvāsā Iva Śailendraṃ Cittaṃ Tasya Mṛtaṃ Viduḥ ||

13. आपत्कार्पण्यमुत्साहो मदो मान्द्यं महोत्सवः। यं नयन्ति न वैरूप्यं तस्य नष्टं मनो विदुः॥

Āpatkārpaṇyamutsāho Mado Māndyaṃ Mahotsavaḥ ।

Yaṃ Nayanti Na Vairūpyaṃ Tasya Naṣṭaṃ Mano Viduḥ ॥

14. द्विविधचित्तनाशोऽस्ति सरूपोऽरूप एव च । जीवन्मुक्तौ सरूपः स्यादरूपो देहमुक्तिगः ॥

Dvividhacittanāśo'sti Sarūpo'rūpa Eva Ca ।

Jīvanmuktau Sarūpaḥ Syādarūpo Dehamuktigaḥ ॥

15. चित्तसत्तेह दुःखाय चित्तनाशः सुखाय च । चित्तसत्तं क्षयं नीत्वा चित्तं नाशमुपानयेत् ॥

Cittasatteha Duḥkhāya Cittanāśaḥ Sukhāya Ca ।

Cittasattaṃ Kṣayaṃ Nītvā Cittaṃ Nāśamupānayet ॥

16. मनस्तां मूढतां विद्धि यदा नश्यति सानघ । चित्तनाशाभिधानं हि तत्स्वरूपमितीरितम् ॥

Manastāṃ Mūḍhatāṃ Viddhi Yadā Naśyati Sānagha ।

Cittanāśābhidhānaṃ Hi Tatsvarūpamitīritam ॥

17. मैत्र्यादिभिर्गुणैर्युक्तं भवत्युत्तमवासनम् । भूयो जन्मविनिर्मुक्तं जीवन्मुक्तस्य तन्मनः ॥

Maitryādibhirguṇairyuktaṃ Bhavatyuttamavāsanam ।

Bhūyo Janmavinirmuktaṃ Jīvanmuktasya Tanmanaḥ ॥

18. सरूपोऽसौ मनोनाशो जीवन्मुक्तस्य विद्यते । निदाघाऽरूपनाशस्तु वर्तते देहमुक्तिके ॥

Sarūpo'sau Manonāśo Jīvanmuktasya Vidyate ।

Nidāghā'rūpanāśastu Vartate Dehamuktike ॥

19. विदेहमुक्त एवासौ विद्यते निष्कलात्मकः । समग्राग्र्यगुणाधारमपि सत्त्वं प्रलीयते ॥

Videhamukta Evāsau Vidyate Niṣkalātmakaḥ ।

Samagrāgryaguṇādhāramapi Sattvaṃ Pralīyate ॥

20. विदेहमुक्तौ विमले पदे परमपावने । विदेहमुक्तिविषये तस्मिन्सत्त्वक्षयात्मके ॥

Videhamuktau Vimale Pade Paramapāvane ।

Videhamuktiviṣaye Tasminsattvakṣayātmake ॥

21. चित्तनाशे विरूपाख्ये न किंचिदिह विद्यते । न गुणा नागुणास्तत्र न श्रीर्नाश्रीर्न लोकता ॥

Cittanāśe Virūpākhye Na Kiṃcidiha Vidyate ।

Na Guṇā Nāguṇāstatra Na Śrīrnāśrīrna Lokatā ॥

22. न चोदयो नास्तमयो न हर्षामर्षसंविदः। न तेजो न तमः किंचिन्न सन्ध्यादिनरात्रयः।
न सत्तापि न चासत्ता न च मध्यं हि तत्पदम्॥

Na Codayo Nāstamayo Na Harṣāmarṣasaṃvidaḥ ।

Na Tejo Na Tamaḥ Kiṃcinna Sandhyādinarātrayaḥ ।

Na Sattāpi Na Cāsattā Na Ca Madhyaṃ Hi Tatpadam ॥

23. ये हि पारं गता बुद्धेः संसाराडम्बरस्य च। तेषां तदास्पदं स्फारं पवनानामिवाम्बरम्॥

Ye Hi Pāraṃ Gatā Buddheḥ Saṃsārāḍambarasya Ca ।

Teṣāṃ Tadāspadaṃ Sphāraṃ Pavanānāmivāmbaram ॥

24. संशान्तदुःखमजडात्मकमेकसुप्तमानन्दमन्थरमपेतरजस्तमो यत्।
आकाशकोशतनवोऽतनवो महान्त स्तस्मिन्पदे गलितचित्तलवा भवन्ति॥

Saṃśāntaduḥkhamajaḍātmakamekasupta-
Mānandamantharamapetarajastamo Yat ।
Ākāśakośatanavo'tanavo Mahānta-
Stasminpade Galitacittalavā Bhavanti ॥

25. हे निदाघ महाप्राज्ञ निर्वासनमना भव। बलाच्चेतः समाधाय निर्विकल्पमना भव॥

He Nidāgha Mahāprājña Nirvāsanamanā Bhava ।

Balāccetaḥ Samādhāya Nirvikalpamanā Bhava ॥

26. यज्जगद्भासकं भानं नित्यं भाति स्वतः स्फुरत्।
स एव जगतः साक्षी सर्वात्मा विमलाकृतिः॥

Yajjagadbhāsakaṃ Bhānaṃ Nityaṃ Bhāti Svataḥ Sphurat ।

Sa Eva Jagataḥ Sākṣī Sarvātmā Vimalākṛtiḥ ॥

27. प्रतिष्ठा सर्वभूतानां प्रज्ञानघनलक्षणः। तद्विद्याविषयं ब्रह्म सत्यज्ञानसुखाद्वनम्॥

Pratiṣṭhā Sarvabhūtānāṃ Prajñānaghanalakṣaṇaḥ ।

Tadvidyāviṣayaṃ Brahma Satyajñānasukhādvanam ॥

28. एकं ब्रह्माहमस्मीति कृतकृत्यो भवेन्मुनिः॥

Ekaṃ Brahmāhamasmīti Kṛtakṛtyo Bhavenmuniḥ ॥

29. सर्वाधिष्ठानमद्वन्द्वं परं ब्रह्म सनातनम् । सच्चिदानन्दरूपं तदवाङ्मनसगोचरम् ॥

Sarvādhiṣṭhānamadvandvaṃ Paraṃ Brahma Sanātanam |

Saccidānandarūpaṃ Tadavāṅmanasagocaram ||

30. न तत्र चन्द्रार्कवपुः प्रकाशते न वान्ति वातः सकलाश्च देवताः ।
स एव देवः कृतभावभूतः स्वयं विशुद्धो विरजः प्रकाशते ॥

Na Tatra Candrārkavapuḥ Prakāśate Na Vānti Vātaḥ Sakalāśca Devatāḥ

Sa Eva Devaḥ Kṛtabhāvabhūtaḥ Svayaṃ Viśuddho Virajaḥ Prakāśate ||

31. भिद्यते हृदयग्रन्थिश्छिद्यन्ते सर्वसंशयाः। क्षीयन्ते चास्य कर्माणि तस्मिन्दृष्टे परावरे ॥

Bhidyate Hṛdayagranthiśchidyante Sarvasaṃśayāḥ |

Kṣīyante Cāsya Karmāṇi Tasmindṛṣṭe Parāvare ||

32. द्वौ सुपर्णौ शरीरेऽस्मिञ्जीवेशाख्यौ सह स्थितौ ।
तयोर्जीवः फलं भुङ्क्ते कर्मणो न महेश्वरः ॥

Dvau Suparṇau Śarīre'smiñjīveśākhyau Saha Sthitau |

Tayorjīvaḥ Phalaṃ Bhuṅkte Karmaṇo Na Maheśvaraḥ ||

33. केवलं साक्षिरूपेण विना भोगो महेश्वरः । प्रकाशते स्वयं भेदः कल्पितो मायया तयोः ।
चिच्चिदाकारतो भिन्ना न भिन्ना चित्त्वहानितः ॥

Kevalaṃ Sākṣirūpeṇa Vinā Bhogo Maheśvaraḥ |

Prakāśate Svayaṃ Bhedaḥ Kalpito Māyayā Tayoḥ |

Ciccidākārato Bhinnā Na Bhinnā Cittvahānitaḥ ||

34. तर्कतश्च प्रमाणाच्च चिदेकत्वव्यवस्थितेः । चिदेकत्वपरिज्ञाने न शोचति न मुह्यति ॥

Tarkataśca Pramāṇācca Cidekatvavyavasthiteḥ |

Cidekatvaparijñāne Na Śocati Na Muhyati ||

35. अधिष्ठानं समस्तस्य जगतः सत्यचिद्घनम् । अहमस्मीति निश्चित्य वीतशोको भवेन्मुनिः ॥

Adhiṣṭhānaṃ Samastasya Jagataḥ Satyacidghanam |

Ahamasmīti Niścitya Vītaśoko Bhavenmuniḥ ||

36. स्वशरीरे स्वयंज्योतिस्वरूपं सर्वसाक्षिणम् । क्षीणदोषाः प्रपश्यन्ति नेतरे माययावृताः ॥

Svaśarīre Svayaṃjyotisvarūpaṃ Sarvasākṣiṇam ।

Kṣīṇadoṣāḥ Prapaśyanti Netare Māyayāvṛtāḥ ॥

37. तमेव धीरो विज्ञाय प्रज्ञां कुर्वीत ब्राह्मणः । नानुध्यायाद्बहूञ्छब्दान्वाचो विग्लापनं हि तत् ॥

Tameva Dhīro Vijñāya Prajñāṃ Kurvīta Brāhmaṇaḥ ।

Nānudhyāyādbahūñchabdānvāco Viglāpanaṃ Hi Tat ॥

38. बालेनैव हि तिष्ठासेन्निर्विद्य ब्रह्मवेदनम् । ब्रह्मविद्यां च बाल्यं च निर्विद्य मुनिरात्मवान् ॥

Bālenaiva Hi Tiṣṭhāsennirvidya Brahmavedanam ।

Brahmavidyāṃ Ca Bālyaṃ Ca Nirvidya Munirātmavān ॥

39. अन्तर्लीनसमारम्भः शुभाशुभमहाङ्कुरम्। संसृतिव्रततेर्बीजं शरीरं विद्धि भौतिकम् ॥

Antarlīnasamārambhaḥ Śubhāśubhamahāṅkuram ।

Saṃsṛtivratataterbījaṃ Śarīraṃ Viddhi Bhautikam ॥

40 भावाभावदशाकोशं दुःखरत्नसमुद्गकम् । चित्तमाशावशानुगम् ॥

Bhāvābhāvadaśākośaṃ Duḥkharatnasamudgakam ।

Bījamasya Śarīrasya Cittamāśāvaśānugam ॥

41. द्वे बीजे चित्तवृक्षस्य वृत्तिव्रततिधारिणः । एकं प्राणपरिस्पन्दो द्वितीयो दृढभावना ॥

Dve Bīje Cittavṛkṣasya Vṛttivratatidhāriṇaḥ ।

Ekaṃ Prāṇaparispando Dvitīyo Dṛḍhabhāvanā ॥

42. यदा प्रस्पन्दन्ते प्राणो नाडीसंस्पर्शनोद्यतः। तदा संवेदनमयं चित्तमाशु प्रजायते ॥

Yadā Praspandante Prāṇo Nāḍīsaṃsparśanodyataḥ ।

Tadā Saṃvedanamayaṃ Cittamāśu Prajāyate ॥

43. सा हि सर्वगता संवित्प्राणस्पन्देन बोध्यते । संवित्संरोधनंश्रेयः प्राणादिस्पन्दनं वरम् ॥

Sā Hi Sarvagatā Saṃvitprāṇaspandena Bodhyate ।

Saṃvitsaṃrodhanaṃ Śreyaḥ Prāṇādispandanaṃ Varam ॥

44. योगिनश्चित्तशान्त्यर्थं कुर्वन्ति प्राणरोधनम् | प्राणायामैस्तथा ध्यानैः प्रयोगैर्युक्तिकल्पितैः

Yoginaścittaśāntyarthaṃ Kurvanti Prāṇarodhanam ।

Prāṇāyāmaistathā Dhyānaiḥ Prayogairyuktikalpitaiḥ ॥

25. चित्तोपशान्तिफलदं परमं विद्धि कारणम् । सुखदं संविदः स्वास्थ्यं प्राणसंरोधनं विदुः

Cittopaśāntiphaladaṃ Paramaṃ Viddhi Kāraṇam |

Sukhadaṃ Saṃvidaḥ Svāsthyaṃ Prāṇasaṃrodhanaṃ Viduḥ ||

26. दृढभावनया त्यक्तपूर्वापरविचारणम्। यदादानं पदार्थस्य वासना सा प्रकीर्तिता ॥

Dṛḍhabhāvanayā Tyaktapūrvāparavicāraṇam |

Yadādānaṃ Padārthasya Vāsanā Sā Prakīrtitā ||

27. यदा न भाव्यते किंचिद्धेयोपादेयरूपि यत् । स्थीयते सकलं त्यक्त्वा तदा चित्तं न जायते ॥

Yadā Na Bhāvyate Kiṃciddheyopādeyarūpi Yat |

Sthīyate Sakalaṃ Tyaktvā Tadā Cittaṃ Na Jāyate ||

28. अवासनत्वात्सततं यदा न मनुते मनः । अमनस्ता तदोदेति परमोपशमप्रदा ॥

Avāsanatvātsatataṃ Yadā Na Manute Manaḥ |

Amanastā Tadodeti Paramopaśamapradā ||

29. यदा न भाव्यते भावः क्वचिज्जगति वस्तुनि। तदा हृदम्बरे शून्ये कथं चित्तं प्रजायते ॥

Yadā Na Bhāvyate Bhāvaḥ Kvacijjagati Vastuni |

Tadā Hṛdambare Śūnye Kathaṃ Cittaṃ Prajāyate ||

30. यदभावनमास्थाय यदभावस्य भावनम् । यद्यथा वस्तुदर्शित्वं तदचित्तत्वमुच्यते ॥

Yadabhāvanamāsthāya Yadabhāvasya Bhāvanam |

Yadyathā Vastudarśitvaṃ Tadacittatvamucyate ||

31. सर्वमन्तः परित्यज्य शीतलाशयवर्ति यत् । वृत्तिस्थमपि तच्चित्तमसद्रूपमुदाहृतम्॥

Sarvamantaḥ Parityajya Śītalāśayavarti Yat |

Vṛttisthamapi Taccittamasadrūpamudāhṛtam ||

32. भ्रष्टबीजोपमा येषां पुनर्जननवर्जिता। वासनारसनाहीना जीवन्मुक्ता हि ते स्मृताः ॥

Bhraṣṭabījopamā Yeṣāṃ Punarjananavarjitā |

Vāsanārasanāhīnā Jīvanmuktā Hi Te Smṛtāḥ ||

33. सत्त्वरूपपरिप्राप्तचित्तास्ते ज्ञानपारगाः । अचित्ता इति कथ्यन्ते देहान्ते व्योमरूपिणः

Sattvarūpaparipräptacittāste Jñānapāragāḥ |

Acittā Iti Kathyante Dehānte Vyomarūpiṇaḥ ||

34. संवेद्यसम्परित्यागात्प्राणस्पन्दनवासने। समूलं नश्यतः क्षिप्रं मूलच्छेदादिव द्रुमः॥

Saṃvedyasamparityāgātprāṇaspandanavāsane |

Samūlaṃ Naśyataḥ Kṣipraṃ Mūlacchedādiva Drumaḥ ||

35. पूर्वदृष्टमदृष्टं वा यदस्याः प्रतिभासते। संविदस्तत्प्रयत्नेन मार्जनीयं विजानता॥

Pūrvadṛṣṭamadṛṣṭaṃ Vā Yadasyāḥ Pratibhāsate |

Saṃvidastatprayatnena Mārjanīyaṃ Vijānatā ||

36. तदमार्जनमात्रं हि महासंसारतां गतम्। तत्प्रमार्जनमात्रं तु मोक्ष इत्यभिधीयते॥

Tadamārjanamātraṃ Hi Mahāsaṃsāratāṃ Gatam |

Tatpramārjanamātraṃ Tu Mokṣa Ityabhidhīyate ||

37. अजडो गलितानन्दस्त्यक्तसंवेदनो भव॥

Ajaḍo Galitānandastyaktasaṃvedano Bhava ||

38. संविद्वस्तुदशालम्बः सा यस्येह न विद्यते। सोऽसंविदजडः प्रोक्तः कुर्वन्कार्यशतान्यपि॥

Saṃvidvastudaśālambaḥ Sā Yasyeha Na Vidyate |

So'saṃvidajaḍaḥ Proktaḥ Kurvankāryaśatānyapi ||

39. संवेद्येन हृदाकाशे मनागपि न लिप्यते। यस्यासावजडा संविज्जीवन्मुक्तः स कथ्यते॥

Saṃvedyena Hṛdākāśe Manāgapi Na Lipyate |

Yasyāsāvajaḍā Saṃvijjīvanmuktaḥ Sa Kathyate ||

40. यदा न भाव्यते किंचिन्निर्वासनतयात्मनि। बालमूकादिविज्ञानमिव च स्थीयते स्थिरम्॥

Yadā Na Bhāvyate Kiṃcinnirvāsanatayātmani |

Bālamūkādivijñānamiva Ca Sthīyate Sthiram ||

41. तदा जाड्यविनिर्मुक्तमसंवेदनमाततम्। आश्रितं भवति प्राज्ञो यस्माद्भूयो न लिप्यते

Tadā Jāḍyavinirmuktamasaṃvedanamātatam |

Āśritaṃ Bhavati Prājño Yasmādbhūyo Na Lipyate ||

42. समस्ता वासनास्त्यक्त्वा निर्विकल्पसमाधितः । तन्मयत्वादनाद्यन्ते तदप्यन्तर्विलीयते ॥

Samastā Vāsanāstyaktvā Nirvikalpasamādhitaḥ |

Tanmayatvādanādyante Tadapyantarvilīyate ||

43. तिष्ठन्गाच्छन्स्पृशञ्जिघ्रन्नपि तल्लेपवर्जितः । अजडो गलितानन्दस्त्यक्तसंवेदनः सुखी ॥

Tiṣṭhangacchanspṛśañjighrannapi Tallepavarjitaḥ |

Ajaḍo Galitānandastyaktasaṃvedanaḥ Sukhī ||

44. एतां दृष्टिमवष्टभ्य कष्टचेष्टायुतोऽपि सन् । तरेद्दुःखाम्बुधेः पारमपारगुणसागरः ॥

Etāṃ Dṛṣṭimavaṣṭabhya Kaṣṭaceṣṭāyuto'pi San |

Taredduḥkhāmbudheḥ Pāramapāraguṇasāgaraḥ ||

45. विशेषं सम्परित्यज्य सन्मात्रं यदलेपकम् । एकरूपं महारूपं सत्तायास्तत्पदं विदुः ॥

Viśeṣaṃ Samparityajya Sanmātraṃ Yadalepakam |

Ekarūpaṃ Mahārūpaṃ Sattāyāstatpadaṃ Viduḥ ||

46. कालसत्ता कलासत्ता वस्तुसत्तेयमित्यपि । विभागकलनां त्यक्त्वा सन्मात्रैकपरो भव ॥

Kālasattā Kalāsattā Vastusatteyamityapi |

Vibhāgakalanāṃ Tyaktvā Sanmātraikaparo Bhava ||

47. सत्तासामान्यमेवैकं भावयन्केवलं विभुः । परिपूर्णः परानन्दि तिष्ठापूरितदिग्भरः ॥

Sattāsāmānyamevaikaṃ Bhāvayankevalaṃ Vibhuḥ |

Paripūrṇaḥ Parānandi Tiṣṭhāpūritadigbharaḥ ||

48. सत्तासामान्यपर्यन्ते यत्तत्कलनयोज्झितम् । पदमाद्यमनाद्यन्तं तस्य बीजं न विद्यते ॥

Sattāsāmānyaparyante Yattatkalanayojjhitam |

Padamādyamanādyantaṃ Tasya Bījaṃ Na Vidyate ||

49. तत्र संलीयते संविन्निर्विकल्पं च तिष्ठति । भूयो न वर्तते दुःखे तत्र लब्धपदः पुमान् ॥

Tatra Saṃlīyate Saṃvinnirvikalpaṃ Ca Tiṣṭhati |

Bhūyo Na Vartate Duḥkhe Tatra Labdhapadaḥ Pumān ||

50. तद्धेतुः सर्वभूतानां तस्य हेतुर्न विद्यते । स सारः सर्वसाराणां तस्मात्सारो न विद्यते ॥

Taddhetuḥ Sarvabhūtānāṃ Tasya Heturna Vidyate ।

Sa Sāraḥ Sarvasārāṇāṃ Tasmātsāro Na Vidyate ॥

51. तस्मिंश्चिद्दर्पणे स्फारे समस्ता वस्तुदृष्टयः। इमास्ताः प्रतिबिम्बन्ति सरसीव तटद्रुमाः॥

Tasmiṃściddarpaṇe Sphāre Samastā Vastudṛṣṭayaḥ ।

Imāstāḥ Pratibimbanti Sarasīva Taṭadrumāḥ ॥

52. तदमलमरजं तदात्मतत्त्वं तदवगतावुपशान्तिमेति चेतः।
अवगतविगतैकतत्स्वरूपो भवभयमुक्तपदोऽसि सम्यगेव॥

Tadamalamarajaṃ Tadātmatattvaṃ Tadavagatāvupaśāntimeti Cetaḥ ।

Avagatavigataikatatsvarūpo Bhavabhayamuktapado'si Samyageva ॥

53. एतेषां दुःखबीजानां प्रोक्तं यद्यन्मयोत्तरम्। तस्य तस्य प्रयोगेण शीघ्रं तत्प्राप्यते पदम्

Eteṣāṃ Duḥkhabījānāṃ Proktaṃ Yadyanmayottaram ।

Tasya Tasya Prayogeṇa Śīghraṃ Tatprāpyate Padam ॥

54. सत्तासामान्यकोटिस्थे द्रागित्येव पदे यदि। पौरुषेण प्रयत्नेन बलात्संत्यज्य वासनाम्॥

Sattāsāmānyakoṭisthe Drāgityeva Pade Yadi ।

Pauruṣeṇa Prayatnena Balātsaṃtyajya Vāsanām ॥

55. स्थितिं बध्नासि तत्त्वज्ञ क्षणमप्यक्षयात्मिकाम्। क्षणेऽस्मिन्नेव तत्साधु पदमासादयस्यलम्

Sthitiṃ Badhnāsi Tattvajña Kṣaṇamapyakṣayātmikām ।

Kṣaṇe'sminneva Tatsādhu Padamāsādayasyalam ॥

56. सत्तासामान्यरूपे वा करोषि स्थितिमादरात्। तत्किंचिदधिकेनेह यत्नेनाप्नोषि तत्पदम्॥

Sattāsāmānyarūpe Vā Karoṣi Sthitimādarāt ।

Tatkiṃcidadhikeneha Yatnenāpnoṣi Tatpadam ॥

57. संवित्तत्त्वे कृतध्यानो निदाघ यदि तिष्ठसि। तद्यत्नेनाधिकेनोच्चैरासादयसि तत्पदम्॥

Saṃvittattve Kṛtadhyāno Nidāgha Yadi Tiṣṭhasi ।

Tadyatnenādhikenoccairāsādayasi Tatpadam ॥

58. वासनासम्परित्यागे यदि यत्नं करोषि भोः। यावद्विलीनं न मनो न तावद्वासनाक्षयः॥

Vāsanāsamparityāge Yadi Yatnaṃ Karoṣi Bhoḥ |
Yāvadvilīnaṃ Na Mano Na Tāvadvāsanākṣayaḥ ||

59. न क्षीणा वासना यावच्चित्तं तावन्न शाम्यति। यावन्न तत्त्वविज्ञानं तावच्चित्तशमः कुतः ॥

Na Kṣīṇā Vāsanā Yāvaccittaṃ Tāvanna Śāmyati |
Yāvanna Tattvavijñānaṃ Tāvaccittaśamaḥ Kutaḥ ||

60. यावन्न चित्तोपशमो न तावत्तत्त्ववेदनम्। यावन्न वासनानाशस्तावत्तत्त्वागमः कुतः।
यावन्न तत्त्वसम्प्राप्तिर्न तावद्वासनक्षयः ॥

Yāvanna Cittopaśamo Na Tāvattattvavedanam |
Yāvanna Vāsanānāśastāvattattvāgamaḥ Kutaḥ |
Yāvanna Tattvasamprāptirna Tāvadvāsanakṣayaḥ ||

61. तत्त्वज्ञानं मनोनाशो वासनाक्षय एव च। मिथः कारणतां गत्वा दुःसाधानि स्थितान्यतः

Tattvajñānaṃ Manonāśo Vāsanākṣaya Eva Ca |
Mithaḥ Kāraṇatāṃ Gatvā Duḥsādhāni Sthitānyataḥ ||

62. भोगेच्छां दूरतस्त्यक्त्वा त्रयमेतत्समाचर ॥

Bhogecchāṃ Dūratastyaktvā Trayametatsamācara ||

63. वासनाक्षयविज्ञानमनोनाशा महामते। समकालं चिराभ्यस्ता भवन्ति फलदा मताः ॥

Vāsanākṣayavijñānamanonāśā Mahāmate |
Samakālaṃ Cirābhyastā Bhavanti Phaladā Matāḥ ||

64. त्रिभिरेभिः समभ्यस्तैर्हृदयग्रन्थयो दृढाः। निःशेषमेव त्रुट्यन्ति बिसच्छेदाद्गुणाइव ॥

Tribhirebhiḥ Samabhyastairhṛdayagranthayo Dṛḍhāḥ |
Niḥśeṣameva Truṭyanti Bisacchedādguṇā Iva ||

65. वासनासम्परित्यागसमं प्राणनिरोधनम्। विदुस्तत्त्वविदस्तस्मात्तदप्येवं समाहरेत् ॥

Vāsanāsamparityāgasamaṃ Prāṇanirodhanam |
Vidustattvavidastasmāttadapyevaṃ Samāharet ||

66. वासनासम्परित्यागाच्चित्तं गच्छत्यचित्तताम्। प्राणस्पन्दनिरोधाच्च यथेच्छसि तथा कुरु

Vāsanāsamparityāgāccittaṃ Gacchatyacittatām |

Prāṇaspandanirodhācca Yathecchasi Tathā Kuru ||

67. प्राणायामदृढाध्यासैर्युक्त्या च गुरुदत्तया। आसनाशनयोगेन प्राणस्पन्दो निरुध्यते॥

Prāṇāyāmadṛḍhādhyāsairyuktyā Ca Gurudattayā |

Āsanāśanayogena Prāṇaspando Nirudhyate ||

68. निःसङ्गव्यवहारत्वाद्भवभावनवर्जनात्। शरीरनाशदर्शित्वाद्वासना न प्रवर्तते॥

Niḥsaṅgavyavahāratvādbhavabhāvanavarjanāt |

Śarīranāśadarśitvādvāsanā Na Pravartate ||

69. यः प्राणपवनस्पन्दश्चित्तस्पन्दः स एव हि। प्राणस्पन्दजये यत्नः कर्तव्यो धीमतोच्चकैः॥

Yaḥ Prāṇapavanaspandaścittaspandaḥ Sa Eva Hi |

Prāṇaspandajaye Yatnaḥ Kartavyo Dhīmatoccakaiḥ ||

70. न शक्यते मनो जेतुं विना युक्तिमनिन्दिताम्। शुद्धां संविदमाश्रित्यवीतरागः स्थिरो भव

Na Śakyate Mano Jetuṃ Vinā Yuktimaninditām |

Śuddhāṃ Saṃvidamāśrityavītarāgaḥ Sthiro Bhava ||

71. संवेद्यवर्जितमनुत्तममाद्यमेकं संविदत्पदं विकलनं कलयन्महात्मन्।
हृद्येव तिष्ठ कलनारहितः क्रियां तु कुर्वन्नकर्तृपदमेत्य शमोदितश्रीः॥

Saṃvedyavarjitamanuttamamādyamekaṃ
Saṃvidatpadaṃ Vikalanaṃ Kalayanmahātman |
Hṛdyeva Tiṣṭha Kalanārahitaḥ Kriyāṃ Tu
Kurvannakartṛpadametya Śamoditaśrīḥ ||

72. मनागपि विचारेण चेतसः स्वस्य निग्रहः। पुरुषेण कृतो येन तेनाप्तं जन्मनः फलम्॥

Manāgapi Vicāreṇa Cetasaḥ Svasya Nigrahaḥ |

Puruṣeṇa Kṛto Yena Tenāptaṃ Janmanaḥ Phalam ||

इति चतुर्थोऽध्यायः॥ *Iti Caturtho'dhyāyaḥ ||*

Fifth Chapter

1. गच्छतस्तिष्ठतो वापि जाग्रतः स्वपतोऽपि वा। न विचारपरं चेतो यस्यासौ मृत उच्यते॥

Gacchatastiṣṭhato Vāpi Jāgrataḥ Svapato'pi Vā ।
Na Vicāraparaṃ Ceto Yasyāsau Mṛta Ucyate ॥

2. सम्यग्ज्ञानसमालोकः पुमाऽज्ञेयसमः स्वयम्। न बिभेति न चादत्ते वैवश्यं न च दीनताम्॥

Samyagjñānasamālokaḥ Pumā'jñeyasamaḥ Svayam ।
Na Bibheti Na Cādatte Vaivaśyaṃ Na Ca Dīnatām ॥

3. अपवित्रमपथ्यं च विषसंसर्गदूषितम्। भुक्तं जरयति ज्ञानी क्लिन्नं नष्ठं च मृष्टवत्॥

Apavitramapathyaṃ Ca Viṣasaṃsargadūṣitam ।
Bhuktaṃ Jarayati Jñānī Klinnaṃ Naṣṭhaṃ Ca Mṛṣṭavat ॥

4. सञ्ण्गत्यागं विदुर्मोक्षं सङ्गत्यागादजन्मता। सङ्गं त्यज त्वं भावानां जीवन्मुक्तो भवानघ

Saññgatyāgaṃ Vidurmokṣaṃ Saṅgatyāgādajanmatā ।
Saṅgaṃ Tyaja Tvaṃ Bhāvānāṃ Jīvanmukto Bhavānagha ॥

5. भावाभावे पदार्थानां हर्षामर्षविकारदा। मलिना वासना यैषा साऽसङ्ग इति कथ्यते॥

Bhāvābhāve Padārthānāṃ Harṣāmarṣavikāradā ।
Malinā Vāsanā Yaiṣā Sā'saṅga Iti Kathyate ॥

6. जीवन्मुक्तशरीराणामपुनर्जन्मकारिणी। मुक्ता हर्षविषादाभ्यां शुद्धा भवति वासना॥

Jīvanmuktaśarīrāṇāmapunarjanmakāriṇī ।
Muktā Harṣaviṣādābhyāṃ Śuddhā Bhavati Vāsanā ॥

7. दुःखैर्न ग्लानिमायासि हृदि हृष्यसि नो सुखैः। आशावैवश्यमुत्सृज्य निदाघाऽसङ्गतां व्रज

Duḥkhairna Glānimāyāsi Hṛdi Hṛṣyasi No Sukhaiḥ ।
Āśāvaivaśyamutsṛjya Nidāghā'saṅgatāṃ Vraja ॥

8. दिक्कालाद्यनवच्छिन्नमदृष्टोभयकोटिकम्। चिन्मात्रमक्षयं शान्तमेकं ब्रह्मास्मि नेतरत्

Dikkālādyanavacchinnamadṛṣṭobhayakoṭikam ।
Cinmātramakṣayaṃ Śāntamekaṃ Brahmāsmi Netarat ॥

9. इति मत्वाहमित्यन्तर्मुक्तामुक्तवपुःपुमान्। एकरूपः प्रशान्तात्मा मौनी स्वात्मसुखो भव॥

Iti Matvāhamityantarmuktāmuktavapuḥ Pumān ।
Ekarūpaḥ Praśāntātmā Maunī Svātmasukho Bhava ॥

10. नास्ति चित्तं न चाविद्या न मनो न च जीवकः । ब्रह्मैवैकमनाद्यन्तमब्धिवत्प्रविजृम्भते ॥

Nāsti Cittaṃ Na Cāvidyā Na Mano Na Ca Jīvakaḥ |

Brahmaivaikamanādyantamabdhivatpravijṛmbhate ||

11. देहे यावदहंभावो दृश्येऽस्मिन्यावदात्मता । यावन्ममेदमित्यास्था तावच्चित्तादिविभ्रमः ॥

Dehe Yāvadahaṃbhāvo Dṛśye'sminyāvadātmatā |

Yāvanmamedamityāsthā Tāvaccittādivibhramaḥ ||

12. अन्तर्मुखतया सर्वं चिद्वह्नौ त्रिजगत्तृणम् । जुह्वन्तोऽन्तर्निवर्तन्ते मुने चित्तादिविभ्रमाः ॥

Antarmukhatayā Sarvaṃ Cidvahnau Trijagattṛṇam |

Juhvanto'ntarnivartante Mune Cittādivibhramāḥ ||

13. चिदात्मास्मि निरंशोऽस्मि परापरविवर्जितः । रूपं स्मरन्निजं स्फारं मा स्मृत्या संमितो भव॥

Cidātmāsmi Niraṃśo'smi Parāparavivarjitaḥ |

Rūpaṃ Smarannijaṃ Sphāraṃ Mā Smṛtyā Saṃmito Bhava ||

14. अध्यात्मशास्त्रमन्त्रेण तृष्णाविषविषूचिका । क्षीयते भावितेनान्तः शरदा मिहिका यथा ॥

Adhyātmaśāstramantreṇa Tṛṣṇāviṣaviṣūcikā |

Kṣīyate Bhāvitenāntaḥ Śaradā Mihikā Yathā ||

15. परिज्ञाय परित्यागो वासानानं य उत्तमः । सत्तासामान्यरूपत्वात्तत्कैवल्यपदं विदुः ॥

Parijñāya Parityāgo Vāsānānaṃ Ya Uttamaḥ |

Sattāsāmānyarūpatvāttatkaivalyapadaṃ Viduḥ ||

16. यन्नास्ति वासना लीना तत्सुषुप्तं न सिद्धये । निर्बीजा वासना यत्र तत्तुर्यं सिद्धिदं स्मृतम् ॥

Yannāsti Vāsanā Līnā Tatsuṣuptaṃ Na Siddhaye |

Nirbījā Vāsanā Yatra Tatturyaṃ Siddhidaṃ Smṛtam ||

17. वासनायास्तथा वह्नेरृणव्याधिद्विषामपि । स्नेहवैरविषाण च शेषः स्वल्पोऽपि बाधते ॥

Vāsanāyāstathā Vahnerṛṇavyādhidviṣāmapi |

Snehavairaviṣāṇa Ca Śeṣaḥ Svalpo'pi Bādhate ||

18. निर्दग्धवासनाबीजः सत्तासामान्यरूपवान् । सदेहो वा विदेहो वा न भूयो दुःखभाग्भवेत् ॥

Nirdagdhavāsanābījaḥ Sattāsāmānyarūpavān |

Sadeho Vā Videho Vā Na Bhūyo Duḥkhabhāgbhavet ||

19. एतावदेवाविद्यात्वं नेदं ब्रह्मेति निश्चयः । एष एव क्षयस्तस्या ब्रह्मेदमिति निश्चयः ॥

Etāvadevāvidyātvaṃ Nedaṃ Brahmeti Niścayaḥ |

Eṣa Eva Kṣayastasyā Brahmedamiti Niścayaḥ ||

20. ब्रह्म चिद्ब्रह्म भुवनं ब्रह्म भूतपरम्परा। ब्रह्माहं ब्रह्म चिच्छत्रुर्ब्रह्म चिन्मित्रबान्धवाः ॥

Brahma Cidbrahma Bhuvanaṃ Brahma Bhūtaparamparā |

Brahmāhaṃ Brahma Cicchatrurbrahma Cinmitrabāndhavāḥ ||

21. ब्रह्मैव सर्वमित्येव भाविते ब्रह्म वै पुमान्। सर्वत्रावस्थितं शान्तं चिद्ब्रह्मेत्यनुभूयते॥

Brahmaiva Sarvamityeva Bhāvite Brahma Vai Pumān |

Sarvatrāvasthitaṃ Śāntaṃ Cidbrahmetyanubhūyate ||

22. असंस्कृताध्वगालोके मनस्यन्यत्र संस्थिते। या प्रतीतिरनागसका तच्चिदब्रह्मास्मि सर्वगम्

Asaṃskṛtādhvagāloke Manasyanyatra Saṃsthite |

Yā Pratītiranāgasakā Taccidbrahmāsmi Sarvagam ||

23. प्रशान्तसर्वसंकल्पं विगताखिलकौतुकम्। विगताशेषसंरंभंचिदात्मानं समाश्रय ॥

Praśāntasarvasaṃkalpaṃ Vigatākhilakautukam |

Vigatāśeṣasaṃraṃbhaṃ Cidātmānaṃ Samāśraya ||

24. एवं पूर्णधियो धीराः समा नीरागचेतसः । न नन्दन्ति न निन्दन्ति जीवितं मरणं तथा ॥

Evaṃ Pūrṇadhiyo Dhīrāḥ Samā Nīrāgacetasaḥ |

Na Nandanti Na Nindanti Jīvitaṃ Maraṇaṃ Tathā ||

25. प्राणोऽयमनिशं ब्रह्मस्पन्दशक्तिः सदागतिः । सबाह्याभ्यन्तरे देहेप्राणोऽसावूर्ध्वगः स्थितः ॥

Prāṇo'yamaniśaṃ Brahmaspandaśaktiḥ Sadāgatiḥ |

Sabāhyābhyantare Dehéprāṇo'sāvūrdhvagaḥ Sthitaḥ ||

26. अपानोऽप्यनिशं ब्रह्मस्पन्दशक्तिः सदागतिः । सबाह्याभ्यन्तरे देहे अपानोऽयमवाक्स्थितः॥

Apāno'pyaniśaṃ Brahmaspandaśaktiḥ Sadāgatiḥ |

Sabāhyābhyantare Dehe Apāno'yamavāksthitaḥ ||

27. जाग्रतः स्वपतश्चैव प्राणायामोऽयमुत्तमः । प्रवर्तते ह्यभिज्ञस्य तं तावच्छ्रेयसे शृणु ॥

Jāgrataḥ Svapataścaiva Prāṇāyāmo'yamuttamaḥ |

Pravartate Hyabhijñasya Taṃ Tāvacchreyase Śṛṇu ||

28. द्वादशाङ्गुलपर्यन्तं बाह्यमाक्रमतां ततः । प्राणाङ्गनामा संस्पर्शो यः स पूरक उच्यते ॥

Dvādaśāṅgulaparyantaṃ Bāhyamākramatāṃ Tataḥ |

Prāṇāṅganāmā Saṃsparśo Yaḥ Sa Pūraka Ucyate ||

29. अपानश्चन्द्रमा देहमाप्याययति सुव्रत । प्राणः सूर्योऽग्निरथ वा पचत्यनत्रिदं वपुः ॥

Apānaścandramā Dehamāpyāyayati Suvrata |

Prāṇaḥ Sūryo'gniratha Vā Pacatyanatridaṃ Vapuḥ ||

30. प्राणक्षयसमीपस्थमपानोदयकोटिगम् । अपानप्राणयोरैक्यं चिदात्मानं समाश्रय ॥

Prāṇakṣayasamīpasthamapānodayakoṭigam |

Apānaprāṇayoraikyaṃ Cidātmānaṃ Samāśraya ||

31. अपानोऽस्तंगतो यत्र प्राणो नाभ्युदितः क्षणम् । कलाकलङ्करहितं तच्चित्तत्त्वं समाश्रय

Apāno'staṃgato Yatra Prāṇo Nābhyuditaḥ Kṣaṇam |

Kalākalaṅkarahitaṃ Taccittattvaṃ Samāśraya ||

32. नापानोऽस्तंगतो यत्र प्राणश्चास्तमुपागतः । नासाग्रगमनावर्तं तच्चित्तत्त्वमुपाश्रय ॥

Nāpāno'staṃgato Yatra Prāṇaścāstamupāgataḥ |

Nāsāgragamanāvartaṃ Taccittattvamupāśraya ||

33. आभासमात्रमेवेदं न सनासज्जगत्त्रयम् । इत्यन्यकलनात्यागं सम्यग्ज्ञानं विदुर्बुधाः ॥

Ābhāsamātramevedaṃ Na Sanāsajjagattrayam |

Ityanyakalanātyāgaṃ Samyagjñānaṃ Vidurbudhāḥ ||

34. आभासमात्रकं ब्रह्मंश्चित्तदर्शकलङ्कितम् । ततस्तदपि संत्यज्य निराभासो भवोत्तम ॥

Ābhāsamātrakaṃ Brahmaṃścittadarśakalaṅkitam |

Tatastadapi Saṃtyajya Nirābhāso Bhavottama ||

35. भयप्रदमकल्याणं धैर्यसर्वस्वहारिणम् । मनःपिशाचमुत्सार्य योऽसि सोऽसि स्थिरो भव

Bhayapradamakalyāṇaṃ Dhairyasarvasvahāriṇam |

Manaḥpiśācamutsārya Yo'si So'si Sthiro Bhava ||

36. चिद्व्योमेव किलास्तीह परापरविवर्जितम् । सर्वत्रासंभवच्चैत्यं यत्कल्पान्तेऽवशिष्यते ॥

Cidvyomeva Kilāstīha Parāparavivarjitam |

Sarvatrāsaṃbhavaccaityaṃ Yatkalpānte'vaśiṣyate ||

37. वाञ्छाक्षणे तु या तुष्टिस्तत्र वाञ्छैव कारणम् । तुष्टिस्त्वतुष्टिपर्यन्ता तस्माद्वाञ्छां परित्यज॥

Vāñchākṣaṇe Tu Yā Tuṣṭistatra Vāñchaiva Kāraṇam |

Tuṣṭistvatuṣṭiparyantā Tasmādvāñchāṃ Parityaja ||

38. आशा यातु निराशात्वमभावं यातु भावना । अमनस्त्वं मनो यातु तवासङ्गेन जीवतः ॥

Āśā Yātu Nirāśātvamabhāvaṃ Yātu Bhāvanā |

Amanastvaṃ Mano Yātu Tavāsaṅgena Jīvataḥ ||

39. वासनारहितैरन्तरिन्द्रियैराहरन्क्रिया । न विकारमवाप्नोषि खवत्क्षोभशतैरपि ॥

Vāsanārahitairantarindriyairāharankriyā |

Na Vikāramavāpnoṣi Khavatkṣobhaśatairapi ||

40. चित्तोन्मेषनिमेषाभ्यां संसारप्रलयोदयौ । वासनाप्राणसंरोधमनुन्मेषं मनः कुरु ॥

Cittonmeṣanimeṣābhyāṃ Saṃsārapralayodayau |

Vāsanāprāṇasaṃrodhamanunmeṣaṃ Manaḥ Kuru ||

41. प्राणोन्मेषनिमेषाभ्यां संसृतेः प्रलयोदयौ । तमभ्यासप्रयोगाभ्यामुन्मेषरहितं कुरु ॥

Prāṇonmeṣanimeṣābhyāṃ Saṃsṛteḥ Pralayodayau |

Tamabhyāsaprayogābhyāmunmeṣarahitaṃ Kuru ||

42. मौर्ख्योन्मेषनिमेषाभ्यां कर्मणां प्रलयोदयौ । तद्विलीनं कुरु बलाद्गुरुशास्त्रार्थसंगमैः॥

Maurkhyonmeṣanimeṣābhyāṃ Karmaṇāṃ Pralayodayau |

Tadvilīnaṃ Kuru Balādguruśāstrārthasaṃgamaiḥ ||

43. असंवित्स्पन्दमात्रेण याति चित्तमचित्तताम् । प्राणानां वा निरोधेन तदेव परमं पदम् ॥

Asaṃvitspandamātreṇa Yāti Cittamacittatām |

Prāṇānāṃ Vā Nirodhena Tadeva Paramaṃ Padam ||

44. दृश्यदर्शनसंबन्धे यत्सुखं पारमार्थिकम् । तदन्तैकान्तसंवित्त्या ब्रह्मदृष्ट्यावलोकय ॥

Dṛśyadarśanasaṃbandhe Yatsukhaṃ Pāramārthikam |

Tadantaikāntasaṃvittyā Brahmadṛṣṭyāvalokaya ||

45. यत्र नाभ्युदितं चित्तं तद्वै सुखमकृत्रिमम् । क्षयातिशयनिर्मुक्तं नोदेति न च शाम्यति ॥

Yatra Nābhyuditaṃ Cittaṃ Tadvai Sukhamakṛtrimam |

Kṣayātiśayanirmuktaṃ Nodeti Na Ca Śāmyati ||

46. यस्य चित्तं न चित्ताख्यं चित्तं चित्तत्त्वमेव हि । तदेव तुर्यावस्थायं तुर्यातीतं भवत्यतः ॥

Yasya Cittaṃ Na Cittākhyaṃ Cittaṃ Cittattvameva Hi |

Tadeva Turyāvasthāyaṃ Turyātītaṃ Bhavatyataḥ ||

47. संन्यस्तसर्वसंकल्पः समः शान्तमना मुनिः । संन्यासयोगयुक्तात्मा ज्ञानवान्मोक्षवान्भव

Saṃnyastasarvasaṃkalpaḥ Samaḥ Śāntamanā Muniḥ |

Saṃnyāsayogayuktātmā Jñānavānmokṣavānbhava ||

48. सर्वसंकल्पसंशान्तंप्रशान्तघनवासनम् । न किंचिद्भावनाकारं यत्तद्ब्रह्म परं विदुः ॥

Sarvasaṃkalpasaṃśāntaṃ Praśāntaghanavāsanam |

Na Kiṃcidbhāvanākāraṃ Yattadbrahma Paraṃ Viduḥ ||

49. सम्यग्ज्ञानावरोधेन नित्यमेकसमाधिना । सांख्य एवावबुद्धा ये ते सांख्या योगिनः परे ॥

Samyagjñānāvarodhena Nityamekasamādhinā |

Sāṃkhya Evāvabuddhā Ye Te Sāṃkhyā Yoginaḥ Pare ||

50. प्राणाद्यनिलसंशान्तौ युक्त्या ये पदमागताः । अनामयमनाद्यन्तं ते स्मृता योगयोगिनः ॥

Prāṇādyanilasaṃśāntau Yuktyā Ye Padamāgatāḥ |

Anāmayamanādyantaṃ Te Smṛtā Yogayoginaḥ ||

51. उपादेयं तु सर्वेषां शातं पदमकृत्रिमम् । एकार्थाभ्यसनं प्राणरोधश्चेतः परिक्षयः ॥

Upādeyaṃ Tu Sarveṣāṃ Śātaṃ Padamakṛtrimam |

Ekārthābhyasanaṃ Prāṇarodhaścetaḥ Parikṣayaḥ ||

52. एकस्मिन्नेव संसिद्धे संसिद्ध्यन्ति परस्परम् । अविनाभाविनी नित्यं जन्तूनां प्राणचेतसी ॥

Ekasminneva Saṃsiddhe Saṃsiddhyanti Parasparam I

Avinābhāvinī Nityaṃ Jantūnāṃ Prāṇacetasī II

53. आधाराधेयवच्चैते एकभावे विनश्यतः । कुरुतः स्वविनाशेन कार्यं मोक्षाख्यमुत्तमम् ॥

Ādhārādheyavaccaite Ekabhāve Vinaśyataḥ I

Kurutaḥ Svavināśena Kāryaṃ Mokṣākhyamuttamam II

54. सर्वमेतद्धिया त्यक्त्वा यदि तिष्ठसि निश्चलः । तदाहंकारविलये त्वमेव परमं पदम् ॥

Sarvametaddhiyā Tyaktvā Yadi Tiṣṭhasi Niścalaḥ I

Tadāhaṃkāravilaye Tvameva Paramaṃ Padam II

55. महाचिदेकैवेहास्ति महासत्तेति योच्यते । निष्कलंका समा शुद्धा निरहंकाररूपिणी ॥

Mahācidekaivehāsti Mahāsatteti Yocyate I

Niṣkalaṃkā Samā Śuddhā Nirahaṃkārarūpiṇī II

56. सकृद्विभाता विमला नित्योदयवती समा । सा ब्रह्म परमात्मेति नामभिः परिगीयते ॥

Sakṛdvibhātā Vimalā Nityodayavatī Samā I

Sā Brahma Paramātmeti Nāmabhiḥ Parigīyate II

57. सैवाहमिति निश्चित्य निदाघ कृतकृत्यवान् । न भूतं न भविष्यच्च चिन्तयामि कदाचन ॥

Saivāhamiti Niścitya Nidāgha Kṛtakṛtyavān I

Na Bhūtaṃ Na Bhaviṣyacca Cintayāmi Kadācana II

58. दृष्टिमालम्ब्य तिष्ठामि वर्तमानामिहात्मना । इदमद्य मया लब्धमिदं प्राप्स्यामि सुन्दरम्

Dṛṣṭimālambya Tiṣṭhāmi Vartamānāmihātmanā I

Idamadya Mayā Labdhamidaṃ Prāpsyāmi Sundaram II

59. न स्तौमि न च निन्दामि आत्मनोऽन्यन्नहि क्वचित् ।
न तुष्यामि शुभप्राप्तौ न खिद्याम्यशुभागमे ॥

Na Staumi Na Ca Nindāmi Ātmano'nyannahi Kvacit I

Na Tuṣyāmi Śubhaprāptau Na Khidyāmyaśubhāgame II

60. प्रशान्तचापलं वीतशोकमस्तसमीहितम् । मनो मम मुने शान्तं तेन जीवाम्यनामयः ॥

Praśāntacāpalaṃ Vītaśokamastasamīhitam |

Mano Mama Mune Śāntaṃ Tena Jīvāmyanāmayaḥ ||

61. अयं बन्धुः परश्चायं ममायमयमन्यकः । इति ब्रह्मन्न जानामि संस्पर्शं न ददाम्यहम् ॥

Ayaṃ Bandhuḥ Paraścāyaṃ Mamāyamayamanyakaḥ |

Iti Brahmanna Jānāmi Saṃsparśaṃ Na Dadāmyaham ||

62. वासनामात्रसंत्यागाज्जरामरणवर्जितम् । सवासनं मनो ज्ञानं ज्ञेयं निर्वासनं मनः ॥

Vāsanāmātrasaṃtyāgājjarāmaraṇavarjitam |

Savāsanaṃ Mano Jñānaṃ Jñeyaṃ Nirvāsanaṃ Manaḥ ||

63. चित्ते त्यक्ते लयं याति द्वैतमेतच्च सर्वतः । शिष्यते परमं शान्तमेकमगच्छमनामयम् ॥

Citte Tyakte Layaṃ Yāti Dvaitametacca Sarvataḥ |

Śiṣyate Paramaṃ Śāntamekamagacchamanāmayam ||

64. अनन्तमजमव्यक्तमजरं शान्तमच्युतम् । अद्वितीयमनाद्यन्तं यदाद्यमुपलम्भनम् ॥

Anantamajamavyaktamajaraṃ Śāntamacyutam |

Advitīyamanādyantaṃ Yadādyamupalambhanam ||

65. एकमाद्यन्तरहितं चिन्मात्रममलं ततम् । खादप्यतितरां सूक्ष्मं तद्ब्रह्मास्मि न संशयः ॥

Ekamādyantarahitaṃ Cinmātramamalaṃ Tatam |

Khādapyatitarāṃ Sūkṣmaṃ Tadbrahmāsmi Na Saṃśayaḥ ||

66. दिक्कालाद्यनवच्छिन्नं स्वच्छं नित्योदितं ततम् । सर्वार्थमयमेकार्थं चिन्मात्रममलं भव ॥

Dikkālādyanavacchinnaṃ Svacchaṃ Nityoditaṃ Tatam |

Sarvārthamayamekārthaṃ Cinmātramamalaṃ Bhava ||

67. सर्वमेकमिदं शान्तमादिमध्यान्तवर्जितम् । भावाभावमजं सर्वमिति मत्वा सुखी भव ॥

Sarvamekamidaṃ Śāntamādimadhyāntavarjitam |

Bhāvābhāvamajaṃ Sarvamiti Matvā Sukhī Bhava ||

68. न बद्धोऽस्मि न मुक्तोऽस्मि ब्रह्मैवास्मि निरामयम् ।
द्वैतभावविमुक्तोऽस्मि सच्चिदानन्दलक्षणः । एवं भावय यत्नेन जीवन्मुक्तो भविष्यसि ॥

Na Baddho'smi Na Mukto'smi Brahmaivāsmi Nirāmayam ।

Dvaitabhāvavimukto'smi Saccidānandalakṣaṇaḥ ।

Evaṃ Bhāvaya Yatnena Jīvanmukto Bhaviṣyasi ॥

69. पदार्थवृन्दे देहादिधिया संत्यज्य दूरतः । आशीतलान्तःकरणो नित्यमात्मपरो भव ॥

Padārthavṛnde Dehādidhiyā Saṃtyajya Dūrataḥ ।

Āśītalāntaḥkaraṇo Nityamātmaparo Bhava ॥

70. इदं रम्यमिदं नेति बीजं ते दुःखसंततेः । तस्मिन्साम्याग्निना दग्धे दुःखस्यावसरः कुतः ॥

Idaṃ Ramyamidaṃ Neti Bījaṃ Te Duḥkhasaṃtateḥ ।

Tasminsāmyāgninā Dagdhe Duḥkhasyāvasaraḥ Kutaḥ ॥

71. शास्त्रसज्जनसम्पर्कैः प्रज्ञामादौ विवर्धयेत् ॥

Śāstrasajjanasamparkaiḥ Prajñāmādau Vivardhayet ॥

72. ऋतं सत्यं परं ब्रह्म सर्वसंसारभेषजम् । अत्यर्थममलं नित्यमादिमध्यान्तवर्जितम् ॥

Ṛtaṃ Satyaṃ Paraṃ Brahma Sarvasaṃsārabheṣajam ।

Atyarthamamalaṃ Nityamādimadhyāntavarjitam ॥

73. तथा स्थूलमनाकाशमसंस्पृश्यमचाक्षुषम्। न रसं न च गन्धाख्यमप्रमेयमनूपमम् ॥

Tathā Sthūlamanākāśamasaṃspṛśyamacākṣuṣam ।

Na Rasaṃ Na Ca Gandhākhyamaprameyamanūpamam ॥

74. आत्मानं सच्चिदानन्दमनन्तं ब्रह्म सुव्रत। अहमस्मीत्यभिध्यायेद्ध्येयातीतं विमुक्तये ॥

Ātmānaṃ Saccidānandamanantaṃ Brahma Suvrata ।

Ahamasmītyabhidhyāyeddhyeyātītaṃ Vimuktaye ॥

75. समाधिः संविदुत्पत्तिः परजीवैकतं प्रति। नित्यः सर्वगतो ह्यात्मा कूटस्थो दोषवर्जितः ॥

Samādhiḥ Saṃvidutpattiḥ Parajīvaikataṃ Prati ।

Nityaḥ Sarvagato Hyātmā Kūṭastho Doṣavarjitaḥ ॥

76. एकः सन्भिद्यते भ्रान्त्या मायया न स्वरूपतः । तस्मादद्वैत एवास्ति न प्रपञ्चो न संसृतिः

Ekaḥ Sanbhidyate Bhrāntyā Māyayā Na Svarūpataḥ ।

Tasmādadvaita Evāsti Na Prapañco Na Saṃsṛtiḥ ॥

77. यथाकाशो घटाकाशो महाकाश इतीरितः । तथा भ्रान्तेर्द्विधा प्रोक्तो ह्यात्मा जीवेश्वरात्मना॥

Yathākāśo Ghaṭākāśo Mahākāśa Itīritaḥ ।

Tathā Bhrānterdvidhā Prokto Hyātmā Jīveśvarātmanā ॥

78. यदा मनसि चैतन्यं भाति सर्वत्रगं सदा । योगिनोऽऽव्यवधानेन तदा सम्पद्यते स्वयम् ॥

Yadā Manasi Caitanyaṃ Bhāti Sarvatragaṃ Sadā ।

Yogino''vyavadhānena Tadā Sampadyate Svayam ॥

79. यदा सर्वाणि भूतानि स्वात्मन्येव हि पश्यति । सर्वभूतेषु चात्मानं ब्रह्म सम्पद्यते सदा ॥

Yadā Sarvāṇi Bhūtāni Svātmanyeva Hi Paśyati ।

Sarvabhūteṣu Cātmānaṃ Brahma Sampadyate Sadā ॥

80. यदा सर्वाणि भूतानि समाधिस्थो न पश्यति । एकीभूतः परेणासौ तदा भवति केवलः ॥

Yadā Sarvāṇi Bhūtāni Samādhistho Na Paśyati ।

Ekībhūtaḥ Pareṇāsau Tadā Bhavati Kevalaḥ ॥

81. शास्त्रसज्जनसम्पर्कवैराग्याभ्यासरूपिणी । प्रथमा भूमिकैषोक्ता मुमुक्षुत्वप्रदायिनी॥

Śāstrasajjanasamparkavairāgyābhyāsarūpiṇī ।

Prathamā Bhūmikaiṣoktā Mumukṣutvapradāyinī ॥

82. विचारणा द्वितीया स्यात्तृतीया साङ्गभावना ।
विलापिनी चतुर्थी स्याद्वासना विलयात्मिका ॥

Vicāraṇā Dvitīyā Syāttṛtīyā Sāṅgabhāvanā ।

Vilāpinī Caturthī Syādvāsanā Vilayātmikā ॥

83. शुद्धसंविन्मनानन्दरूपा भवति पञ्चमी । अर्धसुप्तप्रबुद्धाभो जीवन्मुक्तोऽत्र तिष्ठति ॥

Śuddhasaṃvinmanānandarūpā Bhavati Pañcamī ।

Ardhasuptaprabuddhābho Jīvanmukto'tra Tiṣṭhati ॥

84. असंवेदनरूपा च षष्ठी भवति भूमिका। आनन्दैकघनाकारा सुषुप्तसदृशी स्थितिः ॥

Asaṃvedanarūpā Ca Ṣaṣṭhī Bhavati Bhūmikā ।

Ānandaikaghanākārā Suṣuptasadṛśī Sthitiḥ ॥

85. तुर्यावस्थोपशान्ता सा मुक्तिरेव हि केवला। समता स्वच्छता सौम्या सप्तमी भूमिका भवेत्

Turyāvasthopaśāntā Sā Muktireva Hi Kevalā |

Samatā Svacchatā Saumyā Saptamī Bhūmikā Bhavet ||

86. तुर्यातीता तु यावस्था परा निर्वाणरूपिणी। सप्तमी सा परा प्रौढा विषयो नैव जीवताम् ॥

Turyātītā Tu Yāvasthā Parā Nirvāṇarūpiṇī |

Saptamī Sā Parā Prauḍhā Viṣayo Naiva Jīvatām ||

87. पूर्वावस्थात्रयं तत्र जाग्रदित्येव संस्थितम्। चतुर्थी स्वप्न इत्युक्ता स्वप्नाभं यत्र वै जगत् ॥

Pūrvāvasthātrayaṃ Tatra Jāgradityeva Saṃsthitam |

Caturthī Svapna Ityuktā Svapnābhaṃ Yatra Vai Jagat ||

88. आनन्दैकघनाकारा सुषुप्ताख्या तु पञ्चमी। असंवेदनरूपा तु षष्ठी तुर्यपदाभिधा॥

Ānandaikaghanākārā Suṣuptākhyā Tu Pañcamī |

Asaṃvedanarūpā Tu Ṣaṣṭhī Turyapadābhidhā ||

89. तुर्यातीतपदावस्था सप्तमी भूमिकोत्तमा। मनोवचोभिरग्राह्या स्वप्रकाशसदात्मिका ॥

Turyātītapadāvasthā Saptamī Bhūmikottamā |

Manovacobhiragrāhyā Svaprakāśasadātmikā ||

90. अन्तः प्रत्याहृतिवशाच्चैत्यं चेन्न विभावितम्। मुक्त एव न सन्देहो महासमतया तया ॥

Antaḥ Pratyāhṛtivaśāccaityaṃ Cenna Vibhāvitam |

Mukta Eva Na Sandeho Mahāsamatayā Tayā ||

91. न म्रिये न च जीवामि नाहं सन्नाप्यसन्मयः। अहं न किंचिच्चिदिति मत्वा धीरो न शोचति

Na Mriye Na Ca Jīvāmi Nāhaṃ Sannāpyasanmayaḥ |

Ahaṃ Na Kiṃcicciditi Matvā Dhīro Na Śocati ||

92. अलेपकोऽहमजरो नीरागः शान्तवासनः। निरंशोऽस्मि चिदाकाशमिति मत्वा न शोचति ॥

Alepako'hamajaro Nīrāgaḥ Śāntavāsanaḥ |

Niraṃśo'smi Cidākāśamiti Matvā Na Śocati ||

93. अहंमत्या विरहितः शुद्धो बुद्धोऽजरोऽमरः। शान्तः शमसमाभास इति मत्वा न शोचति ॥

Ahaṃmatyā Virahitaḥ Śuddho Buddho'jaro'maraḥ |

Śāntaḥ Śamasamābhāsa Iti Matvā Na Śocati ||

94. तृणाग्रेष्वम्बरे भानौ नरनागामरेषु च । यत्तिष्ठति तदेवाहमिति मत्वा न शोचति ॥

Tṛṇāgreṣvambare Bhānau Naranāgāmareṣu Ca |

Yattiṣṭhati Tadevāhamiti Matvā Na Śocati ||

95. भावनां सर्वभावेभ्यः समुत्सृज्य समुत्थितः । अवशिष्टं परं ब्रह्म केवलोऽस्मीति भावय ॥

Bhāvanāṃ Sarvabhāvebhyaḥ Samutsṛjya Samutthitaḥ |

Avaśiṣṭaṃ Paraṃ Brahma Kevalo'smīti Bhāvaya ||

96. वाचामतीतविषयो विषयाशादशोज्झितः । परानन्दरसाक्षुब्धो रमते स्वात्मनात्मनि ॥

Vācāmatītaviṣayo Viṣayāśādaśojjhitaḥ |

Parānandarasākṣubdho Ramate Svātmanātmani ||

97. सर्वकर्मपरित्यागी नित्यतृप्तो निराश्रयः । न पुण्येन न पापेन नेतरेण च लिप्यते ॥

Sarvakarmaparityāgī Nityatṛpto Nirāśrayaḥ |

Na Puṇyena Na Pāpena Netareṇa Ca Lipyate ||

98. स्फटिकः प्रतिबिम्बेन यथा नायाति रञ्जनम् ।
तज्ज्ञः कर्मफलेनान्तस्तथा नायाति रञ्जनम् ॥

Sphaṭikaḥ Pratibimbena Yathā Nāyāti Rañjanam |

Tajjñaḥ Karmaphalenāntastathā Nāyāti Rañjanam ||

99. विहरञ्जनतावृन्दे देवकीर्तन पूजनैः । खेदाह्लादौ न जानाति प्रतिबिम्बगतैरिव ॥

Viharañjanatāvṛnde Devakīrtana Pūjanaiḥ |

Khedāhlādau Na Jānāti Pratibimbagatairiva ||

100. निस्स्तोत्रो निर्विकारश्च पूज्यपूजाविवर्जितः । संयुक्तश्च वियुक्तश्च सर्वाचारनयक्रमैः ॥

Nisstotro Nirvikāraśca Pūjyapūjāvivarjitaḥ |

Saṃyuktaśca Viyuktaśca Sarvācāranayakramaiḥ ||

101. तनुं त्यजतु वा तीर्थे श्वपचस्य गृहेऽथ वा । ज्ञानसम्पत्तिसमये मुक्तोऽसौ विगताशयः ॥

Tanuṃ Tyajatu Vā Tīrthe Śvapacasya Gṛhe'tha Vā |

Jñānasampattisamaye Mukto'sau Vigatāśayaḥ ||

102. संकल्पत्वं हि बन्धस्य कारणं तत्परित्यज । मोक्षो भवेदसंकल्पात्तदभ्यासं धिया कुरु ॥

Saṃkalpatvaṃ Hi Bandhasya Kāraṇaṃ Tatparityaja |

Mokṣo Bhavedasaṃkalpāttadabhyāsaṃ Dhiyā Kuru ||

103. सावधानो भव त्वं च ग्राह्यग्राहकसंगमे। अजस्रमेव संकल्पदशाः परिहरञ्शनैः ॥

Sāvadhāno Bhava Tvaṃ Ca Grāhyagrāhakasaṃgame |

Ajasrameva Saṃkalpadaśāḥ Pariharañśanaiḥ ||

104. मा भव ग्राह्यभावात्मा ग्राहकात्मा च मा भव ।
भावनामखिलां त्यक्त्वा यच्छिष्टं तन्मयो भव ॥

Mā Bhava Grāhyabhāvātmā Grāhakātmā Ca Mā Bhava |

Bhāvanāmakhilāṃ Tyaktvā Yacchiṣṭaṃ Tanmayo Bhava ||

105. किंचिच्चेद्रोचते तुभ्यं तद्बद्धोऽसि भवस्थितौ ।
न किंचिद्रोचते चेत्ते तन्मुक्तोऽसि भवस्थितौ ॥

Kiṃciccedrocate Tubhyaṃ Tadbaddho'si Bhavasthitau |

Na Kiṃcidrocate Cette Tanmukto'si Bhavasthitau ||

106. अस्मात्पदार्थनिचयाद्यावत्स्थावरजङ्गमात् । तृणादेर्देहपर्यन्तान्मा किंचित्तत्र रोचताम् ॥

Asmātpadārthanicayādyāvatsthāvarajaṅgamāt |

Tṛṇāderdehaparyantānmā Kiṃcittatra Rocatām ||

107. अहंभावानहंभावौत्यक्त्वा सदसती तथा । यदसक्तं समं स्वच्छं स्थितं तत्तुर्यमुच्यते॥

Ahaṃbhāvānahaṃbhāvau Tyaktvā Sadasatī Tathā |

Yadasaktaṃ Samaṃ Svacchaṃ Sthitaṃ Tatturyamucyate ||

108. या स्वच्छा समता शान्ता जीवन्मुक्तव्यवस्थितिः ।
साक्ष्यवस्था व्यवहृतौ सा तुर्या कलनोच्यते ॥

Yā Svacchā Samatā Śāntā Jīvanmuktavyavasthitiḥ |

Sākṣyavasthā Vyavahṛtau Sā Turyā Kalanocyate ||

109. नैतज्जाग्रन्न च स्वप्नः संकल्पानामसंभवात्। सुषुप्तभावो नाऽप्येतदभावाज्जडतास्थितेः॥

Naitajjāgranna Ca Svapnaḥ Saṃkalpānāmasaṃbhavāt |

Suṣuptabhāvo Nā'pyetadabhāvājjaḍatāsthiteḥ ||

110. शान्तसम्यक्प्रबुद्धानां यथास्थितमिदं जगत् । विलीनं तुर्यमित्याहुरबुद्धानां स्थितं स्थिरम् ॥

Śāntasamyakprabuddhānāṃ Yathāsthitamidaṃ Jagat |

Vilīnaṃ Turyamityāhurabuddhānāṃ Sthitaṃ Sthiram ||

111. अहंकारकलात्यागे समतायाः समुद्गमे । विशरारौ कृते चित्ते तुर्यावस्थोपतिष्ठते ॥

Ahaṃkārakalātyāge Samatāyāḥ Samudgame |

Viśarārau Kṛte Citte Turyāvasthopatiṣṭhate ||

112. सिद्धान्तोऽध्यात्मशास्त्राणां सर्वापह्नव एव हि ।
नाविद्यास्तीह नो माया शान्तं ब्रह्मेदमक्लमम् ॥

Siddhānto'dhyātmaśāstrāṇāṃ Sarvāpahnava Eva Hi |

Nāvidyāstīha No Māyā Śāntaṃ Brahmedamaklamam ||

113. शान्त एव चिदाकाशे स्वच्छे शमसमात्मनि । समग्रशक्तिखचिते ब्रह्मेति कलिताभिधे ॥

Śānta Eva Cidākāśe Svacche Śamasamātmani |

Samagraśaktikhacite Brahmeti Kalitābhidhe ||

114. सर्वमेव परित्यज्य महामौनी भवानघ । निर्वाणवान्निर्मननः क्षीणचित्तः प्रशान्तधीः ॥

Sarvameva Parityajya Mahāmaunī Bhavānagha |

Nirvāṇavānnirmananaḥ Kṣīṇacittaḥ Praśāntadhīḥ ||

115. आत्मन्येवास्व शान्तात्मा मूकान्धबधिरोपमः ।
नित्यमन्तर्मुखः स्वच्छः स्वात्मनान्तः प्रपूर्णधीः ॥

Ātmanyevāsva Śāntātmā Mūkāndhabadhiropamaḥ |

Nityamantarmukhaḥ Svacchaḥ Svātmanāntaḥ Prapūrṇadhīḥ ||

116. जाग्रत्येव सुषुप्तस्थः कुरु कर्माणि वै द्विज । अन्तः सर्वपरित्यागी बहिः कुरु यथागतम् ॥

Jāgratyeva Suṣuptasthaḥ Kuru Karmāṇi Vai Dvija |

Antaḥ Sarvaparityāgī Bahiḥ Kuru Yathāgatam ||

117. चित्तसत्ता परं दु ःखं चित्तत्यागः परं सुखम् । अतश्चित्तं चिदाकाशे नय क्षयमवेदनात् ॥

Cittasattā Paraṃ Duḥkhaṃ Cittatyāgaḥ Paraṃ Sukham ।

Ataścittaṃ Cidākāśe Naya Kṣayamavedanāt ॥

118. दृष्ट्वा रम्यमरम्यं वा स्थेयं पाषाणवत्सदा । एतावतात्मयत्नेन जिता भवति संसृतिः ॥

Dṛṣṭvā Ramyamaramyaṃ Vā Stheyaṃ Pāṣāṇavatsadā ।

Etāvatātmayatnena Jitā Bhavati Saṃsṛtiḥ ॥

119. वेदान्ते परमं गुह्यं पुराकल्पप्रचोदितम् । नाप्रशान्ताय दातव्यं न चाशिष्याय वै पुनः ॥

Vedānte Paramaṃ Guhyaṃ Purākalpapracoditam ।

Nāpraśāntāya Dātavyaṃ Na Cāśiṣyāya Vai Punaḥ ॥

120. अन्नपूर्णोपनिषदं योऽधीते गुर्वनुग्रहात् । स जीवन्मुक्ततां प्राप्य ब्रह्मैव भवति स्वयम् ॥

Annapūrṇopaniṣadaṃ Yo'dhīte Gurvanugrahāt ।

Sa Jīvanmuktatāṃ Prāpya Brahmaiva Bhavati Svayam ॥

इत्युपनिषत् ॥ *Ityupaniṣat* ॥

इति पञ्चमोऽध्यायः ॥ *Iti Pañcamo'dhyāyaḥ* ॥

शान्ति मन्त्रः । *Śānti Mantraḥ* ।

ॐ भद्रं कर्णेभिः शृणुयाम देवाः । भद्रं पश्येमाक्षभिर्यजत्राः ।

Oṃ Bhadraṃ Karṇebhiḥ Śṛṇuyāma Devāḥ ॥

Bhadraṃ Paśyemākṣabhiryajatrāḥ ॥
स्थिरैरङ्गैस्तुष्टुवाँसस्तनूभिः । व्यशेम देवहितं यदायुः ।

SthirairaṅgaistuṣṭuvāgͫSastanūbhiḥ ॥ *Vyaśema Devahitaṃ Yadāyuḥ* ॥
स्वस्ति न इन्द्रो वृद्धश्रवाः । स्वस्ति नः पूषा विश्ववेदाः ।

Svasti Na Indro Vṛddhaśravāḥ ॥ *Svasti Naḥ Pūṣā Viśvavedāḥ* ॥
स्वस्ति नस्तार्क्ष्यो अरिष्टनेमिः । स्वस्ति नो बृहस्पतिर्दधातु ॥

Svasti Nastārkṣyo Ariṣṭanemiḥ ॥ *Svasti No Bṛhaspatirdadhātu* ॥
ॐ शान्तिः शान्तिः शान्तिः ॥ *Oṃ Śāntiḥ Śāntiḥ Śāntiḥ* ॥

इत्यन्नपूर्णोपनिषत्समाप्ता ॥ *Ityannapūrṇopaniṣatsamāptā* ॥

Tripurātāpinyupaniṣat
त्रिपुरातापिन्युपनिषत्

This *Upaniṣat* also belongs to Atharva Veda.

त्रिपुरातापिनीविद्यावेद्यचिच्छक्तिविग्रहम्। वस्तुतश्चिन्मात्ररूपं परं तत्त्वं भजाम्यहम् ॥

Tripurātāpinīvidyāvedyacicchaktivigraham ।

Vastutaścinmātrarūpaṃ Paraṃ Tattvaṃ Bhajāmyaham ॥

शान्ति मन्त्रः । *Śānti Mantraḥ* ।

ॐ भद्रं कर्णेभिः शृणुयाम देवाः ।भद्रं पश्येमाक्षभिर्यजत्राः ।

Oṃ Bhadraṃ Karṇebhiḥ Śṛṇuyāma Devāḥ ॥

Bhadraṃ Paśyemākṣabhiryajatrāḥ ॥
स्थिरैरङ्गैस्तुष्टुवाँसस्तनूभिः । व्यशेम देवहितं यदायुः ।

Sthirairaṅgaistuṣṭuvāǵ̐Sastanūbhiḥ ॥ *Vyaśema Devahitaṃ Yadāyuḥ* ॥
स्वस्ति न इन्द्रो वृद्धश्रवाः । स्वस्ति नः पूषा विश्ववेदाः ।

Svasti Na Indro Vṛddhaśravāḥ ॥ *Svasti Naḥ Pūṣā Viśvavedāḥ* ॥
स्वस्ति नस्तार्क्ष्यो अरिष्टनेमिः । स्वस्ति नो बृहस्पतिर्दधातु ॥

Svasti Nastārkṣyo Ariṣṭanemiḥ ॥ *Svasti No Bṛhaspatirdadhātu* ॥
ॐ शान्तिः शान्तिः शान्तिः ॥ *Oṃ Śāntiḥ Śāntiḥ Śāntiḥ* ॥

हरिः ॐ ॥ *Haiḥ Oṃ* ॥

1. अथैतस्मिन्नन्तरे भगवान्प्राजापत्यं वैष्णवं विलयकारणं रूपमाश्रित्य त्रिपुराभिधा भगवतीत्येवमादिशक्त्या भूर्भुवः स्वस्त्रीणि स्वर्गभूपातालानि त्रिपुराणि हरमायात्मकेन ह्रीङ्कारेण हृल्लेखाख्या भगवती त्रिकूटावसाने निलये विलये धाम्नि महसा घोरेण प्राप्नोति। सैवेयं भगवती त्रिपुरेति व्यापठ्यते। तत्सवितुर्वरेण्यं भर्गो देवस्य धीमहि। धियो यो नः प्रचोदयात् परो रजसे सावदोम्। जातवेदसे सुनवाम सोममरातीयतो निदहाति वेद।
स नः पर्षदति दुर्गाणि विश्वा नावेव सिन्धुं दुरितात्यग्निः ।
त्र्यम्बकं यजामहे सुगन्धिं पुष्टिवर्धनम्। उर्वारुकमिव बन्धना न्मृत्योर्मुक्षीय मामृतात्।
शताक्षरी परमा विद्या त्रयीमयी साष्टार्णा त्रिपुरा परमेश्वरी।
आद्यानि चत्वारि पदानि परब्रह्मविकासीनि। द्वितीयानि शक्त्याख्यानि।
तृतीयानि शैवानि। तत्र लोका वेदाः शास्त्राणि पुराणानि धर्माणि वै चिकित्सितानि

ज्योतींषि शिवशक्तियोगादित्येवं घटना व्यापठ्यते ।
अथैतस्य परं गह्वरं व्याख्यास्यामो महामनुसमुद्भवं तदिति ।
ब्रह्म शाश्वतम् । परो भगवान्निर्लक्षणो निरञ्जनो निरुपाधिराधिरहितो देवः ।
उन्मीलते पश्यति विकासते चैतन्यभावं कामयत इति ।
स एको देवः शिवरूपी दृश्यत्वेन विकासते यतिषु यज्ञेषु योगिषु कामयते ।
कामं जायते स एष निरञ्जनोऽकामत्वेनोज्जृम्भते ।
अकचटतपयशान्सृजते । तस्मादीश्वरः कामोऽभिधीयते ।
तत्परिभाषया कामः ककारं व्याप्नोति ।
काम एवेदं तत्तदिति ककारो गृह्यते । भस्मात्तत्पदार्थ इति य एवं वेद ।
सवितुर्वरेण्यमिति षूङ् प्राणिप्रसवे सविता प्राणिनः सूते प्रसूते शक्तिम् ।
सूते त्रिपुरा शक्तिराद्येयं त्रिपुरा परमेश्वरी महाकुण्डलिनी देवी ।
जातवेदसमण्डलं योऽधीते सर्वं व्याप्यते । त्रिकोणशक्तिरेकारेण महाभागेन प्रसूते ।
तस्मादेकार एव गृह्यते । वरेण्यं श्रेष्ठं भजनीयमक्षरं नमस्कार्यम् ।
तस्माद्वरेण्यमेकाराक्षरं गृह्यत इति य एवं वेद । भर्गो देवस्य धीमहीत्येवं व्याख्यास्यामः ।
धकारो धारणा । धियैव धार्यते भगवान्परमेश्वरः ।
भर्गो देवो मध्यवर्ति तुरीयमक्षरं साक्षात्तुरीयं सर्वं सर्वान्तर्भूतम् ।
तुरीयाक्षरमीकारं पदानां मध्यवर्तीत्येवं व्याख्यातं भर्गोरूपं व्याचक्षते ।
तस्माद्भर्गो देवस्य धीमहीत्येवमीकाराक्षरं गृह्यते ।
महीत्यस्य व्याख्यानं महत्त्वं जडत्वं काठिन्यं विद्यते यस्मिन्नक्षतेरेतन्महि लकारः परं धाम ।
काठिन्याढ्यं ससागरं सपर्वतं स सप्तद्वीपं सकाननमुज्ज्वलद्रूपंमण्डलमेवोक्तं लकारेण ।
पृथ्वी देवी महीत्यनेन व्याचक्षते । धियो यो नः प्रचोदयात् ।
परमात्मा सदाशिव आदिभूतः परः । स्थाणुभूतेन लकारेण ज्योतिर्लिङ्गमात्मानं धियो बुद्धयः
परे वस्तुनि ध्यानेच्छारहितं निर्विकल्पके प्रचोदयात्प्रेरयेदित्युच्चारणरहितं चेतसैव
चिन्तयित्वा भावयेदिति । परो रजसे सावदोमिति तदवसाने परं
ज्योतिरमलं हृदि दैवतं चैतन्यं चिल्लिङ्गं हृदयागारवासिनी
हृल्लेखेत्यादिना स्पष्टं वाग्भवकूटं पञ्चाक्षरं पञ्चभूतजनकं पञ्चकलामयं व्यापठ्यत इति । य
एवं वेद । अथ तु परं कामकलाभूतं कामकूटमाहुः । तत्सवितुर्वरेण्य मित्यादिद्वात्रिंशदक्षरीं
पठित्वा तदिति परमात्मा सदाशिवोऽकशरं विमलं निरुपाधितादात्म्यप्रतिपादनेन हकाराक्षरं
शिवरूपं निरक्षरमक्षरं व्यालिख्यत इति । तत्परागव्यावृत्तिमादाय शक्तिं दर्शयति ।
तत्सवितुरिति पूर्वेणाध्वना सूर्याधश्चन्द्रिकां व्यालिख्य मूलादिब्रह्मरन्ध्रगं
साक्षरमद्वितीयमाचक्षत इत्याह भगवन्तं देवं शिवशक्त्यात्मकमेवोदितम् ।
शिवोऽयं परमं देवं शक्तिरेषा तु जीवज्जा ।

सूर्याचन्द्रमसोर्योगाद्धंसस्ततत्पदमुच्यते॥

Athaitasminnantare Bhagavānprājāpatyaṃ Vaiṣṇavaṃ Vilayakāraṇaṃ Rūpamāśritya Tripurābhidhā Bhagavatītyevamādiśaktyā Bhūrbhuvaḥ Svastrīṇi Svargabhūpātālāni Tripurāṇi Haramāyātmakena Hīṅkāreṇa Hṛllekhākhyā Bhagavatī Trikūṭāvasāne Nilaye Vilaye Dhāmni Mahasā Ghoreṇa Prāpnoti | Saiveyaṃ Bhagavatī Tripureti Vyāpaṭhyate |

Tatsaviturvareṇyaṃ Bhargo Devasya Dhīmahi |

Dhiyo Yo Naḥ Pracodayāt Paro Rajase Sāvadom | Jātavedase Sunavāma Somamarātīyato Nidahāti Veda | Sa Naḥ Parṣadati Durgāṇi Viśvā Nāveva Sindhuṃ Duritātyagniḥ | Tryambakaṃ Yajāmahe Sugandhiṃ Puṣṭivardhanam | Urvārukamiva Bandhanā Nmṛtyormukṣīya Māmṛtāt |

Śatākṣarī Paramā Vidyā Trayīmayī Sāṣṭārṇā Tripurā Parameśvarī |

Ādyāni Catvāri Padāni Parabrahmavikāsīni |

Dvitīyāni Śaktyākhyāni | Tṛtīyāni Śaivāni |

Tatra Lokā Vedāḥ Śāstrāṇi Purāṇāni Dharmāṇi Vai Cikitsitāni Jyotīṃṣi Śivaśaktiyogādityevaṃ Ghaṭanā Vyāpaṭhyate |

Athaitasya Paraṃ Gahvaraṃ Vyākhyāsyāmo Mahāmanusamudbhavaṃ Taditi | Brahma Śāśvatam | Paro Bhagavānnirlakṣaṇo Nirañjano Nirupādhirādhirahito Devaḥ | Unmīlate Paśyati Vikāsate Caitanyabhāvaṃ Kāmayata Iti | Sa Eko Devaḥ Śivarūpī Dṛśyatvena Vikāsate Yatiṣu Yajñeṣu Yogiṣu Kāmayate |

Kāmaṃ Jāyate Sa Eṣa Nirañjano'kāmatvenojjṛmbhate |

Akacaṭatapayaśānsṛjate | Tasmādīśvaraḥ Kāmo'bhidhīyate |

Tatparibhāṣayā Kāmaḥ Kakāraṃ Vyāpnoti |

Kāma Evedaṃ Tattaditi Kakāro Gṛhyate |

Bhasmāttatpadārtha Iti Ya Evaṃ Veda |

Saviturvareṇyamiti Ṣūṅ Prāṇiprasave Savitā Prāṇinaḥ Sūte Prasūte Śaktim |

Sūte Tripurā Śaktirādyeyaṃ Tripurā Parameśvarī Mahākuṇḍalinī Devī |

Jātavedasamaṇḍalaṃ Yo'dhīte Sarvaṃ Vyāpyate |

Trikoṇaśaktirekāreṇa Mahābhāgena Prasūte I

Tasmādekāra Eva Gṛhyate I

Vareṇyaṃ Śreṣṭhaṃ Bhajanīyamakṣaraṃ Namaskāryam I

Tasmādvareṇyamekārākṣaraṃ Gṛhyata Iti Ya Evaṃ Veda I

Bhargo Devasya Dhīmahītyevaṃ Vyākhyāsyāmaḥ I

Dhakāro Dhāraṇā I Dhiyaiva Dhāryate Bhagavānparameśvaraḥ I Bhargo Devo Madhyavarti Turīyamakṣaraṃ Sākṣātturīyaṃ Sarvaṃ Sarvāntarbhūtam I Turīyākṣaramīkāraṃ Padānāṃ Madhyavartītyevaṃ Vyākhyātaṃ Bhargorūpaṃ Vyācakṣate I

Tasmādbhargo Devasya Dhīmahītyevamīkārākṣaraṃ Gṛhyate I Mahītyasya Vyākhyānaṃ Mahattvaṃ Jaḍatvaṃ Kāṭhinyaṃ Vidyate Yasminnakṣateretanmahi Lakāraḥ Paraṃ Dhāma I Kāṭhinyāḍhyaṃ Sasāgaraṃ Saparvataṃ Sa Saptadvīpaṃ Sakānanamujjvaladrūpaṃ Maṇḍalamevoktaṃ Lakāreṇa I

Pṛthvī Devī Mahītyanena Vyācakṣate I Dhiyo Yo Naḥ Pracodayāt I

Paramātmā Sadāśiva Ādibhūtaḥ Paraḥ I Sthāṇubhūtena Lakāreṇa Jyotirliṅgamātmānaṃ Dhiyo Buddhayaḥ Pare Vastuni Dhyānecchārahitaṃ Nirvikalpake Pracodayātprerayedityuccāraṇarahitaṃ Cetasaiva Cintayitvā Bhāvayediti I Paro Rajase Sāvadomiti Tadavasāne Paraṃ Jyotiramalaṃ Hṛdi Daivataṃ Caitanyaṃ Cilliṅgaṃ Hṛdayāgāravāsinī Hṛllekhetyādinā Spaṣṭaṃ Vāgbhavakūṭaṃ Pañcākṣaraṃ Pañcabhūtajanakaṃ Pañcakalāmayaṃ Vyāpaṭhyata Iti I

Ya Evaṃ Veda I Atha Tu Paraṃ Kāmakalābhūtaṃ Kāmakūṭamāhuḥ I Tatsaviturvareṇya-Mityādidvātriṃśadakṣarīṃ Paṭhitvā Taditi Paramātmā Sadāśivo'kaśaraṃ Vimalaṃ Nirupādhitādātnya Pratipādanena Hakārākṣaraṃ Śivarūpaṃ Nirakṣaramakṣaraṃ Vyālikhyata Iti I Tatparāgavyāvṛttimādāya Śaktiṃ Darśayati I Tatsavituriti Pūrveṇādhvanā Sūryādhaścandrikāṃ Vyālikhya Mūlādibrahmarandhragaṃ Sākṣaramadvitīyamācakṣata Ityāha Bhagavantaṃ Devaṃ Śivaśaktyātmakamevoditam I

Śivo'yaṃ Paramaṃ Devaṃ Śaktireṣā Tu Jīvajjā |

Sūryācandramasoryogāddhaṃsastatatpadamucyate ||

2. तस्मादुज्जृम्भते कामः कामात्कामः परः शिवः। कार्णोऽयं कामदेवोऽयं वरेण्यं भर्ग उच्यते

Tasmādujjṛmbhate Kāmaḥ Kāmātkāmaḥ Paraḥ Śivaḥ |

Kārṇo'yaṃ Kāmadevo'yaṃ Vareṇyaṃ Bharga Ucyate ||

3. तत्सवितुर्वरेण्यं भर्गो देवः क्षीरं सेचनीयमक्षरं समधुघ्नमक्षरं परमात्मजीवात्मनोर्योगात्तदिति स्पष्टमक्षरं तृतीयं ह इति तदेव सदाशिव एव निष्कल्मष आद्यो देवोऽन्त्यमक्षरं व्याक्रियते। परमं पदं धीति धारणं विद्यते जडत्वधारणं महीति लकारः शिवाधस्तात्तु लकारार्थः स्पष्टमन्त्यमक्षरं परमं चैतन्यं धियो यो नः प्रचोदयात्परो रजसे सावदोमित्येवं कूटं कामकलालयं षडध्वपरिवर्तको वैष्णवं परमं धामैति भगवांश्चैतस्माद्य एवं वेद।
अथैतस्मादपरं तृतीयं शक्तिकूटं प्रतिपद्यते।
द्वात्रिंशदक्षर्या गायत्र्या तत्सवितुर्वरेण्यं तस्मादात्मन आकाश आकाशाद्वायुः स्फुरति तदधीनं वरेण्यं समुदीयमानं सवितुर्वा योग्यो जीवात्मपरमात्म समुद्भवस्तं प्रकाशशक्तिरूपं जीवाक्षरं स्पष्टमापद्यते। भर्गो देवस्य धीत्यनेनाधाररूपशिवात्माक्षरं गण्यते।
महीत्यादिनाशेषं काम्यं रमणीयं दृश्यं शक्तिकूटं स्पष्टीकृतमिति।
एवं पञ्चदशाक्षरं त्रैपुरं योऽधीते स सर्वान्कामानवाप्नोति।
स सर्वांल्लोकाञ्जयति। स सर्वा वाचो विजृम्भयति।
स रुद्रत्वं प्राप्नोति। स वैष्णवं धाम भित्त्वा परं ब्रह्म प्राप्नोति।
य एवं वेद। इत्याद्यां विद्यामभिधायैतस्याः शक्तिकूटं शक्तिशिवाद्यं लोपामुद्रेयम्।
द्वितीये धामनि पूर्वेणैव मनुना बिन्दुहीना शक्तिभूतहृल्लेखा क्रोधमुनिनाधिष्ठिता।
तृतीये धामनि पूर्वस्या एव विद्याया यद्वाग्भवकूटं तेनैव मानवीं चान्द्रीं कौबेरीं विद्यामाचक्षते।
मदनाधः शिवं वाग्भवम्। तदूर्ध्वं कामकलामयम्। शक्त्यूर्ध्वं शक्तिमिति मानवी विद्या।
चतुर्थे धामनि शिवशक्त्याख्यमन्यत्तृतीयं चेयं चान्द्री विद्या।
पञ्चमे धामनि ध्येयेयं चान्द्री कामाधः शिवाद्यकामा।
सैव कौबेरि षष्ठे धामनि व्याचक्षत इति। य एवं वेद।
हित्वेकारं तुरीयस्वरं सर्वादौ सूर्याचन्द्रमस्केन कामेश्वर्येवागस्त्यसंज्ञा।
सप्तमे धामनि तृतीयमेतस्या एव पूर्वोक्तायाः कामाद्यं द्विधाधः कं मदनकलाद्यं शक्तिबीजं वाग्भवाद्यं तयोरर्धावशिरस्कं कृत्वा नन्दिविद्येयम्। अष्टमे धामनि वाग्भवमागस्त्यं वागर्थकलामयं कामकलाभिधं सकलमायाशक्तिः प्रभाकरी विद्येयम्।
नवमे धामनि पुनरागस्त्यं वाग्भवं शक्तिमन्मथशिवशक्तिमन्मथोर्वीमायाकामकलालयं

चन्द्रसूर्यानङ्गधूर्जटिमहिमालयं तृतीयं षण्मुखीयं विद्या।
दशमे धामनि विद्याप्रकाशितया भूय एवागस्त्यविद्यां पठित्वा भूय एवेमामन्त्यमायां परमशिवविद्येयमेकादशे धामनि भूय एवागस्त्यं पठित्वा एतस्या एव वाग्भवं यद्धनजं कामकलालयं च तत्सहजं कृत्वा लोपामुद्रायाः शक्तिकूटराजं पठित्वा वैष्णवी विद्या द्वादशे धामनि व्याचक्षत इति। य एवं वेद।

Tatsaviturvareṇyaṃ Bhargo Devaḥ Kṣīraṃ Secanīyamakṣaraṃ Samadhughnamakṣaraṃ Paramātmajīvātmanoryogāttaditi Spaṣṭamakṣaraṃ Tṛtīyaṃ Ha Iti Tadeva Sadāśiva Eva Niṣkalmaṣa Ādyo Devo'ntyamakṣaraṃ Vyākriyate |

Paramaṃ Padaṃ Dhīti Dhāraṇaṃ Vidyate Jaḍatvadhāraṇaṃ Mahīti Lakāraḥ Śivādhastāttu Lakārārthaḥ Spaṣṭamantyamakṣaraṃ Paramaṃ Caitanyaṃ Dhiyo Yo Naḥ Pracodayātparo Rajase Sāvadomityevaṃ Kūṭaṃ Kāmakalālayaṃ Ṣaḍadhvaparivartako Vaiṣṇavaṃ Paramaṃ Dhāmaiti Bhagavāṃścaitasmādya Evaṃ Veda |

Athaitasmādaparaṃ Tṛtīyaṃ Śaktikūṭaṃ Pratipadyate | Dvātriṃśadakṣaryā Gāyatryā Tatsaviturvareṇyaṃ Tasmādātmana Ākāśa Ākāśādvāyuḥ Sphurati Tadadhīnaṃ Vareṇyaṃ Samudīyamānaṃ Saviturvā Yogyo Jīvātmaparamātma-Samudbhavastaṃ Prakāśaśaktirūpaṃ Jīvākṣaraṃ Spaṣṭamāpadyate |

Bhargo Devasya Dhītyanenādhārarūpaśivātmākṣaraṃ Gaṇyate | Mahītyādināśeṣaṃ Kāmyaṃ Ramaṇīyaṃ Dṛśyaṃ Śaktikūṭaṃ Spaṣṭīkṛtamiti | Evaṃ Pañcadaśākṣaraṃ Traipuraṃ Yo'dhīte Sa Sarvānkāmānavāpnoti | Sa Sarvāṃllokāñjayati | Sa Sarvā Vāco Vijṛmbhayati | Sa Rudratvaṃ Prāpnoti | Sa Vaiṣṇavaṃ Dhāma Bhittvā Paraṃ Brahma Prāpnoti | Ya Evaṃ Veda | Ityādyāṃ Vidyāmabhidhāyaitasyāḥ Śaktikūṭaṃ Śaktiśivādyaṃ Lopāmudreyam |

Dvitīye Dhāmani Pūrveṇaiva Manunā Binduhīnā Śaktibhūtahṛllekhā Krodhamuninādhiṣṭhitā | Tṛtīye Dhāmani Pūrvasyā Eva Vidyāyā Yadvāgbhavakūṭaṃ Tenaiva Mānavīṃ Cāndrīṃ Kauberīṃ Vidyāmācakṣate | Madanādhaḥ Śivaṃ Vāgbhavam |

Tadūrdhvaṃ Kāmakalāmayam | Śaktyūrdhvaṃ Śaktimiti Mānavī Vidyā |

Caturthe Dhāmani Śivaśaktyākhyamanyattṛtīyaṃ Ceyaṃ Cāndrī Vidyā |

Pañcame Dhāmani Dhyeyeyaṃ Cāndrī Kāmādhaḥ Śivādyakāmā |

Saiva Kauberi Ṣaṣṭhe Dhāmani Vyācakṣata Iti | Ya Evaṃ Veda |
Hitvekāraṃ Turīyasvaraṃ Sarvādau Sūryācandramaskena

Kāmeśvaryevāgastyasaṃjñā | Saptame Dhāmani
Tṛtīyametasyā Eva Pūrvoktāyāḥ Kāmādyaṃ Dvidhādhaḥ Kaṃ
Madanakalādyaṃ Śaktibījaṃ Vāgbhavādyaṃ Tayorardhāvaśiraskaṃ

Kṛtvā Nandividyeyam | Aṣṭame Dhāmani Vāgbhavamāgastyaṃ
Vāgarthakalāmayaṃ Kāmakalābhidhaṃ

Sakalamāyāśaktiḥ Prabhākarī Vidyeyam |
Navame Dhāmani Punarāgastyaṃ Vāgbhavaṃ
Śaktimanmathaśivaśaktimanmathorvīmāyākāmakalālayaṃ

Candrasūryānaṅgadhūrjaṭimahimālayaṃ Tṛtīyaṃ Ṣaṇmukhīyaṃ Vidyā |
Daśame Dhāmani Vidyāprakāśitayā Bhūya Evāgastyavidyāṃ Paṭhitvā
Bhūya Evemāmantyamāyāṃ Paramaśivavidyeyamekādaśe Dhāmani
Bhūya Evāgastyaṃ Paṭhitvā Etasyā Eva Vāgbhavaṃ Yaddhanajaṃ
Kāmakalālayaṃ Ca Tatsahajaṃ Kṛtvā Lopāmudrāyāḥ Śaktikūṭarājaṃ

Paṭhitvā Vaiṣṇavī Vidyā Dvādaśe Dhāmani Vyācakṣata Iti |

Ya Evaṃ Veda |

तान्होवाच । भगवान्सर्वे यूयं श्रुत्वा पूर्वां कामाख्यां तुरीयरूपां तुरीयातीतां सर्वोत्कटां सर्वमन्त्रासनगतां पीठोपपीठदेवतापरिवृतां सकलकलाव्यापिनीं देवतां सामोदां सपरागां सहृदयां सामृतां सकलां सेन्द्रियां सदोदितां परां विद्यां स्पष्टीकृत्वा हृदये निधाय विज्ञायानिलयं गमयित्वा त्रिकूटां त्रिपुरां परमां मायां श्रेष्ठां परां वैष्णवीं संनिधाय हृदयकमलकर्णिकायां परां भगवतीं लक्ष्मीं मायां सदोदितां महावश्यकरीं मदनोन्मादनकारिणीं धनुर्बाणधारिणीं वाग्विजृम्भिणीं चन्द्रमण्डलमध्यवर्तिनीं चन्द्रकलां सप्तदशीं महानित्योपस्थितां पाशाङ्कुशमनोज्ञ-पाणिपल्लवां समुद्यदर्कनिभां त्रिनेत्रां विचिन्त्य देवीं महालक्ष्मीं सर्वलक्ष्मीमयीं सर्वलक्षणसम्पन्नां हृदये चैतन्यरूपिणीं निरञ्जनां त्रिकूटाख्यां स्मितमुखीं सुन्दरीं महामायां सर्वसुभगां महाकुण्डलिनीं त्रिपीठमध्यवर्तिनीमकथादिश्रीपीठे परां भैरवीं चित्कलां महात्रिपुरां देवीं ध्यायेन्महाध्यान-योगेनेयमेवं वेदेति महोपनिषत् ॥ इति प्रथमोपनिषत् ॥

Tānhovāca | Bhagavānsarve Yūyaṃ Śrutvā Pūrvāṃ Kāmākhyāṃ

Turīyarūpāṃ Turīyātītāṃ Sarvotkaṭāṃ Sarvamantrāsanagatāṃ Pīṭhopapīṭhadevatāparivṛtāṃ Sakalakalāvyāpinīṃ Devatāṃ Sāmodāṃ Saparāgāṃ Sahṛdayāṃ Sāmṛtāṃ Sakalāṃ Sendriyāṃ Sadoditāṃ Parāṃ Vidyāṃ Spaṣṭīkṛtvā Hṛdaye Nidhāya Vijñāyānilayaṃ Gamayitvā Trikūṭāṃ Tripurāṃ Paramāṃ Māyāṃ Śreṣṭhāṃ Parāṃ Vaiṣṇavīṃ Saṃnidhāya Hṛdayakamalakarṇikāyāṃ Parāṃ Bhagavatīṃ Lakṣmīṃ Māyāṃ Sadoditāṃ Mahāvaśyakarīṃ Madanonmādanakāriṇīṃ Dhanurbāṇadhāriṇīṃ Vāgvijṛmbhiṇīṃ Candramaṇḍalamadhyavartinīṃ Candrakalāṃ Saptadaśīṃ Mahānityopasthitāṃ Pāśāṅkuśamanojña-Pāṇipallavāṃ Samudyadarkanibhāṃ Trinetrāṃ Vicintya Devīṃ Mahālakṣmīṃ Sarvalakṣmīmayīṃ Sarvalakṣaṇasampannāṃ Hṛdaye Caitanyarūpiṇīṃ Nirañjanāṃ Trikūṭākhyāṃ Smitamukhīṃ Sundarīṃ Mahāmāyāṃ Sarvasubhagāṃ Mahākuṇḍalinīṃ Tripīṭhamadhyavartinīmakathādiśrīpīṭhe Parāṃ Bhairavīṃ Citkalāṃ Mahātripurāṃ Devīṃ Dhyāyenmahādhyāna-Yogeneyamevaṃ Vedeti Mahopaniṣat || Iti Prathamopaniṣat || 1 ||

Second *Upaniṣat*

अथातो जातवेदसे सुनवाम सोममित्यादि पठित्वा त्रैपुरी व्यक्तिर्लक्ष्यते । जातवेदस इत्येकर्चसूक्तस्याद्यमध्यमावसानेषु तत्र स्थानेषु विलीनं बीजसागररूपं व्याचक्ष्वेत्यृषय ऊचुः । तान्होवाच भगवाञ्जातवेदसे सुनवाम सोमं तदत्यग्रवाणीं विलोमेन पठित्वा प्रथमस्याद्यं तदेवं दीर्घं द्वितीयस्याद्यं सुनवाम सोममित्यनेन कौलं वामं श्रेष्ठं सोमं महासौभाग्यमाचक्षते । स सर्वसम्पत्तिभूतं प्रथमं निवृत्तिकारणं द्वितीयं स्थितिकारणं तृतीयं सर्गकारणमित्यनेन करशुद्धिं कृत्वा त्रिपुराविद्यां स्पष्टीकृत्वा जातवेदसे सुनवाम सोममित्यादि पठित्वा महाविद्येश्वरी विद्यामाचक्षते त्रिपुरेश्वरीं जातवेदस इति । जाते आद्यक्षरे मातृकायाः शिरसि बैन्दवममृतरूपिणीं कुण्डलिनीं त्रिकोणरूपिणीं चेति वाक्यार्थः । एवं प्रथमस्याद्यं वाग्भवम् । द्वितीयं कामकलालयम् । जात इत्यनेन परमात्मनो जृम्भणम् । जात इत्यादिना परमात्मा शिव उच्यते । जातमात्रेण कामी कामयते काममित्यादिना पूर्णं व्याचक्षते । तदेव सुनवाम गोत्रारूढं मध्यवर्तिनामृतमध्येनार्णेन मन्त्रार्णान्स्पष्टीकृत्वा । गोत्रेति नामगोत्रायामित्यादिना स्पष्टं कामकलालयं शेषं वाममित्यादिना । पूर्वेणाध्वना विद्येयं सर्वरक्षाकरी व्याचक्षते । एवमेतेन विद्यां त्रिपुरेशीं स्पष्टीकृत्वा जातवेदस इत्यादिना जातो देव एक ईश्वरः परमो ज्योतिर्मन्त्रतो वेति तुरीयं वरं दत्त्वा बिन्दुपूर्णज्योतिःस्थानं कृत्वा प्रथमस्याद्यं द्वितीयं च

तृतीयं च सर्वरक्षाकरीसंबन्धं कृत्वा विद्यामात्मासनरूपिणीं स्पष्टीकृत्वा जातवेदसे सुनवाम सोममित्यादि पठित्वा रक्षाकरीं विद्यां स्मृत्वाद्यन्तयोर्धाम्नोः शक्तिशिवरूपिणीं विनियोज्य स इति शक्त्यात्मकं वर्णं सोममिति शैवात्मकं धाम जानीयात्।

यो जानीते स सुभगो भवति। एवमेतां चक्रासनगतां त्रिपुरवासिनीं सदोदितां शिवशक्त्यात्मिकमवेदितां जातवेदाः शिव इति सेति शक्त्यात्माक्षरमिति शिवादिशक्त्यन्तरालभूतां त्रिकूटादिचारिणीं सूर्याचन्द्रनमस्कां मन्त्रासनगतां त्रिपुरं महालक्ष्मीं सदोदितां स्पष्टीकृत्वा जातवेदसे सुनवाम सोममित्यादि पठित्वा पूर्वं सदात्मासनरूपां विद्यां स्मृत्वा वेद इत्यादिना विश्वाहसं ततोदयबैन्दवमुपरि विन्यस्य सिद्धासनस्थां त्रिपुरां मालिनीं विद्यां स्पष्टीकृत्वा जातवेदसे सुनवाम सोममित्यादि पठित्वा त्रिपुरां सुन्दरीं श्रित्वा कले अक्षरे विचिन्त्य मूर्तिभूतां मूर्तिरूपिणीं सर्वविद्येश्वरीं त्रिपुरां विद्यां स्पष्टीकृत्वा जातवेदस इत्यादि पठित्वा त्रिपुरां लक्ष्मीं श्रित्वाग्निं निदहाति सैवेयमग्न्यानने ज्वलतीति विचिन्त्य त्रिज्योतिषमीश्वरीं त्रिपुरामम्बां विद्यां स्पष्टीकुर्यात्।

एवमेतेन स नः पर्षदति दुर्गाणि विश्वेत्यादिपरप्रकाशिनी प्रत्यग्भूता कार्या।

विद्येयमाह्वानकर्माणि सर्वतो धीरेति व्याचक्षते।

एवमेतद्विद्याष्टकं महामाया देव्यङ्गभूतं व्याचक्षते।

देवा ह वै भगवन्तमब्रुवन्महाचक्रनायकं नो ब्रूहीति सार्वकामिकं सर्वाराध्यं सर्वरूपं विश्वतोमुखं मोक्षद्वारं यद्योगिन उपविश्य परं ब्रह्म भित्त्वा निर्वाणमुपविशन्ति।

तान्होवाच भगवाञ्श्रीचक्रं व्याख्यास्याम इति।

त्रिकोणं त्र्यस्रं कृत्वा तदन्तर्मध्यवृत्तमानयष्टिरेखामाकृष्य विशालं नीत्वाग्रतो योनिं कृत्वा पूर्वयोन्यग्ररूपिणीं मानयष्टिं कृत्वा तां सर्वोर्ध्वां नीत्वा योनिं कृत्वाद्यं त्रिकोणं चक्रं भवति।

द्वितीयमन्तरालं भवति। तृतीयमष्टयोन्यङ्कितं भवति।

अथाष्टारचक्राद्यन्तविदिक्कोणाग्रतो रेखां नीत्वा साध्याद्याकर्षणबद्धरेखां नीत्वेत्येवमथोर्ध्वं सम्पुटयोन्यङ्कितं कृत्वा कक्षाभ्य ऊर्ध्वगरेखाचतुष्टयं कृत्वा यथाक्रमेण मानयष्टिद्वयेन दशयोन्यङ्कितं चक्रं भवति।

अनेनैव प्रकारेण पुनर्दशारचक्रं भवति। मध्यत्रिकोणाग्रचतुष्टया द्रेखाचराग्रकोणेषु संयोज्य तद्दशारां शतोनीतां मानयष्टिरेखां योजयित्वा चतुर्दशारं चक्रं भवति।

ततोऽष्टपत्रसंवृतं चक्रं भवति। षोडशपत्रसंवृतं चक्रं चतुर्द्वारं भवति।

ततः पार्थिवं चक्रं चतुर्द्वारं भवति। एवं सृष्टियोगेन चक्रं व्याख्यातम्।

नवात्मकं चक्रं प्रातिलोम्येन वा वच्मि। प्रथमं चक्रं त्रैलोक्यमोहनं भवति।

साणिमाद्यष्टकं भवति। समात्रष्टकं भवति। ससर्वसंक्षोभिण्यादिदशकं भवति।

सप्रकटं भवति। त्रिपुरयाधिष्ठितं भवति। ससर्वसंक्षोभिणीमुद्रया जुष्टं भवति।

द्वितीयं सर्वाशापरिपूरकं चक्रं भवति । सकामाद्याकर्षिणीषोडशकं भवति ।
सगुप्तं भवति । त्रिपुरेश्वर्याधिष्ठितं भवति । सर्वविद्राविणीमुद्रया जुष्टं भवति ।
तृतीयं सर्वसंक्षोभणं चक्रं भवति । सानङ्गकुसुमाद्यष्टकं भवति । सगुप्ततरं भवति ।
त्रिपुरसुन्दर्याधिष्ठितं भवति । सर्वाकर्षिणीमुद्रया जुष्टं भवति ।
तुरीयं सर्वसौभाग्यदायकं चक्रं भवति । ससर्वसंक्षोभिण्यादिद्विसप्तकं भवति ।
ससम्प्रदायं भवति । त्रिपुरवासिन्याधिष्ठितं भवति ।
ससर्ववशंकरिणीमुद्रया जुष्टं भवति । तुरीयान्तं सर्वार्थसाधकं चक्रं भवति ।
ससर्वसिद्धिप्रदादिदशकं भवति । सकलकौलं भवति । त्रिपुरामहालक्ष्म्याधिष्ठितं भवति ।
महोन्मादिनीमुद्रया जुष्टं भवति । षष्ठं सर्वरक्षाकरं चक्रं भवति । ससर्वज्ञत्वादिदशकं भवति ।
सनिगर्भं भवति । त्रिपुरमालिन्याधिष्ठितं भवति । महाङ्कुशमुद्रया जुष्टं भवति ।
सप्तमं सर्वरोगहरं चक्रं भवति । सर्ववशिन्याद्यष्टकं भवति । सरहस्यं भवति ।
त्रिपुरसिद्ध्याधिष्ठितं भवति । सखेचरीमुद्रया जुष्टं भवति ।
अष्टमं सर्वसिद्धिप्रदं चक्रं भवति । सायुधचतुष्टयं भवति । सपरापररहस्यं भवति ।
त्रिपुराम्बयाधिष्ठितं भवति । बीजमुद्रयाधिष्ठितं भवति ।
नवमं चक्रनायकं सर्वानन्दमयं चक्रं भवति ।
सकामेश्वर्यादित्रिकं भवति । सातिरहस्यं भवति । महात्रिपुर सुन्दर्याधिष्ठितं भवति ।
योनिमुद्रया जुष्टं भवति । संक्रामन्ति वै सर्वाणि च्छन्दांसि चकाराणि ।
तदेव चक्रं श्रीचक्रम् । तस्य नाभ्यामग्निमण्डले सूर्याचन्द्रमसौ ॥
तत्रोंकारपीठं पूजयित्वा तत्राक्षरं बिन्दुरूपं तदन्तर्गत व्योमरूपिणीं विद्यां परमां स्मृत्वा
महात्रिपुरसुन्दरीमावाह्य। क्षीरेण स्नापिते देवि चन्दनेन विलेपिते ।
बिल्वपत्रार्चिते देवि दुर्गेऽहं शरणं गतः ।
इत्येकयर्चा प्रार्थ्य मायालक्ष्मी तन्त्रेण पूजयेदिति भगवानब्रवीत् ।
एतैर्मन्त्रैर्भगवतीं यजेत् । ततो देवी प्रीता भवति । स्वात्मानं दर्शयति ।
तस्माद्य एतैर्मन्त्रैर्यजति स ब्रह्म पश्यति । स सर्वं पश्यति ।
सोऽमृतत्वं च गच्छति । य एवं वेदेति महोपनिषत् ॥

Athāto Jātavedase Sunavāma Somamityādi Paṭhitvā Traipurī Vyaktirlakṣyate | Jātavedasa Ityekarcasūktasyādyamadhyamāvasāneṣu Tatra Sthāneṣu Vilīnaṃ Bījasāgararūpaṃ Vyācakṣvetyṛṣaya Ūcuḥ | Tānhovāca Bhagavāñjātavedase Sunavāma Somaṃ Tadatyamravāṇīṃ Vilomena Paṭhitvā Prathamasyādyaṃ Tadevaṃ Dīrghaṃ Dvitīyasyādyaṃ Sunavāma Somamityanena Kaulaṃ Vāmaṃ Śreṣṭhaṃ Somaṃ Mahāsaubhāgyamācakṣate |

Sa Sarvasampattibhūtaṃ Prathamaṃ Nivṛttikāraṇaṃ Dvitīyaṃ Sthitikāraṇaṃ Tṛtīyaṃ Sargakāraṇamityanena Karaśuddhiṃ Kṛtvā Tripurāvidyāṃ Spaṣṭīkṛtvā Jātavedase Sunavāma Somamityādi Paṭhitvā Mahāvidyeśvarī-Vidyāmācakṣate Tripureśvarīṃ Jātavedasa Iti । Jāte Ādyakṣare Mātṛkāyāḥ Śirasi Baindavamamṛtarūpiṇīṃ Kuṇḍalinīṃ Trikoṇarūpiṇīṃ Ceti Vākyārthaḥ । Evaṃ Prathamasyādyaṃ Vāgbhavam । Dvitīyaṃ Kāmakalālayam । Jāta Ityanena Paramātmano Jṛmbhaṇam । Jāta Ityādinā Paramātmā Śiva Ucyate । Jātamātreṇa Kāmī Kāmayate Kāmamityādinā Pūrṇaṃ Vyācakṣate । Tadeva Sunavāma Gotrārūḍhaṃ Madhyavartināmṛtamadhyenārṇena Mantrārṇānspaṣṭīkṛtvā । Gotreti Nāmagotrāyāmityādinā Spaṣṭaṃ Kāmakalālayaṃ Śeṣaṃ Vāmamityādinā । Pūrveṇādhvanā Vidyeyaṃ Sarvarakṣākarī Vyācakṣate । Evametena Vidyāṃ Tripureśīṃ Spaṣṭīkṛtvā Jātavedasa Ityādinā Jāto Deva Eka Īśvaraḥ Paramo Jyotirmantrato Veti Turīyaṃ Varaṃ Dattvā Bindupūrṇajyotiḥsthānaṃ Kṛtvā Prathamasyādyaṃ Dvitīyaṃ Ca Tṛtīyaṃ Ca Sarvarakṣākarīsaṃbandhaṃ Kṛtvā Vidyāmātmāsanarūpiṇīṃ Spaṣṭīkṛtvā Jātavedase Sunavāma Somamityādi Paṭhitvā Rakṣākarīṃ Vidyāṃ Smṛtvādyantayordhāmnoḥ Śaktiśivarūpiṇīṃ Viniyojya Sa Iti Śaktyātmakaṃ Varṇaṃ Somamiti Śaivātmakaṃ Dhāma Jānīyāt । Yo Jānīte Sa Subhago Bhavati । Evametāṃ Cakrāsanagatāṃ Tripuravāsinīṃ Sadoditāṃ Śivaśaktyātmikamaveditāṃ Jātavedāḥ Śiva Iti Seti Śaktyātmākṣaramiti Śivādiśaktyantarālabhūtāṃ Trikūṭādicāriṇīṃ Sūryācandranamaskāṃ Mantrāsanagatāṃ Tripuraṃ Mahālakṣmīṃ Sadoditāṃ Spaṣṭīkṛtvā Jātavedase Sunavāma Somamityādi Paṭhitvā Pūrvaṃ Sadātmāsanarūpāṃ Vidyāṃ Smṛtvā Veda Ityādinā Viśvāhasaṃtatodayabaindavamupari Vinyasya Siddhāsanasthāṃ Tripurāṃ Mālinīṃ Vidyāṃ Spaṣṭīkṛtvā Jātavedase Sunavāma Somamityādi Paṭhitvā Tripurāṃ Sundarīṃ Śritvā Kale Akṣare Vicintya Mūrtibhūtāṃ Mūrtirūpiṇīṃ Sarvavidyeśvarīṃ Tripurāṃ Vidyāṃ Spaṣṭīkṛtvā Jātavedasa Ityādi Paṭhitvā Tripurāṃ Lakṣmīṃ Śritvāgniṃ Nidahāti Saiveyamagnyānane Jvalatīti Vicintya Trijyotiṣamīśvarīṃ Tripurāmambāṃ Vidyāṃ Spaṣṭīkuryāt । Evametena Sa Naḥ Parṣadati Durgāṇi Viśvetyādiparaprakāśinī Pratyagbhūtā Kāryā ।

Vidyeyamāhvānakarmāṇi Sarvato Dhīreti Vyācakṣate ।

Evametadvidyāṣṭakaṃ Mahāmāyā-Devyaṅgabhūtaṃ Vyācakṣate ।
Devā Ha Vai Bhagavantamabruvanmahācakranāyakaṃ No Brūhīti Sārvakāmikaṃ Sarvārādhyaṃ Sarvarūpaṃ Viśvatomukhaṃ Mokṣadvāraṃ Yadyogina Upaviśya Paraṃ Brahma Bhittvā Nirvāṇamupaviśanti ।

Tānhovāca Bhagavāñśrīcakraṃ Vyākhyāsyāma Iti ।
Trikoṇaṃ Tryasraṃ Kṛtvā Tadantarmadhyavṛttamānayaṣṭirekhāmākṛṣya Viśālaṃ Nītvāgrato Yoniṃ Kṛtvā Pūrvayonyagrarūpiṇīṃ Mānayaṣṭiṃ Kṛtvā Tāṃ Sarvordhvāṃ Nītvā Yoniṃ Kṛtvādyaṃ Trikoṇaṃ Cakraṃ Bhavati ।

Dvitīyamantarālaṃ Bhavati । *Tṛtīyamaṣṭayonyaṅkitaṃ Bhavati* ।
Athāṣṭāracakrādyantavidikkoṇāgrato Rekhāṃ Nītvā Sādhyādyākarṣaṇabaddharekhāṃ Nītvetyevamathordhva-Sampuṭayonyaṅkitaṃ Kṛtvā Kakṣābhya Ūrdhvagarekhācatuṣṭayaṃ Kṛtvā Yathākrameṇa Mānayaṣṭidvayena Daśayonyaṅkitaṃ Cakraṃ Bhavati । *Anenaiva Prakāreṇa Punardaśāracakraṃ Bhavati* ।
Madhyatrikoṇāgracatuṣṭayā-Drekhācarāgrakoṇeṣu Saṃyojya Taddaśārāṃśatonītāṃ Mānayaṣṭirekhāṃ Yojayitvā Caturdaśāraṃ Cakraṃ Bhavati ।

Tato'ṣṭapatrasaṃvṛtaṃ Cakraṃ Bhavati ।

Ṣoḍaśapatrasaṃvṛtaṃ Cakraṃ Caturdvāraṃ Bhavati ।

Tataḥ Pārthivaṃ Cakraṃ Caturdvāraṃ Bhavati ।

Evaṃ Sṛṣṭiyogena Cakraṃ Vyākhyātam ।

Navātmakaṃ Cakraṃ Prātilomyena Vā Vacmi ।

Prathamaṃ Cakraṃ Trailokyamohanaṃ Bhavati ।

Sāṇimādyaṣṭakaṃ Bhavati । *Samātraṣṭakaṃ Bhavati* ।

Sasarvasaṃkṣobhiṇyādidaśakaṃ Bhavati । *Saprakaṭaṃ Bhavati* ।

Tripurayādhiṣṭhitaṃ Bhavati ।

Sasarvasaṃkṣobhiṇīmudrayā Juṣṭaṃ Bhavati ।

Dvitīyaṃ Sarvāśāparipūrakaṃ Cakraṃ Bhavati ।

Sakāmādyākarṣiṇīṣoḍaśakaṃ Bhavati | *Saguptaṃ Bhavati* |
Tripureśvaryādhiṣṭhitaṃ Bhavati |
Sarvavidrāviṇīmudrayā Juṣṭaṃ Bhavati |
Tṛtīyaṃ Sarvasaṃkṣobhaṇaṃ Cakraṃ Bhavati |
Sānaṅgakusumādyaṣṭakaṃ Bhavati | *Saguptataraṃ Bhavati* |
Tripurasundaryādhiṣṭhitaṃ Bhavati |
Sarvākarṣiṇīmudrayā Juṣṭaṃ Bhavati |
Turīyaṃ Sarvasaubhāgyadāyakaṃ Cakraṃ Bhavati |
Sasarvasaṃkṣobhiṇyādidvisaptakaṃ Bhavati |
Sasampradāyaṃ Bhavati | *Tripuravāsinyādhiṣṭhitaṃ Bhavati* |
Sasarvavaśaṃkariṇīmudrayā Juṣṭaṃ Bhavati |
Turīyāntaṃ Sarvārthasādhakaṃ Cakraṃ Bhavati |
Sasarvasiddhipradādidaśakaṃ Bhavati | *Sakalakaulaṃ Bhavati* |
Tripurāmahālakṣmyādhiṣṭhitaṃ Bhavati |
Mahonmādinīmudrayā Juṣṭaṃ Bhavati |
Ṣaṣṭhaṃ Sarvarakṣākaraṃ Cakraṃ Bhavati |
Sasarvajñatvādidaśakaṃ Bhavati | *Sanigarbhaṃ Bhavati* |
Tripuramālinyādhiṣṭhitaṃ Bhavati |
Mahāṅkuśamudrayā Juṣṭaṃ Bhavati |
Saptamaṃ Sarvarogaharaṃ Cakraṃ Bhavati |
Sarvavaśinyādyaṣṭakaṃ Bhavati | *Sarahasyaṃ Bhavati* |
Tripurasiddhyādhiṣṭhitaṃ Bhavati |
Sakhecarīmudrayā Juṣṭaṃ Bhavati |
Aṣṭamaṃ Sarvasiddhipradaṃ Cakraṃ Bhavati |
Sāyudhacatuṣṭayaṃ Bhavati | *Saparāpararahasyaṃ Bhavati* |
Tripurāmbayādhiṣṭhitaṃ Bhavati |
Bījamudrayādhiṣṭhitaṃ Bhavati |
Navamaṃ Cakranāyakaṃ Sarvānandamayaṃ Cakraṃ Bhavati |

Sakāmeśvaryāditrikaṃ Bhavati | Sātirahasyaṃ Bhavati |

Mahātripura-Sundaryādhiṣṭhitaṃ Bhavati |

Yonimudrayā Juṣṭaṃ Bhavati |

Saṃkrāmanti Vai Sarvāṇi Cchandāṃsi Cakārāṇi |

Tadeva Cakraṃ Śrīcakram |

Tasya Nābhyāmagnimaṇḍale Sūryācandramasau ||

Tatroṃkārapīṭhaṃ Pūjayitvā Tatrākṣaraṃ Bindurūpaṃ Tadantargata-Vyomarūpiṇīṃ Vidyāṃ Paramāṃ Smṛtvā Mahātripurasundarīmāvāhya |

Kṣīreṇa Snāpite Devi Candanena Vilepite |

Bilvapatrārcite Devi Durge'haṃ Śaraṇaṃ Gataḥ |

Ityekayarcā Prārthya Māyālakṣmī Tantreṇa Pūjayediti Bhagavānabravīt |

Etairmantrairbhagavatīṃ Yajet | Tato Devī Prītā Bhavati |

Svātmānaṃ Darśayati | Tasmādya Etairmantrairyajati Sa Brahma Paśyati | Sa Sarvaṃ Paśyati | So'mṛtatvaṃ Ca Gacchati |

Ya Evaṃ Vedeti Mahopaniṣat ||

इति द्वितीयोपनिषत् ॥ *Iti Dvitīyopaniṣat* ॥ 2 ॥

Third *Upaniṣat*

देवा ह वै मुद्राः सृजेमेति भगवन्तमब्रुवन्।

तान्होवाच भगवानवनिकृतजानुमण्डलं विस्तीर्य पद्मासनं कृत्वा मुद्राः सृजतेति।

स सर्वानाकर्षयति यो योनिमुद्रामधीते। स सर्वं वेत्ति। स सर्वफलमश्नुते।

स सर्वान्भञ्जयति। स विद्वेषिणं स्तम्भयति।

मध्यमे अनामिकोपरि विन्यस्य कनिष्ठिकाङ्गुष्ठतोऽधीते

मुक्तयोस्तर्जन्योर्दण्ड वदधस्ता देवं विधा प्रथमा सम्पद्यते।

सैव मिलितमध्यमा द्वितीया। तृतीयाङ्कुशाकृतिरिति।

प्रातिलोम्येन पाणी सङ्घर्षयित्वाङ्गुष्ठौ साग्रिमौ समाधाय तुरीया।

परस्परं कनीयसेदं मध्यमाबद्धे अनामिके दण्डिन्यौ तर्जन्यावालिङ्ग्यावष्टभ्य

मध्यमानख मिलिताङ्गुष्ठौ पञ्चमी। सैवाग्रेऽङ्कुशाकृतिः षष्ठी।

दक्षिणशये वामबाहुं कृत्वान्योन्यानामिके कनीयसीमध्यगते

मध्यमे तर्जन्याक्रान्ते सरलास्वङ्गुष्ठौ खेचरी सप्तमी ।
सर्वोर्ध्वे सर्वसंहति स्वमध्यमानामिकान्तरे कनीयसि
पार्श्वयोस्तर्जन्यावङ्कुशाद्वये युक्ता साङ्गुष्ठयोगतोऽन्योन्यं सममञ्जलिं कृत्वाष्टमी ।
परस्परमध्यमापृष्ठवर्तिन्यावनामिके तर्जन्याक्रान्ते समे मध्यमे आदायाङ्गुष्ठौ
मध्यवर्तिनौ नवमी प्रतिपद्यत इति ।
सैवेयं कनीयसे समे अन्तरितेऽङ्गुष्ठौ समावन्तरितौ कृत्वा त्रिखण्डापद्यत इति ।
पञ्च बाणाः पञ्चाद्या मुद्राः स्पष्टाः । क्रोमङ्कुशा । हसख्फ्रें खेचरी ।
हंस्रौ बीजाष्टमी वाग्भवाद्या नवमी दशमी च सम्पद्यत इति । य एवं वेद ।
अथातः कामकलाभूतं चक्रं व्याख्यास्यामो ह्रीं क्लीमैंब्लूं स्त्रौमेते पञ्च कामाः
सर्वचक्रं व्यावर्तन्ते । मध्यमं कामं सर्वावसाने सम्पुटीकृत्य ब्लूङ्कारेण सम्पुटं
व्याप्तं कृत्वा द्विरैन्दवेन मध्यवर्तिना साध्यं बद्ध्वा भूर्जपत्रे यजति ।
तच्चक्रं यो वेत्ति स सर्वं वेत्ति । स सकलांल्लोकानाकर्षयति । स सर्वं स्तम्भयति ।
नीलीयुक्तं चक्रं शत्रून्मारयति । गतिं स्तम्भयति ।
लाक्षायुक्तं कृत्वा सकललोकं वशीकरोति ।
नवलक्षजपं कृत्वा रुद्रत्वं प्राप्नोति । मातृकया वेष्टितं कृत्वा विजयी भवति ।
भगाङ्ककुण्डं कृत्वाग्निमाधाय पुरुषो हविषा हुत्वा योषितो वशीकरोति ।
वर्तुले हुत्वा श्रियमतुलं प्राप्नोति । चतुरस्रे हुत्वा वृष्टिर्भवति ।
त्रिकोणे हुत्वा शत्रून्मारयति । गतिं स्तम्भयति । पुष्पाणि हुत्वा विजयी भवति ।
महारसैर्हुत्वा परमानन्दनिर्भरो भवति ।
गणानां त्वा गणपतिं हवामहे कविं कवीनामुपमश्रवस्तमम् ।
ज्येष्ठराजं ब्रह्मणां ब्रह्मणस्पत आ नः श्रुण्वन्नूतिभिः सीद सादनम् ।
इत्येवमाद्यमक्षरं तदन्त्यबिन्दुपूर्णमित्यनेनाङ्गं स्पृशति ।
गं गणेशाय नम इति गणेशं नमस्कुर्वीत ।
ॐ नमो भगवते भस्माङ्गरागायोग्रतेजसे हनहन दहदह पचपच मथमथ
विध्वंसयविध्वंसय हलभञ्जन शूलमूले व्यञ्जनसिद्धिं कुरुकुरु
समुद्रं पूर्वप्रतिष्ठिअतं शोषयशोषय स्तम्भयस्तम्भय परमन्त्र परयन्त्र परतन्त्र परदूत परकटक
परच्छेदनकर विदारयविदारय च्छिन्धिच्छिन्धि ह्रीं फट् स्वाहा ।
अनेन क्षेत्राध्यक्षं पूजयेदिति । कुलकुमारि विद्महे मन्त्रकोटिसुधीमहि ।
तन्नः कौलिः प्रचोदयात् ।
इति कुमार्यर्चनं कृत्वा यो वै साधकोऽभिलिखति सोऽमृतत्वं गच्छति ।
स यश आप्नोति । स परमायुष्यमथ वा परं ब्रह्म भित्त्वा तिष्ठति ।
य एवं वेदेति महोपनिषत् । इति तृतीयोपनिषत् ॥

Devā Ha Vai Mudrāḥ Sṛjemeti Bhagavantamabruvan |
Tānhovāca Bhagavānavanikṛtajānumaṇḍalaṃ Vistīrya Padmāsanaṃ Kṛtvā Mudrāḥ Sṛjateti |
Sa Sarvānākarṣayati Yo Yonimudrāmadhīte | Sa Sarvaṃ Vetti |
Sa Sarvaphalamaśnute | Sa Sarvānbhañjayati |
Sa Vidveṣiṇaṃ Stambhayati | Madhyame Anāmikopari Vinyasya Kaniṣṭhikāṅguṣṭhato'dhīte Muktayostarjanyordaṇḍavadadhastādevaṃvidhā Prathamā Sampadyate | Saiva Militamadhyamā Dvitīyā | Tṛtīyāṅkuśākṛtiriti | Prātilomyena Pāṇī Saṅgharṣayitvāṅguṣṭhau Sāgrimau Samādhāya Turīyā | Parasparaṃ Kanīyasedaṃ Madhyamābaddhe Anāmike Daṇḍinyau Tarjanyāvāliṅgyāvaṣṭabhya Madhyamānakha-Militāṅguṣṭhau Pañcamī | Saivāgre'ṅkuśākṛtiḥ Ṣaṣṭhī | Dakṣiṇaśaye Vāmabāhuṃ Kṛtvānyonyānāmike Kanīyasīmadhyagate Madhyame Tarjanyākrānte Saralāsvaṅguṣṭhau Khecarī Saptamī | Sarvordhve Sarvasaṃhṛti Svamadhyamānāmikāntare Kanīyasi Pārśvayostarjanyāvaṅkuśādhye Yuktā Sāṅguṣṭhayogato'nyonyaṃ Samamañjaliṃ Kṛtvāṣṭamī | Parasparamadhyamāpṛṣṭhavartinyāvanāmike Tarjanyākrānte Same Madhyame Ādāyāṅguṣṭhau Madhyavartinau Navamī Pratipadyata Iti |
Saiveyaṃ Kanīyase Same Antarite'ṅguṣṭhau Samāvantaritau Kṛtvā Trikhaṇḍāpadyata Iti | Pañca Bāṇāḥ Pañcādyā Mudrāḥ Spaṣṭāḥ | Kromaṅkuśā | Hasakhphreṃ Khecarī | Haṃsrau Bījāṣṭamī Vāgbhavādyā Navamī Daśamī Ca Sampadyata Iti | Ya Evaṃ Veda | Athātaḥ Kāmakalābhūtaṃ Cakraṃ Vyākhyāsyāmo Hrīṃ Klīmaiṃ Blūæṃ Sraumete Pañca Kāmāḥ Sarvacakraṃ Vyāvartante | Madhyamaṃ Kāmaṃ Sarvāvasāne Sampuṭīkṛtya Blūṅkāreṇa Sampuṭaṃ Vyāptaṃ Kṛtvā Dviraindavena Madhyavartinā Sādhyaṃ Baddhvā Bhūrjapatre Yajati |
Taccakraṃ Yo Vetti Sa Sarvaṃ Vetti | Sa Sakalāæṃllokānākarṣayati |
Sa Sarvaṃ Stambhayati | Nīlīyuktaṃ Cakraṃ Śatrūnmārayati |

Gatiṃ Stambhayati | Lākṣāyuktaṃ Kṛtvā Sakalalokaṃ Vaśīkaroti |

Navalakṣajapaṃ Kṛtvā Rudratvaṃ Prāpnoti |

Mātṛkayā Veṣṭitaṃ Kṛtvā Vijayī Bhavati |

Bhagāṅkakuṇḍaṃ Kṛtvāgnimādhāya Puruṣo Haviṣā Hutvā Yoṣito Vaśīkaroti | Vartule Hutvā Śriyamatulaṃ Prāpnoti |

Caturasre Hutvā Vṛṣṭirbhavati | Trikoṇe Hutvā Śatrūnmārayati |

Gatiṃ Stambhayati | Puṣpāṇi Hutvā Vijayī Bhavati |

Mahārasairhutvā Paramānandanirbharo Bhavati |

Gaṇānāṃ Tvā Gaṇapatiṃ Havāmahe Kaviṃ Kavīnāmupamaśravastamam | Jyeṣṭharājaṃ Brahmaṇāṃ Brahmaṇaspata Ā Naḥ Śruṇvannūtibhiḥ Sīda Sādanam |

Ityevamādyamakṣaraṃ Tadantyabindupūrṇamityanenāṅgaṃ Spṛśati |

Gaṃ Gaṇeśāya Nama Iti Gaṇeśaṃ Namaskurvīta |

Oṃ Namo Bhagavate Bhasmāṅgarāgāyogratejase Hanahana Dahadaha Pacapaca Mathamatha Vidhvaṃsayavidhvaṃsaya Halabhañjana Śūlamūle Vyañjanasiddhiṃ Kurukuru Samudraṃ Pūrvapratiṣṭhiataṃ Śoṣayaśoṣaya Stambhayastambhaya Paramantra Parayantraparatantraparadūtaparakaṭakaparacchedanakara Vidārayavidāraya Cchindhicchindhi Hrīṃ Phaṭ Svāhā |

Anena Kṣetrādhyakṣaṃ Pūjayediti | Kulakumāri Vidmahe Mantrakoṭisudhīmahi | Tannaḥ Kauliḥ Pracodayāt |

Iti Kumāryarcanaṃ Kṛtvā Yo Vai Sādhako'bhilikhati So'mṛtatvaṃ Gacchati | Sa Yaśa Āpnoti | Sa Paramāyuṣyamatha Vā Paraṃ Brahma Bhittvā Tiṣṭhati | Ya Evaṃ Vedeti Mahopaniṣat |

Iti Tṛtīyopaniṣat || 3 ||

Fourth *Upaniṣat*

देवा ह वै भगवन्तमब्रुवन्देव गायत्रं हृदयं नो व्याख्यातं त्रैपुरं सर्वोत्तमम् ।

जातवेदससूक्तेनाख्यातं नस्त्रैपुराष्टकम् । यदिष्ट्वा मुच्यते योगी जन्मसंसारबन्धनात् ।

अथ मृत्युंजयं नो ब्रूहीत्येवं ब्रुवतां सर्वेषां देवानां श्रुत्वेदं वाक्यमथातस्त्र्यम्बकेनानुष्टुभेन मृत्युंजयं दर्शयति । कस्मात्त्र्यम्बकमिति । त्रयाणां पुराणामम्बकं स्वामिनं तस्मादुच्यते त्र्यम्बकमिति ।

अथ कस्मादुच्यते यजामह इति ।
यजामहे सेवामहे वस्तु महेत्यक्षरद्वयेन कूटत्वेनाक्षरैकेण मृत्युं जयमित्युच्यते ।
तस्मादुच्यते यजामह इति । अथ कस्मादुच्यते सुगन्धिमिति ।
सर्वतो यश आप्नोति । तस्मादुच्यते सुगन्धिमिति । अथ कस्मादुच्यते पुष्टिवर्धनमिति ।
यत्सर्वांल्लोकान्सृजति यत्सर्वांल्लोकांस्तारयति यत्सर्वांल्लोकान्व्याप्नोति
तस्मादुच्यते पुष्टिवर्धनमिति । अथ कस्मादुच्यते उर्वारुकमिव बन्धनान्मृत्योर्मुक्षीयेति ।
संलग्नत्वादुर्वारुकमिव मृत्योः संसारबन्धनात्संलग्नत्वाद्बद्धत्वान्मोक्षीभवति मुक्तो भवति ।
अथ कस्मादुच्यते मामृतादिति अमृतत्वं प्राप्नोत्यक्षरं प्राप्नोति स्वयं रुद्रो भवति ।
देवा ह वै भगवन्तमूचुः सर्वं नो व्याख्यातम् ।
अथ कैर्मन्त्रैः स्तुता भगवती स्वात्मानं दर्शयतितान्सर्वाञ्छैवान्वैष्णवान्सौरान्गाणेशान्नो
ब्रूहीति । स होवाच भगवांस्त्र्यम्बकेनानुष्टुभेन मृत्युं जयमुपासयेत् ।
पूर्वेणाध्वना व्याप्तमेकाक्षरमिति स्मृतम् ।
ॐ नमः शिवायेति याजुषमन्त्रोपासको रुद्रत्वं प्राप्नोति । कल्याणं प्राप्नोति ।
य एवं वेद । तद्विष्णोः परमं पदं सदा पश्यन्ति सूरयः । दिवीव चक्षुराततम् ।
विष्णोः सर्वतोमुखस्य स्नेहो यथा पललपिण्डमोतप्रोतमनुव्याप्तं
व्यतिरिक्तं व्याप्नुत इति व्याप्नुवतो विष्णोस्तत्परमं पदं परं व्योमेति
परमं पदं पश्यन्ति वीक्षन्ते । सूरयो ब्रह्मादयो देवास इति सदा हृदय अदधते ।
तस्माद्विष्णोः स्वरूपं वसति तिष्ठति भूतेश्विति वासुदेव इति ।
ॐ नम इति त्रीण्यक्षराणि । भगवत इति चत्वारि ।
वासुदेवायेति पञ्चाक्षराणि । एतद्वै वासुदेवस्य द्वादशार्णमभ्येति ।
सोपप्लवं तरति । स सर्वमायुरेति ।
विन्दते प्राजापत्यं रायस्पोषं गौपत्यं च तमश्नुते प्रत्यगानन्दं ब्रह्मपुरुषं प्रणवस्वरूपमकार उकारो
मकार इति । तानेकधा संभवति तदोमिति ।
हंसः शुचिषद्वसुरन्तरिक्षसद्धोता वेदिषदतिथिर्दुरोणसत् ।
नृषद्वरसदृतसद्व्योमसदब्जा गोजा ऋतजा अद्रिजा ऋतं बृहत् ।
हंस इत्येतन्मनोरक्षरद्वितीयेन प्रभापुञ्जेन सौरेण धृतमब्जा गोजा ऋतजा अद्रिजा ऋतं
सत्या-प्रभा-पुञ्जि-न्युषा-सन्ध्या-प्रज्ञाभिः शक्तिभिः पूर्वं सौरमधीयानः सर्वं फलमश्नुते ।
स व्योम्नि परमे धामनि सौरे निवसते ।
गणानां त्वति त्रैष्टुभेन पूर्वेणाध्वना मनुनैकार्णेन गणाधिपमभ्यर्च्य गणेशत्वं प्राप्नोति ।
अथ गायत्री सावित्री सरस्वत्यजपा मातृका प्रोक्ता तया सर्वमिदं व्याप्तम् ।
ऐं वागीश्वरि विद्महे क्लीं कामेश्वरी धीमहि । सौस्तन्नः शक्तिः प्रचोदयादिति ।
गायत्री प्रातः सावित्री मध्यन्दिने सरस्वती सायमिति निरन्तरमजपा ।

हंस इत्येव मातृका। पञ्चाशद्वर्णविग्रहेणा कारादिक्षकारान्तेन व्याप्तानि भुवनानि शास्त्राणि च्छन्दांसीत्येवं भगवतीं सर्वं व्याप्नोतीत्येव तस्यै वै नमोनम इति।
तान्भगवानब्रवीदेतैर्मन्त्रैर्नित्यं देवीं यः स्तौति स सर्वं पश्यति।
सोऽमृतत्वं च गच्छति। य एवं वेदेत्युपनिषत्॥

Devā Ha Vai Bhagavantamabruvandeva Gāyatraṃ Hṛdayaṃ No Vyākhyātaṃ Traipuraṃ Sarvottamam | Jātavedasasūktenākhyātaṃ Nastraipurāṣṭakam | Yadiṣṭvā Mucyate Yogī Janmasaṃsārabandhanāt | Atha Mṛtyuṃjayaṃ No Brūhītyevaṃ Bruvatāṃ Sarveṣāṃ Devānāṃ Śrutvedaṃ Vākyamathātastryambakenānuṣṭubhena Mṛtyuṃjayaṃ Darśayati | Kasmāttryambakamiti | Trayāṇāṃ Purāṇāmambakaṃ Svāminaṃ Tasmāducyate Tryambakamiti | Atha Kasmāducyate Yajāmaha Iti | Yajāmahe Sevāmahe Vastu Mahetyakṣaradvayena Kūṭatvenākṣaraikeṇa Mṛtyuṃjayamityucyate | Tasmāducyate Yajāmaha Iti | Atha Kasmāducyate Sugandhimiti | Sarvato Yaśa Āpnoti | Tasmāducyate Sugandhimiti | Atha Kasmāducyate Puṣṭivardhanamiti | Yatsarvāṃllokānsṛjati Yatsarvāṃllokāṃstārayati Yatsarvāṃllokānvyāpnoti Tasmāducyate Puṣṭivardhanamiti | Atha Kasmāducyate Urvārukamiva Bandhanānmṛtyormukṣīyeti | Saṃlagnatvādurvārukamiva Mṛtyoḥ Saṃsāra Bandhanāt Saṃlagnatvād Baddhatvānmokṣībhavati Mukto Bhavati | Atha Kasmāducyate Māmṛtāditi Amṛtatvaṃ Prāpnotyakṣaraṃ Prāpnoti Svayaṃ Rudro Bhavati |

Devā Ha Vai Bhagavantamūcuḥ Sarvaṃ No Vyākhyātam | Atha Kairmantraiḥ Stutā Bhagavatī Svātmānaṃ Darśayati Tānsarvāñchaivānvaiṣṇavānsaurāngāṇeśānno Brūhīti | Sa Hovāca Bhagavāṃstryambakenānuṣṭubhena Mṛtyuṃjayamupāsayet | Pūrveṇādhvanā Vyāptamekākṣaramiti Smṛtam | Oṃ Namaḥ Śivāyeti Yājuṣamantropāsako

Rudratvaṃ Prāpnoti | Kalyāṇaṃ Prāpnoti | Ya Evaṃ Veda | Tadviṣṇoḥ Paramaṃ Padaṃ Sadā Paśyanti Sūrayaḥ | Divīva Cakṣurātatam | Viṣṇoḥ Sarvatomukhasya Sneho Yathā Palalapiṇḍamotaprotamanuvyāptaṃ Vyatiriktaṃ Vyāpnuta Iti Vyāpnuvato Viṣṇostatparamaṃ Padaṃ Paraṃ Vyometi Paramaṃ Padaṃ Paśyanti Vīkṣante |

Sūrayo Brahmādayo Devāsa Iti Sadā Hṛdaya Adadhate |

Tasmādviṣṇoḥ Svarūpaṃ Vasati Tiṣṭhati Bhūteśviti Vāsudeva Iti |

Oṃ Nama Iti Trīṇyakṣarāṇi | Bhagavata Iti Catvāri |

Vāsudevāyeti Pañcākṣarāṇi | Etadvai Vāsudevasya Dvādaśārṇamabhyeti | Sopaplavaṃ Tarati | Sa Sarvamāyureti | Vindate Prājāpatyaṃ Rāyaspoṣaṃ Gaupatyaṃ Ca Tamaśnute Pratyagānandaṃ Brahmapuruṣaṃ Praṇavasvarūpamakāra Ukāro Makāra Iti | Tānekadhā Saṃbhavati Tadomiti |

Haṃsaḥ Śuciṣadvasurantarikṣasaddhotā Vediṣadatithirduroṇasat |

Nṛṣadvarasadṛtasadvyomasadabjā Gojā Ṛtajā Adrijā Ṛtaṃ Bṛhat | Haṃsa Ityetanmanorakṣaradvitīyena Prabhāpuñjena Saureṇa Dhṛtamabjā Gojā Ṛtajā Adrijā Ṛtaṃ Satyā-Prabhā-Puñji-Nyuṣā-Sandhyā-Prajñābhiḥ Śaktibhiḥ Pūrvaṃ Sauramadhīyānaḥ Sarvaṃ Phalamaśnute |

Sa Vyomni Parame Dhāmani Saure Nivasate |

Gaṇānāṃ Tvati Traiṣṭubhena Pūrveṇādhvanā Manunaikārṇena Gaṇādhipamabhyarcya Gaṇeśatvaṃ Prāpnoti | Atha Gāyatrī Sāvitrī Sarasvatyajapā Mātṛkā Proktā Tayā Sarvamidaṃ Vyāptam |

Aiṃ Vāgīśvari Vidmahe Klīṃ Kāmeśvarī Dhīmahi |

Saustannaḥ Śaktiḥ Pracodayāditi | Gāyatrī Prātaḥ Sāvitrī Madhyandine Sarasvatī Sāyamiti Nirantaramajapā | Haṃsa Ityeva Mātṛkā | Pañcāśadvarṇavigraheṇā-Kārādikṣakārāntena Vyāptāni Bhuvanāni Śāstrāṇi Cchandāṃsītyevaṃ Bhagavatīṃ Sarvaṃ Vyāpnotītyeva Tasyai Vai Namonama Iti | Tānbhagavānabravīdetairmantrairnityaṃ Devīṃ Yaḥ Stauti Sa Sarvaṃ Paśyati |

So'mṛtatvaṃ Ca Gacchati | Ya Evaṃ Vedetyupaniṣat ||

इति तुरीयोपनिषत्॥ *Iti Turīyopaniṣat* || 4||

Fifth *Upanishṣat*

1. देवा ह वै भगवन्तमब्रुवन्स्वामिन्नः कथितं स्फुटं क्रियाकाण्डं सविषयं त्रैपुरमिति।
अथ परमनिर्विशेषं कथयस्वेति। तान्होवाच भगवांस्तुरीययामाययान्त्ययानिर्दिष्टं परमं ब्रह्मेति।
परमपुरुषं चिद्रूपं परमात्मेति।
श्रोता मन्ता द्रष्टादेष्टा स्प्रष्टाघोष्टा विज्ञाता प्रज्ञाता सर्वेषां पुरुषाणामन्तःपुरुषः
स आत्मा स विज्ञेय इति। न तत्र लोका अलोका न तत्र देवा अदेवाः
पशवोऽपशवस्तापसो न तापसः पौल्कसो न पौल्कसो विप्रा न विप्राः।
स इत्येकमेव परं ब्रह्म विभ्राजते निर्वाणम्।
न तत्र देवा ऋषयः पितर ईशते प्रतिबुद्धः सर्वविद्येति।
तत्रैते श्लोका भवन्ति। अतो निर्विषयं नित्यं मनः कार्यं मुमुक्षुणा।
यतो निर्विषयो नाम मनसो मुक्तिरिष्यते॥ १॥

Devā Ha Vai Bhagavantamabruvansvāminnaḥ Kathitaṃ Sphuṭaṃ Kriyākāṇḍaṃ Saviṣayaṃ Traipuramiti | Atha Paramanirviśeṣaṃ Kathayasveti | Tānhovāca Bhagavāṃsturīyayā Māyayāntyayā Nirdiṣṭaṃ Paramaṃ Brahmeti | Paramapuruṣaṃ Cidrūpaṃ Paramātmeti | Śrotā Mantā Draṣṭādeṣṭā Spraṣṭāghoṣṭā Vijñātā Prajñātā Sarveṣāṃ Puruṣāṇāmantaḥpuruṣaḥ Sa Ātmā Sa Vijñeya Iti | Na Tatra Lokā Alokā Na Tatra Devā Adevāḥ Paśavo'paśavastāpaso Na Tāpasaḥ Paulkaso Na Paulkaso Viprā Na Viprāḥ | Sa Ityekameva Paraṃ Brahma Vibhrājate Nirvāṇam | Na Tatra Devā Ṛṣayaḥ Pitara Īśate Pratibuddhaḥ Sarvavidyeti | Tatraite Ślokā Bhavanti |

Ato Nirviṣayaṃ Nityaṃ Manaḥ Kāryaṃ Mumukṣuṇā |

Yato Nirviṣayo Nāma Manaso Muktiriṣyate ||

2. मनो हि द्विविधं प्रोक्तं शुद्धं चाशुद्धमेव च। अशुद्धं कामसंकल्पं शुद्धं कामविवर्जितम्॥

Mano Hi Dvividhaṃ Proktaṃ Śuddhaṃ Cāśuddhameva Ca |

Aśuddhaṃ Kāmasaṃkalpaṃ Śuddhaṃ Kāmavivarjitam ||

3. मन एव मनुष्याणां कारणं बन्धमोक्षयोः । बन्धनं विषयासक्तं मुक्त्यै निर्विषयं मनः ॥

Mana Eva Manuṣyāṇāṃ Kāraṇaṃ Bandhamokṣayoḥ |

Bandhanaṃ Viṣayāsaktaṃ Muktyai Nirviṣayaṃ Manaḥ ||

4. निरस्तविषयासङ्गं संनिरुध्य मनो हृदि । यदा यात्यमनीभावस्तदा तत्परमं पदम् ॥

Nirastaviṣayāsaṅgaṃ Saṃnirudhya Mano Hṛdi |

Yadā Yātyamanībhāvastadā Tatparamaṃ Padam ||

5. तावदेव निरोद्धव्यं यावधृदिगतं क्षयम् । एतज्ज्ञानं च ध्यानं च शेषोऽन्यो ग्रन्थविस्तरः ॥

Tāvadeva Niroddhavyaṃ Yāvadhṛdigataṃ Kṣayam |

Etajjñānaṃ Ca Dhyānaṃ Ca Śeṣo'nyo Granthavistaraḥ ||

6. नैव चिन्त्यं न चाचिन्त्यं न चिन्त्यं चिन्त्यमेव च । पक्षपातविनिर्मुक्तं ब्रह्म सम्पद्यते ध्रुवम् ॥

Naiva Cintyaṃ Na Cācintyaṃ Na Cintyaṃ Cintyameva Ca |

Pakṣapātavinirmuktaṃ Brahma Sampadyate Dhruvam ||

7. स्वरेण सल्लयेद्योगी स्वरं संभावयेत्परम् । अस्वरेण तु भावेन न भावो भाव इष्यते ॥

Svareṇa Sallayedyogī Svaraṃ Saṃbhāvayetparam |

Asvareṇa Tu Bhāvena Na Bhāvo Bhāva Iṣyate ||

8. तदेव निष्कलं ब्रह्म निर्विकल्पं निरञ्जनम् । तद्ब्रह्माहमिति ज्ञात्वा ब्रह्म सम्पद्यते क्रमात्

Tadeva Niṣkalaṃ Brahma Nirvikalpaṃ Nirañjanam |

Tadbrahmāhamiti Jñātvā Brahma Sampadyate Kramāt ||

9. निर्विकल्पमनन्तं च हेतुदृष्टान्तवर्जितम् । अप्रमेयमनाद्यन्तं यज्ज्ञात्वा मुच्यते बुधः ॥

Nirvikalpamanantaṃ Ca Hetudṛṣṭāntavarjitam |

Aprameyamanādyantaṃ Yajjñātvā Mucyate Budhaḥ ||

10. न निरोधो न चोत्पत्तिर्न बद्धो न च साधकः । न मुमुक्षुर्नवै मुक्त इत्येषा परमार्थता ॥

Na Nirodho Na Cotpattirna Baddho Na Ca Sādhakaḥ |

Na Mumukṣurna Vai Mukta Ityeṣā Paramārthatā ||

11. एक एवात्मा मन्तव्यो जाग्रत्स्वप्नसुषुप्तिषु। स्थानत्रयव्यतीतस्य पुनर्जन्म न विद्यते ॥

Eka Evātmā Mantavyo Jāgratsvapnasuṣuptiṣu ।

Sthānatrayavyatītasya Punarjanma Na Vidyate ॥

12. एक एव हि भूतात्मा भूतेभूते व्यवस्थितः । एकधा बहुधा चैव दृश्यते जलचन्द्रवत् ॥

Eka Eva Hi Bhūtātmā Bhūtebhūte Vyavasthitaḥ ।

Ekadhā Bahudhā Caiva Dṛśyate Jalacandravat ॥

13. घटसंवृतमाकाशं नीयमाने घटे यथा । घटो नीयेत नाकाशं तथा जीवो नभोपमः ॥

Ghaṭasaṃvṛtamākāśaṃ Nīyamāne Ghaṭe Yathā ।

Ghaṭo Nīyeta Nākāśaṃ Tathā Jīvo Nabhopamaḥ ॥

14. घटवद्विविधाकारं भिद्यमां पुनः पुनः । तद्भेदे च न जानाति स जानाति च नित्यशः ॥

Ghaṭavadvividhākāraṃ Bhidyamāṃ Punaḥ Punaḥ ।

Tadbhede Ca Na Jānāti Sa Jānāti Ca Nityaśaḥ ॥

15. शब्दमायावृतो यावत्तावत्तिष्ठति पुष्कले। भिन्ने तमसि चैकत्वमेक एवानुपश्यति ॥

Śabdamāyāvṛto Yāvattāvattiṣṭhati Puṣkale ।

Bhinne Tamasi Caikatvameka Evānupaśyati ॥

16. शब्दार्णमपरं ब्रह्म तस्मिन्क्षीणे यदक्षरम् । तद्विद्वानक्षरं ध्यायेद्यदीच्छेच्छान्तिमात्मनः ॥

Śabdārṇamaparaṃ Brahma Tasminkṣīṇe Yadakṣaram ।

Tadvidvānakṣaraṃ Dhyāyedyadīcchecchāntimātmanaḥ ॥

17. द्वे ब्रह्मणी हि मन्तव्ये शब्दब्रह्म परं च यत् । शब्दब्रह्मणि निष्णातः परं ब्रह्माधिगच्छति ॥

Dve Brahmaṇī Hi Mantavye Śabdabrahma Paraṃ Ca Yat ।

Śabdabrahmaṇi Niṣṇātaḥ Paraṃ Brahmādhigacchati ॥

18. ग्रन्थमभ्यस्य मेधावी ज्ञानविज्ञानतत्परः । पलालमिव धान्यार्थी त्यजेद् ग्रन्थमशेषतः॥

Granthamabhyasya Medhāvī Jñānavijñānatatparaḥ ।

Palālamiva Dhānyārthī Tyajedgranthamaśeṣataḥ ॥

19. गवामनेकवर्णानां क्षीरस्याप्येकवर्णता । क्षीरवत्पश्यति ज्ञानी लिङ्गिनस्तु गवां यथा ॥

Gavāmanekavarṇānāṃ Kṣīrasyāpyekavarṇatā |

Kṣīravatpaśyati Jñānī Liṅginastu Gavāṃ Yathā ||

20. ज्ञाननेत्रं समाधाय स महत्परमं पदम् । निष्कलं निश्चलं शान्तं ब्रह्माहमिति संस्मरेत्॥

Jñānanetraṃ Samādhāya Sa Mahatparamaṃ Padam |

Niṣkalaṃ Niścalaṃ Śāntaṃ Brahmāhamiti Saṃsmaret ||

21. इत्येकं परब्रह्मरूपं सर्वभूताधिवासं तुरीयं जानीते सोऽक्षरे परमे व्योमन्यधिवसति ।
य एतां विद्यां तुरीयां ब्रह्मयोनिस्वरूपां तामिहायुषे शरणमहं प्रपद्ये ।
आकाशाद्यनुक्रमेण सर्वेषां वा एतद्भूतानामाकाशः परायणम् ।
सर्वाणि ह वा इमानि भूतान्याकाशादेव जायन्ते ।
आकाश एव लीयन्ते । तस्मादेव जातानि जीवन्ति । तस्मादाकाशजं बीजं विन्द्यात् ।
तदेवाकाशपीठं स्पार्शनं पीठं तेजःपीठममृतपीठं रत्नपीठं जानीयात् ।
यो जानीते सोऽमृतत्वं च गच्छति । तस्मादेतां तुरीयां श्रीकामराजीयामेकादशधा
भिन्नमेकाक्षरं ब्रह्मेति यो जानीते स तुरीयं पदं प्राप्नोति ।
य एवं वेदेति महोपनिषत् ॥

Ityekaṃ Parabrahmarūpaṃ Sarvabhūtādhivāsaṃ Turīyaṃ Jānīte So'kṣare Parame Vyomanyadhivasati | Ya Etāṃ Vidyāṃ Turīyāṃ Brahmayonisvarūpāṃ Tāmihāyuṣe Śaraṇamahaṃ Prapadye | Ākāśādyanukrameṇa Sarveṣāṃ Vā Etadbhūtānāmākāśaḥ Parāyaṇam | Sarvāṇi Ha Vā Imāni Bhūtānyākāśādeva Jāyante | Ākāśa Eva Līyante | Tasmādeva Jātāni Jīvanti | Tasmādākāśajaṃ Bījaṃ Vindyāt | Tadevākāśapīṭhaṃ Spārśanaṃ Pīṭhaṃ Tejaḥpīṭhamamṛtapīṭhaṃ Ratnapīṭhaṃ Jānīyāt | Yo Jānīte So'mṛtatvaṃ Ca Gacchati | Tasmādetāṃ Turīyāṃ Śrīkāmarājīyāmekādaśadhā Bhinnamekākṣaraṃ Brahmeti Yo Jānīte Sa Turīyaṃ Padaṃ Prāpnoti | Ya Evaṃ Vedeti Mahopaniṣat ||

इति पञ्चमोपनिषत् ॥ *Iti Pañcamopaniṣat ||*

शान्ति मन्त्रः । *Śānti Mantraḥ* ।

ॐ भद्रं कर्णेभिः शृणुयाम देवाः । भद्रंपश्येमाक्षभिर्यजत्राः ।

Oṃ Bhadraṃ Karṇebhiḥ Śṛṇuyāma Devāḥ ॥

Bhadraṃ Paśyemākṣabhiryajatrāḥ ॥
स्थिरैरङ्गैस्तुष्टुवाँसस्तनूभिः । व्यशेम देवहितं यदायुः ।

Sthirairaṅgaistuṣṭuvāg̃Sastanūbhiḥ ॥ *Vyaśema Devahitaṃ Yadāyuḥ* ॥
स्वस्ति न इन्द्रो वृद्धश्रवाः । स्वस्ति नः पूषा विश्ववेदाः ।

Svasti Na Indro Vṛddhaśravāḥ ॥ *Svasti Naḥ Pūṣā Viśvavedāḥ* ॥
स्वस्ति नस्तार्क्ष्यो अरिष्टनेमिः । स्वस्ति नो बृहस्पतिर्दधातु ॥

Svasti Nastārkṣyo Ariṣṭanemiḥ ॥ *Svasti No Bṛhaspatirdadhātu* ॥
ॐ शान्तिः शान्तिः शान्तिः ॥ *Oṃ Śāntiḥ Śāntiḥ Śāntiḥ* ॥

॥ इति श्रीत्रिपुरातापिन्युपनिषत्समाप्ता ॥
॥ *Iti Śrītripurātāpinyupaniṣatsamāptā* ॥

*****

Bhāvanopaniṣat

भावनोपनिषत्

This also belongs to *Atharva Veda*. This is normally chant during *Pūrnāhuti* of *Candī Homa*-s. In some schools this is also called as *Śrīcakropaniṣat*. Still, there is one other *Upaniṣat* called, *Śrīcakropaniṣat* and that has been discussed separately in this book.

स्वाविद्यापदतत्कार्यं श्रीचक्रोपरि भासुरम् । बिन्दुरूपशिवाकारं रामचन्द्रपदं भजे ॥

Svāvidyāpadatatkāryaṃ Śrīcakropari Bhāsuram |

Bindurūpaśivākāraṃ Rāmacandrapadaṃ Bhaje ||

शान्ति मन्त्रः । *Śānti Mantraḥ* |

ॐ भद्रं कर्णेभिः शृणुयाम देवाः । भद्रं पश्येमाक्षभिर्यजत्राः ।

Oṃ Bhadraṃ Karṇebhiḥ Śṛṇuyāma Devāḥ ||

Bhadraṃ Paśyemākṣabhiryajatrāḥ ||

स्थिरैरङ्गैस्तुष्टुवाँसस्तनूभिः । व्यशेम देवहितं यदायुः ।

SthirairaṅgaistuṣṭuvāgͫSastanūbhiḥ || *Vyaśema Devahitaṃ Yadāyuḥ* ||

स्वस्ति न इन्द्रो वृद्धश्रवाः । स्वस्ति नः पूषा विश्ववेदाः ।

Svasti Na Indro Vṛddhaśravāḥ || *Svasti Naḥ Pūṣā Viśvavedāḥ* ||

स्वस्ति नस्तार्क्ष्यो अरिष्टनेमिः । स्वस्ति नो बृहस्पतिर्दधातु ॥

Svasti Nastārkṣyo Ariṣṭanemiḥ || *Svasti No Bṛhaspatirdadhātu* ||

ॐ शान्तिः शान्तिः शान्तिः ॥ *Oṃ Śāntiḥ Śāntiḥ Śāntiḥ* ||

हरिः ॐ । *Hariḥ Oṃ* |

आत्मानमखण्डमण्डलाकारमवृत्य सकलब्रह्माण्डमण्डलं स्वप्रकाशं ध्यायेत् ।

ॐ श्रीगुरुः सर्वकारणभूता शक्तिः । तेन नवरन्ध्ररूपो देहः । नवशक्तिरूपं श्रीचक्रम् ।

वाराही पितृरूपा । कुरुकुल्ला बलिदेवता माता । पुरुषार्थाः सागराः । देहो नवरत्नद्वीपः ।

त्वगादिसप्तधातुभिरनेकैः संयुक्ताः सङ्कल्पाः कल्पतरवः । तेजः कल्पकोद्यानम् ।

रसनया भाव्यमाना मधुराम्लतिक्तकटुकषायलवणभेदाः षड्रसाः षड्तवः क्रियाशक्तिः पीठम् ।

कुण्डलिनी ज्ञानशक्तिर्गृहम् । इच्छाशक्तिर्महात्रिपुरसुन्दरी ।

ज्ञाता होता ज्ञानमग्निः (ज्ञानमर्घ्यम्) ज्ञेयं हविः ।

ज्ञातृ ज्ञान ज्ञेया नाम भेद भावनं श्रीचक्र पूजनम् ।

नियतिसहिताः शृङ्गारादयो नव रसा अणिमादयः ।
कामक्रोधलोभमोहमदमात्सर्यपुण्यपापमया ब्राह्म्याद्यष्टशक्तयः ।
(आधरनवकम् मुद्राशक्तयः ।)

Ātmānamakhaṇḍamaṇḍalākāramavṛtya Sakalabrahmāṇḍamaṇḍalaṃ Svaprakāśaṃ Dhyāyet | Oṃ Śrīguruḥ Sarvakāraṇabhūtā Śaktiḥ | Tena Navarandhrarūpo Dehaḥ | Navaśaktirūpaṃ Śrīcakram | Vārāhī Pitṛrūpā | Kurukullā Balidevatā Mātā | Puruṣārthāḥ Sāgarāḥ | Deho Navaratnadvīpaḥ | Tvagādisaptadhātubhiranekaiḥ Saṃyuktāḥ Saṅkalpāḥ Kalpataravaḥ | Tejaḥ Kalpakodyānam | Rasanayā Bhāvyamānā Madhurāmlatiktakaṭukaṣāyalavaṇabhedāḥ Ṣaḍrasāḥ Ṣaḍṛtavaḥ Kriyāśaktiḥ Pīṭham | Kuṇḍalinī Jñānaśaktirgṛham | Icchāśaktirmahātripurasundarī | Jñātā Hotā Jñānamagniḥ (Jñānamarghyam) Jñeyaṃ Haviḥ | Jñātṛjñānajñeyānāmabhedabhāvanaṃ Śrīcakrapūjanam | Niyatisahitāḥ Śṛṅgārādayo Nava Rasā Aṇimādayaḥ | Kāmakrodhalobhamohamadamātsaryapuṇyapāpamayā Brāhmyādyaṣṭaśaktayaḥ | (Ādharanavakam Mudrāśaktayaḥ |)

पृथिव्यप्तेजोवाय्वाकाशश्रोत्रत्वक्चक्षुर्जिह्वाघ्राणवाक्पाणिपादपायूपस्थमनोविकाराः (कामाकर्षिण्यादि) षोडष शक्तयः ।
वचनादानगमनविसर्गानन्दहानो(पादानो)पेक्षा(ख्य) भुद्धयोऽनङ्गकुसुमादिशक्तयोऽष्टौ।
अलम्बुसा कुहूर्विश्वोदरी वरुणा हस्तिजिह्वा यशस्वत्यश्विनी गान्धारी पूषा शङ्खिनी सरस्वतीडा पिङ्गला सुषुम्ना चेति चतुर्दश नाड्यः । सर्वसंक्षोभिण्यादिचतुर्दशारगा देवताः ।
प्राणापानव्यानोदानसमाननागकूर्मकृकरदेवदत्तधनञ्जया इति दश वायवः ।
सर्वसिद्धिप्रदा देव्यो बहिर्दशारगा देवताः ।
एतद्वायुदशकसंसर्गोपाधिभेधेन रेचकपूरकशोषकदाहप्लावका (रेचकः पाचकः शोषको दाहकः प्लावका इति) प्राणमुख्यत्वेन पञ्चधोऽस्ति (जठराग्निर्भवति) ।

Pṛthivyaptejovāyvākāśaśrotratvakcakṣurjihvāghrāṇavākpāṇipādapāyūpasthamanovikārāḥ (Kāmākarṣiṇyādi) Ṣoḍaṣa Śaktayaḥ | Vacanādānagamanavisargānandahāno(Pādāno)Pekṣā(Khya)-

Bhuddhayo'naṅgakusumādiśaktayo'ṣṭau |
Alambusā Kuhūrviśvodarī Varuṇā Hastijihvā Yaśasvatyaśvinī Gāndhārī Pūṣā Śaṅkhinī Sarasvatīḍā Piṅgalā Suṣumnā Ceti Caturdaśa Nāḍyaḥ | Sarvasaṃkṣobhiṇyādicaturdaśāragā Devatāḥ |Prāṇā Pāna Vyāno Dāna Samānanāga Kūrmakṛkara Devadattadhanañjayā Iti Daśa Vāyavaḥ | Sarvasiddhipradā Devyo Bahirdaśāragā Devatāḥ | Etadvāyudaśakasaṃsargopādhibhedhena Recaka Pūrakaśoṣakadāha Plāvakā (Recakaḥ Pācakaḥ Śoṣako Dāhakaḥ Plāvakā Iti) Prāṇamukhyatvena Pañcadho'sti (Jaṭharāgnirbhavati) |

क्षारको दारकः क्षोभको मोहको जृम्भक इत्यपालनमुख्यत्वेन पञ्चविधोऽस्ति।
तेन मनुष्याणां मोहको दाहको (नागप्राधान्येन पञ्चबिधास्ते मनुष्याणां देहगा)
भक्ष्यभोज्यशोष्यलेह्यपेयात्मकं चतुर्विधमन्नं (पञ्चविधमन्नं) पाचयति।
एता दश वह्निकलाः सर्वज्ञत्वाद्यन्तर्दशारगा देवताः।

Kṣārako Dārakaḥ Kṣobhako Mohako Jṛmbhaka Ityapālanamukhyatvena Pañcavidho'sti | Tena Manuṣyāṇāṃ Mohako Dāhako (Nāgaprādhānyena Pañcabidhāste Manuṣyāṇāṃ Dehagā) Bhakṣyabhojyaśoṣyalehyapeyātmakaṃ Caturvidhamannaṃ (Pañcavidhamannaṃ) Pācayati | Etā Daśa Vahnikalāḥ Sarvajñatvādyantardaśāragā Devatāḥ |

शीतोष्णसुखदुःखेच्छासत्त्वरजस्तमोगुणावशिन्यादिशक्तयोऽष्टौ।
शब्दस्पर्शरूपरसगन्धाः पञ्चतन्मात्राः पञ्चपुष्पबाणा मन इक्षु धनुः।
वश्यो वाणो रागः पाशः। द्वेषोऽङ्कुशः।
अव्यक्तमहत्तत्त्वमहदहङ्कार इति कामेश्वरी-वज्रेश्वरी भगमालिन्योऽन्तस्त्रिकोणाग्रगा देवताः
(निरुपाधिकसंविदेव कामेश्वर। सदानन्दपूर्णं स्वात्मेव परदेवता ललिता।
लौहित्यमेतस्य सर्वस्य विमर्श। अनन्यचित्तत्वेन च सिद्धिः।
भावनायाः क्रिया उपचरः। अहं त्वमस्ति नास्ति कर्तव्यमकर्तव्यमुपासितव्यमिति
विकल्पानामात्मनि विलापनम् होमः भवनाविषयाणामभेदभवना तर्पणम्।)
पञ्चदशतिथिरूपेण कालस्य परिणामावलोकनस्थितिः पञ्चदशनित्याः।
श्रद्धानुरूपा धीर्देवता। तयोः कामेश्वरी सदानन्दघना परिपूर्णस्वात्मैक्यरूपा देवता।
सलिलमिति लौहित्यकारणं सत्त्वम्। कर्तव्यमकर्तव्यमिति भावनायुक्त उपचारः।
अस्ति नास्तीति कर्तव्यतानूपचारः। बाह्याभ्यन्तःकरणानां रूपग्रहणयोग्यतास्त्त्वित्यावाहनम्।

तस्य बाह्याभ्यन्तःकरणानामेकरूपविषयग्रहणमासनम् ।
रक्तशुक्लपदैकीकरणं पाद्यम् । उज्ज्वलदामोदानन्दासनदानमर्घ्यम् ।
स्वच्छं स्वतःसिद्धमित्याचमनीयम् । चिच्चन्द्रमयीति सर्वाङ्गस्रवणं स्नानम् ।
चिदग्निस्वरूपपरमानन्दशक्तिस्फुरणं वस्त्रम् । प्रत्येकं सप्तविंशतिधा भिन्नत्वेनेच्छाज्ञान
क्रियात्मकब्रह्मग्रन्थिमद्रसतन्तुब्रह्मनाडी ब्रह्मसूत्रम् ।
स्वव्यतिरिक्तवस्तुसङ्गरहितस्मरणां विभूषणम् ।
सच्चित्सुखपरिपूर्णतास्मरणं गन्धः । समस्तविषयाणां मनसः स्थैर्येणानुसंधानं कुसुमम् ।
तेषामेव सर्वदा स्वीकरणं धूपः । पवनावच्छिन्नोर्ध्वज्वलनसच्चिदुल्काकाशदेहो दीपः ।
समस्तयातायातवर्ज्यं नैवेद्यम् । अवस्थात्रयाणामेकीकरणं ताम्बूलम् ।
मूलाधारादाब्रह्मरन्ध्रपर्यन्तं ब्रह्मरन्ध्रादामूलाधारपर्यन्तं गतागतरूपेण प्रादक्षिण्यम् ।
तुर्यावस्था नमस्कारः । देहशून्यप्रमातृतानिमज्जनं बलिहरणम् ।
सत्यमस्ति लर्तव्यमकर्तव्यमौदासीन्यनित्यात्मविलापनं होमः ।
स्वयं तत्पादुकानिमज्जनं परिपूर्णध्यानम् ।

Śītoṣṇasukhaduḥkhecchāsattvarajastamoguṇā Vaśinyādiśaktayo'ṣṭau | Śabdasparśarūparasagandhāḥ Pañcatanmātrāḥ Pañcapuṣpabāṇā Mana Ikṣudhanuḥ | Vaśyo Vāṇo Rāgaḥ Pāśaḥ | Dveṣo'ṅkuśaḥ | Avyaktamahattattvamahadahaṅkāra Iti Kāmeśvarī-Vajreśvarī-Bhagamālinyo'ntastrikoṇāgragā Devatāḥ | (Nirupādhikasaṃvideva Kāmeśvara | Sadānandapūrṇa Svātmeva Paradevatā Lalitā | Lauhityametasya Sarvasya Vimarśa | Ananyacittatvena Ca Siddhiḥ | Bhāvanāyāḥ Kriyā Upacaraḥ | Ahaṃ Tvamasti Nāsti Kartavyamakartavyamupāsitavyamiti Vikalpānāmātmani Vilāpanam Homaḥ | Bhavanāviṣayāṇāmabhedabhavanā Tarpaṇam |) Pañcadaśatithirūpeṇa Kālasya Pariṇāmāvalokanasthitiḥ Pañcadaśanityāḥ | Śraddhānurūpā Dhīrdevatā | Tayoḥ Kāmeśvarī Sadānandaghanā Paripūrṇasvātmaikyarūpā Devatā | Salilamiti Lauhityakāraṇaṃ Sattvam | Kartavyamakartavyamiti Bhāvanāyukta Upacāraḥ | Asti Nāstīti Kartavyatānūpacāraḥ | Bāhyābhyantaḥkaraṇānāṃ Rūpagrahaṇayogyatāsttvityāvāhanam | Tasya Bāhyābhyantaḥkaraṇānāmekarūpaviṣayagrahaṇamāsanam |

Raktaśuklapadaikīkaraṇaṃ Pādyam ।

Ujjvaladāmodānandāsanadānamarghyam ।

Svacchaṃ Svataḥsiddhamityācamanīyam ।

Ciccandramayīti Sarvāṅgasravaṇaṃ Snānam ।

Cidagnisvarūpaparamānandaśaktisphuraṇaṃ Vastram ।
Pratyekaṃ Saptaviṃśatidhā Bhinnatvenecchājñānakriyātmakabrahmagranthimadrasatantubrahma nāḍī Brahmasūtram । *Svavyatiriktavastusaṅgarahitasmaraṇāṃ Vibhūṣaṇam* । *Saccitsukhaparipūrṇatāsmaraṇaṃ Gandhaḥ* ।

Samastaviṣayāṇāṃ Manasaḥ Sthairyeṇānusaṃdhānaṃ Kusumam ।

Teṣāmeva Sarvadā Svīkaraṇaṃ Dhūpaḥ ।

Pavanāvacchinnotdhvajvalanasaccidulkākāśadeho Dīpaḥ ।

Samastayātāyātavarjyaṃ Naivedyam ।

Avasthātrayāṇāmekīkaraṇaṃ Tāmbūlam ।
Mūlādhārādābrahmarandhraparyantaṃ Brahmarandhrādāmūlādhāraparyantaṃ Gatāgatarūpeṇa Prādakṣiṇyam । *Turyāvasthā Namaskāraḥ* ।

Dehaśūnyapramātṛtānimajjanaṃ Baliharaṇam ।
Satyamasti Lartavyamakartavyamaudāsīnyanityātmavilāpanaṃ Homaḥ । *Svayaṃ Tatpādukānimajjanaṃ Paripūrṇadhyānam* ।

एवं मुहूर्तत्रयं (मुहूर्तद्वितयं मुहूर्तमात्रं वा) भावनापरो जीवन्मुक्तो भवति स एव शिवयोगीति गद्यते । आदिमतेनान्तश्चक्रभावनाः । तस्य देवतात्मैक्यसिद्धिः ।
चिन्तितकार्याण्ययत्नेन सिद्ध्यन्ति । स एव शिवयोगीति कथ्यते ।
कादिहादिमतोक्तेन भावना प्रतिपादिता । जीवन्मुक्तो भवति ।
य एवं वेद । इत्युपनिषत् । (सोऽथर्वशिरोऽधीते ।)

Evaṃ Muhūrtatrayaṃ (Muhūrtadvitayaṃ Muhūrtamātraṃ Vā) Bhāvanāparo Jīvanmukto Bhavati Sa Eva Śivayogīti Gadyate । *Ādimatenāntaścakrabhāvanāḥ* ।

Tasya Devatātmaikyasiddhiḥ । *Cintitakāryāṇyayatnena Siddhyanti* ।

Sa Eva Śivayogīti Kathyate | Kādihādimatoktena Bhāvanā Pratipāditā | Jīvanmukto Bhavati | Ya Evaṃ Veda | Ityupaniṣat |

(So'tharvaśiro'dhīte |)

शान्ति मन्त्रः | *Śānti Mantraḥ* |

ॐ भद्रं कर्णेभिः शृणुयाम देवाः । भद्रं पश्येमाक्षभिर्यजत्राः ।

Oṃ Bhadraṃ Karṇebhiḥ Śṛṇuyāma Devāḥ ||

Bhadraṃ Paśyemākṣabhiryajatrāḥ ||

स्थिरैरङ्गैस्तुष्टुवाँसस्तनूभिः । व्यशेम देवहितं यदायुः ।

Sthirairaṅgaistuṣṭuvāg̐Sastanūbhiḥ || *Vyaśema Devahitaṃ Yadāyuḥ* ||

स्वस्ति न इन्द्रो वृद्धश्रवाः । स्वस्ति नः पूषा विश्ववेदाः ।

Svasti Na Indro Vṛddhaśravāḥ || *Svasti Naḥ Pūṣā Viśvavedāḥ* ||

स्वस्ति नस्ताक्ष्र्यो अरिष्टनेमिः । स्वस्ति नो बृहस्पतिर्दधातु ॥

Svasti Nastārkṣyo Ariṣṭanemiḥ || *Svasti No Bṛhaspatirdadhātu* ||

ॐ शान्तिः शान्तिः शान्तिः ॥ *Oṃ Śāntiḥ Śāntiḥ Śāntiḥ* ||

Ityatharvaṇavede Bhāvanopaniṣatsampūrṇā ||

Atharvaṇa Dvitīyopaniṣat

अथर्वण द्वितीयोपनिषत्

In *Śrī Vamakeśwara Tantra*, there is a hymn called *Śrī Devī Khadgamāla Stotra*, in the form of a dialogue between Goddess *Umā* and Lord *Śivā*. It is a hymn with a total of 1000 characters. Hence it is called "*Sahasrākśarī Vidyā*". When Sengalipuram *Śrī Anantarāma Dīkśitar* used to say about *Śrī Devī Khadgamāla Stotra*, "Didn't by chanting *Śrī Devī Khadkamāla Stotra*, *Śrī Devī* come and stand live?".

This hymn is normally used during the *Śrī Cakra Navavārna* Puja. The names in these are the names of the deities in each of the 9 enclosures in the *Śrī Cakra*. Those names are given here as an *Upaniṣat*.

Pooja is also performed with these names of *Śrī Devī* as *archana*. The names of all the deities mentioned in each of the enclosures, *Siddhi Devi, Ashta Matas, Gupta Yoginis, Gupta Dhara Yoginis*, Traditional *Yoginis, Kulothirna Yoginis, Nikarpa Yoginis*, and so on, can be found in this this Stotra. That is the glory of it.

One can get the benefit of performing Sri Chakra Puja by reciting this hymn. Whatever satisfaction is caused to the Pitru deities, by the Pitru karmas performed in crores of births, equal result will be bestowed by Sri Devi by reciting this hymn once and for all. How glorious!

शान्ति मन्त्रः । *Śānti Mantraḥ* ।

ॐ भद्रं कर्णेभिः शृणुयाम देवाः । भद्रं पश्येमाक्षभिर्यजत्राः ।

Oṃ Bhadraṃ Karṇebhiḥ Śṛṇuyāma Devāḥ ॥

Bhadraṃ Paśyemākṣabhiryajatrāḥ ॥

स्थिरैरङ्गैस्तुष्टुवाँसस्तनूभिः । व्यशेम देवहितं यदायुः ।

Sthirairaṅgaistuṣṭuvāg̐Sastanūbhiḥ ॥ *Vyaśema Devahitaṃ Yadāyuḥ* ॥

स्वस्ति न इन्द्रो वृद्धश्रवाः । स्वस्ति नः पूषा विश्ववेदाः ।

Svasti Na Indro Vṛddhaśravāḥ ॥ *Svasti Naḥ Pūṣā Viśvavedāḥ* ॥

स्वस्ति नस्ताक्ष्र्यो अरिष्टनेमिः । स्वस्ति नो बृहस्पतिर्दधातु ॥

Svasti Nastārkṣyo Ariṣṭanemiḥ ‖ *Svasti No Bṛhaspatirdadhātu* ‖

ॐ शान्तिः शान्तिः शान्तिः ॥ *Oṃ Śāntiḥ Śāntiḥ Śāntiḥ* ‖

ॐ ऐं ह्रीं श्रीं ऐं क्लीं सौः ॐ नमस्त्रिपुरसुन्दरि,

हृदयदेवि, शिरोदेवि, शिखादेवि, कवचदेवि, नेत्रदेवि, अस्त्रदेवि,

कामेश्वरि, भगमालिनि, नित्यक्लिन्ने, भेरुण्डे, वह्निवासिनि, महावज्रेश्वरि, शिवदूति, त्वरिते, कुलसुन्दरि, नित्ये, नीलपताके, विजये, सर्वमङ्गले, ज्वालामालिनि, चित्रे, महानित्ये,

परमेश्वरपरमेश्वरि, मित्रेशमयि, षष्ठीशमयि, उड्डीशमयि, चर्यानाथमयि, लोपामुद्रामयि, अगस्त्यमयि,

कालतापशमयि, धर्माचार्यमयि, मुक्तकेशीश्वरमयि, दीपकलानाथमयि,

विष्णुदेवमयि, प्रभाकरदेवमयि, तेजोदेवमयि, मनोजदेवमयि, कल्याणदेवमयि, वासुदेवमयि, रत्नदेवमयि, श्रीरामानन्दमयि,

अणिमासिद्धे, लघिमासिद्धे, गरिमासिद्धे, महिमासिद्धे, ईशित्वसिद्धे, वशित्वसिद्धे, प्राकाम्यसिद्धे, भुक्तिसिद्धे,

इच्छासिद्धे, प्राप्तिसिद्धे, सर्वकामसिद्धे, ब्राह्मि, माहेश्वरि, कौमारि, वैष्णवि, वाराहि, माहेन्द्रि, चामुण्डे,

महालक्ष्मि, सर्वसङ्क्षोभिणि, सर्वविद्राविणि, सर्वाकर्षिणि, सर्ववशङ्करि, सर्वोन्मादिनि, सर्वमहाङ्कुशे, सर्वखेचरि,

सर्वबीजे, सर्वयोने, सर्वत्रिखण्डे, त्रैलोक्यमोहन चक्रस्वामिनि, प्रकटयोगिनि,

कामाकर्षिणि, बुद्ध्याकर्षिणि, अहंकाराकर्षिणि, शब्दाकर्षिणि, स्पर्शाकर्षिणि, रूपाकर्षिणि, रसाकर्षिणि, गन्धाकर्षिणि,

चित्ताकर्षिणि, धैर्याकर्षिणि, स्मृत्याकर्षिणि, नामाकर्षिणि,
बीजाकर्षिणि, आत्माकर्षिणि, अमृताकर्षिणि, शरीराकर्षिणि,
सर्वाशापरिपूरकचक्रस्वामिनि, गुप्तयोगिनि,

अनङ्गकुसुमे, अनङ्गमेखले, अनङ्गमदने, अनङ्गमदनातुरे,
अनङ्गरेखे, अनङ्गवेगिनि, अनङ्गाङ्कुशे, अनङ्गमालिनि,
सर्वसङ्क्षोभणचक्रस्वामिनि, गुप्ततरयोगिनि,

सर्वसङ्क्षोभिणि, सर्वविद्राविनि, सर्वाकर्षिणि,
सर्वह्लादिनि, सर्वसम्मोहिनि, सर्वस्तम्भिनि, सर्वजृम्भिणि,

सर्ववशङ्करि, सर्वरञ्जनि, सर्वोन्मादिनि, सर्वार्थसाधिके,
सर्वसम्पत्तिपूरिणि, सर्वमन्त्रमयि, सर्वद्वन्द्वक्षयङ्करि,
सर्वसौभाग्यदायकचक्रस्वामिनि, सम्प्रदाययोगिनि,

सर्वसिद्धिप्रदे, सर्वसम्पत्प्रदे, सर्वप्रियङ्करि,
सर्वमङ्गलकारिणि, सर्वकामप्रदे, सर्वदुःखविमोचनि,

सर्वमृत्युप्रशमनि, सर्वविघ्ननिवारिणि, सर्वाङ्गसुन्दरि,
सर्वसौभाग्यदायिनि, सर्वार्थसाधकचक्रस्वामिनि,
कुलोत्तीर्णयोगिनि,

सर्वज्ञे, सर्वशक्ते, सर्वैश्वर्यप्रदायिनि, सर्वज्ञानमयि,
सर्वव्याधिविनाशिनि, सर्वाधारस्वरूपे, सर्वपापहरे,

सर्वानन्दमयी, सर्वरक्षास्वरूपिणि, सर्वेप्सितफलप्रदे,
सर्वरक्षाकरचक्रस्वामिनि, निगर्भयोगिनि,

वशिनि, कामेश्वरि, मोदिनि, विमले, अरुणे, जयिनि,
सर्वेश्वरि, कौलिनि, सर्वरोगहरचक्रस्वामिनि, रहस्ययोगिनि,

बाणिनि, चापिनि, पाशिनि, अङ्कुशिनि, महाकामेश्वरि, महावज्रेश्वरि, महाभगमालिनि, सर्वसिद्धिप्रदचक्रस्वामिनि, अतिरहस्ययोगिनि,

श्री श्रीमहाभट्टारिके, सर्वानन्दमयचक्रस्वामिनि, परापरातिरहस्ययोगिनि,

त्रिपुरे, त्रिपुरेशि, त्रिपुरसुन्दरि, त्रिपुरवासिनि, त्रिपुराश्रीः, त्रिपुरमालिनि, त्रिपुरासिद्धे, त्रिपुराम्ब, महात्रिपुरसुन्दरि

महामहेश्वरि, महामहाराज्ञि, महामहाशक्ते, महामहागुप्ते, महामहाज्ञप्ते, महामहानन्दे, महामहास्कन्धे, महामहाशये, महामहा श्रीचक्रनगरसाम्राज्ञि, नमस्ते नमस्ते नमस्ते नमः ।

Om Aim Hrīm Śrīm Aim Klīm Sou:

Om Namas Tripurasundari, Hrudaya Devi, Śiro Devi, Śikā Devi, Kavaca Devi, Netra Devi, Astra Devi, Kāmeśvari, Baga Mālini, Nityaklinne, Beruṇḍe, Vahnivāsini, Mahāvajreśvari, Śivadhūti, Tvarite, Kulasundari, Nitye, Nīlapatāke, Vijaye, Sarvamaṅgaḷe, Jvālāmālini, Citre, Mahānitye, Parameśvara-Parameśvari, Mitreśamayi, Ṣaṣṭīśamayi, Oḍyāṇamayi, Caryā Nādamayi, Lopāmurāmayi, Agastyamayi, Kālātāpanamayi, Dharmācāryamayi, Muktakeśīśvaramayi, Dīpakalānātamayi, Viṣṇudevamayi, Prabhākaradevamayi, Tejodevamayi, Manojadevamayi,

Aṇimā Siddhe, Laghimā Siddhe, Mahimā Siddhe, Īṣitva Siddhe, Vaṣitva Siddhe, Prākāmya Siddhe, Buddhi Siddhe, Icchā Siddhe, Prāpti Siddhe, Mokśa Siddhe, Brahma Śakte, Śveta Varṇe, Śikhi Vāhanā, Śyāma Varṇā, Śyāmaḷā, Śyāma Varṇā, Krişṇa Varṇā, Pīta Varṇā, Brāhmi, Māheświari, Koumāri, Vaiṣṇavi, Vārāhi, Māhendri, *Cāmuṇḍe, Mahālakśmi,*

Sarva Samkśobiṇi, Sarva Vidrāviṇi, Sarvākarṣiṇi, Sarva Vaśaṅkari, Sarvonmādini, Sarvamahāṅkuśe, Sarva Keśari, Sarva Bīje, Sarva Yone, Sarva Trikaṇḍe, Prakaţa Yogini, Bouddha Darśanāṅgi, Trailokya Mohana Chakrasvāmini,

Kāmākarṣiṇi, Buddhi Ākarṣiṇi, Ahaṅkārākarṣiṇi, Śabdākarṣiṇi, Sparśākarṣiṇi, Rūpākarṣiṇi, Rasākarṣiṇi, Gandākarṣiṇi, Siddhākarṣiṇi, Dairyākarṣiṇi, Smrutyākarṣiṇi, Nāmākarṣiṇi, Bījākarṣiṇi, Ātmākarṣiṇi,

Amrutākarṣiṇi, Śarīrākarṣiṇi, Gupta Yogini, Sarvāvāśā Paripūraka Chakra Svāmini,

Ananga Kusume, Ananga Mekale, Ananga Madane, Ananga Madanā Ture, Ananga Rekhe, Ananga Veginī, Anangānguśe, Ananga Malini, Gupta Tara Yogini, Sarva Saṅkśobaṇa Chakra Svāminī, Pūrvāmnāya Digdevate, Sruşţirūpe,

Sarva Saṅkśobiṇi, Sarva Vidrāviṇi, Sarvākarṣiṇi, Sarvāhlādini, Sarva Sammohini, Sarva Stambini, Sarva Jrumbiṇi, Sarva Vaśaṅkari, Sarva Ranjani, Sarvonmādini, Sarvārthasādini, Sarva Sampatthi Pūrani, Sarva Mantramayī, Sarva Dvandva Kśayaṅkari, Sampradāya Yogini, Sarva Darşanāṅgi, Sarva Sowbhāgya Dāyaka Chakra Svāminī,

Sarva Siddhi Pradhe, Sarva Sampath Pradhe, Sarva Priaṅkari, Sarva Maṅgala Kāriṇi, Sarva Kāma Pradhe, Sarva Dukkha Vimośani, Sarva Mrutyu Praśamani, Sarva Vigna Nivāriṇi, Sarvāṅga Sundari, Sarva Soubhāgya Dāyini, Kulottīrṇa Yogini, Sarvārta Sādaka Chakra Svāminī,

Sarva Jnānamayi, Sarvajne, Sarva Śakte, Sarvaiśvarya Pradhe, Sarva Gnānamayi, Sarva Vyādhi Nivāriṇī, Sarvādhāra Swarūpe, Sarva Pāpahare, Sarvānandamayī, Sarva Rakśā Swarūpiṇī, Sarvepsita *Phalaprade, Nigarba Yogini, Vaiṣṇava Darśanāṅgi, Sarva Rakśākara Chakra Svāminī,*

Vaśini, Kāmeśi, Modini, Vimale, Aruṇe, Jayinī, Sarveśvari, Koulini, Rahasya Yogini, Śākta Darśanāṅgi, Sarva Rogahara Chakra Svāminī, Paścimāmnāyeśi,

Danur Bāṇa Pāśāṅkuśa Devate, Kāmeśi, Vajreśi, *Bagamālini, Atirahasya Yogini, Śaiva Darśanāṅgi, Sarva Siddhiprada Chakra Svāminī, Uttarāmnāyeśi,*

Samhārarūpe, Śuddhapare, Bindu Pīţagate, Mahātripura Sundari, Parāparāti Rahasya Yoginī, Śambava Darśanāṅgi, Sarvānandamaya Chakra Svāminī,

Tripure, Tripureśī, Tripura Sundarī, Tripura Vāsinī, Tripurāśrī:, Tripura Mālinī, Tripura Siddhe, Tripurāmbā, Mahā Tripura Sundarī, Sarva Chakraste, Anuttarāmnāyākya Svarūpe, Mahā Tripura Bhairavī,

Caturvida Guṇarūpe, Kule, Akule, Kulākule, Mahā Koulini, Sarvottare, Sarva Darśanāṅgi, Navāsana Stite, Navākśari, Nava Mitunakrute, Maheśa Mādava Vidātru Manmata Skanda Nandi Indra Manu Candra Gupera Agastrya Krodha Baṭṭārika Vidyātmike, Kalyāṇa Tatvatraya Rūpe, Śiva Śivātmike, Pūrṇa Brahma Śakte, Mahā Tripura Sundarī, Tava Pādukām Pūjayāmi Tarpayāmi Nama:

Śrīm Hrīm Aim Om (*Svāhā*) ll

शान्ति मन्त्रः । *Śānti Mantraḥ* ।

ॐ भद्रं कर्णेभिः शृणुयाम देवाः । भद्रं पश्येमाक्षभिर्यजत्राः ।

Oṃ Bhadraṃ Karṇebhiḥ Śṛṇuyāma Devāḥ ll

Bhadraṃ Paśyemākṣabhiryajatrāḥ ll
स्थिरैरङ्गैस्तुष्टुवाँसस्तनूभिः । व्यशेम देवहितं यदायुः ।

Sthirairaṅgaistuṣṭuvāg̃Sastanūbhiḥ ll *Vyaśema Devahitaṃ Yadāyuḥ* ll
स्वस्ति न इन्द्रो वृद्धश्रवाः । स्वस्ति नः पूषा विश्ववेदाः ।

Svasti Na Indro Vṛddhaśravāḥ ll *Svasti Naḥ Pūṣā Viśvavedāḥ* ll
स्वस्ति नस्तार्क्ष्यो अरिष्टनेमिः । स्वस्ति नो बृहस्पतिर्दधातु ॥

Svasti Nastārkṣyo Ariṣṭanemiḥ ll *Svasti No Bṛhaspatirdadhātu* ll
ॐ शान्तिः शान्तिः शान्तिः ॥ *Oṃ Śāntiḥ Śāntiḥ Śāntiḥ* ll
इत्याथर्वणद्वितीयोपनिषत् समाप्ता ।
Iti Atharvaṇa Dvitīyopaniśat Samāptā ।

(The Gods of the nine enclosures of Sri Chakra / the first enclosure of the Sri Chakra)

*****

Allāh Upaniṣat

अल्ला उपनिशत्

This is another *Upaniśat* based on the *Atharva Veda*. Everyone will be surprised when they hear the name *Allāh Upaniśat*. The Samskruta word '*Allāh*' means 'mother'. Hence the actual name is *Amma Upaniśat*. It is like a Vedic *Gaṇapāta* style.

It is variously said that such an *Upaniśat* did not exist at first and that it was added later. However, an *Upaniśat* like this is given here to show that it is currently in practice.

शान्ति मन्त्रः । *Śānti Mantraḥ* ।

ॐ भद्रं कर्णेभिः शृणुयाम देवाः । भद्रं पश्येमाक्षभिर्यजत्राः ।

Oṃ Bhadraṃ Karṇebhiḥ Śṛṇuyāma Devāḥ ॥

Bhadraṃ Paśyemākṣabhiryajatrāḥ ॥
स्थिरैरङ्गैस्तुष्टुवाँसस्तनूभिः । व्यशेम देवहितं यदायुः ।

Sthirairaṅgaistuṣṭuvāg̃Sastanūbhiḥ ॥ *Vyaśema Devahitaṃ Yadāyuḥ* ॥
स्वस्ति न इन्द्रो वृद्धश्रवाः । स्वस्ति नः पूषा विश्ववेदाः ।

Svasti Na Indro Vṛddhaśravāḥ ॥ *Svasti Naḥ Pūṣā Viśvavedāḥ* ॥
स्वस्ति नस्ताक्ष्र्यो अरिष्टनेमिः । स्वस्ति नो बृहस्पतिर्दधातु ॥

Svasti Nastārkṣyo Ariṣṭanemiḥ ॥ *Svasti No Bṛhaspatirdadhātu* ॥
ॐ शान्तिः शान्तिः शान्तिः ॥ *Oṃ Śāntiḥ Śāntiḥ Śāntiḥ* ॥

हरिः ॐ । *Hariḥ Oṃ* ।

1. दिव्यानि धत्ते धत्ते दिव्यानि दिव्यानि धत्ते ।
धत्त इलल इलले धत्ते धत्त इलले ।
धत्त इति दत्ते । इलले वरुणो वरुण इलल इलले वरुणः ।
इलल इति इलले । वरुणो राजा राजा वरुणो वरुणो राजा ।
राजा पुनर्दुः पुनर्दू राजा राजा पुनर्दुः ।
पुनर्दुरिति पुनः दु :। ह्व्यामि मित्रो मित्रो ह्व्यामि ह्व्यामि मित्रो ।
मित्र इलामिलां मित्रो मित्र इलाम् । इलामिलल इलल इलामिलामिलले ।
इलल इलामिला मिलल इलल इलाम् । इलां वरुणो वरुण इलामिलां वरुणः ।

वरुणो मित्रो मित्रो वरुणो वरुणो मित्र: ।
मित्र स्तेज स्कामस्तेज स्कामो मित्रो मित्र स्तेज स्काम: । तेज स्काम इति तेज: काम: ॥

Divyāni Dhattĕ Dhattĕ Divyāni Divyāni Dhattĕ |

Dhatta Ilal Ilalĕ Dhatte Dhatta Ilalĕ |

Dhatta Iti Datte | Ilale Varuṇo Varuṇ Ilal Ilale Varuṇaḥ |

Ilal Iti Ilale | Varuṇo Rājā Rājā Varuṇo Varuṇo Rājā |

Rājā Punarduḥ Punardū Rājā Rājā Punarduḥ |

Punarduriti Punaḥ Duḥ | Hvyāmi Mitrŏ Mitrŏ Hvyāmi Hvyāmi Mitrŏ |

Mitra Ilāmilāan Mitrŏ Mitra Ilām | Ilāmilal Ilal Ilāmilāmilalĕ |

Ilal Ilāmilā Milal Ilal Ilām | Ilāan Varuṇŏ Varuṇ Ilāmilāan Varuṇaḥ |

Varuṇŏ Mitro Mitro Varuṇŏ Varuṇŏ Mitraḥ |

Mitra Stej Skāmastej Skāmŏ Mitro Mitra Stej Skāmaḥ |

Tej Skām Iti Tejaḥ Kāmaḥ ||

2. अया मिला मिला मया मया मिलां। इलां त्वं त्व मिला मिलां त्वम्।
त्व मर्यम मर्यमं त्वं त्व मर्यमम्। अर्यमं वरुणो वरुणो ऽर्यम मर्यमं वरुण: ।
वरुणो दध्म दध्म वरुणो वरुणो दध्म। दध्म दीर्घायु र्दीर्घायु र्दध्म दध्म दीर्घायु:।
दीर्घायु र्वहते वहते दीर्घायु र्दीर्घायु र्वहते। दीर्घायु रिति दीर्घायु:।
वहते सुय: सुयो वहते वहते सुय:। सुय इति सुय:।
होतार मिन्द्र इन्द्रो होतारं होतार मिन्द्र: । इन्द्रो होतारं होतार मिन्द्र इन्द्रो होतारम्।
इन्द्रो महा सुरेन्द्रो महा सुरेन्द्र इन्द्र इन्द्रो महा सुरेन्द्र:।
महा सुरेन्द्र: सप्त ऋषय: सप्त ऋषयो महा सुरेन्द्रो महा सुरेन्द्र: सप्त ऋषय: ।
सप्त ऋषय: सं सं सप्त ऋषय: सप्त ऋषय: सम्। सप्त ऋषय इति सप्त ऋषय: ।
सं तुष्ट तुष्ट सं सं तुष्ट। तुष्ट देवा देवास् तुष्ट तुष्ट देवा: । देवा इति देवा: ॥

Ayā Milā Milā Mayā Mayā Milāan | Ilāan Tvan Tva Milā Milāan Tvam |

Tva Maryam Maryaman Tvan Tva Maryamam |

Aryaman Varuṇŏ Varuṇŏ 'Ryam Maryaman Varuṇaḥ |

Varuṇŏ Dadhma Dadhma Varuṇŏ Varuṇŏ Dadhma | Dadhma Dīrghāyu Rdīrghāyu Rdadhma Dadhma Dīrghāyuḥ |

Dīrghāyu Rvahate Vahate Dīrghāyu Rdīrghāyu Rvahate |

Dīrghāyu Riti Dīrghāyuḥ I

Vahatĕ Suyaḥ Suyo Vahate Vahate Suyaḥ I *Suya Iti Suyaḥ* I

Hotār Mindra Indro Hotāran Hotār Mindraḥ I

Indro Hotāran Hotār Mindra Indrŏ Hotāram I

Indro Mahā Surendro Mahā Surendra Indra Indro Mahā Surendraḥ I
Mahā Surendraḥ Sapta Ṛuṣhayaḥ Sapta Ṛuṣhayo Mahā Surendro Mahā Surendraḥ Sapta Ṛuṣhayaḥ I

Sapta Ṛuṣhayaḥ San San Sapta Ṛuṣhayaḥ Sapta Ṛuṣhayaḥ Sam I

Sapta Ṛuṣhaya Iti Sapta Ṛuṣhayaḥ I

San Tuṣhṭa Tuṣhṭa San San Tuṣhṭa I

Tuṣhṭa Devā Devās Tuṣhṭa Tuṣhṭa Devāḥ I *Devā Iti Devāḥ* II

3. इलामिला मिलामिला मिलाम् । इलेला कबर्हो ऽकबर्ह इलेला कबर्हो ऽकबर्हो इलेला कबर्हो ऽकबर्ह इलेला कबर्हो ऽकबर्ह इलेला कबर्हो ऽकबर्हः ।
अकबर्हो ऽस्म्यकबर्हो ऽस्म्यकबर्हो ऽस्म्यकबर्हो ऽस्म्यकबर्हो ऽस्मि ॥

Ilāmilā Milāmilā Milām I *Ilelā Kabarho 'Kabarha Ilelā Kabarhŏ 'Kabarhŏ*

Ilelā Kabarhŏ 'Kabarha Ilelā Kabarhŏ 'Kabarha Ilelā Kabarhŏ 'Kabarha: I
Akabarhŏ 'Smyakabarhŏ 'Smyakabarhŏ 'Smyakabarhŏ 'Smyakabarhŏ 'Smi II

शान्ति मन्त्रः I *Śānti Mantraḥ* I

ॐ भद्रं कर्णेभिः शृणुयाम देवाः । भद्रंपश्येमाक्षभिर्यजत्राः ।

Oṃ Bhadraṃ Karṇebhiḥ Śṛṇuyāma Devāḥ II

Bhadraṃ Paśyemākṣabhiryajatrāḥ II
स्थिरैरङ्गैस्तुष्टुवाँसस्तनूभिः । व्यशेम देवहितं यदायुः ।

Sthirairaṅgaistuṣṭuvāg̃Sastanūbhiḥ II *Vyaśema Devahitaṃ Yadāyuḥ* II
स्वस्ति न इन्द्रो वृद्धश्रवाः । स्वस्ति नः पूषा विश्ववेदाः ।

Svasti Na Indro Vṛddhaśravāḥ II *Svasti Naḥ Pūṣā Viśvavedāḥ* II
स्वस्ति नस्ताक्ष्यो अरिष्टनेमिः । स्वस्ति नो बृहस्पतिर्दधातु ॥

Svasti Nastārkṣyo Ariṣṭanemiḥ || *Svasti No Bṛhaspatirdadhātu* ||
ॐ शान्तिः शान्तिः शान्तिः || *Oṃ Śāntiḥ Śāntiḥ Śāntiḥ* ||

इति अल्ला-उपनिषत् समाप्ता || *Iti Allāh Upaniśat Samāpatā* ||

*****

Kāmarājakīlitoddhāropaniṣat

कामराजकीलितोद्धारोपनिषत्

This is also another *Upaniṣat* from *Atharva Veda.*

शान्ति मन्त्रः । *Śānti Mantraḥ* ।

ॐ भद्रं कर्णेभिः शृणुयाम देवाः । भद्रं पश्येमाक्षभिर्यजत्राः ।

Oṃ Bhadraṃ Karṇebhiḥ Śṛṇuyāma Devāḥ ॥

Bhadraṃ Paśyemākṣabhiryajatrāḥ ॥
स्थिरैरङ्गैस्तुष्टुवाँसस्तनूभिः । व्यशेम देवहितं यदायुः ।

Sthirairaṅgaistuṣṭuvāg̃Sastanūbhiḥ ॥ *Vyaśema Devahitaṃ Yadāyuḥ* ॥
स्वस्ति न इन्द्रो वृद्धश्रवाः । स्वस्ति नः पूषा विश्ववेदाः ।

Svasti Na Indro Vṛddhaśravāḥ ॥ *Svasti Naḥ Pūṣā Viśvavedāḥ* ॥
स्वस्ति नस्तार्क्ष्यो अरिष्टनेमिः । स्वस्ति नो बृहस्पतिर्दधातु ॥

Svasti Nastārkṣyo Ariṣṭanemiḥ ॥ *Svasti No Bṛhaspatirdadhātu* ॥
ॐ शान्तिः शान्तिः शान्तिः ॥ *Oṃ Śāntiḥ Śāntiḥ Śāntiḥ* ॥

हरिः ॐ ॥ *Hariḥ Oṃ* ॥

1. अथोवाच कामराजम् । तदुपासनात् कुशलं लभेत् ।
श्रियं लभेत् । गुर्वीं वाणीं लभेत् । सर्वयुवतीनां प्रियो भवेत् ।
प्रथमं कामस्ततः शक्तिस्तदनु तुरीयं द्वावेतौ परैतानि पञ्चाक्षराणि भवन्ति ।
ततः शून्यं च द्वौ दिवाकरहरौ । तदनु गोत्रभृन्माया ।
एतानि षडक्षराणि भवन्ति । ततश्चन्द्रः प्रजापतिशक्रौ ।
ततो माया । एतानि चतुरक्षराणि भवन्ति ।
आद्यं वाग्भवं द्वितीयं कामराजं तृतीयं शक्तिबीजं शुक्लं तरुगदिवाकराभं
शशिकान्तं क्रमेण स्मरेत् । कफारादित्वात्कीलिता । कोटिजपात् सिद्धिर्न जायते ।
यदा मन्मथकलादिर्भवति तदा निष्कीलिता भवेत् । सिद्धिदा भवेत् ।
सा वीर्यवती भवेत् । त्रैलोक्यं वशमानयेत् । पूजनाद्दौर्भाग्यनाशो भवेत् ।
जपात् सिद्धीश्वरो भवेत् । इति शिवम् ॥

Athovāca Kāmarājam । *Tadupāsanāt Kuśalaṃ Labhet* । *Śriyaṃ Labhet* ।

Gurvīṃ Vāṇīṃ Labhet । *Sarvayuvatīnāṃ Priyo Bhavet* ।

Prathamaṃ Kāmastataḥ Śaktistadanu Turīyaṃ Dvāvetau Paraitāni Pañcākṣarāṇi Bhavanti | Tataḥ Śūnyaṃ Ca Dvau Divākaraharau | Tadanu Gotrabhṛnmāyā | Etāni Ṣaḍakṣarāṇi Bhavanti | Tataścandraḥ Prajāpatiśakrau | Tato Māyā | Etāni Caturakṣarāṇi Bhavanti | Ādyaṃ Vāgbhavaṃ Dvitīyaṃ Kāmarājaṃ Tṛtīyaṃ Śaktibījaṃ Śuklaṃ Tarugadivākarābhaṃ Śaśikāntaṃ Krameṇa Smaret | Kaphārāditvātkīlitā | Koṭijapāt Siddhirna Jāyate | Yadā Manmathakalādirbhavati Tadā Niṣkīlitā Bhavet | Siddhidā Bhavet | Sā Vīryavatī Bhavet | Trailokyaṃ Vaśamānayet | Pūjanāddaurbhāgyanāśo Bhavet | Japāt Siddhīśvaro Bhavet | Iti Śivam || 1

2. अथाद्यं शाम्भवं द्वितायं शाक्तं चेति गुरुमुखात्ज्ञातव्यम्। अन्यथा शापमाप्नुयात्। उपासना द्विविधा। शाम्भवं शाक्तं चेति। एवं लोपनाल्लोपा। प्रथमं शम्भुचन्द्रौ। तदनु दिवाकरेन्द्रौ। ततः पराबीजं वाग्भवम्। ततः कामराजं शिवचन्द्रकामशम्भुहरयः। पराबीजं शक्तिः। कामपरामध्ये देवराजमेतच्छक्तिकूटम्। एतेन पञ्चादशाक्षराणि भवन्ति। शम्भुप्रधानत्वाच्छाम्भवम्। पूर्णोहं शिवोऽहमद्वैतरूपोऽहं नित्यानन्दरूपोऽहं इति स्मरेत्। नापि पूजायां व्रतनियमः। सर्वदा जपं चरेत्। विनोदतः कामिनीमध्ये कामि नीर्दृष्ट्वा च सदानन्दरूपो भवेत्। दिव्याङ्गरागैर्देहं भूषयेत् सुगन्धमाल्याम्बरालङ्काराद्यैः। मांसाद्यैः शुद्धैः सुमधुरैर्भोजयेत्। भपञ्चकेन पूजा कार्या। सदा कौलिको भवेत्। कुलाचागत् सर्वसिद्धीश्वरो भवेत्। एकाकी शक्तियुक्तो भवेत्। मादनं भुक्त्वा शक्तिभुग्भवेत्। शक्तिचक्रं पूजयेत्। भोगेन शिवं मोक्षमाप्नुयात्। शक्तिहर्षोत्पादनाच्छक्तिः प्रीता भवति। इति शिवम्॥

Athādyaṃ Śāmbhavaṃ Dvitāyaṃ Śāktaṃ Ceti Gurumukhāt Jñātavyam | Anyathā Śāpamāpnuyāt | Upāsanā Dvividhā | Śāmbhavaṃ Śāktaṃ Ceti | Evaṃ Lopanāllopā |

Prathamaṃ Śambhucandrau | Tadanu Divākarendrau |

Tataḥ Parābījaṃ Vāgbhavam | Tataḥ Kāmarājaṃ

Śivacandrakāmaśambhuharayaḥ | Parābījaṃ Śaktiḥ |

Kāmaparāmadhye Devarājametacchaktikūṭam |

Etena Pañcādaśākṣarāṇi Bhavanti |

Śambhupradhānatvācchāmbhavam |

Pūrṇo'haṃ Śivo'hamadvaitarūpo'haṃ Nityānandarūpo'haṃ Iti Smaret |

Nāpi Pūjāyāṃ Vrataniyamaḥ | Sarvadā Japaṃ Caret |

Vinodataḥ Kāminīmadhye Kāmi Nīrdṛṣṭvā Ca Sadānandarūpo Bhavet |

Divyāṅgarāgaurdehaṃ Bhṛṣayet Sugandhamālyāmbarālaṅkārādyaiḥ |

Māṃsādyaiḥ Śuddhaiḥ Sumadhurairbhojayet |

Bhapañcakena Pūjā Kāryā | Sadā Kauliko Bhavet |

Kulācāgat Sarvasiddhīśvaro Bhavet | Ekākī Śaktiyukto Bhavet |

Mādanaṃ Bhuktvā Śaktibhugbhavet | Śakticakraṃ Pūjayet |

Bhogena Śivaṃ Mokṣamāpnuyāt |

Śaktiharṣotpādanācchaktiḥ Prītā Bhavati | Iti Śivam || 2

3. अथ वकुलैरर्चयेत्। रक्तपुष्पैरर्चयेत्। तदभावे जलैस्तदभाबे मानसीं भक्तिमाचरेत्। इति शिवम् ॥

Atha Vakulairarcayet | Raktapuṣpairarcayet | Tadabhāve

Jalaistadabhābe Mānasīṃ Bhaktimācaret | Iti Śivam || 3

शान्ति मन्त्रः | *Śānti Mantraḥ* |

ॐ भद्रं कर्णेभिः शृणुयाम देवाः। भद्रं पश्येमाक्षभिर्यजत्राः।

Oṃ Bhadraṃ Karṇebhiḥ Śṛṇuyāma Devāḥ ||

Bhadraṃ Paśyemākṣabhiryajatrāḥ ||
स्थिरैरङ्गैस्तुष्टुवाँसस्तनूभिः। व्यशेम देवहितं यदायुः।

Sthirairaṅgaistuṣṭuvāg̃Sastanūbhiḥ || Vyaśema Devahitaṃ Yadāyuḥ ||
स्वस्ति न इन्द्रो वृद्धश्रवाः। स्वस्ति नः पूषा विश्ववेदाः।

Svasti Na Indro Vṛddhaśravāḥ || *Svasti Naḥ Pūṣā Viśvavedāḥ* ||
स्वस्ति नस्ताक्ष्र्यो अरिष्टनेमिः । स्वस्ति नो बृहस्पतिर्दधातु ॥

Svasti Nastārkṣyo Ariṣṭanemiḥ || *Svasti No Bṛhaspatirdadhātu* ||

ॐ शान्तिः शान्तिः शान्तिः ॥ *Oṃ Śāntiḥ Śāntiḥ Śāntiḥ* ||

इत्याथर्वणशाखायां कामराजकीलितोद्धारोपनिषत् समाप्ता ।

Ityātharvaṇaśākhāyāṃ Kāmarājakīlitoddhāropaniṣat Samāptā |

*****

Kālikopaniṣat

कालिकोपनिषत्

This is also another *Upaniṣat* from *Atharva Veda*.

शान्ति मन्त्रः । *Śānti Mantraḥ* ।

ॐ भद्रं कर्णेभिः शृणुयाम देवाः । भद्रंपश्येमाक्षभिर्यजत्राः ।

Oṃ Bhadraṃ Karṇebhiḥ Śṛṇuyāma Devāḥ ॥

Bhadraṃ Paśyemākṣabhiryajatrāḥ ॥
स्थिरैरङ्गैस्तुष्टुवाँस्सस्तनूभिः । व्यशेम देवहितं यदायुः ।

Sthirairaṅgaistuṣṭuvāg̐Sastanūbhiḥ ॥ *Vyaśema Devahitaṃ Yadāyuḥ* ॥
स्वस्ति न इन्द्रो वृद्धश्रवाः । स्वस्ति नः पूषा विश्ववेदाः ।

Svasti Na Indro Vṛddhaśravāḥ ॥ *Svasti Naḥ Pūṣā Viśvavedāḥ* ॥
स्वस्ति नस्ताक्ष्यों अरिष्टनेमिः । स्वस्ति नो बृहस्पतिर्दधातु ॥

Svasti Nastārkṣyo Ariṣṭanemiḥ ॥ *Svasti No Bṛhaspatirdadhātu* ॥
ॐ शान्तिः शान्तिः शान्तिः ॥ *Oṃ Śāntiḥ Śāntiḥ Śāntiḥ* ॥

हरिः ॐ ॥ *Hariḥ Oṃ* ॥

अथ देनं ब्रह्मरन्ध्रे ब्रह्मरूपिणीमाप्नोति । सुभगां त्रिगुणितां मुक्तासुभगां कामरेफेन्दिरासमस्तरूपिणीमेतानि त्रिगुणितानि तदनु कूर्चबीजं व्योमषष्ठस्वरां विन्दुमेलनरूपां तद्द्वयं मायाद्वयं दक्षिणे कालिके चेत्यभिमुखगतां तदनु बाञ्जसप्तकमुच्चार्य बृहद्भानुजायामुच्चरेत्।

Atha Denaṃ Brahmarandhre Brahmarūpiṇīmāpnoti । *Subhagāṃ Triguṇitāṃ Muktāsubhagāṃ Kāmarephendirāsamastarūpiṇīmetāni Triguṇitāni Tadanu Kūrcabījaṃ Vyomaṣaṣṭhasvarāṃ Vindumelanarūpāṃ Taddvayaṃ Māyādvayaṃ Dakṣiṇe Kālike Cetyabhimukhagatāṃ Tadanu Bāñjasaptakamuccārya Bṛhadbhānujāyāmuccaret* ।

स तु शिवमयो भवेत् । सर्वसिद्धिश्वरो भवेत् । गतिस्तस्यास्तीति । नान्यस्य गतिरस्ताति । स तु वागीश्वरः । स तु नारीश्वरः । स तु देवेश्वरः । स तु सर्वेश्वरः । अभिनवजलदसङ्काशा घनस्तनी भटिहवेदष्टा शवागना कालिका ध्येया ।

Sa Tu Śivamayo Bhavet | Sarvasiddhiśvaro Bhavet | Gatistasyāstīti | Nānyasya Gatirastāti | Sa Tu Vāgīśvaraḥ | Sa Tu Nārīśvaraḥ | Sa Tu Deveśvaraḥ | Sa Tu Sarveśvaraḥ | Abhinavajaladasaṅkāśā Ghanastanī Bhaṭihavedaṣṭā Śavāganā Kālikā Dhyeyā |

त्रिणेणं पञ्चकोणं नवकोणं पद्मम्। तस्मिन् देवी सर्वाङ्गेऽभ्यर्च्य तदिदं र्वाङ्गं काली कापालिनी कुल्ला कुरुकुल्ला विरोधिनी विप्रचित्ता उग्रा उग्रप्रभा दीप्ता नीला घना बलाका भात्रा मुद्राऽमिता चैव पञ्चदशकोणगाः।

Triṇeṇaṃ Pañcakoṇaṃ Navakoṇaṃ Padmam |
Tasmin Devī Sarvāṅge'bhyarcya Tadidaṃ Rvāṅgaṃ Kālī Kāpālinī Kullā Kurukullā Virodhinī Vipracittā Ugrā Ugraprabhā Dīptā Nīlā Ghanā Balākā Bhātrā Mudrā'mitā Caiva Pañcadaśakoṇagāḥ |

ब्राह्मी नारायणी माहेश्वरी कौमारी। अपराजिता वाराही नारसिंहिका चेत्यष्टपत्रगाः।
पोडशम्वरभेदेन प्रथमेन मन्वविभागः। तन्मूलेनावाहनं तेनैव पूजनम्।
य एवं मन्त्रराजं नियमेन वा लक्षमावर्तयति स पाप्मानं हन्ति।
स ब्रह्मत्वं भजति। सः अमृतत्वं भजति। स आयुरारोग्यमैश्वर्यं भजति।
सदा पञ्चमकारेण पूजयेत्। सदा गुरुभक्तो भवेत्।
सदा देवभक्तो भवेत्। धर्मिष्ठतां पुष्टिमहतवाचं विप्रा लभन्ते।
मन्त्रजापिनो ह्यात्मा विद्याप्रपूरितो भवति। स जीवन्मुक्तो भवति।

Brāhmī Nārāyaṇī Māheśvarī Kaumārī |
Aparājitā Vārāhī Nārasiṃhikā Cetyaṣṭapatragāḥ |
Poḍaśamvarabhedena Prathamena Manvavibhāgaḥ |
Tanmūlenāvāhanaṃ Tenaiva Pūjanam |
Ya Evaṃ Mantrarājaṃ Niyamena Vā Lakṣamāvartayati Sa Pāpmānaṃ Hanti | Sa Brahmatvaṃ Bhajati | Saḥ Amṛtatvaṃ Bhajati |
Sa Āyurārogyamaiśvaryaṃ Bhajati | Sadā Pañcamakāreṇa Pūjayet |
Sadā Gurubhakto Bhavet | Sadā Devabhakto Bhavet |
Dharmiṣṭhatāṃ Puṣṭimahatavācaṃ Viprā Labhante |
Mantrajāpino Hyātmā Vidyāprapūrito Bhavati | Sa Jīvanmukto Bhavati |

स सर्वशास्त्रं जानाति। स सर्वपुण्यकारी भवति।

स सर्वयज्ञयाजी भवति। राजानो दासतां यान्ति। जप्त्वा स सर्वमेतं मन्त्रराजं स्वयं शिव एवाहमित्यणिमादिविभूतीनामीश्वरः कालिकां लभेत्॥

Sa Sarvaśāstraṃ Jānāti | Sa Sarvapuṇyakārī Bhavati | Sa Sarvayajñayājī Bhavati | Rājāno Dāsatāṃ Yānti | Japtvā Sa Sarvametaṃ Mantrarājaṃ Svayaṃ Śiva Evāhamityaṇimādivibhūtīnāmīśvaraḥ Kālikāṃ Labhet ||

आवयोः पात्रभूतः सन् सुकृती त्यक्तकल्मषः। जीवन्मुक्तः स विज्ञेयो यस्मै लब्धा हि दक्षिणा॥

Āvayoḥ Pātrabhūtaḥ San Sukṛtī Tyaktakalmaṣaḥ |
Jīvanmuktaḥ Sa Vijñeyo Yasmai Labdhā Hi Dakṣiṇā ||

दशांशं होमयेत्तदनु तर्पयेत्। अथ हैके यज्ञान्कामानद्वैतज्ञानादीननिरुद्धसरस्वतीति। अथ हैषः कालिकामनुजापी यः सदा शुद्धात्मा ज्ञानवैराग्ययुक्तः शाम्भवीदीक्षासु रक्तः शाक्तासु। यदि वा ब्रह्मचारी रात्रौ नग्नः सर्वदा मधुनाऽशक्तो मनसा जपपूजादिनियमवान्। योषित्प्रियकरो भगोदकेन तर्पणं तेनैव पूजनं कुर्यात्। सर्वदा कालिकारूपमात्मानं विभावयेत्। स सर्वदा योषिदासक्तो भवेत्। स सर्वहत्या तरति तेन मधुदानेन। अथ षञ्चमकारेण सर्वमायादिविद्यां पशुधनधान्यं सर्वेशत्वं च कवित्वं च।

Daśāṃśaṃ Homayettadanu Tarpayet | Atha Haike Yajñānkāmānadvaitajñānādīnaniruddhasarasvatīti | Atha Haiṣaḥ Kālikāmanujāpī Yaḥ Sadā Śuddhātmā Jñānavairāgyayuktaḥ Śāmbhavīdīkṣāsu Raktaḥ Śāktāsu | Yadi Vā Brahmacārī Rātrau Nagnaḥ Sarvadā Madhunā'śakto Manasā Japapūjādiniyamavān | Yoṣitpriyakaro Bhagodakena Tarpaṇaṃ Tenaiva Pūjanaṃ Kuryāt | Sarvadā Kālikārūpamātmānaṃ Vibhāvayet | Sa Sarvadā Yoṣidāsakto Bhavet | Sa Sarvahatyā Tarati Tena Madhudānena | Atha Ṣañcamakāreṇa Sarvamāyādividyāṃ Paśudhanadhānyaṃ Sarveśatvaṃ Ca Kavitvaṃ Ca |

नान्यः परमः पन्था विद्यते मोक्षाय ज्ञानाय धर्माधर्माय। तत्सर्वं भूतं भव्यं यत्किञ्चिद्दृश्यमानंस्थावरजङ्गमं तत्सर्वं कालिकातन्त्रे ओतं प्रोतं वेद। य एवं मनुजापी स पाप्मानं तरति। स भ्रूणहत्यां तरति। सोऽगम्यागमनं तरति। स सर्वसुखमाप्नोति। स सर्वं जानाति।

स सर्वसंन्यासई भवति । स विरक्तो भवति । ल्स सर्ववेदाध्यायी भवति ।
स सर्वमन्त्रजापी भवति । स सर्वशास्रवेत्ता भवति ।
स सर्वज्ञानकारी भवति । स आवयोर्मित्रभूतो भवति । इत्याह भगवान् शिवः ।
निर्विकल्पेन मनसा स वन्द्यो भवति ॥

Nānyaḥ Paramaḥ Panthā Vidyate Mokṣāya Jñānāya Dharmādharmāya |
Tatsarvaṃ Bhūtaṃ Bhavyaṃ Yatkiñciddṛśyamānaṃ
Sthāvarajaṅgamaṃ Tatsarvaṃ Kālikātantre Otaṃ Protaṃ Veda |
Ya Evaṃ Manujāpī Sa Pāpmānaṃ Tarati | Sa Bhrūṇahatyāṃ Tarati |
So'gamyāgamanaṃ Tarati | Sa Sarvasukhamāpnoti | Sa Sarvaṃ Jānāti |
Sa Sarvasaṃnyāsaī Bhavati | Sa Virakto Bhavati |
Lsa Sarvavedādhyāyī Bhavati | Sa Sarvamantrajāpī Bhavati |
Sa Sarvaśāsravettā Bhavati | Sa Sarvajñānakārī Bhavati |
Sa Āvayormitrabhūto Bhavati | Ityāha Bhagavān Śivaḥ |
Nirvikalpena Manasā Sa Vandyo Bhavati ||

अथ हैनाम् । *Atha Hainām |*

मूलाधारे स्मरेद्दिव्यं त्रिकोणं तेजसां निधिम् ।
शिखा आनीय तस्याग्नेरथ तूर्ध्वं व्यवस्थिता ॥

Mūlādhāre Smareddivyaṃ Trikoṇaṃ Tejasāṃ Nidhim |
Śikhā Ānīya Tasyāgneratha Tūrdhvaṃ Vyavasthitā ||

नलितोयदमध्यस्था विद्युल्लेखेव भास्वरा । नीवारशूकवत्तन्वी पीता भास्वत्यणूपमा ॥

Nalitoyadamadhyasthā Vidyullekheva Bhāsvarā |
Nīvāraśūkavattanvī Pītā Bhāsvatyaṇūpamā ||

तस्याः शिखाया मध्ये परमात्मा व्यवस्थितः । स ब्रह्मा स शिवः सेन्द्रः सोक्षरः परमः स्वराट् ॥

Tasyāḥ Śikhāyā Madhye Paramātmā Vyavasthitaḥ |
Sa Brahmā Sa Śivaḥ Sendraḥ Sokṣaraḥ Paramaḥ Svarāṭ ||

स एव विष्णुः स प्राणः स कालोऽग्निः स चन्द्रमाः ।
इति कुण्डलिनीं ध्यात्वा सर्वपापैः प्रमुच्यते ॥

Sa Eva Viṣṇuḥ Sa Prāṇaḥ Sa Kālo'gniḥ Sa Candramāḥ |

Iti Kuṇḍalinīṃ Dhyātvā Sarvapāpaiḥ Pramucyate ||

महापातकेभ्यः पूतो भूत्वा सर्वमन्त्रसिद्धिं कृत्वा भैरवो भवेत्।
महाकालभैरवोऽस्य ऋषिः। अनुष्टुप् छन्दः (उष्णिक् छन्दः)
कालिका देवता। ह्रीं बीजं ह्रूं शक्तिः क्रीं कीलकं अनिरुद्धसरस्वती देवता।
कवित्वे पाण्डित्यार्थे (धर्मार्थकाममोक्षार्थे) जपे विनियोगः।

Mahāpātakebhyaḥ Pūto Bhūtvā Sarvamantrasiddhiṃ Kṛtvā Bhairavo Bhavet | Mahākālabhairavo'sya Ṛṣiḥ |

Anuṣṭup Chandaḥ (Uṣṇik Chandaḥ) Kālikā Devatā |

Hrīṃ Bījaṃ Hrūṃ Śaktiḥ Krīṃ Kīlakaṃ Aniruddhasarasvatī Devatā |

Kavitve Pāṇḍityārthe (Dharmārthakāmamokṣārthe) Jape Viniyogaḥ |

इत्येवमृषिच्छन्दोदैवतं ज्ञात्वा मन्त्र साफल्यमश्नुते।

Ityevamṛṣicchandodaivataṃ Jñātvā Mantra Sāphalyamaśnute |

अथर्वविद्यां प्रथममेकं द्वयं त्रयं वा नामद्वयसम्पुटितं कृत्वा योजयेत्।
गतिम्तम्याम्तीति। नान्यस्य गतिरम्तीति। ॐ सत्यम्।

Atharvavidyāṃ Prathamamekaṃ Dvayaṃ Trayaṃ Vā Nāmadvayasamputitaṃ Kṛtvā Yojayet | Gatimtamyāmtīti |

Nānyasya Gatiramtīti | Oṃ Satyam |

ॐ तत्सत् ॥ *Oṃ Tatsat* ॥

अथ हैनं गुरुं परितोष्यैनं मन्त्रराजं गृह्णीयात्। मन्त्रराजं गुरुस्तमपि शिष्याय सत्कुलीनाय विद्याभक्ताय सुवेषां स्त्रियं स्पृष्ट्वा स्वयं निशायां निरुपद्रवः परिपूज्य एकाकी शिवगेहे लक्षं तदर्धं वा जपित्वा दद्यात्। ॐ ॐ सत्यं सत्यं सत्यम्।

Atha Hainaṃ Guruṃ Paritoṣyainaṃ Mantrarājaṃ Gṛhṇīyāt |
Mantrarājaṃ Gurustamapi Śiṣyāya Satkulīnāya Vidyābhaktāya Suveṣāṃ Striyaṃ Spṛṣṭvā Svayaṃ Niśāyāṃ Nirupadravaḥ Paripūjya Ekākī

Śivagehe Lakṣaṃ Tadardhaṃ Vā Japitvā Dadyāt |

Oṃ Oṃ Satyaṃ Satyaṃ Satyam |

नान्यप्रकारेण सिद्धिर्भवति ।

Nānyaprakāreṇa Siddhirbhavati |

अथाह वै कालिकामनोस्तारामनोस्त्रिपुरामनोः सर्वदुर्गामनोर्वा स्वरूपसिद्धिरेवमिति शिवम् ॥

Athāha Vai Kālikāmanostārāmanostripurāmanoḥ

Sarvadurgāmanorvā Svarūpasiddhirevamiti Śivam ||

शान्ति मन्त्रः | *Śānti Mantraḥ* |

ॐ भद्रं कर्णेभिः शृणुयाम देवाः । भद्रं पश्येमाक्षभिर्यजत्राः ।

Oṃ Bhadraṃ Karṇebhiḥ Śṛṇuyāma Devāḥ ||

Bhadraṃ Paśyemākṣabhiryajatrāḥ ||

स्थिरैरङ्गैस्तुष्टुवाँसस्तनूभिः । व्यशेम देवहितं यदायुः ।

Sthirairaṅgaistuṣṭuvāg̃Sastanūbhiḥ || *Vyaśema Devahitaṃ Yadāyuḥ* ||

स्वस्ति न इन्द्रो वृद्धश्रवाः । स्वस्ति नः पूषा विश्ववेदाः ।

Svasti Na Indro Vṛddhaśravāḥ || *Svasti Naḥ Pūṣā Viśvavedāḥ* ||

स्वस्ति नस्तार्क्ष्यो अरिष्टनेमिः । स्वस्ति नो बृहस्पतिर्दधातु ॥

Svasti Nastārkṣyo Ariṣṭanemiḥ || *Svasti No Bṛhaspatirdadhātu* ||

ॐ शान्तिः शान्तिः शान्तिः ॥ *Oṃ Śāntiḥ Śāntiḥ Śāntiḥ* ||

इत्याथर्वणे सौभाग्यकाण्डे कालिकोपनिषत् समाप्ता ।

Ityātharvaṇe Saubhāgyakāṇḍe Kālikopaniṣat Samāptā |

Kālīmedhādīkṣitopaniṣat

कालीमेधादीक्षितोपनिषत्

This is also another *Upaniṣat* from *Atharva Veda.*

शान्ति मन्त्रः । *Śānti Mantraḥ* ।

ॐ भद्रं कर्णेभिः शृणुयाम देवाः । भद्रं पश्येमाक्षभिर्यजत्राः ।

Oṃ Bhadraṃ Karṇebhiḥ Śṛṇuyāma Devāḥ ||

Bhadraṃ Paśyemākṣabhiryajatrāḥ ||
स्थिरैरङ्गैस्तुष्टुवाँसस्तनूभिः । व्यशेम देवहितं यदायुः ।

Sthirairaṅgaistuṣṭuvāg̃Sastanūbhiḥ || *Vyaśema Devahitaṃ Yadāyuḥ* ||
स्वस्ति न इन्द्रो वृद्धश्रवाः । स्वस्ति नः पूषा विश्ववेदाः ।

Svasti Na Indro Vṛddhaśravāḥ || *Svasti Naḥ Pūṣā Viśvavedāḥ* ||
स्वस्ति नस्तार्क्ष्यो अरिष्टनेमिः । स्वस्ति नो बृहस्पतिर्दधातु ॥

Svasti Nastārkṣyo Ariṣṭanemiḥ || *Svasti No Bṛhaspatirdadhātu* ||
ॐ शान्तिः शान्तिः शान्तिः ॥ *Oṃ Śāntiḥ Śāntiḥ Śāntiḥ* ||

हरिः ॐ ॥ *Hariḥ Oṃ* ॥

अथाह वै देवानां पत्नीं भजते । तस्योपासकोऽन्यां गच्छन्
ॐ अथैनां मेधादीक्षितरूपिणीं भावयेत् । स शिवो भवेत् ।
स कालीरूपो भवेत् । सोऽयं मेधास्पर्शमणिकालीं दीक्षयेत् ।
ततश्चिन्तामणिकालीं दीक्षयेत् । ततः सिद्धकाल्यधिकारी भवेत् । ततो विद्याराज्ञीं जपेत् ।
ततः कामकलाकालीं परारूपिणीं जपेत् । ततश्चरणदीक्षारूपिणीं हंसकालीं यजेत् ।
रक्तशुक्लमिश्रनिर्वाणरूपिणीं यजेत् । सर्वनिर्वाणदीक्षितो भवेत् ।
ततः शाम्भवादीक्षितो भवेत् । गुह्यकाल्यधिष्ठितो भवेत् ।
शिवो भवेत् । स परारूपो भवेत् । परात् पररूपो भवेत् ।
परात् परातीतरूपो भवेत् । चित्परारूपो भवेत् । चित्परात् परारूपो भवेत् ।
चित्परात् परातीतरूपो भवेत् । ब्रह्मविष्णुरुद्रेश्वरसदाशिवमहाकालचित्पराम्बारूपो भवेत् ।
स ब्रह्मत्वं गच्छति । मेधादीक्षां लभेत् ।
मेधादीक्षातः परा दीक्षा न विद्यत इत्याह भगवान् शिवः । स्पर्शविद्यया देहशुद्धिर्भवेत् ।
ततश्चिन्तामाणिविद्याधिकारी विद्याराज्ञीं लभेत् ।
विद्याराज्यधिकारी तु षोढां जपेत् । तुर्याषोढाधिकारी कामकलां जपेत् ।

कामकलाधिकारी चरणरूपिणीं जपेत्। हंसदीक्षितो भवेत्।
चरणाधिकारी षट्छाम्भवसम्पन्नो भवेत्। गुह्यकाल्यधिष्ठितो भवेत्।
ततो मेधां चरेत्। जीवको हि भूङ्गत्वं गच्छति। भूरङ्गीभूत्वा षट् चक्राणि निर्भिन्द्यात्।
ततः परागभुग्भवेत्। परकायप्रवेशवान वयस्स्थैर्यं चरेत्। कामरूपत्वं गच्छति।
षष्टिसिद्धीश्वरो भवेदिति शिवप्रोक्तं वेद ॥

Athāha Vai Devānāṃ Patnīṃ Bhajate | Tasyopāsako'nyāṃ Gacchan Oṃ
Athaināṃ Medhādīkṣitarūpiṇīṃ Bhāvayet | Sa Śivo Bhavet |
Sa Kālīrūpo Bhavet | So'yaṃ Medhāsparśamaṇikālīṃ Dīkṣayet |
Tataścintāmaṇikālīṃ Dīkṣayet | Tataḥ Siddhakālyadhikārī Bhavet |
Tato Vidyārājñīṃ Japet | Tataḥ Kāmakalākālīṃ Parārūpiṇīṃ Japet |
Tataścaraṇadīkṣārūpiṇīṃ Haṃsakālīṃ Yajet |
Raktaśuklamiśranirvāṇarūpiṇīṃ Yajet |
Sarvanirvāṇadīkṣito Bhavet | Tataḥ Śāmbhavādīkṣito Bhavet |
Guhyakālyadhiṣṭhito Bhavet | Śivo Bhavet | Sa Parārūpo Bhavet |
Parāt Pararūpo Bhavet | Parāt Parātītarūpo Bhavet |
Citparārūpo Bhavet | Citparāt Parārūpo Bhavet |
Citparāt Parātītarūpo Bhavet |
Brahmaviṣṇurudreśvarasadāśivamahākālacitparāmbārūpo Bhavet |
Sa Brahmatvaṃ Gacchati | Medhādīkṣāṃ Labhet |
Medhādīkṣātaḥ Parā Dīkṣā Na Vidyata Ityāha Bhagavān Śivaḥ |
Sparśavidyayā Dehaśuddhirbhavet |
Tataścintāmāṇividyādhikārī Vidyārājñīṃ Labhet |
Vidyārājyadhikārī Tu Ṣoḍhāṃ Japet |
Turyāṣoḍhādhikārī Kāmakalāṃ Japet |
Kāmakalādhikārī Caraṇarūpiṇīṃ Japet | Haṃsadīkṣito Bhavet |
Caraṇādhikārī Ṣaṭchāmbhavasampanno Bhavet |
Guhyakālyadhiṣṭhito Bhavet | Tato Medhāṃ Caret |
Jīvako Hi Bhūṅgatvaṃ Gacchati |

Bhūraṅgībhūtvā Ṣaṭ Cakrāṇi Nirbhindyāt | Tataḥ Parāgabhugbhavet |

Parakāyapraveśavāna Vayassthairyaṃ Caret |

Kāmarūpatvaṃ Gacchati |

Ṣaṣṭisiddhīśvaro Bhavediti Śivaproktaṃ Veda ||

शान्ति मन्त्रः | *Śānti Mantraḥ* |

ॐ भद्रं कर्णेभिः शृणुयाम देवाः । भद्रं पश्येमाक्षभिर्यजत्राः ।

Oṃ Bhadraṃ Karṇebhiḥ Śṛṇuyāma Devāḥ ||

Bhadraṃ Paśyemākṣabhiryajatrāḥ ||
स्थिरैरङ्गैस्तुष्टुवाँसस्तनूभिः । व्यशेम देवहितं यदायुः ।

SthirairaṅgaistuṣṭuvāğSastanūbhiḥ || Vyaśema Devahitaṃ Yadāyuḥ ||
स्वस्ति न इन्द्रो वृद्धश्रवाः । स्वस्ति नः पूषा विश्ववेदाः ।

Svasti Na Indro Vṛddhaśravāḥ || Svasti Naḥ Pūṣā Viśvavedāḥ ||
स्वस्ति नस्तार्क्ष्यो अरिष्टनेमिः । स्वस्ति नो बृहस्पतिर्दधातु ॥

Svasti Nastārkṣyo Ariṣṭanemiḥ || Svasti No Bṛhaspatirdadhātu ||
ॐ शान्तिः शान्तिः शान्तिः ॥ *Oṃ Śāntiḥ Śāntiḥ Śāntiḥ ||*

इत्याथर्वणे सौभाग्यकाण्डे कालीमेधादीक्षितोपनिषत् समाप्ता ।

Ityātharvaṇe Saubhāgyakāṇḍe Kālīmedhādīkṣitopaniṣat Samāptā |

Gāyatrīrahasyopaniṣat

गायत्रीरहस्योपनिषत्

This is also another Upaniṣat from Atharva Veda.

शान्ति मन्त्रः । *Śānti Mantraḥ* ।

ॐ भद्रं कर्णेभिः शृणुयाम देवाः । भद्रं पश्येमाक्षभिर्यजत्राः ।

Oṃ Bhadraṃ Karṇebhiḥ Śṛṇuyāma Devāḥ ॥

Bhadraṃ Paśyemākṣabhiryajatrāḥ ॥
स्थिरैरङ्गैस्तुष्टुवाँसस्तनूभिः । व्यशेम देवहितं यदायुः ।

Sthirairaṅgaistuṣṭuvāg̃Sastanūbhiḥ ॥ *Vyaśema Devahitaṃ Yadāyuḥ* ॥
स्वस्ति न इन्द्रो वृद्धश्रवाः । स्वस्ति नः पूषा विश्ववेदाः ।

Svasti Na Indro Vṛddhaśravāḥ ॥ *Svasti Naḥ Pūṣā Viśvavedāḥ* ॥
स्वस्ति नस्तार्क्ष्यो अरिष्टनेमिः । स्वस्ति नो बृहस्पतिर्दधातु ॥

Svasti Nastārkṣyo Ariṣṭanemiḥ ॥ *Svasti No Bṛhaspatirdadhātu* ॥
ॐ शान्तिः शान्तिः शान्तिः ॥ *Oṃ Śāntiḥ Śāntiḥ Śāntiḥ* ॥

हरिः ॐ ॥ *Hariḥ Oṃ* ॥

ॐ स्वस्ति सिद्धम् । ॐ नमो ब्रह्मणे ।
ॐ नमस्कृत्य याज्ञवल्क्य ऋषिः स्वयंभुवं परिपृच्छति ।
हे ब्रह्मन् गायत्र्या उत्पत्तिः श्रोतुमिच्छामि । अथातो वसिष्ठः स्वयंभुवं परिपृच्छति ।
यो ब्रह्मा स ब्रह्मोवाच । ब्रह्मज्ञानोत्पत्तेः प्रकृतिं व्याख्यास्यामः ।
को नाम स्वयंभू पुरुष इति । तेनाङ्गुलीमथ्यमानात् सलिलमभवत् ।
सलिलात् फेनमभवत् । फेनाद्बुद्बुदमभवत् बुद्बुदादण्डमभवत् । अण्डाद्ब्रह्माभवत् ।
ब्रह्मणो वायुरभवत् । वायोरग्निरभवत् ।अग्नेरोङ्कारोऽभवत् । ओङ्काराद्व्याहृतिरभवत् ।
व्याहृत्या गायत्र्यभवत् । गायत्र्या सावित्र्यभवत् । सावित्र्या सरस्वत्यभवत् ।
सरस्वत्या सर्वे वेदा अभवन् । सर्वेभ्यो वेदेभ्यः सर्वे लोका अभवन् ।
सर्वेभ्यो लोकेभ्यः सर्वे प्राणिनोऽभवन् ।

Oṃ Svasti Siddham । *Oṃ Namo Brahmaṇe* ।

Oṃ Namaskṛtya Yājñavalkya Ṛṣiḥ Svayaṃbhuvaṃ Paripṛcchati ।

He Brahman Gāyatryā Utpattiḥ Śrotumicchāmi ।

Athāto Vasiṣṭhaḥ Svayaṃbhuvaṃ Paripṛcchati |

Yo Brahmā Sa Brahmovāca |

Brahmajñānotpatteḥ Prakṛtiṃ Vyākhyāsyāmaḥ |

Ko Nāma Svayaṃbhū Puruṣa Iti |

Tenāṅgulīmathyamānāt Salilamabhavat | Salilāt Phenamabhavat |

Phenādbudbudamabhavat | Budbudādaṇḍamabhavat |

Aṇḍādbrahmābhavat | Brahmaṇo Vāyurabhavat | Vāyoragnirabhavat |

Agneroṅkāro'bhavat | Oṅkārādvyāhṛtirabhavat |

Vyāhṛtyā Gāyatryabhavat |Gāyatryā Sāvitryabhavat |

Sāvitryā Sarasvatyabhavat | Sarasvatyā Sarve Vedā Abhavan |

Sarvebhyo Vedebhyaḥ Sarve Lokā Abhavan |

Sarvebhyo Lokebhyaḥ Sarve Prāṇino'bhavan |

अथातो गायत्री व्याहृतयश्च प्रवर्तन्ते।
का च गायत्री काश्च व्याहृतयः।
किं भूः किं भुवः किं सुवः किं महः किं जनः किं तपः
किं सत्यं किं तत् किं सवितुः किं वरेण्यं किं भर्गः
किं देवस्य किं धीमहि किं धियः किं यः किं नः किं प्रचोदयात्।

Athāto Gāyatrī Vyāhṛtayaśca Pravartante |

Kā Ca Gāyatrī Kāśca Vyāhṛtayaḥ |

Kiṃ Bhūḥ Kiṃ Bhuvaḥ Kiṃ Suvaḥ Kiṃ Mahaḥ Kiṃ Janaḥ Kiṃ Tapaḥ
Kiṃ Satyaṃ Kiṃ Tat Kiṃ Savituḥ Kiṃ Vareṇyaṃ Kiṃ Bhargaḥ
Kiṃ Devasya Kiṃ Dhīmahi Kiṃ Dhiyaḥ Kiṃ Yaḥ Kiṃ Naḥ

Kiṃ Pracodayāt |

ॐ भूरिति भुवो लोकः। भुव इत्यन्तरिक्षलोकः।स्वरिति स्वर्गलोकः।
मह इति महर्लोकः। जन इति जनोलोकः। तप इति तपोलोकः। सत्यमिति सत्यलोकः।
तदिति तदसौ तेजोमय तेजोऽग्निर्देवता। सवितुरिति सविता सावित्रमादित्यो वै।
वरेण्यमित्यत्र प्रजापतिः। भर्ग इत्यापो वै भर्गः।
देवस्य इतीन्द्रो देवो द्योतत इति स इन्द्रस्तस्मात् सर्वपुरुषो नाम रुद्रः।
धीमहीत्यन्तरात्मा। धिय इत्यन्तरात्मा परः।

य इति सदाशिवपुरुषः । नो इत्यस्माकं स्वधर्मे ।
प्रचोदयादिति प्रचोदित काम इमान् लोकान् प्रत्याश्रयते यः परो धर्म इत्येषा गायत्री ।
सा च किं गोत्रा कत्यक्षरा कतिपादा । कति कुक्षयः ।

Oṃ Bhūriti Bhuvo Lokaḥ | Bhuva Ityantarikṣalokaḥ |

Svariti Svargalokaḥ | Maha Iti Maharlokaḥ | Jana Iti Janolokaḥ |

Tapa Iti Tapolokaḥ | Satyamiti Satyalokaḥ |

Taditi Tadasau Tejomaya Tejo'gnirdevatā |

Savituriti Savitā Sāvitramādityo Vai | Vareṇyamityatra Prajāpatiḥ |

Bharga Ityāpo Vai Bhargaḥ | Devasya Itīndro Devo Dyotata Iti

Sa Indrastasmāt Sarvapuruṣo Nāma Rudraḥ |

Dhīmahītyantarātmā | Dhiya Ityantarātmā Paraḥ |

Ya Iti Sadāśivapuruṣaḥ | No Ityasmākaṃ Svadharme |
Pracodayāditi Pracodita Kāma Imān Lokān
Pratyāśrayate Yaḥ Paro Dharma Ityeṣā Gāyatrī |

Sā Ca Kiṃ Gotrā Katyakṣarā Katipādā | Kati Kukṣayaḥ |

कानि शीर्षाणि । सांख्यायनगोत्रा स चतुर्विंशत्यक्षरा
गायत्री त्रिपादा चतुष्पादा । पुनस्तस्याश्चत्वारः पादाः षट् कुक्षिकाः पञ्च शीर्षाणि भवन्ति ।
के च पादाः काश्च कुक्षयः कानि शीर्षाणि ।
ऋग्वेदोऽस्याः प्रथमः पादो भवति । यजुर्वेदो द्वितीयः पादः ।
सामवेदस्तृतीयः पादः । अथर्ववेदश्चतुर्थः पादः ।
पूर्वा दिक् प्रथमा कुक्षिर्भवति । दक्षिणा द्वितीया कुक्षिर्भवति ।
पश्चिमा तृतीया कुक्षिर्भवति । उत्तरा चतुर्थी कुक्षिर्भवति ।
ऊर्ध्वं पञ्चमी कुक्षिर्भवति । अधः षष्ठी कुक्षिर्भवति ।
व्याकरणोऽस्याः प्रथमः शीर्षो भवति । शिक्षा द्वितीयः।
कल्पस्तृतीयः । निरुक्तश्चतुर्थः । ज्योतिषामयनमिति पञ्चमः ।
का दिक् को वर्णः किमायतनं कः स्वरः किं लक्षणम्
कानि अक्षरदैवतानि क ऋषयः कानि छन्दांसि का शक्तयः कानि तत्त्वानि के चावयवाः ।
पूर्वायां भवतु गायत्री । मध्यमायां भवतु सावित्री ।
पश्चिमायां भवतु सरस्वती । रक्तागायत्री । श्वेता सावित्री । कृष्णा सरस्वती ।
पृथिव्यन्तरिक्षं द्यौरायतनानि । अकारोकारमकाररूपोदात्तादिस्वरात्मिका ।

पूर्वा सन्ध्या हंसवाहिनी ब्राह्मी। मध्यमा वृषभवाहिनी माहेश्वरी।
पश्चिमा गरुडवाहिनी वैष्णवी। पूर्वाह्णकालिका सन्ध्या गायत्री कुमारी
रक्ता रक्ताङ्गी रक्तवासिनीरक्तगन्धमाल्यानुलेपनी
पाशाकुशाङ्क्षमालाकमण्डलुवरहस्ता हंसारूढा ब्रह्मदैवत्या ऋग्वेदसहिता
आदित्यपथगामिनी भूमण्डलवासिनी।
मध्याह्नकालिका सन्ध्या सावित्री युवती श्वेताङ्गी
श्वेतवासिनीश्वेतगन्धमाल्यानुलेपनी त्रिशूलडमरुहस्ता
वृषभारूढा रुद्रदैवत्यायजुर्वेदसहिता आदित्यपथगामिनी भुवोलोके व्यवस्थिता।
सायं सन्ध्या सरस्वती वृद्धा कृष्णाङ्गी कृष्णवासिनी कृष्णगन्धमाल्यानुलेपना
शङ्खचक्रगदाभयहस्ता गरुडारूढा विष्णुदैवत्या सामवेदसहिता आदित्यपथगामिनी
स्वर्गलोकव्यवस्थिता। अग्निवायुसूर्यरूपाऽऽवहनीयगार्हपत्यदक्षिणाग्निरूपा ऋग्यजु सामरूपा
भूर्भुवःस्वरिति व्याहृतिरूपा प्रातर्मध्याह्नतृतीयसवनात्मिका सत्त्वरजस्तमोगुणात्मिका
जाग्रत्स्वप्नसुषुप्तरूपा वसुरुद्रादित्यरूपा गायत्रीत्रिष्टुब्जगतीरूपा ब्रह्मशङ्करविष्णुरूपेच्छा
ज्ञानक्रियाशक्तिरूपा स्वराड्विराड्वषड्ब्रह्मरूपेति।
प्रथममाग्नेयं द्वितीयं प्राजापत्यं तृतीयं सौम्यं चतुर्थमीशानं पञ्चममादित्यं षष्ठं गार्हपत्यं
सप्तमं मैत्रमष्टमं भगदैवतं नवममार्यमणं दशमं सावित्रमेकादशं त्वाष्ट्रं
द्वादशं पौष्णं त्रयोदशमैद्राग्नं चतुर्दशं वायव्यं पञ्चदशं वामदेवं षोडषं मैत्रावरुं
सप्तदशं भ्रातृव्यमष्टादशं वैष्णवमेकोनविंशं वामनंविंशं वैश्वदेवमेकविंशं रौद्रंद्वाविंशं कौबेरं
त्रयोविंशमाश्विनं चतुर्विंशं ब्राह्ममिति प्रत्यक्षरदैवतानि।
प्रथमं वासिष्ठं द्वितीयं भारद्वाजं तृतीयं गार्ग्यं चतुर्थमुपमन्यवं पञ्चमं भार्गवं षष्ठं शाण्डिल्यं
सप्तमं लोहितमाष्टमं वैष्णवं नवमं शातातपं दशमं सनत्कुमारमेकादशं वेदव्यासं द्वाशं
शुकं त्रयोदशं पाराशर्यं चतुर्दशं पौण्ड्रकं पञ्चदशं क्रतुंषोडशं दाक्षं सप्तदशं
काश्यपमष्टादशमात्रेयम् एकोनविंशमगस्त्यं विंशमौद्दालकमेकविंशमाङ्गिरसं द्वाविंशं नामिकेतुं
त्रयोविंशं मौद्गल्यं चतुर्विंशमाङ्गिरसवैश्वामित्रमिति प्रत्यक्षराणामृषयो भवन्ति।
गायत्रीत्रिष्टुब्जगत्यनुष्टुप्पङ्क्तिर्बृहत्युष्णिगदितिरिति त्रिरावृत्तेन छन्दांसि प्रतिपाद्यन्ते।

Kāni Śīrṣāṇi | Sāṃkhyāyanagotrā Sa Caturviṃśatyakṣarā

Gāyatrī Tripādā Catuṣpādā | Punastasyāścatvāraḥ Pādāḥ Ṣaṭ Kukṣikāḥ

Pañca Śīrṣāṇi Bhavanti | Ke Ca Pādāḥ Kāśca Kukṣayaḥ Kāni Śīrṣāṇi |

Ṛgvedo'syāḥ Prathamaḥ Pādo Bhavati | Yajurvedo Dvitīyaḥ Pādaḥ |

Sāmavedastṛtīyaḥ Pādaḥ | Atharvavedaścaturthaḥ Pādaḥ |

Pūrvā Dik Prathamā Kukṣirbhavati | Dakṣiṇā Dvitīyā Kukṣirbhavati |

Paścimā Tṛtīyā Kukṣirbhavati । Uttarā Caturthī Kukṣirbhavati ।

Ūrdhvaṃ Pañcamī Kukṣirbhavati । Adhaḥ Ṣaṣṭhī Kukṣirbhavati ।

Vyākaraṇo'syāḥ Prathamaḥ Śīrṣo Bhavati । Śikṣā Dvitīyaḥ ।

Kalpastṛtīyaḥ । Niruktaścaturthaḥ । Jyotiṣāmayanamiti Pañcamaḥ ।

Kā Dik Ko Varṇaḥ Kimāyatanaṃ Kaḥ Svaraḥ Kiṃ Lakṣaṇam, Kāni Akṣaradaivatāni Ka Ṛṣayaḥ Kāni Chandāṃsi Kā Śaktayaḥ

Kāni Tattvāni Ke Cāvayavāḥ । Pūrvāyāṃ Bhavatu Gāyatrī ।

Madhyamāyāṃ Bhavatu Sāvitrī । Paścimāyāṃ Bhavatu Sarasvatī ।

Raktā Gāyatrī । Śvetā Sāvitrī । Kṛṣṇā Sarasvatī ।

Pṛthivyantarikṣaṃ Dyaurāyatanāni ।

Akārokāramakārarūpodāttādisvarātmikā ।

Pūrvā Sandhyā Haṃsavāhinī Brāhmī ।

Madhyamā Vṛṣabhavāhinī Māheśvarī ।

Paścimā Garuḍavāhinī Vaiṣṇavī ।

Pūrvāhṇakālikā Sandhyā Gāyatrī Kumārī Raktā Raktāṅgī Raktavāsinīraktagandhamālyānulepanī Pāśākuśāṅkṣamālākamaṇḍaluvarahastā Haṃsārūḍhā Brahmadaivatyā Ṛgvedasahitā

Ādityapathagāminī Bhūmaṇḍalavāsinī ।

Madhyāhnakālikā Sandhyā Sāvitrī Yuvatī Śvetāṅgī Śvetavāsinīśvetagandhamālyānulepanī Triśūlaḍamaruhastā Vṛṣabhārūḍhā Rudradaivatyāyajurvedasahitā Ādityapathagāminī

Bhuvoloke Vyavasthitā ।

Sāyaṃ Sandhyā Sarasvatī Vṛddhā Kṛṣṇāṅgī Kṛṣṇavāsinī Kṛṣṇagandhamālyānulepanā Śaṅkhacakragadābhayahastā Garuḍārūḍhā Viṣṇudaivatyā Sāmavedasahitā Ādityapathagāminī

Svargalokavyavasthitā ।

Agnivāyusūryarūpā''vahanīyagārhapatyadakṣiṇāgnirūpā Ṛgyaju Sāmarūpā Bhūrbhuvaḥsvariti Vyāhṛtirūpā Prātarmadhyāhnatṛtīyasavanātmikā Sattvarajastamoguṇātmikā Jāgratsvapnasuṣuptarūpā Vasurudrādityarūpā Gāyatrītriṣṭubjagatīrūpā Brahmaśaṅkaraviṣṇurūpecchā-

Jñānakriyāśaktirūpā Svarāḍvirāḍvaṣaḍbrahmarūpeti ।

Prathamamāgneyaṃ Dvitīyaṃ Prājāpatyaṃ Tṛtīyaṃ Saumyaṃ Caturthamīśānaṃ Pañcamamādityaṃ Ṣaṣṭhaṃ Gārhapatyaṃ Saptamaṃ Maitramaṣṭamaṃ Bhagadaivataṃ Navamamāryamaṇaṃ Daśamaṃ Sāvitramekādaśaṃ Tvāṣṭraṃ Dvādaśaṃ Pauṣṇaṃ Trayodaśamaidrāgnaṃ Caturdaśaṃ Vāyavyaṃ Pañcadaśaṃ Vāmadevaṃ Ṣoḍaṣaṃ Maitrāvaruṇaṃ Saptadaśaṃ Bhrātṛvyamaṣṭādaśaṃ Vaiṣṇavamekonaviṃśaṃ Vāmanaṃ Viṃśaṃ Vaiśvadevamekaviṃśaṃ Raudraṃ Dvāviṃśaṃ Kauberaṃ Trayoviṃśamāśvinaṃ Caturviṃśaṃ Brāhmamiti Pratyakṣaradaivatāni | Prathamaṃ Vāsiṣṭhaṃ Dvitīyaṃ Bhāradvājaṃ Tṛtīyaṃ Gārgyaṃ Caturthamupamanyavaṃ Pañcamaṃ Bhārgavaṃ Ṣaṣṭhaṃ Śāṇḍilyaṃ Saptamaṃ Lohitamāṣṭamaṃ Vaiṣṇavaṃ Navamaṃ Śātātapaṃ Daśamaṃ Sanatkumāramekādaśaṃ Vedavyāsaṃ Dvādaśaṃ Śukaṃ Trayodaśaṃ Pārāśaryaṃ Caturdaśaṃ Pauṇḍrakaṃ Pañcadaśaṃ Kratuṃ Ṣoḍaśaṃ Dākṣaṃ Saptadaśaṃ Kāśyapamaṣṭādaśamātreyam-Ekonaviṃśamagastyaṃ Viṃśamauddālakamekaviṃśamāṅgirasaṃ Dvāviṃśaṃ Nāmiketuṃ Trayoviṃśaṃ Maudgalyaṃ Caturviṃśamāṅgirasa Vaiśvāmitramiti Pratyakṣarāṇāmṛṣayo Bhavanti | Gāyatrītriṣṭubjagatyanuṣṭuppaṅktirbṛhatyuṣṇigaditiriti Trirāvṛttena Chandāṃsi Pratipādyante |

प्रह्लादिनी प्रज्ञाविश्वभद्रा विलासिनी प्रभा शान्ता मा कान्ति स्पर्शा दुर्गा सरस्वती विरूपा विशालाक्षी शालिनी व्यापिनी विमला तमोऽपहारिणीसूक्ष्मावयवा पद्मालया विरजा विश्वरूपा भद्रा कृपासर्वतोमुखीति चतुर्विंशतिशक्तयो निगद्यन्ते। पृथिव्यप्तेजोवाय्वाकाशगन्धरसरूपस्पर्शशब्दवाक्यानि पादपायूपस्थत्वक्चक्षु श्रोत्रजिह्वाघ्राणमनोबुद्ध्यहङ्कार चित्तज्ञानानीति प्रत्यक्षराणां तत्त्वानि प्रतीयन्ते। चम्पकातसीकुङ्कुमपिङ्गलेन्द्रनीलाग्निप्रभोद्यत्सूर्य विद्युत्तारक सरोज गौर मरतक शुक्ल कुन्देन्दु शङ्ख पाण्डु नेत्रनीलोत्पलचन्दनागुरुकस्तूरीगोरोचनघनसारसन्निभं प्रत्यक्षरमनुस्मृत्य समस्तपातकोपपातकमहापातका-गम्यागमनगोहत्याब्रह्महत्याभ्रूणहत्यावीरहत्या-पुरुष हत्या ऽऽजन्म कृत हत्या स्त्रीहत्या गुरुहत्या पितृहत्या- प्राणहत्याचराचरहत्याऽभक्ष्यभक्षणप्रतिग्रह-स्वकर्मविच्छेदनस्वाम्यार्तिहीनकर्मकरणपरधनापहरण शूद्रान्नभोजन शत्रु मारण चण्डाली गमनादिसमस्त-पापहरणार्थं संस्मरेत्।

Prahlādinī Prajñāviśvabhadrā Vilāsinī Prabhā Śāntā Mā Kānti Sparśā Durgā Sarasvatī Virūpā Viśālākṣī Śālinī Vyāpinī Vimalā

Tamo'pahāriṇīsūkṣmāvayavā Padmālayā Virajā Viśvarūpā Bhadrā Kṛpāsarvatomukhīti Caturviṃśatiśaktayo Nigadyante |
Pṛthivyaptejovāyvākāśagandharasarūpasparśaśabdavākyāni Pādapāyūpasthatvakcakṣuśrotrajihvāghrāṇamanobuddhyahaṅkāra-Cittajñānānīti Pratyakṣarāṇāṃ Tattvāni Pratīyante |
Campakātasīkuṅkumapiṅgalendranīlāgniprabhodyatsūrya-Vidyuttārakasarojagauramaratakaśuklakundenduśaṅkhapāṇḍu-Netranīlotpalacandanāgurukastūrīgorocanaghanasārasannibhaṃ Pratyakṣaramanusmṛtya Samastapātakopapātakamahāpātakā-Gamyāgamanagohatyābrahmahatyābhrūṇahatyāvīrahatyā-Puruṣahatyā''janmakṛtahatyāstrīhatyāguruhatyāpitṛhatyā-Prāṇahatyācarācarahatyā'bhakṣyabhakṣaṇapratigraha-Svakarmavicchedanasvāmyārtihīnakarmakaraṇaparadhanāpaharaṇa-Śūdrānnabhojanaśatrumāraṇacaṇḍālīgamanādisamasta-Pāpaharaṇārthaṃ Saṃsmaret |

मूर्धा ब्रह्मा शिखान्तो विष्णुर्ललाटं रुद्रचक्षुषी चन्द्रादित्यौकर्णौ शुक्रबृहस्पती नासापुटे अश्विनौ दन्तोष्ठावुभे सन्ध्ये मुखं मरुतः स्तनौ वस्वादयो हृदयं पर्जन्य उदरमाकाशो नाभिरग्निः कटिरिन्द्राग्नी जघनं प्राजापत्यमूरू कैलासमूलंजानुनी विश्वेदेवौ जङ्घे शिशिरः गुल्फानि पृथिवीवनस्पत्यादीनि नखानि महती अस्थीनि नवग्रहा असृक्केतुर्मांसमृतुसन्धयः कालद्वयास्फालनं संवत्सरोनिमेषोऽहोरात्रमिति वाग्देवीं गायत्रीं शरणमहं प्रपद्ये।

Mūrdhā Brahmā Śikhānto Viṣṇurlalāṭaṃ Rudracakṣuṣī Candrādityau Karṇau Śukrabṛhaspatī Nāsāpuṭe Aśvinau Dantoṣṭhāvubhe Sandhye Mukhaṃ Marutaḥ Stanau Vasvādayo Hṛdayaṃ Parjanya Udaramākāśo Nābhiragniḥ Kaṭirindrāgnī Jaghanaṃ Prājāpatyamūrū Kailāsamūlaṃ Jānunī Viśvedevau Jaṅghe Śiśiraḥ Gulphāni Pṛthivīvanaspatyādīni Nakhāni Mahatī Asthīni Navagrahā Asṛkketurmāṃsamṛtusandhayaḥ Kāladvayāsphālanaṃ Saṃvatsaro Nimeṣo'horātramiti Vāgdevīṃ Gāyatrīṃ Śaraṇamahaṃ Prapadye |

य इदं गायत्रीरहस्यमधीते तेन क्रतुसहस्त्रमिष्टं भवति।
य इदं गायत्रीरहस्यमधीते दिवसकृतं पापं नाशयति।
प्रातरमध्याह्नयोः षण्मासकृतानि पापानि नाशयति।
सायं प्रातरधीयानो जन्मकृतं पापं नाशयति।
य इदं गायत्रीरहस्यं ब्राह्मणः पठेत् तेन गायत्र्याःषष्टिसहस्त्रलक्षाणि जप्तानि भवन्ति।
सर्वान् वेदानधीतो भवति। सर्वेषु तीर्थेषु स्नातो भवति। अपेयपानात् पूतो भवति।

अभक्ष्यभक्षणात् पूतो भवति। वृषलीगमनात् पूतो भवति।
अब्रह्मचारी ब्रह्मचारी भवति। पङ्क्तिषु सहस्रपानात् पूतो भवति।
अष्टौ ब्राह्मणान् ग्राहयित्वा ब्रह्मलोकं स गच्छति। इत्याह भगवान् ब्रह्मा॥

Ya Idaṃ Gāyatrīrahasyamadhīte Tena Kratusahasramiṣṭaṃ Bhavati |

Ya Idaṃ Gāyatrīrahasyamadhīte Divasakṛtaṃ Pāpaṃ Nāśayati |

Prātaramadhyāhnayoḥ Ṣaṇmāsakṛtāni Pāpāni Nāśayati |

Sāyaṃ Prātaradhīyāno Janmakṛtaṃ Pāpaṃ Nāśayati |
Ya Idaṃ Gāyatrīrahasyaṃ Brāhmaṇaḥ Paṭhet Tena Gāyatryāḥ

Ṣaṣṭisahasralakṣāṇi Japtāni Bhavanti | Sarvān Vedānadhīto Bhavati |

Sarveṣu Tīrtheṣu Snāto Bhavati | Apeyapānāt Pūto Bhavati |

Abhakṣyabhakṣaṇāt Pūto Bhavati | Vṛṣalīgamanāt Pūto Bhavati |

Abrahmacārī Brahmacārī Bhavati |

Paṅktiṣu Sahasrapānāt Pūto Bhavati |

Aṣṭau Brāhmaṇān Grāhayitvā Brahmalokaṃ Sa Gacchati |

Ityāha Bhagavān Brahmā ||

शान्ति मन्त्रः | *Śānti Mantraḥ* |

ॐ भद्रं कर्णेभिः शृणुयाम देवाः। भद्रं पश्येमाक्षभिर्यजत्राः।

Oṃ Bhadraṃ Karṇebhiḥ Śṛṇuyāma Devāḥ ||

Bhadraṃ Paśyemākṣabhiryajatrāḥ ||
स्थिरैरङ्गैस्तुष्टुवाँसस्तनूभिः। व्यशेम देवहितं यदायुः।

Sthirairaṅgaistuṣṭuvāg̃Sastanūbhiḥ || Vyaśema Devahitaṃ Yadāyuḥ ||
स्वस्ति न इन्द्रो वृद्धश्रवाः। स्वस्ति नः पूषा विश्ववेदाः।

Svasti Na Indro Vṛddhaśravāḥ || Svasti Naḥ Pūṣā Viśvavedāḥ ||
स्वस्ति नस्तार्क्ष्यो अरिष्टनेमिः। स्वस्ति नो बृहस्पतिर्दधातु॥

Svasti Nastārkṣyo Ariṣṭanemiḥ || Svasti No Bṛhaspatirdadhātu ||
ॐ शान्तिः शान्तिः शान्तिः॥ *Oṃ Śāntiḥ Śāntiḥ Śāntiḥ ||*

इति गायत्रीरहस्योपनिषत् समाप्ता॥ *Iti Gāyatrīrahasyopaniṣat Samāptā ||*

*****

Gāyatryupaniṣat

गायत्र्युपनिषत्

This is also another *Upaniṣat* from *Atharva Veda.*

शान्ति मन्त्रः । *Śānti Mantraḥ* ।

ॐ भद्रं कर्णेभिः शृणुयाम देवाः । भद्रं पश्येमाक्षभिर्यजत्राः ।

Oṃ Bhadraṃ Karṇebhiḥ Śṛṇuyāma Devāḥ ॥

Bhadraṃ Paśyemākṣabhiryajatrāḥ ॥
स्थिरैरङ्गैस्तुष्टुवाँसस्तनूभिः । व्यशेम देवहितं यदायुः ।

SthiraiRaṅgaistuṣṭuvāg̐Sastanūbhiḥ ॥ *Vyaśema Devahitaṃ Yadāyuḥ* ॥
स्वस्ति न इन्द्रो वृद्धश्रवाः । स्वस्ति नः पूषा विश्ववेदाः ।

Svasti Na Indro Vṛddhaśravāḥ ॥ *Svasti Naḥ Pūṣā Viśvavedāḥ* ॥
स्वस्ति नस्तार्क्ष्यो अरिष्टनेमिः । स्वस्ति नो बृहस्पतिर्दधातु ॥

Svasti Nastārkṣyo Ariṣṭanemiḥ ॥ *Svasti No Bṛhaspatirdadhātu* ॥
ॐ शान्तिः शान्तिः शान्तिः ॥ *Oṃ Śāntiḥ Śāntiḥ Śāntiḥ* ॥

हरिः ॐ ॥ *Hariḥ Oṃ* ॥

ॐ भूमिरन्तरिक्ष द्यौरित्यष्टावक्षराणि ।

Oṃ Bhūmirantarikṣa Dyaurityaṣṭāvakṣarāṇi ।

अष्टाक्षर ह वा एक गायत्र्यै पदमेतदु हास्या एतत्स यावदेतेषु लोकेषु तावद्ध जयति । योऽस्या एतदेव पद वेद ऋचो यजूषि सामानीत्यष्टाक्षर ह वा एक गायत्र्यै पदमेतदु हास्या एतत्स यावतीय त्रयी विद्या तावद्ध जयति । योऽस्या एतदेव पद वेद प्राणोऽपानो व्यान इत्यष्टावक्षराण्यष्टाक्षर ह वा एक गायत्र्यै पदमेतदु हास्या एतत्स यावदिद प्राणिति तावद्ध जयति । योऽस्या एतदेव पद वेदाथास्या एतदेव तुरीय दर्शित पद परोरजाय एष तपतीति यद्वै चतुर्थ तत्तुरीय दर्शित पदमिति ददर्श इव ह्येष परोरजा इति सर्वमु ह्येष रज उपर्युपरि तपत्येव ह वा एष श्रिया यशसा तपति ।

Aṣṭākṣara Ha Vā Eka Gāyatryai Padametadu Hāsyā Etatsa Yāvadeteṣu Lokeṣu Tāvaddha Jayati ।
Yo'syā Etadeva Pada Veda Ṛco Yajūṣi SāmānītyaṣṭākṣaraHa Vā Eka Gāyatryai Padametadu Hāsyā Etatsa Yāvatīya Trayī Vidyā

Tāvaddha Jayati ।

Yo'syā Etadeva Pada Veda Prāṇo'pāno Vyāna Ityaṣṭāvakṣarāṇyaṣṭākṣara Ha Vā Eka Gāyatryai Padametadu Hāsyā Etatsa Yāvadida Prāṇiti Tāvaddha Jayati ।

Yo'syā Etadeva Pada Vedāthāsyā Etadeva Turīya Darśita Pada Parorajāya Eṣa Tapatīti Yadvai Caturtha Tatturīya Darśita Padamiti Dadarśa Iva Hyeṣa Parorajā Iti Sarvamu Hyeṣa Raja Uparyupari Tapatyeva Ha Vā Eṣa Śriyā Yaśasā Tapati ।

योऽस्या एतदेव पद वेद सैषा गायत्री एतस्मिस्तुरीये दर्शिते पदे परोरजसि प्रतिष्ठिता तद्वै तत्सत्ये प्रतिष्ठित चक्षुर्हिवै सत्य तस्माद्यदिदानीं द्वौ विवदमानावेयाता अहमद्राक्षमहमश्रौषमिति ।

य एव ब्रूयादहमद्राक्षमिति तस्या एव श्रद्धव्या य एतद्वै तत् सत्य बले प्रतिष्ठित तस्मादाहुर्बलसत्यादौ ज्ञेय एव वैषा गायत्र्यध्यात्म प्रतिष्ठिता सा हैषा गायस्तते प्राणा वै गायास्तान् प्राणास्तते उद्यद्गायस्तते तस्माद्गायत्री नाम स यावेमामूमत्वा हैषैवमास यस्मा इत्याह तस्य प्रमाण त्रायते ता हैके सावित्री मनुष्टुभमन्वाहुरनुष्टुभैतद्वाचमनु ब्रूम इति न तथा कुर्याद्गायत्रीमेवानुब्रूयाद्यदि ह वापि बह्विव प्रतिगृह्णाति ।

Yo'syā Etadeva Pada Veda Saiṣā Gāyatrī Etasmisturīye Darśite Pade Parorajasi Pratiṣṭhitā Tadvai Tatsatye Pratiṣṭhita Cakṣurhi Vai Satya Tasmādyadidānīṃ Dvau Vivadamānāveyātā Ahamadrākṣamahamaśrauṣamiti ।

Ya Eva Brūyādahamadrākṣamiti Tasyā Eva Śraddhavyā Ya Etadvai Tat Satya Bale Pratiṣṭhita Tasmādāhurbalasatyādau Jñeya Eva Vaiṣā Gāyatryadhyātma Pratiṣṭhitā Sā Haiṣā Gāyastate Prāṇā Vai Gāyāstān Prāṇāstate Udyadgāyastate Tasmādgāyatrī Nāma Sa Yāvemāmūmatvā Haiṣaivamāsa Yasmā Ityāha Tasya Pramāṇa Trāyate Tā Haike Sāvitrī-Manuṣṭubhamanvāhuranuṣṭubhaitadvācamanubrūma Iti Na Tathā Kuryādgāyatrīmevānubrūyādyadi Ha Vāpi Bahviva Pratigṛhṇāti ।

इहेव तद्गायत्र्या एकचन पद प्रति य इमास्त्रीन् लोकान् पूर्णान् प्रतिगृह्णीयात् सोऽस्या एतत्प्रथमपदमाप्नुयात् अथ यावतीय त्रयी विद्या यस्तावत्प्रतिगृह्णीयात् सोऽस्या एतद्द्वितीयमाप्नुयात् । अथ यावदिद प्राणिति यस्यावत् प्रतिगृह्णीयात् ।

तस्या उपस्थान गायत्र्यैकपदी द्विपदी त्रिपदीचतुष्पद्यपदा सा न हि पद्यः यस्ते तुरीयायपदाय दर्शिताय परोरजसे सावदोमिति समधीयीतन हैवास्मै सकाम समृद्ध्यते ।

Iheva Tadgāyatryā Ekacana Pada Prati Ya Imāstrīn Lokān Pūrṇān Pratigṛhṇīyāt So'syā Etatprathamapadamāpnuyāt Atha Yāvatīya Trayī Vidyā Yastāvatpratigṛhṇīyāt So'syā Etaddvitīyamāpnuyāt ।

Atha Yāvadida Prāṇiti Yasyāvat Pratigṛhṇīyāt ।

Tasyā Upasthāna Gāyatryaikapadī Dvipadī Tripadīcatuṣpadyapadā Sā Na Hi Padyaḥ Yaste Turīyāyapadāya Darśitāya Parorajase Sāvadomiti Samadhīyītana Haivāsmai Sakāma Samṛddhyate ।

यस्मा एवमुपतिष्ठते ह मद प्रापमिति एतद्धवै तज्जनको वैदेहो वुरिलमाश्रितराश्विमुवाच।
यत्तु होतर्गा कथ हलीभूतो वहसीति ।
मुख ह्यस्या ससभ्रम विदाचकारेति होवाच तस्या अग्निरेव मुख यदिह वापि वह्निमानग्नावभ्यादधाति सर्वमेतत्स हत्येवविद्यद्यपवह्नीव पाप करोति सर्वमेवैतत्सम्यग्विशुद्धो यतोऽजरोऽमरः स भवतीति ॥

Yasmā Evamupatiṣṭhate Ha Mada Prāpamiti Etaddhavai Tajjanako Vaideho Vurilamāśritarāśvimuvāca ।

Yattu Hotargā Katha Halībhūto Vahasīti ।

Mukha Hyasyā Sasabhrama Vidācakāreti Hovāca Tasyā Agnireva Mukha Yadiha Vāpi Vahnimānagnāvabhyādadhāti Sarvametatsa Hatyevavidyadyapavahnīva Pāpa Karoti Sarvamevaitatsamyagviśuddho Yato'jaro'maraḥ Sa Bhavatīti ।।

शान्ति मन्त्र: । *Śānti Mantraḥ* ।

ॐ भद्रं कर्णेभिः शृणुयाम देवाः । भद्रं पश्येमाक्षभिर्यजत्राः ।

Oṃ Bhadraṃ Karṇebhiḥ Śṛṇuyāma Devāḥ ॥

Bhadraṃ Paśyemākṣabhiryajatrāḥ ॥
स्थिरैरङ्गैस्तुष्टुवाँसस्तनूभिः । व्यशेम देवहितं यदायुः ।

SthirairaṅgaistuṣṭuvāğSastanūbhiḥ ॥ *Vyaśema Devahitaṃ Yadāyuḥ* ॥

स्वस्ति न इन्द्रो वृद्धश्रवाः । स्वस्ति नः पूषा विश्ववेदाः ।

Svasti Na Indro Vṛddhaśravāḥ ॥ *Svasti Naḥ Pūṣā Viśvavedāḥ* ॥

स्वस्ति नस्तार्क्ष्यो अरिष्टनेमिः । स्वस्ति नो बृहस्पतिर्दधातु ॥

Svasti Nastārkṣyo Ariṣṭanemiḥ ॥ *Svasti No Bṛhaspatirdadhātu* ॥

ॐ शान्तिः शान्तिः शान्तिः ॥ *Oṃ Śāntiḥ Śāntiḥ Śāntiḥ* ॥

इति गायत्र्युपनिषत् समाप्ता ॥ *Iti Gāyatryupaniṣat Samāptā* ||

*****

Guhyakālyupāniṣat

गुह्यकाल्युपानिषत्

This is also another *Upaniṣat* from *Atharva Veda.*

शान्ति मन्त्रः । *Śānti Mantraḥ* ।

ॐ भद्रं कर्णेभिः शृणुयाम देवाः । भद्रं पश्येमाक्षभिर्यजत्राः ।

Oṃ Bhadraṃ Karṇebhiḥ Śṛṇuyāma Devāḥ ॥

Bhadraṃ Paśyemākṣabhiryajatrāḥ ॥
स्थिरैरङ्गैस्तुष्टुवाँसस्तनूभिः । व्यशेम देवहितं यदायुः ।

SthirairaṅgaistuṣṭuvāğSastanūbhiḥ ॥ *Vyaśema Devahitaṃ Yadāyuḥ* ॥
स्वस्ति न इन्द्रो वृद्धश्रवाः । स्वस्ति नः पूषा विश्ववेदाः ।

Svasti Na Indro Vṛddhaśravāḥ ॥ *Svasti Naḥ Pūṣā Viśvavedāḥ* ॥
स्वस्ति नस्तार्क्ष्यो अरिष्टनेमिः । स्वस्ति नो बृहस्पतिर्दधातु ॥

Svasti Nastārkṣyo Ariṣṭanemiḥ ॥ *Svasti No Bṛhaspatirdadhātu* ॥
ॐ शान्तिः शान्तिः शान्तिः ॥ *Oṃ Śāntiḥ Śāntiḥ Śāntiḥ* ॥

हरिः ॐ ॥ *Hariḥ Oṃ* ॥

1. अथर्ववेदमध्ये तु शाखा मुख्यतमा हि षट् । स्वयम्भुवा याः कथिताः पुत्रायाथर्वणे पुरा ॥

Atharvavedamadhye Tu Śākhā Mukhyatamā Hi Ṣaṭ ।
Svayambhuvā Yāḥ Kathitāḥ Putrāyātharvaṇe Purā ॥

2. तासु गुह्योपनिषदस्तिष्ठन्ति वरवर्णिनि । नामानि शृणु शाखानां तत्राद्या वारतन्तवी ॥

Tāsu Guhyopaniṣadastiṣṭhanti Varavarṇini ।

Nāmāni Śṛṇu Śākhānāṃ Tatrādyā Vāratantavī || ॥

3. मौञ्जायनी द्वितीया तु तृतीया तार्णबैन्दवी । चतुर्थी शौनकी प्रोक्ता पञ्चमी पैप्पलादिका ॥

Mauñjāyanī Dvitīyā Tu Tṛtīyā Tārṇabaindavī ।
Caturthī Śaunakī Proktā Pañcamī Paippalādikā ॥

4. षष्ठी सौमन्तवी ज्ञेया सारात् सारतमा इमाः । गुह्योपनिषदो गूढाः सन्ति शाखासु षट्स्वपि ॥

Ṣaṣṭhī Saumantavī Jñeyā Sārāt Sāratamā Imāḥ |
Guhyopaniṣado Gṛḍhāḥ Santi Śākhāsu Ṣaṭsvapi ||

5. ता एकीकृत्य सर्वास्तु मयाऽस्यां विनिवेशिताः । संहितायां साधकानामुद्धाराय वरानने ॥

Tā Ekīkṛtya Sarvāstu Mayā'syāṃ Viniveśitāḥ |
Saṃhitāyāṃ Sādhakānāmuddhārāya Varānane ||

6. तास्ते वदामि यत प्रोक्तं ध्यानं कुर्वन्ति देवताः ।
विराट्ध्यानं हि तज्ज्ञेयं महापातकनाशनम् ॥

Tāste Vadāmi Yata Proktaṃ Dhyānaṃ Kurvanti Devatāḥ |
Virāṭdhyānaṃ Hi Tajjñeyaṃ Mahāpātakanāśanam ||

7. ब्रह्माण्डाद्बहिरूर्ध्वं हि महत्तत्त्वमहङ्कृतिः । रूपाणि पञ्च तन्मात्राः पुरुषः प्रकृरतिर्नव ॥

Brahmāṇḍādbahirūrdhvaṃ Hi Mahattattvamahaṅkṛtiḥ |
Rūpāṇi Pañca Tanmātrāḥ Puruṣaḥ Prakṛratirnava ||

8. महापातालपादान्तलम्बा तस्या जयं स्मरेत् ।
व्ब्रह्माण्डार्धं कपालं हि शिरस्तम्या विभावयेत् ॥

Mahāpātālapādāntalambā Tasyā Jayaṃ Smaret |
Vbrahmāṇḍārdhaṃ Kapālaṃ Hi Śirastamyā Vibhāvayet ||

9. देवलोको ललाटं च पट्विंशल्लक्षयोजनम्। मेरुः समिन्तदण्डोऽम्या ग्रहरत्नसमाकुलः ॥

Devaloko Lalāṭaṃ Ca Paṭviṃśallakṣayojanam |
Meruḥ Samintadaṇḍo'myā Graharatnasamākulaḥ ||

10. अन्तर्वीथी नागवीथी भ्रुवावम्याः प्रकीर्तिते । शिवलोकश्च वैकुण्ठलोकः कर्णावुभौ मतौ ॥

Antarvīthī Nāgavīthī Bhruvāvamyāḥ Prakīrtite |
Śivalokaśca Vaikuṇṭhalokaḥ Karṇāvubhau Matau ||

11. लोहितं तिलकं ध्यायेन्नासा मन्दाकिनी तथा ।
चक्षुषी चन्द्रसूर्यौ च पक्ष्माणि किरणास्तथा ॥

Lohitaṃ Tilakaṃ Dhyāyennāsā Mandākinī Tathā |
Cakṣuṣī Candrasūryau Ca Pakṣmāṇi Kiraṇāstathā ||

12. गण्डौ न्यातां तपोलोकसत्यलोकौ यथाक्रमम् । जनोलोकमहर्लोकौ कपोलौ परिकीर्तितौ ॥

Gaṇḍau Nyātāṃ Tapolokasatyalokau Yathākramam |
Janolokamaharlokau Kapolau Parikīrtitau ||

13. स्यातां हिमाद्रिकौमासौ तम्यां देव्यास्तु कृण्डले ।
स्वर्लोकश्च भुवर्लोको देव्या ओष्ठाधरौ मतौ ॥

Syātāṃ Himādrikaumāsau Tamyāṃ Devyāstu Kṛṇḍale |
Svarlokaśca Bhuvarloko Devyā Oṣṭhādharau Matau ||

14. दिक्पतीनां ग्रहाणां च लोकाश्चाथ रदावली । गन्धर्वसिद्धसाध्यानां पितृरकिन्नररक्षसाम् ॥

Dikpatīnāṃ Grahāṇāṃ Ca Lokāścātha Radāvalī |
Gandharvasiddhasādhyānāṃ Pitṛrakinnararakṣasām ||

15. पिशाचयक्षाप्सरसां मरीचीयायिनां तथा । विद्याधराणामाज्योष्मपाणां सोमैकपायिनाम् ॥

Piśācayakṣāpsarasāṃ Marīcīyāyināṃ Tathā |
Vidyādharāṇāmājyoṣmapāṇāṃ Somaikapāyinām ||

16. सप्तर्षीणां ध्रुवस्यापि लोका ऊर्ध्वरदावली । मुखं च रोदसी ज्ञेयं द्यौर्लोकश्चिबुकं तथा ॥

Saptarṣīṇāṃ Dhruvasyāpi Lokā Ūrdhvaradāvalī |
Mukhaṃ Ca Rodasī Jñeyaṃ Dyaurlokaścibukaṃ Tathā ||

17. ब्रह्मलोको गलः प्रोक्तो वायव प्राणरूपिणः । वनस्पतय ओषध्यो लोमानि परिचक्षते ॥

Brahmaloko Galaḥ Prokto Vāyava Prāṇarūpiṇaḥ |
Vanaspataya Oṣadhyo Lomāni Paricakṣate ||

18. विद्युद्दृष्टिरहोरात्रंनिमेषोन्मेषसंज्ञकम् । विश्वं तु हृदयं प्रोक्तं पृथिवी पाद उच्यते ॥

Vidyuddṛṣṭirahorātraṃ Nimeṣonmeṣasaṃjñakam |
Viśvaṃ Tu Hṛdayaṃ Proktaṃ Pṛthivī Pāda Ucyate ||

19. तलं तलातलं चैव पातालं सुतलं तथा । रसातलं नागलोकाः पादाङ्गुल्यः प्रकीर्तिताः ॥

Talaṃ Talātalaṃ Caiva Pātālaṃ Sutalaṃ Tathā |
Rasātalaṃ Nāgalokāḥ Pādāṅgulyaḥ Prakīrtitāḥ ||

20. वेदा वाचः स्यन्दमाना नदा नद्योऽमिता मताः । कलाः काष्ठा मुहूर्ताश्च ऋतवोऽयनमेव च ॥

Vedā Vācaḥ Syandamānā Nadā Nadyo'mitā Matāḥ ।
Kalāḥ Kāṣṭhā Muhūrtāśca Ṛtavo'yanameva Ca ॥

21. पक्षा मासास्तथा चाब्दाश्चत्वारोऽपि युगाः प्रिये। कफोणिर्मणिबन्धश्च तदूरुकटिबन्धनाः ॥

Pakṣā Māsāstathā Cābdāścatvāro'pi Yugāḥ Priye ।
Kaphoṇirmaṇibandhaśca Tadūrukaṭibandhanāḥ ॥

22. प्रपदाश्च स्फिचश्चैव सर्वाङ्गानि प्रचक्षते। वैश्वानरः कालमृत्युर्जिह्वात्रयमिदं स्मृतम् ॥

Prapadāśca Sphicaścaiva Sarvāṅgāni Pracakṣate ।
Vaiśvānaraḥ Kālamṛtyurjihvātrayamidaṃ Smṛtam ॥

23. आब्रह्मस्तम्बपर्यन्तं तनुमस्याः प्रचक्षते। प्रलयो भोजने कालस्तृप्तिस्तेन च नासिका ॥

Ābrahmastambaparyantaṃ Tanumasyāḥ Pracakṣate ।
Pralayo Bhojane Kālastṛptistena Ca Nāsikā ॥

24. ज्ञेयः पार्श्वपरीवर्तो महाकल्पान्तरोद्भवः। विराड्रूपवोस्य ते ध्यानमिति संक्षेपतोऽर्पितम्

Jñeyaḥ Pārśvaparīvarto Mahākalpāntarodbhavaḥ ।
Virāḍrūpavosya Te Dhyānamiti Saṃkṣepato'rpitam ॥

25. तस्याः स्वरूपविज्ञानं सपर्या परिकीर्तिता। तदेव हि श्रुतिप्रोक्तमवधारय पार्वति ॥

Tasyāḥ Svarūpavijñānaṃ Saparyā Parikīrtitā ।
Tadeva Hi Śrutiproktamavadhāraya Pārvati ॥

26. यथोर्णनाभिः सूत्राणि सृजत्यपि गिलत्यपि। यथा पृथिव्यामोषध्यः सम्भवन्ति गिलन्त्यपि

Yathorṇanābhiḥ Sūtrāṇi Sṛjatyapi Gilatyapi ।
Yathā Pṛthivyāmoṣadhyaḥ Sambhavanti Gilantyapi ॥

27. पुरुषात् केशलोमानि जायन्ते च क्षरनत्यपि। उत्पद्यन्ते विलीयन्ते तथा तस्यां जगत्यपि

Puruṣāt Keśalomāni Jāyante Ca Kṣaranatyapi ।
Utpadyante Vilīyante Tathā Tasyāṃ Jagatyapi ॥

28. ज्वलतः पावकाद्यद्वत् स्फुलिङ्गाः कोटिकोटिशः।
निर्गत्य च विनश्यन्ति विश्वं तस्यास्तथा प्रिये ॥

Jvalataḥ Pāvakādyadvat Sphuliṅgāḥ Koṭikoṭiśaḥ ।
Nirgatya Ca Vinaśyanti Viśvaṃ Tasyāstathā Priye ॥

29. ऋचो यजूंषि सामानि दीक्षा यज्ञाः सदक्षिणाः । अध्वर्युर्यजमानश्च भुवनानि चतुर्दश ॥

Ṛco Yajūṃṣi Sāmāni Dīkṣā Yajñāḥ Sadakṣiṇāḥ ।
Adhvaryuryajamānaśca Bhuvanāni Caturdaśa ॥

30. ब्रह्मविष्ण्वादिका देवा मनुष्याः पशवो यतः । प्राणापानौ व्रीहयश्च सत्यं श्रद्धा विधिस्तपः ॥

Brahmaviṣṇvādikā Devā Manuṣyāḥ Paśavo Yataḥ ।
Prāṇāpānau Vrīhayaśca Satyaṃ Śraddhā Vidhistapaḥ ॥

31. समुद्रा गिरयो नद्यः सर्वे स्थावरजङ्गमाः । विसृज्येमानि सर्गादौ त्वं प्रकाशयसे ततः ॥

Samudrā Girayo Nadyaḥ Sarve Sthāvarajaṅgamāḥ ।
Visṛjyemāni Sargādau Tvaṃ Prakāśayase Tataḥ ॥

32. जङ्गमानि विधायान्धे विशत्यप्रतिभूतकम् । नवद्वारं पुरं कृत्वा गवाक्षाणीन्द्रियाण्यपि ॥

Jaṅgamāni Vidhāyāndhe Viśatyapratibhūtakam ।
Navadvāraṃ Puraṃ Kṛtvā Gavākṣāṇīndriyāṇyapi ॥

33. सा पश्यत्यत्ति वहति स्पृशति क्रीडतीच्छति । शृणोति जिघ्रति तथा रमते विरमत्यपि ॥

Sā Paśyatyatti Vahati Spṛśati Krīḍatīcchati ।
Śṛṇoti Jighrati Tathā Ramate Viramatyapi ॥

34. तया मुक्तं पुरं तद्धि मतमित्यभिधीयते ॥
Tayā Muktaṃ Puraṃ Taddhi Matamityabhidhīyate ॥

35. ये तपः क्षीणदोषास्ते नैव पश्यन्ति भाविताम् ।
ज्योतिर्मयीं शरीरेऽन्तिर्ध्यायमानां महात्मभिः ॥

Ye Tapaḥ Kṣīṇadoṣāste Naiva Paśyanti Bhāvitām ।
Jyotirmayīṃ Śarīre'ntirdhyāyamānāṃ Mahātmabhiḥ ॥

36. बृहच्च तद्दिव्यमचिन्त्यरूपं सूक्ष्माच्च तत् सूक्ष्मतरं विभाति ।
दूरात् सुदूरे तदिहास्ति किञ्चित् पश्येत्त्विहैतन्निहितं गुहायाम् ॥

Bṛhacca Taddivyamacintyarūpaṃ Sūkṣmācca Tat Sūkṣmataraṃ Vibhāti ।
Dūrāt Sudūre Tadihāsti Kiñcit Paśyettvihaitannihitaṃ Guhāyām ॥

37. न चक्षुषा गृह्यते नापि वाचा नान्यैर्योगैर्न हि सा कर्मणा वा ।
ज्ञानप्रसादेन विशुद्धसत्त्वः ततस्तु तां पश्यति निष्कलां च ॥

Na Cakṣuṣā Gṛhyate Nāpi Vācā Nānyairyogairna Hi Sā Karmaṇā Vā |
Jñānaprasādena Viśuddhasattvaḥ Tatastu Tāṃ Paśyati Niṣkalāṃ Ca ||

38. यथा नद्यः स्यन्दमानाः समुद्रे गच्छन्त्यस्तं नामरूपे विहाय।
तथा विद्वान् नामरूपाद्विमुक्तः परात् परां जगदम्बामुपैति॥
Yathā Nadyaḥ Syandamānāḥ Samudre Gacchantyastaṃ Nāmarūpe Vihāya |
Tathā Vidvān Nāmarūpādvimuktaḥ Parāt Parāṃ Jagadambāmupaiti ||

39. सर्वे वेदा यत्पदमामनन्ति तपांसि सर्वाणि च यद्वदन्ति।
यदिच्छन्तो ब्रह्मचर्यं चरन्ति तत्ते पदं सङ्ग्रहेण ब्रवीमि॥

Sarve Vedā Yatpadamāmananti Tapāṃsi Sarvāṇi Ca Yadvadanti |
Yadicchanto Brahmacaryaṃ Caranti Tatte Padaṃ Saṅgraheṇa Bravīmi ||

40. सैवैतत्। *Saivaitat* |

एषैवालम्बनं श्रेष्ठं सैषैवालम्बनं परम्। एषैवालम्बनं ज्ञात्वा ब्रह्मलोके महीयते॥

Eṣaivālambanaṃ Śreṣṭhaṃ Saiṣaivālambanaṃ Param |
Eṣaivālambanaṃ Jñātvā Brahmaloke Mahīyate ||

41. इन्द्रियेभ्यः परा ह्यर्था ह्यर्थेभ्यश्च परं मनः। मनसस्तु परा बुद्धिर्बुद्धेरात्मा महान् परः॥
Indriyebhyaḥ Parā Hyarthā Hyarthebhyaśca Paraṃ Manaḥ |
Manasastu Parā Buddhirbuddherātmā Mahān Paraḥ ||

42. महतः परमव्यक्तमव्यक्तात् पुरुषः परः। पुरुषात्तु परा देवी सा काष्ठा सा परा गतिः॥

Mahataḥ Paramavyaktamavyaktāt Puruṣaḥ Paraḥ |
Puruṣāttu Parā Devī Sā Kāṣṭhā Sā Parā Gatiḥ ||

43. यथोदकं गिरौ सृष्टं समुद्रेषु विधावति। एवं धर्मान् पृथक पश्यंस्तामेवानुविधावति॥

Yathodakaṃ Girau Sṛṣṭaṃ Samudreṣu Vidhāvati |
Evaṃ Dharmān Pṛthaka Paśyaṃstāmevānuvidhāvati ||

44. एका गुह्या सर्वभूतान्तरात्मा एक रूपं बहुधा या करोति।
तामात्मस्थां येऽनुपश्यन्ति धीराः तेषां सुखं शाश्वतं नेतरेषाम्॥

Ekā Guhyā Sarvabhūtāntarātmā Eka Rūpaṃ Bahudhā Yā Karoti |
Tāmātmasthāṃ Ye'nupaśyanti Dhīrāḥ Teṣāṃ Sukhaṃ Śāśvataṃ Netareṣām ||

45. न तत्र सूर्यो भाति न चन्द्रतारकं नेमा विद्युतो भान्ति कुतोऽयमग्निः।
तामेव भान्तीमनुभाति सर्वं तस्या भासा सर्वमिदं विभाति ॥

Na Tatra Sūryo Bhāti Na Candratārakaṃ Nemā Vidyuto Bhānti Kuto'yamagniḥ |
Tāmeva Bhāntīmanubhāti Sarvaṃ Tasyā Bhāsā Sarvamidaṃ Vibhāti ||

46. यस्याः परं नापरमस्ति किञ्चित् यस्या नाणीयो न ज्यायोऽस्ति किञ्चित्।
वृक्ष इव स्तब्धा दिवि तिष्ठत्येका यदन्तः पूर्णामवगत्य पूर्णः ॥

Yasyāḥ Paraṃ Nāparamasti Kiñcit Yasyā Nāṇīyo Na Jyāyo'sti Kiñcit |
Vṛkṣa Iva Stabdhā Divi Tiṣṭhatyekā Yadantaḥ Pūrṇāmavagatya Pūrṇaḥ ||

47. सर्वाननशिरोग्रीवा सर्वभूतगुहाशया। सर्वत्रस्था भगवती तस्मात् सर्वगता शिवा ॥

Sarvānanaśirogrīvā Sarvabhūtaguhāśayā |
Sarvatrasthā Bhagavatī Tasmāt Sarvagatā Śivā ||

48. सर्वतः पाणिपादान्ता सर्वतोऽक्षिशिरोमुखा। सर्वतः श्रुतिमत्येषा सर्वमावृत्य तिष्ठति ॥

Sarvataḥ Pāṇipādāntā Sarvato'kṣiśiromukhā |
Sarvataḥ Śrutimatyeṣā Sarvamāvṛtya Tiṣṭhati ||

49. सर्वेन्द्रियगुणाभासा सर्वेन्द्रियविवर्जिता। सर्वेषां प्रभुरीशानी सर्वेषां शरणं सुहृत् ॥

Sarvendriyaguṇābhāsā Sarvendriyavivarjitā |
Sarveṣāṃ Prabhurīśānī Sarveṣāṃ Śaraṇaṃ Suhṛt ||

50. नवद्वारे पुरे देवी हंसी लीलायतां बहिः। ध्येया सर्वस्य लोकस्य स्थावरस्य चरस्य च ॥

Navadvāre Pure Devī Haṃsī Līlāyatāṃ Bahiḥ |
Dhyeyā Sarvasya Lokasya Sthāvarasya Carasya Ca ||

51. अपाणिपादा जननी ग्रहीत्री पश्यत्यचक्षुः सा श्रुणोत्यर्णा।
सा वेत्ति वेद्यं न च तस्यास्तु वेत्ता तामाहुरग्र्यां महतीं महीयसीम् ॥

Apāṇipādā Jananī Grahītrī Paśyatyacakṣuḥ Sā Śruṇotyarṇā |
Sā Vetti Vedyaṃ Na Ca Tasyāstu Vettā Tāmāhuragryāṃ Mahatīṃ Mahīyasīm ||

52. सा चैवाग्निः सा च सूर्यः सा वायुः सा च चन्द्रमा ।
सा चैव शुकः सा ब्रह्म सा चापः सा प्रजापतिः ।
सा चैव स्त्री सा च पुमान् सा कुमारः कुमारिका ॥

Sā Caivāgniḥ Sā Ca Sūryaḥ Sā Vāyuḥ Sā Ca Candramā |
Sā Caiva Śukaḥ Sā Brahma Sā Cāpaḥ Sā Prajāpatiḥ |
Sā Caiva Strī Sā Ca Pumān Sā Kumāraḥ Kumārikā ||

53. ऋचो अक्षरे परमे व्योमन् यस्यां देवा अधिरुद्रा निषेदुः ।
यस्तां न वेद किमृचा करिष्यति ये तां विदुस्तु इमे समासते ॥

Ṛco Akṣare Parame Vyoman Yasyāṃ Devā Adhirudrā Niṣeduḥ |
Yastāṃ Na Veda Kimṛcā Kariṣyati Ye Tāṃ Vidustu Ime Samāsate ||

54. छन्दांसि यज्ञाः क्रतवो व्रतानि भृतं भव्यं यच्च वेदा वदन्ति ।
सर्वं देवी सृजते विश्वमेतत् तस्याश्चान्यो मायया सन्निरुद्धः ॥
Chandāṃsi Yajñāḥ Kratavo Vratāni Bhṛtaṃ Bhavyaṃ Yacca Vedā Vadanti |
Sarvaṃ Devī Sṛjate Viśvametat Tasyāścānyo Māyayā Sanniruddhaḥ ||

55. मायां तु प्रकृतिं विद्यात् प्रभुं तस्या महेश्वरीम् । अस्या अवयवैः सूक्ष्मैर्व्याप्तं सर्वमिदं जगत्॥

Māyāṃ Tu Prakṛtiṃ Vidyāt Prabhuṃ Tasyā Maheśvarīm |
Asyā Avayavaiḥ Sūkṣmairvyāptaṃ Sarvamidaṃ Jagat ||

56. या देवानां प्रभवा चोद्भवा च विश्वाधिपा सर्वभूतेषु गूढा ।
हिरण्यगर्भं जनयामास पूर्वं सा नो बुद्ध्या शुभया संयुनक्तुम्॥

Yā Devānāṃ Prabhavā Codbhavā Ca Viśvādhipā Sarvabhūteṣu Gūḍhā |
Hiraṇyagarbhaṃ Janayāmāsa Pūrvaṃ Sā No Buddhyā Śubhayā Saṃyunaktum ||

57. सूक्ष्मातिसूक्ष्मं सलिलस्य मध्ये विश्वस्य स्रष्ट्रीमनेकाननाख्याम् ।
विश्वस्य चैकां परिवेष्टयित्रीं ज्ञात्वा गुह्यां शान्तिमत्यन्तमेति ॥

Sūkṣmātisūkṣmaṃ Salilasya Madhye Viśvasya Sraṣṭrīmanekānanākhyām |
Viśvasya Caikāṃ Pariveṣṭayitrīṃ Jñātvā Guhyāṃ Śāntimatyantameti ||

58. सा ह्येव काले भुवनस्य गोप्त्री विश्वाधिपा सर्वभूतेषु गूढा।
यम्यां मुक्ता ब्रह्मर्षयोऽपि देवाः ज्ञात्वा तां मुत्युपाशाञ्छिनत्ति॥

Sā Hyeva Kāle Bhuvanasya Goptrī Viśvādhipā Sarvabhūteṣu Gūḍhā |
Yamyāṃ Muktā Bradmarṣayo'pi Devāḥ Jñātvā Tāṃ Mutyupāśāñchinatti ||

59. घृतात् परं मण्डमिवातिसूक्ष्मं ज्ञात्वा कालीं सर्वभूतेषु गूढाम्।
कल्पान्ते वै सर्वसंहारकर्त्रीं ज्ञात्वा गुह्यां मुच्यते सर्वपापैः॥

Ghṛtāt Paraṃ Maṇḍamivātisūkṣmaṃ Jñātvā Kālīṃ Sarvabhūteṣu Gūḍhām |
Kalpānte Vai Sarvasaṃhārakatrīṃ Jñātvā Guhyāṃ Mucyate Sarvapāpaiḥ ||

60. एषा देवी विश्वयोनिर्महात्मा सदा जनानां हृदि सन्निविष्टा।
हृदा मनीषा मनसाभिक्लृप्ता ये तां विदुरमृतास्ते भवन्ति॥

Eṣā Devī Viśvayonirmahātmā Sadā Janānāṃ Hṛdi Sanniviṣṭā |
Hṛdā Manīṣā Manasābhikḷptā Ye Tāṃ Viduramṛtāste Bhavanti ||

61. यदा तमस्तत्र दिवा न रात्रिः न सन्न चासद्भगवत्येव गुह्या।
तदक्षरं तत्सवितुर्वरेण्यं प्रज्ञा च तस्याः प्रसृता परा सा॥

Yadā Tamastatra Divā Na Rātriḥ Na Sanna Cāsadbhagavatyeva Guhyā |
Tadakṣaraṃ Tatsaviturvareṇyaṃ Prajñā Ca Tasyāḥ Prasṛtā Parā Sā ||

62. नैनामूर्ध्वं न तिर्यक् च न मध्यं परिजग्रभत्।
न तस्याः प्रतिमाभिश्च तस्या नाम महद्यशः

Naināmūrdhvaṃ Na Tiryak Ca Na Madhyaṃ Parijagrabhat |
Na Tasyāḥ Pratimābhiśca Tasyā Nāma Mahadyaśaḥ ||

63. न सन्दृशे तिष्ठति लूपमस्याः न चक्षुषा पश्यति कश्चिदेनाम्।
हृदा मनीषा मनसाभिक्लृप्तां य एनां विदुरमृतास्ते भवन्ति॥

Na Sandṛśe Tiṣṭhati Lrūpamasyāḥ Na Cakṣuṣā Paśyati Kaścidenām |
Hṛdā Manīṣā Manasābhikḷptāṃ Ya Enāṃ Viduramṛtāste Bhavanti ||

64. भूयश्च सृष्ट्वा त्रिदशानथेशी सर्वाधिपत्यं कुरुते भवानी ।
सर्वा दिशश्चोर्ध्वमधश्च तिर्यक् प्रकाशयन्ती भ्राजते गुह्यकाली ॥

Bhūyaśca Sṛṣṭvā Tridaśānatheśī Sarvādhipatyaṃ Kurute Bhavānī |
Sarvā Diśaścordhvamadhaśca Tiryak Prakāśayantī Bhrājate Guhyakālī ||

65. नैव स्त्री न पुमानेषा नैव चेयं नपुंसका। यद्यच्छरीरमादत्ते तेन तेनैव युज्यते ॥

Naiva Strī Na Pumāneṣā Naiva Ceyaṃ Napuṃsakā |
Yadyaccharīramādatte Tena Tenaiva Yujyate ||

66. धर्मावहां पापनुदां भगेशीं ज्ञात्वात्मस्थाममृतां विश्वमातरम् ।
तामीश्वराणां परमां महेश्वरीं तां देवतानां परदेवतां च ।
पतिं पतीनां परमां पुरस्तात् विद्यावतां गुह्यकालीं मनीषाम् ॥
Dharmāvahāṃ Pāpanudāṃ Bhageśīṃ Jñātvātmasthāmamṛtāṃ Viśvamātaram |
Tāmīśvarāṇāṃ Paramāṃ Maheśvarīṃ Tāṃ Devatānāṃ Paradevatāṃ Ca |
Patiṃ Patīnāṃ Paramāṃ Purastāt Vidyāvatāṃ Guhyakālīṃ Manīṣām ||

67. तस्या न कार्यं करणं च विद्यते न तत्समा चाप्यधिका च दृश्यते ।
परास्याः शक्तिर्विविधैव श्रूयते स्वाभाविकी ज्ञानबलक्रिया च ॥
Tasyā Na Kāryaṃ Karaṇaṃ Ca Vidyate Na Tatsamā Cāpyadhikā Ca Dṛśyate |
Parāsyāḥ Śaktirvividhaiva Śrūyate Svābhāvikī Jñānabalakriyā Ca ||

68. कश्चिन्न तस्याः पतिरस्ति लोके न चेशिता नैव तस्याश्च लिङ्गम् ।
सा कारणं कारणकारणाधिपा नास्याश्च कश्चिज्जनिता न चाधिपः ॥

Kaścinna Tasyāḥ Patirasti Loke Na Ceśitā Naiva Tasyāśca Liṅgam |
Sā Kāraṇaṃ Kāraṇakāraṇādhipā Nāsyāśca Kaścijjanitā Na Cādhipaḥ ||

69. एका देवी सर्वभूतेषु गूढा व्याप्नोत्येतत् सर्वभूतान्तरस्था ।
कर्माध्यक्षा सर्वभूताधिवासा साक्षिण्येपा केवला निर्गुणा च ॥

Ekā Devī Sarvabhūteṣu Gūḍhā Vyāpnotyetat Sarvabhūtāntarasthā ।
Karmādhyakṣā Sarvabhūtādhivāsā Sākṣiṇyepā Kevalā Nirguṇā Ca ॥

70. वशिन्येका निष्कियाणां बहूनां एकं बीजं बहुधा या करोति ।
नानारूपा दशवक्त्रं विधत्ते नानारूपान् या च बाहून् बिभर्ति ॥

Vaśinyekā Niṣkiyāṇāṃ Bahūnāṃ Ekaṃ Bījaṃ Bahudhā Yā Karoti ।
Nānārūpā Daśavaktraṃ Vidhatte Nānārūpān Yā Ca Bāhūn Bibharti ॥

71. नित्या नित्यानां चेतना चेतनानां एका बहूनां विदधाति कामान् ।
तत्कारणं साङ्ख्ययोगाधिगम्यं ज्ञात्वा देवीं मुच्यते सर्वपाशैः ॥

Nityā Nityānāṃ Cetanā Cetanānāṃ Ekā Bahūnāṃ Vidadhāti Kāmān ।
Tatkāraṇaṃ Sāṅkhyayogādhigamyaṃ Jñātvā Devīṃ Mucyate Sarvapāśaiḥ ॥

72. या वै विष्णुं पालने सन्नियुङ्क्ते रुद्रं देवं संहृतौ चापि गुह्या ।
तां वै देवीमात्मबुद्धिप्रकाशां मुमुक्षु र्वैशरणमहं प्रपद्ये ॥

Yā Vai Viṣṇuṃ Pālane Sanniyuṅkte Rudraṃ Devaṃ Saṃhṛtau Cāpi Guhyā ।
Tāṃ Vai Devīmātmabuddhiprakāśāṃ Mumukṣurvai Śaraṇamahaṃ Prapadye ॥

73. निष्कला निष्क्रियां शान्तां निरवद्यां निरञ्जनाम् । बह्वाननकरां देवीं गुह्यामेकां समाश्रये ॥

Niṣkalā Niṣkriyāṃ Śāntāṃ Niravadyāṃ Nirañjanāṃ ।
Bahvānanakarāṃ Devīṃ Guhyāmekāṃ Samāśraye ॥

74. इयं हि गुह्योपनिषत् सुगूढा यस्या ब्रह्मा देवता विश्वयोनिः ।
एतां जपंश्चान्वहं भक्तियुक्तः सत्यं सत्यं ह्यमृतः सम्बभूव ॥

Iyaṃ Hi Guhyopaniṣat Sugṛḍhā Yasyā Brahmā Devatā Viśvayoniḥ ।
Etāṃ Japaṃścānvahaṃ Bhaktiyuktaḥ Satyaṃ Satyaṃ Hyamṛrataḥ Sambabhūva ॥

75. वेदवेदान्तयोर्गुह्यं पुराकल्पे प्रचोदितम् । नाप्रशान्ताय दातव्यं नाशिष्याय च वै पुनः ॥

Vedavedāntayorguhyaṃ Purākalpe Pracoditam ।
Nāpraśāntāya Dātavyaṃ Nāśiṣyāya Ca Vai Punaḥ ॥

76. यस्य देव्यां परा भक्तिर्यथा देव्यां तथा गुरौ। तस्यैते कथिता ह्यर्थाः प्रकाशन्ते महात्मनः ॥

Yasya Devyāṃ Parā Bhaktiryathā Devyāṃ Tathā Gurau I
Tasyaite Kathitā Hyarthāḥ Prakāśante Mahātmanaḥ II

77. महाकाल उवाच - *Mahākāla Uvāca* -
गुह्योपनिषदित्येषा गोप्यात् गोप्यतरा सदा। चतुर्भ्यश्चापि वेदेम्य एकीकृत्यात्र योजिता ॥

Guhyopaniṣadityeṣā Gopyāt Gopyatarā Sadā I
Caturbhyaścāpi Vedemya Ekīkṛtyātra Yojitā II

78. उपदिष्टा च सर्गादौ सर्वानेव दिवौकसः। एवंविधं च यद् ध्यानमेवंरूपंच कीर्तितम् ॥

Upadiṣṭā Ca Sargādau Sarvāneva Divaukasaḥ I
Evaṃvidhaṃ Ca Yaddhyānamevaṃrūpaṃ Ca Kīrtitam II

79. सा सपर्या परिज्ञेया विधानमधुना शृणु। सोऽहमस्मीति प्रथमं सोऽहमस्मि द्वितीयकम्

Sā Saparyā Parijñeyā Vidhānamadhunā Śṛṇu I
So'hamasmīti Prathamaṃ So'hamasmi Dvitīyakam II

80. तदस्स्यहं तृतीयं च महावाक्यत्रयं भवेत्। आद्यान्येतानि वाक्यानि छन्दांसि परिचक्षते ॥

Tadassyahaṃ Tṛtīyaṃ Ca Mahāvākyatrayaṃ Bhavet I
Ādyānyetāni Vākyāni Chandāṃsi Paricakṣate II

81. देवता गुह्यकाली च रजःसत्त्वतमोगुणाः। सर्वेषां प्रणवो बीजं हंसः शक्तिः प्रकीर्तिता ॥

Devatā Guhyakālī Ca Rajaḥsattvatamoguṇāḥ I
Sarveṣāṃ Praṇavo Bījaṃ Haṃsaḥ Śaktiḥ Prakīrtitā II

82. मकारश्चाप्यकारश्च ह्यु कारश्चेति कीलकम्। एभिर्वाक्यत्रयैः सर्वं कर्म प्रोतं विधानतः ॥

Makāraścāpyakāraśca Hyukāraśceti Kīlakam I
Ebhirvākyatrayaiḥ Sarvaṃ Karma Protaṃ Vidhānataḥ II

83. अनुक्षणं जपं श्चैव निश्चयः परिकीर्तितः। द्वितीयोपासकानां हि परिपाटीयमीरिता ॥

Anukṣaṇaṃ Japaṃścaiva Niścayaḥ Parikīrtitaḥ I
Dvitīyopāsakānāṃ Hi Paripāṭīyamīritā II

84. एवं चाप्यातुरो यस्तु मनुष्यो भक्तिभावितः। विमुक्तः सर्वपापेभ्यः कैवल्यायोपकल्पते
सर्वाभिः सिद्धिभिस्तस्य किं कार्यं कमलानने ॥

Evaṃ Cāpyāturo Yastu Manuṣyo Bhaktibhāvitaḥ |

Vimuktaḥ Sarvapāpebhyaḥ Kaivalyāyopakalpate |

Sarvābhiḥ Siddhibhistasya Kiṃ Kāryaṃ Kamalānane ||

शान्ति मन्त्र: | *Śānti Mantraḥ* |

ॐ भद्रं कर्णेभिः शृणुयाम देवाः। भद्रं पश्येमाक्षभिर्यजत्राः।

Oṃ Bhadraṃ Karṇebhiḥ Śṛṇuyāma Devāḥ ||

Bhadraṃ Paśyemākṣabhiryajatrāḥ ||

स्थिरैरङ्गैस्तुष्टुवाँसस्तनूभिः। व्यशेम देवहितं यदायुः।

Sthirairaṅgaistuṣṭuvāg̐Sastanūbhiḥ || *Vyaśema Devahitaṃ Yadāyuḥ* ||

स्वस्ति न इन्द्रो वृद्धश्रवाः। स्वस्ति नः पूषा विश्ववेदाः।

Svasti Na Indro Vṛddhaśravāḥ || *Svasti Naḥ Pūṣā Viśvavedāḥ* ||

स्वस्ति नस्तार्क्ष्यो अरिष्टनेमिः। स्वस्ति नो बृहस्पतिर्दधातु ॥

Svasti Nastārkṣyo Ariṣṭanemiḥ || *Svasti No Bṛhaspatirdadhātu* ||

ॐ शान्तिः शान्तिः शान्तिः ॥ *Oṃ Śāntiḥ Śāntiḥ Śāntiḥ* ||

इति श्रीमहाकालसंहितायां गुह्यकाल्युपनिषत् समाप्ता।

Iti Śrīmahākālasaṃhitāyāṃ Guhyakālyupaniṣat Samāptā |

*****

Guhyaṣoḍhānyāsopaniṣat

गुह्यषोढान्यासोपनिषत्

This is also another *Upaniṣat* from *Atharva Veda.*

शान्ति मन्त्रः । *Śānti Mantraḥ* ।

ॐ भद्रं कर्णेभिः शृणुयाम देवाः । भद्रं पश्येमाक्षभिर्यजत्राः ।

Oṃ Bhadraṃ Karṇebhiḥ Śṛṇuyāma Devāḥ ॥

Bhadraṃ Paśyemākṣabhiryajatrāḥ ॥
स्थिरैरङ्गैस्तुष्टुवाँसस्तनूभिः । व्यशेम देवहितं यदायुः ।

SthirairaṅgaistuṣṭuvāgͫSastanūbhiḥ ॥ *Vyaśema Devahitaṃ Yadāyuḥ* ॥
स्वस्ति न इन्द्रो वृद्धश्रवाः । स्वस्ति नः पूषा विश्ववेदाः ।

Svasti Na Indro Vṛddhaśravāḥ ॥ *Svasti Naḥ Pūṣā Viśvavedāḥ* ॥
स्वस्ति नस्तार्क्ष्यो अरिष्टनेमिः । स्वस्ति नो बृहस्पतिर्दधातु ॥

Svasti Nastārkṣyo Ariṣṭanemiḥ ॥ *Svasti No Bṛhaspatirdadhātu* ॥
ॐ शान्तिः शान्तिः शान्तिः ॥ *Oṃ Śāntiḥ Śāntiḥ Śāntiḥ* ॥

हरिः ॐ ॥ *Hariḥ Oṃ* ॥

अथ गुह्यां न्यसेत् । शिवो भवेत् । शक्तिरूपो भवेत् ।
विद्याराज्ञीन्यासमेवं चरेत् । न जपो न पूजा न साधनं न कालनियमो न दिवा न रात्रिः ।
सर्वकालं न्यसेत् । शक्तियुक्तो भवेत् । यथाधिकारवान् न्यसेत् । पूर्णदीक्षां लभेत् ।
षोढारूपो भवेत् । चिन्तामणिर्भवेत् । क्रीं मातृस्थाने न्यसेत् । परात् परतरो भवेत् ।
शिवो भवेदित्येकः । अथ ताराद्वयपुटितां मातृकां मातृकापुटितां तां मातृकास्थाने न्यसेत् ।
परातीतारूपो भवेदिति द्वितीयः । अथ शक्तिकाद्वयपुटितां मातृकां मातृकापुटितां तां न्यसेत् ।
तुर्यारूपो भवेत् । तृतीयकलारूपो भवेत् । कालसङ्कलनात् काली ।
सहेलं सलीलं वा स्मरणाद्वरदानेषु चतुरा । तेनेयं दक्षिणा । सम्बोधनद्वयपुटितां
मातृकां मातृकापुटितं नामद्वयं लिपिस्थाने न्यसेत् । तुर्यात् परारूपो भवेत् ।
चतुर्थीकलारूपो भवेत् । लोकपालसंवादिनी चतुर्थी ।
अथ पञ्चमीं कलां न्यसेत् । पञ्चमीकलारूपो भवेत् ।
सुभगात्रयं कूर्चवह्निललनां वह्नेस्त्रिकोणदैवतस्य लालनाच्छ्रीकण्ठरूपस्तुर्या परातीता ।
एतत्पुटितमातृकापुटितमेतन्मन्त्रं मातृकास्थाने न्यसेदिति पञ्चमी ।

शिवत्वं गच्छति । स सर्वरूपो भवेत् । अथ षष्ठीं कलां न्यसेत् ।
पूर्णां विद्याराज्ञीं लिपिस्थाने न्यसेद्व्यापयेत् । स शिवो भवेत् ।
स सर्वज्ञत्वं गच्छति । स कविर्भवेत् । स संन्यासी भवेत् ।
देवो ह वै भवेत् । विश्वरूपो भवेत् । अयुतं न्यसेत् । ऋषिच्छन्दादि पूर्ववद्भवेत् ।
ब्रह्माण्डगोलकेऽपि या जगतीतले तां सर्वां भुनक्ति ।
यस्याः स्मरणात् सिद्धो निदेशवर्ती च भवेत् तां न्यसेत् । न्यसनं न्यासः ।
सम्यक् न्यासः सन्न्यासः । न तु मुण्डितमुण्डः । तस्य देवादयो नमस्यन्तीति प्रोतं वेद ।

Atha Guhyāṃ Nyaset | Śivo Bhavet | Śaktirūpo Bhavet |
Vidyārājñīnyāsamevaṃ Caret | Na Japo Na Pūjā Na Sādhanaṃ Na Kālaniyamo Na Divā Na Rātriḥ | Sarvakālaṃ Nyaset | Śaktiyukto Bhavet |
Yathādhikāravān Nyaset | Pūrṇadīkṣāṃ Labhet | Ṣoḍhārūpo Bhavet |
Cintāmaṇirbhavet | Krīṃ Mātṛsthāne Nyaset | Parāt Parataro Bhavet |
Śivo Bhavedityekaḥ | Atha Tārādvayapuṭitāṃ Mātṛkāṃ Mātṛkāpuṭitāṃ Tāṃ Mātṛkāsthāne Nyaset | Parātītārūpo Bhavediti Dvitīyaḥ |
Atha Śaktikādvayapuṭitāṃ Mātṛkāṃ Mātṛkāpuṭitāṃ Tāṃ Nyaset |
Turyārūpo Bhavet | Tṛtīyakalārūpo Bhavet | Kālasaṅkalanāt Kālī |
Sahelaṃ Salīlaṃ Vā Smaraṇādvaradāneṣu Caturā | Teneyaṃ Dakṣiṇā |
Sambodhanadvayapuṭitāṃ Mātṛkāṃ Mātṛkāpuṭitaṃ Nāmadvayaṃ Lipisthāne Nyaset . Turyāt Parārūpo Bhavet | Caturthīkalārūpo Bhavet |
Lokapālasaṃvādinī Caturthī | Atha Pañcamīṃ Kalāṃ Nyaset |
Pañcamīkalārūpo Bhavet | Subhagātrayaṃ Kūrcavahnilalanāṃ Vahnestrikoṇadaivatasya Lālanācchrīkaṇṭharūpasturyā Parātītā . Etatpuṭitamātṛkāpuṭitametanmantraṃ Mātṛkāsthāne Nyaseditі Pañcamī | Śivatvaṃ Gacchati | Sa Sarvarūpo Bhavet |
Atha Ṣaṣṭhīṃ Kalāṃ Nyaset |
Pūrṇāṃ Vidyārājñīṃ Lipisthāne Nyasedvyāpayet |
Sa Śivo Bhavet | Sa Sarvajñatvaṃ Gacchati | Sa Kavirbhavet |
Sa Saṃnyāsī Bhavet | Devo Ha Vai Bhavet | Viśvarūpo Bhavet |
Ayutaṃ Nyaset | Ṛṣicchandādi Pūrvavadbhavet |
Brahmāṇḍagolake'pi Yā Jagatītale Tāṃ Sarvāṃ Bhunakti |
Yasyāḥ Smaraṇāt Siddho Nideśavartī Ca Bhavet Tāṃ Nyaset |
Nyasanaṃ Nyāsaḥ | Samyak Nyāsaḥ Sannyāsaḥ |

Na Tu Muṇḍitamuṇḍaḥ । Tasya Devādayo Namasyantīti Protaṃ Veda ।

ॐ शिवम् ॥ *Oṃ Śivam* ॥

शान्ति मन्त्र: । *Śānti Mantraḥ* ।

ॐ भद्रं कर्णेभिः शृणुयाम देवाः । भद्रं पश्येमाक्षभिर्यजत्राः ।

Oṃ Bhadraṃ Karṇebhiḥ Śṛṇuyāma Devāḥ ॥

Bhadraṃ Paśyemākṣabhiryajatrāḥ ॥
स्थिरैरङ्गैस्तुष्टुवाँसस्तनूभिः । व्यशेम देवहितं यदायुः ।

Sthirairaṅgaistuṣṭuvāg̐Sastanūbhiḥ ॥ *Vyaśema Devahitaṃ Yadāyuḥ* ॥
स्वस्ति न इन्द्रो वृद्धश्रवाः । स्वस्ति नः पूषा विश्ववेदाः ।

Svasti Na Indro Vṛddhaśravāḥ ॥ *Svasti Naḥ Pūṣā Viśvavedāḥ* ॥
स्वस्ति नस्तार्क्ष्यो अरिष्टनेमिः । स्वस्ति नो बृहस्पतिर्दधातु ॥

Svasti Nastārkṣyo Ariṣṭanemiḥ ॥ *Svasti No Bṛhaspatirdadhātu* ॥
ॐ शान्तिः शान्तिः शान्तिः ॥ *Oṃ Śāntiḥ Śāntiḥ Śāntiḥ* ॥

इत्याथर्वणे सौभाग्यकाण्डे गुह्यषोढान्यासोपनिषत् समाप्ता ।
Ityātharvaṇe Saubhāgyakāṇḍe Guhyaṣoḍhānyāsopaniṣat Samāptā ।

*****

Tulasyupaniṣat
तुलस्युपनिषत्

This is also another *Upaniṣat* from *Atharva Veda.*

शान्ति मन्त्रः । *Śānti Mantraḥ* ।

ॐ भद्रं कर्णेभिः शृणुयाम देवाः । भद्रं पश्येमाक्षभिर्यजत्राः ।

Oṃ Bhadraṃ Karṇebhiḥ Śṛṇuyāma Devāḥ ॥

Bhadraṃ Paśyemākṣabhiryajatrāḥ ॥
स्थिरैरङ्गैस्तुष्टुवाँसस्तनूभिः । व्यशेम देवहितं यदायुः ।

Sthirairaṅgaistuṣṭuvāg̃Sastanūbhiḥ ॥ *Vyaśema Devahitaṃ Yadāyuḥ* ॥
स्वस्ति न इन्द्रो वृद्धश्रवाः । स्वस्ति नः पूषा विश्ववेदाः ।

Svasti Na Indro Vṛddhaśravāḥ ॥ *Svasti Naḥ Pūṣā Viśvavedāḥ* ॥
स्वस्ति नस्ताक्ष्यों अरिष्टनेमिः । स्वस्ति नो बृहस्पतिर्दधातु ॥

Svasti Nastārkṣyo Ariṣṭanemiḥ ॥ *Svasti No Bṛhaspatirdadhātu* ॥
ॐ शान्तिः शान्तिः शान्तिः ॥ *Oṃ Śāntiḥ Śāntiḥ Śāntiḥ* ॥

हरिः ॐ ॥ *Hariḥ Oṃ* ॥

अध तुलस्युपनिषदं व्याख्यास्यामः । नारद ऋषिः ।
अथर्वाङ्गिराश्छन्दः । अमृता तुलसी देवता ।
सुधाबीजम् । वसुधा शक्तिः । नारायणः कीलकम् ।
Adha Tulasyupaniṣadaṃ Vyākhyāsyāmaḥ | *Nārada Ṛṣiḥ* |
Atharvāṅgirāśchandaḥ | *Amṛtā Tulasī Devatā* |
Sudhābījam | *Vasudhā Śaktiḥ* | *Nārāyaṇaḥ Kīlakam* |

श्यामां श्यामवपुर्धरां ऋक्स्वरूपां यजुर्मनसं ब्रह्माथर्वप्राणां
कल्पहस्तां पुराणपठितां अमृतोद्भवां अमृतरसमञ्जरीं अनन्तां
अनन्तरसभोगदां वैष्णवीं विष्णुवल्लभां मृत्युजन्मनिबर्हिणीं
दर्शनात्पापनाशिनीं स्पर्शनात्पावनीं अभिवन्दनाद् रोगनाशिनीं सेवनात्
मृत्युनाशिनीं वैकुण्ठार्चनात् विपद्धन्त्रीं, भक्षणात् वयुनप्रदां ,
प्रादक्षिण्यात् दारिद्र्यनाशिनीं, मूलमृल्लेपनात् महापापभञ्जिनीं
घ्राणतर्पणात् अन्तर्मलनाशिनीं य एवं वेद स वैष्णवो भवति ।

Śyāmāṃ Śyāmavapurdharāṃ Ṛksvarūpāṃ Yajurmanasaṃ Brahmātharvaprāṇāṃ Kalpahastāṃ Purāṇapaṭhitāṃ Amṛtodbhavāṃ Amṛtarasamañjarīṃ Anantāṃ Anantarasabhogadāṃ Vaiṣṇavīṃ Viṣṇuvallabhāṃ Mṛtyujanmanibarhiṇīṃ Darśanātpāpanāśinīṃ Sparśanātpāvanīṃ Abhivandanād Roganāśinīṃ Sevanāt Mṛtyunāśinīṃ Vaikuṇṭhārcanāt Vipaddhantrīṃ, Bhakṣaṇāt Vayunapradāṃ , Prādakṣiṇyāt Dāridryanāśinīṃ, Mūlamṛllepanāt Mahāpāpabhañjinīṃ Ghrāṇatarpaṇāt Antarmalanāśinīṃ Ya Evaṃ Veda Sa Vaiṣṇavo Bhavati |

1. वृथा न छिन्द्यात् । दृष्ट्वा प्रदक्षिणं कुर्यात् । द्वादश्यां न स्पृशेत् । पर्वणि न विचिन्वेत् । यदि विचन्वति स विष्णुहा भवति । श्री तुलस्यै स्वाहा । विष्णुप्रियायै स्वाहा । अमृतायै स्वाहा । श्री तुलस्यै विद्महे विष्णुप्रियायै धीमहि । तन्नो अमृता प्रचोदयात् ।
अमृतेऽमृतरूपाऽसि अमृतत्वप्रदायिनि । त्वं मामुद्धर संसारात्क्षीरसागर कन्यके ॥

Vṛthā Na Chindyāt | Dṛṣṭvā Pradakṣiṇaṃ Kuryāt |
Dvādaśyāṃ Na Spṛśet | Parvaṇi Na Vicinvet |
Yadi Vicanvati Sa Viṣṇuhā Bhavati | Śrī Tulasyai Svāhā |
Viṣṇupriyāyai Svāhā | Amṛtāyai Svāhā |
Śrī Tulasyai Vidmahe Viṣṇupriyāyai Dhīmahi | Tanno Amṛtā Pracodayāt |
Amṛte'mṛtarūpā'si Amṛtatvapradāyini |
Tvaṃ Māmuddhara Saṃsārāt Kṣīrasāgara Kanyake ||

2. श्रीसखि त्वं सदानन्दे मुकुन्दस्य सदा प्रिये । वरदाभयहस्ताभ्यां मां विलोकय दुर्लभे॥
Śrīsakhi Tvaṃ Sadānande Mukundasya Sadā Priye |
Varadābhayahastābhyāṃ Māṃ Vilokaya Durlabhe ||

3. अवृक्षवृक्षरूपाऽसि वृक्षत्वं मे विनाशय । तुलस्यतुलरूपाऽसि तुलाकोटिनिभेऽजरे ॥
Avṛkṣavṛkṣarūpā'si Vṛkṣatcaṃ Me Vināśaya |
Tulasyatularūpā'si Tulākoṭinibhe'jare ||

4. अतुले त्वत्तुलायां हि हरिरेकोऽस्ति नान्यथा । त्वमेव जगतां धात्री त्वमेव विष्णुवल्लभा ॥
Atule Tvattulāyāṃ Hi Harireko'sti Nānyathā |
Tvameva Jagatāṃ Dhātrī Tvameva Viṣṇuvallabhā ||

5. त्वमेव सुरसंसेव्या त्वमेव मोक्षदायिनी ।
त्वच्छायायां वसेल्लक्ष्मीः त्वन्मूले विष्णुरव्ययः । समन्ताद् देवताः सर्वाः सिद्धचारणपन्नगाः ॥

Tvameva Surasaṃsevyā Tvameva Mokṣadāyinī ।
Tvacchāyāyāṃ Vasellakṣmīḥ Tcanmūle Viṣṇuravyayaḥ ।
Samantād Devatāḥ Sarvāḥ Siddhacāraṇapannagāḥ ॥

6. यन्मूले सर्वतीर्थानि यन्मध्ये ब्रह्म देवताः । यदग्रे वेदशास्राणि तुलसीं तां नमाम्यहम् ॥
Yanmūle Sarvatīrthāni Yanmadhye Brahma Devatāḥ ।
Yadayre Vedaśāsrāṇi Tulasīṃ Tāṃ Namāmyaham ॥

7. तुलसि श्रीसखि शुभे पापहारिणि पुण्यदे। नमस्ते नारदनुते नारायणमनः प्रिये ॥
Tulasi Śrīsakhi Śubhe Pāpahāriṇi Puṇyade ।
Namaste Nāradanute Nārāyaṇamanaḥ Priye ॥

8. ब्रह्मानन्दाश्रुसञ्जाते वृन्दावननिवासिनि । सर्वावयसम्पूर्णे अमृतोपनिषद्रसे ॥
Brahmānandāśrusañjāte Vṛndāvananivāsini ।
Sarvāvayasampūrṇe Amṛtopaniṣadrase ॥

9. त्वं मामुद्धर कल्याणि महापापाब्धिदुस्तरात् । सर्वेषामपि पापानां प्रायश्चित्तं त्वमेव हि ॥
देवानां च ऋषीणां च पितॄणां त्वं सदा प्रिया ॥
Tvaṃ Māmuddhara Kalyāṇi Mahāpāpābdhidustarāt ।
Sarveṣāmapi Pāpānāṃ Prāyaścittaṃ Tvameva Hi ॥
Devānāṃ Ca Ṛṣīṇāṃ Ca Pitṝṇāṃ Tvaṃ Sadā Priyā ॥

10. विना श्रीतुलसीं विप्रा येऽपि श्राद्धं प्रकुर्वते। वृथा भवति तच्छ्राद्धं पितॄणां नोपगच्छति ॥
Vinā Śrītulasīṃ Viprā Ye'pi Śrāddhaṃ Prakurvate ।
Vṛthā Bhavati Tacchrāddhaṃ Pitṝṇāṃ Nopagacchati ॥

11. तुलसीपत्रमुत्सृज्य यदि पूजां करोति वै । आसुरी सा भवेत्पूजा विष्णुप्रीतिकरी न च ॥
Tulasīpatramutsṛjya Yadi Pūjāṃ Karoti Vai ।
Āsurī Sā Bhavetpūjā Viṣṇuprītikarī Na Ca ॥

12. यज्ञं दानं जपं तीर्थं श्राद्धं वै देवतार्चनम् । तर्पणं मार्जनं चान्यन्न कुर्यात् तुलसीं विना ॥
Yajñaṃ Dānaṃ Japaṃ Tīrthaṃ Śrāddhaṃ Vai Devatārcanam ।
Tarpaṇaṃ Mārjanaṃ Cānyanna Kuryāt Tulasīṃ Vinā ॥

13. तुलसीदारुमणिभिर्जपः सर्वार्थसाधकः । एवं न वेद यः कश्चित् स विप्रः श्वपचाधमः ॥

Tulasīdārumaṇibhirjapaḥ Sarvārthasādhakaḥ I
Evaṃ Na Veda Yaḥ Kaścit Sa Vipraḥ Śvapacādhamaḥ II

14. इत्याह भगवान् ब्रह्माणं नारायणः ,ब्रह्मा नारदसनकादिभ्यः,
सनकादयो वेदव्यासाय, वेदव्यासः शुकाय, शुको वामदेवाय, वामदेवो
मुनिभ्यः , मुनयो मनुभ्यः प्रोचुः ।
Ityāha Bhagavān Brahmāṇaṃ Nārāyaṇaḥ, Brahmā Nārada Sanakādibhyaḥ, Sanakādayo Vedavyāsāya, Vedavyāsaḥ Śukāya, Śuko Vāmadevāya, Vāmadevo Munibhyaḥ , Munayo Manubhyaḥ Procuḥ I

य एवं वेद, स स्रीहत्यायाः प्रमुच्यते, स वीरहत्यायाः प्रमुच्यते,
स ब्रह्महत्यायाः प्रमुच्यते, स महाभयात् प्रमुच्यते, स महादुःखात्प्रमुच्यते, देहान्ते
वैकुण्ठमवाप्नोति वैकुण्ठमवाप्नोति । इत्युपनिषत् ।
Ya Evaṃ Veda, Sa Srīhatyāyāḥ Pramucyate, Sa Vīrahatyāyāḥ Pramucyate, Sa Brahmahatyāyāḥ Pramucyate, Sa Mahābhayāt Pramucyate, Sa Mahāduḥkhātpramucyate, Dehānte Vaikuṇṭhamavāpnoti Vaikuṇṭhamavāpnoti I *Ityupaniṣat* I

शान्ति मन्त्र: I *Śānti Mantraḥ* I

ॐ भद्रं कर्णेभिः शृणुयाम देवाः । भद्रंपश्येमाक्षभिर्यजत्राः ।

Oṃ Bhadraṃ Karṇebhiḥ Śṛṇuyāma Devāḥ II

Bhadraṃ Paśyemākṣabhiryajatrāḥ II
स्थिरैरङ्गैस्तुष्टुवाँसस्तनूभिः । व्यशेम देवहितं यदायुः ।

Sthirairaṅgaistuṣṭuvāg̃Sastanūbhiḥ II

Vyaśema Devahitaṃ Yadāyuḥ II
स्वस्ति न इन्द्रो वृद्धश्रवाः । स्वस्ति नः पूषा विश्ववेदाः ।

Svasti Na Indro Vṛddhaśravāḥ II *Svasti Naḥ Pūṣā Viśvavedāḥ* II
स्वस्ति नस्ताक्ष्र्यो अरिष्टनेमिः । स्वस्ति नो बृहस्पतिर्दधातु ॥

Svasti Nastārkṣyo Ariṣṭanemiḥ II *Svasti No Bṛhaspatirdadhātu* II

ॐ शान्तिः शान्तिः शान्तिः ॥ *Oṃ Śāntiḥ Śāntiḥ Śāntiḥ* II

इति तुलस्योपनिषत् समाप्ता । *Iti Tulasyupaniṣat Samāptā* I

*****

Pītāmbaropaniṣat

पीताम्बरोपनिषत्

This is also another *Upaniṣat* from *Atharva Veda.*

शान्ति मन्त्रः । *Śānti Mantraḥ* ।

ॐ भद्रं कर्णेभिः शृणुयाम देवाः । भद्रं पश्येमाक्षभिर्यजत्राः ।

Oṃ Bhadraṃ Karṇebhiḥ Śṛṇuyāma Devāḥ ॥

Bhadraṃ Paśyemākṣabhiryajatrāḥ ॥
स्थिरैरङ्गैस्तुष्टुवाँसस्तनूभिः । व्यशेम देवहितं यदायुः ।

SthirairaṅgaistuṣṭuvāġSastanūbhiḥ ॥ *Vyaśema Devahitaṃ Yadāyuḥ* ॥
स्वस्ति न इन्द्रो वृद्धश्रवाः । स्वस्ति नः पूषा विश्ववेदाः ।

Svasti Na Indro Vṛddhaśravāḥ ॥ *Svasti Naḥ Pūṣā Viśvavedāḥ* ॥
स्वस्ति नस्तार्क्ष्यो अरिष्टनेमिः । स्वस्ति नो बृहस्पतिर्दधातु ॥

Svasti Nastārkṣyo Ariṣṭanemiḥ ॥ *Svasti No Bṛhaspatirdadhātu* ॥
ॐ शान्तिः शान्तिः शान्तिः ॥ *Oṃ Śāntiḥ Śāntiḥ Śāntiḥ* ॥

हरिः ॐ ॥ *Hariḥ Oṃ* ॥

ॐ अथ हैनां ब्रह्मरन्ध्रे सुभगां ब्रह्मास्त्रत्वरूपिणीमाप्नोति ।
ब्रह्मास्त्रां महाविद्यां शाम्भवीं सर्वस्तम्भकरीं सिद्धां चतुर्भुजां दक्षाभ्यां कराभ्यां मुद्गरपाशै वामाभ्यां शत्रुजिह्वावज्रे दधानां पतिवाससं पीतालङ्कारसम्पन्ना दृढीभूतपीनोन्नतपयोधरयुग्माढ्यां तप्तकार्तस्वरकुण्डलद्वयविराजितमुखाम्भोजां ललाटपट्टोल्लसत्पीतचन्द्रार्धमनुबिभ्रतीमुद्यद्दिवाकरोद्योतां स्वर्णसिंहासनमध्यकमलसंस्थांधिया सञ्चिन्त्य तदुपरि त्रिकोणषट्कोणवसुपत्रवृत्तान्तः षोडशदलकमलोपरि भूबिम्बत्रयमनुसन्धाय तत्राद्ययोन्यन्तरे देवीमाहूय ध्यायेत् ।
Oṃ Atha Haināṃ Brahmarandhre Subhagāṃ Brahmāstratvarūpiṇīmāpnoti ।

Brahmāstrāṃ Mahāvidyāṃ Śāmbhavīṃ Sarvastambhakarīṃ Siddhāṃ Caturbhujāṃ Dakṣābhyāṃ Karābhyāṃ Mudgarapāśai Vāmābhyāṃ Śatrujihnāvajre Dadhānāṃ Pativāsasaṃ Pītālaṅkārasampannā Dṛḍhībhūtapīnonnatapayodharayugmāḍhyāṃ Taptakārtasvarakuṇḍaladvayavirājitamukhāmbhojāṃ Lalāṭapaṭṭollasatpītacandrārdhamanubibhratīmudyaddivākarodyotāṃ

Svarṇasiṃhāsanamadhyakamalasaṃsthāṃ Dhiyā Sañcintya Tadupari Trikoṇaṣaṭkoṇavasupatravṛttāntaḥ Ṣoḍaśadalakamalopari Bhūbimbatrayamanusandhāya Tatrādyayonyantare Devīmāhūya Dhyāyet ।

योनिं जगद्योनिं समायमुच्चार्य शिवाते भूमाग्रबिन्दुमिन्दु खण्डमग्निबीजं ततो वरुणाङ्कगुणार्णमत्रियुतं स्थिरामुखि इति सम्बोध्य सर्वदु ष्टानामिदं चाभाष्य वाचमिति मुखमिति पदमिति स्तम्भयेति वोच्चार्य जिह्वां वैशारदी कीलयेति बुद्धिं विनाशयेति प्रोच्चार्य भूमायां वेदाद्यं ततो यज्ञभूगुहायां योजयेत् । स महास्तम्भेश्वरः सर्वेश्वरः ।

Yoniṃ Jagadyoniṃ Samāyamuccārya Śivāte Bhūmāgrabindumindukhaṇḍamagnibījaṃ Tato Varuṇāṅkaguṇārṇamatriyutaṃ Sthirāmukhi Iti Sambodhya Sarvaduṣṭānāmidaṃ Cābhāṣya Vācamiti Mukhamiti Padamiti Stambhayeti Voccārya Jihvāṃ Vaiśāradī Kīlayeti Buddhiṃ Vināśayeti Proccārya Bhūmāyāṃ Vedādyaṃ Tato Yajñabhūguhāyāṃ Yojayet । *Sa Mahāstambheśvaraḥ Sarveśvaraḥ* ।

स मेनास्तम्भं करोति । किं बहुना विवस्वद्धृतिस्तम्भकर्ता सर्ववातस्तम्भकर्तेति । किं दिवाकर्षयति । स सर्वविद्येश्वरः सर्वमन्त्रेश्वरो भूत्वा पूजाया आवर्तनं त्रैलोक्यस्तम्भिन्याः कुर्यात् ।

Sa Menāstambhaṃ Karoti ।

Kiṃ Bahunā Vivasvaddhṛtistambhakartā Sarvavātastambhakarteti ।

Kiṃ Divākarṣayati । *Sa Sarvavidyeśvaraḥ Sarvamantreśvaro Bhūtvā Pūjāyā Āvartanaṃ Trailokyastambhinyāḥ Kuryāt* ।

अङ्गमाद्यं द्वारतो गणेशं वटुकं योगिनीं क्षेत्राधीशं च पूर्वादिकमभ्यर्च्य गुरुपङ्क्तिमीशासुरान्तमन्तः प्राच्यादौ क्रमानुगता बगला स्तम्भिनी जृम्भिणी मोहिनी वश्या अचला चला दु र्धरा अकल्मषा आधारा कल्पना कालकर्षिणी भ्रमरिका मदगमना भोगा योगिका एता ह्यष्टदलानुगताः पूज्याः ।

Aṅgamādyaṃ Dvārato Gaṇeśaṃ Vaṭukaṃ Yoginīṃ Kṣetrādhīśaṃ Ca Pūrvādikamabhyarcya Gurupaṅktimīśāsurāntamantaḥ Prācyādau Kramānugatā Bagalā Stambhinī Jṛmbhiṇī Mohinī Vaśyā Acalā Calā Durdharā Akalmaṣā Ādhārā Kalpanā Kālakarṣiṇī Bhramarikā Madagamanā Bhogā Yogikā Etā Hyaṣṭadalānugatāḥ Pūjyāḥ ।

ब्राह्मी माहेश्वरी कौमारी वैष्णवी वाराही नारसिंही चामुण्डा महालक्ष्मीश्च।
षड्योनिगर्भान्ता डाकिनी राकिनी लाकिनी काकिनी शाकिनी हाकिनी वेद्याद्यम्थिरमायाद्याः
समभ्यर्च्य शक्राग्नियमनिरृतिवरुणवायव्यधनदेशानप्रजापतिनागेशाः परिवाराभिमताः
स्थिरादिवेदाद्याः सवाहनाः सदस्त्रका बाह्यतोऽभ्यर्च्य तां योनिं रतिप्रीतिमनोभवा एताः सर्वाः
समाः पीतांशुकाध्येयाः। तदन्तमूलायां बलादिषोडशानुगताः पूज्याः नीराजनैः।
स हैश्वर्ययुक्तो भवति। य एनां ध्यायति स वाग्मी भवति। सोऽमृतमश्नुते।
सर्वसिद्धिकर्ता भवति। सृष्टिस्थितिसंहारकर्ता भवति। स सर्वेश्वरो भवति।
स तु ऋद्धीश्वरो भवति। स शाक्तः स वैष्णवः स गणपः स शैवः। स जीवन्मुक्तो भवति।
स संन्यासई भवति। न्यसनं न्यासः। सम्यङ्न्यासः सन्न्यासः। न तु मुण्डितमुण्डः।
षट्त्रिंशदस्त्रेश्वरो भवेत् सौभाग्यार्चनेनेति प्रोतं वेद।

Brāhmī Māheśvarī Kaumārī Vaiṣṇavī Vārāhī Nārasiṃhī Cāmuṇḍā Mahālakṣmīśca I *Ṣaḍyonigarbhāntā Ḍākinī Rākinī Lākinī Kākinī Śākinī Hākinī Vedyādyamthiramāyādyāḥ Samabhyarcya Śakrāgniyamanirṛtivaruṇavāyavyadhanadeśānaprajāpatināgeśāḥ Parivārābhimatāḥ Sthirādivedādyāḥ Savāhanāḥ Sadastrakā Bāhyato'bhyarcya Tāṃ Yoniṃ Ratiprītimanobhavā Etāḥ Sarvāḥ Samāḥ Pītāṃśukā Dhyeyāḥ* I

Tadantamūlāyāṃ Balādiṣoḍaśānugatāḥ Pūjyāḥ Nīrājanaiḥ I

Sa Haiśvaryayukto Bhavati I *Ya Enāṃ Dhyāyati Sa Vāgmī Bhavati* I

So'mṛratamaśnute I *Sarvasiddhikartā Bhavati* I

Sṛṣṭisthitisaṃhārakartā Bhavati I *Sa Sarveśvaro Bhavati* I

Sa Tu Ṛddhīśvaro Bhavati I

Sa Śāktaḥ Sa Vaiṣṇavaḥ Sa Gaṇapaḥ Sa Śaivaḥ I

Sa Jīvanmukto Bhavati I *Sa Saṃnyāsaī Bhavati* I *Nyasanaṃ Nyāsaḥ* I

Samyaṅnyāsaḥ Sannyāsaḥ I *Na Tu Muṇḍitamuṇḍaḥ* I

Ṣaṭtriṃśadastreśvaro Bhavet Saubhāgyārcaneneti Protaṃ Veda I

ॐ शिवम्॥ *Oṃ Śivam* ॥

शान्ति मन्त्रः। *Śānti Mantraḥ* I

ॐ भद्रं कर्णेभिः शृणुयाम देवाः। भद्रं पश्येमाक्षभिर्यजत्राः।

Oṃ Bhadraṃ Karṇebhiḥ Śṛṇuyāma Devāḥ ॥

Bhadraṃ Paśyemākṣabhiryajatrāḥ ॥

स्थिरैरङ्गैस्तुष्टुवाँसस्तनूभिः । व्यशेम देवहितं यदायुः ।

Sthirairaṅgaistuṣṭuvāg̃Sastanūbhiḥ ॥ *Vyaśema Devahitaṃ Yadāyuḥ* ॥

स्वस्ति न इन्द्रो वृद्धश्रवाः । स्वस्ति नः पूषा विश्ववेदाः ।

Svasti Na Indro Vṛddhaśravāḥ ॥ *Svasti Naḥ Pūṣā Viśvavedāḥ* ॥

स्वस्ति नस्तार्क्ष्यो अरिष्टनेमिः । स्वस्ति नो बृहस्पतिर्दधातु ॥

Svasti Nastārkṣyo Ariṣṭanemiḥ ॥ *Svasti No Bṛhaspatirdadhātu* ॥

ॐ शान्तिः शान्तिः शान्तिः ॥ *Oṃ Śāntiḥ Śāntiḥ Śāntiḥ* ॥

इति पीताम्बरोपनिषत् समाप्ता । *Iti Pītāmbaropaniṣat Samāptā* ।

*****

Muktikopaniṣat

मुक्तिकोपनिषत्

This is also another *Upaniṣat* from *Atharva Veda*. All the Shakta related *Upaniṣats* lead to liberation. Hence all are called as *Mukti Upaniṣats* However there is also a separate *Upaniṣat* called *Muktikopaniṣat*.

हरिः ॐ ॥ *Hariḥ Oṃ* ॥

ईशाद्यष्टोत्तरशतवेदान्तपटलाशयम् । मुक्तिकोपनिषद्वेद्यं रामचन्द्रपदं भजे ॥

Īśādyaṣṭottaraśatavedāntapaṭalāśayam I
Muktikopaniṣadvedyaṃ Rāmacandrapadaṃ Bhaje II

शान्ति मन्त्रः । *Śānti Mantraḥ* I

हरिः ॐ पूर्णमदः पूर्णमिदं पूर्णात्पूर्णमुदच्यते। पूर्णस्य पूर्णमादाय पूर्णमेवावशिष्यते॥

Hariḥ Oṃ Pūrṇamadaḥ Pūrṇamidaṃ Pūrṇātpūrṇamudacyate I
Pūrṇasya Pūrṇamādāya Pūrṇamevāvaśiṣyate II

ॐ शान्तिः शान्तिः शान्तिः ॥ *Oṃ Śāntiḥ Śāntiḥ Śāntiḥ* ॥

1. ॐ अयोध्यानगरे रम्ये रत्नमण्डपमध्यमे । सीताभरतसौमित्रिशत्रुघ्नाद्यैः समन्वितम् ॥

Oṃ Ayodhyānagare Ramye Ratnamaṇḍapamadhyame I
Sītābharatasaumitriśatrughnādyaiḥ Samanvitam II

2. सनकाद्यैर्मुनिगणैर्वसिष्ठाद्यैः शुकादिभिः । अन्यैर्भागवतैश्चापि स्तूयमानमहर्निशम् ॥

Sanakādyairmunigaṇairvasiṣṭhādyaiḥ Śukādibhiḥ I
Anyairbhāgavataiścāpi Stūyamānamaharniśam II

3. धीविक्रियासहस्राणां साक्षिणं निर्विकारिणम् । स्वरूपध्याननिरतं समाधिविरमे हरिम्

Dhīvikriyāsahasrāṇāṃ Sākṣiṇaṃ Nirvikāriṇam I
Svarūpadhyānaniratam Samādhivirame Harim II

4. भक्त्या शुश्रूषया रामं स्तुवन्पप्रच्छ मारुतिः । राम त्वं परमात्मसि सच्चिदानन्दविग्रहः ॥

Bhaktyā Śuśrūṣayā Rāmaṃ Stuvanpapraccha Mārutiḥ I
Rāma Tvaṃ Paramātmasi Saccidānandavigrahaḥ II

5. इदानीं त्वां रघुश्रेष्ठ प्रणमामि मुहुर्मुहुः। त्वद्रूपं ज्ञातुमिच्छामि तत्त्वतो राम मुक्तये॥

Idānīṃ Tvāṃ Raghuśreṣṭha Praṇamāmi Muhurmuhuḥ |
Tvadrūpaṃ Jñātumicchāmi Tattvato Rāma Muktaye ||

6. अनायासेन येनाहं मुच्येयं भवबन्धनात्। कृपया वद मे राम येन मुक्तो भवाम्यहम्॥

Anāyāsena Yenāhaṃ Mucyeyaṃ Bhavabandhanāt |
Kṛpayā Vada Me Rāma Yena Mukto Bhavāmyaham ||

7. साधु पृष्टं महाबाहो वदामि शृणु तत्त्वतः। वेदान्ते सुप्रतिष्ठोऽहं वेदान्तं समुपाश्रय॥

Sādhu Pṛṣṭaṃ Mahābāho Vadāmi Śṛṇu Tattvataḥ |
Vedānte Supratiṣṭho'haṃ Vedāntaṃ Samupāśraya ||

8. वेदान्ताः के रघुश्रेष्ठ वर्तन्ते कुत्र ते वद। हनूमञ्छृणु वक्ष्यामि वेदान्तस्थितिमञ्जसा॥

Vedāntāḥ Ke Raghuśreṣṭha Vartante Kutra Te Vada |
Hanūmañchṛṇu Vakṣyāmi Vedāntasthitimañjasā ||

9. निश्वासभूता मे विष्णोर्वेदा जाताः सुविस्तराः। तिलेषु तैलवद्वेदे वेदान्तः सुप्रतिष्ठितः॥

Niśvāsabhūtā Me Viṣṇorvedā Jātāḥ Suvistarāḥ |
Tileṣu Tailavadvede Vedāntaḥ Supratiṣṭhitaḥ ||

10. राम वेदाः कतिविधास्तेषां शाखाश्च राघव। तासूपनिषदाः काः स्युः कृपया वद तत्त्वतः

Rāma Vedāḥ Katividhāsteṣāṃ Śākhāśca Rāghava |
Tāsūpaniṣadāḥ Kāḥ Syuḥ Kṛpayā Vada Tattvataḥ ||

11. श्रीराम उवाच। *Śrīrāma Uvāca |*

ऋग्वेदादिविभागेन वेदाश्चत्वार ईरिताः। तेषां शाखा ह्यनेकाः स्युस्तासूपनिषदस्तथा॥

Ṛgvedādivibhāgena Vedāścatvāra Īritāḥ |
Teṣāṃ Śākhā Hyanekāḥ Syustāsūpaniṣadastathā ||

12. ऋग्वेदस्य तु शाखाः स्युरेकविंशतिसङ्ख्यकाः। नवाधिकशतं शाखा यजुषो मारुतात्मज॥

Ṛgvedasya Tu Śākhāḥ Syurekaviṃśatisaṅkhyakāḥ |
Navādhikaśataṃ Śākhā Yajuṣo Mārutātmaja ||

13. सहस्रसङ्ख्यया जाताः शाखाः साम्नः परन्तप।
अथर्वणस्य शाखाः स्युः पञ्चाशद्भेदतो हरे॥

Sahasrasaṅkhyayā Jātāḥ Śākhāḥ Sāmnaḥ Parantapa |
Atharvaṇasya Śākhāḥ Syuḥ Pañcāśadbhedato Hare ||

14. एकैकस्यास्तु शाखाया एकैकोपनिषन्मता । तासामेकामृचं यश्च पठते भक्तितो मयि ॥

Ekaikasyāstu Śākhāyā Ekaikopaniṣanmatā |
Tāsāmekāmṛcaṃ Yaśca Paṭhate Bhaktito Mayi ||

15. स मत्सायुज्यपदवीं प्राप्नोति मुनिदुर्लभाम्। राम केचिन्मुनिश्रेष्ठा मुक्तिरेकेति चक्षिरे ॥

Sa Matsāyujyapadavīṃ Prāpnoti Munidurlabhām |
Rāma Kecinmuniśreṣṭhā Muktireketi Cakṣire ||

16. केचित्त्वन्नामभजनात्काश्यां तारोपदेशतः । अन्येतु साङ्ख्ययोगेन भक्तियोगेन चापरे ॥

Kecittvannāmabhajanātkāśyāṃ Tāropadeśataḥ |
Anyetu Sāṅkhyayogena Bhaktiyogena Cāpare ||

17. अन्ये वेदान्तवाक्यार्थविचारात्परमर्षयः । सालोक्यादिविभागेन चतुर्धा मुक्तिरीरिता ॥

Anye Vedāntavākyārthavicārātparamarṣayaḥ |
Sālokyādivibhāgena Caturdhā Muktirīritā ||

18. सहोवाच श्रीरामः । *Sahovāca Śrīrāmaḥ* |

कैवल्यमुक्तिरेकैव परमार्थिकरूपिणी । दुराचाररतो वापि मन्नामभजनात्कपे ॥

Kaivalyamuktirekaiva Paramārthikarūpiṇī |
Durācārarato Vāpi Mannāmabhajanātkape ||

19. सालोक्यमुक्तिमाप्नोति न तु लोकान्तरादिकम् ।
काश्यां तु ब्रह्मनालेऽस्मिन्मृतो मत्तारमाप्नुयात् ॥

Sālokyamuktimāpnoti Na Tu Lokāntarādikam |
Kāśyāṃ Tu Brahmanāle'sminmṛto Mattāramāpnuyāt ||

20. पुनरावृत्तिरहितां मुक्तिं प्राप्नोति मानवः । यत्र कुत्रापि वा काश्यां मरणे स महेश्वरः ॥

Punarāvṛttirahitāṃ Muktiṃ Prāpnoti Mānavaḥ |
Yatra Kutrāpi Vā Kāśyāṃ Maraṇe Sa Maheśvaraḥ ||

21. जन्तोर्दक्षिणकर्णे तु मत्तारं समुपादिशेत्। निर्धूताशेषपापौघो मत्सारूप्यं भजत्ययम् ॥

Jantordakṣiṇakarṇe Tu Mattāraṃ Samupādiśet ।
Nirdhūtāśeṣapāpaugho Matsārūpyaṃ Bhajatyayam ॥

22. सैव सालोक्यसारूप्यमुक्तिरत्यभिधीयते। सदाचाररतो भूत्वा द्विजो नित्यमनन्यधीः ॥

Saiva Sālokyasārūpyamuktiratyabhidhīyate ।
Sadācārarato Bhūtvā Dvijo Nityamananyadhīḥ ॥

23. मयि सर्वात्मको भावो मत्सामीप्यं भजत्ययम्।
सैव सालोक्यसारूप्यसामीप्या मुक्तिरिष्यते॥

Mayi Sarvātmako Bhāvo Matsāmīpyaṃ Bhajatyayam ।
Saiva Sālokyasārūpyasāmīpyā Muktiriṣyate ॥

24. गुरूपदिष्टमार्गेण ध्यायन्मद्गुणमव्ययम्। मत्सायुज्यं द्विजः सम्यग्भजेद्भ्रमरकीटवत् ॥

Gurūpadiṣṭamārgeṇa Dhyāyanmadguṇamavyayam ।
Matsāyujyaṃ Dvijaḥ Samyagbhajedbhramarakīṭavat ॥

25. सैव सायुज्यमुक्तिः स्याद्ब्रह्मानन्दकरी शिवा। चतुर्विधा तु या मुक्तिर्मदुपासनया भवेत् ॥

Saiva Sāyujyamuktiḥ Syādbrahmānandakarī Śivā ।
Caturvidhā Tu Yā Muktirmadupāsanayā Bhavet ॥

26. इयं कैवल्यमुक्तिस्तु केनोपायेन सिद्ध्यति। माण्डूक्यमेकमेवालं मुमुक्षूणांविमुक्तये॥

Iyaṃ Kaivalyamuktistu Kenopāyena Siddhyati ।
Māṇḍūkyamekamevālaṃ Mumukṣūṇāṃ Vimuktaye ॥

27. तथाप्यसिद्धं चेज्ज्ञानं दशोपनिषदं पठ। ज्ञानं लब्ध्वा चिरादेव मामकं धाम यास्यसि ॥

Tathāpyasiddhaṃ Cejjñānaṃ Daśopaniṣadaṃ Paṭha ।
Jñānaṃ Labdhvā Cirādeva Māmakaṃ Dhāma Yāsyasi ॥

28. तथापि दृढता न चेद्विद्ज्ञानस्याञ्जनासुत। द्वात्रिंशाख्योपनिषदं समभ्यस्य निवर्तय ॥

Tathāpi Dṛḍhatā Na Cedvidjñānasyāñjanāsuta ।
Dvātriṃśākhyopaniṣadaṃ Samabhyasya Nivartaya ॥

29. विदेहमुक्ताविच्छा चेदष्टोत्तरशतं पठ। तासां क्रम सशान्तिं च श्रुणु वक्ष्यामि तत्त्वतः ॥

Videhamuktāvicchā Cedaṣṭottaraśataṃ Paṭha ।
Tāsāṃ Krama Saśāntiṃ Ca Śruṇu Vakṣyāmi Tattvataḥ ॥

30. ईशकेनकठप्रश्नमुण्डमाण्डूक्यतित्तिरिः। ऐतरेयं च छान्दोग्यं बृहदारण्यकं तथा ॥

Īśakenakaṭhapraśnamuṇḍamāṇḍūkyatittiriḥ |
Aitareyaṃ Ca Chāndogyaṃ Bṛhadāraṇyakaṃ Tathā ||

31. ब्रह्मकैवल्यजाबालश्वेताश्वो हंस आरुणिः। गर्भो नारायणो हंसो बिन्दुर्नादशिरः शिखा ॥

Brahmakaivalyajābālaśvetāśvo Haṃsa Āruṇiḥ |
Garbho Nārāyaṇo Haṃso Bindurnādaśiraḥ Śikhā ||

32. मैत्रायणी कौषीतकी बृहज्जाबालतापनी। कालाग्निरुद्रमैत्रेयी सुबालक्षुरिमन्त्रिका॥

Maitrāyaṇī Kauṣītakī Bṛhajjābālatāpanī |
Kālāgnirudramaitreyī Subālakṣurimantrikā ||

33. सर्वसारं निरालम्बं रहस्यं वज्रसूचिकम्। तेजोनादध्यानविद्यायोगतत्त्वात्मबोधकम् ॥

Sarvasāraṃ Nirālambaṃ Rahasyaṃ Vajrasūcikam |
Tejonādadhyānavidyāyogatattvātmabodhakam ||

34. परिव्राट् त्रिशिखी सीता चूडा निर्वाणमण्डलम्। दक्षिणा शरभं स्कन्दं महानारायणाह्वयम् ॥

Parivrāṭ Triśikhī Sītā Cūḍā Nirvāṇamaṇḍalam |
Dakṣiṇā Śarabhaṃ Skandaṃ Mahānārāyaṇāhvayam ||

35. रहस्यं रामतपनं वासुदेवं च मुद्गलम्। शाण्डिल्यं पैङ्गलं भिक्षु महच्छारीरकं शिखा ॥

Rahasyaṃ Rāmatapanaṃ Vāsudevaṃ Ca Mudgalam |
Śāṇḍilyaṃ Paiṅgalaṃ Bhikṣumahacchārīrakaṃ Śikhā ||

36. तुरीयातीतसंन्यासपरिव्राजाक्षमालिका। अव्यक्तैकाक्षरं पूर्णा सूर्याक्ष्यध्यात्मकुण्डिका ॥

Turīyātītasaṃnyāsaparivrājākṣamālikā |
Avyaktaikākṣaraṃ Pūrṇā Sūryākṣyadhyātmakuṇḍikā

37. सावित्र्यात्मा पाशुपतं परं ब्रह्मावधूतकम्। त्रिपुरातपनं देवीत्रिपुरा कठभावना।
हृदयं कुण्डली भस्म रुद्राक्षगणदर्शनम् ॥

Sāvitryātmā Pāśupataṃ Paraṃ Brahmāvadhūtakam |

Tripurātapanaṃ Devītripurā Kaṭhabhāvanā |
Hṛdayaṃ Kuṇḍalī Bhasma Rudrākṣagaṇadarśanam ||

38. तारसारमहावाक्य पञ्चब्रह्माग्निहोत्रकम्। गोपालतपनं कृष्णं याज्ञवल्क्यं वराहकम् ॥

Tārasāramahāvākya Pañcabrahmāgnihotrakam I
Gopālatapanaṃ Kṛṣṇaṃ Yājñavalkyaṃ Varāhakam II

39. शाट्यायनी हयग्रीवं दत्तात्रेयं च गारुडम् । कलिजाबालिसौभाग्यरहस्यऋचमुक्तिका ॥

Śāṭyāyanī Hayagrīvaṃ Dattātreyaṃ Ca Gāruḍam I
Kalijābālisaubhāgyarahasyaṛcamuktikā II

40. एवमष्टोत्तरशतं भावनात्रयनाशनम् । ज्ञानवैराग्यदं पुंसां वासनात्रयनाशनम् ॥

Evamaṣṭottaraśataṃ Bhāvanātrayanāśanam I
Jñānavairāgyadaṃ Puṃsāṃ Vāsanātrayanāśanam II

41. पूर्वोत्तरेषु विहिततत्तच्छान्तिपुरःसरम् । वेदविद्याव्रतस्नातदेशिकस्य मुखात्स्वयम् ॥

Pūrvottareṣu Vihitatattacchāntipuraḥsaram I
Vedavidyāvratasnātadeśikasya Mukhātsvayam II

42. गृहीत्वाष्टोत्तरशतं ये पठन्ति द्विजोत्तमाः । प्रारब्धक्षयपर्यन्तं जीवन्मुक्ता भवन्ति ते ॥

Gṛhītvāṣṭottaraśataṃ Ye Paṭhanti Dvijottamāḥ I
Prārabdhakṣayaparyantaṃ Jīvanmuktā Bhavanti Te II

43. ततः कालवशादेव प्रारब्धे तु क्षयं गते । वैदेहीं मामकीं मुक्तिं यान्ति नास्त्यत्रसंशयः ॥

Tataḥ Kālavaśādeva Prārabdhe Tu Kṣayaṃ Gate I
Vaidehīṃ Māmakīṃ Muktiṃ Yānti Nāstyatrasaṃśayaḥ II

44. सर्वोपनिषदां मध्ये सारमष्टोत्तरशतम् । सकृच्छ्रवणमात्रेण सर्वाघौघनिकृन्तनम् ॥

Sarvopaniṣadāṃ Madhye Sāramaṣṭottaraśatam I
Sakṛcchravaṇamātreṇa Sarvāghaughanikṛntanam II

45. मयोपदिष्टं शिष्याय तुभ्यं पवननन्दन । इदं शास्त्रं मयादिष्टं गुह्यमष्टोत्तरं शतम् ॥

Mayopadiṣṭaṃ Śiṣyāya Tubhyaṃ Pavananandana I
Idaṃ Śāstraṃ Mayādiṣṭaṃ Guhyamaṣṭottaraṃ Śatam II

46. ज्ञानतोऽज्ञानतो वापि पठतां बन्धमोचकम् । राज्यं देयं धनं देयं याचतः कामपूरणम् ॥

Jñānato'jñānato Vāpi Paṭhatāṃ Bandhamocakam I
Rājyaṃ Deyaṃ Dhanaṃ Deyaṃ Yācataḥ Kāmapūraṇam II

47. इदमष्टोत्तरशतं न देयं यस्य कस्यचित् । नास्तिकाय कृतघ्नाय दुराचाररताय वै ॥

Idamaṣṭottaraśataṃ Na Deyaṃ Yasya Kasyacit |
Nāstikāya Kṛtaghnāya Durācāraratāya Vai ||

48. मद्भक्तिविमुखायापि शास्त्रगर्तेषु मुह्यते। गुरुभक्तिविहीनाय दातव्यं न कदाचन ॥

Madbhaktivimukhāyāpi Śāstragarteṣu Muhyate |
Gurubhaktivihīnāya Dātavyaṃ Na Kadācana ||

49. सेवापराय शिष्याय हितपुत्राय मारुते। मद्भक्ताय सुशीलाय कुलीनाय सुमेधसे ॥

Sevāparāya Śiṣyāya Hitaputrāya Mārute |
Madbhaktāya Suśīlāya Kulīnāya Sumedhase ||

1. सम्यक् परीक्ष्य दातव्यमेवमष्टोत्तरं शतम्। यः पठेच्छृणुयाद्वापि स मामेति न संशयः।
तदेतदृचाभ्युक्तम्। विद्या ह वै ब्राह्मणमाजगाम गोपाय मा शेवधिष्टीऽहमस्मि।
असूयकायानृजवे शठाय मा मा ब्रूया वीर्यवती तथा स्याम्।
यमेव विद्याश्रुतमप्रमत्तं मेधाविनं ब्रह्मचर्योपपन्नम्।
तस्मा इमामुपसन्नाय सम्यक् परीक्ष्य दद्याद्वैष्णवीमात्मनिष्ठाम् ॥ इति ॥

Samyak Parīkṣya Dātavyamevamaṣṭottaraṃ Śatam |

Yaḥ Paṭhecchṛṇuyādvāpi Sa Māmeti Na Saṃśayaḥ |

Tadetadṛcābhyuktam |

Vidyā Ha Vai Brāhmaṇamājagāma Gopāya Mā Śevadhiṣṭī'hamasmi |

Asūyakāyānṛjave Śaṭhāya Mā Mā Brūyā Vīryavatī Tathā Syām |
Yameva Vidyāśrutamapramattaṃ Medhāvinaṃ Brahmacaryopapannam |
Tasmā Imāmupasannāya Samyak Parīkṣya Dadyādvaiṣṇavīmātmaniṣṭhām || Iti ||

1. अथ हैनं श्रीरामचन्द्रं मारुतिः पप्रच्छ ऋग्वेदादिविभागेन पृथक् शान्तिमनुब्रूहीति।
Atha Hainaṃ Śrīrāmacandraṃ Mārutiḥ Papraccha Ṛgvedādivibhāgena Pṛthak Śāntimanubrūhīti |

स होवाच श्रीरामः। *Sa Hovāca Śrīrāmaḥ |*

ऐतरेयकौषीतकीनादबिन्द्वात्मप्रबोधनिर्वाण मुद्गलाक्षमालिकात्रिपुरासौभाग्यबह्वृचा
नामृग्वेदगतानां दशसंख्याकानामुपनिषदां वाङ्मे मनसीति शान्तिः ॥

Aitareyakauṣītakīnādabindvātmaprabodhanirvāṇa-
Mudgalākṣamālikātripurāsaubhāgyabahvṛcā
Nāmṛgvedagatānāṃ Daśasaṃkhyākānāmupaniṣadāṃ
Vāṅme Manasīti Śāntiḥ ||

2. ईशावास्यबृहदारण्यजाबालहंसपरमहंससुबालमन्त्रिकानिरालम्बत्रिशिखी ब्राह्मणमण्डलब्राह्मणाद्वयतारक पैङ्गलभिक्षु तुरीयातीताध्यात्मतारसारयाज्ञवल्क्य शाट्यायनीमुक्तिकानां शुक्लयजुर्वेदगतानामेकोनविंशतिसंख्याकानामुपनिषदां पूर्णमद इति शान्तिः ॥

Īśāvāsyabṛhadāraṇyajābālahaṃsaparamahaṃsasubāla-
Mantrikānirālambatriśikhībrāhmaṇamaṇḍalabrāhmaṇādvayatāraka-
Paiṅgalabhikṣuturīyātītādhyātmatārasārayājñavalkya-
Śāṭyāyanīmuktikānāṃ Śuklayajurvedagatānāmekonaviṃśati-
Saṃkhyākānāmupaniṣadāṃ Pūrṇamada Iti Śāntiḥ ||

3. कठवल्लीतैत्तिरीयकब्रह्मकैवल्यश्वेताश्वतरगर्भ नारायणामृतबिन्द्वमृतनादकालाग्निरुद्र क्षुरिकासर्वसारशुकरहस्यतेजोबिन्दु ध्यानबिन्दुब्रह्मविद्या योगतत्त्वदक्षिणामूर्तिस्कन्द शारीरकयोगशिखैकाक्षर अक्ष्यवधूतकठरुद्रहृदययोगकुण्डलिनीपञ्चब्रह्म-प्राणाग्निहोत्रवराहकलिसन्तरणसरस्वतीरहस्यानां कृष्णयजुर्वेदगतानां द्वात्रिंशत्संख्याकानमुपनिषदां सह नाववत्विति शान्तिः ॥

Kaṭhavallītaittirīyakabrahmakaivalyaśvetāśvataragarbha-
Nārāyaṇāmṛtabindvamṛtanādakālāgnirudrakṣurikā-
Sarvasāraśukarahasyatejobindudhyānabindubrahmavidyā-
Yogatattvadakṣiṇāmūrtiskandaśārīrakayogaśikhaikākṣara-
Akṣyavadhūtakaṭharudrahṛdayayogakuṇḍalinīpañcabrahma-
Prāṇāgnihotravarāhakalisantaraṇasarasvatīrahasyānāṃ
Kṛṣṇayajurvedagatānāṃ Dvātriṃśatsaṃkhyākānamupaniṣadāṃ
Saha Nāvavatviti Śāntiḥ ||

4. केनछान्दोग्यारुणिमैत्रायणिमैत्रेयीवज्रसूचिकायोगचूडामणि-वासुदेवमहत्संन्यासाव्यक्तकुण्डिकासावित्रीरुद्राक्षजाबालदर्शन-जाबालीनां सामवेदगतानां षोडशसंख्याकाना मुपनिषदानामाप्यायन्त्विति शान्तिः ॥

Kenachāndogyāruṇimaitrāyaṇimaitreyīvajrasūcikāyogacūḍāmaṇi-
Vāsudevamahatsaṃnyāsāvyaktakuṇḍikāsāvitrīrudrākṣajābāladarśana-
Jābālīnāṃ Sāmavedagatānāṃ Ṣoḍaśasaṃkhyākānā-
Mupaniṣadānāmāpyāyantviti Śāntiḥ ||

5. प्रश्नमुण्डकमाण्डुक्याथर्वशिरोऽथर्वशिखाबृहज्जाबालनृसिंहतापनीनारदपरिव्राजक
सीताशरभमहानारायण रामरहस्यरामतापनीशाण्डिल्यपरमहंसपरिव्राजक-
अन्नपूर्णासूर्यात्मपाशुपतपरब्रह्मत्रिपुरातपनदेवीभावना ब्रह्मजाबालगणपति
महावाक्यगोपालतपनकृष्णहयग्रीव दत्तात्रेयगारुडानामथर्ववेदगतानामेकत्रिंशत्संख्याकाना
मुपनिषदां भद्रं कर्णेभिरिति शान्तिः ॥

Praśnamuṇḍakamāṇḍukyātharvaśiro'tharvaśikhābṛhajjābāla-
Nṛsiṃhatāpanīnāradaparivrājakasītāśarabhamahānārāyaṇa-
Rāmarahasyarāmatāpanīśāṇḍilyaparamahaṃsaparivrājaka-
Annapūrṇāsūryātmapāśupataparabrahmatripurātapanadevībhāvanā-
Brahmajābālagaṇapatimahāvākyagopālatapanakṛṣṇahayagrīva-
Dattātreyagāruḍānāmatharvavedagatānāmekatriṃśatsaṃkhyākānā-
Mupaniṣadāṃ Bhadraṃ Karṇebhiriti Śāntiḥ ॥

6. मुमुक्षवः पुरुषाः साधनचतुष्टयसम्पन्नाः श्रद्धावन्तः सुकुलभवं श्रोत्रियं शास्त्रवात्सल्य-
गुणवन्तमकुटिलं सर्वभूतहितेरतं दयासमुद्रं सद्गुरुं विधिवदुपसंगम्योपहार
पाणयोऽष्टोत्तरशतोपनिषदं विधिवदधीत्य श्रवणमनननिदिध्यासनानि
नैरन्तर्येण कृत्वा प्रारब्धक्षयाद्देहत्रयभंगं प्राप्योपाधिविनिर्मुक्त-
घटाकाशवत्परिपूर्णता विदेहमुक्तिः। सैव कैवल्यमुक्तिरिति।
अत एव ब्रह्मलोकस्था अपि ब्रह्ममुखाद्वेदान्तश्रवणादि कृत्वा तेन सह कैवल्यं लभन्ते।
अतः सर्वेषां कैवल्यमुक्तिर्ज्ञानमात्रेणोक्ता।
न कर्मसांख्ययोगोपासनादिभिरित्युपनिषत् ॥

Mumukṣavaḥ Puruṣāḥ Sādhanacatuṣṭayasampannāḥ
Śraddhāvantaḥ Sukulabhavaṃ Śrotriyaṃ Śāstravātsalya-
Guṇavantamakuṭilaṃ Sarvabhūtahiterataṃ Dayāsamudraṃ Sadguruṃ
Vidhivadupasaṃgamyopahārapāṇayo'ṣṭottaraśatopaniṣadaṃ
Vidhivadadhītya Śravaṇamanananididhyāsanāni Nairantaryeṇa Kṛtvā
Prārabdhakṣayāddehatrayabhaṃgaṃ Prāpyopādhivinirmukta-
Ghaṭākāśavatparipūrṇatā Videhamuktiḥ । *Saiva Kaivalyamuktiriti* ।
Ata Eva Brahmalokasthā Api Brahmamukhādvedāntaśravaṇādi Kṛtvā
Tena Saha Kaivalyaṃ Labhante ।
Ataḥ Sarveṣāṃ Kaivalyamuktirjñānamātreṇoktā ।
Na Karmasāṃkhyayogopāsanādibhirityupaniṣat ॥

इति प्रथमोऽध्यायः ॥ *Iti Prathamo'dhyāyaḥ* ॥

तथा हैनं श्रीरामचन्द्रं मारुतिः पप्रच्छ । केयं वा तत्सिद्धिः सिद्ध्या वा किं प्रयोजनमिति । सहोवाच श्रीरामः । पुरुषस्य कर्तृत्वभोक्तृत्व सुखदुःखादिलक्षणश्चित्तधर्मः क्लेशरूपत्वाद्बन्धो भवति । तन्निरोधनं जीवन्मुक्तिः । उपाधिविनिर्मुक्त घटाकाशवत्प्रारब्धक्षयाद्विदेहमुक्तिः । जीवन्मुक्तिविदेहमुक्त्योरष्टोत्तरशतोपनिषदः प्रमाणम् । कर्तृत्वादिदुःखनिवृत्तिद्वारा नित्यानन्दावाप्तिः प्रयोजनं भवति ।

तत्पुरुषप्रयत्नसाध्यं भवति । यथा पुत्रकामेष्टिना पुत्रं वाणिज्यादिना वित्तं ज्योतिष्टोमेन स्वर्गं तथा पुरुषप्रयत्नसाध्यवेदान्तश्रवणादिजनितसमाधिना जीवन्मुक्त्यादिलाभो भवति । सर्ववासनाक्षयात्तल्लाभः । अत्र श्लोका भवन्ति ॥

Tathā Hainaṃ Śrīrāmacandraṃ Mārutiḥ Papraccha ।

Keyaṃ Vā Tatsiddhiḥ Siddhyā Vā Kiṃ Prayojanamiti ।

Sahovāca Śrīrāmaḥ । *Puruṣasya Kartṛtvabhoktṛtva-*

Sukhaduḥkhādilakṣaṇaścittadharmaḥ Kleśarūpatvādbandho Bhavati ।

Tannirodhanaṃ Jīvanmuktiḥ । *Upādhivinirmukta*

Ghaṭākāśavatprārabdhakṣayādvidehamuktiḥ ।

Jīvanmuktividehamuktyoraṣṭottaraśatopaniṣadaḥ Pramāṇam ।

Kartṛtvādiduḥkhanivṛttidvārā Nityānandāvāptiḥ Prayojanaṃ Bhavati ।

Tatpuruṣaprayatnasādhyaṃ Bhavati । *Yathā Putrakāmeṣṭinā Putraṃ Vāṇijyādinā Vittaṃ Jyotiṣṭomena Svargaṃ Tathā Puruṣaprayatnasādhyavedāntaśravaṇādijanitasamādhinā*

Jīvanmuktyādilābho Bhavati । *Sarvavāsanākṣayāttallābhaḥ* । *Atra Ślokā Bhavanti* ॥

1. उच्छास्त्रं शास्त्रितं चेति पौरुषं द्विविधं मतम् । अत्रोच्छस्त्रमनर्थाय परमार्थाय शास्त्रितम् ॥

Ucchāstraṃ Śāstritaṃ Ceti Pauruṣaṃ Dvividhaṃ Matam ।
Atrocchastramanarthāya Paramārthāya Śāstritam ॥

2. लोकवासनया जन्तोः शास्त्रवासनयापि च । देहवासनया ज्ञानं यथावन्नैव जायते ॥

Lokavāsanayā Jantoḥ Śāstravāsanayāpi Ca ।
Dehavāsanayā Jñānaṃ Yathāvannaiva Jāyate ॥

3. द्विविधा वासनाव्यूहः शुभश्चैवाशुभश्च तौ । वासनौघेन शुद्धेन तत्र चेदनुनीयसे ॥

Dvividhā Vāsanāvyūhaḥ Śubhaścaivāśubhaśca Tau |
Vāsanaughena Śuddhena Tatra Cedanunīyase ||

4. तत्क्रमेणाशु तेनैव मामकं पदमाप्नुहि। अथ चेदशुभो भावस्त्वां योजयति संकटे।।

Tatkrameṇāśu Tenaiva Māmakaṃ Padamāpnuhi |
Atha Cedaśubho Bhāvastvāṃ Yojayati Saṃkaṭe ||

5. प्राक्तनस्तदसौ यत्नाज्जेतव्यो भवता कपे। शुभाशुभाभ्यां मार्गाभ्यां वहन्ती वासनासरित्।।

Prāktanastadasau Yatnājjetavyo Bhavatā Kape |
Śubhāśubhābhyāṃ Mārgābhyāṃ Vahantī Vāsanāsarit ||

6. पौरुषेण प्रयत्नेन योजनीया शुभे पथि। अशुभेषु समाविष्टं शुभेष्वेवावतारयेत्।।

Pauruṣeṇa Prayatnena Yojanīyā Śubhe Pathi |
Aśubheṣu Samāviṣṭaṃ Śubheṣvevāvatārayet ||

7. अशुभाच्चालितं याति शुभं तस्मादपीतरत्। पौरुषेण प्रयत्नेन लालयेच्चित्तबालकम्।।

Aśubhāccālitaṃ Yāti Śubhaṃ Tasmādapītarat |
Pauruṣeṇa Prayatnena Lālayeccittabālakam ||

8. द्रागभ्यासवशाद्याति यदा ते वासनोदयम्। तदाभ्यासस्य साफल्यं विद्धि त्वममरिमर्दन ।।

Drāgabhyāsavaśādyāti Yadā Te Vāsanodayam |
Tadābhyāsasya Sāphalyaṃ Viddhi Tvamamarimardana ||

9. सन्दिग्धायामपि भृशं शुभामेव समाचर। शुभायां वासनावृद्धौ न दोषाय मरुत्सुत।।

Sandigdhāyāmapi Bhṛśaṃ Śubhāmeva Samācara |
Śubhāyāṃ Vāsanāvṛddhau Na Doṣāya Marutsuta ||

10. वासनाक्षयविज्ञानमनोनाशा महामते। समकालं चिराभ्यस्ता भवन्ति फलदा मताः ।।

Vāsanākṣayavijñānamanonāśā Mahāmate |
Samakālaṃ Cirābhyastā Bhavanti Phaladā Matāḥ ||

11. त्रय एवं समं यावन्नाभ्यस्ताश्च पुनः पुनः। तावन्न पदसम्प्राप्तिर्भवत्यपि समाशतैः ।।

Traya Evaṃ Samaṃ Yāvannābhyastāśca Punaḥ Punaḥ |
Tāvanna Padasamprāptirbhavatyapi Samāśataiḥ ||

12. एकैकशो निषेव्यन्ते यद्येते चिरमप्यलम्। तन्न सिद्धिं प्रयच्छन्ति मन्त्राः संकीर्तिता इव ।।

Ekaikaśo Niṣevyante Yadyete Ciramapyalam ।
Tanna Siddhiṃ Prayacchanti Mantrāḥ Saṃkīrtitā Iva ॥

13. त्रिभिरेतैश्चिराभ्यस्तैर्हृदयग्रन्थयो दृढाः । निःशङ्कमेव त्रुठ्यन्ति बिसच्छेदाद्गुणाइव ॥

Tribhiretaiścirābhyastairhṛdayagranthayo Dṛḍhāḥ ।
Niḥśaṅkameva Truṭhyanti Bisacchedādguṇā Iva ॥

14. जन्मान्तशताभ्यस्ता मिथ्या संसारवासना। सा चिराभ्यासयोगेन विना न क्षीयते क्वचित्

Janmāntaśatābhyastā Mithyā Saṃsāravāsanā ।
Sā Cirābhyāsayogena Vinā Na Kṣīyate Kvacit ॥

15. तस्मात्सौम्य प्रयत्नेन पौरुषेण विवेकिना। भोगेच्छां दूतस्त्यक्त्वा त्रयमेव समाश्रय ॥

Tasmātsaumya Prayatnena Pauruṣeṇa Vivekinā ।
Bhogecchāṃ Dūratastyaktvā Trayameva Samāśraya ॥

16. तस्माद्वासनया युक्तं मनो बद्धं विदुर्बुधाः । सम्यग्वासनया त्यक्तं मुक्तमित्यभिधीयते ।
मनोनिर्वासनीभावमाचराशु महाकपे ॥

Tasmādvāsanayā Yuktaṃ Mano Baddhaṃ Vidurbudhāḥ ।

Samyagvāsanayā Tyaktaṃ Muktamityabhidhīyate ।
Manonirvāsanībhāvamācarāśu Mahākape ॥

17. सम्यगालोचनात्सत्याद्वासना प्रविलीयते। वासनाविलये चेतः शममायाति दीपवत् ॥

Samyagālocanātsatyādvāsanā Pravilīyate ।
Vāsanāvilaye Cetaḥ Śamamāyāti Dīpavat ॥

18. वासनां सम्परित्यज्य मयि चिन्मात्र विग्रहे।
यस्तिष्ठति गतो व्यग्रः सोऽहं सच्चित्सुखात्मकः ॥

Vāsanāṃ Samparityajya Mayi Cinmātra Vigrahe ।
Yastiṣṭhati Gato Vyagraḥ So'haṃ Saccitsukhātmakaḥ ॥

19. समाधिमथ कार्याणि मा करोतु करोतु वा। हृदयेनात्तसर्वेहो मुक्त एवोत्तमाशयः ॥

Samādhimatha Kāryāṇi Mā Karotu Karotu Vā ।
Hṛdayenāttasarveho Mukta Evottamāśayaḥ ॥

20. नैष्कर्म्येण न तस्यार्थस्तस्यार्थोऽस्ति न कर्मभिः । न ससाधनजाप्याभ्यां यस्यनिर्वासनंमनः॥

Naiṣkarmyeṇa Na Tasyārthastasyārtho'sti Na Karmabhiḥ |
Na Sasādhanajāpyābhyāṃ Yasya Nirvāsanaṃ Manaḥ ||

21. संत्यक्तवासनान्मौनादृते नास्त्युत्तमं पदम् ॥

Saṃtyaktavāsanānmaunādṛte Nāstyuttamaṃ Padam ||

22. वासनाहीनमप्येतच्चक्षु रादीन्द्रियं स्वतः । प्रवर्तते बहिः स्वाऽर्थे वासनामात्रकारणम् ॥

Vāsanāhīnamapyetaccakṣurādīndriyaṃ Svataḥ |
Pravartate Bahiḥ Svā'rthe Vāsanāmātrakāraṇam ||

23. अयत्नोपनतेष्वक्षि दृग्द्रव्येषु यथा पुनः । नीरागमेव पतति तद्वत्कार्येषु धीरधीः ॥

Ayatnopanateṣvakṣi Dṛgdravyeṣu Yathā Punaḥ |
Nīrāgameva Patati Tadvatkāryeṣu Dhīradhīḥ ||

24. भावसंवित्प्रकटितामनुरूपा च मारुते । चित्तस्योत्पत्युपरमा वासनां मुनयो विदुः ॥

Bhāvasaṃvitprakaṭitāmanurūpā Ca Mārute |
Cittasyotpatyuparamā Vāsanāṃ Munayo Viduḥ ||

25. दृढाभ्यस्तपदार्थैकभावनादतिचञ्चलम् । चित्तं संजायते जन्मजरामरणकारणम् ॥

Dṛḍhābhyastapadārthaikabhāvanādaticañcalam |
Cittaṃ Saṃjāyate Janmajarāmaraṇakāraṇam ||

26. वासनावशतः प्राणस्पन्दस्तेन च वासना । क्रियते चित्तबीजस्य तेन बीजाङ्कुरक्रमः ॥

Vāsanāvaśataḥ Prāṇaspandastena Ca Vāsanā |
Kriyate Cittabījasya Tena Bījāṅkurakramaḥ ||

27. द्वे बीजे चित्तवृक्षस्य प्राणस्पन्दनवासने । एकस्मिंश्च तयोः क्षीणे क्षिप्रं द्वे अपि नश्यतः ॥

Dve Bīje Cittavṛkṣasya Prāṇaspandanavāsane |
Ekasmiṃśca Tayoḥ Kṣīṇe Kṣipraṃ Dve Api Naśyataḥ ||

28. असङ्गव्यवहारत्वाद्भवभावनवर्जनात् । शरीरनाशदर्शित्वाद्वासना न प्रवर्तते ।
वासनासम्परित्यागाच्चितं गच्छत्यचित्तताम् ॥

Asaṅgavyavahāratvādbhavabhāvanavarjanāt |

Śarīranāśadarśitvādvāsanā Na Pravartate |

Vāsanāsamparityāgāccitaṃ Gacchatyacittatām ||

29. अवासनत्वात्सततं यदा न मनुते मनः । अमनस्ता तदोदेति परमोपशमप्रदा ॥

Avāsanatvātsatataṃ Yadā Na Manute Manaḥ |
Amanastā Tadodeti Paramopaśamapradā ||

30. अव्युत्पन्नमना यावद्भवानज्ञाततत्पदः । गुरुशास्त्रप्रमाणैस्तु निर्णीतं तावदाचर ॥

Avyutpannamanā Yāvadbhavānajñātatatpadaḥ |
Guruśāstrapramāṇaistu Nirṇītaṃ Tāvadācara ||

31. ततः पक्वकषायेण नूनं विज्ञात वस्तुना। शुभोऽप्यसौ त्वया त्याज्यो वासनौघो निराधिना॥

Tataḥ Pakvakaṣāyeṇa Nūnaṃ Vijñāta Vastunā |
Śubho'pyasau Tvayā Tyājyo Vāsanaugho Nirādhinā ||

32. द्विविधचित्तनाशोऽस्ति सरूपोऽरूप एव च। जीवन्मुक्तः सरूपः स्यादरूपो देहमुक्तिगः ॥

Dvividhacittanāśo'sti Sarūpo'rūpa Eva Ca |
Jīvanmuktaḥ Sarūpaḥ Syādarūpo Dehamuktigaḥ ||

33. अस्य नाशमिदानीं त्वं पावने श्रुणु सादरम् ॥

Asya Nāśamidānīṃ Tvaṃ Pāvane Śruṇu Sādaram ||

34. चित्तानाशाभिधानं हि यदा ते विद्यते पुनः। मैत्र्यादिभिर्गुणैर्युक्तं शान्तिमेति न संशयः।
भूयोजन्मविनिर्मुक्तं जीवन्मुक्तस्य तन्मनः ॥

Cittānāśābhidhānaṃ Hi Yadā Te Vidyate Punaḥ |

Maitryādibhirguṇairyuktaṃ Śāntimeti Na Saṃśayaḥ |
Bhūyojanmavinirmuktaṃ Jīvanmuktasya Tanmanaḥ ||

35. सरूपोऽसौ मनोनाशो जीवन्मुक्तस्य विद्यते। अरूपस्तु मनोनाशो वैदेही मुक्तिगो भवेत् ॥

Sarūpo'sau Manonāśo Jīvanmuktasya Vidyate |
Arūpastu Manonāśo Vaidehī Muktigo Bhavet ||

36. सहस्राङ्कुरशाखात्मफलपल्लवशालिनः ॥

Sahasrāṅkuraśākhātmaphalapallavaśālinaḥ ||

37. अस्य संसारवृक्षस्य मनोमूलमिदं स्थितम्। संकल्प एव तन्मन्ये संकल्पोपशमेन तत् ॥

Asya Saṃsāravṛkṣasya Manomūlamidaṃ Sthitam |
Saṃkalpa Eva Tanmanye Saṃkalpopaśamena Tat ||

38. शोषयाशु यथा शोषमेति संसारपादपः । उपाय एक एवास्ति मनसः स्वस्य निग्रहे ॥

Śoṣayāśu Yathā Śoṣameti Saṃsārapādapaḥ |
Upāya Eka Evāsti Manasaḥ Svasya Nigrahe ||

39. मनसोऽभ्युदयो नाशो मनोनाशो महोदयः । ज्ञमनो नाशमभ्येति मनो ज्ञस्य हि शृङ्खला ॥

Manaso'bhyudayo Nāśo Manonāśo Mahodayaḥ |
Jñamano Nāśamabhyeti Mano Jñasya Hi Śṛṅkhalā ||

40. तावन्निशीव वेताला वल्गन्ति हृदि वासनाः । एकतत्त्वदृढाभ्यासाद्यावन्न विजितं मनः ॥

Tāvanniśīva Vetālā Valganti Hṛdi Vāsanāḥ |
Ekatattvadṛḍhābhyāsādyāvanna Vijitaṃ Manaḥ ||

41. प्रक्षीणचित्तदर्पस्य निगृहीतेन्द्रियद्विषः । पद्मिन्य इव हेमन्ते क्षीयन्ते भोगवासनाः ॥

Prakṣīṇacittadarpasya Nigṛhītendriyadviṣaḥ |
Padminya Iva Hemante Kṣīyante Bhogavāsanāḥ ||

42. हस्तं हस्तेन सम्पीड्य दन्तैर्दन्तान्विचूर्ण्य च ।
अङ्गान्यङ्गैः समाक्रम्य जयेदादौ स्वकं मनः ॥

Hastaṃ Hastena Sampīḍya Dantairdantānvicūrṇya Ca |
Aṅgānyaṅgaiḥ Samākramya Jayedādau Svakaṃ Manaḥ ||

43. उपविश्योपविश्यैकां चिन्तकेन मुहुर्मुहुः। न शक्यते मनो जेतुं विना युक्तिमनिन्दिताम् ॥

Upaviśyopaviśyaikāṃ Cintakena Muhurmuhuḥ |
Na Śakyate Mano Jetuṃ Vinā Yuktimaninditām

44. अङ्कुशेन विना मत्तो यथा दुष्टमतङ्गजः। अध्यात्मविद्याधिगमः साधुसंगतिरेव च ॥

Aṅkuśena Vinā Matto Yathā Duṣṭamataṅgajaḥ |
Adhyātmavidyādhigamaḥ Sādhusaṃgatireva Ca ||

45. वासनासम्परित्यागः प्राणस्पन्दनिरोधनम् । एतास्ता युक्तयः पुष्टाः सन्ति चित्तजये किल ॥

Vāsanāsamparityāgaḥ Prāṇaspandanirodhanam |
Etāstā Yuktayaḥ Puṣṭāḥ Santi Cittajaye Kila ||

46. सतीषु युक्तिष्वेतासु हठान्नियमन्ति ये । चेतसो दीपमुत्सृज्य विचिन्वन्ति तमोऽञ्जनैः ॥

Satīṣu Yuktiṣvetāsu Haṭhānniyamanti Ye ।
Cetaso Dīpamutsṛjya Vicinvanti Tamo'ñjanaiḥ ॥

47. विमूढाः कर्तुमुद्युक्ताये हठाच्चेतसो जयम् । ते निबध्नन्ति नागेन्द्रमुन्मत्तं बिसतन्तुभिः

Vimūḍhāḥ Kartumudyuktā Ye Haṭhāccetaso Jayam ।
Te Nibadhnanti Nāgendramunmattaṃ Bisatantubhiḥ ॥

48. द्वे बीजे चित्तवृक्षस्य वृत्तिव्रततिधारणः । एकं प्राणपरिस्पन्दो द्वितीयं दृढभावना ॥

Dve Bīje Cittavṛkṣasya Vṛttivratatidhāraṇaḥ ।
Ekaṃ Prāṇaparispando Dvitīyaṃ Dṛḍhabhāvanā ॥

49. सा हि सर्वगता संवित्प्राणास्पन्देन चाल्यते । चित्तैकाग्र्याद्यतो ज्ञानमुक्तं समुपजायते ॥

Sā Hi Sarvagatā Saṃvitprāṇāspandena Cālyate ।
Cittaikāgryādyato Jñānamuktaṃ Samupajāyate ॥

50. तत्साधनमथो ध्यानं यथावदुपदिश्यते । विनाप्यविकृतिं कृत्स्नां संभवव्यत्ययक्रमात्।
यशोऽरिष्टं च चिन्मात्रं चिदानन्दं विचिन्तय ॥

Tatsādhanamatho Dhyānaṃ Yathāvadupadiśyate ।

Vināpyavikṛtiṃ Kṛtsnāṃ Saṃbhavavyatyayakramāt ।
Yaśo'riṣṭaṃ Ca Cinmātraṃ Cidānandaṃ Vicintaya ॥

51. अपानेऽस्तंगते प्राणो यावन्नाभ्युदितो हृदि । तावत्सा कुंभकावस्था योगिभिर्यानुभूयते ॥

Apāne'staṃgate Prāṇo Yāvannābhyudito Hṛdi ।
Tāvatsā Kuṃbhakāvasthā Yogibhiryānubhūyate ॥

52. बहिरस्तंगते प्राणे यावन्नापान उद्गतः । तावत्पूर्णां समावस्थां बहिष्ठं कुम्भकं विदुः ॥

Bahirastaṃgate Prāṇe Yāvannāpāna Udgataḥ ।
Tāvatpūrṇāṃ Samāvasthāṃ Bahiṣṭhaṃ Kumbhakaṃ Viduḥ ॥

53. ब्रह्माकारमनोवृत्तिप्रवाहोऽहंकृतं विना । सम्प्रज्ञातसमाधिः स्याद् ध्यानाभ्यासप्रकर्षतः ॥

Brahmākāramanovṛttipravāho'haṃkṛtaṃ Vinā ।
Samprajñātasamādhiḥ Syāddhyānābhyāsaprakarṣataḥ ॥

54. प्रशान्तवृत्तिकं चित्तं परमानन्ददायकम् । असम्प्रज्ञातनामायं समाधिर्योगिनां प्रियः ॥

Praśāntavṛttikaṃ Cittaṃ Paramānandadāyakam |
Asamprajñātanāmāyaṃ Samādhiryogināṃ Priyaḥ ||

55. प्रभाशून्यं मनःशून्यं बुद्धिशून्यं चिदात्मकम् । अतद्व्यावृत्तिरूपोऽसौ समाधिर्मुनिभावितः ॥

Prabhāśūnyaṃ Manaḥśūnyaṃ Buddhiśūnyaṃ Cidātmakam |
Atadvyāvṛttirūpo'sau Samādhirmunibhāvitaḥ ||

56. ऊर्ध्वपूर्णमधःपूर्णं मध्यपूर्णं शिवात्मकम् । साक्षाद्विधिमुखो ह्येष समाधिः पारमार्थिकः ॥

Ūrdhvapūrṇamadhaḥpūrṇaṃ Madhyapūrṇaṃ Śivātmakam |
Sākṣādvidhimukho Hyeṣa Samādhiḥ Pāramārthikaḥ ||

57. दृढभावनया त्यक्तपूर्वापरविचारणम् । यदादानं पदार्थस्य वासना सा प्रकीर्तिता ॥

Dṛḍhabhāvanayā Tyaktapūrvāparavicāraṇam |
Yadādānaṃ Padārthasya Vāsanā Sā Prakīrtitā ||

58. भावितं तीव्रसंवेगादात्मना यत्तदेव सः । भवत्याशु कपिश्रेष्ठ विगतेतरवासनः ॥

Bhāvitaṃ Tīvrasaṃvegādātmanā Yattadeva Saḥ |
Bhavatyāśu Kapiśreṣṭha Vigatetaravāsanaḥ ||

59. तादृग्रूपो हि पुरुषो वासनाविवशीकृतः । सम्पश्यति यदैवैतत्सद्वस्त्विति विमुह्यति ॥

Tādṛgrūpo Hi Puruṣo Vāsanāvivaśīkṛtaḥ |
Sampaśyati Yadaivaitatsadvastviti Vimuhyati ||

60. वासनावेगवैचित्र्यात्स्वरूपं न जहाति तत् । भ्रान्तं पश्यति दुर्दृष्टिः सर्वं मदवशादिव ॥

Vāsanāvegavaicitryātsvarūpaṃ Na Jahāti Tat |
Bhrāntaṃ Paśyati Durdṛṣṭiḥ Sarvaṃ Madavaśādiva ||

61. वासना द्विविधा प्रोक्ता शुद्धा च मलिना तथा ।
मलिना जन्महेतुः स्याच्छुद्धा जन्मविनाशिनी ॥

Vāsanā Dvividhā Proktā Śuddhā Ca Malinā Tathā |
Malinā Janmahetuḥ Syācchuddhā Janmavināśinī ||

62. अज्ञानसुघनाकारा घनाहंकारशालिनी । पुनर्जन्मकरी प्रोक्ता मलिना वासना बुधैः ।
पुनर्जन्माङ्कुरं त्यक्त्वा स्थितिः संभृष्टबीजवत् ॥

Ajñānasughanākārā Ghanāhaṃkāraśālinī ।
Punarjanmakarī Proktā Malinā Vāsanā Budhaiḥ ।
Punarjanmāṅkuraṃ Tyaktvā Sthitiḥ Saṃbhṛṣṭabījavat ॥

63. बहुशास्त्रकथाकन्थारोमन्थेन वृथैव किम् । अन्वेष्टव्यं प्रयत्नेन मारुते ज्योतिरान्तरम् ॥

Bahuśāstrakathākanthāromanthena Vṛthaiva Kim ।
Anveṣṭavyaṃ Prayatnena Mārute Jyotirāntaram ॥

64. दर्शनादर्शने हित्वा स्वयं केवलरूपतः । य आस्ते कपिशार्दूल ब्रह्म स ब्रह्मवित्स्वयम् ॥

Darśanādarśane Hitvā Svayaṃ Kevalarūpataḥ ।
Ya Āste Kapiśārdūla Brahma Sa Brahmavitsvayam ॥

65. अधीत्य चतुरो वेदान्सर्वशास्त्राण्यनेकशः । ब्रह्मतत्त्वं न जानाति दर्वी पाकरसं यथा ॥

Adhītya Caturo Vedānsarvaśāstrāṇyanekaśaḥ ।
Brahmatattvaṃ Na Jānāti Darvī Pākarasaṃ Yathā ॥

66. स्वदेहाशुचिगन्धेन न विरज्येत यः पुमान् । विरागकारणं तस्य किमन्यदुपदिश्यते ॥

Svadehāśucigandhena Na Virajyeta Yaḥ Pumān ।
Virāgakāraṇaṃ Tasya Kimanyadupadiśyate ॥

67. अत्यन्तमलिनो देहो देही चात्यन्तनिर्मलः । उभयोरन्तरं ज्ञात्वा कस्य शौचं विधीयते ॥

Atyantamalino Deho Dehī Cātyantanirmalaḥ ।
Ubhayorantaraṃ Jñātvā Kasya Śaucaṃ Vidhīyate ॥

68. बद्धो हि वासनाबद्धो मोक्षः स्याद्वासनाक्षयः । वासनां सम्परित्यज्य मोक्षार्थित्वमपि त्यज॥

Baddho Hi Vāsanābaddho Mokṣaḥ Syādvāsanākṣayaḥ ।
Vāsanāṃ Samparityajya Mokṣārthitvamapi Tyaja ॥

69. मानसीर्वासनाः पूर्वं त्यक्त्वा विषयवासनाः । मैत्र्यादिवासनानाम्नीर्गृहाणामलवासनाः ॥

Mānasīrvāsanāḥ Pūrvaṃ Tyaktvā Viṣayavāsanāḥ ।
Maitryādivāsanānāmnīrgṛhāṇāmalavāsanāḥ ॥

70. ता अप्यतः परित्यज्य ताभिर्व्यवहरन्नपि । अन्तःशान्तः समस्नेहो भव चिन्मात्रवासनः ॥

Tā Apyataḥ Parityajya Tābhirvyavaharannapi |
Antaḥśāntaḥ Samasneho Bhava Cinmātravāsanaḥ ||

71. तामप्यथ परित्यज्य मनोबुद्धिसमन्विताम् । शेषस्थिरसमाधानो मयि त्वं भव मारुते ॥

Tāmapyatha Parityajya Manobuddhisamanvitām |
Śeṣasthirasamādhāno Mayi Tvaṃ Bhava Mārute ||

72. अशब्दमस्पर्शमरूपमव्ययं तथाऽरसं नित्यमगन्धवच्च यत् ।
अनामगोत्रं मम रूपमीदृशं भजस्व नित्यं पवनात्मजार्तिहन् ॥

Aśabdamasparśamarūpamavyayaṃ
Tathā'rasaṃ Nityamagandhavacca Yat |
Anāmagotraṃ Mama Rūpamīdṛśaṃ
Bhajasva Nityaṃ Pavanātmajārtihan ||

73. दृशिस्वरूपं गगनोपमं परं सकृद्विभातं त्वजमेकमक्षरम् ।
अलेपकं सर्वगतं यदद्वयं तदेव चाहं सकलं विमुक्त ॐ ॥

Dṛśisvarūpaṃ Gaganopamaṃ Paraṃ
Sakṛdvibhātaṃ Tvajamekamakṣaram |
Alepakaṃ Sarvagataṃ Yadadvayaṃ
Tadeva Cāhaṃ Sakalaṃ Vimukta Oṃ ||

74. दृशिस्तु शुद्धोऽहमविक्रियात्मको न मेऽस्ति कश्चिद्विषयः स्वभावतः ।
पुरस्तिरश्चोर्ध्वमधश्च सर्वतः सुपूर्णभूमाहमितीहभावय ॥

Dṛśistu Śuddho'hamavikriyātmako
Na Me'sti Kaścidviṣayaḥ Svabhāvataḥ |
Purastiraścordhvamadhaśca Sarvataḥ
Supūrṇabhūmāhamitīha Bhāvaya ||

75. अजोऽमरश्चैव तथाजरोऽमृतः स्वयंप्रभः सर्वगतोऽहमव्ययः ।
न कारणं कार्यमतीत्य निर्मलः सदैव तृप्तोऽहमितीह भावय ॥

Ajo'maraścaiva Tathājaro'mṛtaḥ
Svayaṃprabhaḥ Sarvagato'hamavyayaḥ |
Na Kāraṇaṃ Kāryamatītya Nirmalaḥ
Sadaiva Tṛpto'hamitīha Bhāvaya ||

76. जीवन्मुक्तपदं त्यक्त्वा स्वदेहे कालसात्कृते। विशत्यदेहमुक्तत्वं पवनोऽस्पन्दतामिव

Jīvanmuktapadaṃ Tyaktvā Svadehe Kālasātkṛte ।
Viśatyadehamuktatvaṃ Pavano'spandatāmiva ॥

तदेतदृचाभ्युक्तम्॥ *Tadetadṛcābhyuktam* ॥

तद्विष्णोः परमं पदं सदा पश्यन्ति सूरयः। दिवीव चक्षुराततम्॥
तद्विप्रासो विपन्यवो जागृवांसः समिन्धते। विष्णोर्यत्परमं पदम्॥

Tadviṣṇoḥ Paramaṃ Padaṃ Sadā Paśyanti Sūrayaḥ ।
Divīva Cakṣurātatam ॥
Tadviprāso Vipanyavo Jāgṛvāṃsaḥ Samindhate ।
Viṣṇoryatparamaṃ Padam ॥

ॐ सत्यमित्युपनिषत्। *Oṃ Satyamityupaniṣat* ।

शान्ति मन्त्रः । *Śānti Mantraḥ* ।

हरिः ॐ पूर्णमदः पूर्णमिदं पूर्णात्पूर्णमुदच्यते। पूर्णस्य पूर्णमादाय पूर्णमेवावशिष्यते॥

Hariḥ Oṃ Pūrṇamadaḥ Pūrṇamidaṃ Pūrṇātpūrṇamudacyate ।
Pūrṇasya Pūrṇamādāya Pūrṇamevāvaśiṣyate ॥

ॐ शान्तिः शान्तिः शान्तिः॥ *Oṃ Śāntiḥ Śāntiḥ Śāntiḥ* ॥

हरिः ॐ तत् सत्। *Hariḥ Oṃ Tat Sat* ॥

इति मुक्तिकोपनिषत्समाप्ता॥ *Iti Muktikopaniṣatsamāptā* ॥

Rājaśyāmalārahasyopaniṣat

राजश्यामलारहस्योपनिषत्

This is also another *Upaniṣat* from *Atharva Veda.*

शान्ति मन्त्रः । *Śānti Mantraḥ* ।

ॐ स्वस्ति न इन्द्रो वृद्धश्रवाः स्वस्ति नः पूषा विश्ववेदाः ।
स्वस्ति नस्तार्क्ष्यो अरिष्टनेमिः स्वस्ति नो बृहस्पतिर्दधातु ॥

Oṃ Svasti Na Indro Vṛddhaśravāḥ Svasti Naḥ Pūṣā Viśvavedāḥ |
Svasti Nastārkṣyo Ariṣṭanemiḥ Svasti No Bṛhaspatirdadhātu ||

ॐ शान्तिः शान्तिः शान्तिः ॥ *Oṃ Śāntiḥ Śāntiḥ Śāntiḥ* ||

हरिः ॐ ॥ *Hariḥ Oṃ* ||

ॐ रत्नसानुशिखरेष्वासीनं श्रीराजश्यामलारहस्योपनिषद्वेत्तारं
मतङ्गऋषिं गुरुं कूचिमारः प्रोवाच ।
मतङ्ग भगवन् गुरो राजश्यामलारहस्योपनिषदं मेऽनुब्रूहि।
मतङ्गभगवान् कूचिमारं स होवाच । ते राजश्यामलारहस्योपनिषदमुपदिशामि॥
Oṃ Ratnasānuśikhareṣvāsīnaṃ Śrīrājaśyāmalārahasyopaniṣadvettāraṃ
Mataṅgarṣiṃ Guruṃ Kūcimāraḥ Provāca | *Mataṅga Bhagavan Guro*
Rājaśyāmalārahasyopaniṣadaṃ Me'nubrūhi |
Mataṅgabhagavān Kūcimāraṃ Sa Hovāca |
Te Rājaśyāmalārahasyopaniṣadamupadiśāmi ||

अथातः श्रीराजश्यामलारहस्योपनिपद्रं व्याख्यास्यामः ।
Athātaḥ Śrīrājaśyāmalārahasyopanipadraṃ Vyākhyāsyāmaḥ |

मन्त्रजपाधिकराणस्तोत्राधिकरणपूजाधिकरणमैथुनाधरणैः पञ्चभिर्ब्राह्मणो भोगमोक्षमाप्नोति
गुरोरनुज्ञया श्रीराजश्यामलामन्त्रं नित्यं सहस्रसङ्ख्यया त्रिशतेन
वाऽष्टाविंशदुत्तरशतेन वा जप्त्वा मन्त्रसिद्धिर्भवति ।
शुक्रवारे भार्याजगन्मोहनचक्रे त्रिशतं मन्त्रजपेन मन्त्रसिद्धिः ।
पुरश्चरणमिद्धिर्भवति। नवाशीतिन्यासानां न्यसनेन देवताशरीरी भवति ।
नवाशीतिन्यागानां न्यसनेन सर्वदेवैर्नमस्कृतो भवति ।

नवाशीतिन्यासानां शरीरे न्यसनेन गन्धर्वकन्याभिः पूजितो भवति।
नवाशीतिन्यासानां न्यसनेन देवस्त्रीभोगमाप्नोति। रम्भासम्भोगमाप्नोति।
नवाशीतिन्यासानां न्यसनेन देवतारूपमाप्नोति। देवताशरीरी भूत्वा विमानवान् भवति।
विमानमारुह्य स्वर्गं गच्छति। स्वर्गं प्राप्य तद्भोगमाप्नोति।
जगन्मोहनचक्रे पाटलकुसुमैः सहस्रसङ्ख्यया पूजिता श्रीराजश्यामला कामितार्थप्रदा मङ्गलप्रदा भवति। वर्षर्तौ श्रावणे मासि सर्वरात्रिषु भार्याजगन्मोहनचक्रे चम्पककुसुमैः सहस्रसङ्ख्यया पूजिता श्रीराजश्यामलाऽऽरोग्यप्रदा भवति।
तत्र शुक्रवारे पूजिता महालक्ष्मीप्रदा भवति। शुक्रवारयुतायां पौर्णमास्यां भार्याजगन्मोहनचक्रे शतसङ्ख्यया श्रीराजश्यामलाम्बां पूजयन् देहान्तरे रम्भासम्भोगमश्नुते।
भाद्रपदे मासि महालक्ष्मीव्रतदिनेषु भार्याजगन्मोहनचक्रे श्रीराजश्यामलाम्बां जाजीकुसुमैः पूजयन् मानवो महदैश्वर्यमाप्नोति। शरत्काले सर्वरात्रिषु भार्याजगन्मोहनचक्रे नीलोत्पलैः सहस्रसङ्ख्यया श्यामलां पूजयन् महाभोगमश्नुते।
शुक्रवारयुतायां पौर्णमास्यां भार्याजगन्मोहनचक्रे श्रीराजश्यामलां पूजयन् कल्हारैः शचीभोगमश्नुते।
हेमन्तकाले सर्वरात्रिषु भार्याजगन्मोहनचक्रे जवन्तीकुरवमैः सहस्रसङ्ख्यया पूजयन् वरुणदेवेन कनकच्छत्री भवति।
मार्गशीर्षे पौर्णमास्यां भार्याजगन्मोहनचक्रे कुसुम्भपुष्पैः पूजयन् मानवो देवेन्द्रैश्वर्यमाप्नोति।
माध्यां शुक्रवारयुक्तायां भार्याजगन्मोहनचक्रे द्वन्द्वमल्लिकाकुड्मलैः सहस्रसङ्ख्यया पूजयन् मानवो राजस्त्रीसम्भोगमाप्नोति। सर्वदा पुष्पिण्यां भार्यायां जगन्मोहनचक्रे वसन्तपुष्पैः पूजयन् मानवो देवतात्वमश्नुते।
चतुर्थ्यां शुक्रवारयुक्तायां भार्याजगन्मोहनचक्रे देवतां श्यामलां जपन् परशिवत्वमाप्नोति।
श्रीराजश्यामलाम्बायाः पञ्चदशस्तोत्राणां पारायणेन देवतासन्तुष्टिर्भवति।
मङ्गलप्रदा राजवशङ्करी च भवति। देवतासान्निध्यमाप्नोति।
सन्निधानेन सर्वनिवृत्तिर्भवति। सर्वमङ्गलमाप्नोति। सर्वदेवनमस्कृतो भवति।
सर्वे राजानो वश्या भवन्ति। रम्भादिभिः पूजितो भवति। स्वर्गभोगमाप्नोति।
गुरोरनुज्ञया शुक्रवारे दिवा रात्रौ च चम्पकतैलाद्यैः कृतस्नातां सर्वालङ्कारभूषितां शुभ्रवस्त्रधरां श्रीचन्दनविलिप्ताङ्गीं कस्तूरीतिलकोपेतां कुङ्कुमलिप्तकुचभारां पुष्पदामयुक्तधम्मिल्लां ताम्बूलपूरितमुखींस्वेदबिन्दु ल्लसन्मुखीं बिम्बोष्ठीं कुन्दरदनां कम्बुकण्ठीं मञ्जुहासां यौवनोन्मत्तां कञ्जलोचनां पृथुनितम्बां राजरम्भोरुं सम्पूर्णचन्द्रवदनां सम्भोगेच्छां शुकवाणीं सङ्गीतरसिकां कुरवकरसाञ्चितपाणिपादां वशवर्तिनीं भार्यां पुष्पशय्यायामुत्तानशायिनीं कृत्वा दर्पणवन्निर्मलं जगन्मोहनचक्रं गन्धद्रव्येण धूपदीपैश्च परिमलीकृतं कुङ्कुममिलितैर्मल्लिकाकुड्मलैः शरसङ्ख्यया पूजयन् ब्राह्मणो देवभोगमाप्नोति।

वसन्तनवरात्रिषु भार्याजगन्मोहनचक्रे मल्लिकाकुड्मलैः सहस्रनामभिः रहस्यनामभिश्च पूजिता राजश्यामला राजवशङ्करी भवति। शुक्रवासरयुक्तायां सप्तम्यां रात्रौ भार्याया जगन्मोहनचक्रे प्रथमयामे कल्हारपुष्पैः सहस्रनामभिर्देवतां पूजयन् दवतासालोक्यमाप्नोति। तस्यामेव द्वितीययामे भार्याजगन्मोहनचक्रे पारिजातपुष्पैः सहस्रनामभिः पूजयन् देवतासामीप्यमाप्नोति। तस्यामेव तृतीययामे भार्याजगन्मोहनचक्रे। मन्दारपुष्पैः सहस्रनामभिः पूजयन् देवतासारूप्यमाप्नोति। तस्यामेव चतुर्थयामे जगन्मोहनचक्रे चम्पकपुष्पैः सहस्रनामभिः पूजयन् देवतासायुज्यमाप्नोति। सर्वरात्रिषु जगन्मोहनचक्रे मल्लिकाकुड्मलैः पूजिता श्यामला कामितार्थप्रदा भवति। ग्रीष्मकाले सर्वरात्रिषु श्रीचन्दनविलिप्तभार्याजगन्मोहनचक्रं पूजयन् सर्वसिद्धिमाप्नोति। दूर्वाभिः पूजयन् महदायुष्यमश्नुते। अष्टम्यां शुक्रवासरयुक्तायां रात्रौ जगन्मोहनचक्रे राजश्यामलाम्बां श्रीचन्दनेन पूजयन् मानवो गन्धलिप्तो जगन्मोहको भवति। महानवम्यां शुक्रवासरयुक्तायां रात्रौ जगन्मोहनचक्रे कुङ्कुमाक्षतैर्देवतां पूजयित्वा पूजिताक्षतान् राज्ञ निवेदयेत्। राजा दासभावमाप्नोति। त्रयोदश्यां शुक्रवासरयुक्तायां रात्रौ भार्याजगन्मोहनचक्रं पूजयन् मानवः कामसुन्दरो भवति॥

Mantrajapādhikarāṇastotrādhikaraṇapūjādhikaraṇamaithunā Dharaṇaiḥ Pañcabhirbrāhmaṇo Bhogamokṣamāpnoti | Guroranujñayā Śrīrājaśyāmalāmantraṃ Nityaṃ Sahasrasaṅkhyayā Triśatena Vā'ṣṭāviṃśaduttaraśatena Vā Japtvā Mantrasiddhirbhavati | Śukravāre Bhāryājaganmohanacakre Triśataṃ Mantrajapena Mantrasiddhiḥ | Puraścaraṇamiddhirbhavati |

Navāśītinyāsānāṃ Nyasanena Devatāśarīrī Bhavati |

Navāśītinyāgānāṃ Nyasanena Sarvadevairnamaskṛto Bhavati | Navāśītinyāsānāṃ Śarīre Nyasanena Gandharvakanyābhiḥ Pūjito Bhavati | Navāśītinyāsānāṃ Nyasanena Devastrībhogamāpnoti | Rambhāsambhogamāpnoti |

Navāśītinyāsānāṃ Nyasanena Devatārūpamāpnoti |

Devatāśarīrī Bhūtvā Vimānavān Bhavati |

Vimānamāruhya Svargaṃ Gacchati |

Svargaṃ Prāpya Tadbhogamāpnoti | Jaganmohanacakre Pāṭalakusumaiḥ Sahasrasaṅkhyayā Pūjitā Śrīrājaśyāmalā Kāmitārthapradā Maṅgalapradā Bhavati | Varṣartau Śrāvaṇe Māsi Sarvarātriṣu Bhāryājaganmohanacakre Campakakusumaiḥ Sahasrasaṅkhyayā Pūjitā Śrīrājaśyāmalā''rogyapradā Bhavati |

Tatra Śukravāre Pūjitā Mahālakṣmīpradā Bhavati | Śukravārayutāyāṃ Paurṇamāsyāṃ Bhāryājaganmohanacakre Śatasaṅkhyayā Śrīrājaśyāmalāmbāṃ Pūjayan Dehāntare Rambhāsambhogamaśnute | Bhādrapade Māsi Mahālakṣmīvratadineṣu Bhāryājaganmohanacakre Śrīrājaśyāmalāmbāṃ Jājīkusumaiḥ Pūjayan Mānavo Mahadaiśvaryamāpnoti | Śaratkāle Sarvarātriṣu Bhāryājaganmohanacakre Nīlotpalaiḥ Sahasrasaṅkhyayā Śyāmalāṃ Pūjayan Mahābhogamaśnute | Śukravārayutāyāṃ Paurṇamāsyāṃ Bhāryājaganmohanacakre Śrīrājaśyāmalāṃ Pūjayan Kalhāraiḥ Śacībhogamaśnute | Hemantakāle Sarvarātriṣu Bhāryājaganmohanacakre Javantīkuravamaiḥ Sahasrasaṅkhyayā Pūjayan Varuṇadevena Kanakacchatrī Bhavati | Mārgaśīrṣe Paurṇamāsyāṃ Bhāryājaganmohanacakre Kusumbhapuṣpaiḥ Pūjayan Mānavo Devendraiśvaryamāpnoti | Mādhyāṃ Śukravārayuktāyāṃ Bhāryājaganmohanacakre Dvandvamallikākuḍmalaiḥ Sahasrasaṅkhyayā Pūjayan Mānavo Rājastrīsambhogamāpnoti | Sarvadā Puṣpiṇyāṃ Bhāryāyāṃ Jaganmohanacakre Vasantapuṣpaiḥ Pūjayan Mānavo Devatātvamaśnute | Caturthyāṃ Śukravārayuktāyāṃ Bhāryājaganmohanacakre Devatāṃ Śyāmalāṃ Japan Paraśivatvamāpnoti | Śrīrājaśyāmalāmbāyāḥ Pañcadaśastotrāṇāṃ Pārāyāṇena Devatāsantuṣṭirbhavati | Maṅgalapradā Rājavaśaṅkarī Ca Bhavati | Devatāsānnidhyamāpnoti | Sannidhānena Sarvanivṛttirbhavati | Sarvamaṅgalamāpnoti | Sarvadevanamaskṛto Bhavati |

Sarve Rājāno Vaśyā Bhavanti | Rambhādibhiḥ Pūjito Bhavati |

Svargabhogamāpnoti | Guroranujñayā Śukravāre Divā Rātrau Ca Campakatailādyaiḥ Kṛtasnātāṃ Sarvālaṅkārabhūṣitāṃ Śubhravastradharāṃ Śrīcandanaviliptāṅgīṃ Kastūrītilakopetāṃ Kuṅkumaliptakucabhārāṃ Puṣpadāmayuktadhammillāṃ Tāmbūlapūritamukhīṃ Svedabindullasanmukhīṃ Bimboṣṭhīṃ Kundaradanāṃ Kambukaṇṭhīṃ Mañjuhāsāṃ Yauvanonmattāṃ Kañjalocanāṃ Pṛthunitambāṃ Rājarambhoruṃ Sampūrṇacandravadanāṃ Sambhogecchāṃ Śukavāṇīṃ Saṅgītarasikāṃ Kuravakarasāñcitapāṇipādāṃ Vaśavartinīṃ Bhāryāṃ Puṣpaśayyāyāmuttānaśāyinīṃ Kṛttvā Darpaṇavannirmalaṃ Jaganmohanacakraṃ Gandhadravyeṇa Dhūpadīpaiśca Parimalīkṛtaṃ Kuṅkumamilitairmallikākuḍmalaiḥ Śarasaṅkhyayā Pūjayan Brāhmaṇo

Devabhogamāpnoti |

Vasantanavarātriṣu Bhāryājaganmohanacakre Mallikākuḍmalaiḥ Sahasranāmabhiḥ Rahasyanāmabhiśca Pūjitā Rājaśyāmalā

Rājavaśaṅkarī Bhavati |

Śukravāsarayuktāyāṃ Saptamyāṃ Rātrau Bhāryāyā Jaganmohanacakre Prathamayāme Kalhārapuṣpaiḥ Sahasranāmabhirdevatāṃ Pūjayan

Davatāsālokyamāpnoti |

Tasyāmeva Dvitīyayāme Bhāryājaganmohanacakre Pārijātapuṣpaiḥ

Sahasranāmabhiḥ Pūjayan Devatāsāmīpyamāpnoti |

Tasyāmeva Tṛtīyayāme Bhāryājaganmohanacakre |

Mandārapuṣpaiḥ Sahasranāmabhiḥ Pūjayan Devatāsārūpyamāpnoti |

Tasyāmeva Caturthayāme Jaganmohanacakre Campakapuṣpaiḥ

Sahasranāmabhiḥ Pūjayan Devatāsāyujyamāpnoti |

Sarvarātriṣu Jaganmohanacakre Mallikākuḍmalaiḥ

Pūjitā Śyāmalā Kāmitārthapradā Bhavati |

Grīṣmakāle Sarvarātriṣu Śrīcandanaviliptabhāryājaganmohanacakraṃ

Pūjayan Sarvasiddhimāpnoti |

Dūrvābhiḥ Pūjayan Mahadāyuṣyamaśnute |

Aṣṭamyāṃ Śukravāsarayuktāyāṃ Rātrau Jaganmohanacakre Rājaśyāmalāmbāṃ Śrīcandanena Pūjayan Mānavo

Gandhalipto Jaganmohako Bhavati |
Mahānavamyāṃ Śukravāsarayuktāyāṃ Rātrau Jaganmohanacakre Kuṅkumākṣatairdevatāṃ Pūjayitvā Pūjitākṣatān Rājña Nivedayet |
Rājā Dāsabhāvamāpnoti | Trayodaśyāṃ Śukravāsarayuktāyāṃ Rātrau Bhāryājaganmohanacakraṃ Pūjayan Mānavaḥ Kāmasundaro Bhavati ||

चन्द्रदर्शनयुक्तायां द्वितीयायां शुक्रवार युक्तायां भार्या जगन्मोहनचक्रे राजश्यामलाम्बां श्वेतगन्धाक्षतैः श्वेतपुष्पैश्च पूज्यन् साधको देहान्ते राजा भवति ।
सर्वभोगप्रदा सर्वसौभाग्यप्रदा दीर्घायुष्यप्रदा महायोगप्रदा महामङ्गलप्रदा काम्यप्रदा श्रीराजश्यामला देवेन्द्रभोगप्रदा भवति ।
सर्वकाम्यरहस्यपूजान्ते मैथुनं देवताप्रीतिकरं भवति ।
मोक्षप्रदं भवति । स एव भोगापवर्गः । गुर्वनुज्ञया गुप्तः क्षपणको मुक्तो भवति ।
एवं कान्तायाः पूजिता स्वर्णचक्रे श्यामला मङ्गलप्रदा भवति ।
द्रोहिणां नोपदेशः । क्षपणकानां पञ्चाधिकरणैः परो मोक्षो नान्यथेति य एवं वेद । इत्युपनिषत् ॥

Candradarśanayuktāyāṃ Dvitīyāyāṃ Śukravārayuktāyāṃ Bhāryājaganmohanacakre Rājaśyāmalāmbāṃ Śvetagandhākṣataiḥ Śvetapuṣpaiśca Pūjyan Sādhako Dehānte Rājā Bhavati |
Sarvabhogapradā Sarvasaubhāgyapradā Dīrghāyuṣyapradā Mahāyogapradā Mahāmaṅgalapradā Kāmyapradā Śrīrājaśyāmalā Devendrabhogapradā Bhavati |
Sarvakāmyarahasyapūjānte Maithunaṃ Devatāprītikaraṃ Bhavati |
Mokṣapradaṃ Bhavati | Sa Eva Bhogāpavargaḥ |
Gurvanujñayā Guptaḥ Kṣapaṇako Mukto Bhavati |
Evaṃ Kāntāyāḥ Pūjitā Svarṇacakre Śyāmalā Maṅgalapradā Bhavati |
Drohiṇāṃ Nopadeśaḥ | Kṣapaṇakānāṃ Pañcādhikaraṇaiḥ Paro Mokṣo Nānyatheti Ya Evaṃ Veda | Ityupaniṣat ||

शान्ति मन्त्रः । *Śānti Mantraḥ |*

ॐ स्वस्ति न इन्द्रो वृद्धश्रवाः स्वस्ति नः पूषा विश्ववेदाः ।
स्वस्ति नस्ताक्ष्यों अरिष्टनेमिः स्वस्ति नो बृहस्पतिर्दधातु ॥

Oṃ Svasti Na Indro Vṛddhaśravāḥ Svasti Naḥ Pūṣā Viśvavedāḥ I
Svasti Nastārkṣyo Ariṣṭanemiḥ Svasti No Bṛhaspatirdadhātu II

ॐ शान्तिः शान्तिः शान्तिः ॥ *Oṃ Śāntiḥ Śāntiḥ Śāntiḥ* II

इति राजश्यामलारहस्योपनिषत् समाप्ता ।

Iti Rājaśyāmalārahasyopaniṣat Samāptā I

*****

Vanadurgopaniṣat
वनदुर्गोपनिषत्

This is also another *Upaniṣat* from *Atharva Veda*.

शान्ति मन्त्रः । *Śānti Mantraḥ* ।

ॐ भद्रं कर्णेभिः शृणुयाम देवाः । भद्रं पश्येमाक्षभिर्यजत्राः ।

Oṃ Bhadraṃ Karṇebhiḥ Śṛṇuyāma Devāḥ ॥

Bhadraṃ Paśyemākṣabhiryajatrāḥ ॥
स्थिरैरङ्गैस्तुष्टुवाँसस्तनूभिः । व्यशेम देवहितं यदायुः ।

SthirairaṅgaistuṣṭuvāğSastanūbhiḥ ॥ *Vyaśema Devahitaṃ Yadāyuḥ* ॥
स्वस्ति न इन्द्रो वृद्धश्रवाः । स्वस्ति नः पूषा विश्ववेदाः ।

Svasti Na Indro Vṛddhaśravāḥ ॥ *Svasti Naḥ Pūṣā Viśvavedāḥ* ॥
स्वस्ति नस्तार्क्ष्यो अरिष्टनेमिः । स्वस्ति नो बृहस्पतिर्दधातु ॥

Svasti Nastārkṣyo Ariṣṭanemiḥ ॥ *Svasti No Bṛhaspatirdadhātu* ॥
ॐ शान्तिः शान्तिः शान्तिः ॥ *Oṃ Śāntiḥ Śāntiḥ Śāntiḥ* ॥

हरिः ॐ ॥ *Hariḥ Oṃ* ॥

ॐ अस्य श्रीवनदुर्गामहामन्त्रस्य किरातरूपधर ईश्वर ऋषिः ।
अनुष्टुप् छन्दः । अन्तर्यामी नारायण ईश्वरो वनदुर्गा गायत्री देवता ।
दुं बीजम् । स्वाहा शक्तिः । क्लीं कीलकम् । मम वनदुर्गाप्रसादसिद्ध्य र्थे
धर्मार्थकाममोक्षार्थे जपे विनियोगः । मूलेन व्यापकत्रयं कुर्यात् ।
ह्रीं इति व्यापकत्रयम् । ॐ हंसिनी ह्रां अङ्गुष्ठाभ्यां हृदि ।
ॐ शिखिनी ह्रीं तर्जनीभ्यां शिरसि । ॐ चक्रिणी ह्रूं मध्यमाभ्यां शिखायाम् ।
ॐ त्रिशूलधारिणी ह्रैं अनामिकाभ्यां कवचम् । ॐ पद्मिनी ह्रौं कनिष्ठिकाभ्यां नेत्रयोः ।
ॐ गदिनी ह्रः करतलकरपृष्ठाभ्यामस्त्रम् । ॐ, भूर्भुवः स्वरोमिति दिग्बन्धः ।

Oṃ Asya Śrīvanadurgāmahāmantrasya Kirātarūpadhara Īśvara Ṛṣiḥ ।
Anuṣṭup Chandaḥ । *Antaryāmī Nārāyaṇa Īśvaro Vanadurgā Gāyatrī Devatā* । *Duṃ Bījam* । *Svāhā Śaktiḥ* । *Klīṃ Kīlakam* । *Mama Vanadurgāprasādasiddhyarthe Dharmārthakāmamokṣārthe Jape Viniyogaḥ* । *Mūlena Vyāpakatrayaṃ Kuryāt* । *Hrīṃ Iti Vyāpakatrayam* ।

Oṃ Haṃsinī Hrāṃ Aṅguṣṭhābhyāṃ Hṛdi | Oṃ Śikhinī Hrīṃ Tarjanībhyāṃ Śirasi | Oṃ Cakriṇī Hrūṃ Madhyamābhyāṃ Śikhāyām | Oṃ Triśūladhāriṇī Hraiṃ Anāmikābhyāṃ Kavacam | Oṃ Padminī Hrauṃ Kaniṣṭhikābhyāṃ Netrayoḥ |

Oṃ Gadinī Hraḥ Karatalakarapṛṣṭhābhyāmastram |

Oṃ Bhūrbhuvaḥ Svaromiti Digbandhaḥ |

अथ ध्यानम् *Atha Dhyānam*

1. अरिशङ्खकृपाणखेटबाणान् सधनुश्शूलकतर्जनीर्दधानाम्।
भज तां महिषोत्तमाङ्गसंस्थां नवदूर्वासदृशी श्रियेऽस्तु दुर्गा ॥

Ariśaṅkhakṛpāṇakheṭabāṇān Sadhanuśśūlakatarjanīrdadhānām |
Bhaja Tāṃ Mahiṣottamāṅgasaṃsthāṃ Navadūrvāsadṛśī Śriye'stu Durgā ||

2. हेमप्रख्यामिन्दु खण्डान्तमौलिं शङ्खारिष्टाभीतिहस्तां त्रिणेत्राम् ।
हेमाब्जस्थां पीतवस्त्रां प्रसन्नां देवीं दुर्गां दिव्यरूपां नमामि ॥

Hemaprakhyāmindukhaṇḍāntamauliṃ Śaṅkhāriṣṭābhītihastāṃ Triṇetrām |
Hemābjasthāṃ Pītavastrāṃ Prasannāṃ Devīṃ Durgāṃ Divyarūpāṃ Namāmi ||

वनदुर्गोपनिषत् - *Vanadurgopaniṣat*

3. उद्यद्भास्वत्समाभां विधृतनवजपामिन्दुखण्डावबद्धां
ज्योतिर्मौलिं त्रिणेत्रां विविधमणिरलसत्कुण्डलां पद्मकाञ्चीम् ।
हारग्रैवेयभूषां मणिगुणवलयाद्यैर्विचित्राम्बराढ्यां
अम्बां पाशाङ्कुशाढ्यामभयवरकरां मञ्जुकान्तां नमामि ॥

Udyadbhāsvatsamābhāṃ Vidhṛtanavajapāmindukhaṇḍāvabaddhāṃ
Jyotirmauliṃ Triṇetrāṃ Vividhamaṇiralasatkuṇḍalāṃ Padmakāñcīm |
Hāragraiveyabhūṣāṃ Maṇiguṇavalayādyairvicitrāmbarāḍhyāṃ
Ambāṃ Pāśāṅkuśāḍhyāmabhayavarakarāṃ Mañjukāntāṃ Namāmi ||

4. सिद्धलक्ष्मी राजलक्ष्मीर्जयलक्ष्मीः सरस्वती । श्रीलक्ष्मीर्वरलक्ष्मीश्च प्रसन्ना मम सर्वदा ॥

Siddhalakṣmī Rājalakṣmīrjayalakṣmīḥ Sarasvatī ।
Śrīlakṣmīrvaralakṣmīśca Prasannā Mama Sarvadā ॥

5. मायाकुण्डलिनी क्रिया मधुमती काली कलामालिनी
मातङ्गी विजया जया भगवती देवी शिवा शाम्भवी ।
शक्तिः शङ्करवल्लभा त्रिणयना वाग्वादिनी भैरवी
ह्रीङ्कारी त्रिपुरा परापरमयी माता कुमारीत्यसि ॥

Māyākuṇḍalinī Kriyā Madhumatī Kālī Kalāmālinī
Mātaṅgī Vijayā Jayā Bhagavatī Devī Śivā Śāmbhavī ।
Śaktiḥ Śaṅkaravallabhā Triṇayanā Vāgvādinī Bhairavī
Hrīṅkārī Tripurā Parāparamayī Mātā Kumārītyasi ॥

6. सौवर्णाम्बुजमध्यगां त्रिणयनां सौदामिनीसन्निभां
शङ्खं चक्रवराभयानि दधतीमिन्दोः कलां बिभ्रतीम् ।
ग्रैवेयाङ्गदहारकुण्डलधरामाकखण्डलाद्यैः स्तुतां
ध्यायेद्विन्ध्यनिवासिनीं शशिमुखीं पार्श्वस्थपञ्चाननाम् ॥

Sauvarṇāmbujamadhyagāṃ Triṇayanāṃ Saudāminīsannibhāṃ
Śaṅkhaṃ Cakravarābhayāni Dadhatīmindoḥ Kalāṃ Bibhratīm ।
Graiveyāṅgadahārakuṇḍaladharāmākakhaṇḍalādyaiḥ Stutāṃ
Dhyāyedvindhyanivāsinīṃ Śaśimukhīṃ Pārśvasthapañcānanām ॥

सिंहारूढां श्यामकान्तिं शङ्खचक्रधरां हृदा । दुर्गां देवीं तथा ध्यायेच्छरचापौ च बिभ्रतीम् ॥

Siṃhārūḍhāṃ Śyāmakāntiṃ Śaṅkhacakradharāṃ Hṛdā ।
Durgāṃ Devīṃ Tathā Dhyāyeccharacāpau Ca Bibhratīm ॥

ॐ ॥ मनुः हास्वा यमश यमश तिवगभ न्मेत वा क्यशमक्यश दिय
तस्थिपमुस मे यम्भ षिपिस्व किं षिरुपु ष्ठत्तिउ

Oṃ ॥ *Manuḥ---Hāsvā Yamaśa Yamaśa Tivagabha Nmeta Vā*
Kyaśamakyaśa Diya Tasthipamusa Me Yambha Ṣipisva Kiṃ Ṣirupu Ṣṭhattiu

ॐ क्लीं श्रीं ह्रीं ऐं ॐ । *Oṃ Klīṃ Śrīṃ Hrīṃ Aiṃ Oṃ* ।

ह्रीं महाभीषणे करालवदने विन्ध्यवासिनि ह्रां ह्रीं ह्रूं ह्रैं ह्रौं ह्रम् ।

नादयक्षयोगिनीपरिवृते दुष्टग्रहनाशिनि हुं फट् स्वाहा।
जम्भिनि मोहिनि स्तम्भिनि पूर्वद्वारं बन्धय बन्धय।
ढं म्र्युं अग्निद्वारं बन्धय बन्धय। ढं ढं ढं भ्रों यमद्वारं बन्धय बन्धय।
खं घ्र्यं निरृतिद्वारं बन्धय बन्धय। लं ब्लौं वरुणद्वारं बन्धय बन्धय।
यं श्लीं वायुद्वारं बन्धय बन्धय। क्लीं ग्लौं कुबेरद्वारं बन्धय बन्धय।
ॐ हं ईं ईशानद्वारं बन्धय बन्धय। ॐ हं कं खें ऊर्ध्वद्वारं बन्धय बन्धय।
ग्लौं घ्रों पातालद्वारं बन्धय बन्धय। ईं ईं अधोद्वारं बन्धय बन्धय। सर्वग्रहान् बन्धय बन्धय।
सर्पराजचोरदुष्ट-मृगादिसकलभयं बन्धय बन्धय।
परप्रयोगभूतप्रेतपिशाचभैरवदुर्गाहनुम द्गणेश्वरादिसकलकिल्बिषं बन्धय बन्धय।
भञ्जय भञ्जय। अमुकं मेह-स्तम्भनं वाक्कायसर्वाङ्गं बन्धय बन्धय।
सर्वक्षुद्रोपद्रवं छिन्धि छिन्धि। रे रे घे घे हुं फट् स्वाहा।
ॐ श्रीं ह्रीं क्लीं सौः ॐ नमो भगवति माहेश्वरि अन्नपूर्णेश्वरि मां पालय पालय स्वाहा।

Hrīṃ Mahābhīṣaṇe Karālavadane Vindhyavāsini Hrāṃ Hrīṃ Hrūṃ Hraiṃ Hrauṃ Hram |

Nādayakṣayoginīparivṛte Duṣṭagrahanāśini Huṃ Phaṭ Svāhā |

Jambhini Mohini Stambhini Pūrvadvāraṃ Bandhaya Bandhaya |

Ḍhaṃ Mryuṃ Agnidvāraṃ Bandhaya Bandhaya |

Ḍhaṃ Ḍhaṃ Ḍhaṃ Bhroṃ Yamadvāraṃ Bandhaya Bandhaya |

Khaṃ Ghryaṃ Nirṛtidvāraṃ Bandhaya Bandhaya |

Laṃ Blauṃ Varuṇadvāraṃ Bandhaya Bandhaya |

Yaṃ Ślīṃ Vāyudvāraṃ Bandhaya Bandhaya |

Klīṃ Glauṃ Kuberadvāraṃ Bandhaya Bandhaya |

Oṃ Haṃ Īṃ Īśānadvāraṃ Bandhaya Bandhaya |

Oṃ Haṃ Kaṃ Kheṃ Ūrdhvadvāraṃ Bandhaya Bandhaya |

Glauṃ Ghroṃ Pātāladvāraṃ Bandhaya Bandhaya | Īṃ Īṃ

Adhodvāraṃ Bandhaya Bandhaya | Sarvagrahān Bandhaya Bandhaya |

Sarparājacoraduṣṭa-Mṛgādisakalabhayaṃ Bandhaya Bandhaya |
Paraprayogabhūtapretapiśācabhairavadurgāhanuma-
Dgaṇeśvarādisakalakilbiṣaṃ Bandhaya Bandhaya |

Bhañjaya Bhañjaya | Amukaṃ Meha-Stambhanaṃ Vākkāyasarvāṅgaṃ Bandhaya Bandhaya | Sarvakṣudropadravaṃ Chindhi Chindhi |
Re Re Ghe Ghe Huṃ Phaṭ Svāhā |
Oṃ Śrīṃ Hrīṃ Klīṃ Sauḥ Oṃ Namo Bhagavati
Māheśvari Annapūrṇeśvari Māṃ Pālaya Pālaya Svāhā |

सं सहस्रबाहवे नमः। पूर्वदिश चोराञ्छत्रून बन्धय बन्धय।
ॐ फ्रों च्रीं क्लीं ब्लूं आं ह्रीं क्रों श्रीं हुं सं सहस्रार हुं फट्र स्वाहा। सं सहस्रबाहवे नमः।

Saṃ Sahasrabāhave Namaḥ |

Pūrvadiśa Corāñchatrūna Bandhaya Bandhaya |
Oṃ Phroṃ Crīṃ Klīṃ Blūṃ Āṃ Hrīṃ Kroṃ Śrīṃ Huṃ Saṃ Sahasrāra Huṃ Phaṭ Svāhā | Saṃ Sahasrabāhave Namaḥ |

आग्नेयदिश चोराञ्छत्रून बन्धय बन्धय।
ॐ फ्रों च्रीं क्लीं ब्लूं आं ह्रीं क्रों श्रीं हुं सं सहस्रार हुं फट्र स्वाहा।
सं सहस्रबाहवे नमः। याम्यदिश चोराञ्छत्रून बन्धय बन्धय।
ॐ फ्रों च्रीं क्लीं ब्लूं आं ह्रीं क्रों श्रीं हुं सं सहस्रार हुं फट्र स्वाहा।

Āgneyadiśa Corāñchatrūna Bandhaya Bandhaya |
Oṃ Phroṃ Crīṃ Klīṃ Blūṃ Āṃ Hrīṃ Kroṃ Śrīṃ Huṃ Saṃ Sahasrāra Huṃ Phaṭ Svāhā |

Saṃ Sahasrabāhave Namaḥ |

Yāmyadiśa Corāñchatrūna Bandhaya Bandhaya |
Oṃ Phroṃ Crīṃ Klīṃ Blūṃ Āṃ Hrīṃ Kroṃ Śrīṃ Huṃ Saṃ Sahasrāra Huṃ Phaṭ Svāhā |

सं सहस्रबाहवे नम। निरृतिदिश चोराञ्छत्रून बन्धय बन्धय।
ॐ फ्रों च्रीं क्लीं ब्लूं आं ह्रीं क्रों श्रीं हुं सं सहस्रार हुं फट्र स्वाहा।

Saṃ Sahasrabāhave Nama | Nirṛtidiśa Corāñchatrūna Bandhaya Bandhaya |
Oṃ Phroṃ Crīṃ Klīṃ Blūṃ Āṃ Hrīṃ Kroṃ Śrīṃ Huṃ Saṃ Sahasrāra Huṃ Phaṭ S vāhā |

सं सहस्रबाहवे नमः । वरुणदिश चोराञ्छत्रून बन्धय बन्धय ।
ॐ फ्रों च्रीं क्लीं ब्लूं आं ह्रीं क्रों श्रीं हुं सं सहस्रार हुं फट् स्वाहा ।

Saṃ Sahasrabāhave Namaḥ | Varuṇadiśa Corāñchatrūna Bandhaya Bandhaya |
Oṃ Phroṃ Crīṃ Klīṃ Blūṃ Āṃ Hrīṃ Kroṃ Śrīṃ Huṃ Saṃ Sahasrāra Huṃ Phaṭ Svāhā |

सं सहस्रबाहवे नमः । वायव्यदिश चोराञ्छत्रून बन्धय बन्धय ।
ॐ फ्रों च्रीं क्लीं ब्लूं आं ह्रीं क्रों श्रीं हुं सं सहस्रार हुं फट् स्वाहा ।

Saṃ Sahasrabāhave Namaḥ | Vāyavyadiśa Corāñchatrūna Bandhaya Bandhaya |
Oṃ Phroṃ Crīṃ Klīṃ Blūṃ Āṃ Hrīṃ Kroṃ Śrīṃ Huṃ Saṃ Sahasrāra Huṃ Phaṭ Svāhā |

सं सहस्रब्राहवे नमः । कुबेरदिश चोराञ्छत्रून बन्धय बन्धय ।
ॐ फ्रों च्रीं क्लीं ब्लूं आं ह्रीं क्रों श्रीं हुं सं सहस्रार हुं फट् स्वाहा ।
सं सहस्रबाहवे नमः ।

Saṃ Sahasrabrāhave Namaḥ | Kuberadiśa Corāñchatrūna Bandhaya Bandhaya |
Oṃ Phroṃ Crīṃ Klīṃ Blūṃ Āṃ Hrīṃ Kroṃ Śrīṃ Huṃ Saṃ Sahasrāra Huṃ Phaṭ Svāhā | Saṃ Sahasrabāhave Namaḥ |

ईशानदिश चोराञ्छत्रून बन्धय बन्धय । ॐ फ्रों च्रीं क्लीं ब्लूं आं ह्रीं क्रों श्रीं हुं सं सहस्रार हुं फट् स्वाहा । सं सहस्रबाहवे नमः ।

Īśānadiśa Corāñchatrūna Bandhaya Bandhaya | Oṃ Phroṃ Crīṃ Klīṃ Blūṃ Āṃ Hrīṃ Kroṃ Śrīṃ Huṃ Saṃ Sahasrāra Huṃ Phaṭ Svāhā | Saṃ Sahasrabāhave Namaḥ |

आकाशदिश चोराञ्छत्रून बन्धय बन्धय ।
ॐ फ्रों च्रीं क्लीं ब्लूं आं ह्रीं क्रों श्रीं हुं सं सहस्रार हुं फट् स्वाहा । सं सहस्रबाहवे नमः ।
पातालदिश चोराञ्छत्रून बन्धय बन्धय ।

ॐ फ्रों च्रीं क्लीं ब्लूं आं ह्रीं क्रों श्रीं हुं सं सहस्रार हुं फट् स्वाहा।
सं सहस्रबाहवे नमः। अवान्तरदिश चोराञ्छत्रून बन्धय बन्धय।

Ākāśadiśa Corāñchatrūna Bandhaya Bandhaya | *Oṃ Phroṃ Crīṃ Klīṃ Blūṃ Āṃ Hrīṃ Kroṃ Śrīṃ Huṃ Saṃ Sahasrāra Huṃ Phaṭ Svāhā* |

Saṃ Sahasrabāhave Namaḥ |

Pātāladiśa Corāñchatrūna Bandhaya Bandhaya |
Oṃ Phroṃ Crīṃ Klīṃ Blūṃ Āṃ Hrīṃ Kroṃ Śrīṃ Huṃ Saṃ Sahasrāra Huṃ Phaṭ Svāhā | *Saṃ Sahasrabāhave Namaḥ* |

Avāntaradiśa Corāñchatrūna Bandhaya Bandhaya |

ॐ फ्रों च्रीं क्लीं ब्लूं आं ह्रीं क्रों श्रीं हुं सं सहस्रार हुं फट् स्वाहा।
Oṃ Phroṃ Crīṃ Klīṃ Blūṃ Āṃ Hrīṃ Kroṃ Śrīṃ Huṃ Saṃ Sahasrāra Huṃ Phaṭ Svāhā |
सं सहस्रबाहवे नमः। *Saṃ Sahasrabāhave Namaḥ* |

ॐ ऐं ह्रीं श्रीं ग ग ग गल ह्रीं ऐं क ए ई ल ह्रीं क्लीं ह स क ह ल ह्रीं सौ स क ल ह्रीं ग
क्षिप्रप्रसादगणपतये वर वरद आं ह्रीं क्रों सर्वजन मे वशमानय स्वाहा।
Oṃ Aiṃ Hrīṃ Śrīṃ Ga Ga Ga Gala Hrīṃ Aiṃ Ka E Ī La Hrīṃ Klīṃ Ha Sa Ka Ha La Hrīṃ Sau Sa Ka La Hrīṃ Ga Kṣipraprasādagaṇapataye Vara Varada Āṃ Hrīṃ Kroṃ Sarvajana Me Vaśamānaya Svāhā |

गणानां त्वां गणपतिं हवामहे कविं कवीनामुपमश्रवस्तमम्।
ज्येष्ठराजं ब्रह्मणां ब्रह्मणस्पत आ नः शृण्वन्नूतिभिः सीद सादनम्॥
Gaṇānāṃ Tvāṃ Gaṇapatiṃ Havāmahe Kaviṃ Kavīnāmupamaśravastamam |
Jyeṣṭharājaṃ Brahmaṇāṃ Brahmaṇaspata Ā Naḥ Śṛṇvannūtibhiḥ Sīda Sādanam ||

ॐ ऐं ह्री श्रीं ग ग ग ग ल ह्रीं ऐ क ए ई ल ह्रीं क्लीं ह स क ह ल
ह्रीं सौ स क ल ह्रीं गं क्षिप्रप्रसादगणपतये वर वरद आं ह्रीं क्रों
सर्वजन मे वशमानय स्वाहा। ॐ ऐं ह्रीं श्रीं यदति यच्च दूके भय विन्दति मामिह।

Oṃ Aiṃ Hrī Śrīṃ Ga Ga Ga Ga La Hrīṃ Ai Ka E Ī La Hrīṃ Klīṃ Ha Sa Ka Ha La Hrīṃ Sau Sa Ka La Hrīṃ Gaṃ Kṣipraprasādagaṇapataye Vara Varada Āṃ Hrīṃ Kroṃ Sarvajana Me Vaśamānaya Svāhā । *Oṃ Aiṃ Hrīṃ Śrīṃ Yadati Yacca Dūrake Bhaya Vindati Māmiha* ।

पवमान वितज्जहि। यदुत्थित भगवति तत्सर्वं शमय शमय स्वाहा।

Pavamāna Vitajjahi ।

Yadutthita Bhagavati Tatsarvaṃ Śamaya Śamaya Svāhā ।

ॐ ऐं ह्रीं श्रीं गं ग ग ग ल ह्रीं ऐं क ए ई ल
ह्रीं क्लीं ह स क ह ल ह्रीं सौ स क ल ह्रीं गं क्षिप्रप्रसादगणपतये
वर वरद आं हीं क्रों सर्वजन मे वशमानय स्वाहा।
ॐ तत्सवितुर्वरेण्यं भर्गो देवस्य धीमहि। धियो यो नः प्रचोदयात्॥

Oṃ Aiṃ Hrīṃ Śrīṃ Gaṃ Ga Ga Ga La Hrīṃ Aiṃ Ka E Ī La Hrīṃ Klīṃ Ha Sa Ka Ha La Hrīṃ Sau Sa Ka La Hrīṃ Gaṃ Kṣipraprasādagaṇapataye Vara Varada Āṃ Hīṃ Kroṃ Sarvajana Me Vaśamānaya Svāhā ।

Oṃ Tatsaviturvareṇyaṃ Bhargo Devasya Dhīmahi ।
Dhiyo Yo Naḥ Pracodayāt ॥

ॐ ऐं ह्रीं श्रीं गं ग ग ग ल ह्रीं ऐं क ए ई ल हीं क्लीं ह स क ह
ल ह्रीं सौ स क ल हीं गं क्षिप्रप्रसादगणपतये वर वरद आं ह्रीं
क्रों सर्वजन मे वशमानय स्वाहा। त्रियम्बक यजामहे सुगन्धि पुष्टिवर्धनम्।
उर्वारुकमिव बन्धनान्मृत्योर्मुक्षीय माऽमृतात॥

Oṃ Aiṃ Hrīṃ Śrīṃ Gaṃ Ga Ga Ga La Hrīṃ Aiṃ Ka E Ī La Hīṃ Klīṃ Ha Sa Ka Ha La Hrīṃ Sau Sa Ka La Hrīṃ Gaṃ Kṣipraprasādagaṇapataye Vara Varada Āṃ Hrīṃ Kroṃ Sarvajana Me Vaśamānaya Svāhā ।

Triyambaka Yajāmahe Sugandhi Puṣṭivardhanam ।
Urvārukamiva Bandhanānmṛtyormukṣīya Mā'mṛtāt ॥

ॐ ऐं हीं श्रीं गं ग ग ग ल हीं ऐं क ए ई ल हीं क्लीं ह स क ह
ल ह्रीं सौ स क ल हीं गं क्षिप्रप्रसादगणपतये वर वरद आ ह्रीं
क्रों सर्वजन मे वशमानय स्वाहा।

Oṃ Aiṃ Hrīṃ Śrīṃ Gaṃ Ga Ga Ga La Hrīṃ Aiṃ Ka E Ī La Hrīṃ Klīṃ Ha Sa Ka Ha La Hrīṃ Sau Sa Ka La Hrīṃ Gaṃ Kṣipraprasādagaṇapataye Vara Varada Ā Hrīṃ Kroṃ Sarvajana Me Vaśamānaya Svāhā ।

ॐ जातवेदसे सुनवाम सोममरातीयतो निदहाति वेद ।
स न पर्षदति दुर्गाणि विश्वा नावेव सिन्धु दुरितास्त्यग्नि ॥

Oṃ Jātavedase Sunavāma Somamarātīyato Nidahāti Veda ।
Sa Na Parṣadati Durgāṇi Viśvā Nāveva Sindhu Duritāstyagni ॥

ॐ ऐं ह्रीं श्रीं गं ग ग ग ल ह्रीं ऐं क ए ई ल ह्रीं क्लीं ह स क
ह ल ह्रीं सौ स क ल ह्रीं गं क्षिप्रप्रसादगणपतये वर वरद
आ ह्रीं क्रों सर्वजन मे वशमानय स्वाहा ।
ॐ नमो भस्माङ्गरागाय उग्रतेजसे हन हन दह दह पच पच मथ मथ विध्वसय
विध्वसय हल हल भञ्जय भञ्जय शूलिनि जय जय तेजसा पूर्वा
सिद्धिं कुरु कुरु समुद्र पूर्वादिष्ट शोषय शोषय स्तम्भय स्तम्भय
परमन्त्रपरयन्त्रपरतन्त्रपरभूतप्रकटिनि छिन्धि छिन्धि ह्रीं फट् स्वाहा ।
हेतुकं पूर्वपीठे तु ह्याग्नेय्या त्रिपुरान्तकम् । दक्षिणे चाग्निवेताल नैर्म्मत्या यमजिह्वकम् ॥

Oṃ Aiṃ Hrīṃ Śrīṃ Gaṃ Ga Ga Ga La Hrīṃ Aiṃ Ka E Ī La Hrīṃ Klīṃ Ha Sa Ka Ha La Hrīṃ Sau Sa Ka La Hrīṃ Gaṃ Kṣipraprasādagaṇapataye Vara Varada Ā Hrīṃ Kroṃ Sarvajana Me Vaśamānaya Svāhā । *Oṃ Namo Bhasmāṅgarāgāya Ugratejase Hana Hana Daha Daha Paca Paca Matha Matha Vidhvasaya Vidhvasaya Hala Hala Bhañjaya Bhañjaya Śūlini Jaya Jaya Tejasā Pūrvā Siddhiṃ Kuru Kuru Samudra Pūrvādiṣṭa Śoṣaya Śoṣaya Stambhaya Stambhaya Paramantra Parayantra Paratantra Parabhūta Prakaṭini Chindhi Chindhi Hrīṃ Phaṭ Svāhā* ।

Hetukaṃ Pūrvapīṭhe Tu Hyāgneyyā Tripurāntakam ।
Dakṣiṇe Cāgnivetāla Nairmmatyā Yamajihvakam ॥

कालाख्य वारुणे पीठे वायव्या च करालिनम् । उत्तरे ह्येकपाद च त्वीशान्या भीमरूपिणम् ॥
आकाशे तु निरालम्बं पाताले बडबानलम् । यथा ग्रामे यथा क्षेत्रे रक्षेन्मां वटुकस्तथा ॥

Kālākhya Vāruṇe Pīṭhe Vāyavyā Ca Karālinam ।
Uttare Hyekapāda Ca Tvīśānyā Bhīmarūpiṇam ॥

Ākāśe Tu Nirālambaṃ Pātāle Baḍabānalam ।
Yathā Grāme Yathā Kṣetre Rakṣenmāṃ Vaṭukastathā ॥

ॐ ह्रीं वटुकाय आपदु द्धरणाय कुरु कुरु वटुकाय ह्रीं ॐ वटुकाय स्वाहा ।
सर्वमङ्गलमाङ्गल्ये शिवे सर्वार्थसाधिके । शरण्ये त्र्यम्बके गौरि नारायणि नमोऽस्तु ते ॥
Oṃ Hrīṃ Vaṭukāya Āpaduddharaṇāya Kuru Kuru
Vaṭukāya Hrīṃ Oṃ Vaṭukāya Svāhā ।
Sarvamaṅgalamāṅgalye Śive Sarvārthasādhike ।
Śaraṇye Tryambake Gauri Nārāyaṇi Namo'stu Te ॥

ॐ ह्रीं श्रीं दु दुर्गायै नमः । ॐ ह्रीं प्रयोगविषये ब्रह्माण्यै नमः ।
ॐ ह्रीं वारुणि खल्विनि माहेश्वर्यै नमः । ॐ ह्रीं कुल्यवासिन्यै कुमार्यै नमः ।
ॐ जयन्तपुरवाहिनि वाराह्यै नमः । ॐ अष्टमहाकालि रुद्राण्यै नमः ।
ॐ चित्रकूट इन्द्राण्यै नमः । ॐ एकवृक्षशुम्भिन्यै महालक्ष्म्यै नमः ।
ॐ त्रिपुरहरब्रह्माण्डनायिकायै नमः । ॐ त्रिपुरहरब्रह्मचारिण्ये नमः ।
एतानि क्ष क्ष क्ष त्रैलोक्यवशङ्करीवीजाक्षराणि ।
ॐ ह्रीं कुरु कुरु स्वाहा ।
Oṃ Hrīṃ Śrīṃ Du Durgāyai Namaḥ । *Oṃ Hrīṃ Prayogaviṣaye*
Brahmāṇyai Namaḥ । *Oṃ Hrīṃ Vāruṇi Khalvini Māheśvaryai Namaḥ* ।
Oṃ Hrīṃ Kulyavāsinyai Kumāryai Namaḥ ।
Oṃ Jayantapuravāhini Vārāhyai Namaḥ ।
Oṃ Aṣṭamahākāli Rudrāṇyai Namaḥ ।
Oṃ Citrakūṭa Indrāṇyai Namaḥ ।
Oṃ Ekavṛkṣaśumbhinyai Mahālakṣmyai Namaḥ ।
Oṃ Tripuraharabrahmāṇḍanāyikāyai Namaḥ ।
Oṃ Tripuraharabrahmacāriṇye Namaḥ ।
Etāni Kṣa Kṣa Kṣa Trailokyavaśaṅkarīvījākṣarāṇi ।
Oṃ Hrīṃ Kuru Kuru Svāhā ।

ॐ ह्रां ह्रीं ह्रूं जय जय चामुण्डे चण्डिके
त्रिदशमुकुटकोटिरत्नसङ्घट्टितचरणारविन्द गायत्रि सावित्रि सरस्वति

माहेश्वरि ब्रह्माण्डभण्डोदररूपधारिणि प्रकटितदंष्ट्रोग्ररूपवदने
घोरघोराननने नयनोज्ज्वलज्वालासहस्रपरिवृते
महाट्टहासधवलीकृतदिगन्तरे कोटिदिवाकरसमप्रभे कामरूपिणि
महाविद्यासञ्चयप्रभाभासितसकलदिगन्तरे सर्वायुधपरिपूर्णे
कपालहस्ते गजाननोत्तरीये भूतवेतालपरिवृते प्रकटितवसुन्धरे
मधुकैटभमहिषासुरधूम्रलोचनचण्डमुण्डप्रचण्डरक्तबीजशुम्भनिशुम्भदैत्यनिकृन्तके
कालरात्रि महामाये शिवदूति इन्द्राणि शाङ्करि आग्नेयि यामि नैरृति वारुणि वायवि
कौबेरि ईशानि ब्रह्माणि विष्णुवक्षस्थिते त्रिभुवनधराधरे
ज्येष्ठे रौद्रे चाम्बिके ब्राह्मि माहेश्वरि वैष्णवि वाराहि इन्द्राणि
शाङ्करि चण्डिके शूलिनि महोग्रविषोग्रभक्षितदंष्ट्रिणि
हरितहयबद्धबहुकठोरोत्तमाङ्गनवरत्ननिधि कोशे तत्र
बहुजिह्वापाणिपादशब्दस्पर्शरूपरसगन्धचक्षु ष्मति
महाविन्ध्यस्थिते महाज्वालामणिमहिषोपरी स्थित गन्धर्वविद्याधरस्तुते
ऐङ्कारि ह्रीङ्कारि श्रीङ्कारि क्लीङ्का रिहस्ते आं ह्रीं क्रों यज्ञपात्रं प्रवेशय प्रवेशय ।

Oṃ Hrāṃ Hīṃ Hrūṃ Jaya Jaya Cāmuṇḍe Caṇḍike Tridaśamukuṭakoṭiratnasaṅghaṭṭitacaraṇāravinda Gāyatri Sāvitri Sarasvati Māheśvari Brahmāṇḍabhaṇḍodararūpadhāriṇi Prakaṭitadaṃṣṭrograrūpavadane Ghoraghorānane Nayanojjvalajvālāsahasraparivṛte Mahāṭṭahāsadhavalīkṛtadigantare Koṭidivākarasamaprabhe Kāmarūpiṇi Mahāvidyāsañcayaprabhābhāsitasakaladigantare Sarvāyudhaparipūrṇe Kapālahaste Gajānanottarīye Bhūtavetālaparivṛte Prakaṭitavasundhare Madhukaiṭabhamahiṣāsuradhūmralocanacaṇḍamuṇḍapracaṇḍa-Raktabījaśumbhaniśumbhadaityanikṛntake Kālarātri Mahāmāye Śivadūti Indrāṇi Śāṅkari Āgneyi Yāmi Nairti Vāruṇi Vāyavi Kauberi Īśāni Brahmāṇi Viṣṇuvakṣasthite Tribhuvanadharādhare Jyeṣṭhe Raudre Cāmbike Brāhmi Māheśvari Vaiṣṇavi Vārāhi Indrāṇi Śāṅkari Caṇḍike Śūlini Mahogravisograbhakṣitadaṃṣṭriṇi Haritahayabaddhabahukaṭhorottamāṅganavaratnanidhikośe Tatra Bahujihvāpāṇipādaśabdasparśarūparasagandhacakṣuṣmati Mahāvindhyasthite Mahājvālāmaṇimahiṣoparī Sthita Gandharvavidyādharastute Aiṅkārihrīṅkāriśrīṅkāriklīṅkārihaste Āṃ Hrīṃ Kroṃ Yajñapātraṃ Praveśaya Praveśaya |

द्रा प्रवेशय प्रवेशय। श्रीं कुसुमापय कुसुमापय।

श्रीं सर्व प्रवेशय प्रवेशय। त्रैलोक्यान्तर्वर्तिन्येकाग्रचित्तवशीकृते
ॐ ह्रां ह्रीं ह्रूं ह्रैं ह्रौं ह्रः फ्रां फ्रीं फ्रूं फ्रैं फ्रौं फ्रः हुं हुं ह्रीं ह्रीं फट् फट्।

Drā Praveśaya Praveśaya | Śrīṃ Kusumāpaya Kusumāpaya | Śrīṃ Sarva Praveśaya Praveśaya | Trailokyāntarvartinyekāgracittavaśīkṛte Oṃ Hrāṃ Hrīṃ Hrūṃ Hraiṃ Hrauṃ Hraḥ Phrāṃ Phrīṃ Phrūṃ Phraiṃ Phrauṃ Phraḥ Huṃ Huṃ Hrīṃ Hrīṃ Phaṭ Phaṭ |

एता महाशक्तयः। एताभिररिष्टकारिभूतप्रेतपिशाचान् विध्वंसय विध्वंसय।
अष्टादशबीजयन्त्रनामानि।
ॐ नमो भगवति महाविद्ये मदनराज्ये क्लीं उपनिद ॐ ह्रीं शिवं कुरु स्वाहा।

Etā Mahāśaktayaḥ | Etābhirariṣṭakāribhūtapretapiśācān Vidhvaṃsaya Vidhvaṃsaya | Aṣṭādaśabījayantranāmāni | Oṃ Namo Bhagavati Mahāvidye Madanarājye Klīṃ Upanida Oṃ Hrīṃ Śivaṃ Kuru Svāhā |

ॐ ऐं ह्रीं सकलनरमुखभ्रमरि ॐ क्लीं ह्रीं श्रीं सकलराजमुखभ्रमरि
ॐ क्रौं सौं ह्रीं सकलदेवतामुखभ्रमरि
ॐ ह्रीं क्लीं सकलकामिनीमुखभ्रमरि मनोभञ्जनि ॐ ग्लौं सकललोकमुखभ्रमरि
ॐ ईं सौं सकलदेवतामुखभ्रमरि ॐ ह्रीं क्लीं सकलकामिनीमुखभ्रमरि मनोभञ्जनि
ॐ ग्लौं सकललोकमुखभ्रमरि
ॐ इं सौं सकलदेशमुखभ्रमरि ह्स्ख्फ्रैं त्रैलोक्यचित्तभ्रमरि
ॐ क्षं क्षां क्षिं क्षीं क्षुं क्षूं क्षें क्षैं क्षों क्षौं क्षं क्षः दिग्भवाद्युग्रभैरवादिभूतप्रेतपिशाचचित्तभ्रमरि
दुष्टग्रहमन्त्रयन्त्रतन्त्रभ्रमरि ह्स्ख्ह्स्त्रौं त्रैलोक्यान्तरभ्रमरि
ॐ हुं क्षूं हुं क्लीं राजमन्त्रयन्त्रतन्त्रभ्रमरि ॐ हुं क्षूं हुं क्लीं परमन्त्रयन्त्रतन्त्रभ्रमरि
ॐ हुं क्षूं हुं क्लीं सिद्धमन्त्रयन्त्रतन्त्रभ्रमरि
ॐ ऐं ईं सौं सकलसुरासुरसर्वमन्त्रयन्त्रतन्त्रभ्रमरि सर्वक्षोभिणि
सर्वक्लेदिनि सकलमनोन्मादिनि भक्तत्राणपरायणि
ॐ ह्री रक्तचामुण्डि अमुकमाकर्षयाकर्षय। आं ह्रीं क्रों परमयोगिनि परमकल्याणि पवित्रि
ईश्वरि स्वाहा। गायत्रि हुं फट् स्वाहा।

Oṃ Aiṃ Hrīṃ Sakalanaramukhabhramari
Oṃ Klīṃ Hrīṃ Śrīṃ Sakalarājamukhabhramari
Oṃ Krauṃ Sauṃ Hrīṃ Sakaladevatāmukhabhramari
Oṃ Hrīṃ Klīṃ Sakalakāminīmukhabhramari Manobhañjani

Oṃ Glauṃ Sakalalokamukhabhramari
Oṃ Īṃ Sauṃ Sakaladevatāmukhabhramari
Oṃ Hrīṃ Klīṃ Sakalakāminīmukhabhramari Manobhañjani
Oṃ Glauṃ Sakalalokamukhabhramari
Oṃ Iṃ Sauṃ Sakaladeśamukhabhramari Hskhphraṁ
Trailokyacittabhramari
Oṃ Kṣaṃ Kṣāṃ Kṣiṃ Kṣīṃ Kṣuṃ Kṣūṃ Kṣeṃ Kṣaiṃ Kṣoṃ Kṣauṃ
Kṣaṃ Kṣaḥ Digbhavādyugrabhairavādibhūtapretapiśācacittabhramari
Duṣṭagrahamantrayantratantrabhramari Hskhhstrauṃ
Trailokyāntarabhramari
Oṃ Huṃ Kṣūṃ Huṃ Klīṃ Rājamantrayantratantrabhramari
Oṃ Huṃ Kṣūṃ Huṃ Klīṃ Paramantrayantratantrabhramari
Oṃ Huṃ Kṣūṃ Huṃ Klīṃ Siddhamantrayantratantrabhramari
Oṃ Aiṃ Īṃ Sauṃ Sakalasurāsurasarvamantrayantratantrabhramari
Sarvakṣobhiṇi Sarvakledini Sakalamanonmādini Bhaktatrāṇaparāyaṇi

Oṃ Hrī Raktacāmuṇḍi Amukamākarṣayākarṣaya ।

Āṃ Hrīṃ Kroṃ Paramayogini Paramakalyāṇi Pavitri Īśvari Svāhā ।

Gāyatri Huṃ Phaṭ Svāhā ।

अक्षिस्पन्दं च दु:स्वप्नंभुजस्पन्दं च दुर्मतिम् । दुश्चित्तं दुर्गतिं रोगं सदा नाशय शाङ्करि ॥

Akṣispandaṃ Ca Duḥsvapnaṃ Bhujaspandaṃ Ca Durmatim ।
Duścittaṃ Durgatiṃ Rogaṃ Sadā Nāśaya Śāṅkari ॥

महाविद्यां प्रवक्ष्यामि महादेवेन निर्मिताम् । चिन्तितां च किरातेन मातॄणां चित्तनन्दिनीम् ॥

Mahāvidyāṃ Pravakṣyāmi Mahādevena Nirmitām ।
Cintitāṃ Ca Kirātena Mātṝṇāṃ Cittanandinīm ॥

उत्तमां सर्वविद्यानां सर्वभूतवशङ्करीम् । सर्वपापक्षयकरीं सर्वशत्रुनिवारणीम् ॥

Uttamāṃ Sarvavidyānāṃ Sarvabhūtavaśaṅkarīm ।
Sarvapāpakṣayakarīṃ Sarvaśatrunivāraṇīm ॥

कुलगोत्रकरीं विद्याधनधान्ययशस्करीम् । जृम्भिणीं स्तम्भिनीं देवीमुत्साहबलवर्धनीम् ॥

Kulagotrakarīṃ Vidyādhanadhānyayaśaskarīm ।
Jṛmbhiṇīṃ Stambhinīṃ Devīmutsāhabalavardhanīm ॥

सर्वज्वरोच्चाटनीं च सर्वमन्त्रप्रभञ्जनीम् । सनातनीं मोहिनीं च सर्वविद्याप्रभेदिनीम् ॥

Sarvajvaroccāṭanīṃ Ca Sarvamantraprabhañjanīm |
Sanātanīṃ Mohinīṃ Ca Sarvavidyāprabhedinīm ||

विश्वयोनिं महाशक्तिमायु प्रज्ञाविवर्धनीम् । मातङ्गीं मदिरामोदां वन्दे तां जगदीश्वरीम् ॥

Viśvayoniṃ Mahāśaktimāyu Prajñāvivardhanīm |
Mātaṅgīṃ Madirāmodāṃ Vande Tāṃ Jagadīśvarīm ||

मोहिनीं सर्वलोकानां तां विद्यां शाम्बरीत्रयाम् । अभीष्टफलदां देवीं वन्दे तां जगदीश्वरीम् ॥

Mohinīṃ Sarvalokānāṃ Tāṃ Vidyāṃ Śāmbarītrayām |
Abhīṣṭaphaladāṃ Devīṃ Vande Tāṃ Jagadīśvarīm ||

परकृताभिचारभस्मना यन्त्रीकृतदुष्टत्रिकोणयन्त्रमध्ये पदन्यासारिष्टज्म्रि छिन्धि छिन्धि । अरिष्टकारिण हन हन । कृष्णपक्षरिक्तसन्ध्यामरिष्टयुक्तप्रकृतिकाले योगिनीकालाशनिकृतारिष्ट कृतदृष्टिं ज्म्रिं छिन्धि छिन्धि । अरिष्टकारिणीविभाविनीपरकृतदुष्टग्रहमन्त्रयन्त्रतन्त्रोच्चाटनीप्रेरित-ब्रह्मराक्षसशाकिनीडाकिनीछायावासिनीकङ्कालीहिर-ण्याक्षसन्धिग्रहमुक्तकेश्यादिपिशाचेभ्यो महाभयं छिन्धि छिन्धि ।

Parakṛtābhicārabhasmanā Yantrīkṛtaduṣṭatrikoṇayantramadhye Padanyāsāriṣṭajmri Chindhi Chindhi | Ariṣṭakāriṇa Hana Hana | Kṛṣṇapakṣariktasandhyāmariṣṭayuktaprakṛtikāle Yoginīkālāśanikṛtāriṣṭa Kṛtadṛṣṭiṃ Jmriṃ Chindhi Chindhi |

अरिष्टकारिणीछेदिनीपरकृतसर्वोपद्रवेभ्य सर्पोलूककाककङ्ककपोतादिवृश्चिकाग्निज्वालामण्डलाग्रेण नवकारश्मशानभस्मना परवश्ययन्त्रतन्त्रादिदु ष्टवाक्स्तम्भनंच सभाजयं ब्लू फट्र फट्र ॐ नमो महाविद्यायै स्वाहा ।

Ariṣṭakāriṇīvibhāvinīparakṛtaduṣṭagrahamantrayantratantroccāṭanīprer ita-Brahmarākṣasaśākinīḍākinīchāyāvāsinīkaṅkālīhira-Ṇyākṣasandhigrahamuktakeśyādipiśācebhyo Mahābhayaṃ Chindhi Chindhi |

Ariṣṭakāriṇīchedinīparakṛtasarvopadravebhya Sarpolūkakākakaṅkakapotādivṛścikāgnijvālāmaṇḍalāgreṇa

Navakāraśmaśānabhasmanā
Paravaśyayantratantrādiduṣṭavākstambhanaṃ Ca
Sabhājayaṃ Blū Phaṭ Phaṭ Oṃ Namo Mahāvidyāyai Svāhā ।

ऐकाहिकं द्व्याहिकं त्र्याहिकं चातुर्थिकं पञ्चाहिकं षष्ठाहिकं प्ताहिकमष्टाहिकं नवाहिकं दशाहिकमेकादशाहिकं द्वादशाहिकं त्रयोदशाहिकमर्धमासिकं मासिकं द्विमासिकं त्रिमासिकं षाण्मासिकं सावत्सरिकं वातिकं
पैत्तिकमापस्मारिकं ब्राह्मीकं श्लैष्मिकं सान्निपातिकं सन्ततज्वरं शीतज्वरमुष्णज्वरं विषमज्वरं गण्डपित्ततालुकविस्फोटकादित्वग्रोगादिसर्वरोगान् सर्वविषं जहि जहि ।

Aikāhikaṃ Dvyāhikaṃ Tryāhikaṃ Cāturthikaṃ Pañcāhikaṃ Ṣaṣṭhāhikaṃ Ptāhikamaṣṭāhikaṃ Navāhikaṃ Daśāhikamekādaśāhikaṃ Dvādaśāhikaṃ Trayodaśāhikamardhamāsikaṃ Māsikaṃ Dvimāsikaṃ Trimāsikaṃ Ṣāṇmāsikaṃ Sāvatsarikaṃ Vātikaṃ Paittikamāpasmārikaṃ Brāhmīkaṃ Ślaiṣmikaṃ Sānnipātikaṃ Santatajvaraṃ Śītajvaramuṣṇajvaraṃ Viṣamajvaraṃ Gaṇḍapittatālukavisphoṭakāditvagrogādisarvarogān Sarvaviṣaṃ Jahi Jahi ।

आद्यन्तशून्याः कवयः पुराणाः सूक्ष्मा बृहन्तो ह्यनुशासितारः ।
सर्वान् ज्वरान् घ्नन्तु ममानिरुद्धप्रद्युम्नसङ्कर्षणवासुदेवाः ।
आद्यानिरुद्धाखिलविश्वरूप त्वं पाहि नः सर्वभयादजस्रम् ॥

Ādyantaśūnyāḥ Kavayaḥ Purāṇāḥ Sūkṣmā Bṛhanto Hyanuśāsitāraḥ ।
Sarvān Jvarān Ghnantu Mamāniruddhapradyumna
Saṅkarṣaṇavāsudevāḥ ।
Ādyāniruddhākhilaviśvarūpa Tvaṃ Pāhi Naḥ Sarvabhayādajasram ॥

त्रिपाद्भस्मप्रहरणस्त्रिशिरा रक्तलोचनः । स मे प्रीतः सुखं दद्यात् सर्वामयपतिर्ज्वरः ॥
भस्मायुधाय विद्महे तीक्ष्णदंष्ट्राय धीमहि । तन्नो ज्वरः प्रचोदयात् ।

Tripādbhasmapraharaṇastriśirā Raktalocanaḥ ।
Sa Me Prītaḥ Sukhaṃ Dadyāt Sarvāmayapatirjvaraḥ ॥
Bhasmāyudhāya Vidmahe Tīkṣṇadaṃṣṭrāya Dhīmahi ।
Tanno Jvaraḥ Pracodayāt ।

शिरश्शूलाक्षिशूलकर्णशूमलनासिकाशूलगाण्डशूलकपोलशूलतालु-
शूलौष्ठशूलजिह्वाशूलमुखशूलकण्ठशूलकूर्परशूलावरगल
शूलस्कन्धशूलबाहुशूलकक्षशूलप्रकोष्ठशूलमणिबन्धशूल
करशूलकरपृष्ठशूलकराङ्गुलीशूलहृदयशूलमनःशूलस्तनशूल
पार्श्वशूलकुक्षिशूलनाभिशूलकटिशूलगुदशूलगुह्यशूलमूलशूलौरुशू-
जानुशूलजङ्घाशूलगुल्फशूलपादशूलपादाङ्गुलीशूलविस्फोटकप्रभेदिनि
ह्रीं ॐ नमो भगवति परच्छेदमन्त्रायत्ते भो भो भो दृष्टिशूलमुष्टिशूलमुष्टिपृष्ठशूलमुष्टिपार्श्वशूल
सर्वशूलपरावारङ्गमनायै स्वाहा ।

*Śiraśśūlākṣiśūlakarṇaśūmalanāsikāśūlagāṇḍaśūlakapolaśūlatālu-
Śūlauṣṭhaśūlajihvāśūlamukhaśūlakaṇṭhaśūlakūrparaśūlāvaragala-
Śūlaskandhaśūlabāhuśūlakakṣaśūlaprakoṣṭhaśūlamaṇibandhaśūla-
Karaśūlakarapṛṣṭhaśūlakarāṅgulīśūlahṛdayaśūlamanaḥśūlastanaśūla-
Pārśvaśūlakukṣiśūlanābhiśūlakaṭiśūlagudaśūlaguhyaśūlamūlaśūlauruśūla-
Jānuśūlajaṅghāśūlagulphaśūlapādaśūlapādāṅgulīśūlavisphoṭakaprabhedini Hrīṃ Oṃ Namo Bhagavati Paracchedamantrāyatte Bho Bho Bho
Dṛṣṭiśūlamuṣṭiśūlamuṣṭipṛṣṭhaśūlamuṣṭipārśvaśūla-
Sarvaśūlaparāvāraṅgamanāyai Svāhā |*

ॐ नमो भगवते नायकाय छिन्धि छिन्धि आवेशयावेशय परमेश्वराय अघोररूपाय ह्रीं ज्वल ज्वल मुलुट्मुलूट्ह्रीं फट् फट् स्वाहा ।

Oṃ Namo Bhagavate Nāyakāya Chindhi Chindhi Āveśayāveśaya Parameśvarāya Aghorarūpāya Hrīṃ Jvala Jvala Muluṭmulūṭ Hrīṃ Phaṭ Phaṭ Svāhā |

आत्मरक्षापररक्षाप्रत्यक्षरक्षाऽग्निरक्षावायुरक्षौ दकरक्षा महान्धकारोल्काविद्युदग्न्यनिलचोरशस्त्रास्त्रेभ्यो भयान्मां रक्ष रक्ष ।

Ātmarakṣāpararakṣāpratyakṣarakṣā'gnirakṣāvāyurakṣaudakarakṣā-Mahāndhakārolkāvidyudagnyanilacoraśastrāstrebhyo Bhayānmāṃ Rakṣa Rakṣa |

पथगतांश्चोरान् शत्रून् बन्धय बन्धय । ॐ फ्रों च्रीं क्लीं ब्लूं आं ह्रीं क्रों श्रीं हुं फट् स्वाहा ।
ॐ नमो भगवते कार्तवीर्यार्जुनाय महाभुजपरिवारितसप्तद्वीपाय ।
अस्मद्वसुविलुम्पकान् चोरसमूहान् सहस्रभुजैर्दशदिक्षु बन्धय बन्धय ।
चोरान् ध ध ध ठः ठः ठः हुं फट् स्वाहा । महादेवस्य तेजसा भयङ्करादिष्टदेवतां बन्धयामि ।

महागणेन पञ्चशीर्षेण पाणिना ॐ ब्लूं ग्लौं हं गं ग्लौं हरिद्रागणपतये वरवरदाय सर्वजनहृदयं स्तम्भय स्तम्भय स्वाहा ।

Pathagatāṃścorān Śatrūn Bandhaya Bandhaya |

Oṃ Phroṃ Crīṃ Klīṃ Blūṃ Āṃ Hrīṃ Kroṃ Śrīṃ Huṃ Phaṭ Svāhā |
Oṃ Namo Bhagavate Kārtavīryārjunāya
Mahābhujaparivāritasaptadvīpāya |
Asmadvasuvilumpakān Corasamūhān Sahasrabhujairdaśadikṣu
Bandhaya Bandhaya |

Corān Dha Dha Dha Ṭhaḥ Ṭhaḥ Ṭhaḥ Huṃ Phaṭ Svāhā |

Mahādevasya Tejasā Bhayaṅkarādiṣṭadevatāṃ Bandhayāmi |
Mahāgaṇena Pañcaśīrṣeṇa Pāṇinā Oṃ Blūṃ Glauṃ Haṃ
Gaṃ Glauṃ Haridrāgaṇapataye Varavaradāya Sarvajanahṛdayaṃ
Stambhaya Stambhaya Svāhā |

कलहलपिङ्गलकण्ठमयीं रुद्राङ्गीं रुद्रजटीं महावृक्षनिवासिनीं महामत्तमातङ्गीं स्वरबीजैर्बन्धयामि ।
ॐ श्रीं ह्रीं ऐं ॐ नम उच्छिष्टचाश्णडालि मातङ्गि सर्वजनवशङ्करि क्लीं स्वाहा ।
Kalahalapiṅgalakaṇṭhamayīṃ Rudrāṅgīṃ Rudrajaṭīṃ
Mahāvṛkṣanivāsinīṃ Mahāmattamātaṅgīṃ Svarabījairbandhayāmi |
Oṃ Śrīṃ Hrīṃ Aiṃ Oṃ Nama Ucchiṣṭacāśṇḍāli Mātaṅgi
SarvajanavaśaṅkariKlīṃ Svāhā |

ॐ ऐं ह्रीं श्रीं ऐं क्लीं सौं ॐ नमो भगवति मातङ्गि सर्वजनमनोहारिणि सर्वदुःखरञ्जनि क्लीं ह्रीं श्रीं सर्वराजवशङ्करि सर्वस्त्रीपुरुषवशङ्करि सर्वदुष्टमृगवशङ्करि सर्वसत्त्ववशङ्करि सर्वलोकवशङ्करि अमुकं वशमानय स्वाहा ।
ॐ ऐं ह्रीं श्रीं ॐ आं मातङ्गि ॐ ऐं ह्रीं श्रीं इं ईं मातङ्गि ॐ ऐं ह्रीं श्रीं उं ऊं मातङ्गि
ॐ ऐं ह्रीं श्रीं ऋं ॠं मातङ्गि ॐ ऐं ह्रीं श्रीं ऌं ॡं मातङ्गि
ॐ ऐं ह्रीं श्रीं एं ऐं मातङ्गि ॐ ऐं ह्रीं श्रीं ओं औं मातङ्गि
ॐ ऐं ह्रीं श्री ॐ अः मातङ्गि ॐ स्वर स्वर ।
ब्रह्मदण्ड विस्फुर विस्फुर विष्णुदण्ड विस्फोटय विस्फोटय । रुद्रदण्ड प्रज्वल प्रज्वल ।
वायुदण्ड प्रहर प्रहर । इन्द्रदण्ड भक्षय भक्ष्य । निरृतिदण्ड हिलि हिलि ।
यमदण्ड रक्ष रक्ष । कुबेरदण्ड प्रज्वल प्रज्वल । अग्निदण्ड शमय शमय ।

वरुणदण्ड एह्येहि । नित्यानन्दिनि हंसिनि चक्रिणि शङ्खिनि
गदिनि पद्मिनि त्रिशूलधारिणि हुं फट् । क्रीं क्रीं क्रीं ह्रीं ह्रीं ह्रीम् ।
आयुः प्रज्ञा च सौभाग्य धान्य च धनमेव च । सदा शिव पुत्रवृद्धिं देहि मे चण्डिके शुभे ॥

Oṃ Aiṃ Hrīṃ Śrīṃ Aiṃ Klīṃ Sauṃ Oṃ Namo Bhagavati Mātaṅgi Sarvajanamanohāriṇi Sarvaduḥkharañjani Klīṃ Hrīṃ Śrīṃ Sarvarājavaśaṅkari Sarvastrīpuruṣavaśaṅkari Sarvaduṣṭamṛgavaśaṅkari Sarvasattvavaśaṅkari Sarvalokavaśaṅkari Amukaṃ Vaśamānaya Svāhā |
Oṃ Aiṃ Hrīṃ Śrīṃ Oṃ Āṃ Mātaṅgi Oṃ Aiṃ Hrīṃ Śrīṃ Iṃ Īṃ Mātaṅgi Oṃ Aiṃ Hrīṃ Śrīṃ Uṃ Ūṃ Mātaṅgi
Oṃ Aiṃ Hrīṃ Śrīṃ Ṛṃ Ṛṃ Mātaṅgi Oṃ Aiṃ Hrīṃ Śrīṃ Ḷṃ Ḹṃ Mātaṅgi Oṃ Aiṃ Hrīṃ Śrīṃ Eṃ Aiṃ Mātaṅgi Oṃ Aiṃ Hrīṃ Śrīṃ Oṃ Auṃ Mātaṅgi Oṃ Aiṃ Hrīṃ Śrī Oṃ Aḥ Mātaṅgi Oṃ Svara Svara |
Brahmadaṇḍa Visphura Visphura Viṣṇudaṇḍa Visphoṭaya Visphoṭaya |
Rudradaṇḍa Prajvala Prajvala | Vāyudaṇḍa Prahara Prahara |
Indradaṇḍa Bhakṣaya Bhakṣya | Nirṛtidaṇḍa Hili Hili |
Yamadaṇḍa Rakṣa Rakṣa | Kuberadaṇḍa Prajvala Prajvala |
Agnidaṇḍa Śamaya Śamaya | Varuṇadaṇḍa Ehyehi |
Nityānandini Haṃsini Cakriṇi Śaṅkhini Gadini Padmini Triśūladhāriṇi Huṃ Phaṭ | Krīṃ Krīṃ Krīṃ Hrīṃ Hrīṃ Hrīm |

Āyuḥ Prajñā Ca Saubhāgya Dhānya Ca Dhanameva Ca |
Sadā Śiva Putravṛddhiṃ Dehi Me Caṇḍike Śubhe ||

अथातो मन्त्रपदानि भवन्ति । ॐ छा छायायै स्वाहा । ॐ चं चतुरायै स्वाहा ।
ॐ कुं कुलि स्वाहा । ॐ खुं खुलि स्वाहा । ॐ हिं हिलि स्वाहा ।
ॐ जं जलि स्वाहा । ॐ झं झलि स्वाहा । ॐ ऐं पिलि स्वाहा । ॐ ऐं पिलि पिलि स्वाहा ।
ॐ हर स्वाहा ॥ ॐ हरहर स्वाहा । ॐ गं गन्धर्वाय स्वाहा ।
ॐ यं यक्षाय स्वाहा । ॐ यं यक्षोऽधिपतये स्वाहा । ॐ रं रक्षसे स्वाहा ।
ॐ रं रक्षोऽधिपतये स्वाहा । ॐ भूः स्वाहा ।
ॐ भुवः स्वाहा । ॐ स्व स्वाहा । ॐ उल्कामुखि स्वाहा । ॐ रुं रुद्रजटि स्वाहा ।
ॐ अं ऊं मं ब्रह्मविष्णुरुद्रतेजसे स्वाहा ।
ॐ ह्रीं श्रीं क्लीं नमश्चण्डिकायै महासिद्धलक्ष्म्यै ममेष्टार्थसिद्धये धीमहि ।
तन्नः शक्तिः प्रचोदयात् । ॐ ऐं वद वद वाग्वादिनि क्लीं सौं महाक्षेमं कुरु

कुरु ज्वालामालिनि वह्निवासिनि विद्याया नाभौ हुं फट् स्वाहा।
वर्णात्मिकायै ब्रह्माण्यै नमः। ॐ ऐं ह्रीं श्रीं ऐं अं आं इं ईं उं ऊं ऋं ॠं लृं
लॄं एं ऐं ओं औं अं अः कं खं गं घं ङं चं छं जं झं ञं टं ठं डं ढं णं तं थं दं धं नं पं फं बं भं मं यं रं
लं वं शं षं सं हं क्षं नमः स्वाहा।
ॐ ऐं ह्रीं श्रीं ङं णं नं मं स्वाहा। ॐ ऐं ह्रीं श्रीं गायत्रि सावित्रि सरस्वति हुं फट् स्वाहा।
ये भूतप्रेतपिशाचब्रह्मराक्षसनवग्रहभूतवेतालशाकिनीडाकिनी कूश्माण्डवासवाश्वत्वरराज
पुरुषकलहपुरुषाः कुसुमाम्भोवासिनस्तेषां बाधकं कण्टकं बध्नामि। हस्तौ बध्नामि।
चक्षुषी बध्नामि। श्रोत्रे बध्नामि। मुखं बध्नामि। घ्राणं बध्नामि। जिह्वां बध्नामि।
गतिं बध्नामि। मतिं बध्नामि। बुद्धिं बध्नामि। आकाशं बध्नामि। पातालं बध्नामि।
अन्तरिक्षं बध्नामि। पार्श्वौ बध्नामि। सर्वाङ्गं बध्नामि।
ॐ क्लीं बगलामुखि सर्वदुष्टानां वाचं मुखं पदं स्तम्भय। जिह्वां कीलय। बुद्धिं विनाशय।
ह्रीं ॐ स्वाहा। ॐ नमो भगवति पुण्यपवित्रि महाविद्यासर्वार्थसाधिनि सिद्धलक्ष्मि
वागीश्वरि परमसुन्दरि मां रक्ष रक्ष। ॐ ह्रीं फट् स्वाहा।
ॐ हुं ह्रीं श्रीं क्लीं सौं ऐं ह्रीं ॐ नमो भगवति महामाये कालि कङ्कालि
महाकालि शाङ्करि परमकल्याणि पवित्रि शाम्भवि परञ्ज्योतिःपरमात्मिके
आदिभवान्यानन्दयोगिन्यनादियोगिन्यादिपतियोगिनि रेणुकायोगिन्येकाक्षरि
परब्रह्मणि महाकालि सिद्धिकारिणि शिवरूपिणि सरस्वति मत्तकालि
मन्मथमनोन्मादिन्यादिभवान्यखिलाण्डकोटिब्रह्माण्डनायकि ब्रं ब्रं ब्रह्माण्डनिलये मां मां
माहेश्वरि महामाये वैं वैं वैष्णवि वरमुनिदेवि वां वां वाराह्यादिभेदिनि वं वं वनदुर्गे वरत्रिवेदि स्थं
स्थं स्थलदुर्गे स्थलत्रिवेदि जं जं जलदुर्गे जलत्रिवेदि अं अं अग्निदुर्गे आनन्दवेदि चं चं चण्डदुर्गे
चण्डकपालिनि सां सां सकलदुरितनिवारणि हं हं हंसरूपिण्यट्टहासिनि ऊं ऊं उत्तिष्ठ पुरुषि दु दु
ह्रीं ह्रीं क्रों क्रों मां मां महाविद्ये दु ह्रीं दुर्गायै नमः। नमस्ते अस्तु मा मा हिसी।
द्विषन्त मे नाशय। त मृत्यो मृत्यवे नय। इष्टं रक्ष रक्ष।
अरिष्ट मे भञ्जय भञ्जय स्वाहा।
ॐ ऐं ह्रीं श्रीं आ कृष्णेन रजसा वर्तमानो निवेशयन्नमृतं मर्त्य च।
हिरण्ययेन सविता रथेना दवो याति भुवनानि पश्यन्।
ॐ सूर्याय स्वाहा। ॐ ऐं ह्रीं श्रीं आ प्यायस्व समेतु ते विश्वतः सोम वृष्ण्यम्।
भवा वाजस्य सङ्गथे। ॐ सोमाय स्वाहा।
ॐ ऐं ह्रीं श्रीं अग्निर्मूर्धा दिवः ककुत् पतिःपृथिव्या अयम्।
अपां रेतांसि जिन्वति। ॐ अङ्गारकाय स्वाहा। ॐ ऐं ह्रीं श्रीं उद्बु ध्यध्वं समनसः सखायः
समग्निमिन्ध्वं बहवः सनीलाः।
दधिक्रामग्निमुषसं च देवीमिन्द्रावतोऽवसे नि ह्वये वः। ॐ बुधाय स्वाहा।

ॐ ऐं ह्रीं श्रीं बृहस्पते अति यदर्यो अर्हाद्युमद्विभाति क्रतुमज्जनेषु।
यद्दीदयच्छवसर्तप्रजात तदस्मासु द्रविण धेहि चित्रम्। ॐ बृहस्पतये स्वाहा।
ॐ ऐं ह्रीं श्रीं शुक्रः शुशुक्वाँ उषो न जारः पप्रा समीची दिवो न ज्योतिः।
परि प्रजात कत्वा बभूथ भुवो देवानां पिता पुत्रः सन्। ॐ शुक्राय स्वाहा।
ऐं ह्रीं श्रीं शमग्निरग्निभि करच्छ नस्तपतु सूर्यः। श वातो वात्वरपा अप स्रिधः।
ॐ शनैश्चराय स्वाहा। ॐ ऐं ह्रीं श्रीं कया नश्चित्र आ भुवदूती सदावृधः सखा।
कया शचिष्ठया वृता। ॐ राहवे स्वाहा। ॐ ऐं ह्रीं श्रीं केतुं कृण्वन्नकेतवे पेशो मर्या
अपेशसे। समुषद्भिरजा यथा। ॐ केतवे स्वाहा।

Athāto Mantrapadāni Bhavanti | Oṃ Chā Chāyāyai Svāhā |

Oṃ Caṃ Caturāyai Svāhā | Oṃ Kuṃ Kuli Svāhā |

Oṃ Khuṃ Khuli Svāhā | Oṃ Hiṃ Hili Svāhā |

Oṃ Jaṃ Jali Svāhā | Oṃ Jhaṃ Jhali Svāhā | Oṃ Aiṃ Pili Svāhā |

Oṃ Aiṃ Pili Pili Svāhā | Oṃ Hara Svāhā ||

Oṃ Harahara Svāhā | Oṃ Gaṃ Gandharvāya Svāhā |

Oṃ Yaṃ Yakṣāya Svāhā | Oṃ Yaṃ Yakṣosdhipataye Svāhā |

Oṃ Raṃ Rakṣase Svāhā | Oṃ Raṃ Rakṣo'dhipataye Svāhā |

Oṃ Bhūḥ Svāhā | Oṃ Bhuvaḥ Svāhā | Oṃ Sva Svāhā |

Oṃ Ulkāmukhi Svāhā | Oṃ Ruṃ Rudrajaṭi Svāhā |

Oṃ Aṃ Ūṃ Maṃ Brahmaviṣṇurudratejase Svāhā |
Oṃ Hrīṃ Śrīṃ Klīṃ Namaścaṇḍikāyai Mahāsiddhalakṣmyai
Mameṣṭārthasiddhaye Dhīmahi |

Tannaḥ Śaktiḥ Pracodayāt |
Oṃ Aiṃ Vada Vada Vāgvādini Klīṃ Sauṃ Mahākṣemaṃ Kuru
Kuru Jvālāmālini Vahnivāsini Vidyāyā Nābhau Huṃ Phaṭ Svāhā |

Varṇātmikāyai Brahmāṇyai Namaḥ |
Oṃ Aiṃ Hrīṃ Śrīṃ Aiṃ Aṃ Āṃ Iṃ Ī Uṃ Ūṃ Ṛṃ Ṛṃ Ḷṃ Ḹṃ Eṃ Aiṃ Oṃ
Auṃ Aṃ Aḥ Kaṃ Khaṃ Gaṃ Ghaṃ Ṅa Caṃ Chaṃ Jaṃ Jhaṃ Ñaṃ
Ṭaṃ Ṭhaṃ Ḍaṃ Ḍhaṃ Ṇaṃ Taṃ Tha Daṃ Dhaṃ Naṃ Paṃ Phaṃ Baṃ
Bhaṃ Maṃ Yaṃ Raṃ Laṃ Vaṃ Śaṃ Ṣaṃ Saṃ

Haṃ Kṣaṃ Namaḥ Svāhā |

Oṃ Aiṃ Hrīṃ Śrīṃ Ṅaṃ Ṇaṃ Naṃ Maṃ Svāhā |

Oṃ Aiṃ Hrīṃ Śrīṃ Gāyatri Sāvitri Sarasvati Huṃ Phaṭ Svāhā I
Ye Bhūtapretapiśācabrahmarākṣasanavagrahabhūtavetālaśākinīḍākinī-Kūśmāṇḍavāsavāścatvararājapuruṣakalahapuruṣāḥ
Kusumāmbhovāsinasteṣāṃ Bādhakaṃ Kaṇṭakaṃ Badhnāmi I
Hastau Badhnāmi I *Cakṣuṣī Badhnāmi* I
Śrotre Badhnāmi I *Mukhaṃ Badhnāmi* I *Ghrāṇaṃ Badhnāmi* I *Jihvāṃ Badhnāmi* I *Gatiṃ Badhnāmi* I *Matiṃ Badhnāmi* I *Buddhiṃ Badhnāmi* I
Ākāśaṃ Badhnāmi I *Pātālaṃ Badhnāmi* I *Antarikṣaṃ Badhnāmi* I
Pārśvau Badhnāmi I *Sarvāṅgaṃ Badhnāmi* I
Oṃ Klīṃ Bagalāmukhi Sarvaduṣṭānāṃ Vācaṃ Mukhaṃ Padaṃ Stambhaya I *Jihvāṃ Kīlaya* I *Buddhiṃ Vināśaya* I *Hrīṃ Oṃ Svāhā* I
Oṃ Namo Bhagavati Puṇyapavitri Mahāvidyāsarvārthasādhini Siddhalakṣmi Vāgīśvari Paramasundari Māṃ Rakṣa Rakṣa I
Oṃ Hrīṃ Phaṭ Svāhā I *Oṃ Huṃ Hrīṃ Śrīṃ Klīṃ Sauṃ Aiṃ Hrīṃ Oṃ Namo Bhagavati Mahāmāye Kāli Kaṅkāli Mahākāli Śāṅkari Paramakalyāṇi Pavitri Śāmbhavi Parañjyotiḥparamātmike Ādibhavānyānandayoginyanādiyoginyādipatiyogini Reṇukāyoginyekākṣari Parabrahmaṇi Mahākāli Siddhikāriṇi Śivarūpiṇi Sarasvati Mattakāli Manmathamanonmādinyādibhavānyakhilāṇḍakoṭibrahmāṇḍanāyaki Braṃ Braṃ Brahmāṇḍanilaye Māṃ Māṃ Māheśvari Mahāmāye Vaiṃ Vaiṃ Vaiṣṇavi Varamunidevi Vāṃ Vāṃ Vārāhyādibhedini Vaṃ Vaṃ Vanadurge Varatrivedi Sthaṃ Sthaṃ Sthaladurge Sthalatrivedi Jaṃ Jaṃ Jaladurge Jalatrivedi Aṃ Aṃ Agnidurge Ānandavedi Caṃ Caṃ Caṇḍadurge Caṇḍakapālini Sāṃ Sāṃ Sakaladuritanivāraṇi Haṃ Haṃ Haṃsarūpiṇyaṭṭahāsini Ūṃ Ūṃ Uttiṣṭha Puruṣi Du Du Hrīṃ Hrīṃ Kroṃ Kroṃ Māṃ Māṃ Mahāvidye Du Hrīṃ Durgāyai Namaḥ* I
Namaste Astu Mā Mā Hisī I *Dviṣanta Me Nāśaya* I
Ta Mṛtyo Mṛtyave Naya I *Iṣṭaṃ Rakṣa Rakṣa* I
Ariṣṭa Me Bhañjaya Bhañjaya Svāhā I *Oṃ Aiṃ Hrīṃ Śrīṃ Ā Kṛṣṇena Rajasā Vartamāno Niveśayannamṛtaṃ Martya Ca* I
Hiraṇyayena Savitā Rathenā Davo Yāti Bhuvanāni Paśyan I

Oṃ Sūryāya Svāhā | *Oṃ Aiṃ Hrīṃ Śrīṃ Ā Pyāyasva*

Sametu Te Viśvataḥ Soma Vṛṣṇyam | *Bhavā Vājasya Saṅgathe* |

Oṃ Somāya Svāhā | *Oṃ Aiṃ Hrīṃ Śrīṃ Agnirmūrdhā Divaḥ Kakut*

Patiḥpṛthivyā Ayam | *Apāṃ Retāṃsi Jinvati* | *Oṃ Aṅgārakāya Svāhā* |
Oṃ Aiṃ Hrīṃ Śrīṃ Udbudhyadhvaṃ Samanasaḥ Sakhāyaḥ

Samagnimindhvaṃ Bahavaḥ Sanīlāḥ |

Dadhikrāmagnimuṣasaṃ Ca Devīmindrāvato'vase Ni Hvaye Vaḥ |

Oṃ Budhāya Svāhā | *Oṃ Aiṃ Hrīṃ Śrīṃ Bṛhaspate Ati Yadaryo*

Arhādyumadvibhāti Kratumajjaneṣu |

Yaddīdayacchavasartaprajāta Tadasmāsu Draviṇa Dhehi Citram |

Oṃ Bṛhaspataye Svāhā | *Oṃ Aiṃ Hrīṃ Śrīṃ Śukraḥ Śuśukvām̐ Uṣo Na*

Jāraḥ Paprā Samīcī Divo Na Jyotiḥ |

Pari Prajāta Katvā Babhūtha Bhuvo Devānāṃ Pitā Putraḥ San |

Oṃ Śukrāya Svāhā | *Aiṃ Hrīṃ Śrīṃ Śamagniragnibhi Karaccha*

Nastapatu Sūryaḥ | *Śa Vāto Vātvarapā Apa Sridhaḥ* |

Oṃ Śanaiścarāya Svāhā |

Oṃ Aiṃ Hrīṃ Śrīṃ Kayā Naścitra Ā Bhuvadūtī Sadāvṛdhaḥ Sakhā |

Kayā Śaciṣṭhayā Vṛtā | *Oṃ Rāhave Svāhā* |

Ū-Aiṃ Hrīṃ Śrīṃ Ketuṃ Kṛṇvannaketave Peśo Maryā Apeśase |

Samuṣadbhirajā Yathā | *Oṃ Ketave Svāhā* |

ॐ ऐं ह्रीं श्रीं अं आं इं ईं उं ऊं ऋं ॠं ऌं ॡं एं ऐं ओं औं अं अः कं खं गं घं ङं चं छं जं झं ञं टं ठं डं ढं णं तं थं दं धं नं पं फं बं भं मं यं रं लं वं शं षं सं हं क्षं नमः स्वाहा। ॐ अश्विन्यै स्वाहा। ॐ भरण्यै स्वाहा। ॐ कृत्तिकायै स्वाहा। ॐ रोहिण्यै स्वाहा। ॐ मृगशीर्षाय स्वाहा।

ॐ आर्द्रयै स्वाहा। ॐ पुनर्वसवे स्वाहा। ॐ पुष्याय स्वाहा।

ॐ आश्रेषायै स्वाहा। ॐ मघाय स्वाहा। ॐ पूर्वफल्गुन्यैस्वाहा।

ॐ उत्तरफल्गुन्यै स्वाहा। ॐ हस्ताय स्वाहा। ॐ चित्रायै स्वाहा।

ॐ अभिजित्यै स्वाहा। ॐ विशाखायै स्वाहा। ॐ अनुराधाय स्वाहा। ॐ ज्येष्ठायै स्वाहा।

ॐ मूलाय स्वाहा। ॐ पूर्वाषाढायै स्वाहा। ॐ उत्तराषाढायै स्वाहा।

ॐ श्रोणायै स्वाहा। ॐ श्रविष्ठायै स्वाहा। ॐ शतभिषजे स्वाहा।
ॐ पूर्वप्रोष्ठपदाय स्वाहा। ॐ उत्तरप्रोष्ठपदाय स्वाहा। ॐ रेवत्यै स्वाहा।
ॐ नमो भगवते रुद्राय नमः। ॐ नमो भगवते रुद्राय।

Oṃ Aiṃ Hrīṃ Śrīṃ Aṃ Āṃ Iṃ Īṃ Uṃ Ūṃ Ṛṃ Ṛṃ Ḷṃ Ḹṃ Eṃ Aiṃ Oṃ Auṃ Aṃ Aḥ Kaṃ Khaṃ Gaṃ Ghaṃ Ṅaṃ Caṃ Chaṃ Jaṃ Jhaṃ Ñaṃ Ṭaṃ Ṭhaṃ Ḍaṃ Ḍhaṃ Ṇaṃ Taṃ Thaṃ Daṃ Dhaṃ Naṃ Paṃ Phaṃ Baṃ Bhaṃ Maṃ Yaṃ Raṃ Laṃ Vaṃ Śaṃ Ṣaṃ Saṃ Haṃ Kṣaṃ Namaḥ

Svāhā | Oṃ Aśvinyai Svāhā | Oṃ Bharaṇyai Svāhā |

Oṃ Kṛttikāyai Svāhā | Oṃ Rohiṇyai Svāhā |

Oṃ Mṛgaśīrṣāya Svāhā | Oṃ Ārdrāyai Svāhā | Oṃ Punarvasave Svāhā |

Oṃ Puṣyāya Svāhā | Oṃ Āśreṣāyai Svāhā | Oṃ Maghāya Svāhā |

Oṃ Pūrvaphalgunyai Svāhā | Oṃ Uttaraphalgunyai Svāhā |

Oṃ Hastāya Svāhā | Oṃ Citrāyai Svāhā | Oṃ Abhijityai Svāhā |

Oṃ Viśākhāyai Svāhā | Oṃ Anurādhāya Svāhā | Oṃ Jyeṣṭhāyai Svāhā |

Oṃ Mūlāya Svāhā | Oṃ Pūrvāṣāḍhāyai Svāhā |

Oṃ Uttarāṣāḍhāyai Svāhā | Oṃ Śroṇāyai Svāhā |

Oṃ Śraviṣṭhāyai Svāhā | Oṃ Śatabhiṣaje Svāhā |

Oṃ Pūrvaproṣṭhapadāya Svāhā | Oṃ Uttaraproṣṭhapadāya Svāhā |

Oṃ Revatyai Svāhā | Oṃ Namo Bhagavate Rudrāya Namaḥ |

Oṃ Namo Bhagavate Rudrāya |

यममुखेन पञ्चयोजनविस्तीर्णेन रुद्रो बध्नातु रुद्रमण्डलम्।
रुद्र सपरिवार देवताप्रत्यधिदेवतासहितं रुद्र मण्डलं मम सपरिवारकस्य प्रत्यक्षं बन्धय बन्धय।
सर्वतो मां रक्ष रक्ष। अचल मचलमाक्रम्याक्रम्य महावज्रकवचैरस्त्रैः
राजचोरसर्पसिंहव्याघ्राग्न्याद्युपद्रवं नाशय नाशय।
ॐ ह्रां ह्रीं ह्रूं श्रीं क्लीं ब्लूं फ्रों आं ह्रीं क्रों हुं फट् स्वाहा।

Yamamukhena Pañcayojanavistīrṇena Rudro Badhnātu Rudramaṇḍalam | Rudra Saparivāra Devatāpratyadhidevatāsahitaṃ Rudramaṇḍalaṃ Mama Saparivārakasya Pratyakṣaṃ Bandhaya Bandhaya |

Sarvato Māṃ Rakṣa Rakṣa | Acala- Macalamākramyākramya Mahāvajrakavacairastraiḥ
Rājacorasarpasiṃhavyāghrāgnyādyupadravaṃ Nāśaya Nāśaya |
Oṃ Hrāṃ Hrīṃ Hrūṃ Śrīṃ Klīṃ Blūṃ Phroṃ Āṃ Hrīṃ Kroṃ Huṃ Phaṭ Svāhā |

त्रियम्बकं यजामहे सुगन्धिं पुष्टिवर्धनम्। उर्वारुकमिव बन्धनान्मृत्योर्मुक्षीय मामृतात्।

Triyambakaṃ Yajāmahe Sugandhiṃ Puṣṭivardhanam |

Urvārukamiva Bandhanānmṛtyormukṣīya Māmṛtāt |

यो रुद्रो अग्नो यो अप्सु य ओषधीषु यो रुद्रो विश्वा भुवना विवेश तस्मै
रुद्राय नमो अस्तु। वर्षन्तु ते विभावरि दिवो अभ्रस्य विद्युतः।
रोहन्तु सर्ववीजान्यव ब्रह्म द्विषो जहि। ॐ नमो भगवते रुद्राय नमः।
Yo Rudro Agno Yo Apsu Ya Oṣadhīṣu Yo Rudro Viśvā Bhuvanā Viveśa Tasmai Rudrāya Namo Astu | Varṣantu Te Vibhāvari Divo Abhrasya Vidyutaḥ | Rohantu Sarvavījānyava Brahma Dviṣo Jahi |
Oṃ Namo Bhagavate Rudrāya Namaḥ |

ॐ नमो भगवते रुद्राय। प्राच्यां दिशीन्द्रो देवता। ऐरावतारूढो हेमवर्णो वजाङ्कुशहस्त इन्द्रो बध्नात्विन्द्रमण्डलम्। इन्द्र सपरिवार देवता प्रत्यधिदेवतासहितमिन्द्रमण्डलं मम सपरिवारकस्य प्रत्यक्षं बन्धय बन्धय। सर्वतो मां रक्ष रक्ष। अचलमचलमाक्रम्याद्ध्यय महावज्रकवचैरस्त्रैः राजचोरसर्पसिंहव्याघ्राग्न्याद्युपद्रवं नाशय नाशय।
ॐ ह्रां ह्रीं ह्रूं श्रीं क्लीं ब्लूं फ्रों आं ह्रीं क्रों हुं फट् स्वाहा।

Oṃ Namo Bhagavate Rudrāya | Prācyāṃ Diśīndro Devatā | Airāvatārūḍho Hemavarṇo Vajāṅkuśahasta Indro Badhnātvindramaṇḍalam | Indra Saparivāra Devatā-Pratyadhidevatāsahitamindramaṇḍalaṃ Mama Saparivārakasya Pratyakṣaṃ Bandhaya Bandhaya | Sarvato Māṃ Rakṣa Rakṣa | Acalamacalamākramyāddhyaya Mahāvajrakavacairastraiḥ Rājacorasarpasiṃhavyāghrāgnyādyupadravaṃ Nāśaya Nāśaya | Oṃ Hrāṃ Hrīṃ Hrūṃ Śrīṃ Klīṃ Blūṃ Phroṃ Āṃ Hrīṃ Kroṃ Huṃ Phaṭ Svāhā |

त्रियम्बकं यजामहे सुगन्धिं पुष्टिवर्धनम्। उर्वारुकमिव बन्धनान्मृत्योर्मुक्षीय मामृतात्।

Triyambakaṃ Yajāmahe Sugandhiṃ Puṣṭivardhanam | Urvārukamiva Bandhanānmṛtyormukṣīya Māmṛtāt |

इन्द्रं वो विश्वतस्परि हवामहे जनेभ्यः। अस्माकमस्तु केवलः। वर्षन्तु ते विभावरि दिवो अभ्रस्य विद्युतः। रोहन्तु सर्वबीजान्यव ब्रह्म द्विषो जहि। ॐ नमो भगवते रुद्राय नमः।

Indraṃ Vo Viśvataspari Havāmahe Janebhyaḥ | Asmākamastu Kevalaḥ |
Varṣantu Te Vibhāvari Divo Abhrasya Vidyutaḥ |
Rohantu Sarvabījānyava Brahma Dviṣo Jahi |
Oṃ Namo Bhagavate Rudrāya Namaḥ |

ॐ नमो भगवते रुद्राय। आग्नेय्या दिश्यग्निर्देवता। मेषारूढो रक्तवर्णो ज्वालाहस्तोऽग्निर्बध्नात्वग्निमण्डलम्। अग्ने सपरिवार देवताप्रत्यधिदेवतासहितमग्निमण्डलं मम सपरिवारकस्य प्रत्यक्षं बन्धय बन्धय। सर्वतो मां रक्ष रक्ष। अचलमचलमाक्रम्याक्रम्य महावज्रकवचैरस्त्रैः राजचोरसर्पसिंहव्याघ्राग्न्याद्युपद्रव नाशय नाशय।
ॐ ह्रां ह्रीं ह्रूं श्रीं क्लीं ब्लूं फ्रों आं ह्रीं क्रों हुं फट् स्वाहा।

Oṃ Namo Bhagavate Rudrāya | Āgneyyā Diśyagnirdevatā | Meṣārūḍho Raktavarṇo Jvālāhasto'gnirbadhnātvagnimaṇḍalam | Agne Saparivāra Devatāpratyadhidevatāsahitamagnimaṇḍalaṃ Mama Saparivārakasya Pratyakṣaṃ Bandhaya Bandhaya | Sarvato Māṃ Rakṣa Rakṣa | Acalamacalamākramyākramya Mahāvajrakavacairastraiḥ Rājacorasarpasiṃhavyāghrāgnyādyupadrava Nāśaya Nāśaya | Oṃ Hrāṃ Hrīṃ Hrūṃ Śrīṃ Klīṃ Blūṃ Phroṃ Āṃ Hrīṃ Kroṃ Huṃ Phaṭ Svāhā |

त्रियम्बकं यजामहे सुगन्धिं पुष्टिवर्धनम्। उर्वारुकमिव बन्धनान्मृप्योर्मुक्षीय मामृतात्।

Triyambakaṃ Yajāmahe Sugandhiṃ Puṣṭivardhanam | Urvārukamiva Bandhanānmṛpyormukṣīya Māmṛtāt |

अग्निं दूतं वृणीमहे होतारं विश्ववेदसम्। अस्य यज्ञस्य सुक्रतुम्। वर्षन्तु ते विभावरि दिवो अभ्रस्य विद्युतः। रोहन्तु सर्वबीजान्यव ब्रह्म द्विषो जहि। ॐ नमो भगवते रुद्राय नमः।

Agniṃ Dūtaṃ Vṛṇīmahe Hotāraṃ Viśvavedasam | Asya Yajñasya Sukratum | Varṣantu Te Vibhāvari Divo Abhrasya Vidyutaḥ | Rohantu Sarvabījānyava Brahma Dviṣo Jahi |

Oṃ Namo Bhagavate Rudrāya Namaḥ |

ॐ नमो भगवते रुद्राय। याम्यां दिशि यमो देवता।

Oṃ Namo Bhagavate Rudrāya | Yāmyāṃ Diśi Yamo Devatā |

महिषारूढो नीलवर्ण कालदण्डो यमो बध्नातु यममण्डलम्। यम सपरिवार देवताप्रत्यधिदेवतासहितं यममण्डलं मम सपरिवारकस्य प्रत्यक्षं बन्धय बन्धय। सर्वतो मां रक्ष रक्ष। अचलमचलमाक्रम्याक्रम्य महावज्रकवचैरस्त्रैः राजचोरसर्पसिंहव्याघ्राग्न्याद्युपद्रवं नाशय नाशय।
ॐ ह्रां ह्रीं ह्रूं श्रीं क्लीं ब्लूं फ्रों आं ह्रीं क्रों हुं फट् स्वाहा।

Mahiṣārūḍho
Nīlavarṇa Kāladaṇḍo Yamo Badhnātu Yamamaṇḍalam |
Yama Saparivāra Devatāpratyadhidevatāsahitaṃ Yamamaṇḍalaṃ Mama Saparivārakasya Pratyakṣaṃ Bandhaya Bandhaya |
Sarvato Māṃ Rakṣa Rakṣa | Acalamacalamākramyākramya Mahāvajrakavacairastraiḥ
Rājacorasarpasiṃhavyāghrāgnyādyupadravaṃ Nāśaya Nāśaya |
Oṃ Hrāṃ Hrīṃ Hrūṃ Śrīṃ Klīṃ Blūṃ Phroṃ Āṃ Hrīṃ Kroṃ Huṃ Phaṭ Svāhā |

त्रियम्बकं यजामहे सुगन्धिं पुष्टिवर्धनम्। उर्वारुकमिव बन्धनान्मृत्योर्मुक्षीय मामृतात्।

Triyambakaṃ Yajāmahe Sugandhiṃ Puṣṭivardhanam |
Urvārukamiva Bandhanānmṛtyormukṣīya Māmṛtāt |

यमाय सोमं सुनुत यमाय जुहुता हविः।
यमं ह यज्ञो गच्छत्यग्निदूतो अरकृतः। वर्षन्तु ते विभावरि दिवो अभ्रस्य विद्युतः।
रोहन्तु सर्वबीजान्यव ब्रह्म द्विषो जहि। ॐ नमो भगवते रुद्राय नमः।

Yamāya Somaṃ Sunuta Yamāya Juhutā Haviḥ |

Yamaṃ Ha Yajño Gacchatyagnidūto Arakṛtaḥ ।

Varṣantu Te Vibhāvari Divo Abhrasya Vidyutaḥ ।

Rohantu Sarvabījānyava Brahma Dviṣo Jahi ।

Oṃ Namo Bhagavate Rudrāya Namaḥ ।

ॐ नमो भगवते रुद्राय। नैरृत्या दिशि निरृतिर्देवता।
नरारूढो नीलवर्ण खड्गहस्तो निर्कतिर्बध्नातु निरृतिमण्डलम्।
निरृते सपरिवार देवताप्रत्यधिदेवतासहितं निरृतिमण्डल मम सपरिवारकस्य प्रत्यक्षं बन्धय बन्धय। सर्वतो मां रक्ष रक्ष। अचलमचलमाक्रम्याक्रम्य महावज्रकवचैरस्त्रैः
राजचोरसर्पसिंहव्याघ्राग्न्याद्युपद्रवं नाशय नाशय।
ॐ ह्रां ह्रीं ह्रूं श्रीं क्लीं ब्लूं फ्रों आं ह्रीं क्रों हुं फट् स्वाहा।

Oṃ Namo Bhagavate Rudrāya । *Nairṛtyā Diśi Nirṛtirdevatā* ।

Narārūḍho Nīlavarṇa Khaḍgahasto Nirkatirbadhnātu Nirṛtimaṇḍalam ।
Nirṛte Saparivāra Devatāpratyadhidevatāsahitaṃ Nirṛtimaṇḍala Mama Saparivārakasya Pratyakṣaṃ Bandhaya Bandhaya ।

Sarvato Māṃ Rakṣa Rakṣa ।
Acalamacalamākramyākramya Mahāvajrakavacairastraiḥ
Rājacorasarpasiṃhavyāghrāgnyādyupadravaṃ Nāśaya Nāśaya ।
Oṃ Hrāṃ Hrīṃ Hrūṃ Śrīṃ Klīṃ Blūṃ Phroṃ Āṃ Hrīṃ Kroṃ Huṃ Phaṭ Svāhā ।

त्रियम्बकं यजामहे सुगन्धिं पुष्टिवर्धनम्। उर्वारुकमिव बन्धनान्मृत्योर्मुक्षीय मामृतात्।

Triyambakaṃ Yajāmahe Sugandhiṃ Puṣṭivardhanam ।

Urvārukamiva Bandhanānmṛtyormukṣīya Māmṛtāt ।

मोषुण परापरा निरृतिर्दुर्हणावधीत्। पदीष्ट तृष्णया सह।
वर्षन्तु ते विभावरि दिवो अभ्रस्य विद्युतः। रोहन्तु सर्वबीजान्यव ब्रह्म द्विषो जहि।
ॐ नमो भगवते रुद्राय नमः।

Moṣuṇa Parāparā Nirṛtirdurhaṇāvadhīt । *Padīṣṭa Tṛṣṇayā Saha* ।

Varṣantu Te Vibhāvari Divo Abhrasya Vidyutaḥ ।

Rohantu Sarvabījānyava Brahma Dviṣo Jahi ।

Oṃ Namo Bhagavate Rudrāya Namaḥ |

ॐ नमो भगवते रुद्राय। वारुण्यां दिशि वरुणो देवता।
मकरारूढ श्वेतवर्ण पाशहस्तो वरुणो बध्नातु वरुणमण्डलम्।
वरुण सपरिवार देवताप्रत्यधिदेवतासहितं वरुणमण्डलं मम सपरिवारकस्य प्रत्यक्षं बन्धय बन्धय। सर्वतो मां रक्ष रक्ष। अचलमचलमाक्रम्याक्रम्य महावज्रकवचैरस्त्रैः राजचोरसर्पसिंहव्याघ्राग्न्याद्युपद्रवं नाशय नाशय।
ॐ ह्रां ह्रीं ह्रूं श्रीं क्लीं ब्लूं फ्रों आं ह्रीं क्रों हुं फट् स्वाहा।

Oṃ Namo Bhagavate Rudrāya | *Vāruṇyāṃ Diśi Varuṇo Devatā* | *Makarārūḍha Śvetavarṇa Pāśahasto Varuṇo Badhnātu Varuṇamaṇḍalam* | *Varuṇa Saparivāra Devatāpratyadhidevatāsahitaṃ Varuṇamaṇḍalaṃ Mama Saparivārakasya Pratyakṣaṃ Bandhaya Bandhaya* |
Sarvato Māṃ Rakṣa Rakṣa | *Acalamacalamākramyākramya Mahāvajrakavacairastraiḥ Rājacora Sarpasiṃha Vyāghrāgnyādyupadravaṃ Nāśaya Nāśaya* |
Oṃ Hrāṃ Hrīṃ Hrūṃ Śrīṃ Klīṃ Blūṃ Phroṃ Āṃ Hrīṃ Kroṃ Huṃ Phaṭ Svāhā |

त्रियम्बकं यजामहे सुगन्धिं पुष्टिवर्धनम्।
उर्वारुकमिव बन्धनान्मृत्योर्मुक्षीय मामृतात्। इमं मे वरुण श्रुधी हवमद्या च मृडय।
त्वामवस्युराचके। तत्त्वा यामि ब्रह्मणा वन्दमानस्तदा शास्ते यजमानो हविर्भि।
अहेडमानो वरुणेह बोध्युरुशस मा न आयुः प्र मोषीः।
वर्षन्तु ते विभावरि दिवो अभ्रस्य विद्युतः। रोहन्तु सर्वबीजान्यव ब्रह्म द्विषो जहि।
ॐ नमो भगवते रुद्राय नमः।

Triyambakaṃ Yajāmahe Sugandhiṃ Puṣṭivardhanam |
Urvārukamiva Bandhanānmṛtyormukṣīya Māmṛtāt |
Imaṃ Me Varuṇa Śrudhī Havamadyā Ca Mṛḍaya | *Tvāmavasyurācake* |
Tattvā Yāmi Brahmaṇā Vandamānastadā Śāste Yajamāno Havirbhi |
Aheḍamāno Varuṇeha Bodhyuruśasa Mā Na Āyuḥ Pra Moṣīḥ |
Varṣantu Te Vibhāvari Divo Abhrasya Vidyutaḥ |

Rohantu Sarvabījānyava Brahma Dviṣo Jahi |

Oṃ Namo Bhagavate Rudrāya Namaḥ |

ॐ नमो भगवते रुद्राय। वायव्यां दिशि वायुर्देवता। मृगारूढो धूम्रवर्णो ध्वजहस्तो वायुर्बध्नातु वायुमण्डलम्। वायो सपरिवार देवताप्रत्यधिदेवतासहितं वायुमण्डलं मम सपरिवारकस्य प्रत्यक्षं बन्धय बन्धय। सर्वतो मां रक्ष रक्ष। अचलमचलमाक्रम्याक्रम्य महावज्रकवचैरस्त्रैः राजचोरसर्पसिंहव्याघ्राग्न्याद्युपद्रवं नाशय नाशय।
ॐ हां ह्रीं ह्रूं श्रीं क्लीं ब्लूं फ्रों आं ह्रीं क्रों हुं फट् स्वाहा।

Oṃ Namo Bhagavate Rudrāya | Vāyavyāṃ Diśi Vāyurdevatā |

Mṛgārūḍho Dhūmravarṇo Dhvajahasto Vāyurbadhnātu Vāyumaṇḍalam| Vāyo Saparivāra Devatāpratyadhidevatāsahitaṃ Vāyumaṇḍalaṃ Mama Saparivārakasya Pratyakṣaṃ Bandhaya Bandhaya |

Sarvato Māṃ Rakṣa Rakṣa | Acalamacalamākramyākramya Mahāvajrakavacairastraiḥ Rājacorasarpasiṃhavyāghrāgnyādyupadravaṃ Nāśaya Nāśaya | Oṃ Hāṃ Hrīṃ Hrūṃ Śrīṃ Klīṃ Blūṃ Phroṃ Āṃ Hrīṃ Kroṃ Huṃ Phaṭ Svāhā |

त्रियम्बकं यजामहे सुगन्धिं पुष्टिवर्धनम्। उर्वारुकमिव बन्धनान्मृत्योर्मुक्षीय मामृतात्।

Triyambakaṃ Yajāmahe Sugandhiṃ Puṣṭivardhanam |

Urvārukamiva Bandhanānmṛtyormukṣīya Māmṛtāt |

तव वायवृतस्पते त्वष्टुर्जामातरद्भुत। अवां स्या वृणीमहे।
वर्षन्तु ते विभावरि दिवो अभ्रस्य विद्यतः। रोहन्तु सर्वबीजान्यव ब्रह्म द्विषो जहि।
ॐ नमो भगवते रुद्राय नमः।

Tava Vāyavṛtaspate Tvaṣṭurjāmātaradbhuta | Avāṃ Syā Vṛṇīmahe |

Varṣantu Te Vibhāvari Divo Abhrasya Vidyataḥ |

Rohantu Sarvabījānyava Brahma Dviṣo Jahi |

Oṃ Namo Bhagavate Rudrāya Namaḥ |

ॐ नमो भगवते रुद्राय। कौबेर्यां दिशि कुबेरो देवता। अश्वारूढः पीतवर्णो गदाङ्कुशहस्तः कुबेरो बध्नातु कुबेरमण्डलम्। कुबेर सपरिवार देवताप्रत्यधिदेवतासहितं कुबेरमण्डलं मम सपरिवारकस्य प्रत्यक्षं बन्धय बन्धय। सर्वतो मां रक्ष रक्ष।
अचलमचलमाक्रम्याक्रम्य महावज्र- कवचैरस्त्रैः राजचोरसर्पसिंहव्याघ्राग्न्याद्युपद्रवं नाशय नाशय। ॐ ह्रां ह्रीं ह्रूं श्रीं क्लीं ब्लूं फ्रों आं ह्रीं क्रों हुं फट् स्वाहा।

Oṃ Namo Bhagavate Rudrāya | Kauberyāṃ Diśi Kubero Devatā | Aśvārūḍhaḥ Pītavarṇo Gadāṅkuśahastaḥ Kubero Badhnātu Kuberamaṇḍalam | Kubera Saparivāra Devatāpratyadhidevatāsahitaṃ Kuberamaṇḍalaṃ Mama Saparivārakasya Pratyakṣaṃ Bandhaya Bandhaya | Sarvato Māṃ Rakṣa Rakṣa | Acalamacalamākramyākramya Mahāvajra- Kavacairastraiḥ Rājacorasarpasiṃhavyāghrāgnyādyupadravaṃ Nāśaya Nāśaya | Oṃ Hrāṃ Hrīṃ Hrūṃ Śrīṃ Klīṃ Blūṃ Phroṃ Āṃ Hrīṃ Kroṃ Huṃ Phaṭ Svāhā |

त्रियम्बकं यजामहे सुगन्धिं पुष्टिवर्धनम्। उर्वारुकमिव बन्धनान्मृत्योर्मुक्षीय मामृतात्।
सोमो धेनुं सोमो अर्वन्तमाशुं सोमो वीरं कर्मण्यं ददाति।
सादन्यं विदथ्यं सभेयं पितृश्रवणं यो ददाशदस्मै।
वर्षन्तु ते विभावरि दिवो अभ्रस्य विद्युतः।
रोहन्तु सर्वबीजान्यव ब्रह्म द्विषो जहि। ॐ नमो भगवते रुद्राय नमः।

Triyambakaṃ Yajāmahe Sugandhiṃ Puṣṭivardhanam | Urvārukamiva Bandhanānmṛtyormukṣīya Māmṛtāt | Somo Dhenuṃ Somo Arvantamāśuṃ Somo Vīraṃ Karmaṇyaṃ Dadāti | Sādanyaṃ Vidathyaṃ Sabheyaṃ Pitṛśravaṇaṃ Yo Dadāśadasmai |
Varṣantu Te Vibhāvari Divo Abhrasya Vidyutaḥ |
Rohantu Sarvabījānyava Brahma Dviṣo Jahi |
Oṃ Namo Bhagavate Rudrāya Namaḥ |

ॐ नमो भगवते रुद्राय। ईशान्यां दिशीशानो देवता।
वृषभारूढः श्वेतवर्णस्त्रिशूलहस्त ईशानो बध्नात्वीशानमण्डलम्। ईशान सपरिवार देवताप्रत्यधिदेवतासहितमीशानमण्डलं मम सपरिवारकस्य प्रत्यक्षं बन्धय बन्धय।

सर्वतो मां रक्ष रक्ष। अचलमचलमाक्रम्याक्रम्य महावज्रकवचैरस्त्रैः
राजचोरसर्पसिंहव्याघ्राग्न्याद्युपद्रवं नाशय नाशय।
ॐ ह्रां ह्रीं ह्रूं श्रीं क्लीं ब्लूं फ्रों आं ह्रीं क्रों हुं फट् स्वाहा।

Oṃ Namo Bhagavate Rudrāya | Īśānyāṃ Diśīśāno Devatā |
Vṛṣabhārūḍhaḥ Śvetavarṇastriśūlahasta Īśāno
Badhnātvīśānamaṇḍalam | Īśāna Saparivāra
Devatāpratyadhidevatāsahitamīśānamaṇḍalaṃ Mama Saparivārakasya
Pratyakṣaṃ Bandhaya Bandhaya | Sarvato Māṃ Rakṣa Rakṣa |
Acalamacalamākramyākramya Mahāvajrakavacairastraiḥ
Rājacorasarpasiṃhavyāghrāgnyādyupadravaṃ Nāśaya Nāśaya |
Oṃ Hrāṃ Hrīṃ Hrūṃ Śrīṃ Klīṃ Blūṃ Phroṃ Āṃ Hrīṃ Kroṃ Huṃ Phaṭ
Svāhā |

त्रियम्बकं यजामहे सुगन्धि पुष्टिवर्धनम्। उर्वारुकमिव बन्धनान्मृत्योर्मुक्षीय मामृतात्।
तमीशानं जगतस्तस्थुषस्पतिं धियं जिन्वमवसे हूमहे वयम्।
पूषा नो यथा वेदसामसद्वृधे रक्षिता पायुरदब्ध स्वस्तये।
वर्षन्तु ते विभावरि दिवो अभ्रस्य विद्युतः।
रोहन्तु सर्वबीजान्यव ब्रह्म द्विषो जहि। ॐ नमो भगवते रुद्राय नमः।

Triyambakaṃ Yajāmahe Sugandhi Puṣṭivardhanam |
Urvārukamiva Bandhanānmṛtyormukṣīya Māmṛtāt |
Tamīśānaṃ Jagatastasthuṣaspatiṃ Dhiyaṃ Jinvamavase Hūmahe
Vayam | Pūṣā No Yathā Vedasāmasadvṛdhe Rakṣitā Pāyuradabdha
Svastaye | Varṣantu Te Vibhāvari Divo Abhrasya Vidyutaḥ |
Rohantu Sarvabījānyava Brahma Dviṣo Jahi |
Oṃ Namo Bhagavate Rudrāya Namaḥ |

ॐ नमो भगवते रुद्राय। ऊर्ध्वायां दिशि ब्रह्मा देवता।
हंसारूढो रक्तवर्ण कमण्डलुहस्तो ब्रह्मा बध्नातु ब्रह्ममण्डलम्।
ब्रह्मन् सपरिवार देवताप्रत्यधिदेवतासहितं ब्रह्ममण्डलं मम सपरिवारकस्य प्रत्यक्षं बन्धय
बन्धय। सर्वतो मां रक्ष रक्ष। अचलमचलमाक्रम्याक्रम्य महावज्रकवचैरस्त्रैः
राजचोरसर्पसिंहव्याघ्राग्न्याद्युपद्रवं नाशय नाशय।
ॐ ह्रां ह्रीं ह्रूं श्रीं क्लीं ब्लूं फ्रों आं ह्रीं क्रों हुं फट् स्वाहा।

Oṃ Namo Bhagavate Rudrāya | Ūrdhvāyāṃ Diśi Brahmā Devatā | Haṃsārūḍho Raktavarṇa Kamaṇḍaluhasto Brahmā Badhnātu Brahmamaṇḍalam | Brahman Saparivāra Devatāpratyadhidevatāsahitaṃ Brahmamaṇḍalaṃ Mama Saparivārakasya Pratyakṣaṃ Bandhaya Bandhaya |

Sarvato Māṃ Rakṣa Rakṣa | Acalamacalamākramyākramya Mahāvajrakavacairastraiḥ Rājacorasarpasiṃhavyāghrāgnyādyupadravaṃ Nāśaya Nāśaya |
Oṃ Hrāṃ Hrīṃ Hrūṃ Śrīṃ Klīṃ Blūṃ Phroṃ Āṃ Hrīṃ Kroṃ Huṃ Phaṭ Svāhā |

त्रियम्बकं यजामहे सुगन्धिं पुष्टिवर्धनम्। उर्वारुकमिव बन्धनान्मृत्योर्मुक्षीय मामृतात्।
ब्रह्मा देवानां पदवीः कवीनामृषिर्विप्राणां महिषो मृगाणाम्। श्येनो गृध्राणां स्वधितिर्वनानां
सोमः पवित्रमत्येति रेभन्। वर्षन्तु ते विभावरि दिवो अभ्रस्य विद्युतः।
रोहन्तु सर्वबीजान्यव ब्रह्म द्विषो जहि। ॐ नमो भगवते रुद्राय नमः।

Triyambakaṃ Yajāmahe Sugandhiṃ Puṣṭivardhanam |

Urvārukamiva Bandhanānmṛtyormukṣīya Māmṛtāt | Brahmā Devānāṃ Padavīḥ Kavīnāmṛṣirviprāṇāṃ Mahiṣo Mṛgāṇām | Śyeno Gṛdhrāṇāṃ Svadhitirvanānāṃ Somaḥ Pavitramatyeti Rebhan |

Varṣantu Te Vibhāvari Divo Abhrasya Vidyutaḥ |

Rohantu Sarvabījānyava Brahma Dviṣo Jahi |

Oṃ Namo Bhagavate Rudrāya Namaḥ |

ॐ नमो भगवते रुद्राय। अधस्ताद्दिशि वासुकिर्देवता।
कूर्मारूढो नीलवर्ण पद्महस्तो वासुकिर्बध्नातु वासुकिमण्डलम् वासुके सपरिवार देवता
प्रत्यधिदेवतासहितं वासुकिमण्डलं मम सपरिवारकस्य प्रत्यक्षं बन्धय बन्धय।
सर्वतो मां रक्ष रक्ष। अचलमचलमाक्रम्याक्रम्य महावज्रकवचैरस्त्रैः राजचोर-
सर्पसिंहव्याघ्राग्न्याद्युपद्रवं नाशय नाशय।
ॐ ह्रां ह्रीं ह्रूं श्रीं क्लीं ब्लूं फ्रों आं ह्रीं क्रों हुं फट् स्वाहा।

Oṃ Namo Bhagavate Rudrāya | Adhastāddiśi Vāsukirdevatā | Kūrmārūḍho

Nīlavarṇa Padmahasto Vāsukirbadhnātu Vāsukimaṇḍalam | Vāsuke Saparivāra Devatā Pratyadhidevatāsahitaṃ Vāsukimaṇḍalaṃ Mama Saparivārakasya Pratyakṣaṃ Bandhaya Bandhaya |

Sarvato Māṃ Rakṣa Rakṣa | Acalamacalamākramyākramya Mahāvajrakavacairastraiḥ Rājacora Sarpasiṃhavyāghrāgnyādyupadravaṃ Nāśaya Nāśaya |
Oṃ Hrāṃ Hrīṃ Hrūṃ Śrīṃ Klīṃ Blūṃ Phroṃ Āṃ Hrīṃ Kroṃ Huṃ Phaṭ Svāhā |

त्रियम्बकं यजामहे सुगन्धिं पुष्टिवर्धनम्। उर्वारुकमिव बन्धनान्मृत्योर्मुक्षीय मामृतात्।
नमो अस्तु सर्पेभ्यो ये के च पृथिवीमनु। ये अन्तरिक्षे ये दिवि तेभ्यः सर्पेभ्यो नमः।
वर्षन्तु ते विभावरि दिवो अभ्रस्य विद्युत। रोहन्तु सर्वबीजान्यव ब्रह्म द्विषो जहि।
ॐ नमो भगवते रुद्राय नमः।

Triyambakaṃ Yajāmahe Sugandhiṃ Puṣṭivardhanam | Urvārukamiva Bandhanānmṛtyormukṣīya Māmṛtāt | Namo Astu Sarpebhyo Ye Ke Ca Pṛthivīmanu | Ye Antarikṣe Ye Divi Tebhyaḥ Sarpebhyo Namaḥ |
Varṣantu Te Vibhāvari Divo Abhrasya Vidyuta |
Rohantu Sarvabījānyava Brahma Dviṣo Jahi |
Oṃ Namo Bhagavate Rudrāya Namaḥ |

ॐ नमो भगवते रुद्राय। अवान्तरस्यां दिशि विष्णुर्देवता। गरुडारूढ श्यामवर्ण शङ्खचक्राङ्कितहस्तो विष्णुर्बध्नातु विष्णुमण्डलम्।विष्णो सपरिवार देवताप्रत्यधिदेवतासहितं विष्णुमण्डलं मम सपरिवारकस्य प्रत्यक्ष बन्धय बन्धय।
सर्वतो मां रक्ष रक्ष। अचलमचलमाक्रम्याक्रम्य महावज्रकवचैरस्त्रैः सर्पसिंहव्याघ्राग्न्याद्युपद्रवं नाशय नाशय।
ॐ हां हीं हूं श्रीं क्लीं ब्लूं फ्रों आं हीं क्रों हुं फट् स्वाहा।

Oṃ Namo Bhagavate Rudrāya | Avāntarasyāṃ Diśi Viṣṇurdevatā | Garuḍārūḍha Śyāmavarṇa Śaṅkhacakrāṅkitahasto Viṣṇurbadhnātu Viṣṇumaṇḍalam |
Viṣṇo Saparivāra Devatāpratyadhidevatāsahitaṃ Viṣṇumaṇḍalaṃ Mama Saparivārakasya Pratyakṣa Bandhaya Bandhaya |

Sarvato Māṃ Rakṣa Rakṣa | Acalamacalamākramyākramya Mahāvajrakavacairastraiḥ Sarpasiṃhavyāghrāgnyādyupadravaṃ Nāśaya Nāśaya | Oṃ Hrāṃ Hrīṃ Hrūṃ Śrīṃ Klīṃ Blūṃ Phroṃ Āṃ Hrīṃ Kroṃ Huṃ Phaṭ Svāhā |

त्रियम्बकं यजामहे सुगन्धिं पुष्टिवर्धनम्। उर्वारुकमिव बन्धनामृत्योर्मुक्षीय मामृतात्।
इदं विष्णुर्विचक्रमे त्रेधा निदधे पदम्। समूढमस्य पांसुरे।
वर्षन्तु ते विभावरि दिवो अभ्रस्य विद्युतः। रोहन्तु सर्वबीजान्यव ब्रह्म द्विषो जहि।
ॐ नमो भगवते रुद्राय नमः ।

Triyambakaṃ Yajāmahe Sugandhiṃ Puṣṭivardhanam |

Urvārukamiva Bandhanāmṛtyormukṣīya Māmṛtāt |

Idaṃ Viṣṇurvicakrame Tredhā Nidadhe Padam |

Samūḍhamasya Pāṃsure |

Varṣantu Te Vibhāvari Divo Abhrasya Vidyutaḥ |

Rohantu Sarvabījānyava Brahma Dviṣo Jahi |

Oṃ Namo Bhagavate Rudrāya Namaḥ |

ॐ नमो भगवते रुद्राय। स्निक् च स्नीहितिश्च स्निहितिश्च।
उष्णा च शीता च। उग्रा च भीमा च। सदाम्नी सेदिरनिरा। एतास्ते अग्ने घोरास्तनुव।
ताभिरमु गच्छ स्वाहा। अष्टापिधाना नकुली दन्तैः परिवृता पविः ।
सर्वस्यै वाच ईशाना चारु मामिह वादयेत्॥ ऐं वद वद वाग्वादिनि स्वाहा।
ॐ नमो भगवते रुद्राय नमः।

Oṃ Namo Bhagavate Rudrāya | Snik Ca Snīhitiśca Snihitiśca |

Uṣṇā Ca Śītā Ca | Ugrā Ca Bhīmā Ca | Sadāmnī Sediranirā |

Etāste Agne Ghorāstanuva | Tābhiramu Gaccha Svāhā |

Aṣṭāpidhānā Nakulī Dantaiḥ Parivṛtā Paviḥ |

Sarvasyai Vāca Īśānā Cāru Māmiha Vādayet ||

Aiṃ Vada Vada Vāgvādini Svāhā |

Oṃ Namo Bhagavate Rudrāya Namaḥ |

ॐ नमो भगवते रुद्राय। प्राच्यां दिशीन्द्रः सपरिवारो देवता प्रत्यधिदेवता।

तद्दिक्षु त्रिशूलको नाम राक्षसः । तस्याष्टादशकोटिभूतप्रेतपिशाच ब्रह्म राक्षस शाकिनी डाकिनी काकिनी हाकिनी याकिनी राकिनी लाकिनी वेताल कामिनी ग्रहान् बन्धयामि मम सपरिवारकस्य । सर्वतो मां रक्ष रक्ष । अचलमचलमाक्रम्याक्रम्य महावज्रकवचैरस्त्रैः राजचोरसर्पसिंहव्याघ्राग्न्याद्युपद्रवं नाशय नाशय ।
ॐ, ह्रीं ह्रूं श्रीं क्लीं ब्लूं फ्रों आं ह्रीं क्रों हुं फट् स्वाहा ।

Oṃ Namo Bhagavate Rudrāya | Prācyāṃ Diśīndraḥ Saparivāro Devatā Pratyadhidevatā | Taddikṣu Triśūlako Nāma Rākṣasaḥ | Tasyāṣṭādaśakoṭibhūtapretapiśācabrahmarākṣasaśākinīḍākinī-Kākinīhākinīyākinīrākinīlākinīvetālakāminīgrahān Bandhayāmi Mama Saparivārakasya | Sarvato Māṃ Rakṣa Rakṣa | Acalamacalamākramyākramya Mahāvajrakavacairastraiḥ Rājacorasarpasiṃhavyāghrāgnyādyupadravaṃ Nāśaya Nāśaya |
Oṃ, Hrīṃ Hrūṃ Śrīṃ Klīṃ Blūṃ Phroṃ Āṃ Hrīṃ Kroṃ Huṃ Phaṭ Svāhā |

त्रियम्बकं यजामहे सुगन्धिं पुष्टिवर्धनम् । उर्वारुकमिव बन्धनान्मृत्योर्मुक्षीय मामृतात् ।
लं इन्द्रं वो विश्वतस्परि हवामहे जनेभ्यः । अस्माकमस्तु केवलः ।
वर्षन्तु ते विभावरि दिवो अभ्रस्य विद्युतः । रोहन्तु सर्वबीजान्यव ब्रह्म द्विषो जहि ।
ॐ नमो भगवते रुद्राय नमः ।

Triyambakaṃ Yajāmahe Sugandhiṃ Puṣṭivardhanam |
Urvārukamiva Bandhanānmṛtyormukṣīya Māmṛtāt |
Laṃ Indraṃ Vo Viśvataspari Havāmahe Janebhyaḥ |
Asmākamastu Kevalaḥ | Varṣantu Te Vibhāvari Divo Abhrasya Vidyutaḥ | Rohantu Sarvabījānyava Brahma Dviṣo Jahi |
Oṃ Namo Bhagavate Rudrāya Namaḥ |

ॐ नमो भगवते रुद्राय । आग्नेय्यां दिश्यग्निः सपरिवारो देवता प्रत्यधिदेवता ।
तद्दिक्षु तद्दिक्षु मारीचको नाम राक्षसः । तस्याष्टादशकोटिभूत- प्रेत पिशाच ब्रह्म राक्षस शाकिनी डाकिनी काकिनी हाकिनी याकिनी- राकिनीलाकिनीवेतालकामिनीग्रहान् बन्धयामि मम सपरिवारकस्य । सर्वतो मां रक्ष रक्ष ।
अचलमचलमाक्रम्याक्रम्य महावज्रकवचैरस्त्रैः राज चोर सर्प सिंह व्याघ्राग्न्या द्युपद्रवं नाशय नाशय । ॐ ह्रां ह्रीं ह्रूं श्रीं क्लीं ब्लूं फ्रों आं ह्रीं क्रों हुं फट् स्वाहा ।

Oṃ Namo Bhagavate Rudrāya |

Āgneyyāṃ Diśyagniḥ Saparivāro Devatā Pratyadhidevatā |

Taddikṣu Mārīcako Nāma Rākṣasaḥ | Tasyāṣṭādaśakoṭibhūta-Pretapiśācabrahmarākṣasaśākinīḍākinīkākinīhākinīyākinī-Rākinīlākinīvetālakāminīgrahān Bandhayāmi Mama Saparivārakasya |

Sarvato Māṃ Rakṣa Rakṣa | Acalamacalamākramyākramya Mahāvajrakavacairastraiḥ Rājacorasarpasiṃhavyāghrāgnyādyupadravaṃ Nāśaya Nāśaya |
Oṃ Hrāṃ Hrīṃ Hrūṃ Śrīṃ Klīṃ Blūṃ Phroṃ Āṃ Hrīṃ Kroṃ Huṃ Phaṭ Svāhā |

त्रियम्बकं यजामहे सुगन्धिं पुष्टिवर्धनम्। उर्वारुकमिव बन्धनान्मृत्योर्मुक्षीय मामृतात्।
अग्निं दूतं वृणीमहे होतारं विश्ववेदसम्। अस्य यज्ञस्य सुक्रतुम्।
वर्षन्तु ते विभावरि दिवो अभ्रस्य विद्युतः। रोहन्तु सर्वबीजान्यव ब्रह्म द्विषो जहि।
ॐ नमो भगवते रुद्राय नमः।

Triyambakaṃ Yajāmahe Sugandhiṃ Puṣṭivardhanam |

Urvārukamiva Bandhanānmṛtyormukṣīya Māmṛtāt |

Agniṃ Dūtaṃ Vṛṇīmahe Hotāraṃ Viśvavedasam |

Asya Yajñasya Sukratum |

Varṣantu Te Vibhāvari Divo Abhrasya Vidyutaḥ |

Rohantu Sarvabījānyava Brahma Dviṣo Jahi |

Oṃ Namo Bhagavate Rudrāya Namaḥ |

ॐ नमो भगवते रुद्राय। याम्यां दिशि यमः सपरिवारो देवता प्रत्यधिदेवता।
तद्दिक्ष्वेकपिङ्गलको नाम राक्षसः। तस्याष्टादशकोटि
भूतप्रेतपिशाचब्रह्मराक्षसशाकिनीडाकिनीकाकिनीहाकिनीयाकिनी-
राकिनीलाकिनीवेतालकामिनीग्रहान् बन्धयामि मम सपरिवारकस्य।
सर्वतो मां रक्ष रक्ष।
अचलमचलमाक्रम्याक्रम्य महावज्रकवचैरस्त्रैः राज-चोर सर्प सिंह व्याघ्राग्न्याद्युपद्रव नाशय नाशय। ॐ ह्रां ह्रीं ह्रूं श्रीं क्लीं ब्लूं फ्रों आं ह्रीं क्रों हुं फट् स्वाहा।

Oṃ Namo Bhagavate Rudrāya |

Yāmyāṃ Diśi Yamaḥ Saparivāro Devatā Pratyadhidevatā |
Taddikṣvekapiṅgalako Nāma Rākṣasaḥ | Tasyāṣṭādaśakoṭi
Bhūtapretapiśācabrahmarākṣasaśākinīḍākinīkākinīhākinīyākinī-
Rākinīlākinīvetālakāminīgrahān Bandhayāmi Mama Saparivārakasya |
Sarvato Māṃ Rakṣa Rakṣa | Acalamacalamākramyākramya
Mahāvajrakavacairastraiḥ Rāja-
Corasarpasiṃhavyāghrāgnyādyupadrava Nāśaya Nāśaya |
Oṃ Hrāṃ Hrīṃ Hrūṃ Śrīṃ Klīṃ Blūṃ Phroṃ Āṃ Hrīṃ Kroṃ Huṃ Phaṭ Svāhā |

त्रियम्बकं यजामहे सुगन्धिं पुष्टिवर्धनम्। उर्वारुकमिव बन्धनान्मृत्योर्मुक्षीय मामृतात्।
यमाय सोम सुनुत यमाय जुहुता हविः। यमं ह यज्ञो गच्छत्यग्निदूतो अरकृत।
वर्षन्तु ते विभावरि दिवो अभ्रस्य विद्युतः। रोहन्तु सर्वबीजान्यव ब्रह्म द्विषो जहि।
ॐ नमो भगवते रुद्राय नमः।

Triyambakaṃ Yajāmahe Sugandhiṃ
Puṣṭivardhanam | Urvārukamiva Bandhanānmṛtyormukṣīya Māmṛtāt |
Yamāya Soma Sunuta Yamāya Juhutā Haviḥ |
Yamaṃ Ha Yajño Gacchatyagnidūto Arakṛta |
Varṣantu Te Vibhāvari Divo Abhrasya Vidyutaḥ |
Rohantu Sarvabījānyava Brahma Dviṣo Jahi |
Oṃ Namo Bhagavate Rudrāya Namaḥ |

ॐ नमो भगवते रुद्राय। नैरृत्यां दिशि निरृति सपरिवारो देवता प्रत्यधिदेवता।
तद्दिक्षु सत्यको नाम राक्षसः।
तस्याष्टादशकोटिभूतप्रेतपिशाचब्रह्मराक्षसशाकिनीडाकिनी-
काकिनीहाकिनीयाकिनीराकिनीलाकिनीवेतालकामिनीग्रहान् बन्धयामि मम
सपरिवारकस्य।सर्वतो मां रक्ष रक्ष। अचलमचलमाक्रम्याक्रम्य
महावज्रकवचैरस्त्रैः राजचोर- सर्पसिंहव्याघ्राग्न्याद्युपद्रवं नाशय नाशय।
ॐ ह्रां ह्रीं ह्रूं श्रीं क्लीं ब्लूं फ्रों आं ह्रीं क्रों हुं फट् स्वाहा।

Oṃ Namo Bhagavate Rudrāya | Nairṛtyāṃ Diśi Nirṛti Saparivāro
Devatā Pratyadhidevatā | Taddikṣu Satyako Nāma Rākṣasaḥ |
Tasyāṣṭādaśakoṭibhūtapretapiśācabrahmarākṣasaśākinīḍākinī-

Kākinīhākinīyākinīrākinīlākinīvetālakāminīgrahān Bandhayāmi Mama Saparivārakasya |Sarvato Māṃ Rakṣa Rakṣa | Acalamacalamākramyākramya Mahāvajrakavacairastraiḥ Rājacora-Sarpasiṃhavyāghrāgnyādyupadravaṃ Nāśaya Nāśaya | Oṃ Hrāṃ Hrīṃ Hrūṃ Śrīṃ Klīṃ Blūṃ Phroṃ Āṃ Hrīṃ Kroṃ Huṃ Phaṭ Svāhā |

त्रियम्बकं यजामहे सुगन्धिं पुष्टिवर्धनम्। उर्वारुकमिव बन्धानान्मृत्योर्मुक्षीय मामृतात्।
मोषुण परापरा निरृतिर्दुर्हणावधीत् । पदीष्ट तृष्णया सह।
वर्षन्तु ते विभावरि दिवो अभ्रस्य विद्युतः।
रोहन्तु सर्वबीजान्यव ब्रह्म द्विषो जहि। ॐ नमो भगवते रुद्राय नमः ।

Triyambakaṃ Yajāmahe Sugandhiṃ Puṣṭivardhanam |
Urvārukamiva Bandhānānmṛtyormukṣīya Māmṛtāt |
Moṣuṇa Parāparā Nirṛtirdurhaṇāvadhīt |
Padīṣṭa Tṛṣṇayā Saha | Varṣantu Te Vibhāvari Divo Abhrasya Vidyutaḥ |
Rohantu Sarvabījānyava Brahma Dviṣo Jahi |
Oṃ Namo Bhagavate Rudrāya Namaḥ |

ॐ नमो भगवते रुद्राय। वारुण्यां दिशि वरुण सपरिवारो देवता प्रत्यधिदेवता।
तद्दिक्षु यत्खलो नाम राक्षसः ।
तस्याष्टादशकोटिभूतप्रेतपिशाचब्रह्मराक्षसशाकिनीडाकिनी- सपरिवारकस्य।
काकिनीहाकिनीयाकिनीराकिनीलाकिनीवेतालकामिनीग्रहान् बन्धयामि मम
सर्वतो मां रक्ष रक्ष। अचलमचलमाक्रम्याक्रम्य महावज्रकवचैरस्त्रैः
राजचोरसर्पसिंहव्याघ्राग्न्याद्युपद्रवं नाशय नाशय।
ॐ ह्रां ह्रीं ह्रूं श्रीं क्लीं ब्लूं फ्रों आं ह्रीं क्रों हुं फट् स्वाहा।

Oṃ Namo Bhagavate Rudrāya | Vāruṇyāṃ Diśi Varuṇa Saparivāro Devatā Pratyadhidevatā | Taddikṣu Yatkhalo Nāma Rākṣasaḥ | Tasyāṣṭādaśakoṭibhūtapretapiśācabrahmarākṣasaśākinīḍākinī-Kākinīhākinīyākinīrākinīlākinīvetālakāminīgrahān Bandhayāmi Mama Saparivārakasya | Sarvato Māṃ Rakṣa Rakṣa | Acalamacalamākramyākramya Mahāvajrakavacairastraiḥ Rājacorasarpasiṃhavyāghrāgnyādyupadravaṃ Nāśaya Nāśaya |

Oṃ Hrāṃ Hrīṃ Hrūṃ Śrīṃ Klīṃ Blūṃ Phroṃ Āṃ Hrīṃ Kroṃ Huṃ Phaṭ Svāhā ।

त्रियम्बकं यजामहे सुगन्धिं पुष्टिवर्धनम्। उर्वारुकमिव बन्धनान्मृत्योर्मुक्षीय मामृतात्।
इमं मे वरुण श्रुधी हवमद्या च मृडय। त्वामवस्युराचके।
तत्त्वा यामि ब्रह्मणावन्दमानस्तदा शास्ते यजमानो हविर्भिः।
अहेडमानो वरुणेह बोध्युरुशंसमा न आयुः प्र मोषीः।
वर्षन्तु ते विभावरि दिवो अभ्रस्य विद्युतः। रोहन्तु सर्वबीजान्यव ब्रह्म द्विषो जहि।
ॐ नमो भगवते रुद्राय नमः।

Triyambakaṃ Yajāmahe Sugandhiṃ Puṣṭivardhanam । *Urvārukamiva Bandhanānmṛtyormukṣīya Māmṛtāt* । *Imaṃ Me Varuṇa Śrudhī Havamadyā Ca Mṛḍaya* । *Tvāmavasyurācake* ।
Tattvā Yāmi Brahmaṇāvandamānastadā Śāste Yajamāno Havirbhiḥ ।
Aheḍamāno Varuṇeha Bodhyuruśaṃsa Mā Na Āyuḥ Pra Moṣīḥ ।
Varṣantu Te Vibhāvari Divo Abhrasya Vidyutaḥ ।
Rohantu Sarvabījānyava Brahma Dviṣo Jahi ।
Oṃ Namo Bhagavate Rudrāya Namaḥ ।

ॐ नमो भगवते रुद्राय। वायव्यां दिशि वायुः सपरिवारो देवता प्रत्यधिदेवता।
तद्दिक्षु प्रलम्बको नाम राक्षसः।
तस्याष्टादशकोटिभूतप्रेतपिशाचब्रह्मराक्षसशाकिनीडाकिनी-काकिनीहाकिनीयाकिनीराकिनीलाकिनीवेतालकामिनीग्रहान् बन्धयामि मम सपरिवारकस्य। सर्वतो मां रक्ष रक्ष। अचलमचलमाक्रम्याक्रम्य महावज्रकवचैरस्त्रैः राजचोरसर्पसिंहव्याघ्राग्न्याद्युपद्रवं नाशय नाशय।
ॐ ह्रां ह्रीं ह्रूं श्रीं क्लीं ब्लूं फ्रों आं ह्रीं क्रों हुं फट् स्वाहा।

Oṃ Namo Bhagavate Rudrāya । *Vāyavyāṃ Diśi Vāyuḥ Saparivāro Devatā Pratyadhidevatā* । *Taddikṣu Pralambako Nāma Rākṣasaḥ* ।
Tasyāṣṭādaśakoṭibhūtapretapiśācabrahmarākṣasaśākinīḍākinī-Kākinīhākinīyākinīrākinīlākinīvetālakāminīgrahān Bandhayāmi Mama

Saparivārakasya | Sarvato Māṃ Rakṣa Rakṣa | Acalamacalamākramyākramya Mahāvajrakavacairastraiḥ Rājacorasarpasiṃhavyāghrāgnyādyupadravaṃ Nāśaya Nāśaya |

त्रियम्बकं यजामहे सुगन्धिं पुष्टिवर्धनम्। उर्वारुकमिव बन्धनान्मृत्योर्मुक्षीय मामृतात्।
तव वायवृतस्पते त्वष्टुर्जामातरद्भुत। अवां स्या वृणीमहे।
वर्षन्तु ते विभावरि दिवो अभ्रस्य विद्युतः। रोहन्तु सर्वबीजान्यव ब्रह्म द्विषो जहि।
ॐ नमो भगवते रुद्राय नम।

Oṃ Hrāṃ Hrīṃ Hrūṃ Śrīṃ Klīṃ Blūṃ Phroṃ Āṃ Hrīṃ Kroṃ Huṃ Phaṭ Svāhā |

Triyambakaṃ Yajāmahe Sugandhiṃ Puṣṭivardhanam |

Urvārukamiva Bandhanānmṛtyormukṣīya Māmṛtāt |

Tava Vāyavṛtaspate Tvaṣṭurjāmātaradbhuta | Avāṃ Syā Vṛṇīmahe |

Varṣantu Te Vibhāvari Divo Abhrasya Vidyutaḥ |

Rohantu Sarvabījānyava Brahma Dviṣo Jahi |

Oṃ Namo Bhagavate Rudrāya Nama |

ॐ नमो भगवते रुद्राय। कौबेर्यां दिशि कुबेरः सपरिवारो देवता प्रत्यधिदेवता।
तद्दिक्ष्वश्वालको नाम राक्षसः। तस्याष्टादशकोटिभूतप्रेतपिशाचब्रह्मराक्षसशाकिनीडाकिनी-काकिनीहाकिनीयाकिनीराकिनीलाकिनीवेतालकामिनीग्रहान् बन्धयामि मम सपरिवारकस्य। सर्वतो मां रक्ष रक्ष। अचलमचलमाक्रम्याक्रम्य महावज्रकवचैरस्त्रैः राजचोरसर्पसिंहव्याघ्राग्न्याद्युपद्रवं नाशय नाशय।
ॐ ह्रां ह्रीं ह्रूं श्रीं क्लीं ब्लूं फ्रों आं ह्रीं क्रों हुं फट् स्वाहा।

Oṃ Namo Bhagavate Rudrāya | Kauberyāṃ Diśi Kuberaḥ Saparivāro Devatā Pratyadhidevatā | Taddikṣvaśvālako Nāma Rākṣasaḥ | Tasyāṣṭādaśakoṭibhūtapretapiśācabrahmarākṣasaśākinīḍākinī-Kākinīhākinīyākinīrākinīlākinīvetālakāminīgrahān Bandhayāmi Mama Saparivārakasya | Sarvato Māṃ Rakṣa Rakṣa | Acalamacalamākramyākramya Mahāvajrakavacairastraiḥ Rājacorasarpasiṃhavyāghrāgnyādyupadravaṃ Nāśaya Nāśaya | Oṃ Hrāṃ Hrīṃ Hrūṃ Śrīṃ Klīṃ Blūṃ Phroṃ Āṃ Hrīṃ Kroṃ Huṃ Phaṭ Svāhā |

त्रियम्बकं यजामहे सुगन्धिं पुष्टिवर्धनम्। उर्वारुकमिव बन्धनान्मृत्योर्मुक्षीय मामृतात्।
सोमो धेनु सोमो अर्वन्तमाशु सोमो वीरं कर्मण्यं ददाति।
सादन्यं विदथ्यं सभेयं पितृश्रवणं यो ददाशदस्मे। वर्षन्तु ते विभावरि दिवो अभ्रस्य विद्युतः।
रोहन्तु सर्वबीजान्यव ब्रह्म द्विषो जहि।
ॐ नमो भगवते रुद्राय नमः।

Triyambakaṃ Yajāmahe Sugandhiṃ Puṣṭivardhanam | Urvārukamiva Bandhanānmṛtyormukṣīya Māmṛtāt | Somo Dhenu Somo Arvantamāśu Somo Vīraṃ Karmaṇyaṃ Dadāti | Sādanyaṃ Vidathyaṃ Sabheyaṃ Pitṛśravaṇaṃ Yo Dadāśadasme |

Varṣantu Te Vibhāvari Divo Abhrasya Vidyutaḥ |

Rohantu Sarvabījānyava Brahma Dviṣo Jahi |

Oṃ Namo Bhagavate Rudrāya Namaḥ |

ॐ नमो भगवते रुद्राय। ईशान्यां दिशीशानः सपरिवारो देवता प्रत्यधिदेवता।
तद्दिक्षून्मत्तको नाम राक्षसः।
तस्याष्टादशकोटिभूतप्रेतपिशाचब्रह्मराक्षसशाकिनीडाकिनी-
काकिनीहाकिनीयाकिनीराकिनीलाकिनीवेत्तालकामिनीग्रहान् बन्धयामि मम
सपरिवारकस्य। सर्वतो मां रक्ष रक्ष। अचलमचलमाक्रम्याक्रम्य
महावज्रकवचैरस्त्रैः राजचोरसर्पसिंहव्याघ्राग्न्याद्युपद्रवं नाशय नाशय।
ॐ ह्रां ह्रीं ह्रूं श्रीं क्लीं ब्लूं फ्रों आं ह्रीं क्रों हुं फट् स्वाहा।

Oṃ Namo Bhagavate Rudrāya | Īśānyāṃ Diśīśānaḥ Saparivāro Devatā Pratyadhidevatā | Taddikṣūnmattako Nāma Rākṣasaḥ | Tasyāṣṭādaśakoṭibhūtapretapiśācabrahmarākṣasaśākinīḍākinī-Kākinīhākinīyākinīrākinīlākinīvettālakāminīgrahān Bandhayāmi Mama Saparivārakasya | Sarvato Māṃ Rakṣa Rakṣa | Acalamacalamākramyākramya Mahāvajrakavacairastraiḥ Rājacorasarpasiṃhavyāghrāgnyādyupadravaṃ Nāśaya Nāśaya | Oṃ Hrāṃ Hrīṃ Hrūṃ Śrīṃ Klīṃ Blūṃ Phroṃ Āṃ Hrīṃ Kroṃ Huṃ Phaṭ Svāhā |

त्रियम्बकं यजामहे सुगन्धिं पुष्टिवर्धनम्। उर्वारुकमिव बन्धनान्मुत्योर्मुक्षीय मामृतात्।
तमीशानं जगतस्तस्थुषस्पतिं धियं जिन्वमवसे हूमहे वयम्।

पूषा नो यथा वेदसामसद्वृधे रक्षिता पायुरदब्धः स्वस्तये ।
वर्षन्तु ते विभावरि दिवो अभ्रस्य विद्युतः ।
रोहन्तु सर्वबीजान्यव ब्रह्म द्विषो जहि । ॐ नमो भगवते रुद्राय नमः ।

Triyambakaṃ Yajāmahe Sugandhiṃ Puṣṭivardhanam |
Urvārukamiva Bandhanānmutyormukṣīya Māmṛtāt |
Tamīśānaṃ Jagatastasthuṣaspatiṃ Dhiyaṃ Jinvamavase Hūmahe Vayam |
Pūṣā No Yathā Vedasāmasadvṛdhe Rakṣitā Pāyuradabdhaḥ Svastaye |
Varṣantu Te Vibhāvari Divo Abhrasya Vidyutaḥ |
Rohantu Sarvabījānyava Brahma Dviṣo Jahi |
Oṃ Namo Bhagavate Rudrāya Namaḥ |

ॐ नमो भगवते रुद्राय । ऊर्ध्वायां दिशि ब्रह्मा सपरिवारो देवता प्रत्यधिदेवता ।
तद्दिक्ष्वाकाशवासी नाम राक्षसः ।
तस्याष्टादशकोटिभूतप्रेतपिशाचब्रह्मराक्षसशाकिनीडाकिनी-
काकिनीहाकिनीयाकिनीराकिनीलाकिनीवेतालकामिनीग्रहान् बन्धयामि मम
सपरिवारकस्य । सर्वतो मां रक्ष रक्ष । अचलमचलमाक्रम्याक्रम्य
महावज्रकवचैरस्त्रैः राजचोरसर्पसिंहव्याघ्राग्न्याद्युपद्रवं नाशय नाशय ।
ॐ ह्रां ह्रीं ह्रूं श्रीं क्लीं ब्लूं फ्रों आं ह्रीं क्रों हुं फट् स्वाहा ।

Oṃ Namo Bhagavate Rudrāya | Ūrdhvāyāṃ Diśi Brahmā Saparivāro Devatā Pratyadhidevatā | Taddikṣvākāśavāsī Nāma Rākṣasaḥ |
Tasyāṣṭādaśakoṭibhūtapretapiśācabrahmarākṣasaśākinīḍākinī-Kākinīhākinīyākinīrākinīlākinīvetālakāminīgrahān Bandhayāmi Mama Saparivārakasya | Sarvato Māṃ Rakṣa Rakṣa |
Acalamacalamākramyākramya Mahāvajrakavacairastraiḥ Rājacorasarpasiṃhavyāghrāgnyādyupadravaṃ Nāśaya Nāśaya |
Oṃ Hrāṃ Hrīṃ Hrūṃ Śrīṃ Klīṃ Blūṃ Phroṃ Āṃ Hrīṃ Kroṃ Huṃ Phaṭ Svāhā |

त्रियम्बकं यजामहे सुगन्धिं पुष्टिवर्धनम् । उर्वारुकमिव बन्धनान्मृत्योर्मुक्षीय मामृतात् ।
ब्रह्मा देवानां पदवीः कवीनामृषिर्विप्राणां महिषो मृगाणाम् ।
श्येनो गृध्राणां स्वधितिर्वनानां सोम पवित्रमत्येति रेभन् ।

वर्षन्तु ते विभावरि दिवो अभ्रस्य विद्युतः। रोहन्तु सर्वबीजान्यव ब्रह्म द्विषो जहि।
ॐ नमो भगवते रुद्राय नमः।

Triyambakaṃ Yajāmahe Sugandhiṃ Puṣṭivardhanam |
Urvārukamiva Bandhanānmṛtyormukṣīya Māmṛtāt |
Brahmā Devānāṃ Padavīḥ Kavīnāmṛṣirviprāṇāṃ Mahiṣo Mṛgāṇām |
Śyeno Gṛdhrāṇāṃ Svadhitirvanānāṃ Soma Pavitramatyeti Rebhan |
Varṣantu Te Vibhāvari Divo Abhrasya Vidyutaḥ |
Rohantu Sarvabījānyava Brahma Dviṣo Jahi |
Oṃ Namo Bhagavate Rudrāya Namaḥ |

ॐ नमो भगवते रुद्राय। अधस्ताद्दिशि वासुकि सपरिवारो देवता प्रत्यधिदेवता।
तद्दिक्षु पातालवासी नाम राक्षसः।
तस्याष्टादशकोटिभूतप्रेतपिशाचब्रह्मराक्षसशाकिनीडाकिनी-
काकिनीहाकिनीयाकिनीराकिनीलाकिनीवेतालकामिनीग्रहान् बन्धयामि मम
सपरिवारकस्य। सर्वतो मां रक्ष रक्ष। अचलमचलमाक्रम्याक्रम्य
महावज्रकवचैरस्त्रैः राजचोरसर्पसिंहव्याघ्राग्न्याद्युपद्रवं नाशय नाशय।
ॐ ह्रां ह्रीं ह्रूं श्रीं क्लीं ब्लूं फ्रों आं ह्रीं क्रों हुं फट् स्वाहा।

Oṃ Namo Bhagavate Rudrāya | Adhastāddiśi Vāsuki Saparivāro Devatā Pratyadhidevatā | Taddikṣu Pātālavāsī Nāma Rākṣasaḥ | Tasyāṣṭādaśakoṭibhūtapretapiśācabrahmarākṣasaśākinīḍākinī-Kākinīhākinīyākinīrākinīlākinīvetālakāminīgrahān Bandhayāmi Mama Saparivārakasya | Sarvato Māṃ Rakṣa Rakṣa | Acalamacalamākramyākramya Mahāvajrakavacairastraiḥ Rājacorasarpasiṃhavyāghrāgnyādyupadravaṃ Nāśaya Nāśaya | Oṃ Hrāṃ Hrīṃ Hrūṃ Śrīṃ Klīṃ Blūṃ Phroṃ Āṃ Hrīṃ Kroṃ Huṃ Phaṭ Svāhā |

त्रियम्बकं यजामहे सुगन्धिं पुष्टिवर्धनम्। उर्वारुकमिव बन्धनान्मृत्योर्मुक्षीय मामृतात्।
नमो अस्तु सपेभ्यो ये के च पृथिवीमनु। ये अन्तरिक्षे ये दिवि तेभ्य सर्वेभ्यो नमः।
वर्षन्तु ते विभावरि दिवो अभ्रस्य विद्युत। रोहन्तु सर्वबीजान्यव ब्रह्म द्विषो जहि।
ॐ नमो भगवते रुद्राय नमः।

Triyambakaṃ Yajāmahe Sugandhiṃ Puṣṭivardhanam |

Urvārukamiva Bandhanānmṛtyormukṣīya Māmṛtāt |

Namo Astu Sapebhyo Ye Ke Ca Pṛthivīmanu |

Ye Antarikṣe Ye Divi Tebhya Sarvebhyo Namaḥ |

Varṣantu Te Vibhāvari Divo Abhrasya Vidyuta |

Rohantu Sarvabījānyava Brahma Dviṣo Jahi |

Oṃ Namo Bhagavate Rudrāya Namaḥ |

ॐ नमो भगवते रुद्राय। अवान्तरस्यां दिशि विष्णुः सपरिवारो देवता प्रत्यधिदेवता। तद्दिक्षु भीमको नाम राक्षसः। तस्याष्टादशकोटिभूतप्रेतपिशाचब्रह्मराक्षसशाकिनीडाकिनी-काकिनीहाकिनीयाकिनीराकिनीलाकिनीवेतालकामिनीग्रहान् बन्धयामि मम सपरिवारकस्य। सर्वतो मां रक्ष रक्ष। अचलमचलमाक्रम्याक्रम्य महावज्रकवचैरस्त्रैः राजचोर- सर्पसिंहव्याघ्राग्न्याद्युपद्रवं नाशय नाशय। ॐ ह्रां ह्रीं ह्रूं श्रीं क्लीं ब्लूं फ्रों आं ह्रीं क्रों हुं फट् स्वाहा।

Oṃ Namo Bhagavate Rudrāya | *Avāntarasyāṃ Diśi Viṣṇuḥ Saparivāro Devatā Pratyadhidevatā* | *Taddikṣu Bhīmako Nāma Rākṣasaḥ* | *Tasyāṣṭādaśakoṭibhūtapretapiśācabrahmarākṣasaśākinīḍākinī-Kākinīhākinīyākinīrākinīlākinīvetālakāminīgrahān Bandhayāmi Mama Saparivārakasya* | *Sarvato Māṃ Rakṣa Rakṣa* | *Acalamacalamākramyākramya Mahāvajrakavacairastraiḥ Rājacora-Sarpasiṃhavyāghrāgnyādyupadravaṃ Nāśaya Nāśaya* | *Oṃ Hrāṃ Hrīṃ Hrūṃ Śrīṃ Klīṃ Blūṃ Phroṃ Āṃ Hrīṃ Kroṃ Huṃ Phaṭ Svāhā* |

त्रियम्बकं यजामहे सुगन्धिं पुष्टिवर्धनम्। उर्वारुकमिव बन्धनान्मृत्योर्मुक्षीय मामृतात्। इदं विष्णुर्विचक्रमे त्रेधा निदधे पदम्। समूढमस्य पांसुरे। वर्षन्तु ते विभावरि दिवो अभ्रस्य विद्युतः। रोहन्तु सर्वबीजान्यव ब्रह्म द्विषो जहि। ॐ नमो भगवते रुद्राय नमः।

Triyambakaṃ Yajāmahe Sugandhiṃ Puṣṭivardhanam |

Urvārukamiva Bandhanānmṛtyormukṣīya Māmṛtāt |

Idaṃ Viṣṇurvicakrame Tredhā Nidadhe Padam |

Samūḍhamasya Pāṃsure ।

Varṣantu Te Vibhāvari Divo Abhrasya Vidyutaḥ ।

Rohantu Sarvabījānyava Brahma Dviṣo Jahi ।

Oṃ Namo Bhagavate Rudrāya Namaḥ ।

ॐ नमो भगवते रुद्राय। ॐ कालि हुं कालि मं कालि पुलकिते पुलकिते
उच्चाटन्युच्चाटनि ॐ कालि भवानि राजपुरुषस्त्रीपुरुषवशङ्करि स्वाहा।
ॐ नमो भगवति इन्द्राणि मम शत्रुप्राणिनां रक्तपायिनि ह्रां ग्रस ग्रस।
गृह्ण गृह्ण। दुष्टग्रहज्वालामालिनि मोहिनि स्तम्भय स्तम्भय।
सर्वदुष्टप्रदुष्टान् शोषय शोषय। मारय मारय। मम शत्रूणां शिरोलुण्ठनं कुरु कुरु।
ठः ठः ठः स्वाहा। हुं झटि स्वाहा।

Oṃ Namo Bhagavate Rudrāya । *Oṃ Kāli Huṃ Kāli Maṃ Kāli Pulakite Pulakite Uccāṭanyuccāṭani Oṃ Kāli Bhavāni Rājapuruṣastrīpuruṣavaśaṅkari Svāhā* ।
Oṃ Namo Bhagavati Indrāṇi Mama Śatruprāṇināṃ Raktapāyini Hrāṃ Grasa Grasa ।

Gṛhṇa Gṛhṇa । *Duṣṭagrahajvālāmālini Mohini Stambhaya Stambhaya* ।

Sarvaduṣṭapraduṣṭān Śoṣaya Śoṣaya ।

Māraya Māraya । *Mama Śatrūṇāṃ Śiroluṇṭhanaṃ Kuru Kuru* ।

Ṭhaḥ Ṭhaḥ Ṭhaḥ Svāhā । *Huṃ Jhaṭi Svāhā* ।

त्रियम्बकं यजामहे सुगन्धिं पुष्टिवर्धनम्। उर्वारुकमिव बन्धनान्मृत्योर्मुक्षीय मामृतात्।
उत्त्वा मदन्तु स्तोमाः कृणुष्व राधो अद्रिव। अव ब्रह्म द्विषो जहि।
वर्षन्तु ते विभावरि दिवो अभ्रस्य विद्युतः। रोहन्तु सर्वबीजान्यव ब्रह्म द्विषो जहि।
ॐ नमो भगवते रुद्राय नमः।

Triyambakaṃ Yajāmahe Sugandhiṃ Puṣṭivardhanam ।

Urvārukamiva Bandhanānmṛtyormukṣīya Māmṛtāt ।

Uttvā Madantu Stomāḥ Kṛṇuṣva Rādho Adriva ।

Ava Brahma Dviṣo Jahi ।

Varṣantu Te Vibhāvari Divo Abhrasya Vidyutaḥ ।

Rohantu Sarvabījānyava Brahma Dviṣo Jahi |

Oṃ Namo Bhagavate Rudrāya Namaḥ |

ॐ नमो भगवते रुद्राय। प्राच्यां दिशि ॐ नमो भगवति इन्द्राणि
वज्रहस्ताभ्यां मम सपरिवारकस्य प्रत्यक्षं बन्धय बन्धय।
सर्वतो मां रक्ष रक्ष। ह्रां ग्रस ग्रस। गृह्ण गृह्ण। हुं झटि स्वाहा।
त्रियम्बकं यजामहे सुगन्धिं पुष्टिवर्धनम्।
उर्वारुकमिव बन्धनान्मृत्योर्मुक्षीय मामृतात्। इन्द्रं वो विश्वतस्परि हवामहे जनेभ्यः।
अस्माकमस्तु केवलः। वर्षन्तु ते विभावरि दिवो अभ्रस्य विद्युतः।
रोहन्तु सर्वबीजान्यव ब्रह्म द्विषो जहि। ॐ नमो भगवते रुद्राय नमः।

Oṃ Namo Bhagavate Rudrāya | *Prācyāṃ Diśi Oṃ Namo Bhagavati Indrāṇi Vajrahastābhyāṃ Mama Saparivārakasya Pratyakṣaṃ Bandhaya Bandhaya* | *Sarvato Māṃ Rakṣa Rakṣa* | *Hrāṃ Grasa Grasa* | *Gṛhṇa Gṛhna* | *Huṃ Jhaṭi Svāhā* |

Triyambakaṃ Yajāmahe Sugandhiṃ Puṣṭivardhanam |

Urvārukamiva Bandhanānmṛtyormukṣīya Māmṛtāt |

Indraṃ Vo Viśvataspari Havāmahe Janebhyaḥ | *Asmākamastu Kevalaḥ* |

Varṣantu Te Vibhāvari Divo Abhrasya Vidyutaḥ |

Rohantu Sarvabījānyava Brahma Dviṣo Jahi |

Oṃ Namo Bhagavate Rudrāya Namaḥ |

ॐ नमो भगवते रुद्राय। आग्नेय्यां दिशि ॐ नमो भगवति आग्नेयि
ज्वालाहस्ताभ्यां मम सपरिवारकस्य प्रत्यक्षं बन्धय बन्धय।
सर्वतो मां रक्ष रक्ष। ह्रां ग्रस ग्रस। गृह्ण गृह्ण। हुं झटि स्वाहा।
त्रियम्बकं यजामहे सुगन्धिं पुष्टिवर्धनम्।
उर्वारुकमिव बन्धनान्मृत्योर्मुक्षीय मामृतात्। अग्निं दूतं वृणीमहे होतारं विश्ववेदसम्।
अस्य यज्ञस्य सुक्रतुम्। वर्षन्तु ते विभावरि दिवो अभ्रस्य विद्युतः।
रोहन्तु सर्वबीजान्यव ब्रह्म द्विषो जहि। ॐ नमो भगवते रुद्राय नमः।

Oṃ Namo Bhagavate Rudrāya | *Āgneyyāṃ Diśi Oṃ Namo Bhagavati Āgneyi Jvālāhastābhyāṃ Mama Saparivārakasya Pratyakṣaṃ Bandhaya Bandhaya* |

Sarvato Māṃ Rakṣa Rakṣa | Hrāṃ Grasa Grasa | Gṛhṇa Gṛhna |

Huṃ Jhaṭi Svāhā |

Triyambakaṃ Yajāmahe Sugandhiṃ Puṣṭivardhanam |

Urvārukamiva Bandhanānmṛtyormukṣīya Māmṛtāt |

Agniṃ Dūtaṃ Vṛṇīmahe Hotāraṃ Viśvavedasam |

Asya Yajñasya Sukratum |

Varṣantu Te Vibhāvari Divo Abhrasya Vidyutaḥ |

Rohantu Sarvabījānyava Brahma Dviṣo Jahi |

Oṃ Namo Bhagavate Rudrāya Namaḥ |

ॐ नमो भगवते रुद्राय। याम्यां दिशि ॐ नमो भगवति यामि
कालदण्डहस्ताभ्यां मम सपरिवारकस्य प्रत्यक्षं बन्धय बन्धय।
सर्वतो मां रक्ष रक्ष। ह्रां ग्रस ग्रस। गृह्ण गृह्ण। हुं झटि स्वाहा।
त्रियम्बकं यजामहे सुगन्धिं पुष्टिवर्धनम्।
उर्वारुकमिव बन्धनान्मृत्योर्मुक्षीय मामृतात्। यमाय सोमं सुनुत यमाय जुहुता हविः।
यमं ह यज्ञो गच्छत्यग्निदूतो अरङ्कृतः। वर्षन्तु ते विभावरि दिवो अभ्रस्य विद्युतः।
रोहन्तु सर्वबीजान्यव ब्रह्म द्विषो जहि।
ॐ नमो भगवते रुद्राय नमः।

Oṃ Namo Bhagavate Rudrāya | Yāmyāṃ Diśi Oṃ Namo Bhagavati Yāmi Kāladaṇḍahastābhyāṃ Mama Saparivārakasya Pratyakṣaṃ Bandhaya Bandhaya | Sarvato Māṃ Rakṣa Rakṣa | Hrāṃ Grasa Grasa | Gṛhna Gṛhṇa | Huṃ Jhaṭi Svāhā |

Triyambakaṃ Yajāmahe Sugandhiṃ Puṣṭivardhanam |

Urvārukamiva Bandhanānmṛtyormukṣīya Māmṛtāt |

Yamāya Somaṃ Sunuta Yamāya Juhutā Haviḥ |

Yamaṃ Ha Yajño Gacchatyagnidūto Araṅkṛtaḥ |

Varṣantu Te Vibhāvari Divo Abhrasya Vidyutaḥ |

Rohantu Sarvabījānyava Brahma Dviṣo Jahi |

Oṃ Namo Bhagavate Rudrāya Namaḥ |

ॐ नमो भगवते रुद्राय। नैरृत्यां दिशि ॐ नमो भगवति निरृति खड्गहस्ताभ्यां मम सपरिवारकस्य प्रत्यक्षं बन्धय बन्धय। सर्वतो मां रक्ष रक्ष। ह्रां ग्रस ग्रस। गृह्ण गृह्ण। हुं झटि स्वाहा। त्रियम्बकं यजामहे सुगन्धिं पुष्टिवर्धनम्।
उर्वारुकमिव बन्धनान्मृत्योर्मुक्षीय मामृतात्। मोषुणः परापरा निरृतिर्दुर्हणावधीत्।
पदीष्ट तृष्णया सह। वर्षन्तु ते विभावरि दिवो अभ्रस्य विद्युतः।
रोहन्तु सर्वबीजान्यव ब्रह्म द्विषो जहि। ॐ नमो भगवते रुद्राय नमः।

Oṃ Namo Bhagavate Rudrāya | Nairṛtyāṃ Diśi Oṃ Namo Bhagavati Nirṛti Khaṅgahastābhyāṃ Mama Saparivārakasya Pratyakṣaṃ Bandhaya Bandhaya | Sarvato Māṃ Rakṣa Rakṣa | Hrāṃ Grasa Grasa | Gṛhṇa Gṛhṇa | Huṃ Jhaṭi Svāhā |

Triyambakaṃ Yajāmahe Sugandhiṃ Puṣṭivardhanam |

Urvārukamiva Bandhanānmṛtyormukṣīya Māmṛtāt |

Moṣuṇaḥ Parāparā Nirṛtidurhaṇāvadhīt | Padīṣṭa Tṛṣṇayā Saha |

Varṣantu Te Vibhāvari Divo Abhrasya Vidyutaḥ |

Rohantu Sarvabījānyava Brahma Dviṣo Jahi |

Oṃ Namo Bhagavate Rudrāya Namaḥ |

ॐ नमो भगवते रुद्राय। वारुण्यां दिशि ॐ नमो भगवति वारुणि पाशहस्ताभ्यां मम सपरिवारकस्य प्रत्यक्षं बन्धय बन्धय।
सर्वतो मां रक्ष रक्ष। ह्रां ग्रस ग्रस। गृह्ण गृह्ण। हुं झटि स्वाहा।
त्रियम्बकं यजामहे सुगन्धिं पुष्टिवर्धनम्। उर्वारुकमिव बन्धनान्मृत्योर्मुक्षीय मामृतात्।
इमं मे वरुण श्रुधी हवमद्या च मृडय। त्वामवस्युराचके।
तत्त्वा यामि ब्रह्मणा वन्दमानस्तदाशास्ते यजमानो हविर्भिः।
अहेडमानो वरुणेह बोध्युरुशंसमा न आयुः प्र मोषीः।
वर्षन्तु ते विभावरि दिवो अभ्रस्य विद्युतः। रोहन्तु सर्वबीजान्यव ब्रह्म द्विषो जहि।
ॐ नमो भगवते रुद्राय नमः।

Oṃ Namo Bhagavate Rudrāya | Vāruṇyāṃ Diśi Oṃ Namo Bhagavati Vāruṇi Pāśahastābhyāṃ Mama Saparivārakasya Pratyakṣaṃ Bandhaya Bandhaya |

Sarvato Māṃ Rakṣa Rakṣa | Hrāṃ Grasa Grasa | Gṛhna Gṛhna |

Huṃ Jhaṭi Svāhā | Triyambakaṃ Yajāmahe Sugandhiṃ

Puṣṭivardhanam | Urvārukamiva Bandhanānmṛtyormukṣīya Māmṛtāt |

Imaṃ Me Varuṇa Śrudhī Havamadyā Ca Mṛḍaya | Tvāmavasyurācake |
Tattvā Yāmi Brahmaṇā Vandamānastadāśāste
Yajamāno Havirbhiḥ |

Aheḍamāno Varuṇeha Bodhyuruśaṃsa Mā Na Āyuḥ Pra Moṣīḥ |

Varṣantu Te Vibhāvari Divo Abhrasya Vidyutaḥ |

Rohantu Sarvabījānyava Brahma Dviṣo Jahi |

Oṃ Namo Bhagavate Rudrāya Namaḥ |

ॐ नमो भगवते रुद्राय। वायव्यां दिशि ॐ नमो भगवति वायवि ध्वजहस्ताभ्यां मम
सपरिवारकस्य प्रत्यक्षं बन्धय बन्धय। सर्वतो मां रक्ष रक्ष। ह्रां ग्रस ग्रस। गृह्ण गृह्ण।
हुं झटि स्वाहा। त्रियम्बकं यजामहे सुगन्धिं पुष्टिवर्धनम्।
उर्वारुकमिव बन्धनान्मृत्योर्मुक्षीय मामृतात्। तव वायवृतस्पते त्वष्टुर्जामातरद्भुत।
अवां स्या वृणीमहे। वर्षन्तु ते विभावरि दिवो अभ्रस्य विद्युतः।
रोहन्तु सर्वबीजान्यव ब्रह्म द्विषो जहि। ॐ नमो भगवते रुद्राय नमः।

Oṃ Namo Bhagavate Rudrāya | Vāyavyāṃ Diśi Oṃ Namo Bhagavati
Vāyavi Dhvajahastābhyāṃ Mama Saparivārakasya Pratyakṣaṃ
Bandhaya Bandhaya | Sarvato Māṃ Rakṣa Rakṣa | Hrāṃ Grasa Grasa |

Gṛhṇa Gṛhṇa | Huṃ Jhaṭi Svāhā |

Triyambakaṃ Yajāmahe Sugandhiṃ Puṣṭivardhanam |

Urvārukamiva Bandhanānmṛtyormukṣīya Māmṛtāt |

Tava Vāyavṛtaspate Tvaṣṭurjāmātaradbhuta | Avāṃ Syā Vṛṇīmahe |

Varṣantu Te Vibhāvari Divo Abhrasya Vidyutaḥ |

Rohantu Sarvabījānyava Brahma Dviṣo Jahi |

Oṃ Namo Bhagavate Rudrāya Namaḥ |

ॐ नमो भगवते रुद्राय। कौबेर्यां दिशि ॐ नमो भगवति कौबेरि
गदाङ्कुशहस्ताभ्यां मम सपरिवारकस्य प्रत्यक्षं बन्धय बन्धय।
सर्वतो मां रक्ष रक्ष। ह्रां ग्रस ग्रस। गृह्ण गृह्ण। हुं झटि स्वाहा।
त्रियम्बकं यजामहे सुगन्धिं पुष्टिवर्धनम्। उर्वारुकमिव बन्धनान्मृत्योर्मुक्षीय मामृतात्।
सोमो धेनुं सोमो अर्वन्तमाशुं सोमो वीरं कर्मण्यं ददाति।

सादन्यं विदथ्यं सभेयं पितृश्रवणं यो ददाशदस्मै । वर्षन्तु ते विभावरि दिवो अभ्रस्य विद्युतः। रोहन्तु सर्वबीजान्यव ब्रह्म द्विषो जहि। ॐ नमो भगवते रुद्राय नमः।

Oṃ Namo Bhagavate Rudrāya | Kauberyāṃ Diśi Oṃ Namo Bhagavati Kauberi Gadāṅkuśahastābhyāṃ Mama Saparivārakasya Pratyakṣaṃ Bandhaya Bandhaya | Sarvato Māṃ Rakṣa Rakṣa | Hrāṃ Grasa Grasa | Gṛhna Gṛhṇa | Huṃ Jhaṭi Svāhā |

Triyambakaṃ Yajāmahe Sugandhiṃ Puṣṭivardhanam |

Urvārukamiva Bandhanānmṛtyormukṣīya Māmṛtāt |

Somo Dhenuṃ Somo Arvantamāśuṃ Somo Vīraṃ Karmaṇyaṃ Dadāti |

Sādanyaṃ Vidathyaṃ Sabheyaṃ Pitṛśravaṇaṃ Yo Dadāśadasmai |

Varṣantu Te Vibhāvari Divo Abhrasya Vidyutaḥ |

Rohantu Sarvabījānyava Brahma Dviṣo Jahi |

Oṃ Namo Bhagavate Rudrāya Namaḥ |

ॐ नमो भगवते रुद्राय। ईशान्यां दिशि ॐ नमो भगवति ईशानि त्रिशूलहस्ताभ्यां मम सपरिवारकस्य प्रत्यक्षं बन्धय बन्धय। सर्वतो मां रक्ष रक्ष। ह्रां ग्रस ग्रस। गृह्ण गृह्ण। हुं झटि स्वाहा। त्रियम्बकं यजामहे सुगन्धिं पुष्टिवर्धनम्।
उर्वारुकमिव वन्धनान्मृत्योर्मुक्षीय मामृतात्। तमीशानं जगतस्तस्थुषस्पतिं धियं जिन्वमवसे हूमहे वयम्। पूषा नो यथा वेदसामसद्वृधे रक्षिता पायुरदब्धः स्वस्तये।
वर्षन्तु ते विभावरि दिवो अभ्रस्य विद्युतः। रोहन्तु सर्वबीजान्यव ब्रह्म द्विषो जहि।
ॐ नमो भगवते रुद्राय नमः।

Oṃ Namo Bhagavate Rudrāya | Īśānyāṃ Diśi Oṃ Namo Bhagavati Īśāni Triśūlahastābhyāṃ Mama Saparivārakasya Pratyakṣaṃ Bandhaya Bandhaya | Sarvato Māṃ Rakṣa Rakṣa | Hrāṃ Grasa Grasa | Gṛhṇa Gṛhna | Huṃ Jhaṭi Svāhā |

Triyambakaṃ Yajāmahe Sugandhiṃ Puṣṭivardhanam |

Urvārukamiva Vandhanānmṛtyormukṣīya Māmṛtāt |

Tamīśānaṃ Jagatastasthuṣaspatiṃ Dhiyaṃ Jinvamavase Hūmahe Vayam | Pūṣā No Yathā Vedasāmasadvṛdhe Rakṣitā Pāyuradabdhaḥ Svastaye |

Varṣantu Te Vibhāvari Divo Abhrasya Vidyutaḥ ।

Rohantu Sarvabījānyava Brahma Dviṣo Jahi ।

Oṃ Namo Bhagavate Rudrāya Namaḥ ।

ॐ नमो भगवते रुद्राय। ऊर्ध्वायां दिशि ॐ नमो भगवति ब्रह्माणि
स्रुक्स्रुवकमण्डल्वक्षसूत्रहस्ताभ्यांमम सपरिवारकस्य प्रत्यक्षं बन्धय बन्धय।
सर्वतो मां रक्ष रक्ष। ह्रां ग्रस ग्रस। गृह्ण गृह्ण। हुं झटि स्वाहा।
त्रियम्बकं यजामहे सुगन्धिं पुष्टिवर्धनम्। उर्वारुकमिव बन्धनान्मृत्योर्मुक्षीय मामृतात्।
ब्रह्मा देवानां पदवीः कवीनामृषिर्विप्राणां महिषो मृगाणाम्।
श्येनो गृध्राणां स्वधितिर्वनानां सोमः पवित्रमत्येति रेभन्।
वर्षन्तु ते विभावरि दिवो अभ्रस्य विद्युतः। रोहन्तु सर्वबीजान्यव ब्रह्म द्विषो जहि।
ॐ नमो भगवते रुद्राय नमः।

Oṃ Namo Bhagavate Rudrāya । *Ūrdhvāyāṃ Diśi Oṃ Namo Bhagavati Brahmāṇi Sruksruvakamaṇḍalvakṣasūtrahastābhyāṃ Mama Saparivārakasya Pratyakṣaṃ Bandhaya Bandhaya* ।

Sarvato Māṃ Rakṣa Rakṣa । *Hrāṃ Grasa Grasa* । *Gṛhṇa Gṛhna* ।

Huṃ Jhaṭi Svāhā ।

Triyambakaṃ Yajāmahe Sugandhiṃ Puṣṭivardhanam ।

Urvārukamiva Bandhanānmṛtyormukṣīya Māmṛtāt ।

Brahmā Devānāṃ Padavīḥ Kavīnāmṛṣirviprāṇāṃ Mahiṣo Mṛgāṇām ।

Śyeno Gṛdhrāṇāṃ Svadhitirvanānāṃ Somaḥ Pavitramatyeti Rebhan ।

Varṣantu Te Vibhāvari Divo Abhrasya Vidyutaḥ ।

Rohantu Sarvabījānyava Brahma Dviṣo Jahi ।

Oṃ Namo Bhagavate Rudrāya Namaḥ ।

ॐ नमो भगवते रुद्राय। अधस्ताद्दिशि ॐ नमो भगवति पातालवासिनि
विषगलहस्ताभ्यां मम सपरिवारकस्य प्रत्यक्षं बन्धय बन्धय।
सर्वतो मां रक्ष रक्ष। ह्रां ग्रस ग्रस। गृह्ण गृह्ण। हुं झटि स्वाहा।
त्रियम्बकं यजामहे सुगन्धिं पुष्टिवर्धनम्।
उर्वारुकमिव बन्धनान्मृत्योर्मुक्षीय मामृतात्। नमो अस्तु सर्वेभ्यो ये के च
पृथिवीमनु। ये अन्तरिक्षे ये दिवि तेभ्यः सर्पेभ्यो नमः।

वर्षन्तु रोहन्तु सर्वबीजान्यव ब्रह्म द्विषो जहि।
ॐ नमो भगवते रुद्राय नमः।

Oṃ Namo Bhagavate Rudrāya | Adhastāddiśi Oṃ Namo Bhagavati Pātālavāsini Viṣagalahastābhyāṃ Mama Saparivārakasya Pratyakṣaṃ Bandhaya Bandhaya | Sarvato Māṃ Rakṣa Rakṣa | Hrāṃ Grasa Grasa |
Gṛhṇa Gṛhṇa | Huṃ Jhaṭi Svāhā |
Triyambakaṃ Yajāmahe Sugandhiṃ Puṣṭivardhanam |
Urvārukamiva Bandhanānmṛtyormukṣīya Māmṛtāt |
Namo Astu Sarvebhyo Ye Ke Ca Pṛthivīmanu |
Ye Antarikṣe Ye Divi Tebhyaḥ Sarpebhyo Namaḥ |
Varṣantu Te Vibhāvari Divo Abhrasya Vidyutaḥ |
Rohantu Sarvabījānyava Brahma Dviṣo Jahi |
Oṃ Namo Bhagavate Rudrāya Namaḥ |

ॐ नमो भगवते रुद्राय। अवान्तरस्यां दिशि ॐ नमो भगवति महालक्ष्मि पद्मारूढे पद्महस्ताभ्यां मम सपरिवारकस्य प्रत्यक्षं बन्धय बन्धय।
सर्वतो मां रक्ष रक्ष। ह्रां ग्रस ग्रस। गृह्ण गृह्ण। हुं झटि स्वाहा।
त्रियम्बकं यजामहे सुगन्धिं पुष्टिवर्धनम्।
उर्वारुकमिव बन्धनान्मृत्योर्मुक्षीय मामृतात्। इदं विष्णुर्विचक्रमे त्रेधा निदधे पदम्।
समूढमस्य पांसुरे। वर्षन्तु ते विभावरि दिवो अभ्रस्य विद्युतः।
रोहन्तु सर्वबीजान्यव ब्रह्म द्विषो जहि। ॐ नमो भगवते रुद्राय नमः।

Oṃ Namo Bhagavate Rudrāya | Avāntarasyāṃ Diśi Oṃ Namo Bhagavati Mahālakṣmi Padmārūḍhe Padmahastābhyāṃ Mama Saparivārakasya Pratyakṣaṃ Bandhaya Bandhaya |
Sarvato Māṃ Rakṣa Rakṣa | Hrāṃ Grasa Grasa | Gṛhṇa Gṛhṇa |
Huṃ Jhaṭi Svāhā |
Triyambakaṃ Yajāmahe Sugandhiṃ Puṣṭivardhanam |
Urvārukamiva Bandhanānmṛtyormukṣīya Māmṛtāt |
Idaṃ Viṣṇurvicakrame Tredhā Nidadhe Padam |
Samūḍhamasya Pāṃsure |

Varṣantu Te Vibhāvari Divo Abhrasya Vidyutaḥ |

Rohantu Sarvabījānyava Brahma Dviṣo Jahi |

Oṃ Namo Bhagavate Rudrāya Namaḥ |

ॐ नमो भगवते रुद्राय। ॐ नमो भगवति कौमारि शक्तिहस्तेन
सर्वतो मां रक्ष रक्ष। हुं झटि स्वाहा। त्रियम्बकं यजामहे सुगन्धिं पुष्टिवर्धनम्।
उर्वारुकमिव बन्धनान्मृत्योर्मुक्षीय मामृतात्।
इन्द्रं वो विश्वतस्परि हवामहे जनेभ्यः। अस्माकमस्तु केवलः।
वर्षन्तु ते विभावरि दिवो अभ्रस्य विद्युतः। रोहन्तु सर्वबीजान्यव ब्रह्म द्विषो जहि।
ॐ नमो भगवते रुद्राय नमः।

Oṃ Namo Bhagavate Rudrāya | *Oṃ Namo Bhagavati Kaumāri*

Śaktihastena Sarvato Māṃ Rakṣa Rakṣa | *Huṃ Jhaṭi Svāhā* |

Triyambakaṃ Yajāmahe Sugandhiṃ Puṣṭivardhanam |

Urvārukamiva Bandhanānmṛtyormukṣīya Māmṛtāt |

Indraṃ Vo Viśvataspari Havāmahe Janebhyaḥ | *Asmākamastu Kevalaḥ* |

Varṣantu Te Vibhāvari Divo Abhrasya Vidyutaḥ |

Rohantu Sarvabījānyava Brahma Dviṣo Jahi |

Oṃ Namo Bhagavate Rudrāya Namaḥ |

ॐ नमो भगवते रुद्राय। ॐ नमो भगवति वाराहि असिहस्तेन सर्वतो मां रक्ष रक्ष।
हुं झटि स्वाहा। त्रियम्बकं यजामहे सुगन्धिं पुष्टिवर्धनम्।
उर्वारुकमिव बन्धनान्मृत्योर्मुक्षीय मामृतात्।
अग्निं दूतं वृणीमहे होतारं विश्ववेदसम्। अस्य यज्ञस्य सुक्रतुम्।
वर्षन्तु ते विभावरि दिवो अभ्रस्य विद्युतः। रोहन्तु सर्वबीजान्यव ब्रह्म द्विषो जहि।
ॐ नमो भगवते रुद्राय नमः।

Oṃ Namo Bhagavate Rudrāya | *Oṃ Namo Bhagavati Vārāhi Asihastena*

Sarvato Māṃ Rakṣa Rakṣa | *Huṃ Jhaṭi Svāhā* |

Triyambakaṃ Yajāmahe Sugandhiṃ Puṣṭivardhanam |

Urvārukamiva Bandhanānmṛtyormukṣīya Māmṛtāt |

Agniṃ Dūtaṃ Vṛṇīmahe Hotāraṃ Viśvavedasam |

Asya Yajñasya Sukratum |

Varṣantu Te Vibhāvari Divo Abhrasya Vidyutaḥ |

Rohantu Sarvabījānyava Brahma Dviṣo Jahi |

Oṃ Namo Bhagavate Rudrāya Namaḥ |

ॐ नमो भगवते रुद्राय। ॐ नमो भगवति सिद्धचामुण्डेश्वरि शङ्खचक्रहस्ताभ्यां सर्वतो मां रक्ष रक्ष। हुं झटि स्वाहा। त्रियम्बकं यजामहे सुगन्धिं पुष्टिवर्धनम्।
उर्वारुकमिव बन्धनान्मृत्योर्मुक्षीय मामृतात्। यमाय सोमं सुनुत यमाय जुहुता हविः।
यमं ह यज्ञो गच्छत्यग्निदूतो अरकृत। वर्षन्तु ते विभावरि दिवो अभ्रस्य विद्युतः।
रोहन्तु सवर्बीजान्यव ब्रह्म द्विषो जहि। ॐ नमो भगवते रुद्राय नमः।

Oṃ Namo Bhagavate Rudrāya | *Oṃ Namo Bhagavati Siddhacāmuṇḍeśvari Śaṅkhacakrahastābhyāṃ Sarvato Māṃ Rakṣa Rakṣa* | *Huṃ Jhaṭi Svāhā* |

Triyambakaṃ Yajāmahe Sugandhiṃ Puṣṭivardhanam |

Urvārukamiva Bandhanānmṛtyormukṣīya Māmṛtāt |

Yamāya Somaṃ Sunuta Yamāya Juhutā Haviḥ |

Yamaṃ Ha Yajño Gacchatyagnidūto Arakṛta |

Varṣantu Te Vibhāvari Divo Abhrasya Vidyutaḥ |

Rohantu Savarbījānyava Brahma Dviṣo Jahi |

Oṃ Namo Bhagavate Rudrāya Namaḥ |

ॐ नमो भगवते रुद्राय। ॐ नमो भगवति गणेश्वरि परशुहस्तेन सर्वतो मां रक्ष रक्ष।
हुं झटि स्वाहा। त्रियम्बकं यजामहे सुगन्धिं पुष्टिवर्धनम्।
उर्वारुकमिव बन्धनान्मृत्योर्मुक्षीय मामृतात्।
मोषुणः परापरा निरृतिर्दुर्हणावधीत्। पदीष्ट तृष्णया सह।
वर्षन्तु ते विभावरि दिवो अभ्रस्य विद्युतः। रोहन्तु सर्वबीजान्यव ब्रह्म द्विषो जहि।
ॐ नमो भगवते रुद्राय नमः।

Oṃ Namo Bhagavate Rudrāya | *Oṃ Namo Bhagavati Gaṇeśvari Paraśuhastena Sarvato Māṃ Rakṣa Rakṣa* | *Huṃ Jhaṭi Svāhā* |

Triyambakaṃ Yajāmahe Sugandhiṃ Puṣṭivardhanam |

Urvārukamiva Bandhanānmṛtyormukṣīya Māmṛtāt |

Moṣuṇaḥ Parāparā Nirṛtirdurhaṇāvadhīt | Padīṣṭa Tṛṣṇayā Saha |

Varṣantu Te Vibhāvari Divo Abhrasya Vidyutaḥ |

Rohantu Sarvabījānyava Brahma Dviṣo Jahi |

Oṃ Namo Bhagavate Rudrāya Namaḥ |

ॐ नमो भगवते रुद्राय। ॐ नमो भगवति क्षेत्रपालिनि
विषज्वालाहस्ताभ्यां सर्वतो मां रक्ष रक्ष। हुं झटि स्वाहा। त्रियम्बकं यजामहे सुगन्धिं
पुष्टिवर्धनम्। उर्वारुकमिव बन्धनान्मृत्योर्मुक्षीय मामृतात्।
इमं मे वरुण श्रुधी हवमद्या च मृडय। त्वामवस्युराचके।
तत्त्वा यामि ब्रह्मणा वन्दमानस्तदाशास्ते यजमानो हविर्भिः।
अहेडमानो वरुणेह बोध्युरुशस मा न आयुः प्र मोषीः।
वर्षन्तु ते विभावरि दिवो अभ्रस्य विद्युतः। रोहन्तु सर्वबीजान्यव ब्रह्म द्विषो जहि।
ॐ नमो भगवते रुद्राय नमः।

Oṃ Namo Bhagavate Rudrāya | Oṃ Namo Bhagavati Kṣetrapālini

Viṣajvālāhastābhyāṃ Sarvato Māṃ Rakṣa Rakṣa | Huṃ Jhaṭi Svāhā |

Triyambakaṃ Yajāmahe Sugandhiṃ Puṣṭivardhanam |

Urvārukamiva Bandhanānmṛtyormukṣīya Māmṛtāt |

Imaṃ Me Varuṇa Śrudhī Havamadyā Ca Mṛḍaya | Tvāmavasyurācake |

Tattvā Yāmi Brahmaṇā Vandamānastadāśāste Yajamāno Havirbhiḥ |

Aheḍamāno Varuṇeha Bodhyuruśasa Mā Na Āyuḥ Pra Moṣīḥ |

Varṣantu Te Vibhāvari Divo Abhrasya Vidyutaḥ |

Rohantu Sarvabījānyava Brahma Dviṣo Jahi |

Oṃ Namo Bhagavate Rudrāya Namaḥ |

ॐ नमो भगवते रुद्राय। ॐ नमो भगवति नारसिंहि दशननखाग्रैः सर्वतो मां रक्ष रक्ष।
हुं झटि स्वाहा। त्रियम्बकं यजामहे सुगन्धिं पुष्टिवर्धनम्।
उर्वारुकमिव बन्धनान्मृत्योर्मुक्षीय मामृतात्।
तव वायवृतस्पते त्वष्टुर्जामातरद्भुत। अवां स्या वृणीमहे।
वर्षन्तु ते विभावरि दिवो अभ्रस्य विद्युतः। रोहन्तु सर्वबीजान्यव ब्रह्म द्विषो जहि।
ॐ नमो भगवते रुद्राय नमः।

Oṃ Namo Bhagavate Rudrāya | Oṃ Namo Bhagavati Nārasiṃhi Daśananakhāgraiḥ Sarvato Māṃ Rakṣa Rakṣa | Huṃ Jhaṭi Svāhā | Triyambakaṃ Yajāmahe Sugandhiṃ Puṣṭivardhanam | Urvārukamiva Bandhanānmṛtyormukṣīya Māmṛtāt | Tava Vāyavṛtaspate Tvaṣṭurjāmātaradbhuta | Avāṃ Syā Vṛṇīmahe | Varṣantu Te Vibhāvari Divo Abhrasya Vidyutaḥ | Rohantu Sarvabījānyava Brahma Dviṣo Jahi | Oṃ Namo Bhagavate Rudrāya Namaḥ |

ॐ नमो भगवते रुद्राय। ॐ नमो भगवति बगळामुखि ब्रह्मास्त्रेण सर्वतो मां रक्ष रक्ष।
हुं झटि स्वाहा। त्रियम्बकं यजामहे सुगन्धिं पुष्टिवर्धनम्।
उर्वारुकमिव बन्धनान्मृत्योर्मुक्षीय मामृतात्॥
सोमो धेनुं सोमो अर्वन्तमाशु सोमो वीरं कर्मण्यं ददाति।
सादन्यं विदथ्यं सभेयं पितृश्रवणं यो ददाशदस्मै। वर्षन्तु ते विभावरि दिवो अभ्रस्य विद्युतः।
रोहन्तु सर्वबीजान्यव ब्रह्म द्विषो जहि।
ॐ नमो भगवते रुद्राय नमः।

Oṃ Namo Bhagavate Rudrāya | Oṃ Namo Bhagavati Bagaḷāmukhi Brahmāstreṇa Sarvato Māṃ Rakṣa Rakṣa | Huṃ Jhaṭi Svāhā | Triyambakaṃ Yajāmahe Sugandhiṃ Puṣṭivardhanam | Urvārukamiva Bandhanānmṛtyormukṣīya Māmṛtāt || Somo Dhenuṃ Somo Arvantamāśu Somo Vīraṃ Karmaṇyaṃ Dadāti | Sādanyaṃ Vidathyaṃ Sabheyaṃ Pitṛśravaṇaṃ Yo Dadāśadasmai | Varṣantu Te Vibhāvari Divo Abhrasya Vidyutaḥ | Rohantu Sarvabījānyava Brahma Dviṣo Jahi | Oṃ Namo Bhagavate Rudrāya Namaḥ |

ॐ नमो भगवते रुद्राय। ॐ नमो भगवत्यन्नपूर्णेश्वरि कनकदर्विहस्तेन सर्वतो मां रक्ष रक्ष।
हुं झटि स्वाहा। त्रियम्बकं यजामहे सुगन्धिं पुष्टिवर्धनम्।
उर्वारुकमिव बन्धनान्मृत्योर्मुक्षीय मामृतात्।
तमीशानं जगतस्तस्थुषस्पतिं धियं जिन्वमवसे हूमहे वयम्।

पूषा नो यथा वेदसामसद्वृधे रक्षिता पायुरदब्धस्वस्तये ।
वर्षन्तु ते विभावरि दिवो अभ्रस्य विद्युतः । रोहन्तु सर्वबीजान्यव ब्रह्म द्विषो जहि ।
ॐ नमो भगवते रुद्राय नमः ।

Oṃ Namo Bhagavate Rudrāya । Oṃ Namo Bhagavatyannapūrṇeśvari Kanakadarvihastena Sarvato Māṃ Rakṣa Rakṣa । Huṃ Jhaṭi Svāhā ।

Triyambakaṃ Yajāmahe Sugandhiṃ Puṣṭivardhanam ।

Urvārukamiva Bandhanānmṛtyormukṣīya Māmṛtāt ।

Tamīśānaṃ Jagatastasthuṣaspatiṃ Dhiyaṃ Jinvamavase Hūmahe Vayam ।

Pūṣā No Yathā Vedasāmasadvṛdhe Rakṣitā Pāyuradabdha Svastaye ।

Varṣantu Te Vibhāvari Divo Abhrasya Vidyutaḥ ।

Rohantu Sarvabījānyava Brahma Dviṣo Jahi ।

Oṃ Namo Bhagavate Rudrāya Namaḥ ।

ॐ नमो भगवते रुद्राय ।
भगवति भवरोगात् पीडितं दुष्कृतौघात् सुतदुहितृकळत्रोपद्रवैर्व्याप्यमानम् ।
विलसदमृतदृष्ट्या वीक्ष्य विभ्रान्तचित्त सकलभुवनमातस्त्राहि मां त्वं नमस्ते ॥
ॐ ह्रीं श्रीं भगवत्यै नमः । ॐ नमो भगवति पद्मारूढे पद्महस्ताभ्यां सर्वतो मां रक्ष रक्ष ।
हुं झटि स्वाहा ।
लक्ष्मीं क्षीरसमुद्रराजतनयां श्रीरङ्गधामेश्वरीं दासीभूतसमस्तदेववनितां लोकैकदीपाङ्कुराम् ।
श्रीमत्कामकटाक्षलब्धविभवब्रह्मेन्द्रगङ्गाधरां तां त्रैलोक्यकुटुम्बिनीं सरसिजां वन्दे मुकुन्दप्रियाम् ॥ ॐ ह्रीं श्रीं क्लीं श्रीं सिद्धलक्ष्म्यै स्वाहा ।
सुवर्णं धर्म परिवेद वेनम् । इन्द्रस्यात्मानं दशधा चरन्तं स्वाहा ।
ॐ नमो भगवत्यै सर्वतो भूर्भुवः स्वरोमिति दिग्बन्धः ।
ॐ ह्रीं दुर्गे स्वाहा । वन्दे रुद्रप्रियां नित्यमुत्पन्नां कामरूपिणीम् ।
उल्कामुखीं रुद्रजटीं नागपुष्पशिरोरुहाम् ॥ मं महिषमर्दिनि स्वाहा ।
ॐ ह्रीं दुं हुं फट् स्वाहा । प्रयोगबीजानि । ॐ क्लीं ह्रीं श्रीं ऐं ग्लौं
ॐ ह्रीं क्रौं गं ॐ नमो भगवते महागणपतये स्मरणमात्रसन्तुष्टाय
सर्वविद्याप्रकाशकाय सर्वकामप्रदाय भवबन्धविमोचनाय ह्रीं
सर्वभूतबन्धनाय क्रों साध्याकर्षणाय क्लीं जगत्त्रयवशीकरणाय सौः
सर्वमनःक्षोभणाय श्रीं महासम्पत्प्रदाय ग्लौं भूमण्डलाधिपत्यप्रदाय

महाज्ञानप्रदाय चिदानन्दात्मने गौरीनन्दनाय महायोगिने शिवप्रियाय
सर्वानन्दवर्धनाय सर्वविद्याप्रकाशनप्रदाय द्रां चिरञ्जीविने ब्लूं सम्मोहनाय ॐ मोक्षप्रदाय।
फट् वशीकुरु वशीकुरु। वौषडाकर्षणाय हुं विद्वेषणाय विद्वेषय विद्वेषय।
फट् उच्चाटयोच्चाटय। ठः ठः स्तम्भय स्तम्भय। खें खें मारय मारय।
शोषय शोषय। परमन्त्रयन्त्रतन्त्राणि छेदय छेदय।
दुष्टग्रहान्निवारय निवारय। दु:खं हर हर। व्याधिं नाशय नाशय।
नमः सम्पन्नाय सम्पन्नाय स्वाहा। सर्वपल्लवस्वरूपाय महाविद्याय
गं गणपतये स्वाहा। यन्मन्त्रेक्षितलाञ्छिताभमनघं मृत्युश्च
वज्राशिषो भूतप्रेतपिशाचकाः प्रति हता निर्घातपातादिव।
उत्पन्नं च समस्तदुःखदुरितं ह्यु च्चाटनोत्पादकं वन्देऽभीष्टगणाधिपं
भयहरं विघ्नौघनाशं परम्॥

Oṃ Namo Bhagavate Rudrāya | Bhagavati Bhavarogāt Pīḍitaṃ
Duṣkṛtaughāt Sutaduhitṛkaḷatropadravairvyāpyamānam |
Vilasadamṛtadṛṣṭyā Vīkṣya Vibhrāntacitta Sakalabhuvanamātastrāhi
Māṃ Tvaṃ Namaste || Oṃ Hrīṃ Śrīṃ Bhagavatyai Namaḥ |
Oṃ Namo Bhagavati Padmārūḍhe Padmahastābhyāṃ Sarvato
Māṃ Rakṣa Rakṣa | Huṃ Jhaṭi Svāhā |
Lakṣmīṃ Kṣīrasamudrarājatanayāṃ Śrīraṅgadhāmeśvarīṃ
Dāsībhūtasamastadevavanitāṃ Lokaikadīpāṅkurām |
Śrīmatkāmakaṭākṣalabdhavibhavabrahmendragaṅgādharāṃ Tāṃ
Trailokyakuṭumbinīṃ Sarasijāṃ Vande Mukundapriyām ||
Oṃ Hrīṃ Śrīṃ Klīṃ Śrīṃ Siddhalakṣmyai Svāhā |
Suvarṇaṃ Dharma Pariveda Venam |
Indrasyātmānaṃ Daśadhā Carantaṃ Svāhā |
Oṃ Namo Bhagavatyai Sarvato Bhūrbhuvaḥ Svaromiti Digbandhaḥ |
Oṃ Hrīṃ Durge Svāhā |
Vande Rudrapriyāṃ Nityamutpannāṃ Kāmarūpiṇīm |
Ulkāmukhīṃ Rudrajaṭīṃ Nāgapuṣpaśiroruhām ||
Maṃ Mahiṣamardini Svāhā | Oṃ Hrīṃ Duṃ Huṃ Phaṭ Svāhā |
Prayogabījāni | Oṃ Klīṃ Hrīṃ Śrīṃ Aiṃ Glauṃ

Oṃ Hrīṃ Krauṃ Gaṃ Oṃ Namo Bhagavate Mahāgaṇapataye Smaraṇamātrasantuṣṭāya Sarvavidyāprakāśakāya Sarvakāmapradāya Bhavabandhavimocanāya Hrīṃ Sarvabhūtabandhanāya Kroṃ Sādhyākarṣaṇāya Klīṃ Jagattrayavaśīkaraṇāya Sauḥ Sarvamanaḥkṣobhaṇāya Śrīṃ Mahāsampatpradāya Glauṃ Bhūmaṇḍalādhipatyapradāya Mahājñānapradāya Cidānandātmane Gaurīnandanāya Mahāyogine Śivapriyāya Sarvānandavardhanāya Sarvavidyāprakāśanapradāya Drāṃ Cirañjīvine Blūṃ Sammohanāya Oṃ Mokṣapradāya | Phaṭ Vaśīkuru Vaśīkuru |

Vauṣaḍākarṣaṇāya Huṃ Vidveṣaṇāya Vidveṣaya Vidveṣaya |

Phaṭ Uccāṭayoccāṭaya | Ṭhaḥ Ṭhaḥ Stambhaya Stambhaya |

Kheṃ Kheṃ Māraya Māraya | Śoṣaya Śoṣaya |

Paramantrayantratantrāṇi Chedaya Chedaya |

Duṣṭagrahānnivāraya Nivāraya | Duḥkhaṃ Hara Hara |

Vyādhiṃ Nāśaya Nāśaya |

Namaḥ Sampannāya Sampannāya Svāhā |

Sarvapallavasvarūpāya Mahāvidyāya Gaṃ Gaṇapataye Svāhā |
Yanmantrekṣitalāñchitābhamanaghaṃ Mṛtyuśca
Vajrāśiṣo Bhūtapretapiśācakāḥ Prati Hatā Nirghātapātādiva |
Utpannaṃ Ca Samastaduḥkhaduritaṃ Hyuccāṭanotpādakaṃ
Vande'bhīṣṭagaṇādhipaṃ Bhayaharaṃ Vighnaughanāśaṃ Param ||

ॐ गं गणपतये नमः। ॐ ह्रीं ऐं ईं स्वाहा। ईकारप्रथमाक्षरश्च वदने द्रां द्रीं कुचावेष्टिते क्लीं नाभिस्थमनङ्गराजसदने ब्लूङ्कारमूरुद्वये। सः पादेऽपि च पञ्चबाणसदने बन्धूकपुष्पद्युतिंध्यायेन्नग्ननिवर्तितेन पुलको गङ्गाप्रवाहो द्रवः ॥
ॐ नमो मगवते कामदेवाय द्रां द्रां द्रावणबाणाय द्रीं द्रीं सन्दीपनबाणाय क्लीं क्लीं सम्मोहनबाणाय ब्लूं ब्लूं सन्तापनबाणाय सः सः वशीकरणबाणाय ह्रीं ह्रीं मदनावेशबाणाय सकलजनचिन्तितं द्रावय द्रावय। कम्पय कम्पय। हुं फट्‌ स्वाहा।
ॐ क्लीं नमो भगवते कामदेवाय श्रीं सर्वजनप्रियाय सर्वसम्मोहनाय ज्वल ज्वल प्रज्वल प्रज्वल हन हन वद वद तप तप सम्मोहय सम्मोहय सर्वजनं मे वश्यं कुरु कुरु स्वाहा।
ॐ ह्रीं श्रीं क्ष्म्रीं क्ष्म्रैं सहस्रार हुं फट्‌ स्वाहा। ॐ नमो विष्णवे। ॐ नमो नारायणाय।
ॐ नमो जय जय गोपीजनवल्लभाय स्वाहा। सहस्रारज्वालावर्त क्ष्मीं हन हन हुं फट्‌ स्वाहा।

ॐ तत्सवितुर्वरेण्यं भर्गोदेवस्य धीमहि। धियो यो नः प्रचोदयात्।
ॐ श्रीनारायणस्य चरणौ शरणं प्रपद्ये। श्रीमते नारायणाय नमः।
उग्रं वीरं महाविष्णुं ज्वलन्तं सर्वतोमुखम्। नृसिंहं भीषणं भद्रं मृत्युमृत्युं नमाम्यहम्॥
ॐ ऐं ह्लीं श्रीं दुं हुं फट् कनकवज्रवैडूर्यमुक्तालङ्कृतभूषणे एह्येहि आगच्छागच्छ मम कर्णे प्रविश्य प्रविश्य भूतभविष्यद्वर्तमानकालज्ञानदूदृष्टिदूरस्थश्रवणं ब्रूहि ब्रूहि। अग्निस्तम्भनं शत्रुमुखस्तम्भनं शत्रुबुद्धिस्तम्भनं शत्रुगतिस्तम्भनं परेषां गतिमतिवाग्जिह्वास्त्रभनं कुरु कुरु।
शत्रुकार्यं हन हन। मम कार्यं साधय साधय।
शत्रूणामुद्योगविध्वंसनंकुरु कुरु। वीरचामुण्डि असिकण्टकधारिणि नगरपुरीपट्टणराजधानीसम्मोहिनि असाध्यसाधनि ॐ ह्लीं श्रीं देवि हन हन हुं फट् स्वाहा।
ॐ अमरदुर्गे आं ह्रां सौं ऐं क्लीं हुं सौः ग्लौं श्रीं क्रों एह्येहि भ्रमराम्ब सकलजगन्मोहिनि सकलाण्डजपिण्डजान् भ्रामय भ्रामय। राजप्रजावशङ्करि सम्मोहय सम्मोहय।
महामाये अष्टादशपीठरूपिणि अमलवरयूं स्फुर स्फुर। प्रस्फुर प्रस्फुर।
कोटिसूर्यप्रभाभासुरे चन्द्रजटे मां रक्ष रक्ष। मम शत्रून् भस्मीकुरु भस्मीकुरु।
विश्वमोहिनि हुं फट् स्वाहा। ॐ नमो भगवते रुद्राय नमः।

Oṃ Gaṃ Gaṇapataye Namaḥ | Oṃ Hrīṃ Aiṃ Īṃ Svāhā |
Īkāraprathamākṣaraśca Vadane Drāṃ Drīṃ Kucāveṣṭite
Klīṃ Nābhisthamanaṅgarājasadane Blūṅkāramūrudvaye |
Saḥ Pāde'pi Ca Pañcabāṇasadane Bandhūkapuṣpadyutiṃ
Dhyāyennagnanivartitena Pulako Gaṅgāpravāho Dravaḥ ||
Oṃ Namo Magavate Kāmadevāya Drāṃ Drāṃ Drāvaṇabāṇāya Drīṃ Drīṃ Sandīpanabāṇāya Klīṃ Klīṃ Sammohanabāṇāya Blūṃ Blūṃ Santāpanabāṇāya Saḥ Saḥ Vaśīkaraṇabāṇāya Hrīṃ Hrīṃ
Madanāveśabāṇāya Sakalajanacintitaṃ Drāvaya Drāvaya |
Kampaya Kampaya | Huṃ Phaṭ Svāhā |
Oṃ Klīṃ Namo Bhagavate Kāmadevāya Śrīṃ Sarvajanapriyāya Sarvasammohanāya Jvala Jvala Prajvala Prajvala Hana Hana Vada Vada Tapa Tapa Sammohaya Sammohaya Sarvajanaṃ Me Vaśyaṃ Kuru Kuru
Svāhā | Oṃ Hrīṃ Śrīṃ Kṣmrīṃ Kṣmraiṃ Sahasrāra Huṃ Phaṭ Svāhā |
Oṃ Namo Viṣṇave | Oṃ Namo Nārāyaṇāya |
Oṃ Namo Jaya Jaya Gopījanavallabhāya Svāhā |
Sahasrārajvālāvarta Kṣmīṃ Hana Hana Huṃ Phaṭ Svāhā |
Oṃ Tatsaviturvareṇyaṃ Bhargodevasya Dhīmahi |

Dhiyo Yo Naḥ Pracodayāt | Oṃ Śrīnārāyaṇasya Caraṇau Śaraṇaṃ Prapadye | Śrīmate Nārāyaṇāya Namaḥ |

Ugraṃ Vīraṃ Mahāviṣṇuṃ Jvalantaṃ Sarvatomukham |

Nṛsiṃhaṃ Bhīṣaṇaṃ Bhadraṃ Mṛtyumṛtyuṃ Namāmyaham ||

Oṃ Aiṃ Hrīṃ Śrīṃ Duṃ Huṃ Phaṭ Kanakavajravaiḍūryamuktālaṅkṛtabhūṣaṇe Ehyehi Āgacchāgaccha Mama Karṇe Praviśya Praviśya Bhūtabhaviṣyadvartamānakāla Jñānadūra Dṛṣṭidūrasthaśravaṇaṃ Brūhi Brūhi | Agnistambhanaṃ ŚatrumukhastambhanaṃŚatrubuddhistambhanaṃ Śatrugatistambhanaṃ Pareṣāṃ Gatimativāgjihvāsttrabhanaṃ Kuru Kuru | Śatrukāryaṃ Hana Hana | Mama Kāryaṃ Sādhaya Sādhaya | Śatrūṇāmudyogavidhvaṃsanaṃ Kuru Kuru | Vīracāmuṇḍi Asikaṇṭakadhāriṇi Nagarapurīpaṭṭaṇarājadhānīsammohini Asādhyasādhani Oṃ Hrīṃ Śrīṃ Devi Hana Hana Huṃ Phaṭ Svāhā | Oṃ Amaradurge Āṃ Hrāṃ Sauṃ Aiṃ Klīṃ Huṃ Sauḥ Glauṃ Śrīṃ Kroṃ Ehyehi Bhramarāmba Sakalajaganmohini Sakalāṇḍajapiṇḍajān Bhrāmaya Bhrāmaya | Rājaprajāvaśaṅkari Sammohaya Sammohaya | Mahāmāye Aṣṭādaśaṣīṭharūpiṇi Amalavarayūṃ Sphura Sphura | Prasphura Prasphura | Koṭisūryaprabhābhāsure Candrajaṭe Māṃ Rakṣa Rakṣa | Mama Śatrūn Bhasmīkuru Bhasmīkuru | Viśvamohini Huṃ Phaṭ Svāhā | Oṃ Namo Bhagavate Rudrāya Namaḥ |

ॐ नमो भगवते रुद्राय। शिरो रक्षतु वाराही चैन्द्री रक्षेद्भुजद्वयम्।
चामुण्डा हृदयं रक्षेत् कुक्षिं रक्षतु वारुणी ॥ वैष्णवी पादमाश्रित्य पृष्ठदेशे धनुर्धरा।
यथा ग्रामे तथा क्षेत्रे रक्षेन्मां च पदे पदे ॥
सर्वमङ्गलमाङ्गल्ये शिवे सर्वार्थसाधिके। शरण्ये त्र्यम्बके
गौरि नारायणि नमोऽस्तु ते ॥ ब्राह्मि माहेश्वरि कौमारि वैष्णवि वाराहि
इन्द्राणि चामुण्डे सिद्धिचामुण्डे क्षेत्रमालिके नारसिंहि महालक्ष्मि
सर्वतो दुर्गे हुं फट् स्वाहा। भगवन् सर्वविजय सहस्रारापराजित।
शरणं त्वां प्रपन्नोऽस्मि श्रीकरं श्रीसुदर्शनम्॥ अरुणी वारुणी रक्षेत् सर्वग्रहनिवारणी।

सर्वदारिद्र्यशमनी सर्वराजवशङ्करी ॥
सर्वकर्मकारिणि ॐ भूः स्वाहा । ॐ भुवः स्वाहा । ॐ स्वः स्वाहा ।
ॐ भूर्भुवः स्वः स्वाहा । ॐ आं ह्रीं क्रोम् । फट् फट् जहि महाकृत्ये विधूमाग्निसमप्रभे ।
हन शत्रूंस्त्रिशूलेनक्रुद्धास्ये पिब शोणितम् ॥
देवि देवि महादेवि ह्रीं मम शत्रून् विनाशय विनाशय । अहं न जाने न च पार्वतीशः ।
अष्टौ ब्राह्मणान् ग्राहयित्वा ततो महाविद्या सिध्यति ।
अशिक्षिताय नोपयच्छेत् । एकविंशतिवाराणि परिजप्य शुचिर्भवेत् ।
पत्रं पुष्पं फलं दद्यात् स्त्रियो वा पुरुषस्य वा । अवश्यं वशमित्याहुरात्मना च परेण वा ॥
महाविद्यावतां पुंसां मनःक्षोभं करोति यः । सप्तरात्रौ व्यतीतायां स च शत्रुर्विनश्यति ॥
कुबेरं ते मुखं रौद्रं नन्दिमानन्दमावह । ज्वरं य घोरं द्विषं नाशय नाशय ॥
ॐ नमो भगवतेऽमृतवर्षाय रुद्राय हृदयेऽमृताभिवर्षणाय ।
मम ज्वरदाहशान्तिं कुरु कुरु स्वाहा । ॐ हौं जूं सः मां पालय पालय सः जूं हौं ॐ ।
ॐ नमो भगवते । भो भोः सुदर्शन दुष्टं दारय दारय ।
दुरितं हन हन । पापं मथ मथ । आरोग्यं कुरु कुरु । द्विषन्तं हन हन ।
ठः ठः सहस्रार हुं फट् । भस्मायुधाय विद्महे तीक्ष्णदंष्ट्राय धीमहि । तन्नो ज्वरः प्रचोदयात् ।
समुद्रस्योत्तरे तीरे द्विविदो नाम वानरः । चातुर्थिकं ज्वरं हन्ति लिखित्वा यस्तु पश्यति ॥
यस्ते मन्योरिति च चतुर्दशर्चस्य सूक्तस्य रुद्रो दुर्वासास्तपनपुत्रो मन्युर्देवता ।
अपनिलयन्तामिति बीजम् । संसृष्टमिति शक्तिः ।
शत्रुं क्षपयेति कीलकम् । मम शत्रुक्षयार्थे जपे विनियोगः ।

Oṃ Namo Bhagavate Rudrāya |

Śiro Rakṣatu Vārāhī Caindrī Rakṣedbhujadvayam |

Cāmuṇḍā Hṛdayaṃ Rakṣet Kukṣiṃ Rakṣatu Vāruṇī ||

Vaiṣṇavī Pādamāśritya Pṛṣṭhadeśe Dhanurdharā |

Yathā Grāme Tathā Kṣetre Rakṣenmāṃ Ca Pade Pade ||

Sarvamaṅgalamāṅgalye Śive Sarvārthasādhike |

Śaraṇye Tryambake Gauri Nārāyaṇi Namo'stu Te ||

Brāhmi Māheśvari Kaumāri Vaiṣṇavi Vārāhi Indrāṇi Cāmuṇḍe Siddhicāmuṇḍe Kṣetramālike Nārasiṃhi Mahālakṣmi

Sarvato Durge Huṃ Phaṭ Svāhā |

Bhagavan Sarvavijaya Sahasrārāparājita |

Śaraṇaṃ Tvāṃ Prapanno'smi Śrīkaraṃ Śrīsudarśanam ||

Aruṇī Vāruṇī Rakṣet Sarvagrahanivāraṇī |
Sarvadāridryaśamanī Sarvarājavaśaṅkarī ||

Sarvakarmakāriṇi Oṃ Bhūḥ Svāhā | *Oṃ Bhuvaḥ Svāhā* |
Oṃ Svaḥ Svāhā | *Oṃ Bhūrbhuvaḥ Svaḥ Svāhā* | *Oṃ Āṃ Hrīṃ Krom* |
Phaṭ Phaṭ Jahi Mahākṛtye Vidhūmāgnisamaprabhe |
Hana Śatrūṃstriśūlena Kruddhāsye Piba Śoṇitam ||

Devi Devi Mahādevi Hrīṃ Mama Śatrūn Vināśaya Vināśaya |
Ahaṃ Na Jāne Na Ca Pārvatīśaḥ |
Aṣṭau Brāhmaṇān Grāhayitvā Tato Mahāvidyā Sidhyati |
Aśikṣitāya Nopayacchet | *Ekaviṃśativārāṇi Parijapya Śucirbhavet* |
Patraṃ Puṣpaṃ Phalaṃ Dadyāt Striyo Vā Puruṣasya Vā |
Avaśyaṃ Vaśamityāhurātmanā Ca Pareṇa Vā ||
Mahāvidyāvatāṃ Puṃsāṃ Manaḥkṣobhaṃ Karoti Yaḥ |
Saptarātrau Vyatītāyāṃ Sa Ca Śatrurvinaśyati ||
Kuberaṃ Te Mukhaṃ Raudraṃ Nandimānandamāvaha |
Jvaraṃ Ya Ghoraṃ Dviṣaṃ Nāśaya Nāśaya ||

Oṃ Namo Bhagavate'mṛtavarṣāya Rudrāya Hṛdaye'mṛtābhivarṣaṇāya |
Mama Jvaradāhaśāntiṃ Kuru Kuru Svāhā |
Oṃ Hauṃ Jūṃ Saḥ Māṃ Pālaya Pālaya Saḥ Jūṃ Hauṃ Oṃ |
Oṃ Namo Bhagavate | *Bho Bhoḥ Sudarśana Duṣṭaṃ Dāraya Dāraya* |
Duritaṃ Hana Hana | *Pāpaṃ Matha Matha* | *Ārogyaṃ Kuru Kuru* |
Dviṣantaṃ Hana Hana | *Ṭhaḥ Ṭhaḥ Sahasrāra Huṃ Phaṭ* |
Bhasmāyudhāya Vidmahe Tīkṣṇadaṃṣṭrāya Dhīmahi |
Tanno Jvaraḥ Pracodayāt |
Samudrasyottare Tīre Dvivido Nāma Vānaraḥ |
Cāturthikaṃ Jvaraṃ Hanti Likhitvā Yastu Paśyati ||

Yaste Manyoriti Ca Caturdaśarcasya Sūktasya Rudro Durvāsāstapanaputro Manyurdevatā | Apanilayantāmiti Bījam | Saṃsṛṣṭamiti Śaktiḥ | Śatruṃ Kṣapayeti Kīlakam | Mama Śatrukṣayārthe Jape Viniyogaḥ |

अथ ध्यानम् *Atha Dhyānam-*

1. दंष्ट्राकरालवदनं ज्वालामालाशिरोरुहम् । कपालकर्तिकाहस्तं रुद्रं मन्युं नमाम्यहम् ॥

Daṃṣṭrākarālavadanaṃ Jvālāmālāśiroruham |
Kapālakartikāhastaṃ Rudraṃ Manyuṃ Namāmyaham ||

यस्ते मन्योऽविधद्वज्र सायक सह ओजः पुष्यति विश्वमानुषक् ।
साह्याम दासमार्यं त्वया युजा सहत्कृतेन सहसा सहस्वता ॥

Yaste Manyo'vidhadvajra Sāyaka Saha Ojaḥ Puṣyati Viśvamānuṣak |
Sāhyāma Dāsamāryaṃ Tvayā Yujā Sahatkṛtena Sahasā Sahasvatā || ॥

2. मन्युरिन्द्रो मन्युरेवास देवो मन्युर्होता वरुणो जातवेदा ।
मन्यु विश ईळते मानुषीर्याः पाहि नो मन्यो तपसा सजोषा ॥

Manyurindro Manyurevāsa Devo Manyurhotā Varuṇo Jātavedā |
Manyu Viśa Īḷate Mānuṣīryāḥ Pāhi No Manyo Tapasā Sajoṣā ॥

3. अभीहि मन्यो तवसस्तवीयान् तपसा युजा वि जहि शत्रून् ।
अमित्रहा वृत्रहा दस्युहा च विश्वा वसून्या भरा त्वं न ॥

Abhīhi Manyo Tavasastavīyān Tapasā Yujā Vi Jahi Śatrūn |
Amitrahā Vṛtrahā Dasyuhā Ca Viśvā Vasūnyā Bharā Tvaṃ Na ॥

4. त्वं हि मन्यो अभिभूत्योजा स्वयम्भूर्भामो अभिमातिषाह ।
विश्वचर्षणिः सहुरिः सहावानस्मास्वोजः पृतनासु धेहि ॥

Tvaṃ Hi Manyo Abhibhūtyojā Svayambhūrbhāmo Abhimātiṣāha |
Viśvacarṣaṇiḥ Sahuriḥ Sahāvānasmāsvojaḥ Pṛtanāsu Dhehi ॥

5. अभागः सन्नप परेतो अस्मि तव क्रत्वा तविषस्य प्रचेतः ।
तं त्वा मन्यो अक्रतुर्जिहीळाहं स्वा तनूर्बलदेयाय मेहि ॥

Abhāgaḥ Sannapa Pareto Asmi Tava Kratvā Taviṣasya Pracetaḥ |
Taṃ Tvā Manyo Akraturjihīḷāhaṃ Svā Tanūrbaladeyāya Mehi ||

6. अयं ते अस्म्युप मेह्यर्वाङ् प्रतीचीनः सहुरे विश्वधायः।
मन्यो वज्रिन्नभि मामा ववृत्स्व हनाव दस्यूनुत बोध्यापे ॥

Ayaṃ Te Asmyupa Mehyarvāṅ Pratīcīnaḥ Sahure Viśvadhāyaḥ |
Manyo Vajrinnabhi Māmā Vavṛtsva Hanāva Dasyūnuta Bodhyāpe ||

7. अभि प्रेहि दक्षिणतो भवा मेऽधा वृत्राणि जङ्घनाव भूरि।
जुहोमि ते धरुणं मध्वो अग्रमुभा उपांशु प्रथमा पिबाव ॥

Abhi Prehi Dakṣiṇato Bhavā Me'dhā Vṛtrāṇi Jaṅghanāva Bhūri |
Juhomi Te Dharuṇaṃ Madhvo Agramubhā Upāṃśu Prathamā Pibāva ||

8. त्वया मन्यो सरथमारुजन्तो हर्षमाणासो धृषिता मरुत्व।
तिग्मेषव आयुधा सशिशाना अभि प्र यन्तु नरो अग्निरूपा ॥

Tvayā Manyo Sarathamārujanto Harṣamāṇāso Dhṛṣitā Marutva |
Tigmeṣava Āyudhā Saśiśānā Abhi Pra Yantu Naro Agnirūpā ||

9. अग्निरिव मन्यो त्विषित सहस्व सेनानीर्न सहुरे हूत एधि।
हत्वाय शत्रून् विभजस्व वेद ओजो मिमानो वि मृधो नुदस्व ॥

Agniriva Manyo Tviṣita Sahasva Senānīrna Sahure Hūta Edhi |
Hatvāya Śatrūn Vibhajasva Veda Ojo Mimāno Vi Mṛdho Nudasva ||

10. सहस्व मन्यो अभिमातिमस्मे रुजन् मृणन् प्रमृणन् प्रेहि शत्रून्।
उग्रं ते पाजो नन्वा रुरुध्रे वशी वशं नयस एकज त्वम् ॥

Sahasva Manyo Abhimātimasme Rujan Mṛṇan Pramṛṇan Prehi Śatrūn |
Ugraṃ Te Pājo Nanvā Rurudhre Vaśī Vaśaṃ Nayasa Ekaja Tvam ||

11. एको बहूनामसि मन्यवीळितो विशं विशं युधये सं शिशाधि।
अकृत्तरुक् त्वया युजा वयं द्युमन्तं घोषं विजयाय कृण्महे ॥

Eko Bahūnāmasi Manyavīḷito Viśaṃ Viśaṃ Yudhaye Saṃ Śiśādhi |
Akṛttaruk Tvayā Yujā Vayaṃ Dyumantaṃ Ghoṣaṃ Vijayāya Kṛṇmahe ||

12. विजेषकृदिन्द्र इवानवब्रवोऽस्माकं मन्यो अधिपा भवेह ।
प्रियं ते नाम सहुरे गृणीमसि विद्मा तमुत्सं यत आ बभूव ॥

Vijeṣakṛdindra Ivānavavravo'smākaṃ Manyo Adhipā Bhaveha |
Priyaṃ Te Nāma Sahure Gṛṇīmasi Vidmā Tamutsaṃ Yata Ā Babhūva ||

13. आभूत्या सहजा वज्र सायक सहो बिभर्ष्यभिभूत उत्तरम् ।
क्रत्वा नो मन्यो सह मेद्येधि महाधनस्य पुरुहूत संसृजि ॥

Ābhūtyā Sahajā Vajra Sāyaka Saho Bibharṣyabhibhūta Uttaram |
Kratvā No Manyo Saha Medyedhi Mahādhanasya Puruhūta Saṃsṛji ||

14. संसृष्टं धनमुभयं ममाकृतमस्मभ्यं दत्तां वरुणश्च मन्युः ।
भियं दधाना हृदयेषु शत्रवः पराजितासो अपनिलयन्ताम् ॥

Saṃsṛṣṭaṃ Dhanamubhayaṃ Mamākṛtamasmabhyaṃ Dattāṃ Varuṇaśca Manyuḥ |
Bhiyaṃ Dadhānā Hṛdayeṣu Śatravaḥ Parājitāso Apanilayantām ||

हुं फट् । *Huṃ Phaṭ* |

1. जातवेदसे सुनवाम सोममरातीयतो निदहाति वेदः ।
स नः पर्षदति दुर्गाणि विश्वा नावेव सिन्धु दुरिताऽत्यग्निः ॥

Jātavedase Sunavāma Somamarātīyato Nidahāti Vedaḥ |
Sa Naḥ Parṣadati Durgāṇi Viśvā Nāveva Sindhu Duritā'tyagniḥ ||

2. तामग्निवर्णो तपसा ज्वलन्तीं वैरोचनीं कर्मफलेषु जुष्टाम् ।
दुर्गां देवीं शरणमहं प्रपद्ये सुतरसि तरसे नमः ॥

Tāmagnivarṇo Tapasā Jvalantīṃ Vairocanīṃ Karmaphaleṣu Juṣṭām |
Durgā Devīṃ Śaraṇamahaṃ Prapadye Sutarasi Tarase Namaḥ ||

3. अग्ने त्वं पारया नव्यो अस्मान् स्वस्तिभिरति दुर्गाणि विश्वा ।
पूश्च पृथ्वी बहुला न उर्वी भवा तोकाय तनयाय शयो ॥

Agne Tvaṃ Pārayā Navyo Asmān Svastibhirati Durgāṇi Viśvā |
Pūśca Pṛthvī Bahulā Na Urvī Bhavā Tokāya Tanayāya Śayo ||

4. विश्वानि नो दुर्गहा जातवैदस्सिन्धु न नावा दुरिताऽतिपर्षि ।
अग्ने अत्रिवन्मनसा गृणानोऽस्माकं भूत्वविता तनूनाम् ॥

Viśvāni No Durgahā Jātavaidassindhu Na Nāvā Duritā'tiparṣi |
Agne Atrivanmanasā Gṛṇāno'smākaṃ Bhūtvavitā Tanūnām ||

5. पृतनाजितं सहमानमग्निमुग्रं हुवेव परमात् सधस्थात् ।
स नः पर्षदति दुर्गाणि विश्वा क्षामद्देवो अति दुरिताऽत्यग्निः ॥

Pṛtanājitaṃ Sahamānamagnimugraṃ Huveva Paramāt Sadhasthāt |
Sa Naḥ Parṣadati Durgāṇi Viśvā Kṣāmaddevo Ati Duritā'tyagniḥ ||

6. प्रत्नोषि कमीड्यो अध्वरेषु सनाच्च होता नव्यश्च सत्सि ।
स्वां चाग्ने तनुवं पिप्रियस्वास्मभ्यं च सौभगमा यजस्व ॥

Pratnoṣi Kamīḍyo Adhvareṣu Sanācca Hotā Navyaśca Satsi |
Svāṃ Cāgne Tanuvaṃ Pipriyasvāsmabhyaṃ Ca Saubhagamā Yajasva ||

7. गोभिर्जुष्टमयुजो निषिक्तं तवेन्द्र विष्णोरनु सं चरेम ।
नाकस्य पृष्ठमभि सं वसानो वैष्णवीं लोक इह मादयन्ताम् ॥

Gobhirjuṣṭamayujo Niṣiktaṃ Tavendra Viṣṇoranu Saṃ Carema |
Nākasya Pṛṣṭhamabhi Saṃ Vasāno Vaiṣṇavīṃ Loka Iha Mādayantām ||

8. भास्कराय विद्महे महाद्युतिकराय धीमहि । तन्नो आदित्यः प्रचोदयात् ।
घृणिः सूर्य आदित्यो न प्रभावात्यक्षरम् । मधु क्षरन्ति तद्रसम् ।
सत्यं वै तद्रसमापो ज्योती रसोघ्नुतं ब्रह्म भूर्भुवःस्वरोम् ।
श्रीं श्रीं सोऽहमर्कमहमहं ज्योतिरहं शिवः । आत्मज्योतिरहं शुक्रः सर्वज्योतिरसोप्रमोम् ॥
आदित्यं भास्करं भानुं रविं सूर्यं दिवाकरम् । नामषट्कं स्मरेन्नित्यं महापातकनाशनम् ॥

Bhāskarāya Vidmahe Mahādyutikarāya Dhīmahi |

Tanno Ādityaḥ Pracodayāt |

Ghṛṇiḥ Sūrya Āditvo Na Prabhāvātyakṣaram |

Madhu Kṣaranti Tadrasam | Satyaṃ Vai Tadrasamāpo Jyotī

Rasoghnutaṃ Brahma Bhūrbhuvaḥsvarom |

Śrīṃ Śrīṃ So'hamarkamahamahaṃ Jyotirahaṃ Śivaḥ |

Ātmajyotiraham̱ Śukraḥ Sarvajyotirasopramom ||

Ādityam̱ Bhāskaram̱ Bhānum̱ Ravim̱ Sūrya Divākaram |
Nāmaṣaṭkam̱ Smarennityam̱ Mahāpātakanāśanam ||

कात्यायनाय विद्महे कन्यकुमारि धीमहि। तन्नो दुर्गिः प्रचोदयात्।
ॐ नमो भगवति माहेश्वरि ह्रीं श्रीं क्लीं कल्पलते ममाभीष्टफलं देहि।
प्रतिकूलं मे नश्यतु। अनुकूलं मे अस्तु। महादेव्यै च विद्महे विष्णुपत्न्यै च धीमहि।
तन्नो लक्ष्मीः प्रचोदयात्।
ॐ ब्लीं ह्रीं श्रीं क्लीं ब्रह्मेशानि मां रक्ष रक्ष। पञ्चम्यां च नवम्यां च पञ्चदश्यां विशेषतः।
पठित्वा तु महाविद्यां श्रीकामः सर्वदा पठेत्॥

Kātyāyanāya Vidmahe Kanyakumāri Dhīmahi | Tanno Durgiḥ Pracodayāt | Om̱ Namo Bhagavati Māheśvari Hrīm̱ Śrīm̱ Klīm̱ Kalpalate Mamābhīṣṭaphalam̱ Dehi |

Pratikūlam̱ Me Naśyatu | Anukūlam̱ Me Astu |

Mahādevyai Ca Vidmahe Viṣṇupatnyai Ca Dhīmahi |

Tanno Lakṣmīḥ Pracodayāt |

Om̱ Blīm̱ Hrīm̱ Śrīm̱ Klīm̱ Brahmeśāni Mām̱ Rakṣa Rakṣa |

Pañcamyām̱ Ca Navamyām̱ Ca Pañcadaśyām̱ Viśeṣataḥ |
Paṭhitvā Tu Mahāvidyām̱ Śrīkāmaḥ Sarvadā Paṭhet ||

गन्धद्वारां दुराधर्षो नित्यपुष्टां करीषिणीम्। ईश्वरीं सर्वभूतानां तामिहोपह्वये श्रियम्॥
श्रीर्मे भजतु। अलक्ष्मीर्मे नश्यतु।
यां कल्पयन्ति नोऽरयः क्रूरा कृत्यां वधूमिव। तां ब्रह्मणे च निर्णुमः प्रत्यक्कर्तारमृच्छतु॥
यदन्ति यच्च दूरके भयं विन्दति मामिह। पवमान वि तज्जहि॥
क्षिप्रं कृत्ये निवर्तस्व कर्तुरेव गृहान् प्रति।
नाशयास्य पशूंश्चैव वीरांश्चास्य निबर्हय॥ ॐ स्वाहा।

Gandhadvārām̱ Durādharṣo Nityapuṣṭām̱ Karīṣiṇīm |

Īśvarīm̱ Sarvabhūtānām̱ Tāmihopahnaye Śriyam ||

Śrīrme Bhajatu | Alakṣmīrme Naśyatu |

Yām̱ Kalpayanti No'rayaḥ Krūrā Kṛtyām̱ Vadhūmiva |

Tāṃ Brahmaṇe Ca Nirṇumaḥ Pratyakkartāramṛcchatu ||

Yadanti Yacca Dūrake Bhayaṃ Vindati Māmiha |

Pavamāna Vi Tajjahi ||

Kṣipraṃ Kṛtye Nivartasva Kartureva Gṛhān Prati |

Nāśayāsya Paśūṃścaiva Vīrāṃścāsya Nibarhaya || Oṃ Svāhā |

यदुदितं भगवति तत्सर्वं शमय शमय स्वाहा। ॐ गायत्र्यै स्वाहा।
ॐ सावित्र्यै स्वाहा। ॐ सरस्वत्यै स्वाहा। ॐ अघोरेभ्योऽथ घोरेभ्यो घोरघोरतरेभ्यः।
सर्वेभ्यः सर्वशर्वेभ्यो नमस्ते अस्तु रुद्ररूपेभ्यः।
तत्पुरुषाय विद्महे वक्रतुण्डाय धीमहि। तन्नो दन्तिः प्रचोदयात्।
तत्पुरुषाय विद्महे महासेनाय धीमहि। तन्नः षण्मुखः प्रचोदयात्।
तत्पुरुषाय विद्महेसुवर्णपक्षाय धीमहि। तन्नो गरुडः प्रचोदयात्।
वेदात्मनाय विद्महे हिरण्यगर्भाय धीमहि। तन्नो ब्रह्म प्रचोदयात्।
नारायणाय विद्महे वासुदेवाय धीमहि। तन्नो विष्णुः प्रचोदयात्।
वज्रनखाय विद्महे तीक्ष्णदंष्ट्राय धीमहि। तन्नो नारसिंहः प्रचोदयात्।
भास्कराय विद्महे महाद्युतिकराय धीमहि। तन्नो आदित्यः प्रचोदयात्।
वैश्वानराय विद्महे लालीलाय धीमहि। तन्नो अग्निः प्रचोदयात्।
कात्यायनाय विद्महे कन्यकुमारि धीमहि। तन्नो दुर्गिः प्रचोदयात्।
सदाशिवाय विद्महे सहस्राक्षाय धीमहि। तन्नः साम्बः प्रचोदयात्।
क्षेत्रपालाय विद्महे तीक्ष्णदंष्ट्राय धीमहि। तन्नो भैरवः प्रचोदयात्।
रघुवंश्यायविद्महे सीतावल्लभाय धीमहि। तन्नो रामः प्रचोदयात्।
कुलकुमार्यै विद्महे कौलदेवाय धीमहि। तन्नः कौलः प्रचोदयात्।
कालिकायै विद्महे श्मशानवासिन्यै धीमहि। तन्नोऽघोरः प्रचोदयात्।
ॐ ऐं ह्रीं श्रीं आनन्देश्वराय विद्महे सुधादेव्यै च धीमहि। तन्नो अर्धनारीश्वरः प्रचोदयात्।
एं वागीश्वर्यै च विद्महे क्लीं कामेश्वर्यै च धीमहि। तन्नः क्लीं प्रचोदयात्।
ऐं त्रिपुरादेव्यै च विद्महे क्लीं कामेश्वर्यै च धीमहि। सौः तन्नः शक्तिः प्रचोदयात्।
हंसहंसायविद्महे सोऽहं हंसाय धीमहि। तन्नो हंसः प्रचोदयात्।
यन्त्रराजाय विद्महे महायन्त्राय धीमहि। तन्नो यन्त्रः प्रचोदयात्।
तन्त्रराजाय विद्महे महातन्त्राय धीमहि। तन्नस्तन्त्रः प्रचोदयात्।
मन्त्रराजाय विद्महे महामन्त्राय धीमहि। तन्नो मन्त्रः प्रचोदयात्।
यत इन्द्र भयामहे ततो नो अभयं कृधि। मघवञ्छग्धि तव तन्न
ऊतये विद्विषो विमृधो जहि॥ स्वस्तिदा विशस्पतिर्वृत्रहा विमृधो वशी।

वृषेन्द्रः पुर एतु नः स्वस्तिदा अभयङ्करः ॥

Yaduditaṃ Bhagavati Tatsarvaṃ Śamaya Śamaya Svāhā ।

Oṃ Gāyatryai Svāhā । *Oṃ Sāvitryai Svāhā* । *Oṃ Sarasvatyai Svāhā* ।

Oṃ Aghorebhyo'tha Ghorebhyo Ghoraghoratarebhyaḥ ।

Sarvebhyaḥ Sarvaśarvebhyo Namaste Astu Rudrarūpebhyaḥ ।

Tatpuruṣāya Vidmahe Vakratuṇḍāya Dhīmahi ।

Tanno Dantiḥ Pracodayāt ।

Tatpuruṣāya Vidmahe Mahāsenāya Dhīmahi ।

Tannaḥ Ṣaṇmukhaḥ Pracodayāt ।

Tatpuruṣāya Vidmahesuvarṇapakṣāya Dhīmahi ।

Tanno Garuḍaḥ Pracodayāt ।

Vedātmanāya Vidmahe Hiraṇyagarbhāya Dhīmahi ।

Tanno Brahma Pracodayāt ।

Nārāyaṇāya Vidmahe Vāsudevāya Dhīmahi । *Tanno Viṣṇuḥ Pracodayāt* ।

Vajranakhāya Vidmahe Tīkṣṇadaṃṣṭrāya Dhīmahi ।

Tanno Nārasiṃhaḥ Pracodayāt ।

Bhāskarāya Vidmahe Mahādyutikarāya Dhīmahi ।

Tanno Ādityaḥ Pracodayāt ।

Vaiśvānarāya Vidmahe Lālīlāya Dhīmahi । *Tanno Agniḥ Pracodayāt* ।

Kātyāyanāya Vidmahe Kanyakumāri Dhīmahi ।

Tanno Durgiḥ Pracodayāt ।

Sadāśivāya Vidmahe Sahasrākṣāya Dhīmahi ।

Tannaḥ Sāmbaḥ Pracodayāt ।

Kṣetrapālāya Vidmahe Tīkṣṇadaṃṣṭrāya Dhīmahi ।

Tanno Bhairavaḥ Pracodayāt ।

Raghuvaṃśyāya Vidmahe Sītāvallabhāya Dhīmahi ।

Tanno Rāmaḥ Pracodayāt ।

Kulakumāryai Vidmahe Kauladevāya Dhīmahi ।

Tannaḥ Kaulaḥ Pracodayāt |

Kālikāyai Vidmahe Śmaśānavāsinyai Dhīmahi |

Tanno'ghoraḥ Pracodayāt |

Oṃ Aiṃ Hrīṃ Śrīṃ Ānandeśvarāya Vidmahe Sudhādevyai Ca Dhīmahi |

Tanno Ardhanārīśvaraḥ Pracodayāt |

Eṃ Vāgīśvaryai Ca Vidmahe Klīṃ Kāmeśvaryai Ca Dhīmahi |

Tannaḥ Klīṃ Pracodayāt |

Aiṃ Tripurādevyai Ca Vidmahe Klīṃ Kāmeśvaryai Ca Dhīmahi |

Sauḥ Tannaḥ Śaktiḥ Pracodayāt |

Haṃsahaṃsāya Vidmahe So'haṃ Haṃsāya Dhīmahi |

Tanno Haṃsaḥ Pracodayāt |

Yantrarājāya Vidmahe Mahāyantrāya Dhīmahi |

Tanno Yantraḥ Pracodayāt |

Tantrarājāya Vidmahe Mahātantrāya Dhīmahi |

Tannastantraḥ Pracodayāt |

Mantrarājāya Vidmahe Mahāmantrāya Dhīmahi |

Tanno Mantraḥ Pracodayāt |

Yata Indra Bhayāmahe Tato No Abhayaṃ Kṛdhi |
Maghavañchagdhi Tava Tanna
Ūtaye Vidviṣo Vimṛdho Jahi ||

Svastidā Viśaspatirvṛtrahā Vimṛdho Vaśī |

Vṛṣendraḥ Pura Etu Naḥ Svastidā Abhayaṅkaraḥ ||

सहस्रपरमा देवी शतमूला शताङ्कुरा । सर्वे हरतु मे पापं दूर्वा दुःस्वप्ननाशिनी ॥
काण्डात्काण्डात्प्ररोहन्ती परुषः परुषः परि । एवा नो पूर्वे प्रतनु सहस्रेण शतेन च ॥
या शतेन प्रतनोषि सहस्रेण विरोहसि । तस्यास्ते देवीष्टके विधेम हविषा वयम् ॥
अश्वक्रान्ते रथक्रान्ते विष्णुक्रान्ते वसुन्धरा । शिरसा धारयिष्यामि रक्षस्व मां पदे पदे ॥
ऋतं सत्यं परं ब्रह्म पुरुषं कृष्णपिङ्गलम् । ऊर्ध्वरेतं विरूपाक्षं विश्वरूपाय वै नमो नमः ॥
ॐ ह्रीं फट् स्वाहा । खण्फण्म्रसि । ब्रह्मणा त्वा शपामि ।

ब्रह्मणस्त्वा शपथेन शपामि। घोरेण त्वा भृगूणां चक्षु षा प्रेक्षे।
रौद्रेण त्वाङ्गिरसां मनसा ध्यायामि। अघस्य त्वा धारया विद्यामि।
अधरो मत्पद्यस्वासौ। उत्तुद शिमिजावरि। तल्पेजे तल्प उत्तुद।
गिरीरनु प्रवेशय। मरीचीरुप सनुद। यावदितः पुरस्तादुदयाति सूर्यः।
तावदितौऽमुं नाशय। योऽस्मान् द्वेष्टि। यं च वयं द्विष्मः। खट् फट् जहि।
छिन्धी भिन्धी हन्धी कट्। इति वाचः क्रूराणि। नमस्ते अस्तु मा मा हिंसीः।
द्विषन्तं मेऽभिराय। तं मृत्यो मृत्यवे नय। संसृष्टं धनमुभयं समाकृतमस्मभ्यं दत्तां वरुणश्च मन्युः।
भियं दधाना हृदयेषु शत्रवः पराजितासो अपनिलयन्तां हुं फट्।
ॐ ह्रीं कृष्णवाससे नारसिंहवदने महाभैरवि विद्युज्जवालाजिह्वे करालवदने
प्रत्यङ्गिरे क्श्रीं क्ष्म्रौं ज्वल ज्वल। ॐ नमो नारायणाय।
घृणिः सूर्य आदित्यो सहस्रार हुं फट्। इष्टं रक्ष रक्ष। अरिष्टं भञ्जय भञ्जय स्वाहा।
ब्रह्मा नारदाय नारदो बृहत्सेनाय बृहत्सेनो बृहस्पतये बृहस्पतिरिन्द्रायेन्द्रो भारद्वाजाय भारद्वाजो
जीवितुकामेभ्यः शिष्येभ्यः प्रायच्छत् क्षीं स्वाहा।
नमो ब्रह्मणे नमो अस्त्वग्नये नमः पृथिव्यै नम ओषधीभ्यः।
नमो वाचे नमो वाचस्पतये नमो विष्णवे बृहते करोमि।
ॐ नमो भगवते श्रीं श्रीमन्महागरुडायामृतकलशोद्भवाय वज्रनखाय
वज्रतुण्डवज्रपक्षालङ्कृताय एह्येहि महागरुड हुं फट् स्वाहा।
ॐ ह्रीं दुं सर्पोलूककाककपोतवृश्चिकदंष्ट्राग्निविषंनो भयं
भूतप्रेतपिशाचब्रह्मराक्षससकलकिल्विषादिमहारोगविष निर्विषं कुरु कुरु स्वाहा।
विन्ध्यस्योत्तरे तीरे मारीचो नाम राक्षसः। तत्र मूत्रपुरीषाभ्यां हुताशनं शमय शमय स्वाहा।
ॐ आं ह्रीं क्रों एह्येहि दत्तात्रेयाय स्वाहा। महाविद्यां ज्ञातवतो योऽस्मान् द्वेष्टि योऽरिः
स्मरति यावदेकविंशति कृत्वा तावदधिकं नाशय।

SahasraparamāDevī Śatamūlā Śatāṅkurā |

Sarve Haratu Me Pāpaṃ Dūrvā Duḥsvapnanāśinī ||

Kāṇḍātkāṇḍātprarohantī Paruṣaḥ Paruṣaḥ Pari |

Evā No Pūrve Pratanu Sahasreṇa Śatena Ca ||

Yā Śatena Pratanoṣi Sahasreṇa Virohasi |

Tasyāste Devīṣṭake Vidhema Haviṣā Vayam ||

Aśvakrānte Rathakrānte Viṣṇukrānte Vasundharā |

Śirasā Dhārayiṣyāmi Rakṣasva Māṃ Pade Pade ||

Ṛtaṃ Satyaṃ Paraṃ Brahma Puruṣaṃ Kṛṣṇapiṅgalam |

Ūrdhvaretaṃ Virūpākṣaṃ Viśvarūpāya Vai Namo Namaḥ ||

Oṃ Hrīṃ Phaṭ Svāhā | Khaṇphaṇmrasi | Brahmaṇā Tvā Śapāmi |

Brahmaṇastvā Śapathena Śapāmi |

Ghoreṇa Tvā Bhṛgūṇāṃ Cakṣuṣā Prekṣe |

Raudreṇa Tvāṅgirasāṃ Manasā Dhyāyāmi |

Aghasya Tvā Dhārayā Vidyāmi | Adharo Matpadyasvāsau |

Uttuda Śimijāvari | Talpeje Talpa Uttuda | Girīṃ̐ Ranu Praveśaya |

Marīcīrupa Sanuda | Yāvaditaḥ Purastādudayāti Sūryaḥ |

Tāvaditau'muṃ Nāśaya | Yo'smān Dveṣṭi | Yaṃ Ca Vayaṃ Dviṣmaḥ |

Khaṭ Phaṭ Jahi | Chindhī Bhindhī Handhī Kaṭ | Iti Vācaḥ Krūrāṇi |

Namaste Astu Mā Mā Hiṃsīḥ | Dviṣantaṃ Me'bhirāya |

Taṃ Mṛtyo Mṛtyave Naya | Saṃsṛṣṭaṃ Dhanamubhayaṃ

Samākṛtamasmabhyaṃ Dattāṃ Varuṇaśca Manyuḥ |

Bhiyaṃ Dadhānā Hṛdayeṣu Śatravaḥ Parājitāso Apanilayantāṃ Huṃ

Phaṭ | Oṃ Hrīṃ Kṛṣṇavāsase Nārasiṃhavadane Mahābhairavi

Vidyujjavālājihve Karālavadane Pratyaṅgire Kśrīṃ Kṣmrauṃ Jvala Jvala |

Oṃ Namo Nārāyaṇāya | Dhṛṇiḥ Sūrya Āditya Sahasrāra Huṃ Phaṭ |

Iṣṭaṃ Rakṣa Rakṣa | Ariṣṭaṃ Bhañjaya Bhañjaya Svāhā |

Brahmā Nāradāya Nārado Bṛhatsenāya Bṛhatseno Bṛhaspataye
Bṛhaspatirindrāyendro Bhāradvājāya Bhāradvājo Jīvitukāmebhyaḥ

Śiṣyebhyaḥ Prāyacchat Kṣīṃ Svāhā |

Namo Brahmaṇe Namo Astvagnaye Namaḥ Pṛthivyai Nama

Oṣadhībhyaḥ | Namo Vāce Namo Vācaspataye Namo Viṣṇave Bṛhate

Karomi | Oṃ Namo Bhagavate Śrīṃ

Śrīmanmahāgaruḍāyāmṛtakalaśodbhavāya
Vajranakhāya Vajratuṇḍavajrapakṣālaṅkṛtāya Ehyehi Mahāgaruḍa Huṃ

Phaṭ Svāhā |

Oṃ Hrīṃ Duṃ Sarpolūkakākakapotavṛścikadaṃṣṭrāgniviṣaṃ

No Bhayaṃ Bhūtapretapiśācabrahmarākṣasasakalakilviṣādimahārogaviṣa

Nirviṣaṃ Kuru Kuru Svāhā |

Vindhyasyottare Tīre Mārīco Nāma Rākṣasaḥ |

Tatra Mūtrapurīṣābhyāṃ Hutāśanaṃ Śamaya Śamaya Svāhā |

Oṃ Āṃ Hrīṃ Kroṃ Ehyehi Dattātreyāya Svāhā |

Mahāvidyāṃ Jñātavato Yo'smān Dveṣṭi Yo'riḥ

Smarati Yāvadekaviṃśati Kṛtvā Tāvadadhikaṃ Nāśaya |

ब्रह्मविद्यामिमां दिव्यां नित्यं सेवेत यः सुधीः। ऐहिकामुष्मिकं सौख्यं प्राप्नोत्येव न संशयः॥
अनवद्यां महाविद्यां यो दूषयति मानवः। सोऽवश्यं नाशमाप्नोति षण्मासाभ्यन्तरेण वै॥
अग्रतः पृष्ठतः पार्श्व ऊर्ध्वतो रक्ष सर्वतः। चन्द्रघण्टाविरूपाक्षि त्वां भजे जगदीश्वरीम्॥
एवं विद्यां महाविद्यां त्रिसन्ध्यं स्तौति मानवः। दृष्टा दुष्टजनाः सर्वे तस्य मोहवशं गताः॥
तामग्निवर्णां तपसा ज्वलन्तीं वैरोचनीं कर्मफलेषु जुष्टाम्।
दुर्गां देवीं शरणमहं प्रपद्ये सुतरसि तरसे नमः॥

Brahmavidyāmimāṃ Divyāṃ Nityaṃ Seveta Yaḥ Sudhīḥ |

Aihikāmuṣmikaṃ Saukhyaṃ Prāpnotyeva Na Saṃśayaḥ ||

Anavadyāṃ Mahāvidyāṃ Yo Dūṣayati Mānavaḥ |

So'vaśyaṃ Nāśamāpnoti Ṣaṇmāsābhyantareṇa Vai ||

Agrataḥ Pṛṣṭhataḥ Pārśva Ūrdhvato Rakṣa Sarvataḥ |

Candraghaṇṭāvirūpākṣi Tvāṃ Bhaje Jagadīśvarīm ||

Evaṃ Vidyāṃ Mahāvidyāṃ Trisandhyaṃ Stauti Mānavaḥ |

Dṛṣṭā Duṣṭajanāḥ Sarve Tasya Mohavaśaṃ Gatāḥ ||

Tāmagnivarṇāṃ Tapasā Jvalantīṃ Vairocanīṃ Karmaphaleṣu Juṣṭām |

Durgā Devīṃ Śaraṇamahaṃ Prapadye Sutarasi Tarase Namaḥ ||

मातर्मे मधुकैटभघ्नि महिषप्राणापहारोद्यमे हेलानिर्मितधूम्रलोचनबधे हे चण्डमुण्डार्दिनि।
निश्शेषीकृतरक्तबीजदनुजे नित्ये निशुम्भापहे शुम्भध्वंसिनि कालि सर्वदुरितं दुर्गे नमस्ते हर॥

कालदण्डो करालास्या रक्तलोचनभीषणाम् । कालदण्डपरं मृत्युं विजयां बन्धयाम्यहम् ॥
पञ्चयोजनविस्तीर्णं मृत्योश्च मुखमण्डलम् । तस्माद्रक्ष महाविद्ये भद्रकालि नमोऽस्तु ते ॥
अव ब्रह्म द्विषो जहि । वारिजलोचनसहाये वारिगतिं वारयासुकरनिकरैः ।
पीडितमत्र भ्रान्तं मामनिशं पालय त्वमनवद्ये ॥
अव ब्रह्म द्विषो जहि । ॐ ह्रीं श्रीं क्लीं सिद्धलक्ष्मि स्वाहा ।
ॐ क्लीं ह्रीं श्रीं ॐ आवहन्ती वितन्वाना । कुर्वाणा चीरमात्मनः । वासांसि मम गावश्च ।
अन्नपाने च सर्वदा । ततो मे श्रियमावह । लोमशा पशुभिः सह स्वाहा ।
श्रिये जातः श्रिय आ निरियाय श्रियं वयो जरितृभ्यो दधाति ।
श्रियं वसाना अमृतत्वमायन् भवन्ति सत्या समिथा मितद्रौ ॥
ॐ हीं श्रीं क्लीं ब्लूं फ्रों आं ह्रीं क्रों हुं फट् स्वाहा ।

Mātarme Madhukaiṭabhaghni Mahiṣaprāṇāpahārodyame
Helānirmitadhūmralocanabadhe He Caṇḍamuṇḍārdini ।
Niśśeṣīkṛtaraktabījadanuje Nitye Niśumbhāpahe
Śumbhadhvaṃsini Kāli Sarvaduritaṃ Durge Namaste Hara ।।

Kāladaṇḍo Karālāsyā Raktalocanabhīṣaṇām ।
Kāladaṇḍaparaṃ Mṛtyuṃ Vijayāṃ Bandhayāmyaham ।।

Pañcayojanavistīrṇaṃ Mṛtyośca Mukhamaṇḍalam ।
Tasmādrakṣa Mahāvidye Bhadrakāli Namo'stu Te ।।

Ava Brahma Dviṣo Jahi ।
Vārijalocanasahāye Vārigatiṃ Vārayāsukaranikaraiḥ ।
Pīḍitamatra Bhrāntaṃ Māmaniśaṃ Pālaya Tvamanavadye ।।

Ava Brahma Dviṣo Jahi । *Oṃ Hrīṃ Śrīṃ Klīṃ Siddhalakṣmi Svāhā* ।
Oṃ Klīṃ Hrīṃ Śrīṃ Oṃ Āvahantī Vitanvānā । *Kurvāṇā Cīramātmanaḥ* ।
Vāsāṃsi Mama Gāvaśca । *Annapāne Ca Sarvadā* ।
Tato Me Śriyamāvaha । *Lomaśā Paśubhiḥ Saha Svāhā* ।
Śriye Jātaḥ Śriya Ā Niriyāya Śriyaṃ Vayo Jaritṛbhyo Dadhāti ।

Śriyaṃ Vasānā Amṛtatvamāyan Bhavanti Satyā Samithā Mitadrau ||

Oṃ Hīṃ Śrīṃ Klīṃ Blūṃ Phroṃ Āṃ Hrīṃ Kroṃ Huṃ Phaṭ Svāhā |

सह नाववतु । सह नौ भुनक्तु । सह वीर्यं करवावहै ।
तेजस्वि नावधीतमस्तु मा विद्विषावहै देहमध्यगतो वह्निर्वह्निमध्यगता द्युतिः ।
द्युतिमध्यगता दीप्तिर्दीप्तिमध्यगतः शशी ॥
शशिमध्यगतं देव्याश्चक्रं परमशोभनम् । तन्मध्ये च गतो बिन्दुर्बिन्दुमध्यगतं मनः ॥
मनोमध्यगतो नादो नादमध्यगताः कलाः । कलामध्यगतो जीवो जीवमध्यगता परा ।
जीवः परः परो जीवः सर्व ब्रह्मेति भावयेत् ॥

Saha Nāvavatu | Saha Nau Bhunaktu |

Saha Vīryaṃ Karavāvahai | Tejasvi Nāvadhītamastu Mā Vidviṣāvahai |

Dehamadhyagato Vahnirvahnimadhyagatā Dyutiḥ |

Dyutimadhyagatā Dīptirdīptimadhyagataḥ Śaśī ||

Śaśimadhyagataṃ Devyāścakraṃ Paramaśobhanam |

Tanmadhye Ca Gato Bindurbindumadhyagataṃ Manaḥ ||

Manomadhyagato Nādo Nādamadhyagatāḥ Kalāḥ |

Kalāmadhyagato Jīvo Jīvamadhyagatā Parā |
Jīvaḥ Paraḥ Paro Jīvaḥ Sarva Brahmeti Bhāvayet ||

शान्ति मन्त्रः | *Śānti Mantraḥ |*

ॐ भद्रं कर्णेभिः शृणुयाम देवाः । भद्रं पश्येमाक्षभिर्यजत्राः ।

Oṃ Bhadraṃ Karṇebhiḥ Śṛṇuyāma Devāḥ ||

Bhadraṃ Paśyemākṣabhiryajatrāḥ ||
स्थिरैरङ्गैस्तुष्टुवाँसस्तनूभिः । व्यशेम देवहितं यदायुः ।

Sthirairaṅgaistuṣṭuvāg̃Sastanūbhiḥ || Vyaśema Devahitaṃ Yadāyuḥ ||
स्वस्ति न इन्द्रो वृद्धश्रवाः । स्वस्ति नः पूषा विश्ववेदाः ।

Svasti Na Indro Vṛddhaśravāḥ || Svasti Naḥ Pūṣā Viśvavedāḥ ||
स्वस्ति नस्तार्क्ष्यो अरिष्टनेमिः । स्वस्ति नो बृहस्पतिर्दधातु ॥

Svasti Nastārkṣyo Ariṣṭanemiḥ || *Svasti No Bṛhaspatirdadhātu* ||

ॐ शान्तिः शान्तिः शान्तिः || *Oṃ Śāntiḥ Śāntiḥ Śāntiḥ* ||

इत्याथर्वणरहस्ये वनदुर्गोपनिषत् समाप्ता ||

Ityātharvaṇarahasye Vanadurgopaniṣat Samāptā ||

*****

Śyāmopaniṣat
श्यामोपनिषत्

This is also another *Upaniṣat* from Atharva Veda.

शान्ति मन्त्रः । *Śānti Mantraḥ* ।

ॐ भद्रं कर्णेभिः शृणुयाम देवाः । भद्रं पश्येमाक्षभिर्यजत्राः ।

Oṃ Bhadraṃ Karṇebhiḥ Śṛṇuyāma Devāḥ ॥

Bhadraṃ Paśyemākṣabhiryajatrāḥ ॥
स्थिरैरङ्गैस्तुष्टुवाँसस्तनूभिः । व्यशेम देवहितं यदायुः ।

SthiraiRaṅgaistuṣṭuvāg̃Sastanūbhiḥ ॥ *Vyaśema Devahitaṃ Yadāyuḥ* ॥
स्वस्ति न इन्द्रो वृद्धश्रवाः । स्वस्ति नः पूषा विश्ववेदाः ।

Svasti Na Indro Vṛddhaśravāḥ ॥ *Svasti Naḥ Pūṣā Viśvavedāḥ* ॥
स्वस्ति नस्तार्क्ष्यो अरिष्टनेमिः । स्वस्ति नो बृहस्पतिर्दधातु ॥

Svasti Nastārkṣyo Ariṣṭanemiḥ ॥ *Svasti No Bṛhaspatirdadhātu* ॥
ॐ शान्तिः शान्तिः शान्तिः ॥ *Oṃ Śāntiḥ Śāntiḥ Śāntiḥ* ॥

हरिः ॐ ॥ *Hariḥ Oṃ* ॥

क्रीं अथ हैनां ब्रह्मरन्ध्रे ब्रह्मस्वरूपिणीमाप्नोति सुभगां
शुभधातुकामरेफेन्दिरासमष्टिरूपिणीमेतत्त्रिगुणमादौतदनु
कूर्चबीजद्वयं व्योमषष्ठस्वरबिन्दुमेलनरूपं तदनु भुवनेशीद्वयं भवतु
व्योमज्वलनेन्दिराशून्यमेलनरूपं ततो दक्षिणे कालिके चेत्यपि ततो मुखबीजसप्तकमुच्चार्य
बृहद्भानुजायामुच्चरेत्। अयं स मन्त्रोत्तमः । य इमां सकृज्जपन् स तु देवेश्वरः ।
स तु विश्वेश्वरः । स तु नारीश्वरः । स तु सर्वगुरुः । स तु सर्वनमस्यः । स तु सर्ववेदैरधीतो भवति ।
स सर्वेषु तीर्थेषु स्नातो भवति ।
स स्वयं सदाशिवः । त्रिकोणं त्रिकोणं त्रिकोणं त्रिकोणं पुनश्चैव त्रिकोणं साष्टपत्रं सकेसरं
भूपुरैकेणसंयुतंतस्मिन्देवीं हृल्लेखामङ्गे विन्यस्य ध्यायेत् ।
अभिनवजलदनीला कुटिदंष्ट्रावराभयखड्गमुण्डसहितहस्ताकालिका ध्येया ।
काली कपालिनी कुल्ला कुरुकुल्ला विरोधिनी विप्रचित्तेति बहिः षट्कोणगाः ।
उग्रा उग्रप्रभा दीप्ता नीला घना वलाका मात्रा मुद्रा अमितेति नवकोणगाः ।
ब्राह्मी नारायणी माहेश्वरी चामुण्डा वाराही नारसिंही कौमारी चापराजितेत्यष्टपत्रगाः ।
चतुष्कोणेषु चत्वारो माधवरुद्रविनायकसौराः । दिक्षु दिक्पालाः ।

देवीं सर्वाङ्गेणादौ सम्पूज्य भगोदकेन तर्पणं पञ्चमकारेण पूजनमेतस्याः ।
एवं द्वित्रिक्रमेण कुर्वाणा मुनयो भवन्ति । नारिमित्रादिलक्षणमस्यवर्तते ।
अमुष्या मन्त्रपाठकस्य गतिरस्ति । नान्यस्येह गतिरस्ति ।
एतस्यास्तारामनोर्दुर्गामनोस्सुन्दरीमनोर्वा सिद्धिरिदानीम् । सर्वाः सुप्ता भूताः ।
असिताङ्गी जागर्ति । इमामसिताङ्ग्युपनिषदं योऽधीते अपुत्री पुत्री भवति ।
योऽन्यस्य वरदो दृष्ट्या जगन्मोहयेत् ।
गङ्गादितीर्थक्षेत्राणामग्निष्टोमादियज्ञानां फलभागीयते ॥

Oṃ Krīṃ Atha Haināṃ Brahmarandhre Brahmasvarūpiṇīmāpnoti Subhagāṃ Śubhadhātukāmarephendirāsamaṣṭirūpiṇīmetat Triguṇamādau Tadanu Kūrcabījadvayaṃ Vyomaṣaṣṭhasvarabindumelanarūpaṃ Tadanu Bhuvaneśīdvayaṃ Bhavatu Vyomajvalanendirāśūnyamelanarūpaṃ Tato Dakṣiṇe Kālike Cetyapi Tato Mukhabījasaptakamuccārya Bṛhadbhānujāyāmuccaret |

Ayaṃ Sa Mantrottamaḥ | Ya Imāṃ Sakṛjjapan Sa Tu Deveśvaraḥ |

Sa Tu Viśveśvaraḥ | Sa Tu Nārīśvaraḥ | Sa Tu Sarvaguruḥ |

Sa Tu Sarvanamasyaḥ | Sa Tu Sarvavedairadhīto Bhavati |

Sa Sarveṣu Tīrtheṣu Snāto Bhavati | Sa Svayaṃ Sadāśivaḥ |

Trikoṇaṃ Trikoṇaṃ Trikoṇaṃ Trikoṇaṃ Punaścaiva Trikoṇaṃ Sāṣṭapatraṃ Sakesaraṃ Bhūpuraikeṇa Saṃyutaṃ Tasmindevīṃ Hṛllekhāmaṅge Vinyasya Dhyāyet |

Abhinavajaladanīlā Kuṭidaṃṣṭrāvarābhayakhaḍgamuṇḍasahitahastā Kālikā Dhyeyā |

Kālī Kapālinī Kullā Kurukullā Virodhinī Vipracitteti Bahiḥ Ṣaṭkoṇagāḥ | Ugrā Ugraprabhā Dīptā Nīlā Ghanā Valākā Mātrā Mudrā Amiteti Navakoṇagāḥ | Brāhmī Nārāyaṇī Māheśvarī Cāmuṇḍā Vārāhī Nārasiṃhī Kaumārī Cāparājitetyaṣṭapatragāḥ |

Catuṣkoṇeṣu Catvāro Mādhavarudravināyakasaurāḥ | Dikṣu Dikpālāḥ | Devīṃ Sarvāṅgeṇādau Sampūjya Bhagodakena Tarpaṇaṃ Pañcamakāreṇa Pūjanametasyāḥ |

Evaṃ Dvitrikrameṇa Kurvāṇā Munayo Bhavanti |

Nārimitrādilakṣaṇamasyavartate |

Amuṣyā Mantrapāṭhakasya Gatirasti | Nānyasyeha Gatirasti |

Etasyāstārāmanordurgāmanossundarīmanorvā Siddhiridānīm |

Sarvāḥ Suptā Bhūtāḥ | Asitāṅgī Jāgarti |

Imāmasitāṅgyupaniṣadaṃ Yo'dhīte Aputrī Putrī Bhavati |

Yo'nyasya Varado Dṛṣṭyā Jaganmohayet |

Gaṅgāditīrthakṣetrāṇāmagniṣṭomādiyajñānāṃ Phalabhāgīyate ||

शान्ति मन्त्रः | *Śānti Mantraḥ* |

ॐ भद्रं कर्णेभिः शृणुयाम देवाः । भद्रं पश्येमाक्षभिर्यजत्राः ।

Oṃ Bhadraṃ Karṇebhiḥ Śṛṇuyāma Devāḥ ||

Bhadraṃ Paśyemākṣabhiryajatrāḥ ||

स्थिरैरङ्गैस्तुष्टुवाँसस्तनूभिः । व्यशेम देवहितं यदायुः ।

Sthirairaṅgaistuṣṭuvāg̃Sastanūbhiḥ || *Vyaśema Devahitaṃ Yadāyuḥ* ||

स्वस्ति न इन्द्रो वृद्धश्रवाः । स्वस्ति नः पूषा विश्ववेदाः ।

Svasti Na Indro Vṛddhaśravāḥ || *Svasti Naḥ Pūṣā Viśvavedāḥ* ||

स्वस्ति नस्तार्क्ष्यो अरिष्टनेमिः । स्वस्ति नो बृहस्पतिर्दधातु ॥

Svasti Nastārkṣyo Ariṣṭanemiḥ || *Svasti No Bṛhaspatirdadhātu* ||

ॐ शान्तिः शान्तिः शान्तिः ॥

Oṃ Śāntiḥ Śāntiḥ Śāntiḥ ||

इत्याथर्वणे सौभाग्यकाण्डे श्यामोपनिषत् समाप्ता ।

Ityātharvaṇe Saubhāgyakāṇḍe
Śyāmopaniṣat Samāptā |

*****

Śrīvidyātārakopaniṣat

श्रीविद्यातारकोपनिषत्

This is also another *Upaniṣat* from *Atharva Veda*.

शान्ति मन्त्रः । *Śānti Mantraḥ* ।

ॐ भद्रं कर्णेभिः शृणुयाम देवाः । भद्रं पश्येमाक्षभिर्यजत्राः ।

Oṃ Bhadraṃ Karṇebhiḥ Śṛṇuyāma Devāḥ ॥

Bhadraṃ Paśyemākṣabhiryajatrāḥ ॥
स्थिरैरङ्गैस्तुष्टुवाँसस्तनूभिः । व्यशेम देवहितं यदायुः ।

Sthirairaṅgaistuṣṭuvāg̐Sastanūbhiḥ ॥ *Vyaśema Devahitaṃ Yadāyuḥ* ॥
स्वस्ति न इन्द्रो वृद्धश्रवाः । स्वस्ति नः पूषा विश्ववेदाः ।

Svasti Na Indro Vṛddhaśravāḥ ॥ *Svasti Naḥ Pūṣā Viśvavedāḥ* ॥
स्वस्ति नस्तार्क्ष्यो अरिष्टनेमिः । स्वस्ति नो बृहस्पतिर्दधातु ॥

Svasti Nastārkṣyo Ariṣṭanemiḥ ॥ *Svasti No Bṛhaspatirdadhātu* ॥
ॐ शान्तिः शान्तिः शान्तिः ॥ *Oṃ Śāntiḥ Śāntiḥ Śāntiḥ* ॥

हरिः ॐ ॥ *Hariḥ Oṃ* ॥

प्रथमः पादः । *Prathamaḥ Pādaḥ* ।

अथैनमगस्त्यः पप्रच्छ हयग्रीवं किं तारकं किं तरति ।
स होवाच हयग्रीवः । तारदीर्घानुलम्बिपूर्वकं प्रथमं खण्डं ततो द्वितीयं खण्डं ततस्तृतीयं खण्डं ततश्चतुर्थं खण्डं ब्रह्मात्मसच्चिदानन्दात्मकमन्त्रमित्युपासितव्यम् ।
अकारः प्रथमकूटाक्षरो भवति । उकारो द्वितीयकूटाक्षरो भवति ।
मकारस्तृतीयकूटाक्षरो भवति । अर्धमातृका चतुर्थकूटाक्षरो भवति ।
बिन्दुः पञ्चमकूटाक्षरो भवति । नादः षष्ठकूटाक्षरो भवति ।
तारकत्वात्तारको भवति । तदेव मन्त्रतारकं भवति ।
तदेव मन्त्रतारकब्रह्म त्वं विद्धि । तदेवोपासितव्यम् ।
गर्भजन्ममरणसंसारमहद्भयात्तं तारयति । तारकमित्येतत्तारकं ब्राह्मणो नित्यं महीयते ।
स पाप्मानं तरति । स मृत्युं तरति ।
स ब्रह्महत्यां तरति । स भ्रूणहत्यां तरति । स वीरहत्यां तरति ।
स सर्वं तरति । स संसारं तरति । सोऽविमुक्तमाश्रितो भवति ॥

Athainamagastyaḥ Papraccha Hayagrīvaṃ Kiṃ Tārakaṃ Kiṃ Tarati |

Sa Hovāca Hayagrīvaḥ |

Tāradīrghānulambipūrvakaṃ Prathamaṃ Khaṇḍaṃ
Tato Dvitīyaṃ Khaṇḍaṃ Tatastṛtīyaṃ Khaṇḍaṃ Tataścaturthaṃ
Khaṇḍaṃ Brahmātmasaccidānandātmakamantramityupāsitavyam |

Akāraḥ Prathamakūṭākṣaro Bhavati | *Ukāro Dvitīyakūṭākṣaro Bhavati* |

Makārastṛtīyakūṭākṣaro Bhavati |

Ardhamātṛkā Caturthakūṭākṣaro Bhavati |

Binduḥ Pañcamakūṭākṣaro Bhavati |

Nādaḥ Ṣaṣṭhakūṭākṣaro Bhavati | *Tārakatvāttārako Bhavati* |

Tadeva Mantratārakaṃ Bhavati |

Tadeva Mantratārakabrahma Tvaṃ Viddhi | *Tadevopāsitavyam* |

Garbhajanmamaraṇasaṃsāramahadbhayāttaṃ Tārayati |

Tārakamityetattārakaṃ Brāhmaṇo Nityaṃ Mahīyate |

Sa Pāpmānaṃ Tarati | *Sa Mṛtyuṃ Tarati* |

Sa Brahmahatyāṃ Tarati | *Sa Bhrūṇahatyāṃ Tarati* |

Sa Vīrahatyāṃ Tarati |

Sa Sarvaṃ Tarati | *Sa Saṃsāraṃ Tarati* | *So'vimuktamāśrito Bhavati* ||

अकाराक्षरसम्भूता वाग्भवा विश्वभाविता । उकाराक्षरसम्भूता तेजसः कामराजका ॥

Akārākṣarasambhūtā Vāgbhavā Viśvabhāvitā |
Ukārākṣarasambhūtā Tejasaḥ Kāmarājakā ||

प्राज्ञो मकारसम्भूता तार्तीया च तृतीयका । अर्धमात्रा षोडशी च ब्रह्मानन्दैकविग्रहा ॥

Prājño Makārasambhūtā Tārtīyā Ca Tṛtīyakā |
Ardhamātrā Ṣoḍaśī Ca Brahmānandaikavigrahā ||

तस्याः सान्निध्यवशतो जगदारन्ददायिनी । उत्पत्तिस्थितिसंहारकारिणी सर्वदेहिनाम् ॥

Tasyāḥ Sānnidhyavaśato Jagadārandadāyinī |
Utpattisthitisaṃhārakāriṇī Sarvadehinām ||

त्रिकूटा भवति ज्ञेया मूलप्रकृतिसङ्गता। प्रकृतिः प्रणवत्वाच्च सा त्रिकूटत्रयात्मिका॥

Trikūṭā Bhavati Jñeyā Mūlaprakṛtisaṅgatā |
Prakṛtiḥ Praṇavatvācca Sā Trikūṭatrayātmikā ||

एवं यच्चान्यत् त्रिकालातीतम्। चतुष्कूटात्मिकैव सर्वकूटात्मिका ब्रह्ममयी। तुर्यात्मब्रह्मा सोऽयमात्मा चतुष्पाज्जगतः स्थानं न बहिःप्रज्ञं नोभयतःप्रज्ञं सप्ताङ्ग एकोनविंशतिमुखः। स्थूलभुग्वैश्वानरात्मिकां कामपीठालयां मित्रेशनाथात्मिकां जाग्रद्दशाधिष्ठायिनीमिच्छाशक्त्यात्मिकां कामेश्वरीं प्रथमकूटां मन्यन्ते॥

Evaṃ Yaccānyat Trikālātītam | Catuṣkūṭātmikaiva Sarvakūṭātmikā Brahmamayī |
Turyātmabrahmā So'yamātmā Catuṣpājjagataḥ Sthānaṃ Na Bahiḥprajñaṃ Nobhayataḥprajñaṃ Saptāṅga Ekonaviṃśatimukhaḥ |
Sthūlabhugvaiśvānarātmikāṃ Kāmapīṭhālayāṃ Mitreśanāthātmikāṃ Jāgraddaśādhiṣṭhāyinīmicchāśaktyātmikāṃ Kāmeśvarīṃ Prathamakūṭāṃ Manyante ||

इति प्रथमः पादः। *Iti Prathamaḥ Pādaḥ |*

द्वितीयः पादः। *Dvitīyaḥ Pādaḥ |*

स्वप्नस्थानेऽनन्तः संज्ञासप्ताङ्ग एकोनविंशतिमुखः प्रविभक्तोऽभूत्। तैजसात्मिकां जालन्धरपीठालयां षष्ठीशनाथात्मिकां वज्रेश्वरीं विष्ण्वात्मिकां क्रियारूपां स्वप्नावस्थानस्थितिरूपामिच्छाशक्तिस्वरूपिणीं द्वितीयकूटां मन्यन्ते॥

Svapnasthāne'nantaḥ Saṃjñāsaptāṅga Ekonaviṃśatimukhaḥ Pravibhakto'bhūt |
Taijasātmikāṃ Jālandharapīṭhālayāṃ Ṣaṣṭhīśanāthātmikāṃ Vajreśvarīṃ Viṣṇvātmikāṃ Kriyārūpāṃ Svapnāvasthānasthitirūpāmicchāśaktisvarūpiṇīṃ Dvitīyakūṭāṃ Manyante ||

इति द्वितीयः पादः। *Iti Dvitīyaḥ Pādaḥ |*

तृतीयः पादः। *Tṛtīyaḥ Pādaḥ |*

यत्र सुप्तो न कञ्चन कामं कामयते तत्सुषुप्तम्।

पश्यन्ति यत् सुषुप्तिस्थान एकीभूतप्रज्ञानघन एवानन्देऽभूत्।
इच्छाशक्तिरूपां स्वप्नावस्थानसुषुप्तिदशाधिष्ठायिनीं सानन्दकलां तृतीयकूटां मन्यन्ते ॥

Yatra Supto Na Kañcana Kāmaṃ Kāmayate Tatsuṣuptam | Paśyanti Yat Suṣuptisthāna Ekībhūtaprajñānaghana Evānande'bhūt | Icchāśaktirūpāṃ Svapnāvasthānasuṣuptidaśādhiṣṭhāyinīṃ Sānandakalāṃ Tṛtīyakūṭāṃ Manyante ||

इति तृतीयः पादः । *Iti Tṛtīyaḥ Pādaḥ* |

चतुर्थः पादः । *Caturthaḥ Pādaḥ* |

एषा सर्वेश्वर्येषा सर्वोत्तमैषान्तर्याम्येषा योनिः सर्वेषां प्रभवाप्ययौ हि भूतानाम्। नोभयतःप्रज्ञा प्रज्ञानघनां न प्रज्ञां ना प्रज्ञा मदृष्टाम व्यवहार्या मग्राह्या मलक्षणा मचिन्त्याम व्यपदेश्या मेकात्म- प्रत्ययसारां प्रपञ्चोपशमनीं शान्तां शिवामद्वैतां षोडशाक्षरीं स्फुरत्तादृशाधिष्ठायिनीं चतुर्थखण्डात्मिकां मन्यन्ते । सात्मा विज्ञेया । सदोज्ज्वलाविद्या । तत्कार्यहीना स्वात्मबन्धहरा सर्वदाद्वैतानन्दरूपा सर्बाधिष्ठानसन्मात्रा निरस्ताविद्यातमोमोहाहमेवेति सम्भाव्याहमों तत्सद्यत् परम्ब्रह्म चतुष्कूटा परञ्ज्योतिस्साहमोमित्यात्मानमादाय मनसा चतुष्कूटामेककार्यां तदा चतुष्कूटाहमिति तत्पराः प्रवदन्ति । येन ते संसारिण आत्मना विरागा एव । न संसारिणः । य एवं वेद स मुक्तो भवति स मुक्तो भवति इत्यगस्त्यः ।

Eṣā Sarveśvaryeṣā Sarvottamaiṣāntaryāmyeṣā Yoniḥ Sarveṣāṃ Prabhavāpyayau Hi Bhūtānām | *Nobhayataḥprajñā Prajñānaghanāṃ Na Prajñāṃ Nāprajñāmadṛṣṭāmavyavahāryāmagrāhyāma Lakṣaṇāmacintyāmavyapadeśyāmekātma-Pratyayasārāṃ Prapañcopaśamanīṃ Śāntāṃ Śivāmadvaitāṃ Ṣoḍaśākṣarīṃ Sphurattādṛśādhiṣṭhāyinīṃ Caturthakhaṇḍātmikāṃ Manyante* | *Sātmā Vijñeyā* | *Sadojjvalāvidyā* | *Tatkāryahīnā Svātmabandhaharā Sarvadādvaitānandarūpā Sarbādhiṣṭhānasanmātrā Nirastāvidyātamomohāhameveti Sambhāvyāhamoṃ Tatsadyat Parambrahma Catuṣkūṭā Parañjyotissāhamomityātmānamādāya Manasā Catuṣkūṭāmekakāryāṃ Tadā Catuṣkūṭāhamiti Tatparāḥ Pravadanti* | *Yena Te Saṃsāriṇa Ātmanā Virāgā Eva* | *Na Saṃsāriṇaḥ* | *Ya Evaṃ Veda Sa Mukto Bhavati Sa MuktoBhavati Ityagastyaḥ* |

इत्युपनिषत्॥ *Ityupaniṣat* ॥

इति चतुर्थः पादः । *Iti Caturthaḥ Pādaḥ* ।

शान्ति मन्त्रः । *Śānti Mantraḥ* ।

ॐ भद्रं कर्णेभिः शृणुयाम देवाः। भद्रं पश्येमाक्षभिर्यजत्राः ।

Oṃ Bhadraṃ Karṇebhiḥ Śṛṇuyāma Devāḥ ॥

Bhadraṃ Paśyemākṣabhiryajatrāḥ ॥
स्थिरैरङ्गैस्तुष्टुवाँसस्तनूभिः । व्यशेम देवहितं यदायुः ।

Sthirairaṅgaistuṣṭuvāg̃Sastanūbhiḥ ॥ *Vyaśema Devahitaṃ Yadāyuḥ* ॥
स्वस्ति न इन्द्रो वृद्धश्रवाः । स्वस्ति नः पूषा विश्ववेदाः ।

Svasti Na Indro Vṛddhaśravāḥ ॥ *Svasti Naḥ Pūṣā Viśvavedāḥ* ॥
स्वस्ति नस्ताक्ष्यों अरिष्टनेमिः । स्वस्ति नो बृहस्पतिर्दधातु ॥

Svasti Nastārkṣyo Ariṣṭanemiḥ ॥ *Svasti No Bṛhaspatirdadhātu* ॥
ॐ शान्तिः शान्तिः शान्तिः ॥ *Oṃ Śāntiḥ Śāntiḥ Śāntiḥ* ॥

इति श्रीविद्यातारकोपनिषत् समाप्ता ।

Iti Śrīvidyātārakopaniṣat Samāptā ।

*****

Ṣoḍhopaniṣat

षोढोपनिषत्

This is also another *Upaniṣat* from *Atharva Veda.*

शान्ति मन्त्रः । *Śānti Mantraḥ* ।

ॐ भद्रं कर्णेभिः शृणुयाम देवाः । भद्रं पश्येमाक्षभिर्यजत्राः ।

Oṃ Bhadraṃ Karṇebhiḥ Śṛṇuyāma Devāḥ ॥

Bhadraṃ Paśyemākṣabhiryajatrāḥ ॥
स्थिरैरङ्गैस्तुष्टुवाँसस्तनूभिः । व्यशेम देवहितं यदायुः ।

Sthirairaṅgaistuṣṭuvāg̃Sastanūbhiḥ ॥ *Vyaśema Devahitaṃ Yadāyuḥ* ॥
स्वस्ति न इन्द्रो वृद्धश्रवाः । स्वस्ति नः पूषा विश्ववेदाः ।

Svasti Na Indro Vṛddhaśravāḥ ॥ *Svasti Naḥ Pūṣā Viśvavedāḥ* ॥
स्वस्ति नस्तार्क्ष्यो अरिष्टनेमिः । स्वस्ति नो बृहस्पतिर्दधातु ॥

Svasti Nastārkṣyo Ariṣṭanemiḥ ॥ *Svasti No Bṛhaspatirdadhātu* ॥
ॐ शान्तिः शान्तिः शान्तिः ॥ *Oṃ Śāntiḥ Śāntiḥ Śāntiḥ* ॥

हरिः ॐ ॥ *Hariḥ Oṃ* ॥

अथाह वै श्म शवः शानं शयनं शवानां शयनं श्मशानं तदधिष्ठानो महाकालस्तत्पर्यङ्क समासीनां विश्वव्यापकरूपिणीं कालीं कालादिसन्त्रासात् कालीं चतुर्युगाधिष्ठात्रीं स्वस्मिन् भाव्य षोढां न्यसेत्। स्थानशुद्धिन्यासं विधाय षोढां न्यसेत्।
अथ षोढान्यासी षट्कालित्वं गच्छति।
सेयं षट्कला परा परात्परा परात्परातीता चित्परा चित्परात्परा चित्परात्परातीता।
षण्णां योगे षोढा भवेत्। वैष्णवकलायुक्तां मातृकायुक्तां वैष्णवीं न्यसेदिति प्रथमः।
स परारूपो भवेत्। स भूमिं जयति। स शक्तिरूपो भवेत्।
अथ वै कामकलापुटितां श्रीकलां श्रीकलापुटितां कामकलां लिपिस्थाने न्यसेत्।
द्वितीयारूपो भवेत्। सोऽमृतत्वं गच्छति।
स जलं तरतीति यज्ञे गीर्णं भवति।
आदिकलापुटितां श्रीकलां श्रीकलापुटितामादिकलां मातृस्थाने न्यसेत्।
स सिद्धीश्वरो भवेत्। स वह्निं जयति। दिवारात्रिव्यापी भवेत्।
कूर्चं चन्द्रं कूर्चं चन्द्रमन्तर्दृष्टिमद्दीपनमन्त्रं राज्ञीपुटितमेतेन पुटितां राज्ञीं न्यसेत्।

स खेचरो भवेत्। स वायुपुरगामी भवेत्। स कलावान् भवेत्।
चतुर्थीरूपो भवेत्। अनुलोमविलोमेन मूलमन्त्रं केवलं न्यसेत्।
विद्यान्यासरूपो भवेत्। सर्वं जयति। स पञ्चमीरूपो भवेत्।
स चाकाशं जयति। अष्टोत्तरशतानुलोमविलोमाकृतिक्रमेण देवतां व्यापयेत्।
स ध्वनिरूपो भवेत्। सर्वं जयति। सर्वं जरति।
महापातकोपपातकानि तरति। वयःस्थैर्यकरो भवेत्।
अष्टसिद्धिदाता भवेत्। तद्दर्शनेन देवत्वं भवेत्। षष्ठीकलावान् भवेत्।
विश्वरूपो भवेत्। यं पश्यति तं शिवं कुरुते।
नमस्कारान्मूर्तिस्फोटो भवेत्। स गारूपनाशको भवेत्। स महेन्द्रजालदर्शको भवेत्।
तद्दर्शनात् सिद्धीश्वरो भवेत्। पुटिति छिन्नाकल्पामुग्रायामङ्गषोढां न्यसेत्।
तत्स्पर्शादष्टलोहस्पर्शो भवेत्।
शक्तिकुण्डे जिह्वां नाडीं वा न्यस्य यो जपेत् स कालीरूपो भवेत्।

Athāha Vai Śma Śavaḥ Śānaṃ Śayanaṃ Śavānāṃ Śayanaṃ Śmaśānaṃ Tadadhiṣṭhāno Mahākālastatparyaṅkasamāsīnāṃ Viśvavyāpakarūpiṇīṃ Kālīṃ Kālādisantrāsāt Kālīṃ Caturyugādhiṣṭhātrīṃ Svasmin Bhāvya Ṣoḍhāṃ Nyaset | Sthānaśuddhinyāsaṃ Vidhāya Ṣoḍhāṃ Nyaset |

Atha Ṣoḍhānyāsī Ṣaṭkālitvaṃ Gacchati | Seyaṃ Ṣaṭkalā Parā Parātparā Parātparātītā Citparā Citparātparā Citparātparātītā |

Ṣaṇṇāṃ Yoge Ṣoḍhā Bhavet | Vaiṣṇavakalāyuktāṃ Mātṛkāyuktāṃ Vaiṣṇavīṃ Nyaseditі Prathamaḥ | Sa Parārūpo Bhavet |

Sa Bhūmiṃ Jayati | Sa Śaktirūpo Bhavet |

Atha Vai Kāmakalāpuṭitāṃ Śrīkalāṃ Śrīkalāpuṭitāṃ Kāmakalāṃ Lipisthāne Nyaset | Dvitīyārūpo Bhavet | So'mṛtatvaṃ Gacchati |

Sa Jalaṃ Taratīti Yajñe Gīrṇaṃ Bhavati | Ādikalāpuṭitāṃ Śrīkalāṃ Śrīkalāpuṭitāmādikalāṃ Mātṛsthāne Nyaset | Sa Siddhīśvaro Bhavet |

Sa Vahniṃ Jayati | Divārātrivyāpī Bhavet |

Kūrcaṃ Candraṃ Kūrcaṃ Candramantardṛṣṭimaddīpanamantraṃ Rājñīpuṭitametena Puṭitāṃ Rājñīṃ Nyaset | Sa Khecaro Bhavet |

Sa Vāyupuragāmī Bhavet | Sa Kalāvān Bhavet | Caturthīrūpo Bhavet |

Anulomavilomena Mūlamantraṃ Kevalaṃ Nyaset |

Vidyānyāsarūpo Bhavet | Sarvaṃ Jayati | Sa Pañcamīrūpo Bhavet |

Sa Cākāśaṃ Jayati |

Aṣṭottaraśatānulomavilomākṛtikrameṇa Devatāṃ Vyāpayet |

Sa Dhvanirūpo Bhavet | Sarvaṃ Jayati | Sarvaṃ Jarati |

Mahāpātakopapātakāni Tarati | Vayaḥsthairyakaro Bhavet |

Aṣṭasiddhidātā Bhavet | Taddarśanena Devatvaṃ Bhavet |

Ṣaṣṭhīkalāvān Bhavet | Viśvarūpo Bhavet |

Yaṃ Paśyati Taṃ Śivaṃ Kurute |

Namaskārānmūrtisphoṭo Bhavet | Sa Gārūpanāśako Bhavet |

Sa Mahendrajāladarśako Bhavet | Taddarśanāt Siddhīśvaro Bhavet |

Puṭiti Chinnākalpāmugrāyāmaṅgaṣoḍhāṃ Nyaset |

Tatsparśādaṣṭalohasparśo Bhavet |

Śaktikuṇḍe Jihvāṃ Nāḍīṃ Vā Nyasya Yo Japet Sa Kālīrūpo Bhavet ||

इति शिवम् || *Iti Śivam ||*

शान्ति मन्त्रः | *Śānti Mantraḥ* |

ॐ भद्रं कर्णेभिः शृणुयाम देवाः ।

भद्रं पश्येमाक्षभिर्यजत्राः ।

Oṃ Bhadraṃ Karṇebhiḥ Śṛṇuyāma Devāḥ ||

Bhadraṃ Paśyemākṣabhiryajatrāḥ ||

स्थिरैरङ्गैस्तुष्टुवाँसस्तनूभिः । व्यशेम देवहितं यदायुः ।

Sthirairaṅgaistuṣṭuvāg̃Sastanūbhiḥ || Vyaśema Devahitaṃ Yadāyuḥ ||

स्वस्ति न इन्द्रो वृद्धश्रवाः । स्वस्ति नः पूषा विश्ववेदाः ।

Svasti Na Indro Vṛddhaśravāḥ || Svasti Naḥ Pūṣā Viśvavedāḥ ||

स्वस्ति नस्ताक्ष्र्यो अरिष्टनेमिः । स्वस्ति नो बृहस्पतिर्दधातु ॥

Svasti Nastārkṣyo Ariṣṭanemiḥ || Svasti No Bṛhaspatirdadhātu ||

ॐ शान्तिः शान्तिः शान्तिः || *Oṃ Śāntiḥ Śāntiḥ Śāntiḥ ||*

इत्याथर्वणे सौभाग्यकाण्डे षोढोपनिषत् समाप्ता ।

Ityātharvaṇe Saubhāgyakāṇḍe Ṣoḍhopaniṣat Samāptā |

Sāvitryupaniṣat

सावित्र्युपनिषत्

This is also another *Upaniṣat* from *Atharva Veda.*

शान्ति मन्त्र: । *Śānti Mantraḥ* ।

ॐ सावित्र्युपनिषद्वेद्यचित्सावित्रपदोज्ज्वलम् । प्रतियोगिविनिर्मुक्तं रामचन्द्रपदं भजे ॥
सावित्र्यात्मा पाशुपतं परं ब्रह्मावधूतकम् । त्रिपुरातपनं देवीत्रिपुरा कठभावना ॥
ॐ आप्यायन्तु ममाङ्गानि वाक्प्राणश्चक्षु : श्रोत्रमथो बलमिन्द्रियाणि च ।
सर्वाणि सर्वं ब्रह्मोपनिषदं माहं ब्रह्म निराकुर्यां मा मा ब्रह्म
निराकरोदनिराकरणमस्त्वनिराकरणं मेऽस्तु ।
तदात्मनि निरते य उपनिषत्सु धर्मास्ते मयि सन्तु ते मयि सन्तु ॥

Sāvitryupaniṣadvedyacitsāvitrapadojjvalam ।

Pratiyogivinirmuktaṃ Rāmacandrapadaṃ Bhaje ।।

Sāvitryātmā Pāśupataṃ Paraṃ Brahmāvadhūtakam ।

Tripurātapanaṃ Devītripurā Kaṭhabhāvanā ।।

Oṃ Āpyāyantu Mamāṅgāni Vākprāṇaścakṣuḥ Śrotramatho Balamindriyāṇi Ca । *Sarvāṇi Sarvaṃ Brahmopaniṣadaṃ Māhaṃ Brahma Nirākuryāṃ Mā Mā Brahma Nirākarodanirākaraṇamastva Nirākaraṇaṃ Me'stu* । *Tadātmani Nirate Ya Upaniṣatsu Dharmāste Mayi Santu Te Mayi Santu* ॥

ॐ शान्तिः शान्तिः शान्तिः ॥ *Oṃ Śāntiḥ Śāntiḥ Śāntiḥ* ॥

हरिः ॐ ॥ *Hariḥ Oṃ* ॥

1. कः सविता का सावित्री अग्निरेव सविता पृथिवी सावित्री स यत्राग्निस्तत्पृथिवी यत्र वै पृथिवी तत्राग्निस्ते द्वे योनी तदेकं मिथुनम् ॥

Kaḥ Savitā Kā Sāvitrī Agnireva Savitā Pṛthivī Sāvitrī Sa Yatrāgnistatpṛthivī Yatra Vai Pṛthivī Tatrāgniste Dve Yonī Tadekaṃ Mithunam ॥

2. कः सविता का सवित्री वरुण एव सवितापः सावित्री स यत्र वरुणस्तदापो यत्र वा आपस्तद्वरुणस्ते द्वे योनिस्तदेकं मिथुनम् ॥

Kaḥ Savitā Kā Savitrī Varuṇa Eva Savitāpaḥ Sāvitrī Sa Yatra Varuṇastadāpo Yatra Vā Āpastadvaruṇaste Dve Yonistadekaṃ Mithunam ॥

3. कः सविता का सावित्री वायुरेव सविताकाशः सावित्री स यत्र वायुस्तदाकाशो यत्र वा आकाशस्तद्वायुस्ते द्वे योनिस्तदेकं मिथुनम् ॥

Kaḥ Savitā Kā Sāvitrī Vāyureva Savitākāśaḥ Sāvitrī Sa Yatra Vāyustadākāśo Yatra Vā Ākāśastadvāyuste Dve Yonistadekaṃ Mithunam ॥

4. कः सविता का सावित्री यज्ञ एव सविता छन्दांसि सावित्री स यत्र यज्ञस्तत्र छन्दांसि यत्र वा छन्दांसि स यज्ञस्ते द्वे योनिस्तदेकं मिथुनम् ॥

Kaḥ Savitā Kā Sāvitrī Yajña Eva Savitā Chandāṃsi Sāvitrī Sa Yatra Yajñastatra Chandāṃsi Yatra Vā Chandāṃsi Sa Yajñaste Dve Yonistadekaṃ Mithunam ॥

5. कः सविता का सावित्री स्तनयित्नुरेव सविता विद्युत्सावित्री स यत्र स्तनयित्नुस्तद्विद्युत् यत्र वा विद्युत्तत्र स्तनयित्नुस्ते द्वे योनिस्तदेकं मिथुनम् ॥

Kaḥ Savitā Kā Sāvitrī Stanayitrureva Savitā Vidyutsāvitrī Sa Yatra Stanayitrustadvidyut Yatra Vā Vidyuttatra Stanayitruste Dve Yonistadekaṃ Mithunam ॥

6. कः सविता का सावित्री आदित्य एव सविता द्यौः सावित्री स यत्रादित्यस्तद्द्यौर्यत्र वा द्यौस्तदादित्यस्ते द्वे योनिस्तदेकं मिथुनम् ॥

Kaḥ Savitā Kā Sāvitrī Āditya Eva Savitā Dyauḥ Sāvitrī Sa Yatrādityastaddyauryatra Vā Dyaustadādityaste Dve Yonistadekaṃ Mithunam ॥

7. कः सविता का सावित्री चन्द्र एव सविता नक्षत्राणि सावित्री स यत्र चन्द्रस्तन्नक्षत्राणि यत्र वा नक्षत्राणे स चन्द्रमास्ते द्वे योनिस्तदेकं मिथुनम् ॥ ७॥

Kaḥ Savitā Kā Sāvitrī Candra Eva Savitā Nakṣatrāṇi Sāvitrī Sa Yatra Candrastannakṣatrāṇi Yatra Vā Nakṣatrāṇe Sa Candramāste Dve Yonistadekaṃ Mithunam ॥

8. कः सविता का सावित्री मन एव सविता वाक् सावित्री स यत्र वा मनस्तद्वाक् यत्र वा वाक् तन्मनस्ते द्वे योनिस्तदेकं मिथुनम् ॥

Kaḥ Savitā Kā Sāvitrī Mana Eva Savitā Vāk Sāvitrī Sa Yatra Vā Manastadvāk Yatra Vā Vāk Tanmanaste Dve Yonistadekaṃ Mithunam ॥

9. कः सविता का सावित्री पुरुष एव सविता स्त्री सावित्री स यत्र पुरुषस्तत्स्त्री यत्र वा स्त्री स पुरुषस्ते द्वे योनिस्तदेकं मिथुनम् ॥

Kaḥ Savitā Kā Sāvitrī Puruṣa Eva Savitā Strī Sāvitrī Sa Yatra Puruṣastatstrī Yatra Vā Strī Sa Puruṣaste Dve Yonistadekaṃ Mithunam ॥

10. सावित्र्याः पादत्रयम् तस्या एव (एष) प्रथमः पादो भूस्तत्सवितुवरेण्यमित्यग्निर्वै वरेण्यमापो वरेण्यं चन्द्रमा वरेण्यम् ॥

Sāvitryāḥ Pādatrayam Tasyā Eva (Eṣa) Prathamaḥ Pādo Bhūstat Savitur Vareṇyamityagnirvai Vareṇyamāpo Vareṇyaṃ Candramā Vareṇyam ॥

11. तस्या एव (एष) द्वितीयः पादो भर्गमयोऽपि भुवो भर्गो देवस्य धीमहीत्यग्निर्वै भर्ग आदित्यो वै भर्गश्चन्द्रमा वै भर्गः ॥

Tasyā Eva (Eṣa) Dvitīyaḥ Pādo Bhargamayo'pi Bhuvo Bhargo Devasya Dhīmahītyagnirvai Bharga Ādityo Vai Bhargaścandramā Vai Bhargaḥ ॥

12. तस्या एष तृतीयः पादः स्वर्धियो यो नः प्रचोदयादिति स्त्री चैव पुरुषश्च प्रजनयतः ॥

Tasyā Eṣa Tṛtīyaḥ Pādaḥ Svardhiyo Yo Naḥ Pracodayāditi Strī Caiva Puruṣaśca Prajanayataḥ ॥

13. सावित्रीवेदनफलं पुनर्मृत्युञ्जयः यो वा एतां सावित्रीमेवं वेद स पुनर्मृत्युं जयति ॥

Sāvitrīvedanaphalaṃ Punarmṛtyuñjayaḥ Yo Vā Etāṃ Sāvitrīmevaṃ Veda Sa Punarmṛtyuṃ Jayati ॥

बलातिबलयोर्विराट् पुरुष ऋषिः । गायत्री छन्दः । गायत्री देवता । अकारोकारमकारा बीजाद्याः । क्षु धाऽऽदिनिरसने विनियोगः । क्लामित्यादिषडङ्गम् (षडङ्गन्यासः) ।

Balātibalayorvirāṭ Puruṣa Ṛṣiḥ । Gāyatrī Chandaḥ । Gāyatrī Devatā । Akārokāramakārā Bījādyāḥ । Kṣudhā''dinirasane Viniyogaḥ । Klāmityādiṣaḍaṅgam (Ṣaḍaṅganyāsaḥ) ।

ध्यानम् । *Dhyānam* ।

14. अमृतकरतलाग्रौ (तलार्द्रौ) सर्वसंजीवनाढ्या वघहरणसुदक्षौ वेदसारे मयूखे।
प्रणवमयविकारौ भास्कराकारदेहौ सततमनूभवेऽहं तौ बलातिबलान्तौ ॥ var बलाती
Amṛtakaratalāgrau (Talārdrau) Sarvasaṃjīvanāḍhyā-
Vaghaharaṇasudakṣau Vedasāre Mayūkhe ।
Praṇavamayavikārau Bhāskarākāradehau
Satatamanūbhave'haṃ Tau Balātibalāntau ॥ Var Balātī

ह्रीं वरेण्यं भर्गो देवस्य वरदात्मिके अतिबले सर्वदयामूर्ते
ॐ ह्रीं बले महादेवि ह्रीं महाबले क्लीं चतुर्विधपुरुषार्थसिद्धिप्रदे तत्सवितुर्वरदात्मिके
बले सर्वक्षुच्छ्रमोपनाशिनि धीमहि धियो यो नर्जाते प्रचुर्या
(var बले सर्वक्षुद्भ्रमोपनाशिनि धीमहि धियो यो नर्जाते प्रचुर्यः)
या प्रचोदयादात्मिके प्रणवशिरस्कात्मिके हुं फट् स्वाहा ॥
Oṃ Hrīṃ Bale Mahādevi Hrīṃ Mahābale Klīṃ
Caturvidhapuruṣārthasiddhiprade Tatsaviturvaradātmike
Hrīṃ Vareṇyaṃ Bhargo Devasya Varadātmike Atibale Sarvadayāmūrte
Bale Sarvakṣucchramopanāśini Dhīmahi Dhiyo Yo Narjāte Pracuryā
(Var Bale Sarvakṣudbhramopanāśini Dhīmahi Dhiyo Yo Narjāte
Pracuryaḥ) Yā Pracodayādātmike Praṇavaśiraskātmike
Huṃ Phaṭ Svāhā ॥

15. विद्याफलम् एवं विद्वान् कृतकृत्यो भवति सावित्र्या एव सलोकतां जयतीत्युपनिषत्॥
Vidyāphalam Evaṃ Vidvān Kṛtakṛtyo Bhavati Sāvitryā Eva Salokatāṃ Jayatītyupaniṣat ॥

16. ॐ आप्यायन्तु ममाङ्गानि वाक्प्राणश्चक्षुः श्रोत्रमथो बलमिन्द्रियाणि च ।
सर्वाणि सर्वं ब्रह्मोपनिषदं माहं ब्रह्म निराकुर्यां मा मा ब्रह्म
निराकरोदनिराकरणमस्त्वनिराकरणं मेऽस्तु ।
तदात्मनि निरते य उपनिषत्सु धर्मास्ते मयि सन्तु ते मयि सन्तु ॥

Oṃ Āpyāyantu Mamāṅgāni Vākprāṇaścakṣuḥ Śrotramatho Balamindriyāṇi Ca ।
Sarvāṇi Sarvaṃ Brahmopaniṣadaṃ Māhaṃ Brahma Nirākuryāṃ Mā Mā Brahma Nirākarodanirākaraṇamastvanirākaraṇaṃ Me'stu ।
Tadātmani Nirate Ya Upaniṣatsu Dharmāste Mayi Santu Te Mayi Santu ॥

शान्ति मन्त्रः । *Śānti Mantraḥ* ।

ॐ सावित्र्युपनिषद्वेद्यचित्सावित्रपदोज्ज्वलम् । प्रतियोगिविनिर्मुक्तं रामचन्द्रपदं भजे ॥
सावित्र्यात्मा पाशुपतं परं ब्रह्मावधूतकम् । त्रिपुरातपनं देवीत्रिपुरा कठभावना ॥
ॐ आप्यायन्तु ममाङ्गानि वाक्प्राणश्चक्षुः श्रोत्रमथो बलमिन्द्रियाणि च ।
सर्वाणि सर्वं ब्रह्मोपनिषदं माहं ब्रह्म निराकुर्यां मा मा ब्रह्म
निराकरोदनिराकरणमस्त्वनिराकरणं मेऽस्तु ।
तदात्मनि निरते य उपनिषत्सु धर्मास्ते मयि सन्तु ते मयि सन्तु ॥

Sāvitryupaniṣadvedyacitsāvitrapadojjvalam ।
Pratiyogivinirmuktaṃ Rāmacandrapadaṃ Bhaje ॥

Sāvitryātmā Pāśupataṃ Paraṃ Brahmāvadhūtakam ।
Tripurātapanaṃ Devītripurā Kaṭhabhāvanā ॥

Oṃ Āpyāyantu Mamāṅgāni Vākprāṇaścakṣuḥ Śrotramatho Balamindriyāṇi Ca । Sarvāṇi Sarvaṃ Brahmopaniṣadaṃ Māhaṃ Brahma Nirākuryāṃ Mā Mā Brahma Nirākarodanirākaraṇamastva Nirākaraṇaṃ Me'stu । Tadātmani Nirate Ya Upaniṣatsu Dharmāste Mayi Santu Te Mayi Santu ॥

ॐ शान्तिः शान्तिः शान्तिः ॥ *Oṃ Śāntiḥ Śāntiḥ Śāntiḥ* ॥

॥ इति सावित्र्युपनिषत्समाप्ता ॥ *Iti Sāvitryupaniṣatsamāptā* ॥

*****

Sumukhyupāniṣat

सुमुख्युपानिषत्

This is also another *Upaniṣat* from *Atharva Veda*.

शान्ति मन्त्रः । *Śānti Mantraḥ* ।

ॐ भद्रं कर्णेभिः शृणुयाम देवाः । भद्रं पश्येमाक्षभिर्यजत्राः ।

Oṃ Bhadraṃ Karṇebhiḥ Śṛṇuyāma Devāḥ ॥

Bhadraṃ Paśyemākṣabhiryajatrāḥ ॥
स्थिरैरङ्गैस्तुष्टुवाँसस्तनूभिः । व्यशेम देवहितं यदायुः ।

SthirairaṅgaistuṣṭuvāṁSastanūbhiḥ ॥ *Vyaśema Devahitaṃ Yadāyuḥ* ॥
स्वस्ति न इन्द्रो वृद्धश्रवाः । स्वस्ति नः पूषा विश्ववेदाः ।

Svasti Na Indro Vṛddhaśravāḥ ॥ *Svasti Naḥ Pūṣā Viśvavedāḥ* ॥
स्वस्ति नस्तार्क्ष्यो अरिष्टनेमिः । स्वस्ति नो बृहस्पतिर्दधातु ॥

Svasti Nastārkṣyo Ariṣṭanemiḥ ॥ *Svasti No Bṛhaspatirdadhātu* ॥
ॐ शान्तिः शान्तिः शान्तिः ॥ *Oṃ Śāntiḥ Śāntiḥ Śāntiḥ* ॥

हरिः ॐ ॥ *Hariḥ Oṃ* ॥

अथैनामावाहयाम्यनवद्यां शवाधिरूढां रक्तवस्त्रालङ्कारयुक्तां रक्तपीठोपविष्टां गुञ्जाहारविभूषितहृदयां षोडशसमासमाकारां युवतीं पीनोन्नतघनस्तनीं स्वहृदये चिन्तयित्वोच्छिष्टपदमाभाष्य चण्डालिनीमभिमतां सुमुखीं तदन्ते देवीं चोक्त्वा महापिशाचिनीं तस्माद्धरामग्निमायां बिन्दुमौलिनीं समुच्चार्य ठान्तत्रयं सविसर्गं समुद्धृत्यदेवीं हृदये विभाव्य ईङ्कारस्वरूपं सबिन्दुमुखं युग्मस्तनपदान्तं भावयित्वा यन्त्रं योनिं तदुपरि शिववक्त्रयोनिमष्टपत्रं षोडशाब्जकं वृत्तमेकं चतुरश्रं यन्त्रराजं विचिन्त्यादौ देवीमावाह्य बिन्दौ गन्धाक्षतपुष्पधूपदीपान् संस्कृतान्नं नानाविधं निवेद्याद्यं पलं मीनाद्यन्नं मूलेन मूलां सन्तर्प्य संस्कृतां पुरस्कृतां योनिं देवतायै निवेदयेत् ।

Athaināmāvāhayāmyanavadyāṃ Śavādhirūḍhāṃ Raktavastrālaṅkārayuktāṃ Raktapīṭhopaviṣṭāṃ Guñjāhāravibhūṣitahṛdayāṃ Ṣoḍaśasamāsamākārāṃ Yuvatīṃ Pīnonnataghanastanīṃ Svahṛdaye Cintayitvocchiṣṭapadamābhāṣya Caṇḍālinīmabhimatāṃ Sumukhīṃ Tadante Devīṃ Coktvā Mahāpiśācinīṃ Tasmāddharāmagnimāyāṃ Bindumaulinīṃ

Samuccārya Ṭhāntatrayaṃ Savisargaṃ Samuddhṛtya Devīṃ Hṛdaye Vibhāvya Īṅkārasvarūpaṃ Sabindumukhaṃ Yugmastanapadāntaṃ Bhāvayitvā Yantraṃ Yoniṃ Tadupari Śivavaktrayonimaṣṭapatraṃ Ṣoḍaśābjakaṃ Vṛttamekaṃ Caturaśraṃ Yantrarājaṃ Vicintyādau Devīmāvāhya Bindau Gandhākṣatapuṣpadhūpadīpān Saṃskṛtānnaṃ Nānāvidhaṃ Nivedyādyaṃ Palaṃ Mīnādyannaṃ Mūlena Mūlāṃ Santarpya Saṃskṛtāṃ Puraskṛtāṃ Yoniṃ Devatāyai Nivedayet I

सुकृती चतुरश्रान् देवानिन्द्राग्नियमनिरृतिवरुणवायुकुबेरेशानान् वामावर्तेन सम्पूज्य षोडशाब्जके कलावती कपालिनी कल्याणी नित्या कमला क्रिया कृपा आकुला कुलीना कुमारी कुण्डला आकरा किशोरी कोमला कल्पा कुमुदा एताः पूजयेत्।

Sukṛtī Caturaśrān Devānindrāgniyamanirṛtivaruṇavāyukubereśānān Vāmāvartena Sampūjya Ṣoḍaśābjake Kalāvatī Kapālinī Kalyāṇī Nityā Kamalā Kriyā Kṛpā Ākulā Kulīnā Kumārī Kuṇḍalā Ākarā Kiśorī Komalā Kalpā Kumudā Etāḥ Pūjayet I

अष्टाब्जे ब्राह्मी माहेश्वरी कौमारी वैष्णवी वाराही इन्द्राणी चामुण्डा महालक्ष्मीः।

Aṣṭābje Brāhmī Māheśvarī Kaumārī Vaiṣṇavī Vārāhī Indrāṇī Cāmuṇḍā Mahālakṣmīḥ I

ततो योनिपञ्चके चन्द्रा चन्द्रानना चारुमुखी चामीकरप्रभा चतुरा।

Tato Yonipañcake Candrā Candrānanā Cārumukhī Cāmīkaraprabhā Caturā I

ततो योनौ वामा ज्येष्ठा रौद्री। तदन्ते रतिप्रीतिमनोभवाः पूज्याः।

Tato Yonau Vāmā Jyeṣṭhā Raudrī I
Tadante Ratiprītimanobhavāḥ Pūjyāḥ I

प्रान्ते पूजां सन्तर्प्य पुनर्नैवेद्यं बहुगुणं निवेद्यारात्रिकं निवेद्य परां पूजयन् महाछत्रचामरादिसर्वदेवैर्नमस्कृतामाद्यशक्तिमष्टजातीयां स्वयं भैरवो भूत्वा कुलाकुलामृतैर्देवीं सन्तर्प्य स्वहृदये तां परां विसृज्य सुखेनैव शिवशक्त्यात्मको भावयन् विहरेत्।

Prānte Pūjāṃ Santarpya Punarnaivedyaṃ Bahuguṇaṃ Nivedyārātrikaṃ Nivedya Parāṃ Pūjayan Mahāchatracāmarādisarvadevairnamaskṛtāmādyaśaktimaṣṭajātīyāṃ Svayaṃ Bhairavo Bhūtvā Kulākulāmṛtairdevīṃ Santarpya Svahṛdaye

Tāṃ Parāṃ Visṛjya Sukhenaiva Śivaśaktyātmako Bhāvayan Viharet ।

स सिद्धीश्वरो भवेत् । स सर्वेश्वरो भवेत् । स लोकाध्यक्षो भवेत् । भवो भूत्वा विभावयति ॥

Sa Siddhīśvaro Bhavet । *Sa Sarveśvaro Bhavet* । *Sa Lokādhyakṣo Bhavet* । *Bhavo Bhūtvā Vibhāvayati* ॥

शान्ति मन्त्रः । *Śānti Mantraḥ* ।

ॐ भद्रं कर्णेभिः शृणुयाम देवाः । भद्रं पश्येमाक्षभिर्यजत्राः ।

Oṃ Bhadraṃ Karṇebhiḥ Śṛṇuyāma Devāḥ ॥

Bhadraṃ Paśyemākṣabhiryajatrāḥ ॥

स्थिरैरङ्गैस्तुष्टुवाँसस्तनूभिः । व्यशेम देवहितं यदायुः ।

SthirairaṅgaistuṣṭuvāgͫSastanūbhiḥ ॥ *Vyaśema Devahitaṃ Yadāyuḥ* ॥

स्वस्ति न इन्द्रो वृद्धश्रवाः । स्वस्ति नः पूषा विश्ववेदाः ।

Svasti Na Indro Vṛddhaśravāḥ ॥ *Svasti Naḥ Pūṣā Viśvavedāḥ* ॥

स्वस्ति नस्ताक्ष्यों अरिष्टनेमिः । स्वस्ति नो बृहस्पतिर्दधातु ॥

Svasti Nastārkṣyo Ariṣṭanemiḥ ॥ *Svasti No Bṛhaspatirdadhātu* ॥

ॐ शान्तिः शान्तिः शान्तिः ॥ *Oṃ Śāntiḥ Śāntiḥ Śāntiḥ* ॥

इत्याथर्वणे सौभाग्यकण्डे सुमुख्युपनिषत्समाप्ता ।

Ityātharvaṇe Saubhāgyakaṇḍe Sumukhyupaniṣat Samāptā ।

*****

Haṃsaṣoḍhopaniṣat

हंसषोढोपनिषत्

This is also another *Upaniṣat* from *Atharva Veda.*

शान्ति मन्त्रः । *Śānti Mantraḥ* ।

ॐ भद्रं कर्णेभिः शृणुयाम देवाः । भद्रंपश्येमाक्षभिर्यजत्राः ।

Oṃ Bhadraṃ Karṇebhiḥ Śṛṇuyāma Devāḥ ॥

Bhadraṃ Paśyemākṣabhiryajatrāḥ ॥
स्थिरैरङ्गैस्तुष्टुवाँसस्तनूभिः । व्यशेम देवहितं यदायुः ।

Sthirairaṅgaistuṣṭuvāg̃Sastanūbhiḥ ॥ *Vyaśema Devahitaṃ Yadāyuḥ* ॥
स्वस्ति न इन्द्रो वृद्धश्रवाः । स्वस्ति नः पूषा विश्ववेदाः ।

Svasti Na Indro Vṛddhaśravāḥ ॥ *Svasti Naḥ Pūṣā Viśvavedāḥ* ॥
स्वस्ति नस्तार्क्ष्यो अरिष्टनेमिः । स्वस्ति नो बृहस्पतिर्दधातु ॥

Svasti Nastārkṣyo Ariṣṭanemiḥ ॥ *Svasti No Bṛhaspatirdadhātu* ॥
ॐ शान्तिः शान्तिः शान्तिः ॥ *Oṃ Śāntiḥ Śāntiḥ Śāntiḥ* ॥

हरिः ॐ ॥ *Hariḥ Oṃ* ॥

अथाह वै हंसषोढान्यासी शिवो भवेत् । सर्वसिद्धीश्वरो भवेत् ।
एतत्फलं वक्तुं सदाशिवोऽपि न समर्थः । षोढान्यासस्य विरूपाक्षमहाकाल ऋषिः ।
अनुष्टुप् छन्दः । काली देवता । कालीदेहार्थे विनियोगः । हंसेनाङ्गषट्कम् ।
स निर्वाणरूपो भवेत् ।

Athāha Vai Haṃsaṣoḍhānyāsī Śivo Bhavet । *Sarvasiddhīśvaro Bhavet* ।

Etatphalaṃ Vaktuṃ Sadāśivo'pi Na Samarthaḥ । *Ṣoḍhānyāsasya*

Virūpākṣamahākāla Ṛṣiḥ । *Anuṣṭup Chandaḥ* । *Kālī Devatā* ।

Kālīdehārthe Viniyogaḥ । *Haṃsenāṅgaṣaṭkam* ।

Sa Nirvāṇarūpo Bhavet ।

हंसः कं खं गं घं ङं महामुण्डमालाधारिणि महाकालप्रिये मां रक्ष रक्ष ।
षट्चक्रवासिनि वागीश्वरि जिह्वाग्रे वस । हं नमः शिरसि प्रोतं वेद शिवो भवेत् ।

हंसः चं छं जं झं ञं महात्रिपुरभैरवि पुस्तकाक्षमालाधारिणि शत्रुमुखस्तम्भनं कुरु कुरु स्वाहेति महापद्मे ।

हंसः टं ठं डं ढं णं डां डीं डं डाकिनि मां रक्ष रक्ष स्वाहेत्यनाहते न्यसेत् ।

तृतीयारूपो भवेत् । हंसः तं थं दं धं नं महामारि मारहारिणि हुं हुं दारिद्र्यं हर हर स्वाहा ।

गुं न्यसेत् । स ब्रह्मकालीत्वं गच्छति । चतुर्थत्वं गच्छति ।

हंसः पं फं बं भं मं मार्जारि वीरावलि ममालस्यं नाशय नाशय ।

हंसः यं रं लं वं शं षं सं हं लम्बोदरि मातर्महामङ्गलप्रिये मम जाड्यं छेदय छेदय ।

भ्रंश भ्रंश । भगवति मां रक्ष रक्ष ।

भुवनधारिणि मां धारय धारय । स्वाहापदद्वयं न्यस्य शिवो भवेत् ।

अथ वै षष्ठीं न्यसेत् ।

हंसः लं क्षं महालक्ष्मि राजराजेश्वरि महाकालप्रिये कालखण्डिनि खण्डिनि खण्डय खण्डय खां खीं खूं खैं खों खौं खः खनित्रि समे स्वाहेति सर्वाङ्गे न्यसेत् ।

हंसः पञ्चाशत् व्यापकं कुर्यात् । इति षष्ठी । स शिवो भवेत् । स सोमयाजी भवेत् ।

स विरक्तो भवेत् । स सर्वदीक्षितो भवेत् । सोऽमृतत्वं गच्छति । स सर्वकालत्वं गच्छति ।

स सर्वन्यासकारी भवेत् । अनधीतगतिर्विद्यां लभेत् । कर्तव्याकरणादिकर्ता भवेत् ।

सर्वसिद्धीश्वरो भवेत् । कालीरूपो भवेत् ।

सोऽहं हंस इत्याह भगवान् सदाशिव इति प्रोतं वेद ॥

Haṃsaḥ Kaṃ Khaṃ Gaṃ Ghaṃ Ṅaṃ Mahāmuṇḍamālādhāriṇi Mahākālapriye Māṃ Rakṣa Rakṣa |

Ṣaṭcakravāsini Vāgīśvari Jihvāgre Vasa |

Haṃ Namaḥ Śirasi Protaṃ Veda Śivo Bhavet |

Haṃsaḥ Caṃ Chaṃ Jaṃ Jhaṃ Ñaṃ Mahātripurabhairavi Pustakākṣamālādhāriṇi Śatrumukhastambhanaṃ Kuru Kuru Svāheti Mahāpadme |

Haṃsaḥ Ṭaṃ Ṭhaṃ Ḍaṃ Ḍhaṃ Ṇaṃ Ḍāṃ Ḍīṃ Ḍaṃ Ḍākini Māṃ Rakṣa Rakṣa Svāhetyanāhate Nyaset | Tṛtīyārūpo Bhavet |

Haṃsaḥ Taṃ Thaṃ Daṃ Dhaṃ Naṃ Mahāmāri Mārahāriṇi Huṃ Huṃ Dāridryaṃ Hara Hara Svāhā | Guṃ Nyaset |

Sa Brahmakālītvaṃ Gacchati | Caturthatvaṃ Gacchati |

Haṃsaḥ Paṃ Phaṃ Baṃ Bhaṃ Maṃ Mārjāri Vīrāvali Mamālasyaṃ Nāśaya Nāśaya | Haṃsaḥ Yaṃ Raṃ Laṃ Vaṃ Śaṃ Ṣaṃ Saṃ Haṃ

Lambodari Mātarmahāmaṅgalapriye Mama Jāḍyaṃ Chedaya Chedaya |

Bhraṃśa Bhraṃśa | Bhagavati Māṃ Rakṣa Rakṣa |

Bhuvanadhāriṇi Māṃ Dhāraya Dhāraya |

Svāhāpadadvayaṃ Nyasya Śivo Bhavet |

Atha Vai Ṣaṣṭhīṃ Nyaset | Haṃsaḥ Laṃ Kṣaṃ Mahālakṣmi Rājarājeśvari Mahākālapriye Kālakhaṇḍini Khaṇḍini Khaṇḍaya Khaṇḍaya Khāṃ Khīṃ Khūṃ Khaiṃ Khoṃ Khauṃ Khaḥ Khanitri Same Svāheti

Sarvāṅge Nyaset | Haṃsaḥ Pañcāśat Vyāpakaṃ Kuryāt | Iti Ṣaṣṭhī |

Sa Śivo Bhavet | Sa Somayājī Bhavet |

Sa Virakto Bhavet | Sa Sarvadīkṣito Bhavet | So'mṛtatvaṃ Gacchati |

Sa Sarvakālatvaṃ Gacchati | Sa Sarvanyāsakārī Bhavet |

Anadhītagatirvidyāṃ Labhet | Kartavyākaraṇādikartā Bhavet |

Sarvasiddhīśvaro Bhavet | Kālīrūpo Bhavet | So'haṃ Haṃsa Ityāha Bhagavān Sadāśiva Iti Protaṃ Veda ||

शान्ति मन्त्रः | *Śānti Mantraḥ* |

ॐ भद्रं कर्णेभिः शृणुयाम देवाः । भद्रं पश्येमाक्षभिर्यजत्राः ।

Oṃ Bhadraṃ Karṇebhiḥ Śṛṇuyāma Devāḥ ||

Bhadraṃ Paśyemākṣabhiryajatrāḥ ||
स्थिरैरङ्गैस्तुष्टुवाँसस्तनूभिः । व्यशेम देवहितं यदायुः ।

Sthirairaṅgaistuṣṭuvāg̃Sastanūbhiḥ || Vyaśema Devahitaṃ Yadāyuḥ ||
स्वस्ति न इन्द्रो वृद्धश्रवाः । स्वस्ति नः पूषा विश्ववेदाः ।

Svasti Na Indro Vṛddhaśravāḥ || Svasti Naḥ Pūṣā Viśvavedāḥ ||
स्वस्ति नस्ताक्ष्यों अरिष्टनेमिः । स्वस्ति नो बृहस्पतिर्दधातु ॥

Svasti Nastārkṣyo Ariṣṭanemiḥ || *Svasti No Bṛhaspatirdadhātu* ||

ॐ शान्तिः शान्तिः शान्तिः || *Oṃ Śāntiḥ Śāntiḥ Śāntiḥ* ||

इत्याथर्वणे सौभाग्यकाण्डे हंसषोढोपनिषत् समाप्ता ।

Ityātharvaṇe Saubhāgyakāṇḍe Haṃsaṣoḍhopaniṣat Samāptā |

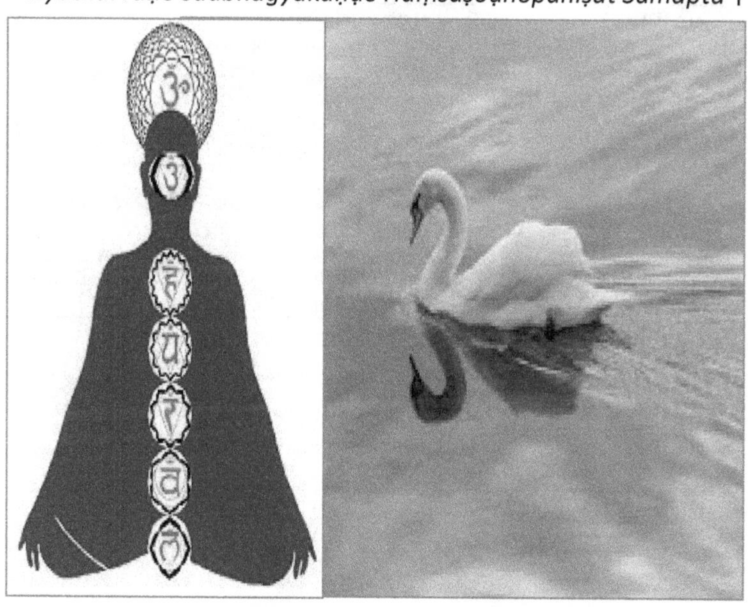

*****

Other Books of the Author

http://ramamurthy.jaagruti.co.in/

#	Title	Remarks	Pages
		Indology Related	
1.	*Shrī Lalitā Sahasranāmam*	English translation of Shrī *Bhāskararāya's Bhāśyam*	750
2.	Power of *Shrī Vidyā*	The secrets demystified – with lucid English rendering and commentaries	80
3.	*Samatā*	An exposition of Similarities in *Lalitā Sahasranāma* with *Soundaryalaharī, Saptaśatī, Viśṇu Sahasranāma* and *Shrīmad Bhagavad Gīta*	172
4.	*Advaita* in *Shākta*	Advaita Philosophy discussed in Shākta related Books	80
5.	*Shrī Lalitā Triśatī*	300 divine names of the celestial Mother – **English** translation of *Shrī Ādhi Śaṅkara*'s *Bhāśyam*	193
6.	Secrets of *Mahāśakti*	Chandi demystified	78
7.	*Daśa Mahā Vidyā*	Ten cosmic forms of the Divine mother	60
8.	ஸ்ரீவித்யா பேதங்கள்	ஸ்ரீவித்யா உபாசனையின் படிகள் - கோவை ஶதச் சண்டீ மலர்	51
9.	ஸ்ரீ தேவீ ஸ்துதிகள்	பல முக்கிய அம்பாள் ஸ்தோத்ரங்கள்	133
10.	Śrī Devī Stutis – श्री देवी स्तुति:	Various important stotras of Sri Devi	
11.	ஷண்மத மந்த்ரங்கள் - षण्मत मन्त्रा:	பொள்ளாச்சி ஸ்ரீ ஸஹஸ்ரசண்டீ மஹாயாக நினைவு மலர்	145
12.	*Śanmata Mantras* - - षण्मत मन्त्रा:	Important Mantras relating to Gods of six religions	87
13.	தேவதா மந்த்ரங்கள்	அக்கரைப்பட்டி ஸஹஸ்ரசண்டீ மஹாயாக நினைவு மலர்	32
14.	ஆதி ஶங்கரரும் ஷண்மதமும்	ஷண்மதங்களைப் பற்றிய ஒரு அறிமுகம்	32
15.	ஸ்ரீ ஷண்மத தேவதா அர்ச்சனை	ஸ்ரீ மஹா கும்பாபிஷேக மலர்	64
16.	*Vaidhīka* Wedding	Typical Wedding process in English	56
17.	வைதீகத் திருமணம்	Typical Wedding process in Tamil	57
18.	ஸ்ரீ லலிதா திரிஶதி	300 divine names of the celestial Mother – Tamil translation of Shrī Ādi *Śaṅkara*'s Bhāśyam	234
19.	ஸ்ரீகுரு பாத பூஜா விதானம்	சித்தகிரி ஸஹஸ்ரசண்டீ மலர்	44
20.	ஸ்ரீவித்யா ஶடாம்னாய மந்த்ரங்கள்	சித்தகிரி ஸஹஸ்ரசண்டீ மலர்	60
21.	*Ekatā*	Oneness among Shiva, Vishnu and Shakti	277
22.	*Vedas* – An Analytical Perspective	A description of Veda, Vedanta, Vedanga, Jyotisha, Shastra, etc.	240

#	Title	Remarks	Pages
23.	*Shrīvidya* Variances	Variances in Srividya Upasana	50
24.	வேதங்கள் – ஒரு பகுப்பாய்வு	A description of Veda, Vedanta, Vedanga, Jyotisha, Shastra, etc.	280
25.	பரமாச்சார்யாள் நோக்கில் ஸ்ரீலலிதாம்பிகா	The explanation given by Paramacharya on some of the names in Lalita Sahasranama	175
26.	*Ṣaṇṇavati* (षण्णवति *Tarpaṇa*	Repaying Debts to Ancestors	42
27.	ஷண்ணவதி (षण्णवति தர்பணம்	முன்னோர் கடன் தீர்த்தல்	48
28.	*Shrī Mahā Pratyangirā Devī*	Holy Divine mother in ferocious form	41
29.	ஸ்ரீ மஹா ப்ரத்யங்கிரா தேவீ	தெய்வீக அன்னையின் பயங்கர வடிவம்	51
30.	*Śrī Chakra Navāvarṇam*	Marvels of *Śrī Chakra*	115
31.	ஸ்ரீ சக்ர நவாவர்ணம்	ஸ்ரீ சக்ரத்தின் அதிசயங்கள்	130
32.	அம்பிகையின் (திரு) அவதாரங்கள்	ஸ்ரீ தேவியின் பல்வேறு அவதாரங்கள்	142
33.	Incarnations of Holy Mother	Different Incarnations of *Śrī Devī*	140
34.	ஸ்ரீ பிரணவானந்தர் - ஒரு சரிதம்	ஒரு அரிய ஸ்வாமிகளின் திவ்ய சரிதம்	90
35.	ஸன்யாஸம் - ஓர் அலசல்	ஹிந்து மத ஸன்யாஸ பேதங்கள் - ஒரு பகுப்பாய்வு	150
36.	Asceticism – an Analysis	A Study of Hindu Sanyasam	150
37.	ஶாக்த உபநிஷதங்கள்	ஸ்ரீ தேவியைப் பற்றிய உபநிஷதங்கள்	400
38.	*Shākta Upaniṣats*	*Upaniṣats* about *Sri Devi*	90
	Applied Samskrutam Based		
39.	*Paribhāshā Stora*-s	An exploration of *Lalitā Sahasranāmam*	96
40.	*Shrī Cakra*, An Esoteric Approach	Mathematical Construction to draw *Shrī Cakra*	64
41.	Number System in Samskrutam	An overview of Mathematics based on Samskrutam	123
42.	*Vedic* Mathematics	30 formulae elucidated	146
43.	Vedic IT	Information Technology and Samskrutam	162
	IT Based		
44.	Orthogonal Array	A Statistical Tool for Software Testing	180
	Banking Based		
45.	Retail Banking	A guide book for Novice	213
46.	Corporate Banking	A guide book for Novice	232
47.	Dictionary of Financial Terms	A Guide Book for all – Demystifying Myriad Global Financial Terms	215
48.	GRC in BFS Industry	(**G**overnance, **R**isk Management and **CO**mpliance by Banking & Finance Industry)	200

Let him be blessed to share his knowledge and experience with others through more books. Let us wish him all the best.

*****

Bibliography

The following books were referred to write this book. Lot many thans to the authors and the publishers. They were very useful.

#	Title	Author
1.	ஸ்ரீ தேவி உபநிஷத்துக்கள்	வாதூல வே. ராமசந்த்ரசர்மா அவர்கள்
2.	வேத சக்தி	ப்ரஹ்மஸ்ரீ அருட்சக்தி நாகராஜ அய்யர்
3.	शाक्ता उपनिषद:	Adyar Library Series – Volume Ten
4.	108 உபநிஷத் ஸாரம் – 3 volumes	அண்ணா
5.	Other books of the same author.	

Om Tat Sat ॐ तत् सत्

CPSIA information can be obtained
at www.ICGtesting.com
Printed in the USA
LVHW071028260623
750792LV00004B/140

9 789382 237662